THE

FOUNTAIN OF LIFE

OPENED;

OR

A DISPLAY OF CHRIST

IN HIS ESSENTIAL MEDIATORIAL GLORY

JOHN FLAVEL

CONTENTS.

SERMON XVI.

SERMON XXIX.

OF THE MANNER OF CHRIST'S DEATH, IN RESPECT OF THE PATIENCE THEREOF.

SERMON XXX.

OF THE INSTRUCTIVENESS OF THE DEATH OF CHRIST, IN HIS SEVEN LAST WORDS; THE FIRST OF WHICH IS HERE ILLUSTRATED.

SERMON XXXI.

THE SECOND EXCELLENT WORD OF CHRIST UPON THE CROSS, ILLUSTRATED.

SERMON XXXII.

THE THIRD OF CHRIST'S LAST WORDS UPON THE CROSS, ILLUSTRATED.

SERMON XXXIII.

THE FOURTH EXCELLENT SAYING OF CHRIST UPON THE CROSS, ILLUSTRATED.

SERMON XXXIV.

THE FIFTH EXCELLENT SAYING OF CHRIST UPON THE CROSS, ILLUSTRATED.

SERMON XXXV.

THE SIXTH EXCELLENT SAYING OF CHRIST UPON THE CROSS, ILLUSTRATED.

SERMON XXXVI.

THE SEVENTH AND LAST WORD WITH WHICH CHRIST BREATHED OUT HIS SOUL, ILLUSTRATED.

SERMON XXXVII.

CHRIST'S FUNERAL ILLUSTRATED, IN ITS MANNER, REASONS, AND
EXCELLENT ENDS.

SERMON XXXVIII.

WHEREIN FOUR WEIGHTY ENDS OF CHRIST'S HUMILIATION ARE
OPENED, AND PARTICULARLY APPLIED.

SERMON XXXIX.

WHEREIN THE RESURRECTION OF CHRIST, WITH ITS INFLUENCES
UPON THE SAINTS' RESURRECTION, IS CLEARLY OPENED, AND
COMFORTABLY APPLIED, BEING THE FIRST STEP OF HIS EX-
ALTATION.

SERMON XL.

THE ASCENSION OF CHRIST ILLUSTRATED, AND VARIOUSLY IM-
PROVED, BEING THE SECOND STEP OF HIS EXALTATION.

SERMON XLI.

THE SESSION OF CHRIST AT GOD'S RIGHT HAND EXPLAINED AND
APPLIED, BEING THE THIRD STEP OF HIS GLORIOUS EXALTATION.

SERMON XLII.

CHRIST'S ADVENT TO JUDGMENT, BEING THE FOURTH AND LAST
DEGREE OF HIS EXALTATION, ILLUSTRATED AND IMPROVED.

THE FOUNTAIN OF LIFE.

SERMON I.

THE EXCELLENCY OF THE SUBJECT.

1 COR. II. 2.

FOR I DETERMINED NOT TO KNOW ANY THING AMONG YOU, SAVE JESUS
CHRIST, AND HIM CRUCIFIED.

THE former verse contains an apology for the plain and familiar manner of the apostle's preaching, which was not (as he there tells them) with excellency of speech, or of wisdom; that is, he studied not to gratify their curiosity with rhetorical strains, or philosophical niceties. In this he gives the reason; " For I determined not to know any thing among you, save Jesus Christ, and him crucified."

" I determined not to know." The meaning is not, that he entirely despised or contemned all other studies and knowledge; but so far only as they stand in competition with, or opposition to the study and knowledge of Jesus Christ. And it is as if he should say, It is my stated, settled judgment; not a hasty, inconsiderate censure, but the product and issue of my most serious inquiries. After I have well weighed the case, turned it round, viewed it exactly on every side, balanced all advantages and disadvantages, pondered all things that are fit to come into consideration about it; this is the result and final determination, that all other knowledge, how profitable, how pleasant soever, is not worthy to be named in the same day with the knowledge of Jesus Christ. This, therefore, I resolve to make the scope and end of my ministry, and the end regulates the mean; such pedantic toys and airy notions as injudicious ears affect, would rather obstruct than promote my grand design among you;

therefore, wholly waving that way, I applied myself to a plain, popular, unaffected dialect, fitted rather to pierce the heart, and convince the conscience, than to tickle the fancy. This is the scope of the words, in which three things fall under consideration:

1. The subject matter of his doctrine, to wit, Jesus Christ. " I determined to know nothing," that is, to study nothing myself, to teach nothing to you, but " Jesus Christ." Christ shall be the centre to which all the lines of my ministry shall be drawn. I have spoken and written of many other subjects in my sermons and epistles, but it is all as consequent upon the preaching and discovery of Jesus Christ: of all the subjects in the world, this is the sweetest; if there be any thing on this side heaven, worthy our time and studies, this is it. Thus he magnifies his doctrine, from the excellency of its subject-matter, accounting all other doctrines but airy things, compared with this.

2. We have here that special respect or consideration of Christ, which he singled out from all the rest of the excellent truths of Christ, to spend the main strength of his ministry upon; and that is, Christ as crucified: and the rather, because hereby he would obviate the vulgar prejudice raised against him upon the account of his cross; for Christ crucified was " to the jews a stumbling-block, and to the greeks foolishness," 1 Cor. i. 23. This also best suited his end, to draw them on to Christ; as Christ above all other subjects, so Christ crucified above all things in Christ. There is, therefore, a great emphasis in this word, " and him crucified."

3. The manner in which he discoursed on this transcendent subject to them, is also remarkable; he not only preached Christ crucified, but he preached him assiduously and plainly. He preached Christ frequently; " and whenever he preached of Christ crucified, he preached him in a crucified style." This is the sum of the words; to let them know that his spirit was intent upon this subject, as if he neither knew, nor cared to speak of any other. All his sermons were so full of Christ, that his hearers might have thought he was acquainted with no other doctrine. Hence observe,

Doct. That there is no doctrine more excel-lent in itself, or more necessary to be preached and studied, than the doctrine of Jesus Christ, and him crucified.

All other knowledge, how much soever it be magnified in the world, is, and ought to be esteemed but dross, in comparison

with the excellency of the knowledge of Jesus Christ, Phil. iii. 8.
" In whom are hid all the treasures of wisdom and knowledge,"
Col. ii. 3.   Eudoxus was so affected with the glory of the sun,
that he thought he was born only to behold it : much more
should a christian judge himself born only to behold and delight in the glory of the Lord Jesus.

The truth of this proposition will be made out by a double
consideration of the doctrine of Christ.

I. Let it be considered absolutely, and then these lovely properties with which it is naturally clothed, will render it superior
to all other sciences and studies.

1. The knowledge of Jesus Christ is the very marrow and
kernel of all the scriptures ; the scope and centre of all divine
revelations.   The ceremonial law is full of Christ, and all the
gospel is full of Christ : the blessed lines of both Testaments
meet in him ; and how they both harmonize, and sweetly concentre in Jesus Christ, is the chief scope of the excellent epistle
to the Hebrews, to discover ; for we may call that epistle the
sweet harmony of both Testaments.   This argues the unspeakable excellency of this doctrine, the knowledge whereof must
needs therefore be a key to unlock the greatest part of the sacred
scriptures.   For it is in the understanding of scripture, much
as it is in the knowledge men have in logic and philosophy : if
a scholar once come to understand the foundation-principle,
upon which, as upon its hinge, the controversy turns, the true
knowledge of that principle shall carry him through the whole
controversy, and furnish him with a solution to every argument.
Even so the right knowledge of Jesus Christ, like a clue, leads
you through the whole labyrinth of the scriptures.

2. The knowledge of Jesus Christ is a fundamental knowledge ; and foundations are most useful, though least seen.
The knowledge of Christ is fundamental to all graces, duties,
comforts, and happiness.

(1.) It is fundamental to all graces ; they all begin in knowledge ; " The new man is renewed in knowledge," Col. iii. 10.
As the old, so the new creation begins in light ; the opening of
the eyes is the first work of the Spirit : and as the beginnings
of grace, so all the after improvements thereof depend upon this
increasing knowledge ; " But grow in grace, and in the knowledge of our Lord and Saviour," 2 Pet. iii. 18.   See how these
two, grace and knowledge, keep equal pace in the soul of a
christian ; in what degree the soul increases, the other increases
answerably.

(2.) The knowledge of Christ is fundamental to all duties ;

the duties, as well as the graces of all christians, are all founded in the knowledge of Christ. Must a christian believe? That he can never do without the knowledge of Christ: faith is so much dependent on his knowledge, that it is denominated by it, " By his knowledge shall my righteous servant justify many," Isa. liii. 11; and hence, John vi. 40, seeing and believing are made the same thing. Would a man exercise hope in God? that he can never do without the knowledge of Christ, for he is the author of that hope, 1 Pet. i. 3; he is also its object, Heb. vi. 19; its ground-work and support, Col. i. 27. And as you cannot believe or hope, so neither can you pray acceptably without a competent degree of this knowledge. The very heathen could say, " Men must not speak of God without light." The true way of conversing with, and enjoying God in prayer, is by acting faith on him through a Mediator. Oh then, how indispensable is the knowledge of Christ, to all who address themselves to God in any duty!

(3.) It is fundamental to all comforts: all the comforts of believers are streams from this fountain. Jesus Christ is the very object matter of a believer's joy, " We rejoice in Christ Jesus," Phil. iii. 3. Take away the knowledge of Christ, and a christian is the most sad and melancholy creature in the world: again, let Christ but manifest himself, and dart the beams of his light into their souls, it will make them kiss the stake, sing in the flames, and shout in the pangs of death, as men that divide the spoil.

(4.) This knowledge is fundamental to the eternal happiness of souls: as we can perform no duty, enjoy no comfort, so neither can we be saved without it; " This is life eternal, that they might know thee the only true God, and Jesus Christ, whom thou hast sent," John xvii. 3. And if it be life eternal to know Christ, then it is eternal damnation to be ignorant of Christ: as Christ is the door that opens heaven, so knowledge is the key that opens Christ. The excellent gifts and renowned parts of the moral heathens, though they purchased to them great esteem and honour among men, yet left them in a state of perdition, because of this great defect, they were ignorant of Christ, 1 Cor. i. 21. Thus you see how fundamental the knowledge of Christ is, essentially necessary to all the graces, duties, comforts, and happiness of souls.

3. The knowledge of Christ is profound and large: all other sciences are but shadows; this is a boundless, bottomless ocean; no creature hath a line long enough to fathom the depth of it; there is height, length, depth, and breadth ascribed to it, Eph.

iii. 18; yea, it passeth knowledge.   There is a manifold wisdom of God in Christ, Eph. iii. 10.   It is indeed simple, pure, and unmixed with any thing but itself, yet it is manifold in degrees, kinds, and administrations; though something of Christ be unfolded in one age, and something in another, yet eternity itself cannot fully unfold him.   I see something, said Luther, which blessed Augustine saw not; and those that come after me, will see that which I see not.   It is in the studying of Christ, as in the planting of a new-discovered country; at first men sit down by the sea-side, upon the skirts and borders of the land; and there they dwell, but by degrees they search further and further into the heart of the country.   Ah, the best of us are yet but upon the borders of this vast continent!

4. The study of Jesus Christ is the most noble subject that ever a soul spent itself upon.   The angels study this doctrine, and stoop down to look into this deep abyss.   What are the truths discovered in Christ, but the very secrets that from eternity lay hid in the bosom of God? Eph. iii. 8, 9.   God's heart is opened to men in Christ, John i. 18; this makes the gospel such a glorious dispensation, because Christ is so gloriously revealed therein, 2 Cor. iii. 9; and the studying of Christ in the gospel, stamps such a heavenly glory upon the contemplating soul, ver. 18.

5. It is the most sweet and comfortable knowledge; to be studying Jesus Christ, what is it but to be digging among all the veins and springs of comfort? and the deeper you dig, the more do these springs flow upon you.   How are hearts enraptured with the discoveries of Christ in the gospel! what ecstasies, meltings, transports, do gracious souls meet there!

II. Let us compare this knowledge with all other knowledge, and thereby the excellency of it will further appear.

1. All other knowledge is natural, but this wholly supernatural; "No man knoweth the Son, but the Father; neither knoweth any the Father, save the Son, and he to whomsoever the Son will reveal him," Matt. xi. 27.   The wisest heathens could never make a discovery of Christ by their deepest searches into nature; the most eagle-eyed philosophers were but children in knowledge, compared with the most illiterate christians.

2. Other knowledge is unattainable by many.   All the helps and means in the world would never enable some christians to attain the learned arts and languages; men of the best wits, and the brightest parts, are most excellent in these; but here is the mystery and excellency of the knowledge of Christ, that men of most blunt, dull, and contemptible parts attain, through the

teaching of the Spirit, to this knowledge, in which the more acute and ingenious are utterly blind; "I thank thee, O Father, Lord of heaven and earth, because thou hast hid these things from the wise and prudent, and hast revealed them unto babes," Matt. xi. 25. "Ye see your calling, brethren, how that not many wise men after the flesh, not many mighty, not many noble, are called: but God hath chosen the foolish things of the world to confound the wise," 1 Cor. i. 26, 27.

3. Other knowledge, though you should attain the highest degree of it, would never bring you to heaven, being defective and lame both in the integrity of parts,—the principal thing, namely Christ, being wanting,—and in the purity of its nature; for the knowing heathens grew vain in their imaginations, Rom. i. 21; and in the efficacy and influence of it on the heart and life; they held the truth in unrighteousness, their lusts were stronger than their light, Rom. i. 18. But this knowledge hath most powerful influences, changing souls into its own image, 2 Cor. iii. 18, and so proves a saving knowledge unto men, 1 Tim. ii. 4. And thus I have in a few particulars pointed out the transcendency of the knowledge of Christ.

The use of all this I shall give you in a few inferences.

INFERENCE 1. The sufficiency of the doctrine of Christ, to make men wise unto salvation. Paul desired to know nothing else; and, indeed, nothing else is of absolute necessity to be known. A little of this knowledge, if saving and effectual upon thy heart, will do the soul more service, than all the vain speculation and profound parts that others so much glory in. Poor christian, be not dejected, because thou seest thyself outstript and excelled by so many in other parts of knowledge; if thou know Jesus Christ, thou knowest enough to comfort and save thy soul. Many learned philosophers are now in hell, and many illiterate christians in heaven.

2. If there be such excellency in the knowledge of Christ, let it humble all, both saints and sinners, that we have no more of this clear and effectual knowledge in us, notwithstanding the excellent advantages we have had for it. Sinners, concerning you I may sigh, and say with the apostle, "Some have not the knowledge of Christ; I speak this to your shame," 1 Cor. xv. 34. This, oh! this is the condemnation. And even for you that are enlightened in this knowledge, how little do you know of Jesus Christ, in comparison of what you might have known of him! What a shame is it, that you should need to be taught the very first truths, "when for the time you might have been teachers of others!" Heb. v. 12—14. "That

your ministers cannot speak unto you as spiritual, but as unto carnal, even as unto babes in Christ," 1 Cor. iii. 1, 2.   Oh how much time is spent in other studies, in vain discourses, frivolous pamphlets, worldly employments! how little in the search and study of Jesus Christ!

3. How sad is their condition that have a knowledge of Christ, and yet as to themselves it had been better they had never had it! Many there be that content themselves with an unpractical, ineffectual, and merely notional knowledge of him; of whom the apostle saith, "It had been better for them not to have known," 2 Pet. ii. 21.   It serves only to aggravate sin and misery; for though it be not enough to save them, yet it puts some weak restraints upon sin, which their impetuous lusts breaking down, exposes them thereby to a greater damnation.

4. This may inform us by what rule to judge both ministers and doctrine.   Certainly that is the highest commendation of a minister, to be " an able minister of the new testament; not of the letter, but of the spirit," 2 Cor. iii. 6.   He is the best preacher, that can in the most lively and powerful manner display Jesus Christ before the people, evidently setting him forth as crucified among them; and that is the best sermon, which is most full of Christ, not of art and language.   I know that a holy dialect well becometh Christ's ministers, they should not be rude and careless in language or method; but surely the excellency of a sermon lies not in that, but in the plainest discoveries and liveliest applications of Jesus Christ.

5. Let all that mind the honour of religion, or the peace and comfort of their own souls, wholly apply themselves to the study of Jesus Christ, and him crucified.   Wherefore spend we ourselves upon other studies, when all excellency, sweetness, and desirableness is centred in this one?   Jesus Christ is fairer than the children of men, the chiefest among ten thousands, "as the apple-tree among the trees of the wood," Cant. ii. 3.   Those things which singly most delight the souls of men, are all found conjoined in Christ.   Oh what a blessed Christ is this! whom to know is eternal life.   From the knowledge of Jesus Christ do bud forth all the fruits of comfort, and that for all seasons and conditions.   Hence he is called " the tree of life, which bears twelve manner of fruits, and yields its fruit every month; and the leaves of the tree are for the healing of the nations," Rev. xxii. 2. In Christ souls have, (1.) All necessaries for food and medicine. (2.) All varieties of fruits, twelve manner of fruits; a distinct sweetness in each and every attribute, promise, ordinance.   (3.) In him are these fruits at all times, he bears fruit every month;

there is precious fruit in Jesus Christ, even in the black month ;
winter fruits as well as summer fruits.   Oh then study Christ,
study to know him more extensively.   There are many excellent
things in Christ, which the most eagle-eyed believer hath not yet
seen: ah ! it is a pity that any thing of Christ should lie hid
from his people.   Study to know Christ more intensely, to get
the experimental taste and lively power of his knowledge upon
your hearts and affections : this is the knowledge that carries
all the sweetness and comfort in it.   Christian, I dare appeal to
thy experience, whether the experimental taste of Jesus Christ,
in ordinances and duties, has not a higher and sweeter relish
than any created enjoyment thou didst ever taste in this world ?
Oh then separate, devote, and wholly give thyself, thy time, thy
strength to this most sweet, transcendent study.

6. Let. me close the whole with a double caution ; one to ourselves, who by our callings and professions are the ministers of
Christ ; another to those that sit under the doctrine of Christ daily.

As to ministers, if this doctrine be the most excellent, necessary, fundamental, profound, noble, and comfortable doctrine, let
us then take heed lest, while we study to be exact in other things,
we be found ignorant in this.   Ye know it is ignominious, by
the common suffrage of the civilized world, for any man to be
unacquainted with his own calling, or not to attend the proper
business of it : it is our calling, as the Bridegroom's friends,
to woo and win souls to Christ, to set him forth to the people
as crucified among them, Gal. iii. 1 ; we must also be able to defend the truths of Christ against undermining heretics, to instil
his knowledge into the ignorant, to answer the cases and scruples
of poor doubting christians.   How many intricate knots have
we to untie !   What pains, what skill is requisite for such as
are employed about our work !   And shall we spend our precious
time in frivolous controversies, philosophical niceties, dry and
barren scholastic notions?   Shall we study every thing but
Christ ? revolve all volumes but the sacred one ?   What is observed even of Bellarmine, that he turned with loathing from
school divinity, because it wanted the sweet juice of piety, may
be a reproof to many among us, who are often too much in love
with worse employment than what he is said to loathe.   Oh let
the knowledge of Christ dwell in us richly.

Let us see that our knowledge of Christ is not a powerless,
barren, unpractical knowledge. Oh that, in its passage from our
understanding to our lips, it might powerfully melt, sweeten, and
delight our hearts !   Remember, brethren, a holy calling never
saved any man, without a holy heart; if our tongues only be

sanctified, our whole man must be condemned. Oh let the keepers of the vineyard look to, and keep their own vineyard! we have a heaven to win or lose, as well as others.

Let us take heed that we withhold not our knowledge of Christ in unrighteousness from the people. Oh that our lips may disperse knowledge and feed many. Remember, I beseech you, the relations wherein you stand, and the obligations resulting thence : remember, the great Shepherd gave himself for, and gave you to the flock ; your time, your gifts are not yours, but God's ; remember the pinching wants of souls, who are perishing for want of Christ ! Did Christ not think it too much to sweat blood, yea, to die for them ? and shall we think it much to watch, study, preach, pray, and do what we can for their salvation ? Oh let the same mind be in you which was also in Christ.

As to the *people* that sit under the doctrine of Christ daily, and have the light of his knowledge shining round about them.

Take heed ye do not reject and despise this light. This may be done two ways. 1. When you despise the means of knowledge by slight and low esteem of it. Surely, if you thus reject knowledge, God will reject you, Hos. iv. 6. It is a despising of the richest gift that ever Christ gave to the church ; and however it be a contempt and slight that begins low, and seems only to vent itself upon the weak parts, such as the artificial discourses, and untaking tones and gestures of the speakers ; yet, believe it, it is a daring sin that flies higher than you are aware : " He that despiseth you, despiseth me ; and he that despiseth me, despiseth Him that sent me," Luke x. 16. You despise the knowledge of Christ, when you despise the directions and loving constraints of that knowledge ; when you refuse to be guided by your knowledge. Your light and your lusts contest and struggle within you ; oh it is sad when your lusts master your light ! You sin not as the heathens sin, who know not God ; but when you sin, you must slight and put by the notices of your own consciences, and offer violence to your own convictions. And what sad work will this make in your souls ! How soon will it lay your consciences waste !

Also, Take heed that you rest not satisfied with that knowledge of Christ you have attained, but go on to perfection. It is the pride and ignorance of many professors, when they have got a few raw and indigested notions, to swell with self-conceit of their excellent attainments. And it is the sin, even of the best of saints, when they see how deep the knowledge of Christ lies, and what pains they must take to dig for it, to throw by the shovel of duty, and cry, Dig we cannot. To your work, christians, to your work; let not your candle go out: devote yourselves to this study, look what intercourses and correspondences are between the two worlds; what communion soever God and souls maintain, it is in this way; count all, therefore, but dross in comparison with that excellency which is in the knowledge of Jesus Christ.

SERMON II.

CHRIST IN HIS ESSENTIAL AND PRIMEVAL GLORY.

PROV. VIII. 30.

THEN I WAS BY HIM, AS ONE BROUGHT UP WITH HIM: AND I WAS DAILY
HIS DELIGHT, REJOICING ALWAYS BEFORE HIM.

THESE words are a part of that excellent commendation of
wisdom, by which in this book Solomon intends two things;
first, Grace or holiness, " Wisdom is the principal thing," Prov.
iv. 7. Secondly, Jesus Christ, the fountain of that grace: and,
as the former is renowned for its excellency, Job xxviii. 14, 15;
so the latter, in this context, wherein the Spirit of God describes
the most blessed state of Jesus Christ, the Wisdom of the Father, from those eternal delights he had with his Father, before
his assumption of our nature: " Then was I by him," &c.
Hence we observe,

> DOCT. THAT THE CONDITION AND STATE OF JESUS
> CHRIST BEFORE HIS INCARNATION, WAS A STATE
> OF THE HIGHEST AND MOST UNSPEAKABLE DE-
> LIGHT AND PLEASURE, IN THE ENJOYMENT OF HIS
> FATHER.

John tells us he was in the bosom of his Father: to lie in
the bosom is the posture of dearest love, as in John xiii. 23;
and therefore in Isa. xlii. 1, the Father calls him, " Mine elect
in whom my soul delighteth;" and he is said, in this state,
wherein I am now describing him, to be rich, 2 Cor. viii. 9; and
" To be equal with God, and to be in the form of God," Phil.
ii. 6, that is, to have all the glory and ensigns of the majesty
of God; and the riches which the apostle speaks of, was no
less than all that God the Father hath; " All that the Father
hath is mine," John xvi. 15; and what he now hath in his
exalted state, is the same that he had before his humiliation,
John xvii. 5. Now to sketch out (as we are able) the unspeakable felicity of that original state of Christ, I shall consider it
three ways, negatively, positively, and comparatively.

I. Let us consider that state negatively, by removing from it all those degrees of abasement and sorrow which his incarnation brought him under : as,

1. He was not then abased to the condition of a creature, which was a low step indeed, for by this, saith the apostle, " he made himself of no reputation," Phil. ii. 7 ; it emptied him of his glory. For God to be made man, is such an abasement as none can express : but then not only to appear in true flesh, but also in the likeness of sinful flesh, as Rom. viii. 3, oh what is this!

2. Christ was not under the law in this state. I confess it was no disparagement to Adam in the state of innocency, or to angels in their state of glory, to be under law to God ; but it was an inconceivable abasement to the absolute independent Being to come under law ; yea, not only under the obedience, but also under the malediction and curse of the law : " But when the fulness of time was come, God sent forth his Son, made of a woman, made under the law," Gal. iv. 4.

3. In this state he was not liable to any of those sorrowful consequences and attendants of that frail and feeble state of humanity, which he afterwards assumed, with the nature. As, (1.) He was unacquainted with griefs ; there was no sorrowing or sighing in that bosom where he lay, though afterwards he became " a man of sorrows and acquainted with grief," Isa. liii. 3. " A man of sorrows," as if he had been constituted and made up of pure and unmixed sorrows ; every day conversing with griefs, as with his intimate companions and acquaintance. (2.) He was never pinched with poverty and wants, while he continued in that bosom, as he was afterwards, when he said, " The foxes have holes, and the birds of the air have nests, but the Son of man hath not where to lay his head," Matt. viii. 20. Ah, blessed Jesus ! thou needest not to have wanted a place to have lain thy head, hadst thou not left that bosom for my sake. (3.) He never underwent reproach and shame in that bosom, there was nothing but glory and honour reflected upon him by his Father, though afterwards " he was despised, and rejected of men," Isa. liii. 3. His Father never looked upon him without smiles and love, delight and joy, though afterwards he became a reproach of men, and despised of the people, Psa. xxii. 6. (4.) While he lay in that bosom of peace and love he never knew what it was to be assaulted with temptations, to be besieged by unclean spirits, as he did afterwards : " Then was Jesus led up of the Spirit into the wilderness to be tempted of the devil," Matt. iv. 1. It was for our sakes that he submitted to those exercises of spirit,

to be " in all points tempted like as we are," Heb. iv. 15, that he might be unto us " a merciful and faithful High Priest," Heb. ii. 17. (5.) He was never sensible of pains and tortures in soul or body, though afterwards he groaned and sweat under them, Isa. liii. 5. The Lord embraced him from eternity, but never wounded him till he stood in our place and room. (6.) There were no hidings or withdrawings of his Father from him; there was not a cloud from eternity upon the face of God, till Jesus Christ had left that bosom. It was a new thing to Christ to cry, " My God, my God, why hast thou forsaken me ?" Matt. xxvii. 46. (7.) There were never any impressions of his Father's wrath upon him, as there were afterwards: God never delivered such a bitter cup into his hands before, as that was, Matt. xxvi. 39. (8.) There was no death, to which he was subject, in that bosom. All these things were new things to Christ; he was above them all, till for our sakes he voluntarily subjected himself unto them. Thus you see what that state was not.

II. Let us consider it positively, what it was, and guess (for indeed we can but guess) by some particular considerations at the glory of it; as,

1. We cannot but conceive it to be a state of matchless happiness, if we consider the persons enjoying and delighting in each other: he was with God, John i. 1. God, you know, is the fountain, ocean, and centre of all delights and joys; " In thy presence is fulness of joy," Psa. xvi. 11. To be wrapt up in the soul and bosom of all delights, as Christ was, must needs be a state of bliss transcending apprehension.

2. Or if we consider the intimacy, dearness, yea, oneness of those great Persons one with another: the nearer the union, the sweeter the communion. Now Jesus Christ was not only near and dear to God, but one with him; " I and my Father are one," John x. 30: one in nature, will, love, and delight. There is indeed a moral union of souls among men by love, but this was a natural oneness; no child is so one with his father, no husband so one with the wife of his bosom, no friend so one with his friend, no soul so one with its body, as Jesus Christ and his Father were one. Oh what matchless delights must necessarily flow from such a blessed union !

3. Consider again the purity of that delight with which the blessed Father and Son embraced each other. The best of creature delights are mixed, debased, and alloyed; if there be something engaging and delightful, there is also something cloying and distasteful. The purer any delight is, the more excellent. Now, there are no crystal streams flowing so purely

from the fountain, no beams of light so unmixed from the sun, as the loves and delights of these holy and glorious persons were : the holy, holy, holy Father, embraced the thrice holy Son with a most holy delight and love.

4. Consider the constancy of this delight ; it was from everlasting, as in verse 23, and from eternity ; it never suffered one moment's interruption. The overflowing fountain of God's delight and love never stopped its course, never ebbed ; but as he speaks in the text, " I was daily his delight, rejoicing always before him."

III. Once more, let us consider it comparatively, and this state will yet appear more glorious, comparing it with either the choicest delights that one creature takes in another, or that God takes in the creature, or that the creatures take in God. Measure these immense delights, between the Father and his Son, by either of these lines, and you shall find them infinitely short : for, (1.) Though the delights that creatures take in each other, be sometimes a great delight ; such was Jacob's delight in Benjamin, whose life is said to be bound up in the lad's life, Gen. xliv. 30, a dear and high expression ; such was that of Jonathan in David, whose soul was knit with his soul, " and he loved him as his own soul," 1 Sam. xviii. 1 ; and such is the delight of one friend in another ; there is a friend that is as a man's own soul, Deut. xiii. 6. Yet all this is but creature delight, and can in no particular equal the delights between the Father and the Son ; for this is but a finite delight, according to the measure and abilities of creatures, but that is infinite, suitable to the infinite perfection of the Divine Being ; this is always mixed, that perfectly pure. (2.) Or if you compare it with the delight that God takes in the creatures, it is confessed that God takes great delight in some creatures. The Lord takes pleasure in his saints, he rejoices over them with singing ; and resteth in his love, Zeph. iii. 17 ; Isa. lxii. 5. But yet there is a great difference between his delight in creatures, and his delights in Christ ; for all his delight in the saints is secondary, and for Christ's sake ; but his delights in Christ are primary, and for his own sake. We are accepted in the Beloved, Eph. 1. 6 ; he is beloved, and accepted for himself. (3.) Compare it once more with the delights that the best of creatures take in God and Christ, and it must be confessed that is a choice delight, and a transcendent love, with which they love and delight in him ; " Whom have I in heaven but thee ? and there is none upon earth that I desire beside thee," Psa. lxxiii. 25. But surely our delight in God is no perfect rule to measure his delight in

Christ by ; for our love to God, at best, is still imperfect. That is the burden and constant complaint of saints, but this is perfect ; ours is inconstant, up and down, ebbing and flowing, but this is constant. So then, the condition and state of Jesus Christ before his incarnation, was a state of the highest and matchless delight, in the enjoyment of his Father. The uses follow.

1. Use of information.

(1.) What an astonishing act of love was this, then, for the Father to give the delight of his soul, out of his very bosom, for poor sinners ! All tongues must needs pause and falter, that attempt the expressions of his grace, expressions being here swallowed up ; "God so loved the world, that he gave his only begotten Son," John iii. 16. Here is a *sic* (so) without a *sicut* (as). *So* loved them : how did he love them? nay, here you must excuse the tongues of angels. Which of us would deliver a child, the child of our delights, an only child, to death, for the greatest inheritance in the world ? what tender parent can endure a parting pull with such a child? When Hagar was taking her last leave (as she thought) of her Ishmael, the text saith, "she went and sat her down over against him, a good way off : for she said, Let me not see the death of the child. And she sat over against him, and lift up her voice, and wept," Gen. xxi. 16. Though she were none of the best of mothers, nor he the best of children, yet she could not give up the child. Oh it was hard to part ! What an outcry did David make, even for an Absalom, wishing he had died for him ! What a hole, as I may say, hath the death of some children made in the hearts of some parents, which will never be closed up in this world ! Yet surely, never did any child lie so close to a parent's heart, as Christ did to his Father's ; and yet he willingly parts with him, though his only one, the Son of his delights ; and that to death, a cursed death, for sinners, for the worst of sinners. Oh the admirable love of God to men ! matchless love ! a love past finding out ! Let all men, therefore, in the business of their redemption, give equal glory to the Father with the Son, John v. 23. If the Father had not loved thee, he had never parted with such a Son for thee.

(2.) From one wonder let our souls turn to another, for they are now in the midst of wonders : adore, and be for ever astonished at the love of Jesus Christ to poor sinners, that ever he should consent to leave such a bosom, and the ineffable delights that were there, for such poor worms as we are. Oh the heights, depths, lengths, and breadths of unmeasurable love ! See Rom. v. 6—8 : read, and wonder. How is the love of Christ commended to poor sinners! As the Father loved him; even so, believers, hath he loved you, John xvii. 23. What manner of love is this! Who ever loved as Christ loves? Who ever denied himself for Christ, as Christ denied himself for us?

(3.) Hence we are informed, That interest in Jesus Christ is the true way to all spiritual preferment in heaven. Do you covet to be in the heart, in the favour and delight of God? Get interest in Jesus Christ, and you shall presently be there. You see among men, all things are carried by interest: persons rise in this world as they are befriended; preferment goes by favour: so it is in heaven, persons are preferred according to their interest in the Beloved, Eph. i. 6. Christ is the great favourite in heaven: his image upon your souls, and his name in your prayers, makes both accepted with God.

(4.) How worthy is Jesus Christ of all our love and delights! You see how infinitely the Father delighteth in him; and shall not our hearts delight in him? Oh that you did but see this lovely Lord Jesus Christ! Why do ye lavish away your precious affections upon vanity? none but Christ is worthy of them. When you spend your precious affections upon other objects, what is it but to dig for dross with golden mattocks? The Lord direct our hearts into the love of Christ. Oh that our hearts, loves, and delights did meet and concentre with the heart of God in this most blessed object! Oh let him that left God's bosom for you, be embosomed by you, though yours be nothing to God's: he that left God's bosom for you, deserves yours.

(5.) If Christ be the beloved of the Father's soul, think what a grievous and insufferable thing it is to the heart of God, to see his dear Son despised, slighted, and rejected by sinners: how God will bear this, that parable, Matt. xxi. 33—41, will inform you: surely he will miserably destroy such wretched sinners. What a dismal word is that, " If any man love not the Lord Jesus Christ, let him be Anathema Maran-atha," 1 Cor. xvi. 22; that is, let the great curse of God lie upon that man till the Lord come. O sinners! you shall one day know the price of this sin; you shall feel what it is to despise a Jesus, that is able to compel love from the hardest heart. Oh that you would slight him no more! Oh that this day your hearts might fall in love with him! I tell you, if you would set your love to sale, none bids so fair for it as Christ.

2. Use of exhortation.

(1.) To saints. If Christ lay eternally in this bosom of love, and yet was content to forsake and leave it for your sakes; then,

[1.] Be you ready to forsake and leave all the comforts you have

on earth for Christ.   Famous Galleacius left all for this enjoyment; Moses left all the glory of Egypt; Peter and the other
apostles left all, Luke xviii. 28.   But what have we to leave
for Christ in comparison with what he left for us?   Surely
Christ is the highest pattern of self-denial in the world.   [2.]
Let this confirm your faith in prayer.   If he, that has such an
interest in the heart of God, intercede with the Father for
you, then never doubt of audience and acceptance with him;
surely you shall be accepted through the Beloved.   Christ
was never denied any thing that he asked, the Father hears
him always, John xi. 42: though you are not worthy, Christ is,
and he ever lives to make intercession for you, Heb. vii. 25.
[3.] Let this encourage thy heart, O saint, in a dying hour, and
not only make thee patient in death, but in a holy manner impatient till thou be gone; for whither is thy soul now going, but
to that bosom of love whence Christ came? " Father, I will
that they also, whom thou hast given me, be with me where I
am," John xvii. 24: and where is he but in that bosom of
glory and love where he lay before the world was? ver. 5.   Oh
then let every believer encourage his soul; comfort ye one
another with these words,—I am leaving the bosom of a creature,
I am going to the bosom of God.

(2.) To sinners, exhorting them to embrace the bosom Son
of God.   Poor fellow-mortals! whatever you are, or have been,
whatever guilt or discouragement at present you lie under, embrace Christ, who is freely offered to you, and you shall be as
dear to God as the holiest and most eminent believer in the
world; but if you still continue to despise and neglect such a
Saviour, sorer wrath is treasured up for you than other sinners,
Heb. x. 28, 29. Oh that these discoveries and overtures of Christ
may never come to such a fatal issue with any of your souls, in
whose eyes his glory hath been this day opened!

SERMON III.

THE COVENANT OF REDEMPTION BETWEEN THE FATHER AND THE REDEEMER.

ISA. LIII. 12.

THEREFORE WILL I DIVIDE HIM A PORTION WITH THE GREAT, AND HE SHALL DIVIDE THE SPOIL WITH THE STRONG, BECAUSE HE HATH POURED OUT HIS SOUL UNTO DEATH: AND HE WAS NUMBERED WITH THE TRANSGRESSORS, AND HE BARE THE SIN OF MANY, AND MADE INTERCESSION FOR THE TRANSGRESSORS.

IN this chapter, the gospel seems to be epitomized; the subject-matter of it is the death of Christ, and the glorious issue thereof. By reading of it, the eunuch of old, and many jews since, have been converted to Christ. Christ is here considered absolutely, and relatively. Absolutely, and so his innocency is industriously vindicated, ver. 9. Though he suffered grievous things, yet not for his own sins, for " he had done no violence, neither was any deceit in his mouth," ver. 9. But relatively considered, in the capacity of a Surety for us: so the justice of God is so fully vindicated in his sufferings; " The Lord hath laid upon him the iniquity of us all," ver. 6. How he came to sustain this capacity and relation of a Surety for us, is in these verses plainly asserted to be by his compact and agreement with his Father, before the worlds were made, ver. 10—12.

In this verse we have, 1. His work. 2. His reward. 3. The relation of each to the other. 1. His work, which was indeed a hard work, to pour out his soul unto death, aggravated by the companions with whom—being numbered with transgressors; the capacity in which—bearing all the sins of the elect, " he bare the sins of many;" and by the manner of his bearing it, namely, meekly, and forgivingly, " he made intercession for the transgressors:" this was his work. 2. The reward or fruit which is promised him for this work, " Therefore will I divide him a portion with the great, and he shall divide the spoil with the strong;" wherein is a plain allusion to conquerors in war, for whom are reserved the richest garments, and most honourable captives to follow the conqueror, as an addition to his magnificence and triumph; these were wont to come after them in chains, Isa. xlv. 14; see Judg. v. 30. 3. The relation between that work and this triumph. Some will have this work to have no other relation to that glory, than a mere antecedent to a consequent; others give it the respect and relation of a meritorious cause to a reward. However, it is plain, that the Father here agrees and promises to give the elect to the Son, if he will undertake their redemption by pouring out his soul unto death; of all which this is the plain result:

> DOCT. THAT THE BUSINESS OF MAN'S SALVATION WAS TRANSACTED UPON COVENANT TERMS, BETWEEN THE FATHER AND THE SON, FROM ALL ETERNITY.

Now, to open this great point, we will here consider,—The persons transacting one with another.—The business transacted. —The quality and manner of the transaction, which is federal. —The articles to which they agree.—How each person performs his engagement to the other.—And, lastly, The antiquity or eternity of this covenant transaction.

I. The persons transacting and dealing with each other in this covenant. And indeed they are great persons, God the Father, and God the Son; the former as a Creditor, and the latter as a Surety. The Father stands upon satisfaction, the Son engages to give it.

II. The business transacted between them; and that was the redemption and recovery of all God's elect: our eternal happiness lay now before them, our dearest and everlasting concerns were now in their hands. The elect (though not yet in being) are here considered as existent, yea, and as fallen, miserable, forlorn creatures: how these may again be restored to happiness without prejudice to the honour, justice, and truth of God; this, this is the business that lay before them.

III. For the manner, or quality of the transaction, it was federal, or of the nature of a covenant; it was by mutual engagements and stipulations, each Person undertaking to perform his part in order to our recovery.

IV. More particularly, we will next consider the articles to which they do both agree; or, what it is that each Person doth for himself promise to the other. And, to let us see how much the Father's heart is engaged in the salvation of poor sinners, there are four things which he promiseth to do for Christ, if he will undertake that work.

1. He promiseth to invest him, and anoint him to a threefold

office, answerable to the misery that lay upon the elect; for, if ever man be restored to that happiness, the blindness of his mind must be cured, the guilt of sin expiated, and his captivity to sin led captive. Christ must, " of God, be made unto us wisdom, and righteousness, and sanctification, and redemption," 1 Cor. i. 30. And he is made so to us as our Prophet, Priest, and King; but he could not put himself into either of these; for if so, he had acted without commission, and consequently all he did had been invalid; " Christ glorified not himself to be made an High Priest, but he that said unto him, Thou art my Son," Heb. v. 5. A commission, therefore, to act authoritatively in these offices being necessary to our recovery, the Father engages to him to seal him such a threefold commission.

He promiseth to invest him with an eternal and royal priesthood; " The Lord hath sworn, and will not repent, Thou art a Priest for ever after the order of Melchisedec," Psa. cx. 4. This Melchisedec being king of righteousness, and king of Salem, that is, Peace, had a royal priesthood; and his descent not being reckoned, it had an adumbration of eternity in it, and so was more fit to typify and shadow forth the priesthood of Christ than Aaron's was, Heb. vii. 17. 24, 25.

He promiseth moreover to make him a Prophet, and that an extraordinary one, even the Prince of prophets; the chief Shepherd, as much superior to all others, as the sun is to the lesser stars; so it is said, " I will give thee for a light to the gentiles, to open the blind eyes," &c. Isa. xlii. 6, 7.

And not only so, but to make him King also, and that of the whole empire of the world; " Ask of me, and I shall give thee the heathen for thine inheritance, and the utmost ends of the earth for thy possession," Psa. ii. 8. Thus the Father promiseth to qualify and furnish the Son completely for the work, by his investiture with this threefold office.

2. He promiseth to crown his work with success, and bring it to a happy issue; " He shall see his seed, he shall prolong his days, and the pleasure of the Lord shall prosper in his hand," Isa. liii. 10. He shall not begin, and not finish; he shall not shed his invaluable blood upon hazardous terms; but shall see and reap the sweet fruits thereof; as the joyful mother forgets her pangs, when she delightfully embraces her living child.

3. The Father promiseth to accept him in his work: " Surely (saith he) my work is with my God," Isa. xlix. 4. And, " I shall be glorious in the eyes of the Lord," ver. 5. His faith hath therein respect to this compact and promise. Accordingly, the Father manifests the satisfaction he had in him, and in his

work, even while he was about it upon the earth, " when there came such a voice from the excellent glory, saying, This is my beloved Son, in whom I am well pleased," 2 Pet. i. 17.

4. As he engaged to reward him highly for his work, by exalting him to singular and super-eminent glory and honour, when he should have despatched and finished it. So you read, " I will declare the decree; the Lord hath said unto me, Thou art my Son, this day have I begotten thee," Psa. ii. 7. It is spoken of the day of his resurrection, when he had just finished his sufferings. And so the apostle expounds and applies it, Acts xiii. 32, 33. For then did the Lord wipe away the reproach of his cross. As if the Father had said, Now thou hast again recovered thy glory, and this day is to thee as a new birth-day.

These are the encouragements and rewards proposed and promised to him by the Father. This was the joy set before him, as the apostle expresses it in Heb. xii. 2, which made him so patiently to " endure the cross, and despise the shame."

And in like manner Jesus Christ gives his engagement to the Father; that, upon these terms, he is content to be made flesh, to divest, as it were, himself of his glory, to come under the obedience and malediction of the law, and not to refuse any, the hardest sufferings it should please his Father to inflict on him. So much is implied in Isa. l. 5—7. " The Lord hath opened mine ear, and I was not rebellious, neither turned away back. I gave my back to the smiters, and my cheeks to them that plucked off the hair; I hid not my face from shame and spitting. For the Lord God will help me, therefore shall I not be confounded; therefore I have set my face like a flint, and I know that I shall not be ashamed." And the sense of this place is well delivered to us in other terms, " Then said I, Lo, I come; I delight to do thy will, O God, thy law is within my heart," Psa. xl. 6—10. Oh see with what a full consent the heart of Christ closeth with the Father's offers and proposals! like some echo, that answers your voice twice or thrice over. So doth Christ here answer his Father's call, " I come; I delight to do thy will; yea, thy law is in my heart."

V. I will briefly show how these articles and agreements were on both parts performed, and that precisely and punctually.

1. The Son having thus consented, accordingly he applies himself to the discharge of his work. He took a body, in it fulfilled all righteousness, even to a tittle, Matt. iii. 15. And, at last, his soul was made an offering for sin, so that he could say, as it is, John xvii. 4, " Father, I have glorified thee on

earth, I have finished the work which thou gavest me to do."
He went through all the parts of his active and passive obedience,
cheerfully and faithfully.

2. The Father made good his engagements to Christ, all
along, with no less faithfulness than Christ did his. He promised to assist, and hold his hand, and so he did; " And
there appeared to him an angel from heaven, strengthening
him," Luke xxii. 43. That was one of the sorest brunts that
ever Christ met with; this was seasonable aid and succour.
He promised to accept him in his work, and that he should be
glorious in his eyes: so he did; for he not only declared it by a
voice from heaven, " Thou art my beloved Son, in thee I am
well pleased," Luke iii. 22; but it was fully declared in his
resurrection and ascension, which were a full discharge and
justification of him. He promised him that " He should see
his seed," Isa. liii. 10, and so he did; for his very birth-dew was
as the dew of the morning; and ever since his blood has been
fruitful in the world. He promised gloriously to reward and
exalt him; and so he hath, and that highly and super-eminently,
" giving him a name above every name in heaven and earth,"
Phil. ii. 9—11. Thus were the articles performed.

VI. When was this compact made between the Father and
the Son? I answer, it bears date from eternity. Before this
world was made, then were his delights in us, while as yet
we had no existence, but only in the infinite mind and purpose
of God, who had decreed this for us in Christ Jesus, as the
apostle speaks, 2 Tim. i. 9. What grace was that which was
given us in Christ before the world began, but this grace of redemption, which was from everlasting thus contrived and designed for us, in that way which hath been here opened? Then
was the counsel, or consultation of peace between them both, as
some take that scripture, Zech. vi. 13.

Next let us apply it to ourselves.

Use 1. The first use that offers itself to us from hence, is
the abundant security that God hath given the elect for their
salvation, and that not only in respect of the covenant of grace
made with them, but also of this covenant of redemption made
with Christ for them; which indeed is the foundation of the
covenant of grace. God's single promise is security enough to
our faith, but his covenant of grace adds further security; but
both these, viewed as the effects and fruits of this covenant of
redemption, make all fast and sure.

2. Moreover, hence we infer the validity and unquestionable
success of Christ's intercession in heaven for believers. You

read, " that he ever liveth to make intercession," Heb. vii. 25, and, that his blood speaks for good things for them, Heb. xii. 24.   Now, that his blood shall obtain what it pleads for in heaven, is undoubted, and that from the consideration of this covenant of redemption.   For here you see that the things he now asks of his Father, are the very same which his Father promised him, and covenanted to give him, before this world was.   So that, besides the interest of the person, the very equity of the matter speaks its success, and requires performance. Whatever he asks for us, is as due to him as the wages of the hireling, when the work is ended.   If the work be done, and done faithfully, as the Father hath acknowledged it is, then the reward is due, and due immediately; and no doubt but he shall receive it from the hands of a righteous God.

3. Hence, in like manner, you may be informed of the consistency of grace with full satisfaction to the justice of God. The apostle tells us, we are saved " according to his own purpose and grace, which was given us in Jesus Christ before the world began," 2 Tim. i. 9, that is, according to the gracious terms of this covenant of redemption; and yet you see notwithstanding, how strictly God stands upon satisfaction from Christ.   So then, grace to us, and satisfaction to justice, are not so inconsistent as some adversaries of the truth would make them; what was debt to Christ, is grace to us.   " Being justified freely by his grace, through the redemption that is in Christ Jesus," Rom. iii. 24.

4. Hence judge of the antiquity of the love of God to believers; what an ancient Friend he hath been to us; who loved us, provided for us, and contrived all our happiness, before we were, yea, before the world was.   We reap the fruits of this covenant now, the seed whereof was sown from eternity; yea, it is not only ancient, but also most free: no excellences of ours could engage the love of God; for as yet we were not.

5. Hence judge, how reasonable it is that believers should embrace the hardest terms of obedience unto Christ, who complied with such hard terms for their salvation.   They were hard and difficult terms indeed, on which Christ received you from the Father's hand; it was, as you have heard, to pour out his soul unto death; " Though he was rich, yet for our sakes he became poor," 2 Cor. viii. 9. Blush, ungrateful believers; oh let shame cover your faces; judge in yourselves now, hath Christ deserved that you should stand with him for trifles, that you should shrink at a few petty difficulties, and complain, this is hard, and that is severe?   Oh if you knew the grace of our Lord Jesus

Christ in this his wonderful condescension for you, you could not do it.

6. Lastly, How greatly are we all concerned to make it sure to ourselves, that we are of this number which the Father and the Son agreed for before the world was; that we were comprehended in Christ's engagement and compact with the Father!

Obj. Yea, but you will say, who can know that?

I answer, We know, without ascending into heaven, or prying into unrevealed secrets, that our names were in that covenant, if, (1.) You are believers indeed; for all such the Father then gave to Christ: " The men that thou gavest me, (for of them he spake immediately before,) they have believed that thou didst send me," John xvii. 6. 8. (2.) If you savingly know God in Jesus Christ, such were given him by the Father: " I have manifested thy name unto the men which thou gavest me," ver. 6. By this they are discriminated from the rest: " The world hath not known thee, but these have known," ver. 25. (3.) If you are men and women of another world : " They are not of the world, even as I am not of the world," ver. 16. May it be said of you, as of dying men, that you are not men and women for this world, that you are crucified and dead to it, Gal. vi. 14, that you are strangers in it ! Heb. xi. 13, 14. (4.) If you keep Christ's word: " Thine they were, and thou gavest them me; and they have kept thy word," John xvii. 6. By keeping his word, understand the receiving of the word, in its sanctifying effects and influences into your hearts, and your perseverance in the profession and practice of it to the end: " Sanctify them through thy truth, thy word is truth," ver. 17. " If ye abide in me, and my words abide in you, ye shall ask what ye will," John xv. 7. Blessed and happy is that soul upon which these blessed characters appear, which our Lord Jesus hath laid so close together, within the compass of a few verses, in the 17th chapter of John. These are the persons the Father delivered unto Christ, and Christ accepted from the Father, in this blessed covenant.

SERMON IV.

THE ADMIRABLE LOVE OF GOD IN GIVING HIS OWN SON FOR US.

JOHN III. 16.

FOR GOD SO LOVED THE WORLD, THAT HE GAVE HIS ONLY BEGOTTEN SON.

IN these words are to be considered,

1. The original spring or fountain of our best mercies—The love of God.

2. The mercy flowing out of this fountain, and that is Christ, The Mercy, as he is emphatically called, Luke i. 72; the marrow, kernel, and substance of all other mercies. "He gave his only begotten Son."

3. The objects of this love, or the persons for whom the eternal Lord delivered Christ, and that is "the world." This must respect the elect of God in the world; such as do, or shall actually believe, as it is exegetically expressed in the next words, "That whosoever believeth in him should not perish." Those whom he calls the world in that, he styles believers in this expression; and the word world is put to signify the elect, because they are scattered through all parts, and are among all ranks of men in the world; these are the objects of this love. It is not angels, but men, that were so loved.

4. The manner in which this never-enough celebrated mercy flows to us, from the fountain of Divine love, and that is most freely and spontaneously. "He gave," not he sold, or barely parted from, but gave. Nor yet doth the Father's giving imply Christ to be merely passive; for as the Father is here said to give him, so the apostle tells us, that he gave himself; "Who loved me, and gave himself for me," Gal. ii. 20. The Father gave him out of good will to men, and he has willingly bestowed himself on that service. Hence we learn this

> DOCT. THAT THE GIFT OF CHRIST IS THE HIGHEST AND FULLEST MANIFESTATION OF THE LOVE OF GOD TO SINNERS, THAT EVER WAS MADE FROM ETERNITY TO THEM.

How is this gift of God to sinners signalized in that sentence of the apostle, "Herein is love; not that we loved God, but

c

that he loved us, and sent his Son to be the propitiation for our sins!" 1 John iv. 10.   Why doth the apostle so magnify this gift in saying, "Herein is love," as if there were love in nothing else?   May we not say, that to have a being, a being among the rational creatures, therein is love?   To have our life carried so many years like a taper in the hand of Providence, through so many dangers, and not yet put out in obscurity, therein is love?   To have food and raiment convenient for us, beds to lie on, relations to comfort us, in all these is love?   Yea, but if you speak comparatively, in all these there is no love, to the love expressed in sending or giving Christ for us: these are great mercies in themselves; but compared to this mercy, they are all swallowed up, as the light of candles when brought into the sunshine.   No, no, herein is love, that God gave Christ for us.   And it is remarkable, that when the apostle would show us, in Rom. v. 8, what is the noblest fruit that most commends to men the root of Divine love that bears it, he shows us this very fruit of it that I am now opening; "But God," saith he, "commendeth his love toward us, in that, while we were yet sinners, Christ died for us:" this is the very flower of that love.

The method into which I will cast this precious point, shall be this: I. To show how Jesus Christ was given by the Father. II. How that gift is the fullest and richest manifestation of the love of God that was ever made to the world. III. And then draw forth the uses of it.

I. How was Jesus Christ given by the Father, and what is implied therein.

1. His designation and appointment unto death for us; for so you read, that it was done "according to the determinate counsel of God," Acts ii. 23.   As the lamb under the law was separated from the flock, and set apart for a sacrifice; though it were still living, yet it was intentionally and preparatively given, and consecrated to the Lord; so Jesus Christ was, by the counsel and purpose of God, thus chosen, and set apart for his service: and therefore in Isa. xlii. 1, God calls him his Elect, or chosen One.

2. His giving Christ, implies a parting with him, or setting him (as the french version hath it) at some distance from himself for a time.   There was a kind of parting between the Father and the Son, when he came to tabernacle in our flesh: so he expresseth it; "I came forth from the Father, and am come into the world; again, I leave the world, and go to the Father," John xvi. 28. This distance that this incarnation and humiliation set him at, was properly as to his humanity, which was really

distant from the glory into which it is now taken up, and in respect of manifestation of delight and love, the Lord seemed to treat him as one at a distance from him.   Oh! this was it that so deeply pierced and wounded his soul, as is evident from that complaint, "My God, my God, why hast thou forsaken me? Why art thou so far from the words of my roaring?   O my God, I cry in the day-time, but thou hearest not," &c. Psa. xxii. 1, 2.

3. God's giving of Christ, implies his delivering him into the hands of justice to be punished; even as condemned persons are, by sentence of law, given or delivered into the hands of executioners.   So Acts ii. 23, "Him, being delivered by the determinate counsel and foreknowledge of God, ye have taken, and by wicked hands have crucified and slain;" and so he is said "to deliver him up to death for us all," Rom. viii. 32.

4. God's giving of Christ, implies his application of him, with all the purchase of his blood, and settling all this upon us, as an inheritance and portion.   "My Father giveth you the true bread from heaven; for the bread of God is he which cometh down from heaven, and giveth life unto the world," John vi. 32, 33.   God hath given him as bread to poor starving creatures, that by faith they might eat and live.   And so he told the samaritan woman, "If thou knewest the gift of God, and who it is that saith unto thee, Give me to drink, thou wouldest have asked of him, and he would have given thee living water," John iv. 10. Bread and water are the two necessaries for the support of natural life; God hath given Christ, you see, to be all that, and more, to the spiritual life.

II. Let us see how this gift of Christ was the highest and fullest manifestation of the love of God, that ever the world saw: and this will be evidenced by the following particulars.

1. If you consider how near and dear Jesus Christ was to the Father: he was his Son, "his only Son," saith the text; the Son of his love, yea, one with himself; the express image of his person; the brightness of his Father's glory: "Unto us a Son is given," Isa. ix. 6, and such a Son as he calls "his dear Son," Col. i. 13.   A late writer tells us, that he hath been informed, that in the famine in Germany, a poor family being ready to perish with famine, the husband proposed to the wife, to sell one of the children for bread, to relieve themselves and the rest: the wife at last consents it should be so; but then they began to think which of the four should be sold; and when the eldest was named, they both refused to part with that, being their first-born, and the beginning of their strength.   Well, then

they came to the second, but could not yield that he should be sold, being the very picture and lively image of his father. The third was named, but that also was a child that best resembled the mother. And when the youngest was thought on, that was the Benjamin, the child of their old age; and so they were content rather to perish altogether in the famine, than to part with a child for relief. And you know how tenderly Jacob took it, when his Joseph and Benjamin were rent from him. What is a child, but a piece of the parent wrapt up in another skin? And yet our dearest children are but as strangers to us, in comparison of the unspeakable dearness that was betwixt the Father and Christ.——Now, that he should ever be content to part with a Son, and such an only One, is such a manifestation of love, as will be admired to all eternity. And then,

2. Let it be considered, To what he gave him, even to death, and that of the cross; to be made a curse for us; to be the scorn and contempt of men; to the most unparalleled sufferings that ever were inflicted or borne by any. It melts our bowels, it breaks our heart, to behold our children striving in the pangs of death: but the Lord beheld his Son struggling under agonies that never any felt before him. He saw him falling to the ground, grovelling in the dust, sweating blood, and amidst those agonies turning himself to his Father, and, with a heart-rending cry, beseeching him, "Father, if it be possible, let this cup pass," Luke xxii. 42. To wrath, to the wrath of an infinite God without mixture; to the very torments of hell was Christ delivered, and that by the hand of his own Father. Sure then that love must needs want a name, which made the Father of mercies deliver his only Son to such miseries for us.

3. It is a special consideration to enhance the love of God in giving Christ, that in giving him he gave the richest jewel in his cabinet, a mercy of the greatest worth, and most inestimable value. Heaven itself is not so valuable and precious as Christ is: "Whom have I in heaven but thee?" Psa. lxxiii. 25. Oh what a fair One! what an only One! what an excellent, lovely One, is Christ! Put the beauty of ten thousand paradises, like the garden of Eden, into one; put all trees, all flowers, all smells, all colours, all tastes, all joys, all sweetness, all loveliness in one; oh what a fair and excellent thing would that be! And yet it should be less to that fair and dearest well-beloved Christ, than one drop of rain to the whole seas, rivers, lakes, and fountains of ten thousand earths. Now, for God to bestow the mercy of mercies, the most precious thing in heaven or earth, upon poor sinners; and, as great, as lovely, as excellent as his Son was,

yet not to account him too good to bestow upon us, what manner of love is this!

4. Once more, let it be considered on whom the Lord bestowed his Son: upon angels? No, but upon men. Upon men his friends? No, but upon his enemies. This is love; and on this consideration the apostle lays a mighty weight, in Rom. v. 8—10. "But God (saith he) commendeth his love towards us, in that while we were yet sinners, Christ died for us.—When we were yet enemies, we were reconciled to God by the death of his Son." Who would part with a son for the sake of his dearest friends? but God gave him to, and delivered him for enemies: O love unspeakable!

5. Let us consider how freely this gift came from him. It was not wrested out of his hand by our importunity; for we as little desired as deserved it. It was surprising, preventing, eternal love, that delivered him to us: "Not that we loved him, but he first loved us," 1 John iv. 19. Thus, as when you weigh a thing, you cast in weight after weight, till the scales break; so doth God, one consideration upon another, to overcome our hearts, and make us admiringly to cry, What manner of love is this! Thus I have showed you what God's giving of Christ is, and what matchless love is manifested in that incomparable gift.

Next we shall apply this, in some practical inferences.

1. Learn hence, the exceeding preciousness of souls, and at what a high rate God values them, that he gave his Son, his only Son out of his bosom, as a ransom for them. Surely this speaks their preciousness: all the world could not redeem them; gold and silver could not be their ransom; so speaks the apostle, "You were not redeemed with corruptible things, as silver and gold, but with the precious blood of Christ," 1 Pet. i. 18. Such an esteem God had for them, that rather than they should perish, Jesus Christ shall be made a man, yea, a curse for them. Oh then, learn to put a due value upon your own souls: do not sell that cheap, which God hath paid so dear for: remember what a treasure you carry about you; the glory that you see in this world is not equivalent in worth to it; "What shall a man give in exchange for his soul?" Matt. xvi. 26.

2. If God has given his own Son for the world, then it follows, that those for whom God gave his own Son may warrantably expect any other temporal mercies from him. This is the apostle's inference, "He that spared not his own Son, but delivered him up for us all; how shall he not, with him, freely give us all things?" Rom. viii. 32. And so 1 Cor. iii. 21—23,

" All is yours, for ye are Christ's," that is, they hold all other things in Christ, who is the capital, and most comprehensive mercy.

To make out the grounds of this comfortable deduction, let these four things be pondered, and duly weighed in your thoughts.

(1.) No other mercy you need or desire, is, or can be so dear to God, as Jesus Christ is: as for the world, and the comforts of it, it is the dust of his feet, he values it not; as you see by his providential disposals of it; having given it to the worst of men. " All the turkish empire," saith Luther, " as great and glorious as it is, is but a crumb which the Master of the family throws to the dogs." Think upon any other outward enjoyment that is valuable in your eyes, and there is not so much comparison between it and Christ, in the esteem of God, as is between your dear children and the lumber of your houses, in your esteem. If then God has parted so freely from that which was infinitely dearer to him than these; how shall he deny these, when they may promote his glory, and your good?

(2.) As Jesus Christ was nearer the heart of God than all these; so Christ is, in himself, much greater and more excellent than all of them. Ten thousand worlds, and the glory of them all, is but the dust of the balance, if weighed with Christ. These things are but poor creatures, but he is over all, God blessed for ever, Rom. ix. 5. They are common gifts, but he is the Gift of God, John iv. 10. They are ordinary mercies, but he is The Mercy, Luke i. 72. As one pearl or precious stone is greater in value than ten thousand common pebbles. Now, if God has so freely given the greater, how can you suppose he should deny the lesser mercies? Will a man give to another a large inheritance, and stand with him for a trifle? how can it be?

(3.) There is no other mercy you want, but you are entitled to it by the gift of Christ; it is, as to right, conveyed to you with Christ. So, in the fore-cited 1 Cor. iii. 21—23, " the world is yours, yea, all is yours; for ye are Christ's." So 2 Cor. i. 20, " For all the promises of God in Christ, in him they are yea, and in him, amen." With him he hath given you all things richly to enjoy, 1 Tim. vi. 17.

(4.) If God has given you this nearer, greater, and all-comprehending mercy, when you were enemies to him, and alienated from him; it is not imaginable he should deny you any inferior mercy, when you are come into a state of reconciliation and amity with him. So the apostle reasons, " For if, when we were enemies, we were reconciled to God by the death of his Son;

much more, being reconciled, we shall be saved by his life,"
Rom. v. 8—10.

3. If the greatest love hath been manifested in giving Christ
to the world, then it follows, that the greatest evil and wickedness is manifested in despising, slighting, and rejecting Christ.
It is sad to abuse the love of God manifested in the least gift of
providence ; but, to slight the richest discoveries of it, even in
that peerless gift, wherein God commends his love in the most
astonishing manner ; this is sin beyond description. Blush, O
heavens, and be astonished, O earth ; yea, be ye horribly afraid !
No guilt like this. But, are there any such in the world ?
Dare any slight this gift of God ? Indeed, if men's words might
be taken, there are few or none that dare do. so ; but if their
lives and practices may be believed, this, this is the sin of the
far greater part of the christianized world. Witness the lamentable stupidity and supineness ; witness the contempt of the
gospel ;- witness the hatred and persecution of his image, laws,
and people.   What is the language of all this, but a vile esteem
of Jesus Christ ?

And now, let me a little expostulate with those ungrateful
souls, that trample under foot the Son of God, that value not
this love that gave him forth.   What is that mercy which you
so contemn and undervalue ? is it so vile and cheap a thing as
your conduct speaks it. to be ? is it indeed worth no more than
this in your eyes ? Surely you will not be long of that opinion !
Will you be of that mind, think you, when death and judgment
shall have thoroughly awakened you ? Oh, no : then a thousand worlds for Christ ! Or think ye, that any beside you in the
world are of your mind ? You are deceived, if you think so ;
" To them that believe he is precious," 1 Pet. ii. 7, through
all the world.   And in the other world they are of a quite contrary mind.   Could you but hear what is said of him in heaven,
in what a dialect the saved of the Lord do extol their Saviour ;
or could you but imagine the self-revenges, the self-torments,
which the damned suffer for their folly, and what a value they
would set upon one tender of Christ, if it might but again be
hoped for ; you would see that such as you are the only despisers of Christ.   Beside, methinks it is astonishing, that you
should despise a mercy in which your own souls are so dearly,
so deeply, so everlastingly concerned, as they are in this gift of
God.   If it were but the soul of another, nay, less, if but the
body of another, and yet less than that, if but another's beast,
whose life you could preserve, you are obliged to do it ; but
when it is thyself, yea, the best part of thyself, thine own in-

valuable soul, that thou ruinest and destroyest thereby, oh, what a monster art thou, to cast it away thus! What! will you slight your own souls? care you not whether they be saved, or whether they be damned? is it indeed an indifferent thing with you which way they fall at death? have you imagined a tolerable hell? is it easy to perish? are you not only turned God's enemies, but your own too? Oh see what monsters sin can turn men and women into! Oh the stupifying, besotting, intoxicating power of sin! But perhaps you think that all these are but uncertain sounds, with which we alarm you; it may be thine own heart will preach such doctrine as this to thee: Who can assure thee of the reality of these things? why shouldst thou trouble thyself with an invisible world, or be so much concerned for what thine eyes never saw, nor didst ever receive the report from any that have seen them? Well, though we cannot now show you these things, yet shortly they shall be shown you; and your own eyes shall behold them. You are convinced and satisfied that many other things are real which you never saw: but be assured, that " if the word spoken by angels was stedfast, and every transgression and disobedience received a just recompence of reward, how shall we escape, if we neglect so great a salvation, which at first began to be spoken to us by the Lord, and was confirmed to us by them that heard him, God also bearing them witness?" Heb. ii. 2—4. But, perhaps you say, if they be certain, yet they are not near; it will be a long time before they come. Poor soul! how dost thou cheat thyself! It may be not one twentieth part so long a time as thy own fancy draws it forth for thee; thou art not certain of the next moment.

And suppose what thou imaginest: what are twenty or forty years when they are past? yea, what are a thousand years to vast eternity? Go trifle away a few days more, sleep out a few nights more, and then lie down in the dust; it will not be long ere the trump of God shall awaken thee, and thine eyes shall behold Jesus coming in the clouds of heaven, and then you will know the price of this sin. Oh, therefore, if there be any sense of eternity upon you, any pity or love for yourselves in you; if you have any concernments more than the beasts that perish, despise not your own offered mercies, slight not the richest gift that ever was yet opened to the world; and a sweeter cannot be opened to all eternity.

SERMON V.

OF CHRIST'S WONDERFUL PERSON.

JOHN I. 14.

AND THE WORD WAS MADE FLESH, AND DWELT AMONG US.

You have heard the covenant of redemption opened. It is such as infinitely exceeds the power of any mere creature to perform. He that undertakes to satisfy God, by obedience for man's sin, must himself be God; and he that performs such a perfect obedience, by doing and suffering all that the law required, in our room, must be man. These two natures must be united in one person, else there could not be a concourse or co-operation of each nature in his mediatorial work. How these natures are united, in the wonderful person of our Immanuel, is the first part of the great mystery of godliness : a subject studied and adored by angels! and the mystery thereof is wrapped up in this text. Wherein we have,

1. The incarnation of the Son of God plainly asserted.
2. That assertion strongly confirmed.

1. In the assertion we have three parts.

(1.) The Person assuming, ο Λογος, the Word, that is, the second Person or Subsistent in the most glorious Godhead; called the Word, either because he is the scope or principal matter, both of the prophetical and promissory word; or because he expounds and reveals the mind and will of God to men, as verse 18. The only begotten Son which is in the bosom of the Father, he hath declared or expounded him.

(2.) The nature assumed, σαρξ, flesh, that is, the entire human nature, consisting of a true human soul and body. For so this word σαρξ, in Rom. iii. 20, and the hebrew word בשׂר which answers to it, by a usual metonomy of a part for the whole, is used, Gen. vi. 12. And the word flesh is rather used here, than man, on purpose to enhance the admirable condescension and abasement of Christ; there being more of vileness, weakness, and opposition to spirit in this word, than in that, as is pertinently noted by some. Hence the whole nature is denominated by that part, and called flesh.

c 3

(3.) The assumption itself, *εγενετο*, he was made; not *fuit*, he was, (as Socinus would render it, designing thereby to overthrow the existence of Christ's glorified body now in heaven,) but *factus est*, he was made, that is, he took or assumed the true human nature into the unity of his Divine person, with all its integral parts and essential properties; and so was made, or became a true and real man, by that assumption. The apostle speaking of the same act, Heb. ii. 16, uses another word, He took on him, or he assumed. And when it is said, he was made flesh, misconceive not, as if there was a mutation of the Godhead into flesh; for this was performed, "not by changing what he was, but by assuming what he was not," as Augustine well expresseth it. As when the scripture, in a like expression, saith, "He was made sin," 2 Cor. v. 21, and made a curse, Gal. iii. 13, the meaning is not, that he was turned into sin, or into a curse; no more may we think here the Godhead was turned into flesh, and lost its own being and nature, because it is said he was made flesh. This is the sum of the assertion.

2. This assertion "that the word was made flesh," is strongly confirmed. He "dwelt among us," and we saw his glory. This was no phantasm, but a most real and indubitable thing. For, *εσκηνωσεν εν ημιν*, pitched his tent, or tabernacled with us. And we are eye-witnesses of it. Parallel to that, "That which was from the beginning, which we have heard, which we have seen with our eyes, which we have looked upon, and our hands have handled, of the Word of life, &c. declare we unto you," 1 John i. 1—3. Hence note,

Doct. THAT JESUS CHRIST DID REALLY ASSUME THE TRUE AND PERFECT NATURE OF MAN, INTO A PERSONAL UNION WITH HIS DIVINE NATURE, AND STILL REMAINS TRUE GOD, AND TRUE MAN, IN ONE PERSON, FOR EVER.

The proposition contains one of the deepest mysteries of godliness, 1 Tim. iii. 16. A mystery, by which apprehension is dazzled, invention astonished, and all expression swallowed up. If ever the tongues of angels were desirable to explicate any word of God, they are so here. The proper use of words is of great importance in this doctrine. We walk upon the brink of danger. The least tread awry may ingulf us in the bogs of error. Arius would have been content, if the council of Nice would but have gratified him in a letter, *ομοουσιος*, and *ομοιουσιος*. The nestorians also desired but a letter, *Θεοδοχος*, *Θεοτοκος*. These seemed but small and modest requests, but, if granted,

had proved no small prejudice to the truth. I desire therefore
the reader would, with greatest attention of mind, apply himself
to these truths. It is a doctrine hard to understand, and dangerous to mistake. I am really of his mind that said,* "It is
better not touch the bottom, than not keep within the circle:"
Melius est nescire centrum, quam non tenere circulum. He did
assume a true human body; that is plainly asserted, Phil. ii. 7,
8, &c. Heb. ii. 14. 16. In one place it is called taking on him
the seed of Abraham, and in the text, flesh. He did also assume a true human soul, this is undeniable by its operations,
passions, and expiration at last, Matt. xxvi. 38, and xxvii. 50.
And that both these natures make but one person, is as evident
from Rom. i. 3, 4, "Jesus Christ was made of the seed of
David according to the flesh, and declared to be the Son of God
with power, according to the Spirit of holiness, by the resurrection from the dead." So Rom. ix. 5, "Of whom, as concerning the flesh, Christ came, who is over all, God blessed for ever.
Amen." But that you may have a sound and clear understanding of this mystery, I will, I. Open the nature; II. The effects;
and III. The reasons or ends of this wonderful union.

I. The nature of this union.

This assumption of which I speak, is that whereby the Second
Person in the Godhead did take the human nature into a personal union with himself, by virtue whereof the manhood subsists
in the Second Person, yet without confusion, both making but
one person, Immanuel, God with us.

So that though we truly ascribe a twofold nature to Christ,
yet not a double person; for the human nature of Christ never
subsisted separately and distinctly, by any personal subsistence
of its own, as it doth in all other men, but from the first moment
of conception, subsisted in union with the Second Person.

To explicate this mystery more particularly, let it be considered:

1. The human nature was united to the Second Person miraculously and extraordinarily, being supernaturally framed in the
womb of the virgin, by the over-shadowing power of the Highest, Luke i. 34, 35. And this was necessary to exempt the assumed nature from the stain and pollution of Adam's sin, which
it wholly escaped; inasmuch as he received it not, as all others
do, in the way of ordinary generation, wherein original sin is
propagated; but this being extraordinarily produced, was a most
pure and holy thing, Luke i. 35. And indeed this perfect shining holiness, in which it was produced, was absolutely necessary,
both in order to its union with the Divine Person, and the design

* Prosper.

of that union; which was both to satisfy for, and to sanctify us. The two natures could not be conjoined in the person of Christ, had there been the least taint of sin upon the human nature. For God can have no fellowship with sin, much less be united to it. Or, supposing such a conjunction with our sinful nature, yet he being a sinner himself, could never satisfy for the sins of others; nor could any unholy thing ever make us holy. "Such an High Priest therefore became us as is holy, harmless, undefiled, separate from sinners," Heb. vii. 26. And such a one he must needs be, whom the Holy Ghost produced in such a peculiar way, το αγιον, that holy thing.

2. As it was produced miraculously, so it was assumed integrally; that is to say, Christ took a complete and perfect human soul and body, with all and every faculty and member pertaining to it. And this was necessary, (as both Austin and Fulgentius have well observed,) that thereby he might heal the whole nature of that leprosy of sin, which hath seized and infected every member and faculty. "He assumed all to sanctify all;" as Damascen expresseth it. He designed a perfect recovery, by sanctifying us wholly in soul, body, and spirit; and therefore assumed the whole in order to it.

3. He assumed our nature, as with all its integral parts, so with all its sinless infirmities. And therefore it is said of him, "That it behoved him," κατα παντα ομοιωθηναι, according to all things (that is, all things natural, not formally sinful, as it is limited by the same apostle, Heb. iv. 15) "to be made like unto his brethren," Heb. ii. 17. But here our divines so carefully distinguish infirmities into personal and natural. Personal infirmities are such as befall particular persons, from particular causes, such as dumbness, blindness, lameness, leprosies, monstrosities, and other deformities. These it was no way necessary that Christ should, nor did he at all assume; but the natural ones, such as hunger, thirst, weariness, sweating, bleeding, mortality, &c. which though they are not in themselves formally and intrinsically sinful, yet are they the effects and consequents of sin. They are so many marks, that sin hath left of itself upon our natures. And on that account Christ is said to be sent "in the likeness of sinful flesh," Rom. viii. 3. Wherein the gracious condescension of Christ for us is marvellously signalized, that he would not assume our innocent nature, as it was in Adam before the fall, while it stood in all its primitive glory and perfection; but after sin had quite defaced, ruined, and spoiled it.

4. The human nature is so united with the Divine, as that

each nature still retains its own essential properties distinct. And this distinction is not, nor can be lost by that union.

II. For the effects, or immediate results of this marvellous union, let these three be well considered.

1. The two natures being thus united in the person of the Mediator, by virtue thereof the properties of each nature are attributed, and do truly agree in the whole person; so that it is proper to say, the Lord of glory was crucified, 1 Cor. ii. 8, and, the blood of God redeemed the church, Acts xx. 28, that Christ was both in heaven and in the earth at the same time, John iii. 13.

Yet we do not believe that one nature doth transfuse or impart its properties to the other, or that it is proper to say the Divine nature suffered, bled, or died; or the human is omniscient, omnipotent, omnipresent; but that the properties of both natures are so ascribed to the person, that it is proper to affirm any of them of him in the concrete, though not abstractly. The right understanding of this would greatly assist in teaching the true sense of the fore-named, and many other dark passages in the scriptures.

2. Another fruit of this hypostatical union, is the singular advancement of the human nature in Christ, far beyond and above what it is capable of in any other person, it being hereby replenished and filled with an unparalleled measure of Divine graces and excellences; in which respect he is said to be " anointed above" or before " his fellows," Psa. xlv. 7, and so becomes the object of adoration and divine worship, Acts vii. 59.

3. Hence, in the last place, follows, as another excellent fruit of this union, the concourse and co-operation of each nature in his mediatorial works; for in them he acts according to both natures: the human nature doing what is human, namely, suffering, sweating, bleeding, dying; and his Divine nature stamping all these with infinite value; and so both sweetly concur unto one glorious work and design of mediation. Papists generally deny that he performs any of these mediatorial works as God, but only as man; but how boldly do they therein contradict these plain scriptures! See 2 Cor. v. 10; Heb. ix. 14, 15.

III. The last thing to be opened is the grounds and reasons of this assumption. And we may say, touching that, (1.) That the human nature was not assumed to any intrinsical perfection of the Godhead, not to make that human nature itself perfect. The Divine did not assume the human nature necessarily, but voluntarily; not out ' of indigence, but bounty; not because it was to be perfected by it, but to perfect it. And so, consequently, to qualify and prepare him for a full discharge of his mediatorship, in the offices of our Prophet, Priest, and King.

Had he not possessed this double nature in the unity of his person, he could not have been our Prophet : for, as God, he knows the mind and will of God, John i. 18, and iii. 13; and as man he is fitted to impart it suitably to us, Deut. xviii. 15—18, compared with Acts xx. 22. As Priest, had he not been man, he could have shed no blood; and if not God, it had been no adequate value for us, Heb. ii. 17; Acts iii. 28. As King, had he not been man, he had been a heterogeneous, and so no fit head for us ; and if not God, he could neither rule nor defend his body the church. These then were the designs and ends of that assumption.

Use 1. Let all christians rightly inform their minds in this truth of so great concernment in religion, and hold it fast against all subtle adversaries, that would wrest it from them. The learned Hooker observes, that the dividing of Christ's person, which is but one, and the confounding of his natures, which are two, hath been the occasion of those errors, which have so greatly disturbed the peace of the church. The arians denied his Deity, levelling him with other mere men. The apollinarians maimed his humanity. The sabellians affirmed, that the Father and Holy Ghost were incarnated as well as the Son ; and were forced upon that absurdity by another error, namely, denying the three distinct persons in the Godhead, and affirming they were but three names. The eutychians confounded both natures in Christ, denying any distinction of them. The seleusians affirmed, that he unclothed himself of his humanity when he ascended, and hath no human body in heaven. The nestorians so rent the two names of Christ asunder, as to make two distinct persons of them.

But ye, beloved, have not so learned Christ. Ye know he is, (1.) True and very God; (2.) True and very man ; that, (3.) These two natures make but one person, being united inseparably; (4.) That they are not confounded or swallowed up one in another, but remain still distinct in the person of Christ. Hold ye the sound words which cannot be condemned. Great things hang upon all these truths. O suffer not a stone to be loosed out of the foundation.

2. Adore the love of the Father, and the Son, who valued your souls so highly, and were willing to save you at such a cost.

The love of the Father is herein admirably conspicuous, who so vehemently willed our salvation, that he was content to degrade the beloved of his soul to so vile and contemptible a state.

And how astonishing is the love of Christ, that would make such a stoop as this to exalt us ! Oh that you would get your hearts suitably impressed and affected with these high impressures of the love both of the Father and the Son ! How is the courage of some noble romans celebrated in history, for the brave adventures they made for the commonwealth; but they could never stoop as Christ did, being so infinitely below him in personal dignity.

3. And here infinite wisdom has also left a famous and everlasting mark of itself; which invites, yea, even chains the eyes of angels and men to itself. Had there been a general council of angels, to advise upon a way of recovering poor sinners, they would all have been at an everlasting demur and loss about it. It could not have entered their thoughts, (though they are most intelligent and sagacious creatures,) that ever mercy, pardon, and grace, should find such a way as this to issue forth from the heart of God to the hearts of sinners. Oh, how wisely is the method of our recovery laid ! so that Christ may be well called, "the power and wisdom of God," 1 Cor. i. 24; forasmuch as in him the Divine wisdom is more glorified than in all the other works of God, upon which he hath impressed it.

4. Hence also we infer the incomparable excellency of the christian religion, that shows poor sinners such a sure foundation to rest their trembling consciences upon. While poor distressed souls look to themselves, they are perpetually puzzled. That is the cry of a distressed natural conscience, " Wherewith shall I come before the Lord?" Mic. vi. 6. The hebrew is אקדם יהוה, How shall I prevent or anticipate the Lord? and so Montanus renders it, In quo præoccupabo Dominum? Conscience sees God arming himself with wrath, to avenge himself for sin ; cries out, Oh, how shall I prevent him ; if he would accept the fruit of my body (those dear pledges of nature) for the sin of my soul, he should have them. But now we see God coming down in flesh, and so intimately uniting our flesh to himself, that it hath no proper subsistence of its own, but is united with the Divine person: hence it is easy to imagine what worth and value must be in that blood ; and how eternal love, springing forth triumphantly from it, flourishes into pardon, grace, and peace. Here is a way in which the sinner may see justice and mercy kissing each other, and the latter exercised freely, without prejudice to the former. All other consciences, through the world, lie either in a deep sleep in the devil's arms, or else are rolling (sea sick) upon the waves of their own fears and dismal presages. Oh, happy are they that have dropped anchor on this

ground, and not only know they have peace, but why they have it.

5. Of how great concernment is it, that Christ should have union with our particular persons, as well as with our common nature! For by this union with our nature alone, never any man was, or can be saved. Yea, let me add, that this union with our natures, is utterly in vain to you, and will do you no good, except he have union with your persons by faith also. It is indeed infinite mercy, that God is come so near you, as to dwell in your flesh; and that he hath fixed upon such an excellent method to save poor sinners. And hath he done all this? is he indeed come home, even to your own doors, to seek peace? doth he veil his insupportable glory under flesh, that he might treat the more familiarly? and yet do you refuse him, and shut your hearts against him? Then hear one word, and let thine ears tingle at the sound of it: thy sin is thereby aggravated beyond the sin of devils, who never sinned against a mediator in their own nature; who never despised, or refused, because, indeed, they were never offered terms of mercy, as you are. And I doubt not but the devils themselves, who now tempt you to reject, will, to all eternity, upbraid your folly for rejecting this great salvation, which in this excellent way is brought down, even to your own doors.

6. If Jesus Christ has assumed our nature, then he is sensibly touched with the infirmities that attend it, and so hath pity and compassion for us, under all our burdens. And indeed this was one end of his assuming it, that he might be able to have compassion on us, as you read, "Wherefore in all things it behoved him to be made like unto his brethren, that he might be a merciful and faithful High Priest, in things pertaining to God, to make reconciliation for the sins of the people. For in that he himself hath suffered, being tempted, he is able to succour them that are tempted," Heb. ii. 17, 18. Oh what a comfort is this to us, that he who is our High Priest in heaven, hath our nature to enable him to take compassion on us!

7. Hence we see, to what a height God intends to build up the happiness of man, in that he hath laid the foundation thereof so deep, in the incarnation of his own Son.

They that intend to build high, lay the foundation low. The happiness and glory of our bodies, as well as our souls, are founded in Christ's taking our flesh upon him: for therein, as in a model or pattern, God intended to show what in time he resolves to make of our bodies; for he will transform our vile bodies, and make them one day conformable to the glorious body of Jesus

Christ, Phil. iii. 21.   This flesh was therefore assumed by
Christ, that in it might be shown, as in a pattern, how God intends to honour and exalt it.   And indeed, a greater honour
cannot be done to the nature of man, than what is already done,
by this grace of union; nor are our persons capable of higher
glory, than what consists in their conformity to this glorious
Head.

8. How wonderful a comfort is it, that he who dwells in our
flesh is God!   What joy may not a poor believer make out
of this!

God and man in one person! Oh! thrice happy conjunction!
As man, he is full of experimental sense of our infirmities, wants,
and burdens; and, as God, he can support and supply them all.
The aspect of faith upon this wonderful Person, how relieving,
how reviving, how abundantly satisfying is it!   God will never
divorce the believing soul, and its comfort, after he hath married
our nature to his own Son, by the hypostatical, and our persons
also, by the blessed mystical union.

SERMON VI.

OF THE AUTHORITY BY WHICH CHRIST, AS MEDIATOR, ACTED.

JOHN VI. 27.

FOR HIM HATH GOD THE FATHER SEALED.

THIS scripture is a part of Christ's excellent reply to an earthly-minded multitude, who followed him, not for any spiritual excellencies that they saw in him, or soul-advantages they expected by him, but for bread. Instead of making his service their meat and drink, they only served him that they might eat and drink. Self is a thing that may creep into the best hearts and actions ; but it only predominates in the hypocrite. These people had sought Christ from place to place, and having at last found him, they salute him with the question, " Rabbi, whence camest thou hither ? " verse 25. Christ's reply is partly dissuasive, and partly directive. He dissuades them from putting the secondary and subordinate, in the place of the principal and ultimate end ; not to prefer their bodies to their souls, their fleshly accommodations to the glory of God. " Labour nor for the meat that perisheth." Wherein he doth not take them off from their lawful labours and callings ; but he dissuades them, first, from minding those things too intently ; and, secondly, he dissuades them from that odious sin of making religion but a pretence for the belly.

And it is partly directive, and that in the main end and business of life. " But labour for that meat which endureth to eternal life ;" to get bread for your souls to live eternally by. And, that he might engage their diligence in seeking it to purpose, he shows them not only where they may have it, ("which the Son of man shall give you,") but also how they may be fully satisfied, that he hath it for them, in the clause I have pitched on ; " For him hath God the Father sealed."

In these words are three parts observable.

1. The Person sealing or investing Christ with authority and power; which is said to be God the Father. Though all the persons in the Godhead are equal in nature, dignity, and power, yet in their operation there is an order observed among them;

the Father sends the Son, the Son is sent by the Father, the Holy Ghost is sent by both.

2. The subject in which God the Father lodges this authority, "Him" that is, the Son of man. God the Father hath so sealed him, as he never sealed any other before him, or that shall arise after him. No name is given in heaven, or earth, but this name, by which we are saved, Acts iv. 12. "The government is upon his shoulder," Isa. ix. 6.

3. Here is further observable, the way and manner of the Father's delegating and committing this authority to Christ; and that is, by sealing him. Where we have both a metonomy, the symbol of authority being put for the authority itself, and a metaphor, sealing, which is a human act, for the ratifying and confirming an instrument, or grant, being here applied to God. Like as princes, by sealed credentials, confirm the authority of those that are sent by them; as the dutch annotators well express the meaning of it. Hence we note,

> DOCT. THAT JESUS CHRIST DID NOT OF HIMSELF UNDERTAKE THE WORK OF OUR REDEMPTION, BUT WAS SOLEMNLY SEALED UNTO THAT WORK BY GOD THE FATHER.

When I say, he did not of himself undertake this work, I mean not that he was unwilling to go about it, for his heart was as fully and ardently engaged in it, as the Father's was : so he tells us, "Lo, I come to do thy will, O God; thy law is in my heart," Psa. xl. 7, 8. But the meaning is, he came not without a due call, and full commission from his Father. And this is the meaning of that scripture, "I proceeded and came from God; neither came I of myself, but he sent me," John viii. 42. And this the apostle plainly expresseth, "And no man taketh this honour to himself, but he that is called of God, as was Aaron : so also Christ glorified not himself to be made an High Priest; but he that said unto him, Thou art my Son," Heb. v. 4, 5. And on the account of these sealed credentials which he received from the Father, he is called the Apostle and High Priest of our profession, Heb. iii. 1, that is, one called and sent forth by the Father's authority.

Our present business, then, is to open Christ's commission, and to view the great seal of heaven by which it was ratified.

And, to preserve a clear method in the explication of this great truth, into which your faith and comfort is resolved, I shall, I. Show what was the work and office to which the Father sealed him. II. What his sealing to this work doth imply. III. How, and by what acts, the Father sealed him to it. IV. Why it was necessary that he should be thus sealed and authorized by his Father.   And then improve it in its proper uses.

I. What was that office, or work, to which his Father sealed him?   I answer, more generally, he was sealed to the whole work of mediation for us, thereby to recover and save all the elect, whom the Father had given him: so John xvii. 2. "It was to give eternal life to as many as was given him:" it was "to bring Jacob again to him," Isa. xlix. 5, or, as the apostle expresses it, "that he might bring us to God," 1 Pet. iii. 18. More particularly, in order to the sure and full effecting of this most glorious design, he was sealed to the offices of a Prophet, Priest, and King, that so he might bring about and compass this work.

1. God sealed him a commission to preach the glad tidings of salvation to sinners.   This commission Christ opened and read in the audience of the people; "And when he had opened the book, he found the place where it was written, The Spirit of the Lord is upon me, because he hath anointed me to preach the gospel to the poor; he hath sent me to heal the broken-hearted, to preach deliverance to the captives, and the recovering of sight to the blind, to set at liberty them that are bruised; to preach the acceptable year of the Lord.   And he closed the book, &c. And he began to say unto them, This day is this scripture fulfilled in your ears," Luke iv. 17—21.

2. He also sealed him to the priesthood, and that the most excellent; authorizing him to execute both the parts of it, namely, oblatory and intercessory.   He called him to offer up himself a sacrifice for us; "I have power (saith he) to lay down my life; this commandment have I received of my Father," John x. 18. And upon that account, his offering up of his blood is, by the apostle, styled an act of obedience, as it is, Phil. ii. 8. "He became obedient unto death," He also called him to intercede for us; "Those priests were made without an oath; but this with an oath by him that said unto him, The Lord sware, and will not repent, Thou art a Priest for ever," Heb. vii. 21. 24, 25: because his sacrifice is virtually continued, in his living for ever to make intercession, as it is, verse 24.   Yea,

3. He called him to his regal office; he was set upon the highest throne of authority by his Father's commission, as it is, Matt. xxviii. 18, "All power in heaven and earth is given to me." To all this was Christ sealed and authorized by his Father.

II. What doth the Father's sealing of Christ to this work and office imply?   There are divers things implied in it: as,

1. The validity and efficacy of all his mediatorial acts. For by virtue of this his sealing whatever he did was fully ratified. And in this very thing lies much of a believer's comfort and security; forasmuch as all acts done without commission and authority (how great, or able soever the person that doth them is, yet) are in themselves null and void. But what is done by commission and authority, is authentic, and most efficacious among men.

2. It imports the great obligations lying upon Jesus Christ to be faithful in the work he was sealed to : for, the Father, in this commission, devolves a great trust upon him, and relies upon him for his most faithful discharge thereof. And, indeed, upon this very account Christ reckons himself specially obliged to pursue the Father's design and end; "I must work the works of him that sent me," John ix. 4. And, "I seek not mine own will, but the will of the Father which hath sent me," John v. 30. Still his eye is upon that work and will of his Father. And he reckons himself under a necessity of punctual and precise obedience to it; and, as a faithful servant, will have his own will swallowed up in his Father's will.

3. It imports Christ's complete qualification and fitness to serve the Father's design and end of our recovery. Had not God known him to be every way fit, and qualified for the work, he would never have sealed him a commission for it. Men may, but God will not seal an unfit or incapable person, for his work. And, indeed, whatever is desirable in a servant, was eminently found in Christ. For faithfulness, none like him. Moses indeed was faithful in every point, but still as a servant ; but Christ as a Son, Heb. iii. 6. He is the faithful and true Witness, Rev. i. 5. For zeal, none like him. The zeal of God's house did eat him up, John ii. 16, 17. He was so intent upon his Father's work that he forgot to eat bread, counting his work his meat and drink, John iv. 32. Yea, and love to his Father carried him on through all his work, and made him delight in the hardest piece of his service ; for he served him as a Son, Heb. iii. 5, 6. All that ever he did was done in love. For wisdom, none like him. The Father knew him to be most wise, and said of him before he was employed, " Behold, my Servant shall deal prudently," Isa. lii. 13. To conclude, for self-denial, never any like him ; he sought not his own glory, but the glory of him that sent him, John viii. 50. Had he not been thus faithful, zealous, full of love, prudent, and self-denying, he had never been employed in this great affair.

4. It implies Christ's sole authority in the church, to appoint

and enjoin what he pleaseth ; and this is his peculiar prerogative. For, the commission God sealed him in the text, is a single, not a joint commission ; he hath sealed him, and none beside him. Indeed there were some that pretended a call and commission from God; but all that came before him, giving themselves out for the Messiah, were thieves and robbers, that came not in at the door, as he did, John x. 8. And he himself foretells, that after him some should arise, and labour to deceive the world with a feigned commission, and a counterfeit seal ; " There shall arise false Christs, and false prophets, and shall show great signs and wonders; insomuch, that if it were possible, they should deceive the very elect," Matt. xxiv. 24. But God never commissioned any besides him, neither is there any other name under heaven, Acts iv. 12. Thus you see how the validity of his acts, his obligation to be faithful, his complete qualifications, and sole authority in the church, are imported in his sealing.

III. Let us inquire how God the Father sealed Jesus Christ to this work ; and we shall find that he was sealed by four acts of the Father.

1. By solemn designation to this work. He singled him out and set him apart for it : and therefore the prophet Isaiah calls him God's elect, chap. xlii. 1. And the apostle Peter, Chosen of God, 1 Pet. ii. 4. This word which we render elect, doth not only signify one that in himself is surpassing, worthy, and excellent, but also one that is set apart and designed, as Christ was, for the work of mediation. And so much is included in John x. 36, where the Father is said to sanctify him, that is, to separate and devote him to this service.

2. He was sealed, not only by solemn designation, but also by supereminent and unparalleled sanctification. He was anointed, as well as appointed to it. The Lord filled him with the Spirit, and that without measure, to qualify him for this service. So Isa. lxi. 1—3. " The Spirit of the Lord is upon me, because he hath anointed me to preach," &c. Yea, the Spirit of the Lord was not only upon him, but he was full of the Spirit, Luke iv. 1, and so full as was never any beside him ; for God " anointed him with the oil of gladness above his fellows," Psa. xlv. 7. Believers are his fellows, or co-partners of this Spirit ; they have an anointing also, but not as Christ had ; in him it dwelt in its fulness, in them according to measure. It was poured out on Christ, our Head, abundantly, and ran down to the hem of his garment. " God gave not the Spirit to him by measure," John iii. 34. God filled Christ's human nature, to the utmost capacity, with all fulness of the Spirit of know-

ledge, wisdom, love, &c. beyond all creatures, for the plenary
and more effectual administration of his mediatorship; he was
full extensively, with all kinds of grace; and full intensively,
with all degrees of grace. "It pleased the Father that in him
should all fulness dwell," Col. i. 19, as light in the sun, or
water in a fountain; so that the holy oil that was poured out
upon the head of kings and priests, whereby they were consecrated to their offices, was but typical of the Spirit, by which
Christ was consecrated, or sealed, to his offices, Exod. xxx. 23
—25. 30—32.

3. Christ was sealed by the Father's immediate testimony
from heaven, whereby he was declared to be the person whom
the Father had solemnly designed and appointed to this work.
And God gave this extraordinary testimony of him at two remarkable seasons; the one was just at his entrance on his
public ministry, Matt. iii. 17; the other but a little before his
sufferings, Matt. xvii. 5. By this God owned, approved, and,
as by a seal, ratified his work.

4. Christ was sealed by the Father, in all those extraordinary
miraculous works wrought by him, by which the Father gave
yet more full and convincing testimonies to the world, that this
was he whom he had appointed to be our Mediator. These
were convictive to the world, that God had sent him, and that
his doctrine was of God. "God anointed Jesus of Nazareth
with the Holy Ghost and power, who went about doing good,
and healing all that were oppressed of the devil; for God was
with him," Acts x. 38. And so, John v. 36, "I have a greater
witness than that of John; for the works which the Father hath
given me to finish, the same works that I do, bear witness of me,
that the Father hath sent me." Therefore he still referred those
that doubted of him, or of his doctrine, to the seal of his Father,
even the miraculous works he wrought in the power of God,
Matt. xi. 3—5. And thus the Father sealed him.

IV. We will inquire why it was necessary Christ should be
sealed by his Father to this work: and there are these three
weighty reasons for it.

1. Else he had not corresponded with the types which prefigured him; and in him it was necessary that they should be
all accomplished. You know, under the law, the kings and
high priests had their inaugurations by solemn unctions; in all
which this consecration, or sealing of Christ to his work, was
shadowed out: and therefore you find, Heb. v. 4, 5. "No man
taketh this honour unto himself, but he that is called of God, as
was Aaron. So also," (mark the necessary correspondence

between Christ and them) " Christ glorified not himself to be made an High Priest ; but he that said unto him, Thou art my Son," Heb. v. 4, 5.

2. Moreover, hereby the hearts of believers are the more engaged to love the Father, inasmuch as it appears hereby that the Father's love and good will to them, was the origin and spring of their redemption. For had not the Father sealed him such a commission, he had not come ; but now he comes in the Father's name, and in the Father's love as well as his name ; and so all men are bound to ascribe equal glory and honour to them both, as it is, John v. 23.

3. And especially Christ would not come without a commission, because, in that case, we should have had no ground for our faith in him. How should we have been satisfied that this is indeed the true Messiah, except he had opened his commission to the world, and showed his Father's seal annexed to it ? If he had come without his credentials from heaven, and only told the world that God had sent him, and that they must take his bare word for it, who could have rested his faith on that testimony ? And that is the true meaning of that place, John v. 31, " If I bear witness of myself, my witness is not true." How so ? You will say, doth not that contradict what he saith, John viii. 14, " Though I bear record of myself, yet my record is true." Therefore you must understand truth, not as it is opposed to reality ; but the meaning is, if I had only given you my bare word for it, and not brought other evidence from my Father, my testimony had not been authentic and valid, according to human laws ; but now all doubtings are precluded.

Let us next improve this in a few inferences.

1. Hence we infer the unreasonableness of infidelity, and how little those who reject Christ can have to pretend for their so doing. You see he hath opened his commission in the gospel, shown the world his Father's hand and seal to it, given as ample satisfaction as reason itself could desire, or expect ; yet even his own received him not, John i. 11. And he knew it before-hand, and therefore complained by the prophet, " Who hath believed our report ?" &c. Isa. liii. 1. Yea, and that he is believed on in the world, is by the apostle put among the great mysteries of godliness, 1 Tim. iii. 16. A man that well considers with what convincing evidence Christ comes, would rather think it a mystery that any should not believe. And it is equally as wonderful to see the facility that is in nature to comply (meanwhile) with any, even the most foolish imposture. Let a false Christ arise, and he shall deceive many, as it is, Matt. xxiv. 24. Of this

Christ complains, and not without great reason, " I am come in my Father's name, and ye receive me not: if another come in his own name, him will ye receive," John v. 43. *q. d.* You are incredulous to none but me: every deceiver, every pitiful cheat, that hath but wit, or rather wickedness, enough to tell you the Lord hath sent him, though you must take his own single word for it, he shall obtain and get disciples ; but though I come in my Father's name, that is, showing you a commission signed and sealed by him, doing those works which none but a God can do, yet ye receive me not.   But in all this we must adore the justice of God, permitting it to be so, giving men up to such unreasonable obstinacy and hardness. It is a sore plague that lies upon the world, and a wonder that we all are not ingulfed in the same infidelity.

2. Hence also we infer, how great an evil it is to intrude into the office of the ministry without a due call.   It is more than Christ himself would do ; he glorified not himself : the honours and advantages attending that office, have invited many to run before they were sent.   But surely this is an insufferable violation of Christ's order.

3. Hence be convinced of the great efficacy that is in all gospel ordinances duly administered ; for Christ having received full commission from his Father, and by virtue thereof having instituted and appointed these ordinances in the church, all the power in heaven is engaged to make them good, to confirm and ratify them.   Hence, in the censures of the church, you have that great expression, " Whatsoever ye bind or loose on earth, shall be bound or loosed in heaven," Matt. xviii. 18. And so, for the word and sacraments, " All power in heaven and earth is given unto me.   Go therefore," &c. Matt. xxviii. 18—20.   They are not the appointments of men ; your faith stands not in the wisdom of men, but in the power of God. That very power God the Father committed to Christ, is the fountain whence all gospel institutions flow.   And he hath promised to be with his officers, not only the extraordinary officers of that age, but with his ministers in succeeding ages to the end of the world.   Oh therefore, when we come to an ordinance, come not with slight thoughts, but with great reverence, and great expectations, remembering Christ is there to make all good.

4. Again, here you have another call to admire the grace and love, both of the Father and Son to your souls : it is not lawful to compare them, but it is duty to admire them.   Was it not wonderful grace in the Father to seal a commission for the death of his Son, for the humbling him as low as hell, and in

that method to save you, when you might have expected he should have sealed your mittimus for hell, rather than a commission for your salvation? He might rather have set his irreversible seal to the sentence of your damnation, than to a commission for his Son's humiliation for you. And no less is the love of Christ to be wondered at, that would accept such a commission as this for us, and receive this seal, understanding fully (as he did) what were the contents of that commission, that the Father delivered him thus sealed, and knowing that there could be no reversing of it afterwards.

Oh then, love the Lord Jesus, all ye his saints, for still you see more and more of his love breaking out upon you. I commend to you a sealed Saviour this day; oh that every one that reads these lines might, in a pang of love, cry out with the enamoured spouse, " Set me as a seal upon thy heart, as a seal upon thy arm; for love is strong as death, jealousy is cruel as the grave; the coals thereof are coals of fire, which have a most vehement flame," Cant. viii. 6.

5. Once more; hath God sealed Christ for you? Then draw forth the comfort of his sealing for you, and be restless till ye also be sealed by him.

(1.) Draw out the comfort of Christ's sealing for you. Remember that hereby God stands engaged, even by his own seal, to allow and confirm whatever Christ hath done in the business of our salvation. And on this ground you may thus plead with God: Lord, thou hast sealed Christ to this office, and therefore I depend upon it, that thou allowest all that he hath done, and all that he hath suffered for me, and wilt make good all that he hath promised me. If men will not deny their own seals, much less wilt thou.

(2.) Get your interest in Christ sealed to you by the Spirit, else you cannot have the comfort of Christ's being sealed for you. Now the Spirit seals two ways, objectively and effectually. The first is, by working those graces in us, which are the conditions of the promises: the latter is, by shining upon his own work, and helping the soul to discern it; which follows the other, both in order of nature, and of time. And these sealings of the Spirit are to be distinguished, both *ex parte subjecti*, or the quality of the person sealed, which always is a believer, Eph. i. 13, for there can be no reflex, till there have been a direct act of faith; and *ex parte materiæ*, by the matter of which that comfort is made; which if it be of the Spirit, is ever consonant to the written word, Isa. viii. 20. And partly by its effects: for it commonly produces in the sealed soul, great care and

caution to avoid sin, Eph. iv. 30.   Great love to God, 1 John
ii. 5.   Readiness to suffer any thing for Christ, Rom. v. 3—5.
Confidence in addresses to God, 1 John v. 13, 14, and great
humility and self-abasement ; as in Abraham, who lay on his
face when God sealed the covenant to him, Gen. xvii. 1—3.
This, oh this brings home the sweet and good of all, when this
seal is superadded to that.

SERMON VII.

OF THE SOLEMN CONSECRATION OF THE MEDIATOR.

JOHN XVII. 19.

AND FOR THEIR SAKES I SANCTIFY MYSELF.

JESUS Christ being fitted with a body, and authorized by a commission, now actually devotes, and sets himself apart to his work. In the former sermon you heard what the Father did; in this you shall hear what the Son hath done towards the further advancement of that glorious design of our salvation: He sanctified himself for our sakes. Wherein observe, Christ's sanctifying of himself; and, The end or design of his so doing.

1. You have Christ's sanctifying of himself. The word *sanctify* is not here to be understood for the cleansing, purifying, or making holy that which was before unclean and unholy, either in a moral sense, as we are cleansed from sin by sanctification; or in a ceremonial sense, as persons and things were sanctified under the law; though here is a plain allusion to those legal rites: but Christ's sanctifying himself imports, (1.) His separation, or setting apart to be an oblation or sacrifice. So Beza explains it, nempe ut sacerdos et victima, as the priest and sacrifice. I sanctify myself, imports, (2.) His consecration, or dedication of himself to this holy use and service. So the dutch annotations, I sanctify myself, that is, I give up myself to a holy sacrifice. And so our english annotations, I sanctify, that is, I consecrate and voluntarily offer myself a holy and unblemished sacrifice to thee for their redemption. And thus under the law, when any day, person, or vessel, was consecrated and dedicated to the Lord, it was so entirely for his use and service, that to use it afterward in any common service, was to profane and pollute it, as you see, Dan. v. 3.

2. The end of his so sanctifying himself, [for their sakes, and that they might be sanctified.] Where you see that the death of Christ wholly respects us; he offered not for himself as other priests did, but for us, that we may be sanctified. Christ is so in love with holiness, that at the price of his blood he will buy it for us. Hence the observation is;

Doct. That Jesus Christ did dedicate, and wholly set himself apart to the work of a Mediator, for the elect's sake.

This point is a glass, wherein the eye of your faith may see Jesus Christ preparing himself to be offered up to God for us, fitting himself to die. And to keep a clear method, I shall open these two things, in the doctrinal part: I. What his sanctifying himself implies: II. How it respects us.

I. What is implied in this phrase, "I sanctify myself." And there are seven things carried in it.

1. This expression, "I sanctify myself," implies the personal union of the two natures in Christ; for what is that which he here calls himself, but the same that was consecrated to be a sacrifice, even his human nature? This was the sacrifice. And this also was himself: so the apostle speaks, "He through the eternal Spirit offered up himself to God without spot," Heb. ix. 14. So that our nature, by that assumption, is become himself. Greater honour cannot be done it, or greater ground of comfort proposed to us. But having spoken of that union in the former sermon, shall remit the reader thither.

2. This sanctifying, or consecrating himself to be a sacrifice for us, implies, the greatness and dreadfulness of that breach which sin made between God and us. You see no less a sacrifice than Christ himself must be sanctified to make atonement. Judge of the greatness of the wound by the breadth of the plaster. "Sacrifice, and offering, and burnt-offering for sin, thou wouldest not; but a body hast thou prepared me," Heb. x. 5. All our repentance, could we shed as many tears for sin as there have fallen drops of rain since the creation, could not have been our atonement: "But God was in Christ, reconciling the world to himself." And had he not sanctified Christ to this end, he would have sanctified himself upon us, in judgment and fury for ever.

3. This his sanctifying himself, implies his free and voluntary undertaking of the work. It is not, I am sanctified, as if he had been merely passive in it, as the lambs that typified him were, when plucked from the fold; but it is an active verb he useth here, I sanctify myself; he would have none think that he died out of a necessity of compulsion, but out of choice : therefore he is said to "offer up himself to God," Heb. x. 14. And, "I lay down my life of myself; no man taketh it from me," John x. 18. And although it is often said his Father sent him, and gave him; yet his heart was as much set on that work, as if

there had been nothing but glory, ease, and comfort in it; he was under no constraint, but that of his own love. Therefore, as when the scripture would set forth the willingness of the Father to this work, it saith, God sent his Son, and God gave his Son; so when it would set forth Christ's willingness to it, it saith, He offered up himself, gave himself, and, here in the text, sanctified himself. A sacrifice that struggled, and came not without force to the altar, was reckoned ominous and unlucky by the heathen: our Sacrifice dedicated himself; he died out of choice, and was a free-will offering.

4. His sanctifying himself implies his pure and perfect holiness; that he had no spot or blemish in him. Those beasts that prefigured him, were to be without blemish, and none else were consecrated to that service. So, and more than so, it behoved Christ to be: "Such an High Priest became us, who is holy, harmless, undefiled, separate from sinners," Heb. vii. 26. And what it became him to be, he was. Therefore in allusion to the lambs offered under the law, the apostle calls him a Lamb without blemish, or spot, 1 Pet. i. 19. Every other man hath a double spot on him, the heart spot, and the life spot; the spot of original, and the spots of actual sins. But Christ was without either, he had not the spot of original sin, for he was not by man; he came in a peculiar way into the world, and so escaped that: nor yet of actual sins; for, as his nature, so his life was spotless and pure, "He did no iniquity," Isa. liii. 9. And though tempted to sin externally, yet he was never defiled in heart or practice.

5. His sanctifying himself for our sakes, speaks the strength of his love and largeness of his heart to poor sinners, thus to set himself wholly and entirely apart for us: so that what he did and suffered, must all of it have a respect and relation to us. He did not (when consecrated for us) live a moment, do an act, or speak a word, but it had some tendency to promote the great design of our salvation. His incarnation respects you; "For to us a child is born, to us a son is given," Isa. ix. 6. And he would never have been the Son of man, but to make you the sons and daughters of God. God would not have come down in the likeness of sinful flesh, in the habit of a man, but to raise up sinful man unto the likeness of God. All the miracles he wrought were for you, to confirm your faith. When he raised up Lazarus, "Because of the people which stand by I said it, that they may believe that thou hast sent me," John xi. 42. While he lived on earth, he lived as one wholly set apart for us: and when he died, he died for us, "he was made a curse for us," Gal. iii.

13.   When he hanged on that cursed tree, he hanged there in our room, and did but fill our place.   When he was buried, he was buried for us; for the end of it was, to perfume our graves, against we come to lie down in them.   And when he rose again, it was, as the apostle saith, "for our justification," Rom. iv. 25. When he ascended into glory, he said it was about our business, that he went to prepare places for us, John xiv. 2.   And now he is there, it is for us that he there lives; for he "ever lives to make intercession for us," Heb. vii. 25.   And when he shall return again to judge the world, he will come for us too.   "He comes (whenever it be) to be glorified in his saints, and admired in them that believe," 2 Thess. i. 10.   He comes to gather his saints home to himself, that where he is, there they all may be in soul and body with him for ever.

6. His sanctifying himself for us plainly speaks the vicarious nature of his death, that it was in our room or stead.   When the priest consecrated the sacrifice, it was set apart for the people. So it is said of the scape goat; "And Aaron shall lay both his hands upon the head of the live goat, and confess over him all the iniquities of the children of Israel, and all their transgressions in all their sins, putting them upon the head of the goat, and shall send him away by the hand of a fit man into the wilderness," Lev. xvi. 21.   Thus Isa. liii. 6, 7.   He stood in our room, to bear our burden.   And as Aaron laid the iniquities of the people upon the goat, so were ours laid on Christ.   His death was in our stead, as well as for our good.   And so much his sanctifying himself "for us" imports.

7. His sanctifying himself imports the extraordinariness of his person; for it speaks him to be both Priest, Sacrifice, and Altar, all in one: a thing unheard of in the world before.   So that his name might well be called Wonderful.   I sanctify myself: I sanctify, according to both natures; myself, that is, my human nature, which was the sacrifice, upon the altar of my Divine nature; for it is the altar that sanctifies the gift.   As the three offices never met in one person before, so these three things never met in one priest before.   The priests indeed consecrated the bodies of beasts for sacrifices, but never offered up their own souls and bodies as a whole burnt-offering, as Christ did.   And thus you have the import of this phrase, I sanctify myself for their sakes.

II. I shall show you briefly the relation that all this hath to us: for unto us the scriptures every where refer it.   So in 1 Cor. v. 7, " Christ our Passover is sacrificed for us." Eph. v. 25, " He loved the church, and gave himself for it."   See Tit. ii.

14. This will be made out, by a threefold consideration of Christ's death. And,

1. Let it be considered, that he was not offered up to God for his own sins; for he was most holy. No iniquity was found in him, Isa. liii. 9. Indeed the priests under the law offered for themselves, as well as the people; but Christ did not so, "He needed not daily, as those high priests, to offer up sacrifice, first for his own sins, and then for the people's," Heb. vii. 27. And indeed had he been a sinner, what value or efficacy could have been in his sacrifice? He could not have been the sacrifice, but would have needed one. Now, if Christ were most holy, and yet put to death, and cruel sufferings, either his death or sufferings must be an act of injustice and cruelty, or it must respect others, whose persons and cause he sustained in that suffering capacity. He could never have suffered or died by the Father's hand, had he not been a sinner by imputation. As the prophet Isaiah speaks, all our sins were made to meet upon him; "He was made sin for us, who knew no sin," 2 Cor. v. 21. So that hence it is evident, that Christ's death, or sacrifice, is wholly a respective or relative thing.

2. It is not to be forgotten here, that the scriptures frequently call the death of Christ a price, 1 Cor. vi. 20, and a ransom, Matt. xx. 28, or counter-price. To whom then doth it relate, but to them that were and are in bondage and captivity? If it was to redeem any, it must be captives: but Christ himself was never in captivity; he was always in his Father's bosom, as you have heard; but we were in cruel bondage and thraldom, under the tyranny of sin and Satan: and it is we only that have the benefit of this ransom.

3. Either the death of Christ must relate to believers, or else he must die in vain. As for the angels, those that stood in their integrity needed no sacrifice, and those that fell, are totally excluded from any benefit by it: he is not a Mediator for them. And among men that have need of it, unbelievers have no share in it, they reject it; such have no part in it. If then he neither died for himself, as I proved before, nor for angels nor unbelievers; either his blood must be shed with respect to believers, or, which is most absurd, and never to be imagined, shed as water upon the ground, and totally cast away: so that you see by all this, it was for our sakes, as the text speaks, that he sanctified himself. And now we may say, Lord, the condemnation was thine, that the justification might be mine; the agony thine, that the victory might be mine; the pain was thine, and the ease is mine; the stripes thine, and the healing balm issuing

from them mine ; the vinegar and gall were thine, that the honey
and sweet might be mine ; the curse was thine, that the blessing might be mine ; the crown of thorns was thine, that the
crown of glory might be mine ; the death was thine, the life
purchased by it mine ; thou paidst the price that I might enjoy
the inheritance.

We come next to the inferences of truth deducible from this
point, which follow.

1. If Jesus Christ did wholly set himself apart for believers,
how reasonable is it that believers should consecrate and set themselves apart wholly for Christ !   Is he all for us, and shall we
be. nothing for him ?   What he was, he was for you ?   Whatever he did, was done for you ; and all that he suffered, was
suffered for you.   Oh then, " I beseech you, brethren, by the
mercies of God, present your bodies," that is, your whole selves,
(for so body is there put to signify the whole person,) I say,
" present your bodies a living sacrifice, holy, acceptable to God,
which is your reasonable service," Rom. xii. 1.   As your good
was Christ's end, so let his glory be your end.   Let Christ be
the "end of your conversation," Heb. xiii. 7.   Oh that all who
profess faith in Christ, could subscribe cordially to that profession. " None of us liveth to himself, and no man dieth to himself ; but whether we live, we live to the Lord ; and whether we
die, we die to the Lord ; so then whether we live or die, we are
the Lord's," Rom. xiv. 8.   This is to be a christian indeed.
What is a christian, but a holy, dedicated thing to the Lord ?
And what greater evidence can there be, that Christ set himself
apart for you, than your setting yourselves apart for him ?

This is the marriage covenant, " Thou shalt be for me, and
not for another : so will I be for thee," Hos. iii. 3.   Ah, what
a life is the life of a christian ; Christ all for you, and you all
for him. Blessed exchange ! Soul, (saith Christ,) all I have is
thine. Lord, (saith the soul,) and all I have is thine.   Soul,
(saith Christ,) my person is wonderful, but what I am, I am for
thee : my life was spent in labour and travail, but it was for thee.
And Lord, (saith the believer,) my person is vile, and not worth
thy accepting ; but such as it is, it is thine ; my soul, with all
and every faculty ; my body, and every member of it, my gifts,
time, and all my talents, are thine.   .

And see that as Christ bequeathed and made over himself to
you, so ye, in like manner, bestow and make over yourselves to
him.   He lived not, neither died (as you hear) for himself, but
you. Oh that you, in like manner, would down with self, and exalt
Christ in the room of it. " Woe, woe is me, (saith one,) that

the holy profession of Christ is made a showy garment by many to bring home a vain fame; and Christ is made to serve men's ends. This is to heat an oven with a king's robes. Except men martyr and slay the body of sin, in holy self-denial, they shall never be Christ's martyrs and faithful witnesses. Oh if I could be master of that house-idol, myself, mine own, mine own wit, will, credit, and ease, how blessed were I! We have need to be redeemed from ourselves, as much as from the devil and the world. Learn to put out yourselves, and to put in Christ for yourselves. I should make a good bargain, and give old for new, if I could turn out self, and substitute Christ my Lord in place of myself; to say, Not I, but Christ; not my will, but Christ's; not my ease, not my lusts, not my credit, but Christ, Christ.—O wretched idol, myself, when shall I see thee wholly expelled, and Christ wholly put in thy room?"

He set himself apart for you believers, and no others; no, not for angels, but for you. Will ye also set yourselves apart peculiarly for Christ? be his, and no other's? Let not Christ and the world share and divide your hearts between them; let not the world step in and say, Half mine. You will never do Christ right, nor answer this grace, till you can say, as it is Psa. lxxiii. 25, "Whom have I in heaven but thee? and on earth there is none that I desire in comparison of thee." None but Christ, none but Christ, is a proper motto for a christian.

He left the highest and best enjoyments, even those in his Father's bosom, to set himself apart for death and suffering for you. Are you ready to leave the bosom of the best and sweetest enjoyments you have in this world, to serve him? If you stand not habitually ready to leave father, mother, wife, children, lands, yea, and life too, to serve him, you are not worthy of him, Matt. x. 37. He was so wholly given up to your service, that he refused not the worst and hardest part of it, even bleeding, groaning, dying work; his love to you sweetened all this to him. Can you say so too? do you "account the reproaches of Christ greater riches than the treasures of Egypt," as Moses did? Heb. xi. 26. He so entirely devoted himself to your work, that he could not be at rest till it was finished: he was so intent upon it, that he "forgot to eat bread," John iv. 31, 32. So it should be with you; his service should be meat and drink to you. To conclude: he was so wholly given up to your work and service, that he would not suffer himself to be in the least diverted, or taken off from it: and if Peter himself counsel him to favour himself, he shall hear, "Get thee behind me, Satan." Oh happy were it if our hearts were but so engaged for Christ! In Galen's time it was proverbial, when they would express the impossibility of a thing, You may as soon take off a christian from Christ. Thus you see what use you should make of Christ's sanctifying himself for you.

2. If Christ hath sanctified or consecrated himself for us; learn hence, what a horrid evil it is, to use Christ or his blood, as a common and unsanctified thing. Yet so some do, as the apostle speaks, Heb. x. 29. The apostate is said to tread upon the Son of God, as if he were no better than the dirt under his feet, and to count his blood an unholy (or common) thing. But woe to them that do so, they shall be counted worthy of something worse than dying without mercy, as the apostle there speaks.

And as this is the sin of the apostate, so it is also the sin of all those that without faith approach, and so profane the table of the Lord, unbelievingly and unworthily handling those awful things. Such " eat and drink judgment to themselves, not discerning the Lord's body," 1 Cor. xi. 29. Whereas the body of Christ was a thing of the deepest sanctification that ever God created; sanctified (as the text tells us) to a far more excellent and glorious purpose than ever any creature in heaven or earth was sanctified. It was therefore the great sin of those Corinthians, not to discern it, and not to behave themselves towards it, when they saw and handled the signs of it, as became so holy a thing. And as it was their great sin, so God declared his just indignation against it, in those sore strokes inflicted for it. As they discerned not the Lord's body, so neither did the Lord discern their bodies from others in the judgments that were inflicted. And, as one well observes, God drew the model and platform of their punishment, from the structure and proportion of their sin. And truly, if the moral and spiritual seeds and originals of many of our outward afflictions and sicknesses were but duly sifted out, possibly we might find a great part of them in this sin.

The just and righteous God will build up the breaches we make upon the honour of his Son, with the ruins of that beauty, strength, and honour which he hath given our bodies. Oh then, when you draw nigh to God in that ordinance, take heed to sanctify his name, by a spiritual discerning of this most holy and most deeply sanctified body of the Lord; sanctified beyond all creatures, angels or men, not only in respect of the Spirit which filled him, without measure, with inherent holiness, but also in respect of its dedication to such a service as this, it being set apart by him to such holy, solemn ends and uses, as you have heard.

And let it, for ever, be a warning to such as have lifted up their hands to Christ in a holy profession, that they never lift up their heel against him afterwards by apostasy. The apostate treads on God's dear Son, and God will tread upon him for it. "Thou hast trodden down all that err from thy statutes," Psa. cxix. 118.

3. What a choice pattern of love to saints have we here before us! Calling all that are in Christ to an imitation of him, even to give up ourselves to their service, as Christ did; not in the same kind, for so none can give himself for them, but as we are capable. You see here how his heart was affected to them, that he would sanctify himself as a sacrifice for them. See to what a height of duty the apostle improves this example of Christ; " Hereby perceive we the love of God, because he laid down his life for us; and we ought also to lay down our lives for the brethren," 1 John iii. 16. Some christians came up fairly to this pattern in primitive times; Priscilla and Aquila laid down their necks for Paul, Rom. xvi. 4, that is, eminently hazarded their lives for him; and he himself could " rejoice, if he were offered up upon the sacrifice and service of their faith," Phil. ii. 17. And in the next times, what was more known, even to the enemies of christianity, than their fervent love one to another ? Ecce quam mutuo se diligunt, et mori volunt pro alterutris ! See how they love one another, and are willing to die one for another !

But alas ! the primitive spirit is almost lost in this degenerate age: instead of laying down life, how few will lay down twelve-pence for them? I remember, it is the observation of a late worthy, upon Matt. v. 44, that he is persuaded there is hardly that man to be found this day alive, that fully understands and fully believes that scripture. Oh, did men think what they do for them is done for Christ himself, it would produce other effects than are yet visible.

4. If Christ sanctified himself, that we might be sanctified by [or in] the truth; then it will follow, That true sanctification is a good evidence that Christ set apart himself to die for us. In vain did he sanctify himself (as to you) unless you be sanctified. Holy souls only can claim the benefit of the great Sacrifice. Oh try then, whether true holiness, (and that is only to be judged by its conformity to its pattern, " As he that called you is holy, so be ye holy," 1 Pet. i. 15,) whether such a holiness as is, and acts (according to its measure) like God's holiness, in the following particulars, be found in you.

(1.) God is universally holy in all his ways; so Psa. cxlv. 17, " His works are holy :" whatever he doth, it is still done as becomes a holy God : he is not only holy in all things, but at all times unchangeably holy. Be ye therefore holy in all things and at all times too, if ever you expect the benefit of Christ's sanctifying himself to die for you.

Oh brethren, let not the feet of your conversation be as the feet of a lame man, which are unequal, Prov. xxvi. 7. Be not sometimes hot, and sometimes cold ; at one time careful, at another time careless ; one day in a spiritual rapture, and the next in a fleshly frolic : but be ye holy "in all manner of conversation," 1 Pet. i. 15, in every creek and turning of your lives ; and let your holiness hold out to the end.

(2.) God is exemplarily holy, Jesus Christ is the great pattern of holiness. Be ye examples of holiness too, unto all that are about you. "Let your light so shine before men, that they may see your good works," Matt. v. 16. As wicked men infect one another by their examples, and diffuse their poison and malignity wherever they come ; so do ye disseminate godliness in all places and companies ; and let those that frequently converse with you, especially those of your own families, receive a deeper dye and tincture of heavenliness every time they come nigh you, as the cloth doth by every new dipping into the vat.

(3.) God delights in nothing but holiness, and holy ones ; he hath set all his pleasure in the saints. Be ye holy herein, as God is holy. Indeed, there is this difference between God's choice and yours ; he chooses not men because they are holy, but that they may be so ; you are to choose them for your delightful companions, that God hath chosen and made holy. "Let all your delights be in the saints, even them that excel in virtue," Psa. xvi. 3.

(4.) God abhors and hates all unholiness ; do ye so likewise, that ye may be like your Father which is in heaven. And when the Spirit of holiness bestows this upon you, a sweeter evidence you cannot have, that Christ was sanctified for you. Holy ones may confidently lay the hand of their faith on the head of this great sacrifice, and say, " Christ our Passover is sacrificed for us."

SERMON VIII.

OF THE NATURE OF CHRIST'S MEDIATION.

1 TIM. II. 5.

AND ONE MEDIATOR BETWEEN GOD AND MEN, THE MAN CHRIST JESUS.

GREAT and long preparations bespeak the solemnity and greatness of the work for which they are designed. A man that had but seen the heaps of gold, silver, and brass, which David amassed in his time, for the building of the temple, might easily conclude before one stone of it was laid, that it would be a magnificent structure. But lo, here is a design of God as far transcending that, as the substance doth the shadow. For, indeed, that glorious temple was but the type and figure of Jesus Christ, John ii. 19, 21, and a weak adumbration of that living, spiritual temple which he was to build, that the great God might dwell and walk in it, 2 Cor. vi. 16. The preparations for that temple were but of few years, but the consultations and preparations for this were from eternity, Prov. viii. 31. And as there were preparations for this work before the world began; so it will be a matter of eternal admiration and praise, when this world shall be dissolved. What this astonishing glorious work is, this text will inform you, as to the general nature of it: it is the work of mediation between God and man, managed by the sole hand of the man Christ Jesus.

In this scripture you have a description of Jesus the Mediator: and he is here described four ways, namely, by his work or office, a Mediator; by the singularity of his mediation, one Mediator; and by the nature and quality of his person, employed in this singular way of mediation, the man; and lastly, his name, Jesus Christ.

1. He is described by the work, or office he is employed about, Μεσιτης, a Mediator, a middle person. So the word imports, a fit and equal person, that comes between two persons that are at variance, to compose the difference and make peace. Such a person is Christ; a days-man, to lay his hand upon both.

2. He is described by the singularity of his mediation, one

Mediator, and but one. Though there be many mediators of reconciliation among men, and many intercessors, in a petitionary way, between God and man; yet but one only Mediator of reconciliation between God and man: and it is as needless and impious to make more mediators than one, as to make more gods than one. There is one God, and one Mediator between God and men. .

3. He is described by the nature and quality of his person, the man Christ Jesus. He is described by his human nature in this place, not only because in this nature he paid that ransom, (which is spoken of in the words immediately following,) but especially for the drawing of sinners to him; seeing he is the man Christ Jesus, one that clothed himself·in their own flesh; and, to encourage the faith of believers, that he tenderly regards all their wants and miseries, and that they may safely trust him with all their concerns, as one that will carefully mind them as his own, and will be for them a merciful and faithful High Priest, in things pertaining to God.

4. He is described by his names; by his appellative name, Christ, and his proper name, Jesus. The name Jesus, notes his work about which he came; and Christ, the offices to which he was anointed, and in the execution of which he is our Jesus. "In the name Jesus, the whole gospel is contained; it is the light, the food, the medicine of the soul," as one speaks.* The note from hence is,

> DOCT. THAT JESUS CHRIST IS THE TRUE AND ONLY MEDIATOR BETWEEN GOD AND MEN.

"Ye are come to Jesus the Mediator of the new covenant," Heb. xii. 24. "And for this cause he is the Mediator of the new testament," &c. Heb. ix. 15. I might show you a whole vein of scriptures running this way; but to keep a profitable and clear method, I shall show, What is the sense of this word μεσιτης, a mediator. What it implies, as it is applied to Christ. How it appears that he is the true and only Mediator between God and men. And, in what capacity he performed his mediatorial work.

· I. What is the sense and import of this word μεσιτης, a mediator? The true sense and importance of it, is a middle person, or one that interposes between two parties at variance, to make peace between them. Christ is such a Mediator, both in respect of his person and office: in respect of his person, he is a Mediator; that is, one that hath the same nature both with

---

* Glassius.

God and us, true God and true man; and in respect of his office or work, which is to interpose, to transact the business of reconciliation between us and God. His being a middle person, fits and capacitates him to stand in the midst between God and us. This, I say, is the proper sense of the word; though μεσιτης, a mediator, is rendered variously; sometimes an umpire or arbitrator; sometimes a messenger that goes between two persons; sometimes an interpreter, imparting the mind of one to another; sometimes a reconciler or peace-maker. And in all these senses Christ is the Μεσιτης, the middle person in his mediation of reconciliation or intercession; that is, either in his mediating, by suffering to make peace, as he did on earth; or to continue and maintain peace, as he doth in heaven, by meritorious intercession. Both these ways he is the only Mediator.

But to be more explicit and clear, I shall,

II. In the next place inquire, what it implies and carries in it, for Christ to be a Mediator between God and us. And there are, mainly, these five things in it.

1. At the first sight, it implies a most dreadful breach between God and men; else no need of a mediator of reconciliation. There was indeed a sweet league of amity once between them, but it was quickly dissolved by sin; the wrath of the Lord was kindled against man, pursuing him to destruction, "Thou hatest all the workers of iniquity," Psa. v. 5. And man was filled with unnatural enmity against his God; " haters of God," Rom. i. 30, this put an end to all friendly intercourse between him and God.

Reader, say not in thy heart, that it is much, that one sin, and that seemingly so small, should make such a breach as this, and cause the God of mercy and goodness so to abhor the works of his hands, and that as soon as he had made man: for it was a heinous and aggravated evil. It was upright, perfect man, created in the image of God, that thus sinned: he sinned when his mind was most bright, clear, and apprehensive; his conscience pure and active; his will free, and able to withstand any temptation; his conscience pure and undefiled: he was a public as well as a perfect man, and well knew that the happiness or misery of his numberless offspring was involved in him. The condition he was placed in, was exceeding happy: no necessity or want could arm and edge temptation: he lived amidst all natural and spiritual pleasures and delights, the Lord most delightfully conversing with him; yea, he sinned while as yet his creation-mercy was fresh upon him; and in this sin was most horrible ingratitude: yea, a casting off the yoke of obedience almost as soon as God had put it on.

2. It implies, a necessity of satisfaction and reparation to the justice of God. For the very design and end of this mediation was to make peace, by giving full satisfaction to the party that was wronged. The photinians, and some others, have dreamed of a reconciliation with God, founded not upon satisfaction, but upon the absolute mercy, goodness, and free-will of God. "But concerning that absolute goodness and mercy of God, reconciling sinners to himself, there is a deep silence throughout the scriptures:" * and whatever is spoken of it, upon that account, is as it works to us through Christ, Eph. i. 3—5; Acts iv. 12; John vi. 40. And we cannot imagine, either how God could exercise mercy to the prejudice of his justice, which must be, if we must be reconciled without full satisfaction; or how such a full satisfaction should be made by any other than Christ. Mercy, indeed, moved in the heart of God to poor man; but from his heart it found no way to vent itself for us, but through the heart-blood of Jesus Christ: and in him the justice of God was fully satisfied, and the misery of the creature fully cured. And so, as Augustine speaks, "God neither lost the severity of his justice in the goodness of mercy, nor the goodness of his mercy in the exactness of his severity."

But if it had been possible that God could have found out a way to reconcile us without satisfaction, yet it is past doubt now, that he hath determined and fixed on this way. And for any now to imagine to reconcile themselves to God by any thing but faith in the blood of this Mediator, is not only most vain in itself, and destructive to the soul, but most insolently derogatory to the wisdom and grace of God. And to such I would say, as Tertullian to Marcion, whom he calls the murderer of truth, "Spare the only hope of the whole world, O thou who destroyest the most necessary glory of our faith!" All that we hope for is but a phantasm without this. Peace of conscience can be rationally settled on no other foundation but this; for God having made a law to govern man, and this law being violated by man, either the penalty must be levied on the delinquent, or satisfaction made by his surety. As good no law, as no penalty for disobedience; and as good no penalty, as no execution. He therefore that will be made a mediator of reconciliation between God and man, must bring God a price in his hand, and that adequate to the offence and wrong done him, else he will not treat about peace; and so did our Mediator.

* Dieteric.

3. Christ being a Mediator of reconciliation and intercession, implies the infinite value of his blood and sufferings, as that which in itself was sufficient to stop the course of God's justice, and render him not only placable, but abundantly satisfied and well pleased, even with those that before were enemies. And so much is said of it, Col. i. 21, 22. "And ye that were sometimes alienated, and enemies in your minds by wicked works, yet now hath he reconciled, in the body of his flesh through death, to present you holy, and unblameable, and unreproveable in his sight." Surely, that which can cause the holy God, justly incensed against sinners, to lay aside all his wrath, and take an enemy into his bosom, and establish such an amity as can never more be broken, but to rest in his love, and to joy over him with singing, as it is, Zeph. iii. 17, this must be a most excellent and efficacious thing.

4. Christ's being a Mediator of reconciliation, implies the ardent tender love and large pity that filled his heart towards poor sinners. For he doth not only mediate by way of entreaty, going between both, and persuading and begging peace ; but he mediates (as you have heard) in the capacity of a surety, by putting himself under an obligation to satisfy our debts. Oh how compassionately did his heart work towards us, that when he saw the arm of justice lifted up to destroy us, would interpose himself, and receive the stroke, though he knew it would smite him dead ! Our Mediator, like Jonah his type, seeing the stormy sea of God's wrath working tempestuously, and ready to swallow us up, cast in himself to appease the storm. I remember how much that noble act of Marcus Curtius is celebrated in the roman history, who being informed by the oracle, that the great breach made by the earthquake could not be closed, except something of worth were cast into it, heated with love to the commonwealth, he went and cast in himself. This was looked upon as a bold and brave adventure. But what was this to Christ ?

5. Christ being a Mediator between God and man, implies as the fitness of his person, so his authoritative call to undertake it. But having discussed this more largely in a former discourse, I shall dismiss it here, and apply myself to the third thing proposed, which is,

III. How it appears that Jesus Christ is the true and only Mediator between God and men. I reply, it is manifest he is so,

1. Because he, and no other, is revealed to us by God. And if God reveal him, and no other, we must receive him, and no other as such. Take but two scriptures at present, that in 1 Cor. viii. 5, " The heathen have many gods, and many lords," that

is, many great gods, supreme powers and ultimate objects of their
worship: and lest these great gods should be defiled by their
immediate and unhallowed approaches to them, they therefore
invented heroes, demigods, intermediate powers, that they were
as agents, or lord mediators between the gods and them, to con-
vey their prayers to the gods, and the blessings of the gods back
again to them. "But unto us (saith he) there is but one God,
the Father, of whom are all things, and we by him," that is, one
supreme essence, the first spring and fountain of blessings, and
one Lord, that is, one Mediator, " by whom are all things, and
we by him." By whom are all things which come from the Father to us, and by whom are all our addresses to the Father.
So Acts iv. 12, " Neither is there salvation in any other: for
there is none other name under heaven given among men, whereby we must be saved." No other name, that is, no other
authority, or rather, no other person authorized under heaven,
that is, the whole world: for heaven is not here opposed to earth,
as though there were other intercessors in heaven besides Christ:
no, no, in heaven and earth God hath given him, and none but
him, to be our Mediator. One sun is sufficient for the whole
world; and one Mediator for all men in the world. So that the
scriptures affirm this is he, and exclude all others.

2. Because he, and no other, is fit for, and capable of this
office. Who but he that hath the Divine and human nature
united in his single person, can be a fit days-man to lay his
hand upon both? Who but he that was God, could support
under such sufferings, as were, by Divine justice, exacted for
satisfaction? Take a person of the greatest spirit, and put him
an hour in the case Christ was in, when he sweat blood in the
garden, or uttered that heart-rending cry upon the cross, and he
had melted under it as a moth.

3. Because he is alone sufficient to reconcile the world to
God by his blood, without accessions from any other. The
virtue of his blood reached back as far as Adam, and reaches
forward to the end of the world; and will be as fresh, vigorous,
and efficacious then, as the first moment it was shed. The sun
makes day before it actually rises, and continues day sometimes
after it is set: so doth Christ, who is the same yesterday, to-day,
and for ever. So that he is the true and only Mediator between
God and men: no other is revealed in scripture; no other is
sufficient for it; no other needed beside him.

IV. The last thing to be explained is, in what capacity he
executed his mediatorial work.

About which we affirm, according to scripture, that he performs that work as God-man, in both natures. Papists, in denying Christ to act as Mediator, according to his Divine nature, do at once spoil the whole mediation of Christ of all its efficacy, dignity, and value, which arise from that nature. They say, the apostle, in my text, distinguishes the Mediator from God, in saying, "there is one God and one Mediator." We reply, that the same apostle distinguishes Christ from man, in Gal. i. 1, " Not by man, but by Jesus Christ." Doth it thence follow that Christ is not true man? Or that according to his Divine nature only, he called Paul? But what need I stay my reader here? Had not Christ, as Mediator, power to lay down his life, and power to take it up again? John x. 17, 18. Had he not, as Mediator, all power in heaven and earth to institute ordinances, and appoint offices? Matt. xxviii. 18; to baptize men with the Holy Ghost and fire? Matt. iii. 11; to keep those whom his Father gave him in this world? John xvii. 12; to raise up the saints again in the last day? John vi. 54. Are these, with many more I might name, the effects of the mere human nature? Or, were they not performed by him as God-man? And besides, how could he, as Mediator, be the object of our faith, and religious adoration, if we are not to respect him as God-man?

But I hasten to the application of this : and the first inference from it is this,

1. That it is a dangerous thing to reject Jesus Christ the only Mediator between God and man. Alas! there is no other to interpose and screen thee from the devouring fire, the everlasting burnings! Oh it is a fearful thing to fall into the hands of the living God! And into his hands you must fall, without an interest in the only Mediator. Which of us can dwell with devouring fire? Who can endure the everlasting burnings? Isa. xxxiii. 14. You know how they singed and scorched the green tree, but what would they do to the dry tree? Luke xxiii. 31. Indeed, if there were another plank to save after the shipwreck, any other way to be reconciled to God, beside Jesus the Mediator, somewhat might be said to excuse this folly ; but you are shut up to the faith of Christ, as to your last remedy, Gal. iii. 23. Oh take heed of despising, or neglecting Christ ! if so, there is none to intercede with God for you ; the breach between him and you can never be composed. I remember, here, the words of Eli, to his profane sons, who caused men to abhor the offerings of the Lord; "If one man sin against another, the judge shall judge him ; but if a man sin against the Lord, who shall entreat for him ?" 1 Sam. ii. 25. The meaning is, common trespasses between men, the civil magistrate takes cognizance of,

and decides the controversy by his authority, so that there is an end of that strife; but if man sin against the Lord, who shall entreat or arbitrate in that case? Eli's sons had despised the Lord's sacrifices, which were sacred types of Christ, and the appointed way that men had then of exercising faith on the Mediator. Now, (saith he,) if a man thus sin against the Lord, by despising the Saviour shadowed out in that way, who shall entreat for him? what hope, what remedy remains?

2. Hence also be informed, how great an evil it is to join any other mediators, either of reconciliation, or meritorious intercession, with Jesus Christ. Oh this is a horrid sin, which both pours the greatest contempt upon Christ, and brings the surest and sorest destruction upon the sinner! I am ashamed my pen should write what mine eyes have seen in the writings of papists, ascribing as much, yea, more to the mediation of Mary than to Christ, with no less than blasphemous impudence. How do they stamp their own sordid works with the peculiar dignity and value of Christ's blood; and therein seek to enter at the gate which God hath shut to all the world, because Jesus Christ the Prince entered in thereby, Ezek. xliv. 2, 3. He entered into heaven in a direct, immediate way, even in his own name, and for his own sake; this gate, saith the Lord, shall be shut to all others; and I wish men would consider it, and fear, lest while they seek entrance into heaven at the wrong door, they do not for ever shut against themselves the true and only door of happiness.

3. If Jesus Christ be the only Mediator of reconciliation between God and men, then reconciled souls should thankfully ascribe all the peace, favours, and comforts they have from God, to their Lord Jesus Christ. Whenever you have had free admission, and sweet entertainment with God in the more public ordinances, or private duties of his worship; when you have had his smiles, his seals, and with hearts warmed with comfort, are returning from those duties, say, O my soul, thou mayest thank thy good Lord Jesus Christ for all this! had not he interposed as a Mediator of reconciliation, I could never have had access to, or friendly communion with God to all eternity.

Immediately upon Adam's sin, the door of communion with God was locked, yea, chained up, and no more coming nigh the Lord: not a soul could have any access to him, either in a way of communion in this world, or of enjoyment in that to come. It was Jesus the Mediator that opened that door again, and in him it is that we have boldness, and access with confidence, Eph. iii. 12. "We can now come to God by a new and living way, consecrated for us through the vail, that is to say, his flesh," Heb. x. 20.   The vail had a double use, as Christ's flesh likewise hath : it hid the glory of the sanctum sanctorum, and also gave entrance into it.   Christ's incarnation so obscures the splendour of the Divine glory and brightness, that we may be able to bear it and converse with it ; and it also gives us admission into it. Oh thank your dear Lord Jesus for your present and future heaven !   Blessed be God for Jesus Christ !

4. If Jesus Christ be the true and only Mediator, both of reconciliation and meritorious intercession between God and men, how safe and secure then is the condition and state of believers ! Surely, as his mediation, by sufferings, hath fully reconciled, so his mediation, by intercession, will everlastingly maintain that state of peace between them and God, and prevent all future breaches.   " Being justified by faith, we have peace with God, through our Lord Jesus Christ," Rom. v. 1.   It is a firm and lasting peace, and the Mediator that made it, is now in heaven to maintain it for ever, " there to appear in the presence of God for us," Heb. ix. 24 ; according to the custom of princes and states, who, being confederated, have their agents residing in each other's courts, who upon all occasions appear in the presence of the prince, in the name and behalf of those whom they represent, and negociate for.

5. Did Jesus Christ interpose between us and the wrath of God, as a Mediator of reconciliation? did he rather choose to receive the stroke upon himself, than to see us ruined by it? How well then doth it become the people of God, in a thankful sense of this grace, to interpose themselves between Jesus Christ and the evils they see likely to fall upon his name and interest in the world ! Oh that there were but such a heart in the people of God ! I remember it is a saying of Jerome, when he heard the revilings and blasphemings of many against Christ, and his precious truths, " Oh that they would turn their weapons from Christ to me, and be satisfied with my blood !"   And much to the same sense is that sweet one of Bernard, " Happy were I, if God would condescend to use me as a shield."   And David could say, " The reproaches of them that reproached thee, fell on me," Psa. lxix. 9.   Ten thousand of our names are nothing to Christ's name : his name is a worthy name ; and no man that gives up his name as a shield to Christ, but shall thereby secure and increase the true honour of it.

SERMON IX.

THE FIRST BRANCH OF CHRIST'S PROPHETICAL OFFICE, CONSIST-
ING IN THE REVELATION OF THE WILL OF GOD.

ACTS III. 22.

A PROPHET SHALL THE LORD YOUR GOD RAISE UP UNTO YOU OF YOUR
BRETHREN, LIKE UNTO ME; HIM SHALL YE HEAR IN ALL THINGS WHAT-
SOEVER HE SHALL SAY UNTO YOU.

HAVING, in the former discourses, shown you the solemn preparations, both on the Father's part, and on the Son's, for the
blessed design of reconciling us by the meritorious mediation of
Christ; and given you a general prospect of that his mediation,
in the former sermon; method now requires, that I proceed to
show how he executes this his mediation, in the discharge of
his blessed offices of Prophet, Priest, and King.

His prophetical office consists of two parts: one external,
consisting in a true and full revelation of the will of God to
men, according to John xvii. 6, "I have manifested thy name
to the men thou gavest me." The other in illuminating the
mind, and opening the heart to receive and embrace that doctrine.
The first part is contained in the words before us; "A prophet
shall the Lord your God raise up," &c.

Which words are those of Moses, recorded in Deut. xviii. 15,
and here, by Peter, pertinently applied to Christ, to convince
the incredulous jews, that he is the true and only Messiah, and
the great Prophet of the church; whose doctrine it was highly
dangerous to contemn, though it came out of the mouths
of such (otherwise contemptible) persons as he and John
were. And it is well observed by Calvin, he singles out this
testimony of Moses, rather than any other, because of the
great esteem they had for Moses, and his writings, beyond any
others.

Now in the words themselves are two general parts: Christ,
according to the prophetical office, described; and, obedience to
him, as such a Prophet, strictly enjoined.

1. You have here a description of Christ in his prophetical
office; "A Prophet shall the Lord your God raise up unto

you of your brethren, like unto me." Where Christ is described,

(1.) By this title, Prophet, and that, Princeps prophetarum, the Prince of the prophets, or the great and chief Shepherd, as he is styled, Heb. xiii. 20 ; 1 Pet. v. 4. It belongs to a prophet to expound the law, declare the will of God, and foretell things to come. All these meet, and that in a singular and eminent manner, in Christ our Prophet, Matt. v. 21, &c.; John i. 18 ; 1 Pet. i. 11.

(2.) He is described by his type ; a Prophet like unto Moses, who therein typified and prefigured him. But is it not said of Moses, in Deut. xxxiv. 10, " that there arose not a prophet since in Israel, like unto Moses, whom the Lord knew face to face ?" True, of mere men there never arose so great a prophet in Israel, as Moses was ; either in respect of his familiarity with God, or of his miracles which he wrought in the power of God : but Moses himself was but a star to this sun. However, in these following particulars, Christ was like him. He was a prophet that went between God and the people, carried God's mind to them, and returned theirs to God, they not being able to hear the voice of God immediately : " According to all that thou desiredst of the Lord thy God in Horeb, in the day of the assembly, saying, Let me not again hear the voice of the Lord my God, neither let me see this great fire any more, that I die not," Deut. xviii. 16. And upon this their request, God makes the promise which is cited in the text; " They have well spoken that which they have spoken : I will raise them up a Prophet like unto thee," &c. ver. 17, 18. Moses was a very faithful prophet, precisely faithful, and exact in all things that God gave him in charge, even to a pin of the tabernacle. " Moses verily was faithful in all his house, as a servant, for a testimony of those things which were to be spoken after : but Christ as a Son over his own house," Heb. iii. 5, 6. Again, Moses confirmed his doctrine by miracles, which he wrought in the presence, and to the conviction of gainsayers. Herein Christ our Prophet is also like unto Moses, who wrought many mighty miracles, which could not be denied, and by them confirmed the gospel which he preached. Lastly, Moses was that prophet which brought God's Israel out of literal Egypt, and Christ his out of spiritual Egypt, whereof that bondage was a figure. Thus he is described by his likeness to Moses, his type.

(3.) He is described by his stock and original, from which, according to his flesh, he sprang; " I will raise him up from among thy brethren." Of Israel, "as concerning the flesh, Christ came," Rom. ix. 5.   And "it is evident that our Lord sprang out of Judah," Heb. vii. 14.   He honoured that nation by his nativity.   Thus the great Prophet is described.

2. Here is a strict injunction of obedience to this Prophet, " Him shall ye hear in all things," &c. By hearing, understand obedience.   So words of sense are frequently put in scripture, to signify those affections that are moved by, and usually follow those senses. And this obedience is required to be yielded to this Prophet only, and universally, and under great penalties.   It is required to be given to him only, for so "him" in the text must be understood, as exclusive of all others.   It is true, we are commanded to obey the voice of his ministers, Heb. xiii. 17.   But still it is Christ speaking by them, to whom we pay our obedience: " He that heareth you, heareth me." We obey them in the Lord, that is, commanding or forbidding in Christ's name and authority. So when God said, " Thou shalt serve him," Deut. vi. 13 ; Christ expounds it exclusively, " Him only shalt thou serve," Matt. iv. 10.   He is the only Lord, Jude 4, and therefore to him only our obedience is required.   And as it is due to him only, so to him universally ; " Him shall ye hear in all things :" his commands are to be obeyed, not disputed. A judgment of discretion indeed is allowed to christians, to judge whether what is told them be the will of Christ or no.   We must " prove what is that holy, good, and acceptable will," Rom. xii. 2.   " His sheep hear his voice, and a stranger they will not follow : they know his voice, but know not the voice of strangers," John x. 4, 5.   But when his will is understood and known, we have no liberty of choice, but are concluded by it, be the duty commanded never so difficult, or the sin forbidden never so tempting : and this is also required severely, under penalty of being destroyed from among the people, and of God's requiring it at our hands, as it is in Deut. xviii. that is, of revenging himself in the destruction of the disobedient.   Hence the observation,

DOCT. THAT JESUS CHRIST IS CALLED AND AP-
POINTED BY GOD TO BE THE GREAT PROPHET AND
TEACHER OF THE CHURCH.

He is anointed to preach good tidings to the meek, and sent to bind up the broken-hearted, Isa. lxi. 1.   When he came to preach the gospel among the people, then was this scripture fulfilled, " Yea, all things are delivered him of his Father ; so that no man knoweth who the Father is, but the Son, and he to whom the Son will reveal him," Matt. xi. 27.   All light is now collected into one body of light, the Sun of righteousness ; and he " enlighteneth every man that cometh into the world," John i. 9. And though he dispensed knowledge variously, in times past, speaking in many ways and divers manners to the fathers; yet now the method and way of revealing the will of God to us is fixed and settled in Christ : In these last times he hath spoken to us by his Son. Twice hath the Lord solemnly sealed him to this office, or approved and owned him in it, by a miraculous voice from the most excellent glory, Matt. iii. 17, and Matt. xvii. 5.

In this point there are two things doctrinally to be discussed and opened, namely, What Christ's being a Prophet to the church implies : and, How he executes and discharges this his office.

I. What is implied in Christ's being a Prophet to the church. And it necessarily imports these three things.

1. The natural ignorance and blindness of men in the things of God. This shows us that " vain man is born as the wild ass's colt."—The world is involved in darkness : the people sit as in the region and shadow of death till Christ arise upon their souls, Matt. iv. 15—17. It is true, in the state of innocency man had a clear apprehension of the will of God, without a Mediator ; but now that light is quenched in the corruption of nature, " and the natural man receiveth not the things of God," 1 Cor. ii. 14. These things of God are not only contrary to corrupt and carnal reason, but they are also above right reason. Grace indeed useth nature, but nature can do nothing without grace. The mind of a natural man hath not only a native blindness, by reason whereof it cannot discern the things of the Spirit, but also a natural enmity, Rom. viii. 7, and it hates the light, John iii. 19, 20. So that until the mind be healed, and enlightened by Jesus Christ, the natural faculty can no more discern the things of the Spirit, than the sensitive faculty can discern the things of reason. The mysteries of nature may be discovered by the light of nature ; but when it comes to supernatural mysteries, there, *Omnis Platonicorum caligavit subtilitus,* as Cyprian some where speaks, The most subtle, searching, penetrating wit and reason, is at a loss.

2. It implies the Divinity of Christ, and proves him to be true God ; forasmuch as no other can reveal to the world, in all ages, the secrets that lay hid in the heart of God, and that with such convincing evidence and authority. He brought his doctrine from the bosom of his Father ; " The only begotten Son, who is in the bosom of the Father, he hath revealed him," John i. 18. The same words which his Father gave him he hath given us, John xvii. 8. He spake to us that which he had seen with

his Father, John viii. 38. What man can tell the bosom counsels and secrets of God?   Who but he that eternally lay in that bosom can expound them?   Besides, other prophets had their times assigned them to rise, shine, and set again by death; "Your fathers, where are they?   And do the prophets live for ever?" Zech. i. 5. But Christ is a fixed and perpetual sun, that gives light in all ages of the world: for he is "the same yesterday, to-day, and for ever," Heb. xiii. 8.   Yea, and the very beams of his Divinity shone with awfulness upon the hearts of them that heard him; so that his very enemies were forced to acknowledge, that "never any man spake like him," John vii. 46.

3. It implies Christ to be the original and fountain of all that light which is ministerially diffused up and down the world by men.   Ministers are but stars, which shine with a borrowed light from the sun: so speaks the apostle, "For God, who commanded the light to shine out of darkness, hath shined into our hearts, to give the light of the knowledge of the glory of God, in the face of Jesus Christ," 2 Cor. iv. 6.   Those that teach men, must be first taught by Christ. What Paul received from the Lord, he delivered to the church, 1 Cor. xi. 23. Jesus Christ is the chief Shepherd, 1 Pet. v. 4; and all the under shepherds receive their gifts and commissions from him.   These things are manifestly implied in Christ's prophetical office.

II. We shall next inquire how he executes and discharges this his office, or how he enlightens and teaches men the will of God.   And this he hath done variously, gradually, plainly, powerfully, sweetly, purely, and fully.

1. Our great Prophet hath revealed unto men the will of God variously; not holding one uniform and constant tenor in the manifestations of the Father's will, but, as the apostle speaks, at sundry times, and in divers manners, Heb. i. 1.   Sometimes he taught the church immediately, and in his own person, John xviii. 20.   He declared God's righteousness in the great congregation, Psa. xxii. 22.   And sometimes mediately, by his ministers and officers, deputed to that service by him.   So he dispensed the knowledge of God to the church before his incarnation; it was Christ that in the time, and by the ministry of Noah, went and preached to the spirits in prison, as it is 1 Pet. iii. 19; that is, to men and women then alive, but now separated from the body, and imprisoned in hell for their disobedience.   And it was Christ that was with the church in the wilderness, instructing and guiding them by the ministry of Moses and Aaron, Acts vii. 37, 38; and so he hath taught the church since his

ascension. He cannot now be personally with us, having other business to do for us in heaven; but, however, he will not be wanting to teach us by his officers, whom, for that end, he hath set and appointed in the church, Eph. iv. 11, 12.

2. He hath dispensed his blessed light to the church gradually. The discoveries of light have been πολυμερως, that is, in many parts or parcels; sometimes more obscure and cloudy; as to the Old Testament believers, by visions, dreams, Urim, Thummim, vocal oracles, types, sacrifices, &c. which, though they were comparatively but a weak, glimmering light, and had no glory compared to that which now shines, 2 Cor. iii. 7—11, yet it was sufficient for the instruction and salvation of the elect in those times; but now is light sprung up gloriously in the gospel dispensation: " And we all with open face, behold as in a glass the glory of the Lord." It is to us not a twilight, but the light of a perfect day; and still is advancing in the several ages of the world. I know more (saith Luther) than blessed Austin knew; and they that come after me, will know more than I know.

3. Jesus Christ, our great Prophet, hath manifested to us the will of God plainly and perspicuously. When he was on earth himself, he taught the people by parables, and " without a parable he spake nothing," Matt. xiii. 34. He clothed sublime and spiritual mysteries in earthly metaphors, bringing them thereby to the low and dull capacities of men, speaking so familiarly to the people about them, as if he had been speaking earthly things to them, John iii. 12. And so (according to his own example) would he have his ministers preach, " using great plainness of speech," 2 Cor. iii. 12. and by manifestation of the truth, " commending themselves to every man's conscience," 2 Cor. iv. 2. Yet not allowing them to be rude and careless in expression, pouring out indigested, crude, immethodical words; no, a holy, serious, strict, and grave expression befits the lips of his ambassadors: and who ever spake more weightily, more logically, persuasively, than that apostle, by whose pen Christ hath admonished us to beware of vain affections and swelling words of vanity? But he would have us stoop to the understandings of the meanest, and not give the people a comment darker than the text; he would have us rather pierce their ears, than tickle their fancies; and break their hearts, than please their ears. Christ was a very plain preacher.

4. Jesus Christ discovered truth powerfully; speaking " as one having authority, and not as the scribes," Matt. vii. 29. They were cold and dull preachers, their words did even freeze

between their lips; but Christ spake with power; there was heat
as well as light in his doctrine: and so there is still, though it be
in the mouth of poor, contemptible men. "The weapons of
our warfare are not carnal, but mighty through God to the casting
down of strong holds," 2 Cor. x. 4: it is still "quick and powerful, sharper than a two-edged sword; and piercing, to the dividing asunder of soul and spirit, and of joints and marrow," Heb.
iv. 12. The blessed apostle imitated Christ; and being filled
with his Spirit, spake home and freely to the hearts of men. So
many words, so many claps of thunder, (as Augustine said of
him,) which made the hearts of sinners shake and tremble in their
breasts. All faithful and able ministers are not alike gifted in
this particular; but, surely, there is a holy seriousness and spiritual grace and majesty in their doctrine, commanding reverence
from their hearers.

5. This Prophet, Jesus Christ, taught the people the mind of
God in a sweet, affectionate, and taking manner: his words made
their hearts burn within them, Luke xxiv. 32. It was prophesied of him, "He shall not cry, nor lift up, nor cause his voice
to be heard on high. A bruised reed he shall not break, and
smoking flax he shall not quench," Isa. xlii. 2, 3. He knew
how to speak a word in season to the weary soul, Isa. l. 4.
He gathered the lambs with his arms, and gently led those
that were with young, Isa. xl. 11. How sweetly did his words
slide to the melting hearts about him! he drew with cords of
love, with the bands of a man: he discouraged none, upbraided
none that were willing to come to him; his familiarity and free
condescensions to the most vile and despicable sinners, were often
made a matter of reproach to him. Such is his gentle and sweet
carriage to his people, that the church is called the Lamb's wife,
Rev. xix. 7.

6. He revealed the mind of God purely to men: his doctrine
had not the least mixture of error to debase it; his most envi-
ously observant hearers could find nothing to charge him with:
he is "the faithful and true Witness," Rev. i. 5; and he hath
commanded his ministers to preserve the simplicity and purity
of the gospel, and not to blend and sophisticate it, 2 Cor. iv. 2.

7. And lastly, He revealed the will of God perfectly and fully,
keeping back nothing needful to salvation. So he tells his disciples, "All things that I have heard of my Father, I have
made known unto you," John xv. 15. He was "faithful as a
Son over his own house," Heb. iii. 6. Thus you have a brief
account of what is implied in this part of Christ's prophetical
office, and how he performed it.

Inference 1. If Jesus Christ, who is now passed into the heavens, be the great Prophet and Teacher of the church; hence we may justly infer the continual necessity of a standing ministry of the church: for by his ministers he now teacheth us, and to that intent hath fixed them in the church, by a firm constitution, there to remain to the end of the world, Matt. xxviii. 20. His ministers supply the want of his personal presence, " We pray you in Christ's stead," 2 Cor. v. 20. These offices he gave the church at his ascension, that is, when he ceased to teach them any longer with his own lips; and so set them in the church, that their succession shall never totally fail: for so the word εθετο, he hath set, 1 Cor. xii. 28, plainly implies. They are set by a sure establishment, a firm and unalterable constitution, even as the times and seasons, which the Father hath put [εθετο] in his own power: it is the same word, and it is well they are so firmly set and fixed there; for how many adversaries in all ages have endeavoured to shake the very office itself! pretending that it is needless to be taught by men, and wresting such scriptures as these to countenance their error: " I will pour out my Spirit upon all flesh: and your sons and daughters shall prophesy," &c. Joel ii. 28, 29. And, " These shall teach no more every man his neighbour, and every man his brother, saying, Know the Lord; for they shall all know me from the least of them to the greatest of them," Jer. xxxi. 34.

As to that of Joel, it is answered, That if an Old Testament prophecy may be understood according to a New Testament interpretation, then that prophecy doth no way oppose, but confirm the gospel ministry. How the apostle understood the prophet in that his prophecy, may be seen in Acts ii. 17, when the Spirit was poured out on the day of Pentecost upon the apostles. And surely he must be a confident person indeed, that thinks not an apostle to be as good an expositor of the prophet, as himself.

And for that text in Jer. xxxi. we say, (1.) That if it conclude against ministerial teachings, it must equally conclude against christian conferences. (2.) We say that cannot be the sense of one scripture which contradicts the plain sense of other scriptures: but so this would, Eph. iv. 11, 12; 1 Cor. xii. 28. (3.) And we say, the sense of that text is not negative, but comparative. Not that they shall have no need to be taught any truth, but no such need to be taught the first truths : That there is a God, and who is this true God: They shall no more " teach every man his brother, saying, Know the Lord; for they shall all know me."

To conclude, God hath given ministers to the church for the work of conversion and edification, "till we all come into the unity of the faith, to a perfect man," Eph. iv. 11, 12.   So that when all the elect are converted, and all those converts become perfect men ; when there is no error in judgment or practice, and no seducer to cause it, then, and not till then, will a gospel ministry be useless.   But (as it has been well observed) there is not a man that opposes a gospel ministry, but the very being of that man is a sufficient argument for the continuance of it.

2. If Christ be the great Prophet of the church, and such a Prophet, then it follows, that the weakest christians need not be discouraged at the dulness and incapacity they find in themselves : for Christ is not only a patient and condescending Teacher, but he can also, as he hath often done, reveal that to babes, which is hid from the wise and learned, Matt. xi. 25. "The testimonies of the Lord are sure, making wise the simple," Psa. xix. 7.   Yea, and such as you are, the Lord delights to choose, that his grace may be the more conspicuous in your weakness, 1 Cor. i. 26, 27.   Well then, be not discouraged ; others may know more in other things than you, but you are not incapable of knowing so much as shall save your souls, if Christ will be your teacher: in other knowledge they excel you ; but if ye know Jesus Christ, and the truth as it is in him, one drop of your knowledge is worth a whole sea of their gifts.   It is better in kind, the one being but natural, the other super-natural, from the saving illuminations and inward teachings of the Spirit : and so is one of those better things that accompany salvation.   It is better in respect of effects ; other knowledge leaves the heart as dry, barren, and unaffected, as if it had its seat in another man's head; but that little you have been taught of Christ, sheds down its gracious influences upon your affections, and slides sweetly to your melting hearts.   So that as one " preferred the most despicable work of a plain rustic christian before all the triumphs of Alexander and Cesar ;" much more ought you to prefer one saving manifestation of the Spirit, to all the powerless illuminations of natural men.

3. If Christ be the great Prophet and Teacher of the church, it follows, that prayer is a proper mean for the increase of know-ledge. Prayer is the golden key that unlocks that treasure. When Daniel was to expound that secret which was contained in the king's dream, about which the chaldean magicians had racked their brains to no purpose ; what course doth Daniel take ? Why, " he went to his house, (saith the text, Dan. ii. 17, 18,) and made the thing known to Hananiah, Mishael, and Azariah

his companions; that they would desire mercies of the God of heaven concerning his secret." And then was the secret revealed to Daniel. Luther was wont to say, "Three things made a divine; meditation, temptation, and prayer." Holy Mr. Bradford was wont to study upon his knees. Those truths that are got by prayer, leave an unusual sweetness upon the heart. If Christ be our Teacher, it becomes all his saints to be at his feet.

4. If Christ be the great Prophet and Teacher of the church, we may thence discern and judge of doctrines, and it may serve us as a test to try them by. For such as Christ is, such are the doctrines that flow from him: every error pretends to derive itself from him; but as Christ was holy, humble, heavenly, meek, peaceful, plain, and simple, and in all things alien, yea, contrary to the wisdom of the world and the gratifications of the flesh; such are the truths which he teaches. They have his character and image engraven on them. Would you know then whether this or that doctrine be from the Spirit of Christ or no? Examine the doctrine itself by this rule. And whatsoever doctrine you find to encourage and countenance sin, to exalt self, to be accommodated to earthly designs and interests, to wrap and bend to the humours and lusts of men, in a word, what doctrine soever makes them that profess it carnal, turbulent, proud, sensual, &c. you may safely reject it, and conclude this never came from Jesus Christ. The doctrine of Christ is after godliness; his truth sanctifies. There is a spiritual taste, by which those that have their senses exercised, can distinguish things that differ. "The spiritual man judgeth all things," 1 Cor. ii. 15. "His ear tries words, as his mouth tasteth meats," Job xxxiv. 3. Swallow nothing (let it come never so speciously) that hath not some relish of Christ and holiness in it. Be sure, Christ never revealed any thing to men, that derogates from his own glory, or prejudices and obstructs the ends of his own death.

5. And as it will serve us for a test of doctrines, so it serves for a test of ministers; and hence you may judge who are authorized and sent by Christ the great Prophet, to declare his will to men. Surely those whom he sends have his Spirit in their hearts, as well as his words in their mouths. And according to the measures of grace received, they faithfully endeavour to fulfil their ministry for Christ, as Christ did for his Father: "As my Father hath sent me, (saith Christ,) so send I you," John xx. 21. They take Christ for their pattern in the whole course of their ministration, and are such as sincerely endeavour to imitate the great Shepherd, in these six particulars following:

(1.) Jesus Christ was a faithful minister, the " faithful and true Witness," Rev. i. 5.   He declared the whole mind of God to men.   Of him it was prophetically said, " I have not hid thy righteousness within my heart ; I have declared thy faithfulness, and thy salvation ; I have not concealed thy loving-kindness and thy truth from the great congregation," Psa. xl. 10.   To the same sense, and almost in the same words, the apostle Paul professed, in Acts xx. 20, " I have kept back nothing that was profitable unto you ;" and, " I have showed you all things," ver. 35.   Not that every faithful minister doth in course of his ministry, anatomize the whole body of truth, and fully expound and apply each particular to the people.   No, that is not the meaning; but with respect to those doctrines which they have opportunity of opening, they do not out of fear, or to accommodate and secure base, low ends, withhold the mind of God, or so corrupt and abuse his words, as to subject truth to their own, or other men's lusts : " They preach not as pleasing men, but God," 1 Thess. ii. 4.   " For if we yet please men, we cannot be the servants of Christ," Gal. i. 10.   Truth must be spoken, though the greatest on earth be offended.

(2.) Jesus Christ was a tender-hearted minister, full of compassion to souls.   He was sent to bind up the broken in heart, Isa. lxi. 1.   He grieved at the hardness of men's hearts, Mark iii. 5.   He mourned over Jerusalem, and said, " O Jerusalem, Jerusalem ! how oft would I have gathered thy children, as a hen gathers her brood under her wings !" Matt. xxiii. 37. His bowels yearned when he saw the multitude, as sheep having no shepherd, Matt. ix. 36.   This tender compassion of Christ must be in all the under shepherds.   " God is my witness, (saith one of them,) how greatly I long after you all, in (or after the pattern of) the bowels of Christ Jesus," Phil. i. 8. He that shows a hard heart, unaffected with the dangers and miseries of souls, can never show a commission from Christ to authorize him for ministerial work.

(3.) Jesus Christ was a laborious, painful minister, he put a necessity on himself to finish his work in his day ; a work infinitely great, in a very little time ; " I must work the works of him that sent me, while it is day : the night cometh, when no man can work," John ix. 4. Oh how much work did Christ do in a little time on earth ! " He went about doing good," Acts x. 38.   He was never idle.   When he sits down at Jacob's well, to rest himself, being weary, presently he falls into his work, preaching the gospel to the samaritan woman.   In this must his ministers resemble him; "striving according to his working, that worketh in them mightily," Col. i. 28, 29.

(4.) Jesus Christ delighteth in nothing more than the success of his ministry; to see the work of the Lord prosper in his hand, this was meat and drink to him. When the seventy returned, and reported the success of their first embassy, "Lord, even the devils are subject to us through thy name!" "Why, (saith Christ,) I beheld Satan fall as lightning from heaven." As if he had said, You tell me no news, I saw it when I sent you at first: I knew the gospel would succeed where it came. "And in that hour Jesus rejoiced in spirit," Luke x. 17, 18. 21. And is it not so with those sent by him? do not they value the success of their ministry at a high rate? "My little children, (saith Paul,) of whom I travail again in birth, till Christ be formed in you," Gal. iv. 19.

(5.) Jesus Christ was a minister that lived up to his doctrine: his life and doctrine harmonized in all things. He pressed to holiness in his doctrine, and was the great pattern of holiness in his life; "Learn of me, I am meek and lowly," Matt. xi. 29. And such his ministers desire to approve themselves; "What ye have heard and seen in me, that do," Phil. iv. 9. He preached to their eyes, as well as ears. His life was a comment on his doctrine. They might see holiness acted in his life, as well as sounded by his lips. He preached the doctrine, and lived the application.

(6.) Jesus Christ was a minister that maintained sweet, secret communion with God, in all his constant public labours. If he had been preaching and healing all the day, yet he would redeem time from his very sleep to spend in secret prayer; "When he had sent the multitude away, he went up into a mountain apart to pray, and was there alone," Matt. xiv. 23. O blessed pattern! Let the keepers of the vineyards remember they have a vineyard of their own to keep, a soul of their own that must be looked after as well as other men's. Those that, in these things, imitate Christ, are surely sent to us from him, and are worthy of double honour: they are a choice blessing to the people.

SERMON X.

LUKE XXIV. 45.

THEN OPENED HE THEIR UNDERSTANDINGS, THAT THEY MIGHT UNDERSTAND THE SCRIPTURES.

KNOWLEDGE of spiritual things is well distinguished into intellectual and practical : the first hath its seat in the mind, the latter in the heart. This latter, divines call a knowledge peculiar to saints ; and, in the apostle's language in Phil. iii. 8, it is, " The eminency, or excellency of the knowledge of Christ." And indeed, there is but little excellency in all those petty notions which furnish the lips with discourse, unless by a sweet and powerful influence they draw the conscience and will to the obedience of Christ. Light in the mind is necessarily antecedent to the sweet and heavenly motions and elevations of the affections: for the further any man stands from the light of truth, the further he must needs be from the warmth of comfort. Heavenly quickenings are begotten in the heart, while the Sun of righteousness spreads the beams of truth into the understanding ; yet all the light of the gospel spreading and diffusing itself in the mind, can never savingly open and change the heart, without another act of Christ upon it ; and what that is the text informs you ; " Then opened he their understandings, that they might understand the scriptures." In which words we have both an act of Christ upon the disciples' understandings, and the immediate end and scope of that act.

1. Christ's act upon their understandings : He opened their understandings. By understanding is not here meant the mind only, in opposition to the heart, will, and affections, but these were opened by and with the mind. The mind is to the heart, as the door to the house ; what comes into the heart, comes in at the understanding, which is introductive to it ; and although truths sometimes go no further than the entry, and never penetrate the heart, yet, here, this effect is undoubtedly included.

Expositors consider this expression as parallel to that in Acts xvi. 14, " The Lord opened the heart of Lydia." And it is well observed, that it is one thing to open the scriptures, that is, to expound them, and give the meaning of them, as Paul is said to do in Acts xxviii. 23, and another thing to open the mind, or heart, as it is here. There are, as a learned man truly observes, two doors of the soul barred against Christ; the understanding, by ignorance; and the heart, by hardness: both these are opened by Christ. The former is opened by the preaching of the gospel, the other by the internal operation of the Spirit. The former belongs to the first part of Christ's prophetical office, opened in the foregoing sermon; the latter, to that special internal part of his prophetical office, which is to be opened in this.

And that it was not a naked act upon their minds only, but that their hearts and minds did work in fellowship, being both touched by this act of Christ, is evident enough by the effects mentioned, ver. 52, 53, " They returned to Jerusalem with great joy, and were continually in the temple, praising and blessing God." It is confessed, that before this time Christ had opened their hearts by conversion; and this opening is therefore to be understood in reference to those particular truths, in which, till now, they were not sufficiently informed, and so their hearts could not be duly affected with them. They were very dark in their apprehensions of the death and resurrection of Christ; and consequently their hearts were sad and dejected about that which had befallen him, ver. 17. But when he opened the scriptures and their understandings and hearts together, then things appeared with another face, and they returned, blessing and praising God.

2. Here is further to be considered, the design and end of this act upon their understandings; " That they might understand the scriptures:" where let it be marked, reader, that the teachings of Christ and his Spirit were never designed to take men off from reading, and studying, and searching the scriptures, as some vain notionists have pretended. God never intended to abolish his word, by giving his Spirit; and they are true fanatics (as Calvin upon this place calls them) that think or pretend so. Hence we observe,

> DOCT. THAT THE OPENING OF THE MIND AND HEART, EFFECTUALLY TO RECEIVE THE TRUTHS OF GOD, IS THE PECULIAR PREROGATIVE AND OFFICE OF JESUS CHRIST.

One of the great miseries under which fallen nature labours, is spiritual blindness. Jesus Christ brings that eye-salve which only can cure it. " I counsel thee to buy of me eye-salve, that thou mayest see," Rev. iii. 18. Those to whom the Spirit hath applied it, can say, as it is 1 John v. 20, " We know that the Son of God is come, and hath given us an understanding, that we may know him that is true ; and we are in him that is true, even in his Son Jesus Christ: this is the true God, and eternal life."

· " For the spiritual illumination of a soul, it is not sufficient that the object be revealed, nor yet that man, the subject of that knowledge, have a due use of his own reason ; but it is further necessary that the grace and special assistance of the Holy Spirit be superadded, to open and mollify the heart, and so give it a due taste and relish of the sweetness of spiritual truth."*

For explication of this part of Christ's prophetical office, I shall, as in the former, show what is included in the opening of their understanding, and by what acts Christ performs it. And,

I. Give you a brief account of what is included in this act of Christ. Take it in the following particulars.

1. It implies the transcendent nature of spiritual things, far exceeding the highest flight and reach of natural reason. Jesus Christ must by his Spirit open the understandings of men, or they can never comprehend such mysteries. Some men have strong natural parts, and by improvement of them are become eagle-eyed in the mysteries of nature. Who more acute than the heathen sages ? Yet, to them the gospel seemed foolishness, 1 Cor. i. 18. Austin confesses, that before his conversion, he often felt his spirit swell with offence and contempt of the gospel ; and he despising it, said, dedignabar esse parvulus ; " he scorned to become a child again." Bradwardine, that profound doctor, professes that when he read Paul's epistles, he contemned them, because in them he found not a metaphysical wit. Surely, it is possible a man may, with Berengarius, be able to dispute de omni scibili, of every point of knowledge ; to unravel nature from the cedar in Lebanon to the hyssop on the wall ; and yet be as blind as a bat in the knowledge of Christ. Yes, it is possible a man's understanding may be improved by the gospel, to a great ability in the literal knowledge of it, so as to be able to expound the scriptures correctly, and enlighten others by them ; as we find in Matt. vii. 22, that the scribes and pharisees were well acquainted with the scriptures of the Old Testament ; and yet notwithstanding Christ truly calls them blind guides, Matt. xxiii. 16. Till Christ open the heart, we

* Reynold. Animal. Homo. p. 25.

can know nothing of him, or of his will, as we ought to know it. So experimentally true is that of the apostle, " The natural man receiveth not the things of the Spirit of God, for they are foolishness to him; neither can he know them, because they are spiritually discerned. But he that is spiritual, judgeth all things; yet he himself is judged of no man," 1 Cor. ii. 14, 15. The spiritual man can judge and discern the carnal man, but the carnal man wants a faculty to judge of the spiritual man : as a man that carries a dark lanthorn, can see another by its light, but the other cannot discern him. Such is the difference between persons whose hearts Christ hath, or hath not opened.

2. Christ's opening the understanding, implies the insufficiency of all external means, how excellent soever they are in themselves, to operate savingly upon men, till Christ by his power opens the soul, and so makes them effectual. What excellent preachers were Isaiah and Jeremiah to the jews ! The former spake of Christ more like an evangelist of the New than a prophet of the Old Testament : the latter was a most convincing and pathetical preacher : yet the one complains, " Who hath believed our report ? and to whom is the arm of the Lord revealed?" Isa. liii. 1. The other laments the ill success of his ministry; " The bellows are burnt, the lead is consumed of fire, the founder melteth in vain," Jer. vi. 29. Under the New Testament, what people ever enjoyed such choice helps and means, as those that lived under the ministry of Christ and the apostles? Yet how many remained still in darkness ! " We have piped to you, but ye have not danced ; we have mourned unto you, but ye have not lamented," Matt. xi. 17. Neither the delightful airs of mercy, nor the doleful ditties of judgment, could affect or move their hearts.

And indeed if you search into the reason of it, you will be satisfied, that the choicest of means can do nothing upon the heart, until Christ by his Spirit open it, because ordinances work not as natural causes do : for then the effect would always follow unless miraculously hindered ; and it would be equally wonderful, that all that hear should not be converted, as that the three children should be in the fiery furnace so long, and yet not be burned: no, it works not as a natural, but as a moral cause, whose efficacy depends on the gracious concurrence of the Spirit. " The wind bloweth where it listeth," John iii. 8. The ordinances are like the pool of Bethesda, John v. 4. At a certain time an angel came down and troubled the waters, and then they had a healing virtue in them. So the Spirit comes down at certain times in the word, and opens the heart; and then it becomes the power of God to salvation. So that when you see souls daily sitting under excellent means of grace, and remain dead still, you may say as Martha did to Christ of her brother Lazarus, Lord, if thou hadst been here they had not remained dead. If thou hadst been in this sermon, it had not been so ineffectual to them.

3. It implies the utter impotency of man to open his own heart, and thereby make the word effectual to his own conversion and salvation. He that at first said, " Let there be light," and it was so, must shine into our hearts, or they will never be savingly enlightened, 2 Cor. iv. 4. 6. A double misery lies upon a great part of mankind, namely, impotency and pride. They have not only lost the liberty and freedom of their wills, but with it have so far lost their understanding and humility as not to own it. But, alas! man is become a most impotent creature by the fall; so far from being able to open his own heart, that he cannot know the things of the Spirit, 1 Cor. ii. 14, cannot believe, John vi. 44, cannot obey, Rom. viii. 7, cannot speak one good word, Matt. xii. 34, cannot think one good thought, 2 Cor. iii. 5, cannot do one good act, John xv. 5. Oh what a helpless thing is a poor sinner! Suitably to this state of impotence, conversion is in scripture called regeneration, John iii. 3, a resurrection from the dead, Eph. ii. 5, a creation, Eph. ii. 10, a victory, 2 Cor. x. 5.

4. Christ's opening the understanding imports his Divine power, whereby he is able to subdue all things to himself. Who but God knows the heart? Who but God can unlock and open it at pleasure? No mere creature, no not the angels themselves, who for their large understandings are called intelligences, can command or open the heart. We may stand and knock at men's hearts, till our own ache; but no opening till Christ come. He can fit a key to all the cross wards of the will, and with sweet efficacy open it, and that without any force or violence to it.

II. In the next place, let us see by what acts Jesus Christ performs this work of his, and what way and method he takes to open the hearts of sinners.

There are two principal ways, by which Christ opens the understandings and hearts of men, namely, by his word and Spirit.

1. By his word; to this end was Paul commissioned and sent to preach the gospel, " To open their eyes, and turn them from darkness to light, and from the power of Satan to God," Acts xxvi. 18. The Lord can, if he pleases, accomplish this

immediately; but though he can do it, he will not do it ordinarily without means, because he will honour his own institutions. There you may observe, that when Lydia's heart was to be opened, " there appeared unto Paul a man of Macedonia, who prayed him, saying, Come over into Macedonia, and help us," Acts xvi. 9. God will keep up his ordinances among men; and though he hath not tied himself, yet he hath tied us to them. Cornelius must send for Peter. God can make the earth produce corn, as it did at first, without cultivation and labour; but he that shall now expect it in the neglect of means, may perish for want of bread.

2. But the ordinances in themselves cannot do it, as I noted before; and therefore Jesus Christ hath sent forth the Spirit, who is his vicegerent, to carry on this work upon the hearts of his elect. And when the Spirit comes down upon the souls in the administration of the ordinances, he effectually opens the heart to receive the Lord Jesus, by the hearing of faith. He breaks in upon the understanding and conscience by powerful convictions and compunctions; as those words, John xvi. 8, import, " He shall convince the world of sin;" convince by clear demonstration, such as enforces assent, so that the soul cannot but yield it to be so; and yet the door of the heart is not opened, till he has also put forth his power upon the will, and, by a sweet and secret efficacy, overcome all its reluctance, and the soul be made willing in the day of his power. When this is done, the heart is opened; saving light now shines in it; and this light set up, the Spirit in the soul is,

(1.) A new light, in which things appear far otherwise than they did before. The names Christ and sin, the words heaven and hell, have another sound in that man's ears, than formerly they had. When he comes to read the same scriptures, which possibly he had read a hundred times before, he wonders he should be so blind as he was, to overlook such great, weighty, and interesting things as he now beholds in them; and saith, Where were mine eyes, that I could never see these things before?

(2.) It is a very affecting light; a light that hath heat and powerful influences with it, which makes deep impressions on the heart. Hence they whose eyes the great Prophet opens, are said to be " brought out of darkness into his marvellous light," 1 Pet. ii. 9. The soul is greatly affected with what it sees. " Did not our hearts burn within us, whilst he talked with us, and opened to us the scriptures?"

(3.) And it is a growing light, like the light of the morning, which " shines more and more unto the perfect day," Prov. iv. 18.   When the Spirit first opens the understanding, he doth not give it at once a full sight of all truths, or a full sense of the power, sweetness, and goodness of any truth ; but the soul in the use of means grows up to a greater clearness day by day: its knowledge grows extensively in measure, and intensively in power and efficacy.   And thus the Lord Jesus by his Spirit opens the understanding.

Now the use of this follows in five practical deductions.

1. If this be the work and office of Jesus Christ, to open the understandings of men ; hence we infer the miseries that lie upon those men, whose understandings, to this day, Jesus Christ hath not opened ; of whom we may say, as it is, Deut. xxix. 4,   To this day Christ hath not given them eyes to see.   Natural blindness, whereby we are deprived of the light of this world, is sad ; but spiritual blindness is much more so.   See how dolefully their case is represented ; " But if our gospel be hid, it is hid to them that are lost : whose eyes the god of this world hath blinded, lest the light of the glorious gospel of Christ, who is the image of God, should shine unto them," 2 Cor. iv. 3, 4 ; he means a total and final concealment of the saving power of the word from them.   What is their condition ?   Truly no better than lost men.   It is hid $\tau o\iota\varsigma$ $\alpha\pi o\lambda\lambda\upsilon\mu\epsilon\nu o\iota\varsigma$, from them that are to perish, or be destroyed.   More particularly, because the point is of deep concernment, let us consider,

(1.) The judgment inflicted, and that is spiritual blindness. A sore misery indeed ! Not a universal ignorance of all truths ; O no ! in natural and moral truths they are oftentimes acute and sharp-sighted men ; but in that part of knowledge which leads to eternal life, John xvii. 2, there they are utterly blinded : as it is said of the jews, upon whom this misery lies, that blindness in part is happened to Israel.

· (2.) The subject of this judgment, the mind, which is the eye of the soul.   If it were put upon the body, it would not be so considerable ; this falls immediately upon the soul, the noblest part of man, and upon the mind, the intellectual, rational faculty, which the philosophers call the leading, directive faculty ; which is to the soul what the natural eye is to the body.   Now the soul being the most active and restless thing in the world, always working, and its leading, directive power blind, judge what a sad and dangerous state such a soul is in ; just like a fiery, high-mettled horse, whose eyes are out, furiously carrying his rider upon rocks, pits, and dangerous precipices.   I remember Chrysostom, speaking of the loss of a soul, saith that the loss of a member of the body is nothing to it: for, saith he, if a man lose an eye, ear, hand, or foot. there is another to supply its want: "God hath given us those members double; but he hath not given us two souls," that if one be lost, yet the other may be saved. Surely it were better for thee, reader, to have every member of thy body made the seat and subject of the most exquisite racking torments, than for spiritual blindness to befall thy soul. Moreover,

(3.) Consider the indiscernibleness of this judgment to the soul on whom it lies: they know it not, no more than a man knows that he is asleep. Indeed it is "the spirit of a deep sleep poured out upon them from the Lord," Isa. xxix. 10. This renders their misery the more remediless: "Because ye say you see, therefore your sin remaineth," John ix. 41. Once more,

(4.) Consider the tendency and effects of it. What doth this tend to but eternal ruin? for hereby we are cut off from the only remedy. The soul that is so blinded, can never see sin, nor a Saviour; but, like the egyptians, during the palpable darkness, sits still, and moves not after its own recovery. And as ruin is that to which it tends, so in order thereto, it renders all the ordinances and duties under which that soul comes, altogether useless and ineffectual to its salvation. He comes to the word, and sees others melted by it, but to him it signifies nothing. Did you but understand the misery of such a state, if Christ should say to you, as he did to the blind man, "What wilt thou that I should do for thee?" you would return as he did, "Lord, that my eyes may be opened," Matt. xx. 32, 33.

2. If Jesus Christ be the great Prophet of the church, then surely he will take special care both of the church and the under shepherds appointed by him to feed them: else both the objects and instruments upon and by which he executes his office, must fail, and consequently this glorious office be in vain. Hence he is said "to walk among the golden candlesticks," Rev. i. 13, and "to hold the stars in his right hand," Rev. ii. 1. Jesus Christ instrumentally opens the understandings of men by the preaching of the gospel; and whilst there is an elect soul to be converted, or a convert to be further illuminated, means shall not fail to accomplish it by.

3. Hence you that are yet in darkness, may be directed to whom to apply yourselves for saving knowledge. It is Christ that hath the sovereign eye-salve, that can cure your blindness; he only hath the key of the house of David; he openeth, and no man shutteth. Oh that I might persuade you to set yourselves in his way, under the ordinances, and cry to him, "Lord, that

my eyes may be opened." Three things are exceedingly encouraging to you so to do.

(1.) God the Father hath put him into this office, for the cure of such as you are: "I will give thee for a light to the gentiles, that thou mayest be my salvation to the end of the earth," Isa. xlix. 6. This may furnish you with an argument to plead for a cure. Why do you not go to God, and say, Lord, didst thou give Jesus Christ a commission to open the blind eyes? Behold me, Lord; such a one am I, a poor, dark, ignorant soul. Didst thou give him to be thy salvation to the ends of the earth? No place nor people excluded from the benefit of that light; and shall I still remain in the shadow of death? Oh that unto me he might be a saving light also!

(2.) It is encouraging to think, that Jesus Christ hath actually opened the eyes of them that were as dark and ignorant as you are. He hath revealed those things to babes, that have been hid from the wise and prudent, Matt. xi. 25. "The law of the Lord is perfect, making wise the simple," Psa. xix. 7. And if you look among those whom Christ hath enlightened, you will not find "many wise after the flesh, many mighty or noble; but the foolish, weak, base, and despised; these are they on whom he hath glorified the riches of his grace," 1 Cor. i. 26, 27.

(3.) And is it not yet further encouraging to you that hitherto he hath mercifully continued you under the means of light? Why is not the light of the gospel put out? Why are times and seasons of grace continued to you, if God have no further design of good to your souls? Be not therefore discouraged, but wait on the Lord in the use of means, that you may yet be healed.

If you ask, What can we do to put ourselves into the way of the Spirit, in order to such a cure? I say, though you cannot do any thing, that can make the gospel effectual, yet the Spirit of God can make those means you are capable of using effectual, if he please to concur with them. And it is a certain truth, that your inability to do what is above your power, doth no ways excuse you from doing what is within the compass of your power to do. Let me therefore advise,

[1.] That you diligently attend upon an able, faithful, and searching ministry. Neglect no opportunity God affords you; for how know you but *that* may be the time of mercy to your soul?

[2.] Satisfy not yourselves with hearing, but consider what you hear. Allow time to reflect upon what God hath spoken to you. What power is there in man more excellent, or more appropriate to the reasonable nature, than its reflective and self-considering power? There is little hope of any good to be done upon your souls, till you begin to go alone, and become thinking men and women : here all conversion begins. I know, a severer task can hardly be imposed upon a carnal heart. It is a hard thing to bring a man and himself together upon this account; but this must be, if ever the Lord do your souls good. "Commune with your own hearts," Psa. iv. 4.

[3.] Labour to see, and ingenuously confess the insufficiency of all your other knowledge to do you good. What if you had never so much skill and knowledge in other mysteries? What if you be never so well acquainted with the letter of the scripture? What if you had an angelical illumination? This can never save thy soul. No, all thy knowledge signifies nothing till the Lord show thee by special light the deplorable sight of thy own heart, and a saving sight of Jesus Christ, thy only remedy.

4. Since then there is a common light, and special saving light, which none but Christ can give, it is therefore the concern of every one of you to try what your light is. "We know, (saith the apostle, 1 Cor. viii. 1,) that we all have knowledge." O but what, and whence is it? Is it the light of life springing from Jesus Christ, that bright and morning Star, or only such as the devils and damned have? These lights differ,

(1.) In their very kind and nature. The one is heavenly, supernatural, and spiritual; the other earthly, and natural, the effect of a better constitution or education, James iii. 15. 17.

(2.) They differ most apparently in their effects and operations. The light that comes in a special way from Christ, is humbling and self-abasing light; by it a man sees the vileness of his own nature and practice, which begets self-loathing in him; but natural light, on the contrary, puffs up, exalts, and makes the heart swell with self-conceitedness, 1 Cor. viii. 1. The light of Christ is practical and operative, still urging the soul, yet lovingly constraining it to obedience. No sooner did it shine into Paul's heart, but presently he asks, " Lord, what wilt thou have me to do?" Acts ix. 6. It brought forth fruit in the colossians, from the first day it came to them, Col. i. 6; but the other spends itself in unpractical notions, and is detained in unrighteousness, Rom. i. 18. The light of Christ is powerfully transformative of its subjects, changing the man, in whom it is, into the same image, from glory to glory, 2 Cor. iii. 18. But common light leaves the heart as dead, as carnal and sensual, as if no light at all were in it. In a word, all saving light endears Jesus Christ to the soul; and as it could not value him before it saw him, so when once he appears to the soul in his own light, he is appreciated and endeared unspeakably : then none but Christ; all is but dung, that he may win Christ: none in heaven but him, nor in earth desirable in comparison of him.   But no such effect flows from natural, common knowledge.

(3.) They differ in their issues. Natural, common knowledge vanishes, as the apostle speaks, 1 Cor. xiii. 8. It is but a May-flower, and dies in its month. " Doth not their excellency that is in them go away ?" Job iv. 21.   But this that springs from Christ is perfected, not destroyed by death : it springs up into everlasting life.   The soul in which it is subjected, carries it away with it into glory. This light is life eternal, John xvii. 3. Now turn in, and compare yourselves with these rules : let not false light deceive you.

5. Lastly, How are they obliged to love, serve, and honour Jesus Christ, whom he hath enlightened with the saving knowledge of himself !   Oh that with hands and hearts lifted up to heaven, ye would adore the free grace of Jesus Christ to your souls !   How many round about you have their eyes closed, and their hearts shut up !   How many are in darkness, and likely to remain so till they come to the blackness of darkness, which is reserved for them.   Oh what a pleasant thing is it for your eyes to see the light of this world ! But what is it for the eye of your mind to see God in Christ ? to see such ravishing sights as the objects of faith are ? and to have such a pledge as this given you of the blessed visions of glory ? for in this light you shall see light.   Bless God, and boast not : rejoice in your light, but be not proud of it ; and beware ye sin not against the best and highest light in this world. If God were so incensed against the heathens for disobeying the light of nature, what is it in you to sin with eyes clearly illuminated with the purest light that shines in this world !   You know, God charges it upon Solomon, 1 Kings xi. 9, that he turned from the way of obedience after the Lord had appeared to him twice. Jesus Christ intended when he opened your eyes, that your eyes should direct your feet.   Light is a special help to obedience, and obedience is a singular help to increase your light.

SERMON XI.

THE NATURE AND NECESSITY OF THE PRIESTHOOD OF CHRIST.

HEB. IX. 23.

IT WAS THEREFORE NECESSARY THAT THE PATTERNS OF THINGS IN THE HEAVENS SHOULD BE PURIFIED WITH THESE; BUT THE HEAVENLY THINGS THEMSELVES WITH BETTER SACRIFICES THAN THESE.

SALVATION (as to the actual dispensation of it) is revealed by Christ as a Prophet, procured by him as a Priest, applied by him as a King. In vain it is revealed, if not purchased; in vain revealed and purchased, if not applied. How it is revealed, both to us, and in us, by our great Prophet, hath been declared. And now, from the prophetical office, we pass on to the priestly office of Jesus Christ, who as our Priest, purchased our salvation. In this office is contained the grand relief for a soul distressed by the guilt of sin. When all other reliefs have been tried, it is the blood of this great Sacrifice, sprinkled by faith upon the trembling conscience, that must cool, refresh, and sweetly compose and settle it. Now, seeing so great a weight hangs upon this office, the apostle industriously confirms and commends it in this epistle, and more especially in this ninth chapter; showing how it was prefigured to the world by the typical blood of the sacrifices, but infinitely excels them all: and as in many other most weighty respects, so principally in this, that the blood of these sacrifices did but purify the types or patterns of the heavenly things; but the blood of this Sacrifice purified or consecrated the heavenly things themselves, signified by those types.

These read, contain an argument to prove the necessity of the offering up of Christ, the great Sacrifice, drawn from the proportion betwixt the types and the things typified. If the sanctuary, mercy-seat, and all things pertaining to the service of the tabernacle, were to be consecrated by blood; those earthly, but sacred types, by the blood of bulls and lambs, &c.; much more the heavenly things shadowed by them, ought to be purified or consecrated by better blood than the blood of beasts. The blood consecrating these, should as much excel the blood that consecrated those, as the heavenly things themselves do, in their own nature, excel those earthly shadows of them. Look, what proportion there is between the type and anti-type, the like proportion also is between the blood that consecrates them; earthly things with common, heavenly things with the most excellent blood.

So then, there are two things to be especially observed here: 1. The nature of Christ's death and sufferings: it had the nature, use, and end of a sacrifice; and it was of all the sacrifices the most excellent. 2. The necessity of his offering it up: it was necessary to correspond with all the types and prefigurations of it under the law; but especially it was necessary for the expiating of sin, the propitiating of a justly incensed God, and the opening a way for us to come to God. The point I shall give you from it is,

DOCT. THAT THE SACRIFICE OF CHRIST, OUR HIGH PRIEST, IS MOST EXCELLENT IN ITSELF, AND MOST NECESSARY FOR US.

Sacrifices are of two sorts; eucharistical, or thank-offerings, in testification of homage, duty, and service, and in token of gratitude for mercies freely received; and ilastical, or expiatory, for satisfaction to justice, and thereby the atoning and reconciling of God. Of this last kind was the sacrifice offered by Jesus Christ for us: to this office he was called by God, Heb. v. 5. In it he was confirmed by the unchangeable oath of God, Psa. cx. 4; for it he was singularly qualified by his incarnation, Heb. x. 6, 7; and all the ends of it he has fully answered, Heb. ix. 11, 12.

My present design is, from this scripture, to open the general nature and absolute necessity of the priesthood of Christ; showing what his priesthood implies in it, and how all this was indispensably necessary in order to our recovery from the deplorable state of sin and misery.

I. We will consider what it supposes and implies; and then, wherein it consists. And there are six things which it either pre-supposes, or necessarily includes in it.

1. At first sight, it supposes man's revolt and fall from God; and a dreadful breach made thereby between God and him; else no need of an atoning sacrifice. "If one died for all, then were all dead," 2 Cor. v. 14, dead in law, under sentence to die, and that eternally. In all the sacrifices, from Adam to Christ, this was still preached to the world, that there was a fearful breach between God and man; and therefore, that justice required our blood should be shed. And the fire flaming on the altar, which wholly burnt up the sacrifice, was a lively emblem of that fiery

indignation that should devour the adversaries. But above all, when Christ, that true and great Sacrifice, was offered up to God, then was the clearest mirror that ever was in the world set before us, therein to see our sin and misery by the fall.

2. His priesthood supposes the unalterable purpose of God to take vengeance for sin; he will not let it pass. I will not pretend to say what God could do in this case, by his absolute power; but I think it is generally yielded, that, by his ordinate power, he could do no less than punish it in the person of the sinner, or of his surety. Those that contend for such a forgiveness, as is an act of charity, like that whereby private persons forgive one another, must at once suppose God to part with his right cedendo de jure suo, and also render the satisfaction of Christ altogether useless, as to the procurement of forgiveness; yea, rather an obstacle, than a means to it. Surely, the nature and truth of God oblige him to punish sin. " He is of purer eyes than to look upon iniquity," Hab. i. 13. And beside, the word is gone out of his mouth, that the sinner shall die.

3. The priesthood of Christ pre-supposes the utter impotency of man to appease God, and recover his favour, by any thing he could do or suffer. Surely God would not come down to assume a body to die, and be offered up for us, if at any cheaper rate it could have been accomplished; there was no other way to recover man and satisfy God. Those that deny the satisfaction of Christ, and talk of his dying to confirm the truth, and give us an example of meekness, patience, and self-denial, affirming these to be the sole ends of his death, do not only therein root up the foundations of their own comfort, peace, and pardon, but most boldly impeach the infinite wisdom. God could have done all this at a cheaper rate: the sufferings of a mere creature are able to attain these ends: the deaths of the martyrs did it. But who by dying can satisfy and reconcile God? what creature can bring him an adequate and proportionable value for sin? yea, for all the sin of all God's elect, from Adam, to the last that shall be found alive at the Lord's coming? Surely, none but Christ can do this.

4. Christ's priesthood implies the necessity of his being God-man. It was necessary he should be a man, in order to his suffering, his compassion, and the derivation of his righteousness and holiness to men. Had he not been a man, he had had no sacrifice to offer, no soul or body to suffer in. The Godhead is immortal, and above all those sufferings and miseries which Christ felt for us. Besides, his being man, fills him with bowels of compassion, and tender sense of our miseries: this makes him a

merciful and faithful High Priest, Heb. iv. 15, and not only fits him to pity, but to sanctify us also; for "he that sanctifieth, and they that are sanctified, are both of one," Heb. ii. 11. 14. 17.   And equally necessary was it that our High Priest should be God, since the value and efficacy of his sacrifice results from thence.

5. The priesthood of Christ implies the extremity of his sufferings. In sacrifices, you know, there was a destruction, a kind of annihilation of the creature to the glory of God. The shedding of the creature's blood, and burning its flesh with fire, was but an umbrage, or faint resemblance of what Christ endured, when he made his soul an offering for sin.

6. It implies the gracious design of God to reconcile us at a dear rate to himself, in that he called and confirmed Christ in his priesthood by an oath, and thereby provided a sacrifice, of infinite value, for the world.   Sins, for which no sacrifice is allowed, are desperate sins; and the case of such sinners is helpless: but if God allow, yea, and provide a sacrifice himself, how plainly doth it speak his intentions of peace and mercy! These things are manifestly pre-supposed, or implied in Christ's priesthood.

This priesthood of Christ is that function, wherein he comes before God, in our name and place, to fulfil the law, and offer up himself to him a sacrifice of reconciliation for our sins; and by his intercession to continue and apply the purchase of his blood to them for whom he shed it: all this is contained in that famous scripture, Heb. x. 7—14.   Or, more briefly, the priesthood of Christ is that whereby he expiated the sins of men, and obtained the favour of God for them, Col. i. 20. 22; Rom. v. 10.   But because I shall insist more largely upon the several parts and fruits of this office, it shall here suffice to speak this much as to its general nature; which was the first thing proposed for explication.

II. The necessity of Christ's priesthood comes next to be opened.   Touching which, I affirm, according to the scriptures, it was necessary, in order to our salvation, that such a Priest should, by such a sacrifice, appear before God for us.

The truth of this assertion will be cleared by these two principles, which are evident in the scripture, namely, That God required full satisfaction, and would not remit one sin without it: and, That fallen man is totally incapable of tendering him any such satisfaction; therefore Christ, who only can, must do it, or we perish.

1. God required full satisfaction, and would not remit one sin

without it. This will be clearly proved, from the nature of sin; and, from the veracity and wisdom of God.

(1.) From the nature of sin, which deserves that the sinner should suffer for it. Penal evil, in a course of justice, follows moral evil. Sin and sorrow ought to go together; there is between these a necessary connexion. "The wages of sin is death," Rom. vi. 23.

(2.) The veracity of God requires it. The word is gone out of his mouth; "In the day that thou eatest thereof, thou shalt surely die," Gen. ii. 17. From that time he was instantly and certainly obnoxious and liable to the death of soul and body. The law pronounces him cursed, "that continues not in all things that are written therein to do them," Gal. iii. 10. Now, though man's threatenings are often vain and insignificant things, yet God's shall surely take place; "not one tittle of the law shall fail, till all be fulfilled," Matt. v. 18. God will be true in his threatenings, though thousands and millions perish.

(3.) The wisdom of God, by which he governs the rational world, admits not of a dispensation or relaxation of the threatenings without satisfaction: for, as good no king, as no laws for government; as good no law, as no penalty; and as good no penalty, as no execution. To this purpose one well observes, " It is altogether indecent, especially to the wisdom and righteousness of God, that that which provoketh the execution, should procure the abrogation of his law; that that should supplant and undermine the law, for the alone preventing whereof the law was before established." How could it be expected, that men should fear and tremble before God, when they should find themselves more scared than hurt by his threats against sin? So then God required satisfaction, and would admit no treaty of peace on any other ground.

Let none here object, that reconciliation upon this only score of satisfaction is derogatory to the riches of grace; or that we allow not God what we do men, namely, to forgive an injury freely, without satisfaction. Free forgiveness to us, and full satisfaction made to God by Jesus Christ for us, are not things inconsistent with each other, as in its proper place shall be more fully cleared to you. And as for denying that to God which we allow to men; you must know, that man and man stand on even ground: man is not capable of being wronged and injured by man, as God is by man, there is no comparison between the nature of the offences. Besides, man only can freely forgive man, in a private capacity, so far as the wrong concerns himself; but he ought not to do so in a public capacity, as he is judge, and bound to execute justice impartially. God is our Law-giver and Judge ; he will not dispense with violations of the law, but strictly stands upon complete satisfaction.

2. Man can render to God no satisfaction of his own, for the wrong done by his sin. He finds no way to compensate and make God amends, either by doing, or by suffering his will.

(1.) Not by doing: this way is shut up to all the world; none can satisfy God, or reconcile himself to him this way ; for it is evident our best works are sinful; "All our righteousness is as filthy rags," Isa. lxiv. 6. And it is strange any should imagine, that one sin should make satisfaction for another. If it be said, not what is sinful in our duties, but what is spiritual, pure, and good, may ingratiate us with God ;—it is obvious to reply, that what is good in any of our duties, is a debt we owe to God, yea, we owe him perfect obedience ; and it is not ima-ginable how we should pay one debt by another ; quit a former by contracting a new engagement. If we do any thing that is good, we are indebted to grace for it, John xv. 5; 2 Cor. iii. 5; 1 Cor. xv. 10. In a word, those that have had as much to plead on that score as any now living, have quitted, and utterly given up all hopes of appeasing and satisfying the justice of God that way. It is likely that holy Job feared God and eschewed evil as much as any of you; yet he saith, "If I justify myself, mine own mouth shall condemn me ; if I say I am per-fect, it shall also prove me perverse. Though I were perfect, yet would I not know my soul ; I would despise my life," Job ix. 20, 21. It is probable that David was a man as much after the heart of God as you ; yet he said, "Enter not into judgment with thy servant ; for in thy sight shall no man be justified," Psa. cxliii. 2. It is likely that Paul lived as holy, heavenly, and fruitful a life as the best of you, and far, far beyond you ; yet he saith, "I know (or am conscious to myself) of nothing, yet am I not hereby justified," 1 Cor. iv. 4. His sincerity might comfort him, but could not justify him. And what need I say more? The Lord hath shut up this way to all the world ; and the scriptures speak it roundly and plainly: "Therefore by the deeds of the law there shall no flesh be justified in his sight," Rom. iii. 20. Compare Gal. iii. 21; Rom. viii. 3.

(2.) And as man can never reconcile himself to God by doing, so neither by suffering : that is equally impossible ; for no suffer-ings can satisfy God, but such as are proportionable to the offence we suffer for. And if so, an infinite suffering must be borne : I say infinite, for sin is an infinite evil, as it wrongs an infinite God. Now sufferings may be said to be infinite, either in respect of their weight, exceeding all bounds and limits; the letting out of the wrath and fury of an infinite God: or in respect of duration, being endless and everlasting. In the first sense, no creature can bear an infinite wrath, it would swallow us up. In the second, it may be borne as the damned do; but then, ever to be suffering, is never to have satisfied. So that no man can be his own priest, to reconcile himself to God by what he can do or suffer. And therefore, one that is able, by doing and suffering, to reconcile him, must undertake it, or we perish. Thus you see plainly and briefly the general nature and necessity of Christ's priesthood.

From both these, several useful, practical deductions offer themselves.

1. This shows, in the first place, the incomparable excellency of the christian religion above all other religions, known to, or professed in the world. What other religions seek, the christian religion alone finds, even a solid foundation for true peace and settlement of conscience. While the jew seeks it in vain in the law; the mahometan in his external and ridiculous observances; and the papist in his own merits; the believer only finds it in the blood of this great Sacrifice: this, and nothing less than this, can pacify a distressed conscience, labouring under the weight of its own guilt. Conscience demands no less to satisfy it, than God demands to satisfy him. The grand inquest of conscience is, Is God satisfied? If he be satisfied, I am satisfied. Woful is the state of that man, that feels the worm of conscience gnawing the most tender part of the soul, and hath no relief against it; that feels the intolerable scalding wrath of God burning within, and hath nothing to cool it. Hear me, you that slight the troubles of conscience, that call them fancies and melancholy whimsies; if you had ever had but one sick night for sin, if you had ever felt that shame, fear, horror, and despair, which are the dismal effects of an accusing and condemning conscience, you would account it an unspeakable mercy to hear of a way for the discharge of a poor sinner from that guilt: you would kiss the feet of that messenger that could bring you tidings of peace; you would call him blessed, that should direct you to an effectual remedy. Now, whoever thou art, that pinest away in thine iniquities, that droopest from day to day under the present wounds and the dismal presages of conscience, know that thy soul and peace can never meet, till thou art persuaded to come to this blood of sprinkling.

The blood of this sacrifice speaks better things than the blood of Abel. The blood of this sacrifice is the blood of God, Acts

xx. 28, invaluably precious blood, 1 Pet. i. 19 One drop of it infinitely excels the blood of all mere creatures, Heb. x. 4—6. Such is the blood that must do thee good.   Lord, I must have such blood (saith conscience) as is capable of giving thee full satisfaction, or it can give me no peace.   The blood of all the cattle upon a thousand hills cannot do this.   What is the blood of beasts to God? The blood of all the men in the world can do nothing in this case.   What is our polluted blood worth?

Yea, Christ's blood is not only the blood of God, but it is blood shed in thy stead, and in thy place and room.   "He was made a curse for us," Gal. iii. 13.   And so it becomes sin-pardoning blood, Heb. ix. 22 ; Eph. i. 7 ; Col. i. 14; Rom. iii. 26 ; and consequently, conscience-pacifying and soul-quieting blood, Col. i. 20 ; Eph. ii. 13, 14 ; Rom. iii. 25.   O bless God, that ever the news of this blood came to thine ears. With hands and eyes lifted up to heaven, admire that grace that cast thy lot in a place where this joyful sound rings in the ears of poor sinners.   Surely the pure light of the gospel shining upon this generation, is a mercy never to be enough prized.

2. Hence also learn the necessity of faith, in order to a state and sense of peace with God : for to what purpose is the blood of Christ our sacrifice shed, unless it be actually and personally applied, and appropriated by faith ? You know, when a sacrifice under the law was brought to be slain, he that brought it was to put his hand upon the head of the sacrifice, and so it was accepted for him, to make an atonement, Lev. i. 4 ; not only to signify, that now it was no more his, but God's, the property being transferred by a kind of manumission ; nor yet that he voluntarily gave it to the Lord as his own free act ; but principally it noted the putting off his sins, and the penalty due to him for them, upon the head of the sacrifice : and so it implied in it an execration, as if he had said, Upon thy head be the evil. So the learned observe, the ancient egyptians were wont expressly to imprecate, when they sacrificed, If any evil be coming upon us or upon Egypt, let it turn and rest upon this head, laying their hand, at these words, on the sacrifice's head.   And upon that ground, saith Herodotus the historian, none of them would eat of the head of any living creature.   You must also lay the hand of faith upon Christ your sacrifice, not to imprecate, but to apply and appropriate him to your own souls, he having been made a curse for you.

To this the whole gospel tends, even to persuade sinners to apply Christ and his blood to their own souls.   To this he invited us, "Come unto me, all ye that labour, and are heavy laden, and I will give you rest," Matt. xi. 28. For this end our sacrifice was lifted up upon the altar; " As Moses lifted up the serpent in the wilderness, so must the Son of man be lifted up: that whosoever believeth in him should not perish, but have everlasting life," John iii. 14, 15. The effects of the law, not only upon the conscience, filling it with torments, but upon the whole person, bringing death upon it, are here shadowed out by the stingings of fiery serpents; and Christ by the brazen serpent, which Moses exalted for the israelites, that were stung, to look unto. And as by looking to it they were healed; so by believing, or looking to Christ in faith, our souls are healed. Those that looked not to the brazen serpent, died infallibly; so must all that look not to Jesus, our sacrifice, by faith. It is true, the death of Christ is the meritorious cause of remission, but faith is the instrumental, applying cause; and as Christ's blood is necessary in its place, so is our faith in its place also. The death of Christ, the offers and tenders of Christ, never saved one soul in themselves, without believing application. But, alas! how do I see sinners, either not at all touched with the sense of sin, and so being whole, need not the physician; or if any be stung and wounded with guilt, how do they lick themselves whole with their own duties and reformations ! Physicians say of wounds, let them be kept clean, and nature will find balsam of its own to heal them. If it were so in spiritual wounds, what need Christ to have left the Father's bosom, and come down to die in the quality and nature of a sacrifice for us ? Oh if men can but have health, pleasure, riches, honours, and any way make a shift to still a disturbing conscience, that it may not check or interrupt them in these enjoyments, they care nothing for Christ. And I am assured, till God show you the face of sin, in the glass of the law, make the scorpions and fiery serpents, that lurk in the law, and in your own consciences, to come hissing about you, and smiting you with their deadly stings, till you have had some sick nights, and sorrowful days for sin, you will never go up and down seeking an interest in the blood of his sacrifice with tears. But, reader, if ever this be thy condition, then wilt thou know the worth of a Christ, then wilt thou have a value for the blood of sprinkling.

3. Is Christ your High Priest, and is his priesthood so indispensably necessary to our salvation ? Then freely acknowledge your utter impotency to reconcile yourselves to God by any thing you can do, or suffer; and let Christ have the whole glory of your recovery ascribed to him. It is highly reasonable that he that laid down the whole price, should have the whole praise.

If any man say or think, he could have made an atonement for himself, he doth therein cast no light reproach upon that profound wisdom which laid the design of our redemption in the death of Christ. But of this I have spoken elsewhere. And therefore,

4. In the last place, I rather choose to persuade you to see your necessity of this Priest, and his most excellent sacrifice; and accordingly to make use of it. The best of you have polluted natures, poisoned in the womb with sin; those natures have need of this sacrifice, they must have the benefit of this blood to pardon and cleanse them, or else be eternally damned. Hear me, ye that never spent a tear for the sin of your nature; if the blood of Christ be not sprinkled upon your natures, it had been better for you, that you had been the generation of beasts, the offspring of dragons or toads. They have a mean, but not a vitiated, sinful nature, as you have.

Your actual sins have need of the Priest, and his sacrifice, to procure remission for them. If he take them not away by the blood of his cross, they can never be taken away; they will lie down with you in the dust; they will rise with you, and follow you to the judgment-seat, crying, We are thy works, and we will follow thee. All thy repentance and tears, couldst thou weep as many as there be drops in the ocean, can never take away sin. Thy duties, even the best of them, need this sacrifice. It is in virtue thereof that they are accepted of God. And were it not that God had respect to Christ's offering, he would not regard, or look towards thee, or any of thy duties. Thou couldst no more come near to God, than thou couldst approach a devouring fire, or dwell with everlasting burnings. Well, then say, I need such a price every way. Love him in all his offices. See the goodness of God in providing such a sacrifice for thee. Meat, drink, and air, are not more necessary to maintain thy natural life, than the death of Christ is to give and maintain thy spiritual life.

Oh then, let thy soul grow big whilst meditating of the grace and excellency of Christ, which is thus displayed and unfolded in every branch of the gospel: and, with a deep sense upon thy heart, let thy lips say, Blessed be God for Jesus Christ.

SERMON XII.

OF THE EXCELLENCY OF OUR HIGH PRIEST'S OBLATION, BEING THE FIRST ACT OR PART OF HIS PRIESTLY OFFICE.

HEB. X. 14.

FOR BY ONE OFFERING, HE HATH PERFECTED FOR EVER THEM THAT ARE SANCTIFIED.

AFTER this more general view and consideration of the priesthood of Christ, method requires that we come to a nearer and more particular consideration of the parts thereof; which are his oblation and intercession, answerable to the double office of the high priest, offering the blood of the sacrifices without the holy place, which typified Christ's oblation; and then once a year bringing the blood before the Lord into the most holy place, presenting it before God, and with it sprinkling the mercy-seat, wherein the intercession of Christ (the other part or act of his priesthood) was in a lively manner typified to us.

My present business is to open and apply the oblation of Christ; the efficacy and excellency whereof is excellently illustrated, by a comparison with all other oblations, in the precedent context, and with a singular encomium commended to us in these words, from the singularity of it. It is but one offering; but once offered, and never more to be repeated : for Christ dieth no more, Rom. vi. 9. He also commends it from the efficacy of it; by it he hath perfected it, that is, not only purchased a possibility of salvation, but all that we need to our full perfection. It brings in a most entire, complete, and perfect righteousness : all that remains to make us perfectly happy, is but the full application of the benefits procured by this oblation for us. Moreover, it is here commended from the extensiveness of it; not being restrained to a few, but applicable to all the saints, in all the ages and places of the world. Lastly, He commends it from its perpetuity; it perfects for ever; that is, it is of everlasting efficacy : it shall abide as fresh, vigorous, and powerful to the end of the world, as it was the first moment it was offered up. All of which runs into this sweet truth :

DOCT. THAT THE OBLATION MADE UNTO GOD BY JESUS CHRIST IS OF UNSPEAKABLE VALUE, AND EVERLASTING EFFICACY, TO PERFECT ALL THEM THAT ARE OR SHALL BE SANCTIFIED, TO THE END OF THE WORLD.

Out of this fountain flow all the blessings that believers either have, or hope for. Had it not been for this, there had been no such things as justification, adoption, salvation, &c. peace with God and hopes of glory, pardon of sin, and Divine acceptance: these and all other our best mercies, had been but so many mere conceits. A man, as one saith, might have happily imagined such things as these, as he may golden mountains, and rivers of liquid gold, and rocks of diamonds: but these things could never have had any real existence, had not Christ offered up himself a sacrifice to God for us. It is " the blood of Christ, who through the eternal Spirit offered up himself without spot to God, that purges the conscience from dead works," Heb. ix. 14, that is, from the sentence of condemnation and death, as it is reflected by conscience, for our works' sake.

His appearing before God as our Priest, with such an offering for us, is that which removes our guilt and fear together: " He appeared to put away sin by the sacrifice of himself," Heb. ix. 26. Now, forasmuch as the point before us is of so great weight in itself, and so fundamental to our safety and comfort, I shall endeavour to give you as distinct and clear an account of it, as can consist with that brevity which I must necessarily use. And therefore, reader, apply thy mind attentively to the consideration of this excellent Priest that appears before God; the sacrifice he offers; the Person before whom he brings, and to whom he offers it; the persons for whom he offers; and the end for which this oblation is made.

I. The Priest that appears before God with an oblation for us, is Jesus Christ, God-man; the dignity of whose person gave an inestimable worth to the offering he made. There were many priests before him, but none like unto him, either for the purity of his person, or the perpetuity of his priesthood: they were sinful men, and offered for their own sins, as well as the sins of the people, Heb. v. 3; " but he was holy, harmless, undefiled, separate from sinners," Heb. vii. 26. He could stand before God, even in the eye of his justice, as a lamb without spot. Though he made his soul an offering for sin, " yet he had done no iniquity, nor was any guile found in his mouth," Isa. liii. 9; and indeed his offering had done us no good, if the least taint of sin had been found on him. They were mortal men, that "continued not by reason of death," Heb. vii. 23, but Christ is a Priest for ever, Psa. cx. 4.

II. The oblation or offering he made, was not the blood of beasts, but his own blood, Heb. ix. 12. And herein he transcended all other priests, that he had something of his own to offer; he had a body given him to be at his own disposal: to this use and purpose "he offered his body," Heb. x. 10; yea, not only his body, but his "soul was made an offering for sin," Isa. liii. 10. We had made a forfeiture of our souls and bodies by sin, and it was necessary the sacrifice of Christ should be answerable to the debt we owed. And when Christ came to offer his sacrifice, he stood not only in the capacity of a priest, but also in that of a surety; and so his soul stood in the stead of ours, and his body in the stead of our bodies. Now the excellency of this oblation will appear in the following adjuncts and properties of it. This oblation being, for the matter of it, the soul and body of Jesus Christ, is therefore,

1. Invaluably precious. So the apostle styles it, "Ye were redeemed with the precious blood of the Son of God," 1 Pet. i. 19: and such it behoved him to offer. For it being offered as an expiatory sacrifice, it ought to be equivalent, in its own intrinsic value, to all the souls and bodies that were to be redeemed by it. And so it was, and more also; for there was a redundancy of value, an overplus of merit, which went to make a purchase for the redeemed. But surely as none but God can estimate the weight and evil of sin, so none but he can comprehend the worth and preciousness of the blood of Christ, shed to expiate it. And being so infinitely precious a thing which was offered up to God, it must,

2. Needs be a most complete and all-sufficient oblation, fully to expiate the sins of all for whom it was offered, in all ages of the world. The virtue of this sacrifice reacheth backward as far as Adam, and reacheth forward to the last person of the elect springing from him. That the efficacy of it thus reacheth back to Adam, is plain: for, on the account thereof, he is styled, "The Lamb slain from the foundation of the world," Rev. xiii. 8. And to the same sense a judicious expositor* understands those words of Christ, "Before Abraham was, I am," John viii. 58. It is therefore but a vain cavil, that some make against the satisfaction of Christ, to render it needless, when they say, many are saved without it, even as many as were saved before the death of Christ. For they say, the effect cannot be

* Calvin, on this place.

before the cause, which is true of physical, but not of moral causes; and such was Christ's satisfaction.   As for example, a captive is freed out of prison from the time that his surety undertakes for him, and promises his ransom ; here the captive is actually delivered, though the ransom that delivered him be not yet actually paid.   So it was in this case ; Christ had engaged to the Father to satisfy for them, and upon that security they were delivered.

And the virtue of this oblation not only reaches those believers, that lived and died before Christ's day, but it extends itself forward to the end of the world.   Hence Christ is said to be " the same yesterday, to-day, and for ever," Heb. xiii. 8.

To the same sense are those words, Heb. xi. 40, rightly paraphrased ; " God having provided some better thing for us, that they without us should not be made perfect :" *q. d.* God hath appointed the accomplishment of the promise of sending the Messiah, to be in the last times, that they (namely, that lived before Christ) should not be perfected, that is, justified and saved by any thing done in their time, but by looking to our time, and Christ's satisfaction made therein ; whereby they and we are perfected together.   No length of time can wear out the virtue of this eternal Sacrifice.   It is as fresh, vigorous, and potent now, as the first hour it was offered.   And though he actually offer it no more, yet he virtually continues it by his intercession now in heaven ; for there he is still a Priest.   And therefore, about sixty years after his ascension, when he gave the Revelation to John, he appears to him in his priestly garment ; " Clothed in a garment down to the feet, and girt about the paps with a golden girdle," Rev. i. 13 ; in allusion to the priestly ephod, and curious girdle.

And as the virtue of this oblation reaches backward and forward, to all ages, and to all believers, so to all the sins of all believers, which are fully purged and expiated by it : this no other oblation could do.   The legal sacrifices were no real expiations, but rather remembrances of sins, Heb. ix. 9. 12 ; x. 3. And all the virtue they had, consisted in their typical relation to this sacrifice, Gal. iii. 23 ; Heb. ix. 13. And, separate from it, were altogether weak, unprofitable, and insignificant things, Heb. vii. 18.   But this blood cleanseth from all sins, 1 John i. 7. It expiates all fully, without exception, and finally, without revocation.   So that by his being made sin for us, we are made not only righteous, but " the righteousness of God in him," 2 Cor. v. 21.

3. Being so precious in itself, and so efficacious to expiate

sin, it must needs be a most grateful oblation to the Lord, highly pleasing and delightful in his eyes.   And so indeed it is said, " He gave himself for us, an offering and a sacrifice to God, for a sweet-smelling savour," Eph. v. 2.   Not that God took any delight or content in the bitter sufferings of Christ, simply and in themselves considered; but with relation to the end for which he was offered, even our redemption and salvation. Hence arose the delight and pleasure God had in it; this made him take pleasure in bruising him, Isa. liii. 10.   God smelled a savour of rest in this sacrifice. The meaning is, that as men are offended with a nauseous smell, and on the contrary delighted with sweet odours and fragrancies; so the blessed God speaking after the manner of man, is offended, and filled with loathing and abhorrence by our sins; but infinitely pleased and delighted in the offering of Christ for them, which came up as an odour of sweet-smelling savour to him, whereof the costly perfumes under the law were types and shadows. This was the oblation.

III. This oblation he brings before God, and to him he offers it up: so speaks the apostle, " Through the eternal Spirit he offered himself without spot to God," Heb. ix. 14.   As Christ sustained the capacity of a surety, so God of a creditor, who exacted satisfaction from him; that is, he required from him, as our surety, the penalty due to us for our sin. And so Christ had to do immediately with God, yea, with a God infinitely wronged, and incensed by sin against us.   To this incensed Majesty, Christ our High Priest approached, as to a devouring fire, with his sacrifice.

IV. The persons for whom, and in whose stead he offered himself to God, were the whole number of God's elect, which were given him of the Father, neither more nor less: so speak the scriptures.   He laid down his life for the sheep, John x. 15, for the church, Acts xx. 28, for the children of God, John xi. 50—52.   It is confessed, there is sufficiency of virtue in this sacrifice to redeem the whole world, and on that account some divines affirm he is called the " Saviour of the world," John iv. 42, *et alibi*. We also acknowledge that the elect being scattered in all parts, and among all ranks of men in the world, and unknown to those that are to tender Jesus Christ to men by the preaching of the gospel; the style of the gospel (as it was necessary) is by such indefinite expressions suited to the general tenders they are to make of him: but that the efficacy and saving virtue of this all-sufficient sacrifice is co-extended with God's election, so that they all, and no others can, or shall reap the special benefits of it, is too clear in the scriptures to be denied, Eph. v. 23; John xvii. 2. 9. 19, 20; John x. 26—28; 1 Tim. iv. 10.

V. The design and end of this oblation was to atone, pacify, and reconcile God, by giving him a full satisfaction for the sins of these his elect: so speaks the apostle, " And having made peace, through the blood of his cross, by him to reconcile all things unto himself; by him, I say, whether they be things in earth, or things in heaven," Col. i. 20. So, " God was in Christ, reconciling the world to himself," 2 Cor. v. 19. Reconciliation is the making up of that breach caused by sin, between us and God, and restoring us again to his favour and friendship. For this end Christ offered up himself to God. So much about the nature and precious worth of Christ's oblation. The uses whereof follow in these five practical inferences.

1. Hence it follows, that actual believers are fully freed from the guilt of their sins, and shall never more come under condemnation. The debt of sin is perfectly abolished, by the virtue of this sacrifice. When Christ became our sacrifice, he both bare, and bare away our sins. They were laid upon him, and then expiated by him: so much is imported in that word, " Christ was once offered to bear the sins of many," Heb. ix. 28. *To bear*, is a full and emphatical word, signifying not only to bear, but to bear away. So John i. 29, " Behold the Lamb of God, that taketh away the sins of the world;" not only declaratively, or by way of manifestation to the conscience; but really, making a purgation of sin, as it is in Hebrews i. 3. Now, how great a mercy is this, " that by him, all that believe should be justified from all things from which they could not be justified by the law of Moses," Acts xiii. 39. " Blessed is he whose transgression is forgiven, whose sin is covered," Psa. xxxii.; or, who can express the mercies, comforts, happiness, of such a state as this? Reader, let me beg thee, if thou be one of this pardoned number, to look over the cancelled bonds, and see what vast sums are remitted to thee. Remember what thou wast in thy natural state: possibly thou wast in that black list, 1 Cor. vi. 9, 10. What, and yet pardoned! fully and finally pardoned, and that freely, as to any hand that thou hadst in the procurement of it! What canst thou do less, than fall down at the feet of free grace, and kiss those feet that moved so freely towards so vile a sinner? It is not long since thy iniquities were upon thee, and thou pinedst away in them. Their guilt could by no creature-power be separated from thy soul. Now they are removed from thee, as far as the

east from the west, Psa. ciii. 12.   So that, when the east and west, which are the two opposite points of heaven, meet, then thy soul and its guilt may meet again together.

2. From this oblation Christ made of himself to God for our sins, we infer the inflexible severity of Divine justice, which could be no other way diverted from us, and appeased, but by the blood of Christ. If Christ had not presented himself to God for us, justice would not have spared us: and if he do appear before God as our Surety, it will not spare him; " He spared not his own Son, but delivered him up to death for us all," Rom. viii. 32.   If forbearance might have been expected from any, surely it might from God, " who is very pitiful, and full of tender mercy," Jam. v. 11; yet God in this case spared not. If one might have expected sparing mercy from any, surely Christ might most of all expect it from his own Father; yet you hear, God spared not his own Son.   Sparing mercy is the lowest degree of mercy, yet it was denied to Christ : though in the garden Christ fell upon the ground, and sweat great drops of blood, and in that unparalleled agony cried, " Father, if it be possible, let this cup pass;" and though he brake out upon the cross, in that heart-rending complaint, " My God, my God, why hast thou forsaken me?" yet no abatement ; justice will not bend in the least ; but having to do with him on this account, resolves upon satisfaction from his blood.

If this be so, what is the case of thy soul, reader, if thou be a man or woman that hast no interest in this sacrifice ? For if these things be done in (Christ) the green tree, what will be done to (thee) the dry tree ? Luke xxiii. 31.   Thus Theophi-lact beautifully paraphrases on that passage : " That is, if God so deal with me, that am not only innocent, but like a green and fruitful tree, full of all delectable fruits of holiness ; yet if the fire of his indignation thus seize upon me, what will be your condition, that are both barren and guilty, void of all good fruit, and full of all unrighteousness," and so like dry, sear wood, fitted as fuel to the fire ? Consider with thyself, man, how canst thou imagine thou canst support that infinite wrath that Christ bore in the room of God's elect ! He had the strength of Deity to support him, " Behold my Servant whom I uphold," Isa. xlii. 1.   He had the fulness of his Spirit to prepare him, Isa. lxi. 1.   He had the ministry of an angel, who came down from heaven to relieve him in his agony, Luke xxii. 43.   He had the ear of his Father to hear him, for he cried, " and was heard in that he feared," Heb. v. 7.   He was assured of the victory, before the combat ; he knew he should be justified, Isa.

L. 8; and yet for all this he was sore amazed, and sorrowful even to death, and his heart was melted like wax in the midst of his bowels. If the case stood thus with Christ, notwithstanding all these advantages he had, to bear the wrath of God for a little time; how dost thou think, a poor worm as thou art, to dwell with everlasting burnings, or contend with devouring fire? Luther saw ground enough for what he said, when he cried out, " I will have nothing to do with an absolute God," that is, with a God out of Christ: for, " it is a fearful thing to fall into the hands of the living God." Woe and alas for evermore to that man who meets a just and righteous God without a Mediator !

Whoever thou art that readest these lines, I beseech thee, by the mercies of God, by all the regard and love thou hast to thy own soul, lose no time, but make quick and sure work of it. Get an interest in this sacrifice quickly; what else will be thy state when vast eternity opens to swallow thee up? what wilt thou do, man, when thine eye-strings and heart-strings are breaking? Oh what a fearful shriek will thy conscience give, when thou art presented before the dreadful God, and no Christ to screen thee from his indignation ! Happy is that man who can say in a dying hour, as William Lyford did, who being desired, a little before his dissolution, to give his friends a little taste of his present hopes, and the grounds of them, cheerfully answered, I will let you know how it is with me: then stretching forth his hand, said, " Here is the grave, the wrath of God, and devouring flame, the just punishment of sin, on the one side; and here am I, a poor sinful soul, on the other side: but this is my comfort, the covenant of grace, which is established upon so many sure promises, hath saved all. There is an act of oblivion passed in heaven: ' I will forgive their iniquities, and their sins will I remember no more.' This is the blessed privilege of all within the covenant, among whom I am one." Oh it is sweet at all times, especially at such a time, to see the reconciled face of God, through Jesus Christ, and hear the voice of peace through the blood of the cross.

3. Hath Christ offered up himself a sacrifice to God for us? Then let us improve, in every condition, this sacrifice, and labour to get hearts duly affected with such a sight as faith can give us of it. Whatever the condition or complaint of any christian is, the beholding the Lamb of God, that taketh away the sin of the world, may give him strong support and sweet relief. Do you complain of the hardness of your hearts, and want of love to Christ? behold him as offered up to God for you; and such a sight (if any in the world will do it) will melt your hard hearts.

" They shall look upon me whom they have pierced, and shall mourn," Zech. xii. 10. It is reported of Johannes Milius, that he was never observed to speak of Christ and his sufferings, but his eyes would drop tears. Art thou too little touched and unaffected with the evil of sin? Is it thy complaint, christian, that thou canst not make sin bear so hard upon thy heart as thou wouldst? Consider but what thou hast now read; realize this sacrifice by faith, and try what efficacy there is in it to make sin for ever bitter as death to thy soul. Suppose thine own father had been stabbed to the heart with a certain knife, and his blood were upon it, wouldst thou delight to see, or endure to use that knife any more? Sin is the knife that stabbed Christ to the heart; this shed his blood. Surely, you can never make light of that which lay so heavy upon the soul and body of Jesus Christ.

Or is your heart pressed down even to despondency, under the guilt of sin, so that you cry, How can such a sinner as I be pardoned? my sin is greater than can be forgiven. " Behold the Lamb of God that taketh away the sin of the world." Remember that no sin can stand before the efficacy of his blood. " The blood of Jesus Christ cleanseth from all sin," 1 John i. 7. This sacrifice makes full satisfaction to God.

Are you at any time staggering through unbelief; filled with unbelieving suspicions of the promises? Look hither, and you shall see them all ratified and established in the blood of the cross, so that hills and mountains shall sooner start from their own bases and foundations, than one tittle of the promise fail, Heb. vi. 17—19.

Do you at any time find your hearts fretting, disquieted, and impatient under every petty cross and trial? See how quietly Christ your sacrifice came to the altar, how meekly and patiently he stood under all the wrath of God and men together. This will silence, convince, and shame you.

In a word, here you will see so much of the grace of God in providing, and the love of Christ in becoming a sacrifice for you: you will see God taking vengeance against sin, but sparing the sinner; you will see Christ standing as the body of sin alone; for " he was made sin for us, that we might be made the righteousness of God in him :" that whatever corruption burdens, this, in the believing application, will support; whatever grace is defective, this will revive it.

Blessed be God for Jesus Christ.

SERMON XIII.

OF THE INTERCESSION OF CHRIST OUR HIGH PRIEST, BEING THE
SECOND ACT OR PART OF HIS PRIESTLY OFFICE.

HEB. VII. 25.

WHEREFORE HE IS ABLE ALSO TO SAVE THEM TO THE UTTERMOST THAT
COME UNTO GOD BY HIM, SEEING HE EVER LIVETH TO MAKE INTERCESSION
FOR THEM.

HAVING despatched the first part or act of Christ's priesthood, consisting in his oblation; we come to the other branch of it, consisting in his intercession, which is nothing else but the virtual continuation of his offering once made on earth.

This second part or branch of his priesthood was typified by the high priest's entering with the blood of the sacrifice and sweet incense into the holy place: " And he shall take a censer full of burning coals of fire from off the altar before the Lord, and his hands full of sweet incense beaten small, and bring it within the vail: and he shall put the incense upon the fire before the Lord, that the cloud of the incense may cover the mercy-seat that is upon the testimony, that he die not: and he shall take of the blood of the bullock, and sprinkle it with his finger upon the mercy-seat eastward," &c. Lev. xvi. 12—14. Christ's offering himself on earth, answered to the killing of the sacrifice without; and his entering into heaven, there to intercede, was that which answered to the priest's going with blood, and his hands full of incense, within the vail. So that this is a part, yea, a special part of Christ's priesthood; and so necessary to it, that if he had not done this, all his work on earth had signified nothing; nor had he been a priest, that is, a complete and perfect priest, if he had remained on earth, Heb. viii. 4, because the very design and end of shedding his blood on earth had been frustrated, which was to carry it before the Lord, into heaven. So that this is the perfective part of the priesthood: he acted the first part on earth, in a state of deep abasement, in the form of a servant; but he acts this in glory, whereto he is taken up, that he may fulfil his design in dying, and give the work of our salvation its last completing act. So much is imported in this scripture, which tells us, by reason hereof, he "is able to save to the uttermost," &c.

These words contain an encouragement to believers, to come to God in the way of faith, drawn from the intercession of Christ in heaven for them. In which you may take notice of these principal parts.

1. The quality of the persons here encouraged, who are described by a direct act of faith, as poor recumbents that are going out of themselves to God by faith; but conscious of great unworthiness in themselves, and thence apt to be discouraged.

2. The encouragement propounded to such believers, drawn from the ability of Jesus Christ, in whose name they go to the Father, to save them to the uttermost, that is, fully, perfectly, completely ; for so this emphatical word, εις το παντελες, signifies, the saving us wholly, thoroughly, completely, and altogether; giving our salvation its last act and completion.

3. The ground or reason of this his saving ability; " Seeing he ever liveth to make intercession;" that is, he hath not only offered up his blood to God upon the cross, as a full price to purchase pardon and grace for believers ; but lives in heaven, and that for ever, to apply unto us, in the way of intercession, all the fruits, blessings, and benefits, that that precious blood of his deserves, and hath procured us a price for them. The words thus opened, the point I shall single out, from among many that lie in them, as most suitable to my design and purpose, is this;

DOCT. THAT JESUS OUR HIGH PRIEST LIVES FOR EVER, IN THE CAPACITY OF A POTENT INTERCESSOR IN HEAVEN, FOR BELIEVERS.

Here we will inquire, I. What it is for Christ to be an Intercessor. II. By what acts he performs that work in heaven. III. Whence the potency and prevalency of his intercession is.

1. What it is for Christ to be an intercessor for us. To intercede, in general, is to go between two parties, to entreat, argue, and plead with one for the other. And of this there are two sorts ; 1. That whereby one christian prays and pleads with God for another, 1 Tim. ii. 1. 2. That whereby Christ, as an act of office, presents himself before God to request for us. Between these two is this difference, that the former is performed not in our own, but in another's name; we can tender no request to God immediately, or for our own sake, either for ourselves, or for others: " Whatsoever ye shall ask the Father in my name, he will give it you," John xvi. 23. But the latter, which is proper to Christ, is an intercession with God for us, in his own

name, and upon the account of his own proper merit. The one is a private act of charity, the other a public act of office; and so he is our Advocate or court Friend, as Satan is our accuser or court adversary. Satan is ο αντιδικος, one that charges us before God, 1 Pet. v. 8, and continually endeavours to make breaches between us and God. Christ is ο παρακλητος, our Advocate, that pleads for us, and continues peace and friendship between us and God; "If any man sin, we have an Advocate with tho Father, Jesus Christ the righteous," 1 John ii. 1.

And thus to make intercession, is the peculiar and incommunicable prerogative of Jesus Christ, none but he can go in his own name to God. And in that sense we may understand that place, " Then said the Lord unto me, This gate shall be shut, it shall not be opened, and no man shall enter in by it, because the Lord the God of Israel hath entered in by it, therefore it shall be shut. It is for the prince, the prince he shall sit in it, to eat bread before the Lord," &c. Ezek. xliv. 2, 3. The great broad gate, called here the prince's gate, signifies that abundant and direct entrance that Christ had into heaven by his own merits, and in his own name; this, saith the Lord, shall be shut, no man shall enter in by it; all other men must come thither, as it were, by side doors, which looked all towards the altar, namely, by virtue of the Mediator, and through the benefit of his death imputed to them.

And yet, though God hath for ever shut up and barred this way to all the children of men, telling us that no man shall ever have access to him in his own name, as Christ the Prince had; how do some, notwithstanding, strive to force open the Prince's gate? So do they, that found the intercession of saints upon their own works and merits, thereby robbing Christ of his peculiar glory ; but all that so approach God, approach a consuming fire; Christ only, in the virtue of his own blood, thus comes before him, to make intercession for us.

II. We will inquire wherein the intercession of Christ in heaven consists, or by what acts he performs his glorious office there. And the scriptures place it in three things:

1. In his presenting himself before the Lord in our names, and upon our account. So we read in Heb. ix. 24, " Christ is entered into heaven itself, now to appear in the presence of God for us." The apostle manifestly alludes to the high priest's appearing in the holy of holies, which was the figure of heaven, presenting to the Lord the names of the twelve tribes of Israel, which were on his breast and shoulders, Exod. xxviii. 9. 12. 28, 29. To which the church is supposed to allude in that request,

" Set me as a seal upon thine heart, as a seal upon thine arm,"
Cant. viii. 6.   Now the very sight of Christ our High Priest
in heaven, prevails exceedingly with God, and turns away his
displeasure from us.   As when God looks upon the rainbow,
which is the sign of the covenant, he remembers the earth in
mercy : so when he looks on Christ, his heart must needs be
towards us, upon his account; and therefore in Rev. iv. 3,
Christ is compared to a rainbow encompassing the throne.

2. Christ performs his intercession-work in heaven, not only
by appearing in the presence of God, but also by presenting his blood and all his sufferings to God, as a moving plea on
our account.   Whether he makes any proper oral intercession
there, as he did on earth, is not so clear.   But sure I am, an
interceding voice is by a usual prosopopeia attributed to his
blood; which in Heb. xii. 24, is said " to speak better things
than that of Abel."   Now Abel's blood, and so Christ's, do cry
unto God, as the hire of the labourers unjustly detained, Jam. v.
4; or the whole creation, which is in bondage, through our sins,
is said to cry and groan in the ears of the Lord, Rom. viii. 22,
not vocally, but efficaciously.   A rare illustration of this efficacious intercession of Christ in heaven, we have in that famous
story of Amintas, who appeared as an advocate for his brother
Æchylus, who was strongly accused, and very likely to be condemned to die.   Now Amintas having performed great services,
and merited highly of the commonwealth, in whose service one of
his hands was cut off in the field; he comes into the court in his
brother's behalf, and said nothing, but only lifted up his arm, and
showed them an arm without a hand, which so moved them, that,
without a word speaking, they freed his brother immediately.
And thus if you look into Rev. v. 6, you shall see in what posture Christ is represented, visionally there, as standing between
God and us : " And I beheld, and, lo, in the midst of the throne
and of the four beasts, and in the midst of the elders, stood a Lamb
as it had been slain ; " that is, bearing in his glorified body the
marks of death and sacrifice.   Those wounds he received for our
sins on earth, are, as it were, still fresh bleeding in heaven : a
moving and prevailing argument it is with the Father, to give us
the mercies he pleads for.

3. And lastly, He presents the prayers of his saints to God,
with his merits ; and desires that they may for his sake be granted.   He causes a cloud of incense to ascend before God with
them, Rev. viii. 3.   All these were excellently typified by the
going in of the high priest before the Lord, with the names of
the children of Israel on his breast, with the blood of the sacri-

fice, and his hands full of incense, as the apostle explains them in Heb. vii. and Heb. ix.

III. And that this intercession of Christ is most potent, successful, and prevalent with God, will be evinced, both from the qualification of this our Advocate, from his great interest in the Father, from the nature of the pleas he useth with God, and from the relation and interest believers have, both in the Father to whom and the Son by whom this intercession is made.

1. Our Intercessor in the heavens is every way able and fit for the work he is engaged in there. Whatever is desirable in an advocate, is in him eminently. It is necessary that he who undertakes to plead the cause of another, especially if it be weighty and intricate, should be wise, faithful, tender-hearted, and one that concerns himself in the success of his business. Our Advocate Christ wants no wisdom to manage his work; he is the Wisdom of God, yea, only wise, Jude 25. And he is no less faithful than wise; therefore he is called " a faithful High Priest, in things pertaining to God," Heb. ii. 17. He assures us we may safely trust our concerns with him, " In my Father's house are many mansions; if it were not so, I would have told you," John xiv. 2. *q. d.* Do you think I could deceive you? men may cheat you, but I will not; your own hearts may and daily do deceive you, but so will not I. And for tender-heartedness, and sensible feelings for your condition, there is none like him: " For we have not an High Priest who cannot be touched with the feeling of our infirmities; but was in all points tempted like as we are, yet without sin," Heb. iv. 15. We have not one that cannot sympathize, so it is in the greek : and on purpose that he might the better sympathize with us, he came as near to our condition as the holiness of his nature could permit. He suffered himself to be in all points tempted like as we are, sin only excepted. And then for his concernment and interest in the success of his suit; he not only reckons, but has really made it his own interest, for now by reason of the mystical union, all our wants and troubles are his, Eph. i. 23; yea, his own glory and completeness, as Mediator, is deeply interested in it; and therefore we need not doubt but he will use all care and diligence in that work. If you say, so he may, and yet not speed for all that, for it depends upon the Father's grant. True; but then,

2. Consider the great interest he hath in the Father, with whom he intercedes. Christ is his dear Son, Col. i. 13, the beloved of his soul, Eph. i. 6. Between him and the Father, with whom he intercedes, there is a unity, not only of nature, but of will; and so he always hears him, John xi. 42. Yea,

and he said to his dear Son, when he came first to heaven, " Ask of me, and I will give thee," Psa. ii. 8.   Moreover,

3. He must needs speed in his suit, if you consider the nature of his intercession, which is just and reasonable for the matter, urgent and continual for the manner of it.   The matter of his request is most equal: what he desires is becoming the holiness and righteousness of God to grant.   And so the justice of God doth not only not oppose, but furthers and pleads for the granting and fulfilling his requests.   Here you must remember, that the Father is under a covenant to do what he asks; for Christ having fully performed the work on his part, the mercies he intercedes for are as due as the hire of the labourer is, when the work is faithfully done.   And as the matter is just, so the manner of his intercession is urgent and continual.   How importunate a suitor he is, may be gathered from that specimen given of his intercession in John xvii.; and for the constancy of it, my text tells us, " he ever lives to make intercession."   And to close all,

4. Consider who they are for whom he makes intercession : the friends of God, the children of God; those that the Father himself loves, and to whom his heart is inclined and ready enough to grant the best and greatest of mercies: which is the meaning of John xvi. 27, " The Father himself loveth you." And it must needs be so, for the first corner-stone of all these mercies was laid by the Father himself in his most free election. He also delivered his Son for us ; and " how shall he not with him freely give us all things ?" Rom. viii. 32.   So then there can remain no doubt upon a considering heart, but that Christ is a prevalent and successful Intercessor in heaven.

Use 1. Doth Christ live for ever in heaven to present his blood to God in the way of intercession for believers ?   How sad then is the case of those that have no interest in Christ's blood ; but instead of pleading for them, it cries to God against them, as the despisers and abusers of it !   Every unbeliever despises it: the apostate treads it under foot.   To be guilty of a man's blood is sad ; but to have the blood of Jesus accusing and crying to God against a soul, is unspeakably terrible.   Surely when he shall make inquisition for blood, when the day of his vengeance is come, he will make it appear by the judgments he will execute, that this is a sin never to be expiated, but vengeance shall pursue the sinner to the bottom of hell.   Ah ! what do men and women do, in rejecting the gracious offer of Christ !   Wo, and alas for that man, against whom this blood cries in heaven !

2. Doth Christ live for ever to make intercession ? Hence let believers fetch relief, and draw encouragement against

all the causes and grounds of their fears and troubles ; for surely this answers them all.

(1.) Hence let them be encouraged against all their sinful infirmities, and lamented weaknesses. It is confessed these are sad things ; they grieve the Spirit of God, sadden your own hearts, cloud your evidences ; but having such a High Priest in heaven, you must never despair. "My little children, these things write I unto you, that you sin not : and if any man sin, we have an Advocate with the Father, Jesus Christ the right-eous," 1 John ii. 1, 2. "My little children." Children, espe-cially little children, when first beginning to take the foot, are apt to stumble at every straw ; so are young and unexperienced christians : but what if they do ? Why though it must be far from them to take encouragement so to do from Christ and his intercession, yet if by surprisal they do sin, let them not be utterly discouraged : for we have an Advocate, he stops what-ever plea may be brought in against us by the devil, or the law, and answers all by his satisfaction : he gets out fresh pardons for new sins. And this Advocate is with "the Father :" he doth not say with his Father, though that had been a singular support in itself, nor yet with our Father, which is a sweet en-couragement singly considered, but with "the Father," which takes in both, to make the encouragement full. Remember, you that are cast down, under the sense of sin, that Jesus, your Friend in the court above, " is able to save to the uttermost." Which is, as one calls it, a reaching word, and extends itself so far, that thou canst not look beyond it. " Let thy soul be set on the highest mount that any creature was ever set on, and enlarged to take in view the most spacious prospect both of sin and misery, and difficulties of being saved, that ever yet any poor humble soul did cast within itself ; yea, join to these, all the hinderances and objections that the heart of man can invent against itself and salvation : lift up thine eyes, and look to the utmost thou canst see ; and Christ, by his intercession, is able to save thee beyond the horizon and utmost compass of thy thoughts, even to the utmost."*

(2.) Hence draw abundant encouragement against all heart-straitenings, and deadness of spirit in prayer. Thou complainest thy heart is dead, wandering, and contracted in duty : oh, but remember Christ's blood speaks, when thou canst not ; it can plead for thee, and that powerfully, when thou art not able to speak a word for thyself : to this sense that scripture speaks, " Who is this that cometh out of the wilderness like pillars of

* Goodwin's Triumph, p. 263.

smoke, perfumed with myrrh, and frankincense, with all powders of the merchant ?" Cant. iii. 6. The duties of christians go up many times, as pillars or clouds of smoke from them, more smoke than fire, prayers smoked and sullied with their offensive corruptions ; but, remember, Christ perfumes them with myrrh, &c. He, by his intercession, gives them a sweet perfume.

(3.) Christ's intercession is a singular relief to all that come unto God by him, against all sinful damps and slavish fears from the justice of God. Nothing more promotes the fear of reverence ; nothing more suppresseth unbelieving despondencies, and destroys the spirit of bondage. So you find it, Heb. x. 19—21. " Having therefore, brethren, boldness to enter into the holiest, by the blood of Jesus, by a new and living way, which he hath consecrated for us through the vail, that is to say, his flesh ; and having a High Priest over the house of God, let us draw near with a true heart, in full assurance of faith."

(4.) The intercession of Christ gives admirable satisfaction and encouragement to all that come to God, against the fears of deserting him again by apostasy. This, my friends, this is your principal security against these matters of fear. With this he relieved Peter ; " Simon, (saith Christ,) Satan hath desired to have you, that he may sift you as wheat ; but I have prayed for thee, that thy faith fail not," Luke xxii. 31, 32 : his temptations are levelled against thy faith ; but fear not, my prayer shall break his designs, and secure thy faith against all his attempts upon it. Upon this powerful intercession of Christ, the apostle builds his triumph against all that threatens to bring him, or any of the saints, again into a state of condemnation. And see how he urges on that triumph, from the resurrection, and session of Christ at the Father's right hand ; and especially from the work of intercession, which he lives there to perform : " Who is he that condemneth ? It is Christ that died ; yea, rather that is risen again, who is even at the right hand of God, who also maketh intercession for us. Who shall separate us from the love of Christ ?" Rom, viii. 34.

(5.) It gives sweet relief against the defects and wants that yet are in our sanctification. We want a great deal of faith, love, heavenly-mindedness, mortification, knowledge. We are short and wanting in all. There are deficiencies, or things wanting, as the apostle calls them, 1 Thess. iii. 10. Well, if grace be but yet in its weak beginnings, and infancy in thy soul, this may encourage you, that by reason of Christ's intercession, it shall live, grow, and expatiate itself in thy heart. He is not only the author, but the finisher of it, Heb. xii. 2. He is ever begging new and fresh mercies for you in heaven; and will never cease till all your wants be supplied. He saves to the uttermost, that is, as I told you before, to the last, perfective, completing act of salvation. So that this is a fountain of relief against all your fears.

3. Doth Christ live for ever to make intercession? Then let those who reap on earth the fruits of that his work in heaven, draw instruction thence about the following duties.

(1.) Do not forget Christ in an exalted state. You see though he be in glory above, at God's right hand, and enthroned King, he doth not forget you: he, like Joseph, remembers his brethren in all his glory. But, alas, how oft doth advancement make us forget him! As the Lord complains in Hosea xiii. 5, 6, "I did know thee in the wilderness, in the land of great drought: but when they came into Canaan, according to their pastures, so were they filled: they were filled, and their heart was exalted: therefore have they forgotten me." As if he had said, O my people, you and I were better acquainted in the wilderness, when you were in a low condition, left to my immediate care, living by daily faith; then you gave me many a sweet visit; but now you are filled, I hear no more of you. Good had it been for some saints, if they had never known prosperity.

(2.) Let the intercession of Christ in heaven for you, encourage you to constancy in the good ways of God. "Seeing then that we have a great High Priest that is passed into the heavens, Jesus the Son of God, let us hold fast our profession," Heb. iv. 14. Here is encouragement to perseverance on a double account. One is, that Jesus, our Head, is already in heaven; and if the head be above water, the body cannot drown. The other is from the business he is there employed about, which is his priesthood; he is passed into the heavens, as our great High Priest, to intercede, and therefore we cannot miscarry.

(3.) Let it encourage you to constancy in prayer: oh do not neglect that excellent duty, seeing Christ is there to present all your petitions to God; yea, to perfume as well as present them. So the apostle infers from Christ's intercession; "Let us therefore come boldly unto the throne of grace, that we may obtain mercy, and find grace to help in time of need," Heb. iv. 16.

(4.) Hence be encouraged to plead for Christ on earth, who continually pleads for you in heaven. If any accuse you, he is there to plead for you: and if any dishonour him on earth, see that you plead his interest, and defend his honour. Thus you have heard what his intercession is, and what benefits we receive by it. Blessed be God for Jesus Christ.

SERMON XIV.

A VINDICATION OF THE SATISFACTION OF CHRIST, AS THE FIRST
EFFECT OR FRUIT OF HIS PRIESTHOOD.

GAL. III. 13.

CHRIST HATH REDEEMED US FROM THE CURSE OF THE LAW, BEING MADE A
CURSE FOR US.

You have seen the general nature, necessity, and parts of Christ's priesthood, namely, oblation and intercession. Before you leave this office, it is necessary you should further take into consideration the principal fruits and effects of his priesthood; which are, complete satisfaction, and the acquisition or purchase of an eternal inheritance. The former, namely, the satisfaction made by his blood, is manifestly contained in this excellent scripture before us, wherein the apostle (having shown before, at ver. 10, that whosoever " continues not in all things written in the law, to do them, is cursed") declares how, notwithstanding the threats of the law, a believer comes to be freed from the curse of it, namely, by Christ's bearing that curse for him, and so satisfying God's justice, and discharging the believer from all obligations to punishment.

More particularly, in these words you have the believer's discharge from the curse of the law, and the way and manner thereof opened.

1. The believer's discharge; " Christ hath redeemed us from the curse of the law." The law of God hath three parts—commands, promises, and threatenings or curses. The curse of the law is its condemning sentence, whereby a sinner is bound over to death, even the death of soul and body. The chain, by which it binds him, is the guilt of sin; and from which none can loose the soul but Christ. This curse of the law is the most dreadful thing imaginable; it strikes at the life of a sinner, yea, his best life, the eternal life of the soul: and when it hath condemned, it is inexorable, no cries nor tears, no reformation nor repentance can loose the guilty sinner; for it requires for its reparation

that which no mere creature can give, even an infinite satisfaction. Now from this curse Christ frees the believer; that is, he dissolves the obligation to punishment, cancels the hand-writing, looses all the bonds and chains of guilt, so that the curse of the law hath nothing to do with him for ever.

2. We have here the way and manner in and by which this is done; and that is by a full price paid down, and that price paid in the room of the sinner, both making up a complete and full satisfaction. He pays a full price, every way adequate and proportionable to the wrong. So much this word, ημας εξηγορασεν, which we translate redeemed, imports; he hath bought us out, or fully bought us; that is, by a full price. And as the price or ransom paid was full, perfect, and sufficient in itself; so it was paid in our room, and upon our account: so saith the text, " By his being made a curse for us;" the meaning is not, that Christ was made the very curse itself, changed into a curse; no more than when the Word is said to be made flesh, the Divine nature was converted into flesh, but it assumed or took flesh; and so Christ took the curse upon himself; therefore it is said, " He was made sin for us who knew no sin," 2 Cor. v. 21, that is, our sin was imputed to our Surety, and laid upon him for satisfaction. And so this word υπερ [for] implies a substitution of one in the place and stead of another. Now the price being full, and paid in lieu of our sins, and thereupon we fully redeemed or delivered from the curse, it follows, as a fair and just deduction, that,

DOCT. THE DEATH OF CHRIST HATH MADE A FULL SATISFACTION TO GOD FOR ALL THE SINS OF HIS ELECT.

" He (to wit, our Surety, Christ) was oppressed, and he was afflicted," saith the prophet, Isa. liii. 7; it may be fitly rendered, (and the words will bear it without the least force,) it was exacted, and answered. So Col. i. 14, " In whom we have redemption through his blood, even the forgiveness of sin." Here we have the benefit, namely, redemption interpreted by way of apposition, " even the remission of sins;" and the matchless price that was laid down to purchase it, the blood of Christ. So again, " By his own blood he entered once into the holy place, having obtained eternal redemption for us," Heb. ix. 12. Here is eternal redemption, the mercy purchased: his own blood, the price that procured it.

Now forasmuch as this doctrine of Christ's satisfaction is so necessary, weighty, and comfortable in itself, and yet so much opposed and intricated by several enemies to it; the method I shall take, shall be,

I. To open the nature of Christ's satisfaction, and show what it is. II. To establish the truth of it, and prove that he made full satisfaction to God for all the sins of the elect. III. To apply it.

I.   What is the satisfaction of Christ, and what doth it imply? I answer, satisfaction is the act of Christ, God-man, presenting himself as our surety, in obedience to God and love to us, to do and to suffer all that the law required of us: thereby freeing us from the wrath and curse due to us for sins.

1. It is the act of God-man; no other was capable of giving satisfaction for an infinite wrong done to God. But by reason of the union of the two natures in his wonderful person, he could do it, and hath done it for us. The human nature supplies what was necessary in its kind; it gave the matter of the sacrifice: the Divine nature stamped the dignity and value upon it, which made it an adequate compensation: so that it was the act of God-man; yet so, that each nature retained its own properties, notwithstanding their joint influence in producing the effect. If the angels in heaven had laid down their lives, or if the blood of all the men in the world had been poured out by justice, this could never have satisfied: because that worth and value which this sacrifice hath, would have still been wanting. "It was God that redeemed the church with his own blood," Acts xx. 28. If God redeem with his own blood, he redeems as God-man, without any dispute.

2. If he satisfy God for us, he must present himself before God, as our surety, in our stead, as well as for our good; else his obedience had signified nothing to us; to this end he was "made under the law," Gal. iv. 4, came under the same obligation with us, and that as a surety, for so he is called, Heb. vii. 22. Indeed his obedience and sufferings could be exacted from him upon no other account. It was not for any thing he had done that he became a curse. It was prophesied of him, "The Messiah shall be cut off, but not for himself," Dan. ix. 26 ; and being dead, the scriptures plainly assert it was for our sins, and upon our account: so "Christ died for our sins, according to the scriptures," 1 Cor. xv. 3.

And it is well observed by our divines, who assert the vicariousness and substitution of Christ in his sufferings, that all those greek particles which we translate [for,] when applied to the sufferings of Christ, do note the meritorious, deserving, procuring cause of those sufferings. So you find, "He offered one sacri-

fice, *υπερ αμαρτιων*, for sins," Heb. x. 12.   "Christ once suffered, *περι*, for sins," 1 Pet. iii. 18.   "He was delivered, *δια*,
for our offences," Rom. iv. 25.   "He gave his life a ransom,
αντι, for many," Matt. xx. 28.   And there are that confidently
affirm this last particle is never used in any other sense in
the whole book of God; as "an eye for an eye, a tooth
for a tooth," that is, one in lieu of another.   And indeed,
this very consideration is that which supports the doctrine of
imputation, the imputation of our sins to Christ, and the imputation of Christ's righteousness unto us, Rom. v. 19.   For
how could our sins be laid on him, but as he stood in our
stead? or his righteousness be imputed to us, but as he was our
surety, performing it in our place? So that to deny Christ's suffering in our stead, is to lose the corner-stone of our justification, and overthrow the very pillar which supports our faith,
comforts, and salvation.   Indeed if this had not been, he would
have been the righteous Lord, but not the Lord our righteousness, as he is styled, Jer. xxxiii. 16.   So that it was but a
vain distinction, to say it was for our good, but not in our stead;
for had he not been in our stead, we could not have had the
good of it.

.3. The internal moving cause of Christ's satisfaction for us,
was his obedience to God, and love to us.   That it was an act
of obedience is plain from Phil. ii. 8, "He became obedient
unto death, even the death of the cross."   Now obedience respects a command, and such a command Christ received to die
for us, as himself tells us, "I lay down my life of myself; I
have power to lay it down, and power to take it again: this
commandment have I received of my Father," John x. 18.   So
that it was an act of obedience with respect to God, and yet a
most free and spontaneous act with respect to himself.   And
that he was moved to it out of pity and love to us, we are assured:
"Christ loved us, and gave himself for us an offering and a sacrifice to God," Eph. v. 2.   Upon this Paul sweetly reflected,
"Who loved me and gave himself for me," Gal. ii. 20.   As
the external moving cause was our misery, so the internal was
his own love and pity for us.

4. The matter of Christ's satisfaction, was his active and
passive obedience to all the law of God required.   I know there
are some that doubt whether Christ's active obedience have any
place here, and so whether it be imputed as any part of our
righteousness.   It is confessed, that scripture most frequently
mentions his passive obedience, as that which made the atonement, and procures our redemption, Matt. xx. 28, and xxvi. 28,

Rom. iii. 24, 25, and elsewhere; but his passive obedience is never mentioned exclusively, as the sole cause, or matter of satisfaction. But in those places where it is mentioned by itself, it is put for his whole obedience, both active and passive, by a usual figure of speech; and in other scriptures it is ascribed to both, as Gal. iv. 4, 5, he is said " to be under the law, to redeem them that were under the law." Now his being " made under the law" to this end, cannot be restrained to his subjection to the curse of the law only, but to the commands of it also. So Rom. v. 19, " As by one man's disobedience, many were made sinners; so by the obedience of one shall many be made righteous." It were a manifest injury to this text also, to restrain it to the passive obedience of Christ only. To be short, this twofold obedience of Christ stands opposed to a twofold obligation that fallen man is under; the one to do what God requires, the other to suffer what he hath threatened for disobedience. Suitably to this double obligation, Christ comes under the commandment of the law, to fulfil it actively, Matt. iii. 15; and under the malediction of the law, to satisfy it passively. And whereas it is objected by some, if he fulfilled the whole law for us by his active, what need then of his passive obedience? We reply, great need; because both these make up that one, entire, and complete obedience, by which God is satisfied, and we justified. The whole obedience of Christ, both active and passive, make up one entire perfect obedience; and therefore there is no reason why one particle, either of the one, or of the other, should be excluded.

5. The effect and fruit of this his satisfaction, is our freedom, ransom, or deliverance from the wrath and curse due to us for our sins. Such was the dignity, value, and completeness of Christ's satisfaction, that in strict justice it merited our redemption and full deliverance; not only a possibility that we might be redeemed and pardoned, but a right whereby to be so. If he be made a curse for us, we must then be redeemed from the curse, according to justice; so the apostle argues, " Whom God hath set forth to be a propitiation through faith in his blood, to declare his righteousness for the remission of sins that are past, through the forbearance of God; to declare, I say, at this time his righteousness: that God might be just, and the justifier of him that believeth in Jesus," Rom. iii. 25, 26. Mark the design and end of God in exacting satisfaction from Christ, it was to declare his righteousness in the remission of sin to believers; and lest we should lose the emphatical word, he doubles it, " to declare, I say, his righteousness." Every one can

see how his mercy is declared in remission : but he would
have us take notice, that his justification of believers is an act of
justice ; and that God, as he is a just God, cannot condemn
the believer, since Christ hath satisfied his debts.   This attribute seemed to be the main bar against remission ; but now it
is become the very ground and reason why God remits.   Oh
how comfortable a text is this ! Doth Satan or conscience set
forth thy sin in all its discouraging circumstances and aggravations ? God hath set forth Christ to be a propitiation.   Must
justice be manifested, satisfied, and glorified ? So it is in the
death of Christ, ten thousand times more than ever it could in
thy damnation.   Thus you have a brief account of the satisfaction made by Jesus Christ.

II. We shall gather up all that hath been said to establish
the truth of Christ's satisfaction ; proving the reality of it, that
it is not an improper, fictitious satisfaction, as some have called
it ; but real, proper, and full, and as such accepted of God.
For his blood is the blood of a Surety, Heb. vii. 22, who came
under the same obligations of the law with us, Gal. iv. 4 ; and
though he had no sin of his own, yet standing before God as our
Surety, the iniquities of us all were laid upon him, Isa. liii. 6 ;
and from him did the Lord, with great severity, exact satisfaction for our sins, Rom. viii. 32, punish them upon his soul,
Matt. xxvii. 46, and upon his body, Acts ii. 23 ; and with this
obedience of his Son, is fully pleased and satisfied, Eph. v. 2,
and hath in token thereof raised him from the dead, and set him
at his own right hand, Eph. i. 20, and for his righteousness'
sake acquitted and discharged believers, who shall never more
come into condemnation, Rom. viii. 1. 34. All this is plain in
scripture ; and our faith in the satisfaction of Christ is not built
on the wisdom of man, but the everlasting sealed truth of God :
yet such is the perverse nature of man, and the pride of his
heart, that whilst he should be humbly adoring the grace of God,
in providing such a Surety for us, he is found accusing the justice
and diminishing the mercy of God, and raising all the objections
which Satan and his own heart can invent, to overturn that
blessed foundation upon which God hath built up his own
honour, and his people's salvation.

III. To apply the doctrine.

Inference 1. If the death of Christ was that which satisfied
God for all the sins of the elect, then certainly there is an infinite evil in sin, since it cannot be expiated but by an infinite
satisfaction.   Fools make a mock at sin, and there are but few
souls in the world that are duly sensible of, and affected with

its evil; but certainly, if God should damn thee to all eternity, thy eternal sufferings could not satisfy for the evil that is in one vain thought. It may be you may think it harsh and severe, that God should hold his creatures under everlasting sufferings for sin, and never be satisfied with them any more. But when you have well considered, that the Being against whom you sin, is the infinitely blessed God, which derives an infinite evil to the sin committed against him; and when you consider how God dealt with the angels that fell, you will alter your minds about it. Oh the depth of the evil of sin! If ever you wish to see how great and horrid an evil sin is, measure it in your thoughts, either by the infinite holiness and excellency of God, who is wronged by it; or by the infinite sufferings of Christ, who died to satisfy for it; and then you will have deeper apprehensions of the evil of sin.

2. If the death of Christ satisfied God, and thereby redeemed the elect from the curse; then the redemption of souls is costly; souls are precious and of great value with God. " Ye know (says the apostle) that ye were not redeemed with corruptible things, as silver and gold, from your vain conversation received by tradition; but with the precious blood of the Son of God, as of a lamb without spot," 1 Pet. i. 18, 19. Only the blood of God is an equivalent price for the redemption of souls. Gold and silver may redeem from turkish, but not from hellish bondage. The whole creation sold to the utmost worth of it, is not a value for the redemption of one soul. Souls are very dear; he that paid for them found them so : yet how cheaply do sinners sell their souls, as if they were but low-priced commodities ! but you that sell your souls cheap, will buy repentance dear.

3. If Christ's death satisfied God for our sins, how unparalleled is the love of Christ to poor sinners ! It is much to pay a pecuniary debt to free another, but who will pay his own blood for another ? We have a noted instance of Zaleucus, that famous locrensian lawgiver, who decreed, that whoever was convicted of adultery, should have both his eyes put out. It so fell out that his own son was brought before him for that crime : hereupon the people interposing, made suit for his pardon. At length the father, partly overcome by their importunities, and not unwilling to show what lawful favour he might to his son, he first put out one of his own eyes, and then one of his son's; and so showed himself both a merciful father and a just lawgiver; so tempering mercy with justice, that both the law was satisfied, and his son spared. This is written by the historian as an

instance of singular love in his father, to pay one half of the penalty for his son. But Christ did not divide, and share in the penalty with us, but bare it all. Zaleucus did it for his son, who was dear to him; Christ did it for enemies, that were fighting and rebelling against him: "While we were yet sinners, Christ died for us," Rom. v. 8.

4. If Christ, by dying, hath made full satisfaction, then God is no loser in pardoning the greatest of sinners, that believe in Jesus; and consequently his justice can be no bar to their justification and salvation. He is just to forgive us our sins, 1 John i. 9. What an argument is here for a poor believer to plead with God! Lord, if thou save me by Jesus Christ, thy justice will be fully satisfied at one full payment; but if thou damn me, and require satisfaction at my hands, thou canst never receive it: I can never make payment, though I lie in hell to eternity. One drop of his blood is more worth than all my polluted blood. Oh how satisfying a thing is this to the conscience of a poor sinner that is objecting the multitude, aggravations, and amazing circumstances of his sins, against the possibility of their being pardoned! Can such a sinner as I be forgiven? Yes, if thou believest in Jesus, thou mayest; for so God will lose nothing in pardoning the greatest transgressors: "Let Israel hope in the Lord; for with the Lord there is mercy, and with him is plenteous redemption," Psa. cxxx. 7; that is, a large stock of merit lying by him in the blood of Christ, to pay him for all that you have done against him.

5. If Christ hath made such a full satisfaction as you have heard, how much is it the concern of every soul, to abandon all thoughts of satisfying God for his own sins, and betake himself to the blood of Christ, the ransomer, by faith, that in that blood they may be pardoned? It would grieve one's heart to see how many poor creatures are drudging and toiling at a task of repentance, and revenge upon themselves, and reformation, and obedience, to satisfy God for what they have done against him: and alas! it cannot be, they do but lose their labour; could they swelter their very hearts out, weep till they can weep no more, cry till their throats be parched, alas, they can never recompense God for one vain thought; for such is the severity of the law, that when it is once offended, it will never be made amends again by all that we can do: it will not discharge the sinner, for all the sorrow in the world. Indeed, if a man be in Christ, sorrow for sin is something, and renewed obedience is something: God looks upon them favourably, and accepts them graciously in Christ: but out of him they signify no more than

the entreaties and cries of a condemned malefactor, to reverse the
legal sentence of the judge.   Reader, be convinced, that one act
of faith in the Lord Jesus pleases God more than all the obedience, repentance, and strivings to obey the law, through thy
whole life, can do.   And thus you have the first special fruits
of Christ's priesthood, in the full satisfaction of God, for all the
sins of believers.

SERMON XV.

OF THE BLESSED INHERITANCE PURCHASED BY THE OBLATION OF
CHRIST, BEING THE SECOND EFFECT OR FRUIT OF HIS PRIEST-
HOOD.

GAL. IV. 4, 5.

BUT WHEN THE FULNESS OF TIME WAS COME, GOD SENT FORTH HIS SON
MADE OF A WOMAN, MADE UNDER THE LAW, TO REDEEM THEM THAT WERE
UNDER THE LAW, THAT WE MIGHT RECEIVE THE ADOPTION OF SONS.

THIS scripture gives us an account of a double fruit of Christ's
death, namely, the payment of our debt, and the purchase of our
inheritance.

1. The payment of our debt, expressed by our redemption, or
buying us out from the obligation and curse of the law, which
hath been considered in the last discourse.

2. The purchase of an inheritance for those redeemed ones,
expressed here by their receiving the adoption of sons; which is
to be our present subject. Adoption is either civil, or divine.
Of the first, the civil law gives this definition: that it is " A
lawful act, an imitation of nature, invented for the comfort of
them that have no children of their own. Divine adoption is
that special benefit whereby God, for Christ's sake, accepteth
us as sons, and makes us heirs of eternal life with him." *

Between this civil and sacred adoption, there is a twofold
agreement, and disagreement. They agree in this, that both
flow from the pleasure and good-will of the adoptant; and in
this, that both confer a right to privileges, which we have not
by nature: but in this they differ, one is an act imitating nature,
the other transcends nature; the one was found out for the comfort of them that had no children; the other for the comfort of
them that had no father. This Divine adoption is, in scripture,
either taken properly for that act or sentence of God, by which
we are made sons, or for the privileges with which the adopted
are invested: and so it is taken Rom. viii. 23, and in this scripture now before us. We lost our inheritance by the fall of
Adam; we receive it, as the text speaks, by the death of Christ,

* Ravanel.

which restores it again to us by a new and better title. The doctrine hence, is this,

> DOCT. THAT THE DEATH OF JESUS CHRIST HATH NOT ONLY SATISFIED FOR OUR DEBTS, BUT OVER AND ABOVE PURCHASED A RICH INHERITANCE FOR THE CHILDREN OF GOD.

" For this end, or cause, he is the Mediator of the new testament, that by means of death, for the redemption of the transgressions that were under the first testament, they which are called might receive the promise of the eternal inheritance," Heb. ix. 15.

We will here, I. See what Christ paid. II. What he purchased. III. For whom.

I. What Christ paid. Our divines comprise the virtue and fruits of the priesthood of Christ in these two things, namely, Solutio debiti, et acquisitio hæreditatis, payment and purchase. Answerably, the obedience of Christ hath a double relation, the relation of a legal righteousness, and of an adequate price. And it hath also in it the relation of a merit over and beyond the law.

Here our divines rightly distinguish between the substance and accidents of Christ's death and obedience. Consider Christ's suffering, as to the substance of it, it was no more than what the law required; for, neither the justice nor love of the Father would permit that Christ should suffer more than what was necessary for him to bear, as our Surety; but, as to the circumstances, the person of the sufferer, the cause and efficacy of his sufferings, &c. it was much more than sufficient, a merit above and beyond what the law required; for, though the law required the death of the sinner, who is but a poor contemptible creature, it did not require that one perfectly innocent should die; it did not require that God should shed his blood; it did not require blood of such value and worth as this was. I say, none of this the law required, though God was pleased, for the advancement and manifestation of his justice and mercy in the highest, to admit, and order this by way of commutation, admitting him to be our ransomer, by dying for us. And, indeed, it was a most gracious relaxation of the law, that admitted of such a commutation as this; for hereby it comes to pass, that justice is fully satisfied, and yet we live and are saved; which, before, was a thing that could not be imagined. Yea, now we are not only redeemed from wrath, by the adequate compensation made for our sins by Christ's blood and sufferings substantially considered;

but entitled to a most glorious inheritance, purchased by his blood, considered as the blood of an innocent, as the blood of God, and therefore as most excellent and efficacious blood, above what the law demanded. By this you see, how rich a treasure lies in Christ, to bestow in a purchase for us, above what he paid to redeem us; even as much as his soul and body were more worth than ours, for whom it was sacrificed; which is so great a sum, that all the angels in heaven, and men on earth, can never compute and sum up, so as to show us the total of it. And this was that inexhaustible treasure that Christ expended, to procure and purchase the fairest inheritance for believers. Having seen the treasure that purchased, let us next inquire into the inheritance purchased by it.

II. This inheritance is so large, that it cannot be surveyed by creatures; nor can the boundaries and limits thereof be described, for it comprehends all things; " All is yours, ye are Christ's, and Christ is God's," 1 Cor. iii. 22, 23. " He that overcomes shall inherit all things," Rev. xxi. 7.

But, to be more particular, I shall distribute the saints' inheritance, purchased by Christ, into three heads; all temporal good things, all spiritual good things, and all eternal good things are theirs.

1. All temporal good things. " He hath given us all things richly to enjoy," 1 Tim. vi. 17. Not that they have the possession, but the comfort and benefit of all things : others have the sting, gall, wormwood, baits and snares of the creature; saints only have the blessing and comfort of it. So that the little that a righteous man hath, is (in this among other respects) better than the treasures of many wicked : which is the true key to open that dark saying of the apostle, " As having nothing, and yet possessing all things," 2 Cor. vi. 10. They only possess, others are possessed by the world. The saints " use the world, and enjoy God" in the use of it. Others are deceived, defiled, and destroyed by the world; but these are refreshed and furthered by it.

2. All spiritual good things are purchased by the blood of Christ for them; as justification, which comprises remission of sins and acceptance of our persons by God: " Being justified freely by his grace, through the redemption that is in Christ," Rom. iii. 24. Sanctification is also purchased for them ; for of " God, he is made unto us, not only wisdom and righteousness, but sanctification also," 1 Cor. i. 30. These two, namely, our justification and sanctification, are two of the most rich and shining robes in the wardrobe of free grace. How glorious and

lovely do they render the soul that wears them! These are like the bracelets and jewels Isaac sent to Rebecca. Adoption into the family of God is purchased for us by his blood; "For ye are all the children of God by faith in Jesus Christ," Gal. iii. 26. Christ, as he is the Son, is *hæres natus*, "the heir by nature;" as he is Mediator, he is *hæres constitutus*, "the heir by appointment," appointed heir of all things, as it is Heb. i. 2. By the sonship of Christ, we, being united to him by faith, become sons; and if sons, then heirs. "O what manner of love is this, that we should be called the sons of God!" 1 John iii. 1. That a poor beggar should be made an heir, yea, an heir of God, and joint heir with Christ! Yea, that very faith, which is the bond of union, and consequently, the ground of all our communion with Christ, is the purchase of his blood also: "To them that have obtained like precious faith with us, through the righteousness of God and our Saviour Jesus Christ," 2 Pet. i. 1. This most precious grace is the dear purchase of our Lord Jesus Christ; yea, all that peace, joy, and spiritual comfort, which are sweet fruits of faith, are with it purchased for us by this blood. So speaks the apostle in Rom. v. 1—3, "Being justified by faith, we have peace with God, through our Lord Jesus Christ," &c. Moreover the Spirit himself, who is the author, fountain, and spring of all graces and comforts, is procured for us by his death and resurrection: "Christ hath redeemed us from the curse of the law, being made a curse for us; for it is written, Cursed is every one that hangeth on a tree: that the blessing of Abraham might come upon the gentiles through Jesus Christ, that we might receive the promise of the Spirit through faith," Gal. iii. 13, 14. That Spirit that first sanctified, and since hath so often sealed, comforted, directed, resolved, guided, and quickened your souls, had not come to perform any of these blessed offices upon your hearts, if Christ had not died.

3. All eternal good things are the purchase of his blood. Heaven, and all the glory thereof, is purchased for believers, with this price. Hence that glory is called "an inheritance incorruptible, undefiled, and that fadeth not away, reserved in heaven for you;" to the lively hope whereof you are begotten again, "by the resurrection of Christ from the dead," 1 Pet. i. 3. Not only present mercies are purchased for us, but things to come also, as it is, 1 Cor. iii. 22.

III. All this is purchased for believers: hence it is called, "the inheritance of the saints in light," Col. i. 12. "All is yours, for ye are Christ's;" that is the tenure, 1 Cor. iii. 22, 23.

So Rom. viii. 30, " Whom he did predestinate, them he also called; and whom he called, them he also justified; and whom he justified, them he also glorified." Only those that are sons, are heirs, Rom. viii. 17. The unrighteous shall not inherit, 1 Cor. vi. 9. " It is the Father's good pleasure, to give the kingdom to the little flock," Luke xii. 32.

Inf. 1. Hath Christ not only redeemed you from wrath, but purchased such an eternal inheritance also by the overplus of his merit for you? Oh how well content should believers then be with their lot of providence in this life, be it what it will! Content did I say? I speak too low; overcome, ravished, filled with praises and thanksgivings; how low, how poor, how afflicted soever for the present they are. Oh let not such things as grumbling, repining, fretting at providence, be found, or once named among the expectants of this inheritance! Suppose you had taken a beggar from your door, and adopted him to be your son, and made him heir of a large inheritance, and after this he should contest and quarrel with you for a trifle; could you bear it? How to work the spirit of a saint into contentment with a low condition here, I have laid down several rules in another discourse,* to which, for the present, I refer the reader.

2. With what weaned affections should the people of God walk up and down this world, content to live, and willing to die! For things present are theirs if they live, and things to come are theirs if they die. Paul expresses himself in a frame of holy indifference, " Which to choose I know not," Phil. i. 22. Many of them that are now in fruition of their inheritance above, had " life in patience, and death in desire," while they tabernacled with us.

And truly the wisdom of God is in this specially remarkable, in giving the new creature such an even temper, as that scripture, 2 Thess. iii. 5, expresses, " The Lord direct your hearts into the love of God and patient waiting for Christ." Love inflames with desire, patience allays that fervour. So that fervent desires (as one happily expresses it) are allayed with meek submission; mighty love with strong patience. And had not God twisted together these two principles in the christian's constitution, he had framed a creature to be a torment to itself, to live upon a very rack.

3. Hence we infer the impossibility of their salvation that know not Christ, nor have interest in his blood. There is but one way to glory for all the world, " No man cometh to the

* A Saint Indeed,—published by the Religious Tract Society.

Father but by me," John xiv. 6. " The blessing of Abraham comes upon the gentiles through faith," Gal. iii. 14. Scripture asserts the impossibility of being or doing any thing that is truly evangelically good, out of Christ; " Without me ye can do nothing," John xv. 5. And, " Without faith it is impossible to please God," Heb. xi. 6. Scripture every where connects salvation with vocation, Rom. viii. 30; and vocation with the gospel, Rom. x. 14. To those that plead for the salvation of heathens, and profane christians, we may apply that tart rebuke of Bernard, that while some labour to make Plato a christian, he feared they therein did prove themselves to be heathens.

4. How greatly are we all concerned to clear up our title to the heavenly inheritance ! It is horrible to see how industrious many are for an inheritance on earth, and how careless for heaven. By which we may plainly see how vilely the noble soul is depressed by sin, and sunk down into flesh, minding only the concernments of the flesh. Hear me, ye that labour for the world, as if heaven were in it ; what will ye do when at death you shall look back over your shoulder, and see what you have spent your time and strength for, shrinking and vanishing away from you ? When you shall look forward, and see vast eternity opening its mouth to swallow you up ; oh then what would you give for a well-grounded assurance of an eternal inheritance !

. Oh, therefore, if you have any regard for your poor souls ; if it be not indifferent to you what becomes of them, whether they be saved, or whether they be damned, " give all diligence to make your calling and election sure," 2 Pet. i. 10. " Work out your own salvation with fear and trembling ; for it is God that worketh in you both to will and to do of his own good pleasure," Phil. ii. 12, 13. Remember it is salvation you work for, and that is no trifle. It is for thy own poor soul that thou art striving ; and what hast thou more ?

Remember, now God offers you his helping nand ; now the Spirit waits upon you in the means, but of the continuance thereof you have no assurance ; for it is of his own good pleasure, and not at yours. To your work, souls, to your work. Ah, strive as men that know what an inheritance in heaven is worth.

And, as for you that have solid evidence that it is yours ; oh, that with hands and eyes lifted up to heaven, you would adore that free grace, that hath entitled a child of wrath to a heavenly inheritance ! Walk as becomes heirs of God, and joint heirs with Christ. Be often looking heaven-ward when wants pinch here.   Oh look to that fair estate you have reserved in heaven for you, and say, I am hastening home; and when I come thither, all my wants shall be supplied.   Consider what it cost Christ to purchase it for thee; and with a deep sense of what he hath laid out for thee, let thy soul say, Blessed be God for Jesus Christ.

SERMON XVI.

OF THE KINGLY OFFICE OF CHRIST, AS IT IS EXECUTED SPIRITUALLY UPON THE SOULS OF THE REDEEMED.

2 COR. X. 5.

CASTING DOWN IMAGINATIONS, AND EVERY HIGH THING THAT EXALTETH IT-SELF AGAINST THE KNOWLEDGE OF GOD, AND BRINGING INTO CAPTIVITY EVERY THOUGHT TO THE OBEDIENCE OF CHRIST.

WE now come to the regal office, by which our glorious Mediator executes the undertaken design of our redemption. Had he not, as our Prophet, opened the way of life and salvation to the children of men, they could never have known it; and if they had clearly known it, yet except, as their Priest, he had offered up himself, to impetrate and obtain redemption for them, they could not have been redeemed virtually by his blood; and if they had been so redeemed, yet had he not lived in the capacity of a King, to apply this purchase of his blood to them, they could have had no actual, personal benefit by his death; for what he revealed as a Prophet, he purchased as a Priest; and what he so revealed and purchased as a Prophet and Priest, he applies as a King; first subduing the souls of his elect to his spiritual government; then ruling them as his subjects, and ordering all things in the kingdom of Providence for their good. So that Christ hath a twofold kingdom, the one spiritual and internal, by which he subdues and rules the hearts of his people; the other providential and external, whereby he guides, rules, and orders all things in the world, in a blessed subordination to their eternal salvation. I am to speak from this text of his spiritual and internal kingdom.

These words hold forth the efficacy of the gospel, in the plainness and simplicity of it, for the subduing of rebellious sinners to Christ: and in them we have these three things to consider.

1. The oppositions made by sinners against the assaults of the gospel, namely, imaginations, or reasonings, as the word λογισμυς, may be fitly rendered. He means the subtleties, slights, excuses, subterfuges, and arguings of fleshly-minded

men; in which they fortify and intrench themselves against the convictions of the word: yea, and there are not only such carnal reasonings, but many proud, high conceits with which poor creatures swell, and scorn to submit to the abasing, humble, self-denying way of the gospel. These are the fortifications erected against Christ by the carnal mind.

2. We have here the conquest which the gospel obtains over sinners, thus fortified against it; it casts down and over-throws these strong holds. Thus Christ spoils Satan of his armour in which he trusted, by showing the sinner that all this can be no defence to his soul against the wrath of God. But that is not all: in the next place,

3. You have here the improvement of the victory. Christ doth not only lead away these enemies spoiled, but brings them into obedience to himself, that is, makes them, after conversion, subjects of his own kingdom, obedient, useful, and serviceable to himself; and so is more than a conqueror. They do not only lay down their arms, and fight no more against Christ, with them; but repair to his camp, and fight for Christ, with those reasons of theirs that were before employed against him: as it is said of Jerom, Origen, and Tertullian, that they came into Canaan laden with egyptian gold; that is, they came into the church full of excellent learning and abilities, with which they eminently served Jesus Christ. " Oh blessed victory, where the conqueror and conquered both triumph together !"* And thus enemies and rebels are subdued, and made subjects of the spiritual kingdom of Christ. Hence the doctrinal note is,

DOCT. THAT JESUS CHRIST EXERCISES A KINGLY POWER OVER THE SOULS OF ALL WHOM THE GOSPEL SUBDUES TO HIS OBEDIENCE.

No sooner were the colossians delivered out of the power of darkness, but they were immediately translated into the kingdom of Christ, the dear Son, Col. i. 13. This kingdom of Christ, which is our present subject, is the internal spiritual kingdom, which is said to be within the saints; " The kingdom of God is within you," Luke xvii. 20, 21. Christ sits as an enthroned King in the hearts, consciences, and affections of his willing people, Psa. cx. 3. And his kingdom consists in " righteousness, peace, and joy in the Holy Ghost," Rom. xiv. 17, and it is properly monarchical, as appears in the margin.

In the prosecution of this point, I will speak doctrinally to these three heads:

* Meyer, in loc.

I. How Christ obtains the throne in the hearts of men. II. How he rules in it, and by what acts he exercises his kingly authority. III. What are the privileges of those souls over whom Christ reigns. And then apply it.

I. We will open the way and manner in which Christ obtains a throne in the hearts of men, and that is by conquest: for though the souls of the elect are his by donation, and right of redemption; the Father gave them to him, and he died for them; yet Satan hath the first possession: and so it fares with Christ, as it did with Abraham, to whom God gave the land of Canaan by promise and covenant, but the canaanites, perizzites, and sons of Anak, had the actual possession of it, and Abraham's posterity must fight for it, and win it by inches, before they enjoy it. The house is conveyed to Christ by him that built it, but the strong man armed keeps the possession of it, till a stronger than he comes and ejects him, Luke xi. 20—22. Christ must fight his way into the soul, though he have a right to enter, as into his dearly purchased possession. And so he doth; for when the time of recovering them is come, he sends forth his armies to subdue them; as it is Psa. cx. 3, "Thy people shall be willing in the day of thy power." The Hebrew may as fitly be rendered, and so is by some, "in the day of thine armies;" when the Lord Jesus sent forth his armies of prophets, apostles, evangelists, pastors, teachers, under the conduct of his Spirit, armed with that two-edged sword, the word of God, which is sharp and powerful, Heb. iv. 12. But that is not all: he causes armies of convictions, and spiritual troubles, to begird and straiten them on every side, so that they know not what to do. These convictions, like a shower of arrows, strike, point-blank, into their consciences; "When they heard this, they were pricked to the heart, and said, Men and brethren, what shall we do?" Acts ii. 37. Christ's arrows are sharp in the hearts of his enemies, whereby the people fall under him, Psa. xlv. 5, 6. By these convictions he batters down all their loose, vain hopes, and levels them with the earth. Now all their weak pleas and defences, from the general mercy of God, the example of others, &c. prove but as paper walls to them. These shake their hearts, even to the very foundation, and overturn every high thought there, that exalts itself against the Lord.

This day, in which Christ sits down before the soul, and summons it by such messengers as these, is a day of distress within; yea, such a day of trouble, that none is like it. But though it be so, yet Satan hath so deeply intrenched himself in the mind and will, that the soul yields not at the first summons, till its provisions within are spent, and all its towers of pride, and walls of vain confidence, be undermined by the gospel, and shaken down about its ears; and then the soul desires a parley with Christ. Oh now it would be glad of terms, any terms, if it may but save its life; let all go as a prey to the conqueror Now it sends many such messengers as these to Christ, who is come now to the very gates of the soul; Mercy, Lord, mercy, oh were I but assured thou wouldst receive, spare, and pardon me, I would open to thee the next moment! Thus the soul is "shut up to the faith of Christ," as it is, Gal. iii. 23, and reduced now to the greatest strait and loss imaginable; and now the merciful King, whose only design is to conquer the heart, hangs forth the white flag of mercy before the soul, giving it hopes it shall be spared, pitied, and pardoned, though so long in rebellion against him, if yet it will yield itself to Christ.

Many staggerings, hesitations, irresolutions, doubts, fears, scruples, half-resolves, reasonings for and against, there are at the council-table of man's own heart, at this time. Sometimes there is no hope; Christ will slay me, if I go forth to him; and then it trembles. But then, who ever found him so that tried him? Other souls have yielded, and found mercy beyond all their expectations. Oh but I have been a desperate enemy against him. Admit it, yet thou hast the word of the King for it; "Let the wicked forsake his way, and the unrighteous man his thoughts; and let him turn to the Lord, and he will have mercy on him; and to our God, for he will abundantly pardon him," Isa. lv. 7. But the time of mercy is past, I have stood out too long. Yet if it were so, how is it that Christ hath not made short work, and cut me off? set fire, hell-fire to my soul, and withdrawn the siege? Still he waiteth that he may be gracious, and is exalted that he may have compassion.

A thousand such debates there are, till at last, the soul considering, if it abide in rebellion, it must needs perish; if it go forth to Christ, it can but perish: and being somewhat encouraged by the messages of grace sent into the soul, at this time, such as in Heb. vii. 25, "Wherefore he is able to save to the uttermost, all that come unto God by him;" and John vi. 37, "He that cometh to me, I will in no wise cast out;" and in Matt. xi. 28. "Come unto me, all ye that labour, and are heavy laden, and I will give you rest." It is, at last, resolved to open to Christ. Now, the will spontaneously opens to Christ; that royal fort submits and yields; all the affections open to him. The will brings Christ the keys of all the rooms in the soul. Concerning the triumphant entrance of Christ into the soul, we may say, as the psalmist rhetorically speaks concerning the triumphant entrance of Israel into Canaan, " The mountains skipped like rams, and the little hills like lambs. What ailed thee, O thou sea, that thou fleddest ? Thou Jordan, that thou wast driven back ?" Psa. cxiv. 5, 6. So here, in the like rhetorical triumph, we may say, the mountains and hills skipped like rams, and the fixed and obstinate will starts from its own basis and centre ; the rocky heart rends in twain. A poor soul comes into the world, full of ignorance, pride, self-love, desperate hardness, and fixed resolutions to go on in its way; and, by an hour's discourse, the tide turns, Jordan is driven back. What ailed thee, thou stout will, that thou surrenderest to Christ ! thou hard heart, that thou relentest, and the waters gush out ? And thus the soul is won to Christ ; he writes down his terms, and the soul willingly subscribes them. Thus it comes in to Christ by free and hearty submission, desiring nothing more than to live under the government of Christ for the time to come.

II. Let us see how Christ rules in the souls of such as submit to him. There are six things in which he exerts his kingly authority over them.

1. He imposes a new law upon them, and enjoins them to be severe and punctual in their obedience to it. The soul was a belialite before, and could endure no restraint; its lusts gave it laws. " We ourselves were sometimes foolish, disobedient, serving divers lusts and pleasures," Tit. iii. 3. Whatever the flesh craved, and the sensual appetite longed after, it must have, cost what it would ; if damnation were the price of it, it would have it, provided it should not be present pay. Now, it must not be any longer " without law to God; but under law to Christ." Those are the articles of peace which the soul willingly subscribes in the day of its admission to mercy, " Take my yoke upon you, and learn of me," Matt. xi. 29. This " law of the spirit of life which is in Christ Jesus makes them free from the law of sin and death," Rom. viii. 2. Here is much strictness, but no bondage ; for the law is not only written in Christ's statute-book, the Bible, but copied out by his Spirit upon the hearts of his subjects, in correspondent principles ; which makes obedience a pleasure, and self-denial easy. Christ's yoke is lined with love, so that it never galls the necks of his people : " His commandments are not grievous," 1 John v. 3. The soul that comes under Christ's government, must receive law from Christ; and under law every thought of the heart must come.

2. He rebukes and chastises souls for the violations and transgressions of his law. That is another act of Christ's regal authority: " Whom he loves he rebukes and chastens," Heb. xii. 6, 7. These chastisements of Christ are either upon their bodies and outward comforts by the rod of providence, or upon their spirits and inward comforts. Sometimes his rebukes are smart upon the outward man; " For this cause many among you are weakly and sick, and many sleep," 1 Cor. xi. 30. They had not that due regard to his body that became them, and he will make their bodies to smart for it. And he had rather their flesh should smart, than their souls should perish. Sometimes he spares their outward, and afflicts their inner man, which is a much smarter rod. He withdraws peace, and takes away joy from the spirits of his people. The hidings of his face are sore rebukes. However, all is for emendation, not for destruction. And it is not the least privilege of Christ's subjects to have a seasonable and sanctified rod to restore them from the ways of sin, Psa. xxiii. 3 ; while others are suffered to go on stubbornly in the way of their own hearts.

3. Another regal act of Christ, is the restraining and keeping back his servants from iniquity, and withholding them from those courses which their own hearts would incline, and lead them to; for, even in them, there is a spirit bent to backsliding, but the Lord in tenderness over them, keeps back their souls from iniquity, and that when they are upon the very brink of sin: " My feet were almost gone, my steps were well nigh slipped," Psa. lxxiii. 2. Then doth the Lord prevent sin, by removing the occasion providentially, or by helping them to resist the temptation, graciously assisting their spirits in the trial, so that no temptation shall befall them; but a way of escape shall be opened, that they may be able to bear it, 1 Cor. x. 13. Thus his people have frequent occasions to bless his name for his preventing goodness, when they are almost in the midst of all evil. And this I take to be the meaning of, " This I say, then, walk in the Spirit, and ye shall not fulfil the lusts of the flesh," Gal. v. 16 ; tempted by them you may be, but fulfil them ye shall not ; my Spirit shall cause the temptation to die, and wither away, in the embryo of it, so that it shall not come to a full birth.

4. He protects them in his ways, and suffers them not to relapse from him into a state of sin, and bondage to Satan any more. Indeed, Satan is restless in his endeavours to reduce them again to his obedience; he never leaves tempting and soliciting for their return; and where he finds a false professor he prevails ; but Christ keeps his own, that they depart not again.

" All that thou hast given me I have kept, and none of them is lost, but the son of perdition," John xvii. 12. They are "kept by the mighty power of God, through faith unto salvation," 1 Pet. i. 5; kept as in a garrison, according to the import of that word. None more assaulted, yet none more safe than the people of God. They are "preserved in Christ Jesus," Jude 1. It is not their own grace that secures them, but Christ's care, and continual watchfulness. This is his covenant with them, " I will put my fear in their hearts, that they shall not depart from me," Jer. xxxii. 40. Thus, as a King, he preserves them.

5. As a King he rewards their obedience, and encourages their sincere service. Though all they do for Christ be duty, yet he hath united their comfort with their duty ; " This I had, because I kept thy precepts," Psa. cxix. 56. They take this encouragement with them to every duty, that he whom they seek "is a bountiful rewarder of such as diligently seek him," Heb. xi. 6. Oh what a good Master do the saints serve! Hear how the King expostulates with his subjects, " Have I been a barren wilderness, or a land of darkness to you?" Jer. ii. 31. *q. d.* Have I been such a hard master to you ? Have you any reason to complain of my service? You have not found the ways or wages of sin like mine.

6. He pacifies all inward troubles, and commands peace when their spirits are tumultuous. This " peace of God rules in their hearts," Col. iii. 15. When the tumultuous affections are up, and in a hurry ; when anger, hatred, and revenge begin to rise in the soul, this hushes and stills all. " I will hearken (saith the church) what God the Lord will speak, for he will speak peace to his people, and to his saints," Psa. lxxxv. 8. He that saith to the raging sea, Be still, and it obeys him ; he only can pacify the disquieted spirit. These are Christ's regal acts. And he exercises them upon the souls of his people, powerfully, sweetly, suitably.

(1.) Powerfully : whether he restrains from sin, or impels to duty, he doth it with a soul-determining efficacy ; for " his kingdom is not in word, but in power," 1 Cor. iv. 20. And yet,

(2.) He rules not by compulsion, but most sweetly. His law is a law of love, written upon their hearts. The church is the Lamb's wife, Rev. xix. 7. " A bruised reed he shall not break, and smoking flax he shall not quench," Isa. xlii. 3. " I beseech you by the meekness and gentleness of Christ," saith the apostle, 2 Cor. x. 1. For he delighteth in free, not in forced obedience. He rules children, not slaves ; and so his kingly power is mixed with fatherly love.

(3.) He rules them suitably to their natures in a rational way; " I drew them with the cords of a man, with bands of love," Hos. xi. 4; that is, in a way proper to convince their'reason, and work upon their affections. And thus his eternal kingdom is administered by his Spirit, who is his vicegerent in our hearts.

III. We will open the privileges pertaining to all the subjects of this spiritual kingdom. And they are such as follow.

1. Those over whom Christ reigns, are certainly and fully set free from the curse of the law. " If the Son makes you free, then are you free indeed," John viii. 36. I say not, they are free from the law as a rule of life; such a freedom were no privilege to them at all: but free from the rigorous exactions, and terrible maledictions of it; to hear our liberty proclaimed from this bondage, is the joyful sound indeed, the most blessed voice that ever our ears heard. And this all that are in Christ shall hear: " If we be led by the Spirit, we are not under the law," Gal. v. 18. " Blessed are the people that hear this joyful sound," Psa. lxxxix. 15.

2. Another privilege of Christ's subjects, is, freedom from the dominion of sin; " Sin shall not reign over them; for they are not under the law, but under grace," Rom. vi. 14. One heaven cannot bear two suns; nor one soul two kings: when Christ takes the throne, sin quits it. It is true, the being of sin is there still; its defiling and troubling power remains still; but its dominion is abolished. O joyful tidings! O welcome day!

3. Another privilege of Christ's subjects, is, protection in all the troubles and dangers to which their souls or bodies are exposed. " This man shall be the peace, when the assyrian shall come into our land, and when he shall tread in our palaces," Mic. v. 5. Kings owe protection to their subjects: none so able, so faithful in that work as Christ; all " thou gavest me, I have kept, and none is lost," John xvii. 12.

4. Another privilege of Christ's subjects, is, a merciful and tender bearing of their burdens and infirmities. They have a meek and patient King; " Tell the daughters of Sion, thy King cometh meek and lowly," Matt. xxi. 5. " Take my yoke, and learn of me, for I am meek and lowly," Matt. xi. 29. The meek Moses could not bear the provocations of the people, Numb. xi. 12, but Christ bears them all: " He carries the lambs in his arms, and gently leads those that are with young," Isa. xl. 11. He is one that can have compassion upon the ignorant, and them that are out of the way.

5. Again, sweet peace, and tranquillity of soul, is the privilege of the subjects of this kingdom: for this kingdom " consists in

peace, and joy in the Holy Ghost," Rom. xiv. 17. And till souls come under his sceptre, they shall never find peace: " Come unto me, ye that are weary, I will give you rest." Yet do not mistake; I say not, they have all actual peace, at all times; no, they often break that peace by sin; but they have the root of peace, the ground-work and cause of peace. If they have not peace, yet they have that which is convertible into peace at any time. They also are in a state of peace; " Being justified by faith, we have peace with God," Rom. v. 10. This is a feast every day, a mercy which they only can duly value, that are in the depths of trouble for sin.

6. Everlasting salvation is the privilege of all over whom Christ reigns. Prince and Saviour are joined together, Acts v. 31. He that can say, " Thou shalt guide me with thy counsel," may add what follows, " and afterwards bring me to glory," Psa. lxxiii. 24. Indeed, the kingdom of grace doth but breed up children for the kingdom of glory. It in fact is the kingdom of heaven here begun; and therefore this, as well as that, bears the name of the kingdom of heaven. The King is the same, and the subjects the same. The subjects of this are shortly to be translated to that kingdom. Thus I have named, and indeed but named, some few of those inestimable privileges of Christ's subjects. We next apply it.

Inference 1. How great is the sin and misery of those who continue in bondage to sin and Satan, and refuse the government of Christ! Satan writes his laws in the blood of his subjects, grinds them with cruel oppression, wears them out with bondage to divers lusts, and rewards their service with everlasting misery. And yet how few are weary of it, and willing to come over to Christ! " Behold, (saith one of Christ's heralds,*) Christ is in the field, sent of God to recover his right and your liberty. His royal standard is pitched in the gospel, and proclamation made, that if any poor sinners, weary of the devil's government, and laden with the miserable chains of his spiritual bondage, shall thus come and repair to Christ, he shall have protection from God's justice, the devil's wrath, and sin's dominion; in a word, he shall have rest, and that glorious," Isa. xi. 10.

And yet how few stir a foot towards Christ, but are willing to have their ears bored, and be perpetual slaves to that cruel tyrant! Oh when will sinners be weary of their bondage, and sigh after deliverance! If any such poor soul shall read these lines, let him know, and I do proclaim it in the name of my royal Master, and give him the word of a King for it, he shall

* Gurnal's Christian Armour, p. 218.

not be rejected by Christ, John vi. 37. Come, poor sinners, come, the Lord Jesus is a merciful King, and never did, nor will hand up that poor penitent, that puts the rope about his own neck, and submits to mercy.

2. How much doth it concern us to inquire and know whose government we are under, and who is king over our souls; whether Christ or Satan be in the throne, and sways the sceptre over our souls! Reader, the work I would now engage thy soul in, is the same that Jesus Christ will thoroughly and effectually do in the great day. Then will he gather out of his kingdom every thing that offends, separate the tares and the wheat, divide the whole world into two ranks or grand divisions, how many divisions and subdivisions soever there be in it now. It nearly concerns thee therefore to know who is Lord and King in thy soul. To help thee in this great work, make use of the following hints; for I cannot fully prosecute these things as I would.

(1.) To whom do you yield your obedience? " His subjects and servants ye are to whom ye obey," Rom. vi. 16. It is but a mockery to give Christ the empty titles of Lord and King, whilst ye give your real service to sin and Satan. What is this but like the jews, to bow the knee to him, and say, Hail, Master, and crucify him? " Then are ye his disciples, if ye do whatsoever he commands you," John xv. 14. Christ doth not deceive you; his pardons, promises, and salvation are real; oh let your obedience be so too! Let it be sincere and universal obedience; this will evidence your unfeigned subjection to Christ. Do not dare to enterprize any thing, till you know Christ's pleasure and will, Rom. xii. 2. Inquire of Christ as David did of the Lord, 1 Sam. xxiii. 9—11. Lord, may I do this or that? or shall I forbear? I beseech thee, tell thy servant.

(2.) Have you the power of godliness, or a form of it only? There be many that do but trifle in religion, and play about the skirts and borders of it; spending their time about jejune and barren controversies: but as to the power of religion, and the life of godliness, which consist in communion with God, and as to duties and ordinances, which promote holiness, and mortify their lusts, they concern not themselves about these things. But surely " the kingdom of God is not in word, but in power," 1 Cor. iv. 20. It is not meat and drink, (that is, dry disputes about meats and drinks,) " but righteousness, and peace, and joy in the Holy Ghost; for he that in these things serveth Christ, is acceptable to God, and approved of men," Rom. xiv. 17, 18. Oh I am afraid when the great host of professors shall be tried by these rules, they will shrink up into a little handful, as Gideon's host did.

(3.) Have you the special saving knowledge of Christ? All his subjects are translated out of the kingdom of darkness, Col. i. 13. The devil is called the ruler of the darkness of this world; his subjects are all blind, else he could never rule them. As soon as their eyes be opened, they run out of his kingdom, and there is no retaining them in subjection to him any longer. Oh inquire then whether you are brought out of darkness into this marvellous light! Do you see your condition, how sad, miserable, wretched it is by nature? do you see your remedy, as it lies only in Christ, and his precious blood? Do you see the true way of obtaining an interest in that blood by faith? does this knowledge run into practice, and put you upon lamenting heartily your misery by sin, thirsting vehemently after Christ and his righteousness, striving continually after a stronger faith and a more intimate union with Christ? This will evidence you indeed to be translated out of the kingdom of darkness into the kingdom of Christ.

(4.) With whom do you delightfully associate yourselves? Who are your chosen companions? You may see to whom you belong by the company you join yourselves to. What have the subjects of Christ to do among the slaves of Satan? If the subjects of one kingdom be in another king's dominion, they love to be together with their own countrymen, rather than the natives of the place; so do the servants of Christ. They are a company of themselves, as it is said, " They went to their own company," Acts iv. 23. I know the subjects of both kingdoms are here mingled, and we cannot avoid the company of sinners except we go out of the world, 1 Cor. v. 10; but yet all your delights should be in the saints and in the excellent of the earth, Psa. xvi. 3.

(5.) Do you live holy and righteous lives? If not, you may claim interest in Christ as your King, but he will never allow your claim. " The sceptre of his kingdom is a sceptre of righteousness," Psa. xlv. 6. If ye oppress, go beyond, and cheat your brethren, and yet call yourselves Christ's subjects! what greater reproach can ye study to cast upon him? What, is Christ the King of cheats? Doth he patronize such things as these? No, no, pull off your vizards, and fall into your own places; you belong to another prince, and not to Christ.

3. Doth Christ exercise such a kingly power over the souls of all them that are subdued by the gospel to him? Oh then let all that are under Christ's government walk as the sub-

jects of such a King. Imitate your King ; the examples of kings are very influential upon their subjects.   Your King hath commanded you not only to take his yoke upon you, but also to learn of him, Matt. xi. 29.   Yea, and "if any man say that he is Christ's, let him walk even as Christ walked," 1 John ii. 6. Your King is meek and patient, Isa. liii. 7 ; as a lamb for meekness : shall his subjects be lions for fierceness ?   Your King was humble and lowly ; " Behold, thy King cometh meek and lowly," Matt. xxi. 5. Will you be proud and lofty ? Doth this become the kingdom of Christ ? Your King was a self-denying King ; he could deny his comforts, ease, honour, life, to serve his Father's design, and accomplish your salvation, 2 Cor. viii. 9 ; Phil. ii. 1—8.   Shall his servants be selfish, and self-seeking persons, that will expose his honour, and hazard their own souls for the trifles of time?   God forbid.   Your King was laborious, and diligent in fulfilling his work, John ix. 4.   Let not his servants be lazy and slothful.   Oh imitate your King, follow his pattern : this will give you comfort now, and boldness in the day of judgment, if as he was, so ye are in this world, 1 John iv. 17.

SERMON XVII.

**OF THE KINGLY OFFICE OF CHRIST, AS IT IS PROVIDENTIALLY
EXECUTED IN THE WORLD, FOR THE REDEEMED.**

EPH. I. 22.

AND HATH PUT ALL THINGS UNDER HIS FEET, AND GAVE HIM TO BE THE
HEAD OVER ALL THINGS TO THE CHURCH.

THE foregoing verses are spent in a thankful and humble adoration of the grace of God, in bringing the ephesians to believe in Christ. This effect of that power that raised their hearts to believe in Christ, is here compared with that other glorious effect of it, even the raising of Christ himself from the dead; both these owe themselves to the same efficient cause. It raised Christ from a low estate, even from the dead, to a high, a very high and glorious state; to be the head both of the world, and of the church; the head of the world by way of dominion, the head of the church by way of union, and special influence, ruling the world for the good of his people in it. " He gave him to be the head over all things to the church."

In this scripture let these four things be seriously regarded.

1. The dignity and authority committed to Christ; " He hath put all things under his feet ;" which implies, full, ample, and absolute dominion in him, and subjection in them over whom he reigns. This power is delegated to him by the Father: for besides the essential, native power and dominion over all, which he hath as God, Psa. xxii. 28, there is a mediatory dispensed authority, which is proper to him as Mediator, which he receives as the reward or fruit of his suffering, Phil. ii. 8.

2. The recipient of this authority is Christ, and Christ primarily, and only: he is the first receptacle of all authority and power. Whatever authority any creature is clothed with, is but ministerial and derivative. Christ is the only Lord, Jude 4, the fountain of all power.

3. The object of this authority is the whole creation; all things are put under his feet: he rules from sea to sea, even to the utmost bounds of God's creation. " Thou hast given him power over all flesh," John xvii. 2 ; all creatures, rational and

irrational, animate and inanimate, angels, devils, men, winds, seas, all obey him.

4. And especially, take notice of the end for which he governs and rules the universal empire; it is for the church, that is, for the advantage, comfort, and salvation of that chosen number he died for. He purchased the church; and that he might have the highest security that his blood should not be lost, God the Father hath put all things into his hand, to order and dispose all as he pleaseth. Hence we deduce this doctrine,

THAT ALL THE AFFAIRS OF THE KINGDOM OF PROVIDENCE ARE ORDERED AND DETERMINED BY JESUS CHRIST, FOR THE SPECIAL ADVANTAGE, AND EVERLASTING GOOD OF HIS REDEEMED PEOPLE.

" As thou hast given him power over all flesh, that he should give eternal life to as many as thou hast given him," John xvii. 2. Hence it comes to pass, that " all things work together for good to them that love God, to them that are called according to his purpose," Rom. viii. 28.

That Jesus Christ hath a providential influence upon all the affairs of this world, is evident, both from scripture assertions, and rational observations, made upon the actings of things here below.

The first chapter of Ezekiel contains an admirable scheme or draught of providence. There you see how all the wheels, that is, the motions and revolutions here on earth, are guided by the spirit that is in them. And, ver. 26, it is all run up into the supreme cause; there you find one like the Son of man, which is Jesus Christ, sitting upon the throne, and giving forth orders from thence for the government of all: and if it were not so, how is it that there are such strong combinations, and predispositions of persons and things to such ends and issues, without any communications of councils, or holding of intelligence with one another? As in Israel's deliverance out of Egypt; and innumerable more instances has appeared. Certainly, if ten men, from several places, should all meet at one place, and about one business, without any fore-appointment among themselves, it would argue their motions were secretly overruled by some invisible agent. How is it that such marvellous effects are produced in the world by causes that carry no proportion to them? Amos v. 9, and 1 Cor. i. 27; and, as often, the most apt and likely means are rendered wholly ineffectual? Psa. xxxiii. 16. In a word, if Christ hath no such providential influence, how are his people in all ages preserved in the midst of so many millions of potent and malicious enemies, amongst whom they live as sheep in the midst of wolves? Luke x. 3. How is it that the bush burns, and yet is not consumed? Exod. iii. 2.

But my business, in this discourse, is not to prove that there is a Providence, which none but atheists deny. I shall rather show by what acts Jesus Christ administers this kingdom, and in what manner; and what use may be made of this subject.

I. He rules and orders the kingdom of Providence, by supporting, permitting, restraining, limiting, protecting, punishing, and rewarding those over whom he reigns providentially.

1. He supports the world, and all creatures in it, by his power. "My Father works hitherto, and I work," John v. 17. "And by him (that is, by Christ) all things consist," Col. i. 17. It is a considerable part of Christ's glory to have a whole world of creatures owing their being and hourly preservation to him. He is "given for a covenant to the people, to establish the earth," Isa. xlix. 8.

2. He permits and suffers the worst of creatures in his dominion, to be and act as they do. Even those that fight against Christ and his people, receive both power and permission from him. Say not, that it is unbecoming the Most Holy to permit such evils, which he could prevent if he pleased. For as he permits no more than he will overrule to his praise, so that very permission of his is holy and just. Christ's working is not confounded with the creature's. Pure sun-beams are not tainted by the noisome vapours of the dunghill on which they shine. His holiness hath no fellowship with their iniquities; nor are their transgressions at all excused by his permissions of them. "He is a rock, his work is perfect, but they have corrupted themselves," Deut. xxxii. 4, 5. And yet should he permit sinful creatures to act out all the wickedness that is in their hearts, there would neither remain peace nor order in the world. And therefore,

3. He powerfully restrains creatures by the bridle of providence, from the commission of those things, to which their hearts are propense enough: "The remainder of wrath thou wilt restrain," Psa. lxxvi. 10; letting forth just so much as shall serve his holy ends, and no more. And truly this is one of the glorious mysteries of Providence, which amazes the serious and considerate soul; to see the spirit of a creature fully set to do mischief; power enough, as one would think, in his hand to do it, and a door of opportunity standing open for it; and yet the effect wonderfully hindered. The strong propensions of the will are inwardly checked, as in the case of Laban, Gen. xxxi. 24; or a diversion and rub is strangely cast in their way, as in the

case of Sennacherib, 2 Kings xix. 7, 8, so that their hands cannot perform their enterprises.   Julian had two great designs before him ; one was to conquer the persians, the other to root out the galileans, as he, by way of contempt, called the christians ; but he would begin with the persians first ; and then make a sacrifice of all the christians to his idols.   He did so, and perished in the first attempt.   Oh the wisdom of Divine Providence!

4. Jesus Christ limits the creatures in their acting, assigning them their boundaries and lines of liberty ; to which they may, but beyond it cannot, go. " Fear none of these things that ye shall suffer ; behold, the devil shall cast some of you into prison, and ye shall have tribulation ten days," Rev. ii. 10.   They would have cast them into their graves, but it shall only be into prisons : they would have stretched out their hands upon them all ; no, but only some of them shall be exposed : they would have kept them there perpetually; no, it must be but for ten days. Four hundred and thirty years were determined upon the people of God in Egypt; and then, even in that very night, God brought them forth ; for then " the time of the promise was come," Acts vii. 17.

5. The Lord Jesus providentially protects his people amidst a world of enemies and dangers.   It was Christ that appeared unto Moses in the flaming bush, and preserved it from being consumed.   The bush signified the people of God in Egypt ; the fire flaming on it, the exquisite sufferings they there endured ; the safety of the bush amidst the flames, the Lord's admirable care and protection of his poor suffering ones.   None so tenderly careful as Christ. " As birds flying, so he defends Jerusalem," Isa. xxxi. 5, that is, as they fly swiftly towards their nests, crying when their young are in danger, so will the Lord preserve his.   They are " preserved in Christ Jesus," Jude 1, as Noah and his family were in the ark.   Hear how a worthy of our own expresses himself on this point.*

" That we are at peace in our houses, at rest in our beds, that we have any quiet in our enjoyments, is from hence alone. Whose person would not be defiled, or destroyed ; whose habitation would not be ruined ; whose blood almost would not be shed, if wicked men had power to perpetrate all their conceived sin ? It may be, the ruin of some of us hath been conceived a thousand times.   We are beholden to this Providence, of obstructing sin, for our lives, our families, our estates, our liberties, and whatsoever is or may be dear to us.   For may we not say sometimes with the psalmist, ' My soul is among lions, and I lie

* Dr. Owen on Indwelling Sin.

even among them that are set on fire, even the sons of men, whose teeth are spears, and their tongue a sharp sword?' Psa. lvii. 4. And how is the deliverance of men contrived from such persons? God breaks their teeth in their mouths, even the great teeth of the young lions, Psa. lviii. 6. He keeps this fire from burning,—some he cuts off and destroys: some he cuts short in their power: some he deprives of the instruments whereby alone they can work: some he prevents in their desired opportunities, or diverts by other objects for their lust; and oftentimes causeth them to spend them among themselves, one upon another. We may say, therefore, with the psalmist, ' O Lord, how manifold are thy works! in wisdom hast thou made them all; the earth is full of thy riches.' Psa. civ. 24."

6. He punishes the evil doers, and repays, by providence, into their own lap, the mischiefs they do, or intend to do, to them that fear him. Pharaoh, Sennacherib, both the Julians, and innumerable more, are the lasting monuments of his righteous retribution. It is true, a sinner may do evil a hundred times, and his days be prolonged; but oft times God hangs up some eminent sinners in chains, as spectacles and warnings to others. Many a heavy blow hath Providence given to the enemies of God, which they were never able to recover. Christ rules, and that with a rod of iron, in the midst of his enemies, Psa. cx. 2.

7. And lastly, He rewards by providence the services done to him and his people. Out of this treasure of providence God repays oftentimes those that serve him, and that with a hundredfold reward now in this life, Matt. xix. 29. This active, vigilant Providence hath its eye upon all the wants, straits, and troubles of the creatures; but especially upon such as religion brings us unto. What huge volumes of experiences might the people of God write upon this subject! and what a pleasant history would it be, to read the strange, constant, wonderful, and unexpected actings of Providence, for them that have left themselves to its care!

II. We shall next inquire how Jesus Christ administers this providential kingdom. And here I must take notice of the means by which, and the manner in which he doth it.

The means, or instruments, he uses in the governing the providential kingdom, (for he is not personally present with us himself,) are either angels or men. " The angels are ministering creatures, sent forth by him for the good of them that shall be heirs of salvation," Heb. i. 14. Luther tells us, they have two offices, "to sing above, and watch beneath." These do us many invisible offices of love. They have dear and tender regards and

love for the saints.   To them, God, as it were, puts forth his
children to nurse, and they are tenderly careful of them whilst
they live, and bring them home in their arms to their Father
when they die.   And as angels, so men are the servants of Providence; yea, bad men as well as good.   Cyrus, on that account,
is called God's servant.   They fulfil his will, whilst they are prose-
cuting their own lusts.   " The earth shall help the woman,"
Rev. xii. 16.   But good men delight to serve Providence; they
and the angels are fellow-servants in one house, and to one
Master, Rev. xix. 10.   Yea, there is not a creature in heaven,
earth, or hell, but Jesus Christ can providentially use it to serve
his ends, and promote his designs.   But whatever the instrument be which Christ uses, of this we may be certain, that his
providential working is holy, judicious, sovereign, profound, irresistible, harmonious, and for the peculiar good of the saints.

1. It is holy.   Though he permits, limits, orders, and overrules many unholy persons and actions, yet he still works like
himself, most holily and purely throughout.   " The Lord is
righteous in all his ways, and holy in all his works," Psa. cxlv.
17.   It is easier to separate light from a sun-beam, than holiness
from the works of God.   The best of men cannot escape sin in
their most holy actions; they cannot touch, but are defiled.
But no sin cleaves to God, whatever he hath to do about it.

2. Christ's providential working is also most wise and judicious.   " The wheels are full of eyes," Ezek. i. 18.   They are
not moved by a blind impetus, but in deep counsel and wisdom.
And, indeed, the wisdom of Providence manifests itself principally in the choice of such states for the people of God, as shall
most effectually promote their eternal happiness.   And herein it
goes quite beyond our understanding and comprehension.   It
makes that medicinal and salutary, which we judge destructive
to our comfort and good, as poison.   I remember, it is a note of
Suarez, speaking of the felicity of the other world: " Then
(saith he) the blessed shall see in God all things and circumstances pertaining to them, excellently accommodated and attem-
pered;" then shall they see that the crossing of their desires
was the saving of their souls; and that otherwise they had
perished.   The most wise Providence looks beyond us.   It eyes
the end, and suits all things thereto, and not to our fond desires.

3. The providence of Christ is most supreme and sovereign.
" Whatsoever he pleaseth, that he doth in heaven and in earth,
and in all places," Psa. cxxxv. 6.   " He is Lord of lords, and
King of kings," Rev. xix. 16.   The greatest monarchs on earth
are but as little bits of clay, as the worms of the earth to him:

they all depend on him, " By me kings reign, and princes decree justice ; by me princes rule, nobles, even all the judges of the earth," Prov. viii. 15, 16.

4. Divine Providence is profound and inscrutable. The judgments of Christ are " a great deep, and his footsteps are not known," Psa. xxxvi. 6. There are hard texts in the works as well as in the words of Christ. The wisest heads have been at a loss in interpreting some events, Jer. xii. 1, 2 ; Job xxi. 7. The angels had the hands of a man under their wings, Ezek. i. 8, that is, they wrought secretly and mysteriously.

5. Divine Providence is irresistible in its designs and motions ; for all providences are but fulfillings and accomplishments of God's immutable decrees. " He works all things according to the counsel of his own will," Eph. i. 11. Hence the instruments by which God executed his wrath, are called " chariots coming from between two mountains of brass," Zech. vi. 1, that is, " the firm and immutable decrees of God." When the jews put Christ to death, they did only what " the hand and counsel of God had before determined to be done," Acts iv. 28. None can oppose or resist Providence. " I will work, and who shall let it ? " Isa. xliii. 13.

6. The providences of Christ are harmonious. There are secret chains and invisible connexions between the works of Christ. We know not how to reconcile promises and providences together, nor yet providences one with another ; but certainly they all work together, Rom. viii. 28, by the influence of the first cause. He doth not do, and undo ; destroy by one providence, what he built by another. But, just as all seasons of the year, the nipping frosts, as well as the halcyon days of summer, conspire and conduce to the harvest ; so it is in providence.

7. The providences of Christ work in a special and peculiar way for the good of the saints. His providential is subordinated to his spiritual kingdom. " He is the Saviour of all men, especially of them that believe," 1 Tim. iv. 10. Things are so laid and ordered, as that their eternal good shall be promoted and secured by all that Christ doth.

Inf. 1. If so, see then, in the first place, to whom you are indebted for your lives, liberties, comforts, and all that you enjoy in this world. Is it not Christ that orders all for you? He is, indeed, in heaven, out of your sight ; but though you see him not, he sees you, and takes care of all your concerns. When one told Silentiarius of a plot laid to take away his life, he answered, " If God take no care of me, how do I live ? " how have I escaped hitherto ? " In all thy ways acknowledge him,"

Prov. iii. 6. It is he that hath appointed that state thou art in, as most proper for thee. It is Christ that doth all for you that is done. He looks down from heaven upon all that fear him; he sees when you are in danger by temptation, and interposes something, you know not how, to hinder it. He sees when you are sad, and orders reviving providences, to refresh you. He sees when corruptions prevail, and orders humbling events to purge them. Whatever mercies you have received, all along the way you have gone hitherto, are the orderings of Christ for you. And you should carefully observe how the promises and providences have kept equal pace with one another, and both gone by step with you until now.

2. Hath God left the government of the whole world in the hands of Christ, and trusted him over all? Then do you also leave all your particular concerns in the hands of Christ too, and know that the infinite wisdom and love, which rule the world, manage every thing that relates to you. It is in a good hand, and infinitely better than if it were in your own. I remember when Melancthon was under some despondencies of spirit about the situation of God's people in Germany, Luther chides him thus for it, " Let Philip cease to rule the world." It is none of our work to steer the course of providence, or direct its motions, but to submit quietly to Him that doth. Yet how apt are we to regret at providences, as if they had no conducency at all to the glory of God, or to our good, Exod. v. 22; yea, to limit the Almighty to our way and time! Thus, the israelites " tempted God, and limited the holy One," Psa. lxxviii. 18. 41. How often also do we, unbelievingly, distrust God, as though he could never accomplish what we profess to expect and believe! " Our bones are dry, our hope is lost; we are cut off for our part," Ezek. xxxvii. 11. So Gen. xviii. 13, 14; Isa. xl. 17. There are but few Abrahams among believers, who "against hope believed in hope, giving glory to God," Rom. iv. 20. And it is but too common for good men to repine and fret at providences, when their wills, lusts, or humours are crossed by it: this was the great sin of Jonah. Brethren, these things ought not to be so : did you but seriously consider, either the design of these providential dealings, which is to bring about the gracious purposes of God upon you, which were laid before this world was, Eph. i. 4; or that it is a lifting up of thy wisdom against his, as if thou couldst better order thine affairs, if thou hadst but the conduct and management of them; or that you have to do herein with a great and dreadful God, in whose hands you are as the clay in the potter's hands, that he may do what he will with you,

and all that is yours, without giving you an account of any of his matters, Job xxxiii. 13 ; I say, if such considerations as these could but have place with you in your troubles and temptations, they would quickly mould your hearts into a better and more quiet frame.

Oh that I could but persuade you to resign all to Christ. He is a skilful workman, Prov. viii. 25—30, and can effect what he pleaseth. It is a good rule, De operibus Dei non est judicandum, ante quintum actum. "Let God work out all that he intends, but have patience till he hath put the last hand to his work, and then find fault with it, if you can." "You have heard of the patience of Job, and have seen the end of the Lord," James v. 11.

3. If Christ be Lord and King over the providential kingdom, and that for the good of his people, let none that are Christ's henceforth stand in a slavish fear of creatures. It is a good note that Grotius hath upon my text ; "It is a great consolation (saith he) that Christ hath so great an empire, and that he governs it for the good of his people, as a head consulting the good of the body." Our Head and Husband, is Lord of all the hosts of heaven and earth ; no creature can move hand or tongue without his leave or order : the power they have is given them from above, John xix. 11, 12. The serious consideration of this truth will make the feeblest spirit cease trembling, and set it a singing ; "The Lord is King of all the earth, sing ye praises with understanding," Psa. xlvii. 7. Hath he not given you abundant security in many express promises, that all shall issue well for you that fear him ? "All things shall work together for good to them that love God," Rom. viii. 28. And verily "it shall be well with them that fear God," even with them that fear before him, Eccl. viii. 12. And suppose he had not, yet the very understanding of our relation to such a King, should, in itself, be sufficient security : for, he is the universal, supreme, absolute, meek, merciful, victorious, and immortal King. He sits in glory, at the Father's right hand ; and his enemies are a footstool for him.* His love to his people is unspeakably tender and fervent, he that touches them, " touches the apple of his eye," Zech. ii. 8. Till this be forgotten, the wrath of man is not feared ; He that fears a man that shall die, forgets the Lord his Maker, Isa. li. 12, 13.

4. If the government of the world be in the hands of Christ, then to acknowledge Christ and engage his blessing in all our affairs and business, is the true and ready way to their success

* See my Saint Indeed.

and prosperity. If all depend upon his pleasure, then sure it is your wisdom to take him along with you to every action and business; it is no lost time that is spent in prayer, wherein we ask his direction, and beg his presence with us : and, take it for a clear truth, that which is not prefaced with prayer, will be followed with trouble. How easily can Jesus Christ dash all your designs, when they are at the very birth and article of execution, and break off, in a moment, all the purposes of your hearts ! It is a proverb among the papists, that mass and meat hinder no man. The turks will pray five times a day, how urgent soever their business be. Blush, you that enterprize your affairs without God.

5. Lastly, Eye Christ in all the events of providence ; see his hand in all that befalls you, whether it be evil or good. " The works of the Lord are great, sought out of all them that have pleasure therein," Psa. cxi. 2. How much good might we get, by observation of the good or evil that befalls us throughout our course !

(1.) In all the *troubles and afflictions* that befall you, eye Jesus Christ : and set your hearts to the study of these four things in affliction.

Study his sovereignty and dominion ; for he creates and forms them : they rise not out of the dust, nor do they befall you casually ; but he raises them up, and gives them their commission ; " Behold, I create evil, and devise a device against you," Jer. xviii. 11. He selects the instrument of your trouble ; he makes the rod as afflictive as he pleaseth ; he orders the continuance and end of your troubles ; and they will not cease to be afflictive to you, till Christ say, Leave off, it is enough. The centurion wisely considered this, when he told him, " I have soldiers under me, and I say to one, Go, and he goeth ; to another, Come, and he cometh," Luke vii. 8 : meaning, that as his soldiers were at his beck and command, so diseases were at Christ's beck, to come and go as he ordered them.

Study the wisdom of Christ in the contrivance of your troubles. His wisdom shines out many ways in them. It is evident in choosing such kinds of trouble for you as are best adapted to work upon, and purge out the corruption that most predominates in you : in the degress of your troubles, suffering them to work to such a height as to reach their end ; but no higher, lest they overwhelm you.

Study the tenderness and compassions of Christ over his afflicted people. Oh think if the devil had but the mixing of my cup, how much more bitter would he make it ! There would not be one drop of mercy in it: but here is much mercy mixed with my troubles. There is mercy in this, that it is no worse. Am I afflicted? "It is of the Lord's mercy I am not consumed," Lam. iii. 22; it might have been hell as well as this. There is mercy in his supports under it; I might have been left, as others have been, to sink and perish under my burdens. Mercy, in deliverance out of it; this might have been everlasting darkness, that should never have had a morning. Oh the tenderness of Christ over his afflicted!

Study the love of Christ to thy soul, in affliction. "Whom I love, I rebuke and chasten," Rev. iii. 19. This is the device of love, to recover thee to thy God, and prevent thy ruin. Oh what an advantage would it be thus to study Christ, in all your evils that befall you!

(2.) Eye and study Christ in all the *good* you receive from the hand of providence. Turn both sides of your mercies, and view them in all their lovely circumstances.

Eye them in their *suitableness:* how conveniently providence hath ordered all things for thee. Thou hast a narrow heart, and a small estate suitable to it: hadst thou more of the world, it would be like a large sail to a little boat, which would quickly pull thee under water: thou hast that which is most suitable to thee of all conditions. Eye the *seasonableness* of thy mercies, how they are timed to an hour. Providence brings forth all its fruits in due season. Eye the *peculiar nature* of thy mercies. Others have common, thou special ones; others have but a single, thou a double sweetness in thy enjoyments, one natural from the matter of it, another spiritual from the way in which, and end for which it comes. Observe the *order* in which Providence sends your mercies. See how one is linked strangely to another, and is a door to let in many. Sometimes one mercy is introductive to a thousand. And lastly, observe the *constancy* of them, "they are new every morning," Lam. iii. 23. How assiduously doth God visit thy soul and body! Think with thyself, if there were but a suspension of the care of Christ for one hour, that hour would be thy ruin.

Could we thus study the providence of Christ in all the good and evil that befalls us in the world, then in every state we should be content, Phil. iv. 11. Then we should never be stopped, but furthered in our way by all that falls out; then would our experience swell to great volumes, which we might carry to heaven with us; and then should we answer all Christ's ends in every state he brings us into. Do this, and say, Thanks be to God for Jesus Christ.

SERMON XVIII.

OF THE NECESSITY OF CHRIST'S HUMILIATION, IN ORDER TO THE
EXECUTION OF ALL THESE HIS BLESSED OFFICES FOR US; AND
PARTICULARLY OF HIS HUMILIATION BY INCARNATION.

PHIL. II. 8.

AND BEING FOUND IN FASHION AS A MAN, HE HUMBLED HIMSELF, AND BE-
CAME OBEDIENT TO DEATH, EVEN THE DEATH OF THE CROSS.

You have heard how Christ was invested with the offices of
Prophet, Priest, and King, for the carrying on the blessed design
of our redemption; the execution of these offices necessarily
required that he should be both deeply abased, and highly
exalted. He cannot, as our Priest, offer up himself a sacrifice
to God for us, except he be humbled, and humbled to death.
He cannot, as a King, powerfully apply the virtue of that his
sacrifice, except he be exalted, yea, highly exalted. Had he
not stooped to the low estate of a man, he had not, as a Priest,
had a sacrifice of his own to offer; he had not been fit, as' a
Prophet, to teach us the will of God, so as that we should be
able to bear it; he had not been, as a King, a suitable head to
the church: and, had he not been highly exalted, that sacrifice
had not been carried within the vail before the Lord. Those
discoveries of God could not have been universal, effectual, and
abiding. The government of Christ could not have secured,
protected, and defended the subjects of his kingdom.

The infinite wisdom foreseeing all this, ordered that Christ
should first be deeply humbled, then highly exalted: both which
states of Christ are presented to us by the apostle in this context.

He that intends to build high, lays the foundation deep and
low. Christ must have a glory in heaven, infinitely transcending
that of angels and men. And, as he must be exalted infinitely
above them, so he must first, in order thereunto, be humbled
and abased as much below them: "His form was marred
more than any man's; and his visage more than the sons of
men." The ground colours are a deep sable, which afterwards
are laid on with all the splendour and glory of heaven.

Method requires that we first speak of his state of humiliation.

And, to that purpose, I have read this scripture to you, which presents you the sun under a total eclipse. He that was beautiful and glorious, Isa. iv. 2, yea, glorious as the only begotten of the Father, John i. 14, yea, the glory, James ii. 1, yea, the splendour and "brightness of the Father's glory," Heb. i. 3, was so vailed, clouded, and debased, that he looked not like himself; a God, no, nor scarce as a man; for, with reference to this humbled state, it is said, "I am a worm, and no man," Psa. xxii. 6; I am become an abject among men, as that word, Isa. liii. 3, signifies. This humiliation of Christ we have here expressed in the nature, degrees, and duration of it.

1. The nature of it, "he humbled himself." The word imports both a real and voluntary abasement. It is not said, he was humbled, but, he humbled himself; he was willing to stoop to this low and abject state for us. And, indeed, the voluntariness of his humiliation made it most acceptable to God, and singularly commends the love of Christ to us that he would choose to stoop to all this ignominy, suffering, and abasement for us.

2. The degrees of his humiliation: it was not only so low as to become a man, a man under law ; but he humbled himself to become "obedient to death, even the death of the cross." Here you see the depth of Christ's humiliation, it was unto death, and aggravated, even the death of the cross, the death of a malefactor.

3. The duration, or continuance of this his humiliation: it continued from the first moment of his incarnation, to the moment of his resurrection from the grave ; so long his humiliation lasted. Hence we derive this proposition ;

THAT THE STATE OF CHRIST, FROM HIS CONCEPTION TO HIS RESURRECTION, WAS A STATE OF DEEP ABASEMENT AND HUMILIATION.

We are now entering upon Christ's humbled state, which I shall describe under three general heads, namely, his humiliation in his incarnation, in his life, and in his death. My present work is to open Christ's humiliation in his incarnation, imported in these words, He was found in fashion as a man. By which you are not to conceive that he only assumed a body, as an assisting form, to appear transiently to us in it, and so lay it down again; but his true and real assumption of our nature, which was a special part of his humiliation ; as will appear by the following particulars.

1. The incarnation of Christ was a most wonderful humilia-

tion of him, inasmuch as thereby he is brought into the rank and order of creatures, who is over all, " God blessed for ever," Rom. ix. 5.   This is the astonishing mystery, that God should be manifest in the flesh, 1 Tim. iii. 16, that the eternal God should truly and properly be called the MAN Christ Jesus, 1 Tim. ii. 5.   It was a wonder to Solomon, that God would dwell in that stately and magnificent temple at Jerusalem: " But will God in very deed dwell with men on earth?   Behold, the heaven, and heaven of heavens cannot contain thee ; how much less this house which I have built !" 2 Chron. vi. 18.   But it is a far greater wonder that God should dwell in a body of flesh, and pitch his tabernacle with us, John i. 14.

The heathen chaldeans told the king of Babel, that the " dwelling of the gods is not with flesh," Dan. ii. 11.   But now God not only dwells with flesh, but dwells in flesh ; yea, was made flesh, and dwelt among us.

For the sun to fall from its sphere, and be degraded into a wandering atom ; for an angel to be turned out of heaven, and be converted into a fly or a worm, had been no such great abasement ; for they were but creatures before, and so they would abide still, though in an inferior order or species of creatures. The distance between the highest and lowest species of creatures, is but a finite distance.   The angel and the worm dwell not so far asunder.   But for the infinite glorious Creator of all things to become a creature, is a mystery exceeding all human understanding.   The distance between God and the highest order of creatures, is an infinite distance.   He is said to humble himself, to behold the things that are done in heaven.   What a humiliation then is it, to behold the things in the lower world ! but to be born into it, and become a man ! Great indeed is the mystery of godliness.   " Behold, (saith the prophet, Isa. xl. 15. 17,) the nations are as the drop of a bucket, and are counted as the small dust of the balance ; he taketh up the isles as a very little thing.   All nations before him are as nothing, and they are accounted to him less than nothing, and vanity."   If, indeed, this great and incomprehensible Majesty will himself stoop to the state and condition of a creature, we may easily believe, that, being once a creature, he would expose himself to hunger, thirst, shame, spitting, death, or any thing but sin.   For that once being a man, he should endure any of these things, is not so wonderful, as that he should become a man.   This was the low step, a deep abasement indeed !

2. It was a marvellous humiliation to the Son of God, not only to become a creature, but an inferior creature, a man, and

not an angel. Had he taken the angelical nature, though it had been a wonderful abasement to him, yet he had staid (if I may so speak) nearer his own home, and been somewhat liker to a God, than now he appeared, when he dwelt with us : for angels are the highest and most excellent of all created beings. For their nature, they are pure spirits ; for their wisdom, intelligences ; for their dignity, they are called principalities and powers ; for their habitations, they are styled the heavenly host ; and for their employment, it is to behold the face of God in heaven. One description both of our holiness and happiness in the coming world, is this, we shall be " equal to the angels," Luke xx. 36. As man is nothing to God, so he is much inferior to the angels ; so much below them, that he is not able to bear the sight of an angel, though in a human shape, Judges xiii. 22. When the psalmist had contemplated the heavens, and viewed the celestial bodies, the glorious luminaries, the moon and stars which God had made, he cries out, " What is man, that thou art mindful of him, or the son of man, that thou visitest him ! thou hast made him a little lower than the angels," Psa. viii. 5, 6. Take man at his best, when he came a perfect and pure piece out of his Maker's hand, in the state of innocency ; yet he was inferior to angels. They always bare the image of God in a more eminent degree than man, as being wholly spiritual substances, and so more lively representing God, than man could do, whose noble soul is immersed in matter, and closed up in flesh and blood. Yet Christ chooseth this inferior order of creatures, and passeth by the angelical nature ; " He took not on him the nature of angels, but the seed of Abraham," Heb. ii. 16.

3. Moreover, Jesus Christ did not only assume the human nature ; but he also assumed its nature, after sin had blotted its original glory, and withered its beauty and excellency. For he came not in our nature before the fall, whilst as yet its glory was fresh in it ; but he came, as the apostle speaks, "in the likeness of *sinful* flesh," Rom. viii. 3, that is, in flesh that had the marks, and miserable effects, and consequents of sin upon it. I say not that Christ assumed sinful flesh, or flesh really defiled by sin. That which was born of the virgin was a holy thing. For by the power of the Highest, that whereof the body of Christ was to be formed, was so sanctified, that no taint or spot of original pollution remained in it. But yet, though it had not intrinsical native uncleanness in it, it had the effects of sin upon it ; yea, it was attended with the whole troop of human infirmities, that sin at first brought into our common nature, such as hun-

ger, thirst, weariness, pain, mortality, and all these natural weaknesses and evils that clog our miserable natures, and make them groan from day to day under them.

By reason whereof, though he was not a sinner, yet he looked like one; and they that saw and conversed with him, took him for a sinner, seeing all these effects of sin upon him. In these things he came as near to sin as his holiness could admit.   Oh what a stoop was this!   To be made in the likeness of flesh, though the *innocent* flesh of Adam, had been much; but to be made in the likeness of *sinful* flesh, the flesh of sinners, rebels; oh what is this! and who can declare it!   And indeed, if he will be a Mediator of reconciliation, it was necessary it should be so.   It behoved him to assume the same nature that sinned, to make satisfaction in it.   Yea, these sinless infirmities were necessary to be assumed with the nature, forasmuch as his bearing them was a part of his humiliation, and went to make up satisfaction for us.   Moreover, by them our High Priest was qualified from his own experience, and filled with tender compassion to us.   Oh the admirable condescensions of a Saviour, to take such a nature! to put on such a garment when so very mean and ragged!

4. And yet more, by this his incarnation he was greatly humbled, inasmuch as this so vailed, clouded, and disguised him, that during the time he lived here, he looked not like himself, as God.   Hereby " he made himself of no reputation," Phil. ii. 7.   By reason hereof he lost all esteem and honour from those that saw him; " Is not this the carpenter's son?" Matt. xiii. 55. To see a poor man travelling up and down the country, in hunger, thirst, weariness, attended with a company of poor men ; one of his company bearing the bag, and that which was put therein, John xiii. 29 ; who that had seen him, would ever have thought this had been the Creator of the world, the Prince of the kings of the earth?   " He was despised, and we esteemed him not."

And think with yourselves now, was not this astonishing self-denial?   It was a black cloud that for so many years darkened and shut up his manifestative glory, that it could not shine out to the world ; only some weak rays of the Godhead shone to some few eyes, through the chinks of his humanity ; as the clouded sun sometimes breaks forth a little, and casts some faint beams, and is muffled up again.   " We saw his glory," says the beloved apostle, " as of the only begotten Son," John i. 14; but the world knew him not. If a prince walk up and down in a disguise, he must expect no more honour than a mean subject. This was the case of our Lord Jesus Christ.

5. Again, Christ was greatly humbled by his incarnation, inasmuch as thereby he was put at a distance from his Father, and that ineffable joy and pleasure he eternally had with him. Think not, reader, but the Lord Jesus lived at a high and unimitable rate of communion with God while he walked here in the flesh: but yet to live by faith, as Christ here did, is one thing; and to be in the bosom of God, as he was before, is another. To cry, and God not hear, as he complains, Psa. xxxii. 3, nay, to be reduced to such distress, as to be forced to cry out so bitterly, as he did, " My God, my God, why hast thou forsaken me ?" Psa. xxii. 1 ; this was a thing Christ was utterly unacquainted with, till he was found in fashion as a man.

6. And lastly, It was a great stoop and condescension of Christ if he would become a man, to take his nature from such obscure parents, and choose such a low and contemptible state in this world as he did. He is born, not of the blood of nobles, but of a poor woman in Israel, espoused to a carpenter : yea, and that, too, under all the disadvantages imaginable ; not in his mother's house, but an inn ; yea, in the stable too. He suited all to that abased state he was designed for ; and came among us under all the humbling circumstances imaginable: " You know the grace of our Lord Jesus Christ, (saith the apostle,) how that though he was rich, yet for our sakes he became poor," 2 Cor. viii. 9. Thus I have shown you some few particulars of Christ's humiliation in his incarnation. Next we shall infer some things from it that are practical.

Inf. 1. Hence we gather the fulness and completeness of Christ's satisfaction, as the sweet first-fruits of his incarnation. Did man offend and violate the law of God? Behold, God himself is become man to repair that breach, and satisfy for the wrong done. The highest honour that ever the law of God received, was to have such a person as the man Christ Jesus is, to stand before its bar, and make reparation to it. This is more than if it had poured out all our blood, and built up its honour upon the ruins of the whole creation.

It is not so much to see all the stars in heaven overcast, as to see one sun eclipsed. The greater Christ was, the greater was his humiliation ; and the greater his humiliation was, the more full and complete was his satisfaction ; and the more completeness there is in Christ's satisfaction, the more perfect and steady is the believer's consolation. If he had not stooped so low, our joy and comfort could not be exalted so high. The depth of the foundation is the strength of the superstructure.

2. Did Christ for our sakes stoop from the majesty, glory, and dignity he was possessed of in heaven, to the mean and contemptible state of a man ?　What a pattern of self-denial is here presented to christians !　What objection against, or excuses to shift off this duty, can remain, after such an example as is here given ?　Brethren, let me tell you, the pagan world was never acquainted with such an argument as this, to press them to self-denial.　Did Christ stoop, and cannot you stoop ? did Christ stoop so much, and cannot you stoop the least ?　Was he content to become any thing, a worm, a reproach, a curse ; and cannot you digest any abasement ?　Do the least slights and neglects rankle your hearts, and poison them with discontent, malice, and revenge ? oh how unlike Christ are you !　Hear, and blush in hearing, what your Lord saith in John xiii. 14. " If I then, your Lord and Master, wash your feet ; ye ought also to wash one another's feet." " The example does not oblige us (as a learned man well observes) to the same individual act, but it obliges us to follow the reason of the example ;" that is, after Christ's example, we must be ready to perform the lowest and meanest offices of love and service to one another.　And indeed to this it obliges most forcibly ; for it is as if a master, seeing a proud, sturdy servant, that grudges at the work he is employed about, as if it were too mean and base, should come and take it out of his hand ; and when he has done it, should say, Doth your lord and master think it not beneath him to do it, and is it beneath you ?

I remember an excellent saying that Bernard hath upon the nativity of Christ : saith he, " What more detestable, what more unworthy, or what deserves severer punishment, than for a poor man to magnify himself, after he hath seen the great and high God so humbled, as to become a little child ?　It is intolerable impudence for a worm to swell with pride, after it hath seen majesty emptying itself ; to see one so infinitely above us, stoop so far beneath us."　Oh how convincing and shaming should it be ! Ah how opposite should pride and haughtiness be to the spirit of a christian ! I am sure nothing is more so to the spirit of Christ.　Your Saviour was lowly, meek, self-denying, and of a most condescending spirit ; he looked not at his own things, but yours, Phil. ii. 4.　And does it become you to be proud and selfish ?　I remember Jerom, in his epistle to Pamachius, a godly young nobleman, advised him to be eyes to the blind, feet to the lame ; yea, saith he, if need be, I would not have you refuse to cut wood and draw water for the saints : and what, saith he, is this to buffeting and spitting upon, to crowning with thorns, scourging and dying! Yet Christ underwent all this, and that for the ungodly.

3. Did Christ stoop so low as to become a man to save us? Then those that perish under the gospel, must needs perish without excuse. What would you have Christ do more to save you? Lo, he hath laid aside the robes of majesty and glory, put on your own garments of flesh, come down from his throne, and brought salvation home to your own doors. Surely, the lower Christ stooped to save us, the lower those shall sink under wrath that neglect so great salvation. The Lord Jesus is brought low, but the unbeliever will lay him yet lower, even under his feet: he will tread the Son of God under foot, Heb. x. 29. For such (as the apostle there speaks) is reserved something worse than dying without mercy. What pleas and excuses others will make at the judgment-seat, I know not; but one thing is evident; you will be speechless.

O poor sinners! Your damnation is just, if you refuse grace brought home by Jesus Christ himself to your very doors. The Lord grant this may not be thy case who readest these lines.

4. Moreover, hence it follows, that none doth, or can love like Christ: His love to man is matchless. The freeness, strength, antiquity, and immutability of it, puts a lustre on it beyond all examples. Surely it was a strong love indeed, that made him lay aside his glory, to be found in fashion as a man, for our salvation. We read of Jonathan's love to David, which passed the love of women; of Jacob's love to Rachel, who for her sake endured the heat of summer, and cold of winter; of David's love to Absalom; of the primitive christian's love to one another, who could die one for another: but neither had they that to deny which Christ had, nor had he those inducements from the object of his love that they had. His love, like himself, is wonderful.

5. Did the Lord Jesus so deeply abase himself for us? What an engagement hath he thereby put on us, to exalt and honour him, who for our sakes was so abased! It was a good saying of Bernard, " By how much the viler he was made for me, by so much the dearer he shall be to me." And oh that all, to whom Christ is dear, would study to exalt and honour him, these four ways.

(1.) By frequent and delightful speaking of him, and for him. When Paul had once mentioned his name, he knows not how to part with it, but repeats it no less than ten times in the compass of ten verses, in 1 Cor. i. 1—10. It was Lambert's motto, " None but Christ, none but Christ." It is said of Johannes

Milius, that after his conversion, he was seldom or never observed to mention the name of Jesus, but tears would drop from his eyes ; so dear was Christ to him.   Mr. Fox never denied any beggar that asked an alms in Christ's name, or for Jesus' sake. Julius Palmer, when all concluded he was dead, being turned as black as a coal, at last moved his scorched lips, and was heard to say, Sweet Jesus, and fell asleep.

Plutarch tells us, that when Titus Flaminius had freed the poor grecians from the bondage with which they had been long ground by their oppressors, and the herald was to proclaim in their audience the articles of peace he had concluded for them, they so pressed upon him, (not being half of them able to hear,) that he was in great danger to have lost his life in the press ; at last, reading them a second time, when they came to understand distinctly how their case stood, they shouted for joy, crying, Σωτηρ, Σωτηρ, " a Saviour, a Saviour," that they made the very heavens ring again with their acclamations, and the very birds fell down astonished.   And all that night the poor grecians, with instruments of music, and songs of praise, danced and sung about his tent, extolling him as a god that had delivered them. But surely you have more reason to be exalting the Author of your salvation, who, at a dearer rate, hath freed you from a more dreadful bondage.   Oh ye that have escaped the eternal wrath of God, by the humiliation of the Son of God, extol your great Redeemer, and for ever celebrate his praises !

(2.) By exercising faith in him, for whatsoever lies in the promises yet unaccomplished.   In this you see the great and most difficult promise fulfilled, " The seed of the woman shall bruise the serpent's head," Gen. iii. 15 ; which contained this mercy of Christ's incarnation for us in it : and seeing that which was most improbable and difficult is come to pass, even Christ come in the flesh, methinks our unbelief should be removed for ever, and all other promises the more easily believed.   It seemed much more improbable and impossible to reason, that God should become a man, and stoop to the condition of a creature, than being a man, to perform all that good which his incarnation and death procured.   Unbelief usually argues from one of these two grounds, Can God do this ? or, Will God do it ? It is questioning either his power or his will ; but after this, let it cease for ever to cavil against either. His power to save should never be questioned by any that know what sufferings and infinite burdens he supported in our nature ; and surely his willingness to save should never be put to a question, by any that consider how low he was content to stoop for our sakes.

(3.) By drawing nigh to God with delight, "through the veil of Christ's flesh," Heb. x. 20. God hath made this flesh of Christ a veil between the brightness of his glory and us ; it serves to rebate the unsupportable glory, and also to give admission to it, as the veil did in the temple. Through this body of flesh, which Christ assumed, are all the outlets of grace from God to us ; and through it, also, must be all our returns to God again. It is made the great medium of our communion with God.

(4.) By applying yourselves to him, under all temptations, wants, and troubles, of what kind soever, as to one that is tenderly sensible of your case, and most willing and ready to relieve you. Oh remember, this was one of the inducements that persuaded him to take your nature, that he might be furnished abundantly with tender compassion for you, from the sense he should have of your infirmities in his own body :* " Wherefore in all things it behoved him to be made like unto his brethren, that he might be a merciful and faithful High Priest, in things pertaining to God, to make reconciliation for the sins of the people," Heb. ii. 17. You know by this argument the Lord pressed the israelites to be kind to strangers; for (saith he) " you know the heart of a stranger," Exod. xxiii. 9. Christ, by being in our nature, knows experimentally what our wants, fears, temptations, and distresses are, and so is able to have compassion. Oh let your hearts work upon this admirable condescension of Christ, till they be filled with it, and your lips say, Thanks be to God for Jesus Christ.

* Haud ignara mali, miseris succurrere disco.—*Virg.*
Like you, an alien in a land unknown,
I learn to pity woes, so like mine own.—*Dryden.*

SERMON XIX.

OF CHRIST'S HUMILIATION IN HIS LIFE.

PHIL. II. 8.

AND BEING FOUND IN FASHION AS A MAN, HE HUMBLED HIMSELF, AND
BECAME OBEDIENT UNTO DEATH, EVEN THE DEATH OF THE CROSS.

THIS scripture hath been once already under consideration, and,
indeed, can never be enough considered: it holds forth the humbled state of the Lord Jesus, during the time of his abode on
earth.   How he was humbled by his incarnation, has been
opened above in the preceding sermon.   How he was humbled
in his life, is the design of this: yet expect not that I should
give you here an exact history of the life of Christ.   The
scriptures speak but little of the private part of his life, and it is
not my design to dilate upon all the memorable passages that
the evangelists (those faithful narrators of the life of Christ)
have preserved for us; but only to observe and improve those
more observable particulars in his life, wherein especially he
was humbled: and such as these that follow.

I. The Lord Jesus was humbled in his very infancy, by his
circumcision according to the law.   For being of the stock of
Israel, he was to undergo the ceremonies, and submit to the
ordinances belonging to that people, and thereby to put an end
to them; for so it became him to fulfil all righteousness.   " And
when eight days were accomplished for the circumcising of the
child, his name was called Jesus," Luke ii. 21.   Hereby the
Son of God was greatly humbled, especially in these two respects.

1. In that hereby he obliged himself to keep the whole law,
though he was the Law-maker; " For I testify again to every
man that is circumcised, that he is a debtor to do the whole
law," Gal. v. 3.   The apostle's meaning is, he is a debtor in
regard of duty, because he that thinks himself bound to keep
one part of the ceremonial law, doth thereby bind himself to keep
it all; for all the parts are inseparably united.   And he that is
a debtor in duty to keep the whole law, quickly becomes a debtor
in regard of penalty, not being able to keep any part of it.   Christ

therefore coming as our Surety, to pay both those debts, the
debt of duty, and the debt of penalty to the law; he, by his
circumcision, obliges himself to pay the whole debt of duty by
fulfilling all righteousness : and though his obedience to it was
so exact and perfect, that he contracted no debt of penalty for
any transgression of his own ; yet he obliges himself to pay the
debt of penalty which he had contracted, by suffering all the
pains due to transgressors.   This was that intolerable yoke that
none were able to bear but Christ, Acts xv. 10.   And it was
no small thing of Christ to bind himself to the law, as a subject
made under it ; for he was the Lawgiver, above all law : and
herein the sovereignty of God (one of the choice flowers in the
crown of heaven) was obscured and veiled by his subjection.

2. Hereby he was represented to the world not only as a
subject, but also as a sinner; for though he was pure and holy,
yet this ordinance passing upon him, seemed to imply as if corruption had indeed been in him, which must be cut off by mortification.   For this was the mystery principally intended by
circumcision : it served to mind and admonish Abraham, and
his seed, of the natural guiltiness, uncleanness, and corruption
of their hearts and nature. So Jer. iv. 4.   Hence the rebellious
and unmortified are called " stiff-necked and uncircumcised in
heart," as it is Acts vii. 51.   And as it served to convince of
natural uncleanness, so it signified and sealed " the putting
off the body of the sins of the flesh," as the apostle expresses
it, Col. ii. 11.   Now, this being the end of God in the institution of this ordinance for Abraham and his ordinary seed, Christ,
in his infancy, by submitting to it, did not only veil his sovereignty by subjection, but was also represented as a sinner to
the world, though most holy and pure in himself.

II. Christ was humbled by persecution, and that in the very
morning of his life; he was banished almost as soon as born.
" Flee into Egypt, (saith the angel to Joseph,) and be thou there
until I bring thee word, for Herod will seek the young child to
destroy him," Matt. ii. 13.   Ungrateful Herod ! was this entertainment for a Saviour? What ! raise a country against him,
as if a destroyer, rather than a Saviour, had landed upon the
coast?   But herein Herod fulfilled the scriptures, whilst vent-
ing his own lusts ; for so it was foretold, Jer. xxxi. 15.   And
this early persecution was not obscurely hinted in the title of
the 22d Psalm, that psalm which looks rather like a history of
the New, than a prophecy of the Old Testament.

III. Our Lord Jesus Christ was yet more humbled in his life,
by that poverty and outward meanness which all along attended

his condition: he lived poor and low, all his days; so speaks the apostle, "Though he was rich, yet for our sakes he became poor," 2 Cor. viii. 9; so poor, that he was never owner of a house to dwell in, but lived all his days in other men's houses, or lay in the open air. His outward condition was more neglected and destitute than that of the birds of the air, or beasts of the earth; so he told that scribe, who professed such readiness to follow him, "The foxes have holes, and the birds of the air have nests; but the Son of man hath not where to lay his head," Matt. viii. 20. Sometimes he feeds upon barley-bread and broiled fish; and sometimes he was hungry, and had nothing to eat, Mark xi. 12.

He came not to be ministered unto, but to minister, Matt. xx. 28; not to amass earthly treasures, but to bestow heavenly ones. His great and heavenly soul neglected and despised those things, which too many of his followers too much admire and prosecute. He spent not a careful thought about those things that eat up thousands and ten thousands of our thoughts. Indeed he came to be humbled, and to teach men by his example the vanity of this world, and pour contempt upon its insnaring glory; and therefore went before us in a chosen and voluntary poverty.

IV. Our Lord Jesus was yet further humbled in his life, by the horrid temptations wherewith Satan assaulted him, than which nothing could be more grievous to his holy heart.* The evangelist gives us an account of this in Luke iv. from the first to the thirteenth verse: in which context you find how the bold and envious spirit meets the Captain of our salvation in the field, comes up with him in the wilderness, when he was solitary, ver. 1, there he keeps him fasting forty days and forty nights, to prepare him to close with his temptation: all this while Satan was pointing and edging that temptation, with which at last he resolves to try the breast of Christ by a home-thrust, ver. 2. By this time Christ being hungry, he assaulted him in a very suitable temptation at first, and with variety of temptations, trying several weapons upon him, afterwards. But when he had made a thrust at him with that first weapon, in which he especially trusted, "Command that these stones may be made bread," ver. 3, and saw how Christ put it by, ver. 4, then he changes postures, and assaults him with temptations to blasphemy, even "to fall down and worship the devil." But when he saw he could fasten nothing on him, that he was as

* It is the fittest and most ordinary season for Satan to tempt, when he sees men hungering and thirsting after temporal things; as the fowler prepares his net especially in the winter season, when the birds have nothing to eat.—*Stapletonis Prompt.* p. 418.

pure fountain-water in a crystal phial, that how much soever agitated and shaken, no dregs, or filthy sediment would rise, but he remained pure still ; I say, seeing this, he makes a politic retreat, quits the field for a season, ver. 13, yet leaves it with a resolution to return to him again. And thus was our blessed Lord Jesus humbled by the temptations of Satan : and what can you imagine more burdensome to him that was brought up from eternity with God, delighting in the holy Father, than to be now shut into a wilderness with the devil, there to be tempted so many days, and have his ears filled, though not defiled, with horrid blasphemy ?

A man would account it no small unhappiness to be shut up five or six weeks together with the devil, though appearing in a human shape, and to hear no language but that of hell spoken all that time ; and the more holy the man is, the more would he be afflicted to hear such blasphemies malignantly uttered against the holy and reverend name of God ; much more to be solicited by the devil to join with him in it. This, I say, would be ac-counted no small misery for a man to undergo. How great a humiliation then must it be to the great God, to be humbled to this ! to see a slave of his house, setting upon himself the Lord ! His jailer coming to take him prisoner, if he can ! A base apostate spirit, daring to attempt such things as these upon him ! Surely this was a deep abasement to the Son of God.

V. Our blessed Lord Jesus was yet more humbled in his life than all this, and that by his own sympathy with others, under all the burdens that made him groan. For he, much more than Paul, could say, Who is afflicted, and I burn not ? He lived all his time as it were in an hospital among the sick and wounded. And so tender was his heart, that every groan for sin, or under the effects of sin, pierced him so, that it was truly said, " himself bare our sicknesses, and took our infirmities," Matt. viii. 16, 17. This was spoken upon the occasion of some poor creatures that were possessed by the devil, being brought to him to be dispossessed. It is said of him, " That when he saw Mary weeping, and the jews also weeping which came with her, he groaned in the Spirit, and was troubled," John xi. 33. And, "Jesus wept," ver. 35. Yea, his heart flowed with pity for them that had not one drop of pity for themselves. Witness his tears wept over Jerusalem, Luke xix. 41, 42. He foresaw the misery that was coming, though they never foresaw, nor feared it. Oh how it pierced him to think of the calamities hanging over that great city ! Yea, he mourned for them that could not mourn for their own sins. Therefore it is said, " He was grieved for the hardness of the people's hearts," Mark iii. 5. So that the commendation of a good physician, that he doth as it were die with every patient, was most applicable to our tender-hearted Physician.   This was one of those things that made him " a man of sorrows, and acquainted with grief." For the more holy any is, the more he is grieved and afflicted for the sin of others; and the more tender any man is, he is pierced with beholding the miseries that lie upon others. Certainly there was never any heart more holy, or more sensible, tender and compassionate than Christ's.

VI. That which yet helped to humble him lower, was the ungrateful, and most base and unworthy entertainment the world gave him.   He was not received or treated like a Saviour, but as the vilest of men. One would think that when he came from heaven, " to give his life a ransom for many," Matt. xx. 28; when he was " not sent to condemn the world, but that the world through him might be saved," John iii. 17; when he came " to destroy the works of the devil," 1 John iii. 8, " to . open the prison-doors, and proclaim liberty to the captives," Isa. lxi. 1 ; I say, when such a Saviour arrived, oh, with what acclamations of joy, and demonstration of thankfulness, should he have been received !   One would have thought they should even kiss the ground he trod upon : but instead of this, he was hated, John xv. 18. He was despised by them, Matt. xiii. 55. So reproached, that he became " the reproach of men," Psa. xxii. 6.   Accused of working his miracles by the power of the devil, Matt. xii. 24.   He was trod upon as a worm, Psa. xxii. 6. They buffeted him, Matt. xxvi. 67 ; smote him on the head, Matt. xxvii. 30 ; arrayed him as a fool, ver. 28, 29 ; spat in his face, ver. 30.   One of his own followers sold him, another forsware him, and all forsook him in his greatest troubles.   All this was a great abasement to the Son of God, who was not thus treated for a day, or in one place, but all his days, and in all places. " He endured the contradiction of sinners against himself." In these particulars I have pointed out to you something of the humble life Christ lived in the world ; from all which some useful inferences will be noted.

1. From the first degree of Christ's humiliation, in submitting to be circumcised, and thereby obliging himself to fulfil the whole law, it follows, that justice itself may set its hand and seal to the acquittance and discharge of believers.   Christ hereby obliged himself to be the law's pay-master, to pay its utmost demand ; to bear that yoke of obedience that never any before him could bear. And as his circumcision obliged him to keep the whole law; so he was most precise and punctual in

the observation of it: so exact that the sharp eye of Divine justice cannot espy the least flaw in it; but acknowledges full payment, and stands ready to sign the believer a full acquittance; " That God may be just, and the justifier of him that believes in Jesus," Rom. iii. 26. Had not Christ been under this obligation, we had never been discharged. Had not his obedience been an entire, complete, and perfect thing, our justification could not have been so. He that hath a precious treasure, will be loth to adventure it in a leaky vessel: woe to the holiest man on earth, if the safety of his precious soul were to be adventured on the bottom of the best duty that ever he performed. But Christ's obedience and righteousness is firm and sound; a bottom that we may safely adventure all in.

2. From the early flight of Christ into Egypt, we infer, that the greatest innocency and piety cannot exempt from persecution and injury. Who more innocent than Christ? And who more persecuted? The world is the world still. " I have given them thy word, and the world hath hated them," John xvii. 14. The world lies in wait as a thief for them that carry this treasure; they who are empty of it may sing before him, he never stops them: but persecution follows piety, as the shadow doth the body. " All that will live godly in Christ Jesus, must suffer persecution," 2 Tim. iii. 12. Whosoever resolves to live holily, must never expect to live quietly. All that will live godly, will exert holiness in their lives, which convinces and galls the consciences of the ungodly. It is this enrages, for there is an enmity and antipathy between them: and this enmity runs in the blood; and it is transmitted with it from generation to generation: " As then he that was born after the flesh persecuted him that was born after the Spirit, even so it is now," Gal. iv. 29. Mark, so it was, and so still it is. *" Cain's club is still carried up and down crimsoned with the blood of Abel," said Bucholtzer; but thus it must be, to conform us unto Christ: and oh that your spirit, as well as your condition, may better harmonize with Christ. He suffered meekly, quietly, and self-denyingly: be ye like him. Let it not be said of you, as it is of the hypocrite, whose lusts are only hid, but not mortified by his duties, that he is like a flint, which seems cold; but if you strike him, he is all fiery. To do well, and suffer ill, is Christ-like.

3. From the third particular of Christ's humiliation, I infer, that such as are full of grace and holiness, may be destitute and empty of creature comforts. What an overflowing fulness of

---

* Multi adhuc sunt, qui clavem sanguine Abelis rubentem circumferunt.—*Bucholtz.*

grace was there in Christ ! and yet to what a low ebb did his outward comforts sometimes fall ! And as it fared with him, so with many others now in glory with him, whilst they were in the way to that glory ; as the apostle says in 1 Cor. iv. 11. " Even to this present hour, we both hunger, and thirst, and are naked, and buffeted, and have no certain dwelling-place." Their souls were richly clothed with robes of righteousness, their bodies naked or meanly clad. Their souls fed on hidden manna, their bodies hungry. Let us be content (saith Luther) with our hard fare ; for do we not feast with angels upon that bread of life ? Remember, when wants pinch hard, that these fix no marks of God's hatred upon you. He hath dealt no worse with you than he did with his own Son. Nay, which of you is not better accommodated than Christ was ? If you be hungry or thirsty, you have some refreshments ; you have beds to lie on : the Son of man had not where to lay his head. And remember you are going to a plentiful country, where all your wants will be supplied ; " poor in the world, rich in faith, and heirs of the kingdom which God hath promised," James ii. 5. The meanness of your present, will add to the lustre of your future condition.

4. From the fourth particular of Christ's humiliation in his life, by Satan's temptations, we infer, that those in whom Satan hath no interest, may have most trouble from him in this world ; " The prince of this world cometh, and hath nothing in me," John xiv. 30. Where he knows he cannot be a conqueror, he will not cease to be a troubler. This bold and daring spirit ventures to assault Christ himself ; for doubtless he was filled with envy at the sight of him, and would do what he could, though to no purpose, to obstruct the blessed design in his hand. And it was the wisdom and love of Christ to admit him to come as near him as might be, and try all his darts upon him ; that by this experience he might himself be filled with pity to succour them that are tempted. And as he set on Christ, so much more will he attack us ; and but too oft comes off a conqueror. Sometimes he shoots the fiery darts of blasphemous injections. These fall as flashes of lightning on the dry thatch, which instantly sets all in a combustion. And just so it is attended with an after thunder-clap of inward horror, that shivers the very heart, and strikes all into confusion within.

Divers rules are prescribed in this case to relieve poor distressed ones. Some advise to think seriously on that which is darted suddenly, and to do with your hearts as men used to do with young horses, that are apt to start at every thing in the way ;

we bring them close to the things they fright at, make them look on them, and smell to them, that time and better acquaintance with such things, may teach them not to start. Others advise to divert the thoughts, as much as may be, to think quite another way. These rules are contrary to one another, and I think avail but little to the relief of a poor soul so distressed.

The best rule, doubtless, is that of the apostle, " Above all, taking the shield of faith, wherewith ye shall be able to quench all the fiery darts of the wicked," Eph. vi. 16. Act your faith, my friends, upon your tempted Saviour, who passed through temptations before you : and particularly exercise faith on three things in Christ's temptations.

(I.) Believingly consider, how great variety of temptations were tried upon Christ; and of what a horrid blasphemous nature that was—Fall down and worship me. (2.) Believingly consider, that Christ came off a perfect conqueror in the day of his trial, beat Satan out of the field. For he saw that what he attempted on Christ was as impossible as to batter the body of the sun with snow-balls. (3.) Lastly, believe that the benefits of those his victories and conquests are for you ; and that for your sakes he permitted the tempter to come so near him: as you find, Heb. ii. 18.

If you say, True, Christ was tempted as well as I ; but there is a vast difference between his temptations and mine ; for the prince of this world came, and found nothing in him, John xiv. 30. He was not internally defiled, though externally assaulted ; but I am defiled by them as well as troubled.

To this I answer, True, it is so, and must be so, or else it had availed nothing to your relief. For had Christ been internally defiled, he had not been a fit Mediator for you ; nor could you have had any benefit, either by his temptations, or sufferings for you. But he being tempted, and yet still escaping the defilement of sin, has not only satisfied for the sins you commit when tempted, but also got an experimental sense of the misery of your condition, which is in him (though now in glory) as a spring of pity and tender compassion to you. Remember, poor tempted christian, " the God of peace shall shortly tread Satan under thy feet," Rom. xvi. 20. Thou shalt set thy foot on the neck of that enemy. Meanwhile, till thou be out of his reach, let me advise thee to go to Jesus Christ, and open the matter to him ; tell him how that base spirit falls upon thee, yea, sets upon thee, even in his presence : entreat him to rebuke and command him off: beg him to consider thy case, and say, Lord, dost thou remember how thy own heart was once grieved, though not defiled, by his assaults? I have grief and guilt together upon me. Ah Lord, I expect pity and help from thee; thou knowest the heart of a stranger, the heart of a poor and tempted one. This will give wonderful relief in this case. O try it!

5. Was Christ yet more humbled, by his own sympathy with others in their distresses? Hence we learn, that a compassionate spirit, towards such as labour under burdens of sin or affliction, is Christ-like, and truly excellent: this was the Spirit of Christ: oh be like him! Put on as the elect of God, bowels of mercy, Col. iii. 12. " Weep with them that weep, and rejoice with them that rejoice," Rom. xii. 15. It was Cain that said, " Am I my brother's keeper?" Blessed Paul was of a contrary temper; " Who is weak, and I am not weak? Who is offended, and I burn not?" 2 Cor. xi. 29. Three things promote sympathy in christians: one is, the Lord's pity for them; he doth as it were suffer with them; " in all their afflictions he was afflicted," Isa. lxiii. 9. Another is, the relation we sustain to God's afflicted people: they are members with us in one body, and the members should have the same care of one another, 1 Cor. xii. 25. The last is, we know not how soon we ourselves may need from others, what others now need from us. " Restore him with the spirit of meekness, considering thyself, lest thou also be tempted," Gal. vi. 1.

6. Did the world add to the humiliation of Christ by their base and vile usage of him? Learn hence, that the judgment which the world gives of persons and their worth, is little to be regarded. Surely it dispenses its smiles and honours very preposterously and unduly, in this respect, among others. The saints are styled persons " of whom the world is not worthy," Heb. xi. 38, that is, it doth not deserve to have such choice spirits as these are left in it, since it knows not how to use or treat them. It was the complaint of Salvian, above eleven hundred years ago; " If any of the nobility (saith he) do but begin to turn to God, presently he loseth the honour of nobility! Oh in how little honour is Christ among (so called) christian people, when religion shall make a man ignoble! So that (as he adds) many are compelled to be evil, lest they should be esteemed vile." And indeed, if the world gives us any help to discover the true worth and excellency of men by, it is by the rule of contraries, for the most part. Where it fixes its marks of hatred, we may usually find that which deserves our respect and love. It should therefore trouble us the less to be under the slights and disrespects of a blind world. " I could be even proud of it, (saith Luther,) that I see I have an ill name from the world." And

Jerom " blessed God that counted him worthy to be hated of the world." Labour to stand right in the judgment of God, and trouble not thyself for the rash censures of men.

7. From the whole of Christ's humiliation in his life, learn to pass through all the troubles of your life with a contented, composed spirit, as Christ your fore-runner did. He was persecuted, and bare it meekly; poor, and never murmured; tempted, and never yielded to the temptation; reviled, and reviled not again. When ye therefore pass through any of these trials, look to Jesus, and consider him. See how he that passed through these things before you, how he conducted himself in like circumstances; yea, not only beat the way by his pattern and example for you, but hath in every one of those conditions left a blessing behind him, for them that follow his steps. Thanks be to God for Jesus Christ.

SERMON XX.

OF CHRIST'S HUMILIATION UNTO DEATH, IN HIS FIRST PREPARATIVE ACT FOR IT.

JOHN XVII. 11.

AND NOW I AM NO MORE IN THE WORLD, BUT THESE ARE IN THE WORLD, AND I COME TO THEE. HOLY FATHER, KEEP THROUGH THINE OWN NAME THOSE WHOM THOU HAST GIVEN ME, THAT THEY MAY BE ONE, AS WE ARE.

WE now come to the last and lowest step of Christ's humiliation, which was in his submitting to death, even the death of the cross. Out of this death of Christ the life of our souls springs up. In the blood of Christ the judicious believer sees multitudes of inestimable blessings. By this crimson fountain I resolve to sit down : and concerning the death of Christ, I shall take distinctly into consideration, the preparations made for it ; the nature and quality of it ; the deportment and conduct of Jesus when dying ; the funeral solemnities with which he was buried ; and lastly, the blessed designs and glorious ends of his death.

The preparatives for his death were six. Three on his own part, and three more by his enemies. The preparations made by himself for it were, the solemn recommendation of his friends to his Father ; the institution of a commemorative sign, to perpetuate and refresh the memory of his death in the hearts of his people, till he come again ; and his pouring out his soul to God by prayer in the garden, which was the posture he chose to be found in, when they should apprehend him.

This scripture contains the first preparative of Christ for death, whereby he sets his house in order, prays for his people, and blesses them before he dies. The love of Christ was ever tender and strong to his people ; but the greatest manifestation of it was at parting. And this he manifested two ways especially ; namely, in leaving singular supports and grounds of comfort with them in his last heavenly sermon, in chap. xiv. xv. xvi. and in pouring out his soul most affectionately to the Father for them in this heavenly prayer, chap. xvii. In this prayer he gives them a specimen of his glorious intercession work, which he was then going to perform in heaven for them. Here his heart overflowed, for he was now leaving them, and going to the Father. The last words of a dying man are remarkable; how much more of a dying Saviour! I shall not launch out into that ocean of precious matter contained in this chapter, but take immediately into consideration the words of the text, wherein I find a weighty petition, strongly followed and set home with many mighty arguments.

1. We have here Christ's petition, or request in behalf of his people, not only those who were with him at the time, but all others that then did, or afterwards should believe on him. And the sum of what he here requests for them is, that his Father would keep them through his name.

Keeping implies danger. And there is a double danger contemplated in this request; danger in respect of sin, and danger in respect of ruin and destruction. To both these the people of God lie open in this world. The means of their preservation from both is the name, that is, the power of God. This name of the Lord is that " strong tower to which the righteous fly, and are safe," Prov. xviii. 10. Alas! it is not your own strength or wisdom that keeps you, but ye are kept by the mighty power of God. This protecting power of God does not, however, exclude our care and diligence, but implies it; therefore it is added, " Ye are kept by the mighty power of God, through faith, unto salvation," 1 Pet. i. 5. God keeps his people, and yet they are to keep themselves in the love of God, Jude 21, to keep their hearts with all diligence, Prov. iv. 23. This is the sum of the petition.

2. The arguments with which he urges and presses this request, are drawn partly from *his own* condition, " I am no more in the world," that is, I am going to die; within a very few hours I shall be separated from them, in regard of my corporeal presence. Partly from *their* condition : " but these are in the world ;" that is, I must leave them in the midst of danger. And partly from the joint interest his Father and himself had in them ; " Keep those that thou hast given me :" with several other most prevalent pleas, which, in their proper places, shall be produced, and displayed, to illustrate and confirm this precious truth, which this scripture affords us,

DOCT. THAT THE FATHERLY CARE AND TENDER LOVE OF OUR LORD JESUS CHRIST, WAS EMINENTLY DISCOVERED IN THAT PLEADING PRAYER HE POURED OUT FOR HIS PEOPLE AT HIS PARTING WITH THEM.

It pertained to the priest and father of the family to bless the rest, especially when he was to be separated from them by death. This was a right in Israel.   When good Jacob was grown old, and the time was come that he should be gathered to his fathers, then "he blessed Joseph, Ephraim and Manasseh, saying, God, before whom my fathers Abraham and Isaac did walk, the God which fed me all my life long unto this day, the angel which redeemed me from all evil, bless the lads," Gen. xlviii. 15, 16.   This was a prophetical and patriarchal blessing : not that Jacob could bless as God blesses ; he could speak the words of blessing, but he knew the effect, the real blessing itself depended upon God : he could, as the mouth of God, pronounce blessings, but could not confer them.   Thus he blessed his children, as his father Isaac had also blessed him before he died, Gen. xxviii. 3 ; and all these blessings were delivered prayer-wise.

Now, when Jesus Christ comes to die, he will bless his children also, and therein will discover how much dear and tender love he had for them : " Having loved his own, which were in the world, he loved them to the end," John xiii. 1.   The last act of Christ in this world, was an act of blessing, Luke xxiv. 50, 51.

I will here open, first, The mercies which Christ requested of the Father for them.   Secondly, The arguments used by him to obtain these mercies.   Thirdly, Why he thus pleaded for them when he was to die.   And lastly, How all this gives full evidence of Christ's tender care and love to his people.

I. We will inquire what those mercies and special favours were, which Christ begged for his people, when he was to die. And we find, among others, these five special mercies desired for them, in this context.

1. The mercy of preservation, both from sin and danger : so in the text, " Keep, through thine own name, those whom thou hast given me :" which is explained, " I pray not that thou shouldest take them out of the world, but that thou shouldest keep them from the evil," ver. 15.   We, in ours, and the saints that are gone, in their respective generations, have reaped the fruit of this prayer.   How else comes it to pass, that our souls are preserved amidst such a world of temptations, and these assisted and favoured by our own corruptions ?   How is it else, that our persons are not ruined and destroyed amidst such multitudes of potent and malicious enemies, that are set on fire of hell ?   Surely the preservation of the burning bush, of the three children amidst the flames, and of Daniel in the den of lions,

are not greater wonders, than these which our eyes daily behold. As the fire would have certainly consumed, and the lions, without doubt, have rended and devoured, had not God, by the interposition of his own hand, stopped and hindered the effect; so would the sin that is in us, and the malice that is in others, quickly ruin our souls and bodies, were it not that the same hand guards and keeps us every moment. To that hand, into which this prayer of Christ delivered your souls and bodies, do you owe all your mercies and salvations, both temporal and spiritual.

2. Another mercy he prays for, is the blessing of union among themselves. This he joins immediately with the first mercy of preservation, and prays for it in the same breath, " That they may be one, as we are," ver. 11. And well might he join them together in one breath ; for this union is not only a choice mercy in itself, but a special means of that preservation he had prayed for before : their union with one another, is a special means to preserve them all.

3. A third mercy that Christ earnestly prayed for, was, that his " joy might be fulfilled in them," ver. 13. He would provide for their joy, even when the hour of his greatest sorrow was at hand; yea, he would not only obtain joy for them, but a full joy : " that my joy might be fulfilled in them." It is as if he had said, O my Father, I am to leave these dear ones in a world of troubles and perplexities ; I know their hearts will be subject to frequent despondencies ; oh let me obtain the cordials of divine joy for them before I go : I would not only have them live, but live joyfully.

4. And as a continued spring to maintain all the forementioned mercies, he prays, that " they all may be sanctified through the word of truth," ver. 17, that is, more abundantly sanctified than yet they were, by a deeper radication of gracious habits and principles in their heart. This is a singular mercy in itself, to have holiness spreading itself over and through their souls, as the light of the morning. Nothing is in itself more desirable. And it is also a great help to their perseverance, union, and spiritual joy, which he had prayed for before, and which are all advanced by their increasing sanctification.

5. And lastly, as the completion and perfection of all mercies, he prays, " that they may be with him, where he is, to behold his glory," ver. 24. This is the best and ultimate privilege they are capable of. The end of his coming down from heaven, and returning thither again, was this, to bring many sons and daughters unto glory. You see Christ asks no trifles, no small

things for his people; no mercies but the best that both worlds afford, will suffice him on their behalf.

II. Let us see how he follows his requests, and with what arguments he pleads with the Father for these things: and, among others, I shall single out six, which are urged in this text, or the immediate context.

1. The first argument is drawn from the joint interest that both himself and his Father have in their persons, for whom he prays, "All mine are thine, and thine are mine," ver. 10. As if he should say, Father, behold, and consider the persons I pray for, they are thy children as well as mine; the very same on whom thou hast set thy eternal love, and in that love hast given them to me; so that they are both thine and mine: great is our interest in them. Oh therefore keep, comfort, sanctify, and save them, for they are thine. What a mighty plea is this! Surely, christians, your Intercessor is skilful in his work, your Advocate wants no eloquence or ability to plead for you.

2. The second argument, and that a powerful one, treads, as I may say, upon the very heel of the former, in the next words, "And I am glorified in them;" *q. d.* My glory and honour are infinitely dear to thee; I know thy heart is entirely set upon the exalting and glorifying of thy Son. Now, what glory have I in the world, but what comes from my people? Others neither can nor will glorify me; nay, I am daily blasphemed and dishonoured by them: these are they from whom my glory and praise in the world must rise. Should these then miscarry and perish, where shall my glory be? and from whom shall I expect it? So that here his property and glory are pleaded with the Father, to prevail for those mercies; and they are both great and valuable things with God. What dearer, what nearer to the heart of God?

3. And yet, to make all fast and sure, he adds, in the beginning of this ver. 11, a third argument, in these words, "And now I am no more in the world." Where we must consider the sense of it, as a proposition, and the force of it, as an argument. This proposition, "I am no more in the world," is not to be taken simply and universally, as if, in no sense, Christ should be any more in this world; but only respectively, as to his corporeal presence; this, which had been a sweet spring of comfort to them, in all their troubles, was, in a little time, to be removed from his people. It might now have been said to the pensive disciples, as the sons of the prophets said to Elisha, a little before Elijah's translation, "Know ye not that your Master shall be taken from your heads to-day?" This comfort-

able enjoyment must be taken from them. And here lies the argument; Father, consider the sadness and trouble I shall leave my poor children under. Whilst I was with them, I was a sweet relief to their souls, whatever troubles they met with; in all doubts, fears, and dangers, they could repair to me; and in their straits and wants I still supplied them: they had my counsels to direct them, my reproofs to restore them, and my comforts to support them; yea, the very sight of me was an unspeakable joy and refreshment to their souls: but now the hour is come, and I must be gone. All the comfort and benefit they had from my presence among them, is cut off: and, except thou do make up all this to them another way, what will become of these children, when their father is gone? what will be the case of the poor sheep, and tender lambs, when the shepherd is smitten?

4. And further, to move and engage the Father's care and love for them, he subjoins another great consideration, in the very next words, drawn from the danger he leaves them in; "But these are in the world." The world is a sinful, infecting, and unquiet place; it lies in wickedness: and a hard thing it will be for such poor, weak, imperfect creatures to escape the pollutions of it; or, if they do, yet the troubles, persecutions, and strong oppositions of it they cannot escape. Seeing therefore I must leave them in the midst of a sinful, troublesome, dangerous world, where they can neither move backward nor forward, without danger of sin or ruin; oh, since the case stands so, look after them, provide for them, and take special care for them all. Consider who they are, and where I leave them. They are thy children, to be left in a strange country; thy soldiers, in the enemies' quarters; thy sheep, in the midst of wolves; thy precious treasure, among thieves.

5. And yet he has not done, for he adds another argument in the next words, "And I come to thee." As his leaving them was an argument, so his coming to the Father is a mighty argument also. There is much in these words, "I come to thee." I thy beloved Son, in which thy soul delighteth; I, to whom thou never deniedst any thing. I am now coming to thee, my Father. I come treading every step of my way to thee in blood, and unspeakable sufferings; and all this for the sake of those dear ones I now pray for; yea, the design and end of my coming to thee, is for them. I am coming to heaven in the capacity of an advocate, to plead with thee for them. And I come to [Thee] my Father, and their Father; my God, and their God. Now then, since I, that am so dear, am coming to thee through such bitter pangs; and all this on their account; since I do but now,

as it were, begin, or give them a little taste of that intercession work, which I shall live for ever to perform for them in heaven ; Father, here, Father, grant what I request.

6. And, to close up all, he tells the Father how careful he had been to observe and perform that trust which was committed to him ; "While I was with them in the world, I kept them in thy name; those that thou gavest me, I have kept, and none of them is lost, but the son of perdition," ver. 12.

And thus lies the argument : Thou hast committed to me a certain number of elect souls, to be redeemed by me ; I undertook the trust, and said, If any of these be lost, at my hand let them be required. In pursuance of which trust, I am now here on the earth, in a body of flesh. I have been faithful in every point. I have redeemed them, (for he speaks of that as finished and done, which was now ready to be done,) I have kept them hitherto ; and now, Father, I commit them to thy care. Lo, here they are, not one is lost, but the son of perdition, who was never given. How great care have I taken for them ! Oh let them not fail now ; let not one of them perish. Thus you see what a nervous, argumentative, pleading prayer Christ poured out to the Father for them at parting.

III. The next inquiry is, why he thus prayed and pleaded with God for them, when he was to die ? And certainly it was not because the Father was unwilling to grant the mercies he desired for them ; for he tells us, " The Father himself loveth you," John xvi. 27, that is, he is inclined enough of his own accord to do you good. But the reasons of this exceeding importunity we may suppose to have been,

1. He foresaw a great trial then at hand ; yea, and all the after-trials of his people as well as that. He knew how much they would be sifted, and put to, in that hour, and power of darkness, that was coming. He knew their faith would be shaken and greatly staggered by the approaching difficulties, when they should see their Shepherd smitten, and themselves scattered, the Son of man delivered into the hands of sinners, and the Lord of life hang dead upon the cross, yea, sealed up in the grave. He foresaw what straits his poor people would fall into, between a busy tempter and an unbelieving heart ; therefore he prays and pleads with such importunity for them, that they might not miscarry.

2. He was now entering upon his intercession work in heaven, and he was desirous in this prayer to give us a specimen, or sample, of that part of his work, before he left us ; that by this we might understand what he would do for us, when he should

be out of sight. For this being his last prayer on earth, it shows us what affections and dispositions he carried hence with him, and satisfies us, that he who was so earnest with God on our behalf, such a mighty pleader here, will not forget us, or neglect our concerns, in the other world. Yet, reader, I would have thee always remember, that the intercession of Christ in heaven is carried much higher than this ; it is performed in a way more suitable to that state of honour to which he is now exalted. Here he used prostrations of body, cries and tears in his prayers : there, his intercession is carried in a more majestic way, and with more state, becoming an exalted Jesus. But yet in this he hath left us a special assistance, to discover much of the frame, temper, and working of his heart now in heaven towards us.

3. And lastly, he would leave this as a standing monument of his father-like care, and love to his people, to the end of the world. And for this it is conceived Christ delivered this prayer so publicly, not withdrawing from the disciples to be private with God, as he did in the garden ; but in their presence. And not only was it publicly delivered, but it was also, by a singular providence, recorded at large by John, though omitted by the other evangelists ; that so it might stand to all generations.

IV. If you ask how this gives evidence of Christ's tender care and love to his people ? which is the last inquiry ; I answer, it appears in these two particulars.

1. His love and care was manifested in the choice of mercies for them. He doth not pray for health, honour, long life, riches, &c.; but for their preservation from sin, spiritual joy in God, sanctification, and eternal glory. No mercies but the very best in God's treasury will content him for his people ; the rest he is content should be dispensed promiscuously by Providence ; but these he will settle as a heritage upon his children. Oh see the love of Christ ! look over all your spiritual inheritance in Christ, compare it with the richest, fairest, largest inheritance on earth ; and see what poor things these are to yours Oh the care of a dear Father ! Oh the love of a tender Saviour !

2. Besides, what an evidence of his tenderness to you, and great care for you, was this, that he should so intently and so affectionately mind, and plead your concerns with God, at such a time as this was, even when a world of sorrow encompassed him on every side ; a cup of wrath mixed, and ready to be put into his hand : at that very time when the clouds of wrath grew black, a storm coming, and such as he never felt before ; when one would have thought, all his care, thoughts, and diligence, should have been employed on his own account, to mind his own suffer-

ings.   No, he doth as it were forget his own sorrows, to mind
our peace and comfort.   O love unspeakable !

Let us further improve this subject by a few deductions. 1.
If this be so, that Christ so eminently discovered his care and
love for his people, in this his parting hour ; then hence we conclude, that the perseverance of the saints is unquestionable. Do
you hear how he pleads, how he fills his mouth with arguments,
how he chooses his words and sets them in order, how he winds
up his spirit to the very highest pitch of zeal and fervency ? and
can you doubt of success ? Can such a Father deny the importunity and pleading of such a Son ? Oh, it can never be ! he
cannot deny him : Christ has the art and skill of prevailing with
God. If the heart or hand of God were hard to be opened, yet
this would open them ; but when the Father himself loves us,
and is inclined to do us good, who can doubt of Christ's success ?
"That which is in motion, is the more easily moved."   The
cause Christ manageth in heaven for us is just and righteous.
The manner in which he pleads is powerful, and therefore the
success of his suit is unquestionable.   Oh think on this, when
dangers surround your souls or bodies, when fears and doubts
are multiplied within ; when thou art ready to say in thy haste,
All men are liars, I shall one day perish by the hand of sin or
Satan ; think on that encouragement Christ gave to Peter, " I
have prayed for thee," Luke xxii. 32.

2. Again, hence we learn, that argumentative prayers are excellent prayers.   The strength of every thing is in its joints;
there lies much of the strength of prayer also. How strongly
jointed, how nervous and argumentative was this prayer of
Christ ! Some there are indeed, that think we need not argue
and plead in prayer with God, but only present the matter of our
prayers to him, and leave Christ (whose office it is) to plead
with the Father ; as if Christ did not present our pleas and arguments, as well as simple desires to God ; as if the choicest
part of our prayers must be kept back, because Christ presents
our prayers to God.   No, no, Christ's pleading is one thing,
ours another : " His and ours are not opposed, but subordinate ;
his pleading doth not destroy, but makes ours successful.   God
call us to plead with him, " Come now, let us reason together,"
Isa. i. 18.   " God (as one * observes) reasons with us by his
word and providences outwardly, and by the motions of his
Spirit inwardly : and we reason with him by framing (through
the help of his Spirit) certain holy arguments, grounded upon
allowed principles, drawn from his nature, name, word, or works."

* Mr. Corbet, of Prayer.

And it is condemned as a very sinful defect in professors, that they did not plead the church's cause with God; "There is none to plead thy cause that thou mayest be bound up," Jer. xxx. 13. What was Jacob's wrestling with the angel, but his holy pleading and importunity with God? and how well it pleased God, let the event speak, "As a prince he prevailed, and had power with God," Gen. xxxii. 24 ; Hos. xii. 4. The Lord, on this account, hath honoured his saints with the title of, His recorders, men fit to plead with him, as that word signifies: "Ye that make mention of the Lord, keep not silence, give him no rest," Isa. lxii. 6. It notes the office of him that recorded all the memorable matters of the king, and used to suggest seasonable items and memorandums of things to be done.

By these holy pleadings, "the King is held in his galleries," as it is Cant. vii. 5. I know we are not heard, either for our much speaking, or our excellent speaking ; it is Christ's pleading in heaven, that makes our pleading on earth available : but yet surely, when the Spirit of the Lord shall suggest proper arguments in prayer, and help the humble suppliant to press them home believingly and affectionately,* when he helps us to weep and plead, to groan and plead, God is greatly delighted with such prayers. "Thou hast said, I will surely do thee good," said Jacob, Gen. xxxii. 12. It is thine own free promise ; I did not go on mine own head, but thou badest me go, and encouragedst me with this promise. Oh this is pleasing to God, when by his Spirit of adoption we can come to God, crying, Abba, Father ; Father, hear, forgive, pity, and help me. Am I not thy child, thy son, or daughter ? To whom may a child be bold to go, with whom may a child have hope to speed, if not with his father ? Father, hear me. The fathers of our flesh are full of compassion, and pity their children, and know how to give good things to them, when they ask them. When they ask bread or clothing, will they deny them ? And is not the Father of spirits more full of compassion, more full of pity ?

3. What an excellent pattern is here, for all that have the charge and government of others committed to them, whether magistrates, ministers, or parents, to teach them how to acquit themselves towards their relations, when they come to die !

Look upon dying Jesus, see how his care and love to his people broke out, when the time of his departure was at hand. Surely, as we are bound to remember our relations every day, and to lay up a stock of prayers for them in the time of our

* The heart cries to God more by groans than by words, and more by tears than by speaking.—*Aug. Mr. R. A. vind.*

health, so it becomes us to imitate Christ in our earnestness with God for them, when we die. Though we die, our prayers do not die with us: they out-live us, and those we leave behind us in the world may reap the benefit of them, when we are turned to dust.

For my own part, I must profess before the world, that I have a high value for this mercy, and do, from the bottom of my heart, bless the Lord, who gave me a religious and tender father, * who often poured out his soul to God for me: he was one that was inwardly acquainted with God; and being full of love to his children, often carried them before the Lord, prayed and pleaded with God for them, wept and made supplications for them. This stock of prayers and blessings left by him before the Lord, I esteem above the fairest inheritance on earth. Oh it is no small mercy to have thousands of fervent prayers lying before the Lord, filed up, as it were, in heaven for us. And oh that we would all be faithful to this duty ! surely our love, especially to the souls of our relations, should not grow cold when our breath does. Oh that we would remember this duty in our lives, and, if God give opportunity and ability, discharge it fully when we die; considering, as Christ did, that we shall be no more, but they are in this world, in the midst of a defiled, tempting, trouble-some world; what temptations and troubles may befall them, we do not know.   Oh imitate Christ your pattern.

4. To conclude; Hence we may see, what a high esteem and valuation Christ has of believers: this was the treasure which he could not quit, he could not die till he had secured it in a safe hand: " I come unto thee, holy Father, keep through thine own name those whom thou hast given me."

Surely believers are dear to Jesus Christ; and good reason, for he has paid dear for them: let his dying language, this last farewell, say how he prized them. "The Lord's portion is his people, Jacob is the lot of his inheritance," Deut. xxxii. 9. " They are a peculiar treasure to him, above all the people of the earth," Exod. xix. 5. Whatever is much upon our hearts when we die, is dear to us indeed. Oh how precious, how dear should Jesus Christ be to us ! Were we first and last upon his heart ; did he mind us, did he pray for us, did he so wrestle with God about us, when the sorrows of death compassed him about? How much are we engaged, not only to love him, and esteem him, whilst we live, but to be in pangs of love for him, when we feel the pangs of death upon us ! The very last whisper of our de-parting souls should be this, Blessed be God for Jesus Christ.

* Mr. Richard Flavel, a faithful and laborious preacher of the gospel, at Haseler in Warwickshire, and afterwards in Willersay in Gloucester-shire, now with God.

SERMON XXI.

THE SECOND PREPARATIVE ACT OF CHRIST, FOR HIS OWN DEATH.

1 COR. XI. 23—25.

THE LORD JESUS THE SAME NIGHT IN WHICH HE WAS BETRAYED TOOK
BREAD: AND WHEN HE HAD GIVEN THANKS, HE BRAKE IT, AND SAID,
TAKE, EAT: THIS IS MY BODY, WHICH IS BROKEN FOR YOU: THIS DO IN
REMEMBRANCE OF ME. AFTER THE SAME MANNER ALSO HE TOOK THE
CUP, WHEN HE HAD SUPPED, SAYING, THIS CUP IS THE NEW TESTAMENT
IN MY BLOOD: THIS DO YE, AS OFT AS YE DRINK IT, IN REMEMBRANCE
OF ME.

CHRIST had no sooner recommended his dear charge to the
Father, but (the time of his death hastening on) he institutes
his last supper, to be the lasting memorial of his death, in all the
churches, until his second coming; therein graciously providing
for the comfort of his people, when he should be removed out
of their sight. This his second act manifests no less love than
the former. It is like the plucking off the ring from his finger,
when ready to lay his neck upon the block, and delivering it to
his dearest friends, to keep that as a memorial of him.

In the text there are four things noted by the apostle, about
this last and lovely act of Christ, namely, the *Author*, *time*,
institution, and *end* of this holy, solemn ordinance.

1. The *Author* of it, the Lord Jesus: it is an effect of his
lordly power and royal authority; "And Jesus came, and
spake unto them, saying, All power is given unto me in heaven
and earth: go ye therefore," Matt. xxviii. 18, 19. The government is upon his shoulders, Isa. ix. 6. He shall bear the glory,
Zech. vi. 13.

2. The *time* when the Lord Jesus appointed this ordinance.
"In the same night in which he was betrayed:" it could not
be sooner, because the passover must first be celebrated; nor
later, for that night he was apprehended. It is therefore emphatically expressed, "in that same night," that night for ever
to be remembered. He gives, that night, a cordial draught to
his disciples before the conflict: he appoints, that night, an ordinance in the church, for the confirmation and consolation of
his people, in all generations, to the end of the world.

3. *The institution itself;* in which we have the memorative, significative, instructive signs, and they are bread and wine; and the glorious mysteries represented and shadowed forth by them, namely, Jesus Christ crucified; the proper New Testament nourishment of believers. Bread and wine are choice creatures, and do excellently shadow forth the flesh and blood of crucified Jesus; and that both in their natural usefulness, and manner of preparation. Their usefulness is very great: bread is necessary to uphold and maintain our natural life; therefore it is called the staff of bread, Isa. iii. 1, because as a feeble man depends and leans upon his staff, so do our feeble spirits upon bread. Wine was made to cheer the heart of man, Judg. ix. 13. They are both useful and excellent creatures; their preparations to become so useful to us, are also remarkable. The corn must be ground in the mill, the grapes torn and squeezed to pieces in the wine-press, before we can either have bread or wine. And when all this is done, they must be received into the body, or they nourish not. So that these were very fit to be set apart for this use and end.

If any object, It is true, they are good creatures, but not precious enough to be the signs of such profound and glorious mysteries: it was worth creating a new creature, to be the sign of the new covenant. Let him that thus objects, ask himself, whether nothing be precious without pomp? The preciousness of these elements is not so much from their own natures, as their use and end; and that makes them precious indeed. A loadstone at sea is much more excellent than a diamond, because more useful. A pennyworth of wax applied to the label of a deed, and sealed, may in a minute have its value raised to thousands of pounds. These elements receive their value and estimation on a like account. Nor should it at all remain a wonder to thee, why Christ should represent himself by such mean and common things, when thou hast well considered that the excellency of the picture, is its similitude and conformity to the original; and that Christ was in a low, sad, and very abased state, when this picture of him was drawn; he was then a man of sorrows. These then, as lively signs, shadow forth a crucified Jesus, represent him to us in his red garments.

4. Lastly take notice of the *use, design, and end* of this institution. " In remembrance," or for a memorial " of me." Oh there is much in this: Christ knew how apt our base hearts would be to lose him, amidst such a throng of sensible objects as we here converse with; and how much that forgetfulness of him and of his sufferings would turn to our prejudice and loss;

therefore he appoints a sign to be remembered by : " As oft as you do this, ye show forth the Lord's death till he come." Hence we observe,

DOCT. THAT THE SACRAMENTAL MEMORIAL CHRIST LEFT WITH HIS PEOPLE, IS A SPECIAL MARK OF HIS CARE AND LOVE FOR THEM.

What ! to order his picture (as it were) to be drawn when he was dying, to be left with his spouse ! To rend his own flesh, and set flowing his own blood, to be meat and drink for our souls ! Oh what manner of love was this ! It is true, his picture in the sacrament is full of scars and wounds : but these are honourable scars, and highly grace and commend it to his spouse, for whose sake he here received them.

" They are marks of love and honour." And he would be so drawn, or rather he so drew himself, that as oft as his people looked upon the portraiture of him, they might remember, and be deeply affected with those things he here endured for their sakes. These are the wounds my dear Husband Jesus received for me. These are the marks of that love which passes the love of creatures. Oh see the love of a Saviour ! Surely the spouse may say of the love of Christ, what David, in his lamentations, said of the love of Jonathan, " Thy love to me was wonderful, passing the love of women." But to prepare the point to be meat indeed, and drink indeed to thy soul, I shall discuss briefly these three things, and hasten to the application.

I. What it is to remember the Lord Jesus in the sacrament.

II. What aptitude there is in that ordinance, so to bring him to our remembrance.

III. How the care and love of Christ is discovered, by leaving such a memorial of himself with us.

I. Remembrance, properly, is the return of the mind to an object, about which it hath been formerly conversant ; and it may so return to a thing it hath conversed with before two ways ; speculatively, and transiently ; or affectionately, and permanently. A speculative remembrance, is only to call to mind the history of such a person, and his sufferings ; that Christ was once put to death in the flesh. An affectionate remembrance, is when we so call Christ and his death to our minds, as to feel the powerful impressions thereof upon our hearts. Thus, " Peter remembered the word of the Lord, and went out, and wept bitterly," Matt. xxvi. 75. His very heart was melted with that remembrance ; his bowels were pained, he could not hold, but went out and wept abundantly. Thus Joseph, when he saw his brother Benjamin, whose sight refreshed the memory of former days and endearments, was greatly affected: " And he lifted up his eyes, and saw his brother Benjamin, his mother's son: and said, Is this your younger brother, of whom ye spake to me? And he said, God be gracious unto thee, my son. And Joseph made haste, for his bowels did yearn upon his brother; and he sought where to weep; and he entered into his chamber, and wept there," Gen. xliii. 29, 30.   Such a remembrance of Christ is that which is here intended. This is indeed a gracious remembrance of Christ: the former hath nothing of grace in it. The time shall come when Judas that betrayed him, and the jews that pierced him, shall historically remember what was done; " Behold, he cometh with clouds; and every eye shall see him, and they also which pierced him; and all kindreds of the earth shall wail because of him," Rev. i. 7. Then, I say, Judas shall remember: This is he whom I perfidiously betrayed. Pilate shall remember: This is he whom I sentenced to be hanged on a tree, though I was convinced of his innocency.   Then the soldiers shall remember: This is that face we spit upon, that head we crowned with thorns; lo, this is he whose side we pierced, whose hands and feet we once nailed to the cross.   But this remembrance will be their torment, not their benefit.   It is not therefore a bare historical, speculative, but a gracious, affectionate, impressive remembrance of Christ, that is here intended: and such a remembrance of Christ supposes and includes,

  1. The saving knowledge of him.   We cannot be said to remember what we never knew; nor to remember savingly, what we never knew savingly.   There have been many previous sweet and gracious transactions, dealings, and intimacies between Christ and his people, from the time of their first happy acquaintance with him: much of that sweetness they have had in former considerations of him, and hours of communion with him, is lost and gone; for nothing is more inconstant than our spiritual comforts: but now at the Lord's table, our old acquaintance is renewed, and the remembrance of his goodness and love revived; " We will remember thy love more than wine; the upright love thee," Cant. i. 4.

  2. Such a remembrance of Christ includes faith in it.   Without discerning Christ at a sacrament, there is no remembrance of him; and, without faith, no discerning Christ there.   But when the precious eye of faith hath spied Christ, under the vail, it presently calls up the affections, saying, " Come see the Lord." These are the wounds he received from me.   This is he that loved me, and gave himself for me.   Awake, my love, rouse up,

my hope, flame out, my desires; come forth, O all ye powers and affections of my soul; come, see the Lord. No sooner doth Christ by his Spirit call to the believer, but faith hears; and discerning the voice, turns about, like Mary, saying, Rabboni, my Lord, my Master.

3. This remembrance of Christ includes suitable impressions made upon the affections, by such a sight and remembrance of him: and therein lies the nature of that precious thing which we call communion with God. Various representations of Christ are made at his table. Sometimes the soul there calls to mind the infinite wisdom, that so contrived and laid the glorious and mysterious design and project of redemption: the effect of this is wonder and admiration. Oh the manifold wisdom of God! Eph. iii. 10. Oh the depth, the heighth, the length, the breadth of this wisdom! I can as easily span the heavens as take the just dimensions of it. Sometimes a representation of the severity of God is made to the soul at that ordinance. Oh how inflexible and severe is the justice of God! What! no abatement; no sparing mercy; no, not to his own Son? This begets a double impression on the heart.

(1.) Just and deep indignation against sin. Oh cursed sin! it was thou usedst my dear Lord so; for thy sake he underwent all this. If thy vileness had not been so great, his sufferings had not been so many. Cursed sin! thou wast the knife that stabbed him, thou the sword that pierced him. Ah what revenge it works! When the believer considers and remembers, that sin put Christ to all that shame and ignominy, and that he was wounded for our transgressions, he is filled with hatred of sin, and cries out, Oh sin, I will revenge the blood of Christ upon thee! thou shalt never live a quiet hour in my heart. And,

(2.) It produces an humble adoration of the goodness and mercy of God, in exacting satisfaction for our sins, by such bloody stripes, from our Surety. Lord, if this wrath had seized on me, as it did on Christ, what had been my condition then? If these things were done in the green tree, what had been the case of the dry tree?

Sometimes extraordinary representations are made of the love of Christ, who assumed a body and soul, on purpose to bear the wrath of God for our sins. And when that surpassing love breaks out in its glory upon the soul, how is the soul transported with it! crying out, What manner of love is this! Here is a love large enough to go round the heavens, and the heaven of heavens! Who ever loved after this rate, to lay down his life for enemies? Oh love unutterable and inconceivable! Sometimes the

fruits of his death are there gloriously displayed : even his satisfaction for sin, and the purchase his blood made of the eternal
inheritance : and this begets thankfulness and confidence in the
soul.   Christ is dead, and his death hath satisfied for my sin.
Christ is dead, therefore my soul shall never die.   Who shall
separate me from the love of God ? These are the fruits, and
this is the nature of that remembrance of Christ here spoken of.

II. What aptitude or fitness is there in this ordinance, to
bring Christ so to remembrance ? Much every way ; for it is a
sign, by him appointed to that end, and hath (as divines well
observe) a threefold use and consideration, namely, as it is memorative, significative, and instructive.

As it is memorative, it has the nature and use of a pledge or
token of love, left by a dying to a dear surviving friend.   And so
the sacrament, as was said before, is like a ring plucked off from
Christ's finger, or a bracelet from his arm ; or rather his picture
from his breast, delivered to us with such words as these ; " As
oft as you look on this, remember me ; let this help to keep me
alive in your remembrance when I am gone, and out of your
sight."

It induces to it also, as it is a significative sign, most aptly
signifying both his bitter sufferings for us, and our strict and intimate union with him ; both which have an excellent usefulness
to move the heart, and its deepest affections, at the remembrance
of it.   The breaking of the bread, and pouring forth the wine,
signify the former ; our eating, drinking, and incorporating them,
is a lively signification of the latter.   Moreover, this ordinance
hath an excellent use and advantage for this affectionate remembrance of Christ, as it is an instructive sign.   And it many ways
instructs us, and enlightens our mind, particularly in these truths.

1. That Christ is the bread on which our souls live, proper
meat and drink for believers, the most excellent new testament
food. It is said, " Man did eat angels' food," Psa. lxxviii. 25 : he
means the manna that fell from heaven, which was so excellent,
that if angels, who are the noblest creatures, did live upon material food, they would choose this above all to feed on.   And
yet this was but a type and weak shadow of Christ, on whom
believers feed.

2. It instructs us that the new testament is now in its full
force, and no substantial alteration can be made in it, since the
Testator is dead, and by his death hath ratified it.   So that all
the excellent promises and blessings of it are now fully confirmed
to the believing soul, Heb. ix. 16, 17.   All these, and many
more choice truths, are we instructed in by this sign : and all

these ways it reminds us of Christ, and helps powerfully to raise, warm, and affect our hearts with that remembrance of him.

III. The last inquiry is, How Christ hath, hereby, left such a special mark of his care for, and love to his people? And that will evidently appear, if you consider these five particulars.

1. This is a special mark of the care and love of Christ, inasmuch as hereby he hath made abundant provision for the confirmation and establishment of the faith of his people to the end of the world. For this being an evident proof that the new testament is in its full force, (" This is the cup of the new testament in my blood," Matt. xxvi. 28,) it tends as much to our satisfaction, as the legal execution of a deed, by which we hold and enjoy our estate. So that when he saith, Take, eat, it is as much as if God should stand before you at the table with Christ, and all the promises in his hand ; and say, I deliver this to thee as my deed. What think you, does not this promote and confirm the faith of a believer ?

2. This is a special mark of Christ's care and love, inasmuch as by this he hath made like abundant provision for the enlargement of the joy and comfort of his people. Believers are at this ordinance, as Mary was at the sepulchre, with fear and great joy, Matt. xxviii. 8. Come, reader, speak thy heart : if thou be one that heartily lovest Jesus Christ, and hast gone many days, possibly years, mourning and lamenting because of the obscurity and cloudiness of thine interest in him ; who hast sought him sorrowing, in this ordinance, and in that, in one duty, and another : if at last Christ should take off that covering (as one calls it) from his face, and be known of thee in breaking of bread : suppose he should, by his Spirit, whisper thus in thine ear as thou sittest at his table, Dost thou indeed so prize, esteem, and value me ? will nothing but Christ and his love content and satisfy thee ? then, know that I am thine : take thine own Christ into the arms of thy faith this day :—would not this create in thy soul, a joy transcendent to all the joys and pleasures in this world ?

3. Here is a signal mark of Christ's care and love, inasmuch as this is one of the highest and best helps for the mortification of the corruption of his people. Nothing tends more to the killing of sin, than this does. One writer calls that table, an altar, on which our corruptions are sacrificed and slain before the Lord. For how can they that there see what Christ suffered for sin, live any longer therein ?

4. Moreover his care and love appear in providing an ordinance so excellently adapted, to excite and blow up his people's

love into a lively flame. When Joseph made himself known to his brethren, "I am Joseph your brother, whom ye sold, be not grieved;" oh what showers of tears and dear affections were there! how did they fall upon each other's necks! so that the egyptians wondered. How does the soul (if I may so speak) passionately love Jesus Christ at such a time! "The fairest among ten thousand." What hath he done, what hath he suffered for me! what great things hath my Jesus given, and what great things hath he forgiven me! A world, a thousand worlds cannot show such another. Here the soul is melted down by love at his feet.

5. To conclude; Christ's care and love are further manifested to his people in this ordinance, as it is one of the strongest bonds of union between them that can be: "We being many, are one bread, and one body; for we are all partakers of that one bread," 1 Cor. x. 17. And though, through our corruptions, it has fallen out, that what was intended for a bond of union has proved a bone of contention; yet, inasmuch as by this it appears how dearly Christ loved them; and as here they are sealed up to the same inheritance, their dividing corruptions here slain, their love to Christ, and consequently to each other, here improved; it is certainly one of the strongest ties in the world, to bind together gracious hearts in a bundle of love. And thus I have despatched the doctrinal part of this point. The improvement of it is in the following inferences.

1. Did Christ leave this ordinance with his church to preserve his remembrance among his people? Then surely he foresaw, that, notwithstanding what he is, and what he has done, suffered, and promised yet to do for his people, they will for all this be still apt to forget him.

One would think that such a Saviour should never be one whole hour together out of his people's thoughts and affections; that wherever they go, they should carry him up and down with them, in their thoughts, desires, and delights; that they should lie down with Christ in their thoughts at night, and when they awake be still with him; that their very dreams in the night should be sweet visions of Christ, and all their words savour of Him. But oh the baseness of these hearts! Here we live and converse in a world of sensible objects, which, like a company of thieves, rob us of our Christ. Woe is me, that it should be so with me, who am under such obligations to love him! Though he be in the highest glory in heaven, he doth not forget us; he hath graven us upon the palms of his hands; we are continually before him. He thinks on us, when we forget him.

The whole honour and glory paid him in heaven by the angels cannot divert his thoughts one moment from us; but every trifle that meets us in the way, is enough to divert our thoughts from him. Why do we not abhor and loathe ourselves for this? What! is it a pain, a burden, to carry Christ in our thoughts about the world? As much a burden, if thy heart be spiritual, as a bird is burdened by carrying his own wings. Will such thoughts intrude unseasonably, and thrust greater things than Christ out of our minds? For shame, christian, for shame, let not thy heart play the wanton, and wander from Christ after every vanity. Never leave praying and striving, till thou canst say, as it is Psa. lxiii. 5, "My soul shall be satisfied as with marrow and fatness, and my mouth shall praise thee with joyful lips; whilst I remember thee on my bed, and meditate on thee in the night watches."

2. Hence also we infer, that sacrament seasons are heart-melting seasons; because therein the most affecting representations of Christ are made. As the gospel offers him to the ear, in the most sweet, affecting sounds of grace; so the sacrament to the eye, in the most pleasing visions that are on this side heaven. There, hearts that will not yield a tear under other ordinances, can pour out floods: "They shall look upon me whom they have pierced, and mourn," Zech. xii. 10. Yet I dare not affirm, that every one whose heart is broken by the believing sight of Christ there, can evidence that it is so by a dropping eye. No, we may say of tears, as it is said of love, Cant. viii. 7. If some christians would give all the treasures of their houses for them, they cannot be purchased: yet they are truly humbled for sin, and seriously affected with the grace of Christ. For the support of such, I would distinguish, and have them to do so also, between what is essential to spiritual sorrow, and what is contingent. Deep displeasure with thyself for sin, hearty resolutions and desires of the complete mortification of it, these are essential to all spiritual sorrow; but tears are accidental, and in some constitutions rarely found. If thou hast the former, trouble not thyself for want of the latter, though it is a mercy when they kindly and undissembledly flow from a heart truly broken.

And surely, to see who it is that thy sins have pierced, how great, how glorious, how wonderful a Person that was, that was so humbled, abased, and brought to the dust, for such a wretched thing as thou art, cannot but tenderly affect the considering soul:

3. Moreover hence it is evident, that the believing and affectionate remembrance of Christ, is of singular advantage at all times to the people of God; for it is the immediate end of one

of the greatest ordinances that ever Christ appointed to the church.

If at any time the heart be dead and hard, this is the likeliest means in the world to dissolve, melt, and quicken it. Look hither, hard heart; hard indeed if this hammer will not break it. Behold the blood of Jesus.

Art thou easily overcome by temptations to sin? This is the most powerful restraint in the world from sin: "How shall we that are dead to sin, live any longer therein?" Rom. vi. 2. We are crucified with Christ, what have we to do with sin? When thy heart is yielding to temptation, think, how can I do this, and crucify the Son of God afresh? As David poured the water brought from the well of Bethlehem, on the ground, though he was athirst, for he said, It is the blood of the men (that is, they hazarded their lives to fetch it); much more should a christian pour out upon the ground, yea, despise and trample under foot, the greatest profit or pleasure of sin; saying, Nay, I will have nothing to do with it, I will on no terms touch it, for it is the blood of Christ: it cost blood, infinite, precious blood to expiate it. If there were a knife in your house that had been thrust to the heart of your father, you would not take pleasure to see that knife, much less to use it.

Are you afraid your sins are not pardoned, but still stand upon account before the Lord? What more relieving, what more satisfying, than to see the cup of the new testament in the blood of Christ, which is "shed for many for the remission of sins?" "Who shall lay any thing to the charge of God's elect? It is Christ that died."

Are you staggered at your sufferings, and hard things you must endure for Christ in this world? Doth the flesh shrink back from these things, and cry, Spare thyself? What is there more likely to fortify thy spirit with resolution and courage, than such a sight as this? Did Christ face the wrath of men, and the wrath of God too? Did he stand with unbroken patience, and stedfast resolution, under such troubles, and shall I shrink for a trifle? Ah, he did not serve me so! I will arm myself with the like mind, 1 Pet. iv. 2.

Is thy faith staggered at the promises? Here is what will help thee against hope to believe in hope, giving glory to God. For this is God's seal added to his covenant, which ratifies and binds fast all that God hath spoken.

Dost thou idle away precious time vainly, and live unusefully to Christ in thy generation? What more apt both to convince and cure thee, than such remembrance of Christ as this? Oh when thou considerest thou art not thine own, thy time, thy talents are not thine own, but Christ's; when thou shalt see thou art bought with such a price, and so art strictly obliged to glorify God, with thy soul and body, which are his, 1 Cor. vi. 20, this will powerfully awaken a dull, sluggish, and lazy spirit! In a word, what grace is there that his remembrance of Christ cannot quicken? What sin cannot it mortify? What duty cannot it animate? Oh it is of singular use in all cases to the people of God!

4. Lastly we infer, Though all other things do, yet Christ never can become uninteresting. Here is an ordinance to preserve his remembrance fresh to the end of the world. The beauty of this Rose of Sharon is never lost or withered. He is the same yesterday, to-day, and for ever. As his body in the grave saw no corruption, so neither can his love, or any of his excellencies. Other beauties have their prime, and their fading time; but Christ abides eternally. Our delight in creatures is often most at first acquaintance; when we come nearer to them, and see more of them, the edge of our delight is abated: but the longer you know Christ, and the nearer you come to him, still the more do you see of his glory. Every farther prospect of Christ entertains the mind with a fresh delight. Blessed be God for Jesus Christ.

SERMON XXII.

LUKE XXII. 41—44.

AND HE WAS WITHDRAWN FROM THEM ABOUT A STONE'S CAST, AND KNEELED DOWN, AND PRAYED, SAYING, FATHER, IF THOU BE WILLING, REMOVE THIS CUP FROM ME: NEVERTHELESS NOT MY WILL, BUT THINE, BE DONE. AND THERE APPEARED AN ANGEL UNTO HIM FROM HEAVEN, STRENGTHENING HIM. AND BEING IN AN AGONY HE PRAYED MORE EARN- ESTLY: AND HIS SWEAT WAS AS IT WERE GREAT DROPS OF BLOOD FALL- ING DOWN TO THE GROUND.

THE hour is now almost come, even that hour of sorrow, which Christ had so often spoken of. Yet a little, a very little while, and the Son of man is betrayed into the hands of sinners. He hath affectionately recommended his children to his Father. He hath set his house in order, and ordained a memorial of his death to be left with his people, as you have heard. There is but one thing more to do, and then the tragedy begins. He recommended us, he must also recommend himself by prayer to the Father; and when that is done, he is ready.

This last act of Christ's preparation for his own death, is contained in this scripture; wherein we have an account,—of his prayer; of the agony attending it; and of his relief in that agony, by an angel, that came and comforted him.

In a praying posture he will be found when the enemy comes; he will be taken upon his knees: he was pleading hard with God in prayer, for strength to carry him through this heavy trial, when they came to take him. And this prayer was a very remarkable prayer, both for the solitariness of it, he withdrew about a stone's cast from his dearest intimates; no ear but his Father's shall hear what he had now to say: and for the vehemency and importunity of it; these were those strong cries that he poured out to God in the days of his flesh, Heb. v. 7. And for the humility expressed in it; he fell upon the ground, he laid himself as it were in the dust, at his Father's feet. And in divers other respects it was a very remarkable prayer, as you will see presently. Hence we note,

Doct. That our Lord Jesus Christ was praying to
his Father in an extraordinary agony, when
they came to apprehend him in the garden.

To open and explain this last act of preparation on Christ's
part for our use, I shall speak of these particulars. First, The
place where he prayed. Secondly, The time when he prayed.
Thirdly, The matter of his prayer. And lastly, The manner
how he prayed.

I. For the circumstance of place, where was this last and remarkable prayer poured out to God? It was in the garden : St.
Matthew tells us it was called Gethsemane, which signifies, (as
Pareus on the place observes,) " the valley of fatness, namely,
of olives, which grew in that valley or garden most plentifully."
This garden lay very near to the city of Jerusalem. The city
had twelve gates, five of which were on the east side of it, among
which the most remarkable was the fountain gate, so called from
the fountain Siloe. Through this gate Christ rode into the city
in triumph, when he came from Bethany. Another was the
sheep-gate, so called from the multitude of sheep driven in at it
for the sacrifice, for it stood close by the temple ; and close by
this gate was the garden called Gethsemane, where they apprehended Christ, and led him through this gate, as a sheep to the
slaughter. Between this garden and the city ran the brook
Cedron, which rose from a hill upon the south, and ran upon
the east part of the city, between Jerusalem and the mount of
olives : and over this brook Christ passed into the garden, John
xviii. 1. To which perhaps the psalmist alludes in Psa.
cx. 7, " He shall drink of the brook in the way ; therefore he
shall lift up the head." For this brook running through the
valley of Jehoshaphat, that fertile soil, together with the filth of
the city which it washed away, gave the waters a black tincture,
and so fitly resembled those grievous sufferings of Christ, in
which he tasted both the wrath of God and men.

Now, Christ went not into this garden to hide, or shelter himself from his enemies. No, that was not his end ; for if so, it
had been the most improper place he could have chosen, it
being the accustomed place where he was wont to pray, and a
place well known to Judas, who was now coming to seek him,
as you may see, John xviii. 2. So that he repairs thither, not
to shun, but to meet the enemy ; to offer himself as a prey to
the wolves, which there found him, and laid hold upon him.
He also resorted thither for an hour or two of privacy before
they came, that he might there freely pour out his soul to God.

II. We shall consider the time when he entered into this garden to pray: and it was in the shutting in of the evening; for it was after the passover and the supper were ended.   Then (as Matthew hath it, chap. xxvi. 36) Jesus went over the brook into the garden, between the hours of nine and ten in the evening, as it is conjectured; and so he had between two and three hours' time to pour out his soul to God. For it was about midnight that Judas and the soldiers came and apprehended him there.   So that it being immediately before his apprehension, it shows us in what frame and posture Christ desired to be found: and by it he left us an excellent pattern what we ought to do, when imminent dangers are near us, even at the door.   It becomes a soldier to die fighting, and a minister to die preaching, and a christian to die praying.   If they come, they will find Christ upon his knees, wrestling mightily with God by prayer. He never spent one moment of the time of his life idly; but these were the last moments he had to live in the world, and here you see how they were filled up and employed.

III. Next let us consider the matter of his prayer, or the things about which he poured out his soul to God in the garden, that evening.   And ver. 42 informs us what that was: he prayed, saying, " Father, if thou be willing, remove this cup from me; nevertheless not my will, but thine be done." These words are involved in many difficulties, as Christ himself was when he uttered them.   By the cup, understand that portion of sorrows then to be given to him by his Father.   Great afflictions and bitter trials are frequently expressed in scripture under the metaphor of a cup.   So, that dreadful storm of wrath upon the wicked, in Psa. xi. 6, " Upon the wicked he shall rain snares, fire and brimstone, and a horrible tempest; this shall be the portion of their cup," that is, the punishment allotted to them by God for their wickedness.   And an exceeding great misery, by a large or deep cup.   So Ezek. xxiii. 32, 33. And when an affliction is compounded of many bitter ingredients, stinging and aggravating considerations and circumstances, then it is said to be mixed.   And from the effect it hath on those that must drink it, is called a cup of trembling, Isa. li. 17. Such a cup now was Christ's cup; a cup of wrath; a large and deep cup, that contained more wrath than ever was drunk by any creature, even the wrath of an infinite God.   A mixed cup, mixed with God's wrath and man's in the extremity.   And all the bitter aggravating circumstances that ever could be imagined; great consternation and amazement; this was the portion of his cup.

By the passing of the cup from him, understand his exemption from suffering that dreadful wrath of God, which he foresaw to be now at hand. For as the coming of the cup to a man doth, in scripture phrase, note his bearing and suffering of evil, as you find it, Lam. iv. 21 : so, on the contrary, the passing away of the cup, notes freedom from, or escaping those miseries. And so Christ's meaning in this conditional request is, Father, if it be thy will, excuse me from this dreadful wrath. My soul is amazed at it. Is there no way to shun it ? Cannot I be excused? Oh, if it be possible, spare me. This is the meaning of it. But then here is the difficulty, how Christ, who knew God had from everlasting determined he should drink it, who had agreed in the covenant of redemption so to do, who came (as himself acknowledges) for that end into the world, John xviii. 37, who foresaw this hour all along, and professed when he spake of this bloody baptism with which he was to be baptized, that he was " straitened till it was accomplished," Luke xii. 50 ; how, I say, to reconcile all this with such a petition, that now when the cup was delivered to him, it might pass from him, or he excused from suffering ; this is the difficulty. What! did he now repent of his engagement ? Doth he now begin to wish to be disengaged, and that he had never undertaken such a work ? Is that the meaning of it ? No, no, Christ never repented of his engagement to the Father, never was willing to let the burden lie on us, rather than on himself ; there was not such a thought in his holy and faithful heart ; but the resolution of this doubt depends upon another distinction, which will clear his meaning in it.

First, You must distinguish of prayers. Some are absolute and peremptory ; and so to have prayed that the cup might pass, would have been chargeable with such absurdities, as were but now mentioned : others are conditional and submissive prayers, " If it may be, if the Lord please." And such was this, If thou be willing ; if not, I will drink it. But you will say, Christ knew what was the mind of God in that case ; he knew what transactions had of old been between his Father and him ; and therefore though he did not pray absolutely, yet it is strange he would pray conditionally it might pass.

Therefore in the second place, You must distinguish of the natures according to which Christ acted. He acted sometimes as God, and sometimes as man. Here he acted according to his human nature ; simply expressing and manifesting in this request the reluctancy it had at such sufferings : wherein he shewed himself.a true man, in shunning that which is destructive to his nature. As Christ had two distinct natures, so two distinct wills. And (as one well observes) in the life of Christ, there was an intermixture of power and weakness, of the Divine glory and human frailty. At his birth a star shone, but he was laid in a manger. The devil tempted him in the wilderness, but there angels ministered to him. He was caught by the soldiers in the garden, but first made them fall back. So here, as man he feared and shunned death; but as God-man he willingly submitted to it.

"It was (as * Deodatus well expresses it) a purely natural desire, mere man, by which for a short moment he apprehended and shunned death and torments; but quickly recalled himself to obedience, by a deliberate will, to submit himself to God."

In a word, as there was nothing of sin in it, it being a pure and sinless affection of nature; so there was much good in it, and that both as it was a part of his satisfaction for our sin, to suffer inwardly such fears, tremblings, and consternations; and as it was a clear evidence, that he was in all things made like unto his brethren, except sin. And lastly, as it serves notably to express the grievousness and extremity of Christ's sufferings, whose very prospect and appearance, at some distance, was so dreadful to him.

IV. Let us consider the manner how he prayed; and that was,

1. Solitarily. He doth not here pray in the audience of his disciples, as he had done before, but went at a distance from them. He had now private business to transact with God. He left some of them at the entering into the garden; and for Peter, James, and John, who went farther with him than the rest, he bids them remain there, while he went and prayed. He did not desire them to pray with him, or for him; no, he must tread the wine-press alone. Nor will he have them with him, possibly lest it should discourage them to see and hear how he groaned, trembled, and cried, as one in an agony, to his Father.

Reader, there are times and cases, when a christian would not be willing that the dearest and most intimate friend he hath in the world should be privy to what passes between him and his God.

2. It was an humble prayer: that is evident by the postures into which he cast himself; sometimes kneeling, and sometimes prostrate upon his face. He lies in the very dust, lower he cannot fall; and his heart was as low as his body. He is meek and lowly indeed.

3. It was a reiterated prayer; he prays, and then returns to the disciples, as a man in extremity turns every way for comfort:

* Deodati Annot. in Matt. xxvi. 39.

so Christ prays, " Father, let this cup pass," but in that request
the Father hears him not; though as to support he was heard.
Being denied deliverance by his Father, he goes and bemoans
himself to his pensive friends, and complains bitterly to them,
" My soul is exceeding sorrowful, even unto death." He would
ease himself a little, by opening his condition to them; but alas!
they rather increase than ease his burden. For he finds them
asleep, which occasioned that gentle reprehension from him,
" What, could ye not watch with me one hour?" Matt. xxvi.
40. What, not watch with me? Who may expect it from
you more than I? Could you not watch? I am going to die
for you, and cannot you watch with me? What! cannot you
watch with me one hour? Alas! what if I had required great
matters from you? What! not an hour, and that the parting
hour too? Christ finds no ease from them, and back again he
goes to that sad place, which he had stained with a bloody sweat,
and prays to the same purpose again. Oh how he returns upon God again and again, as if he resolved to take no denial!
But, however, considering it must be so, he sweetly falls in with
his Father's will, Thy will be done.

4. And lastly, It was a prayer accompanied with a strange
and wonderful agony: so saith verse 44, " And being in an agony,
he prayed more earnestly; and his sweat was as it were great
drops of blood falling down to the ground." Now he was red
indeed in his apparel, as one that trod the wine-press. Consider
what an extraordinary load pressed his soul at that time, even
such as no mere man felt, or was able to stand under, even the
wrath of a great and terrible God, in the extremity of it. " Who
(saith the prophet Nahum, chap. i. 6) can stand before his indignation? And who can abide in the fierceness of his anger? His
fury is poured out like fire, and the rocks are thrown down by him."
The effects of this wrath, as it fell at this time upon the soul
of Christ in the garden, are largely and very emphatically expressed by the several evangelists. Matthew tells us, his soul
was " exceeding sorrowful, even unto death," Matt. xxvi. 38.
" The word * signifies beset with grief round about." And it
is well expressed by that phrase of the psalmist, " The sorrows
of death compassed me about, the pains of hell got hold upon
me." Mark varies the expression, and gives it us in another
word no less significant and full, " He began to be sore amazed,
and very heavy," Mark xiv. 33. †" Sore amazed, it im-

* Περιλυπος, undequaque tristis.—*Beza.*
† Ἐκθαμβεισθαι, medici vocant horripilationem: και αδημονειν, gra-
vissime angebatur.—*Beza.*

ports so high a degree of consternation and amazement, as when the hair of the head stands up through fear." Luke hath another expression for it in the text; He was in an agony. An agony is the labouring and striving of nature in extremity. And John gives it us in another expression, "Now is my soul troubled," John xii. 27. The original word is a very full word; and it is conceived the latins derive that word which signifies hell, from this, by which Christ's troubles are here expressed.[*] This was the load which oppressed his soul, and so straitened it with fear and grief, that his eyes could not vent or ease sufficiently by tears; but the innumerable pores of his body are set open, to give vent by letting out streams of blood. And yet all this while, no hand of man was upon him. This was but a prelude, as it were, to the conflict that was at hand. Now he stood, as it were, arraigned at God's bar, and had to do immediately with him. And you know " it is a fearful thing to fall into the hands of the living God." The uses of this follow in this order.

Inf. 1. Did Christ pour out his soul to God so ardently in the garden, when the hour of his trouble was at hand? Hence we infer, That prayer is a singular preparative for, and relief under the greatest troubles.

It is a happy circumstance, when troubles find us in the way of our duty. The best posture we can wrestle with afflictions in, is to engage them upon our knees. The naturalist tells us, if a lion find a man prostrate, he will do him no harm. Christ hastened to the garden to pray, when Judas and the soldiers were hastening thither to apprehend him. Oh! when we are nigh to danger, it is good for us to draw nigh to our God. Then should we be urging that seasonable request to God, " Be not far from me, for trouble is near; for there is none to help," Psa. xxii. 11. Woe be to him, whom death or trouble finds afar off from God. And as prayer is the best preparative for troubles, so it is the choicest relief under them. Griefs are eased by groans. You know it is some relief if a man can pour out his complaint into the bosom of a faithful friend, though he can but pity him; how much more to pour out our complaints into the bosom of a faithful God, who can both pity and help us! Luther was wont to call prayers the leeches of his cares and sorrows; they suck out the bad blood. It is the title of Psa. cii. " A prayer for the afflicted, when he is overwhelmed, and poureth out his complaint before the Lord." It is no small ease to open our hearts to God.

To go to God when thou art full of sorrow, when thy heart

<hr>

* Τεταρακται, unde Tartarus, quia terret omnia

is ready to burst within thee, as it was with Christ in this day of his trouble; and say, Father, thus and thus the case stands with thy poor child; and so and so it is with me: I will not go up and down complaining from one creature to another, it is to no purpose to do so; nor yet will I leave my complaint upon myself; but I will tell thee, Father, how the case stands with me; for to whom should children make their complaint, but to their Father? Lord, I am oppressed, undertake for me. What thinkest thou, reader, of this? Is it relieving to a sad soul? Yes, yes; if thou be a christian that hast had any experience this way, thou wilt say there is nothing like it; thou wilt bless God for appointing such an ordinance as prayer, and say, Blessed be God for prayer: I know not what I should have done, nor how in all the world I should have waded through the troubles I have passed, if it had not been for the help of prayer.

2. Did Christ withdraw from the disciples to seek God by prayer? Thence it follows, That the company of the best men is not always seasonable. Peter, James, and John, were three excellent men, and yet Christ saith to them, Tarry ye here, while I go and pray yonder. The society of men is useful in its season, but no better than a burden out of season. I have read of a good man, that when his stated time for closet prayer was come, he would say to the company that were with him, whoever they were, "Friends, I must beg your excuse for a while, there is a Friend waits to speak with me." The company of a good man is good, but it ceases to be so, when it hinders the enjoyment of better company. One hour with God is to be preferred to a thousand days' enjoyment of the best men on earth. If thy dearest friends in the world intrude unseasonably between thee and thy God, it is neither rude nor unfriendly to bid them give place to better company; I mean, to withdraw from them, as Christ did from the disciples, to enjoy an hour with God alone. In public and private duties we may admit of the company of others to join with us; and if they be such as fear God, the more the better: but in secret duties, Christ and thou must whisper it over between yourselves; and then the company of the wife of thy bosom, or thy friend, that is as thine own soul, would not be welcome. "When thou prayest, enter into thy closet; and when thou hast shut thy door, pray to thy Father which is in secret," Matt. vi. 6. It is as much as if Christ had said, See all clear; be sure to retire into as great privacy as may be; let no ear but God's hear what thou hast to say to him. This is at once a good note of sincerity, and a great help to spiritual liberty and freedom with God.

3. Did Christ go to God thrice upon the same account? Thence learn, That christians should not be discouraged, though they have sought God once and again, and no answer of peace comes. Christ was not heard the first time, and he goes a second: he was not answered the second, he goes the third and last time, yet was not answered in the thing he desired, namely, that the cup might pass from him; and yet he has no hard thoughts of God, but resolves his will into his Father's. If God deny you in the things you ask, he deals no otherwise with you than he did with Christ. "O my God, (saith he,) I cry in the day-time, but thou hearest not; and in the night, and am not silent." Yet he justifies God, "but thou art holy," Psa. xxii. 3. Christ was not heard in the thing he desired, and yet heard in that he feared, Heb. v. 7. The cup did not pass as he desired, but God upheld him, and enabled him to drink it. He was heard as to support, he was not heard as to exemption from suffering: his will was expressed conditionally; and therefore though he had not the thing he so desired, yet his will was not crossed by the denial.

But now, when *we* have a suit depending before the throne of grace, and cry to God once and again, and no answer comes; how do our hands hang down, and our spirits wax feeble! Then we complain with the church, "When I cry and shout, he shutteth out my prayers. Thou coverest thyself with a cloud, that our prayers cannot pass through," Lam. iii. 8. 44. Then, with Jonah, we conclude "we are cast out of his sight." Alas! we judge by sense according to what we see and feel; and cannot live by faith on God, when he seems to hide himself, put us off, and refuse our requests. It calls for an Abraham's faith, to "believe against hope, giving glory to God." If we cry, and no answer comes presently, our carnal reason draws a headlong, hasty conclusion. Surely I must expect no answer: God is angry with my prayers. The seed of prayer hath lain so long under the clods, and it appears not; surely it is lost, I shall hear no more of it.

Our prayers may be heard, though their answer be for the present suspended. As David acknowledged, when he coolly considered the matter, "I said in my haste, I am cut off from before thine eyes; nevertheless thou heardest the voice of my supplication, when I cried unto thee," Psa. xxxi. 22. No, no, christian; a prayer sent up in faith, according to the will of God, cannot be lost, though it be delayed. We may say of it as David said of Saul's sword, and Jonathan's bow, that they never returned empty.

4. Was Christ so earnest in prayer, that he prayed himself into a very agony?   Let the people of God blush to think how unlike their spirits are to Christ, as to their praying frames.

Oh what lively, sensible, quick, deep, and tender apprehensions and sense of those things about which he prayed, had Christ! Being in an agony, he prayed the more earnestly. I do not say Christ is imitable in this; no, but his fervour in prayer is a pattern for us, and serves severely to rebuke the laziness, dulness, torpor, formality, and stupidity, that are in our prayers. How often do we bring the sacrifice of the dead before the Lord! how often do our lips move, and our hearts stand still! Oh how unlike Christ are we! his prayers were pleading prayers; full of mighty arguments and fervent affections. Oh that his people were in this more like him!

5. Was Christ in such an agony before any hand of man was upon him, merely from the apprehensions of the wrath of God, with which he now contested?   Then surely it is a dreadful thing to fall into the hands of the living God; for our God is a consuming fire.   Ah, what is divine wrath, that Christ staggered when the cup came to him! Could not he bear, and dost thou think to bear it? Did Christ sweat clots of blood at it, and dost thou make light of it? Poor man, if it staggered him, it will confound thee.   If it made him groan, it will make thee howl eternally. Come, sinner, come; dost thou make light of the threatenings of the wrath of God against sin? Dost thou think there is no such matter in it, as these zealous preachers make of it? Come, look here upon my text, which shows thee the face of the Son of God full of purple drops under the sense and apprehension of it. Hark how he cries, " Father, if it be possible, let this cup pass." Oh any thing of punishment rather than this.   Hear what he tells the disciples; " My soul (saith he) is sorrowful even to death: amazed, and very heavy."   But fools make a mock at sin, and the threatenings that lie against it.

6. Did Christ meet death with such a heavy heart? Let the hearts of christians be the lighter for this, when they come to die. The bitterness of death was all squeezed into Christ's cup. He was made to drink up the very dregs of it, that so our death might be the sweeter to us. Alas! there is nothing now left in death that is frightful or troublesome, beside the pain of dissolution, that natural evil of it. I remember it is related of one of the martyrs, that being observed to be exceedingly cheerful and merry when he came to the stake, one asked him, What was the reason his heart was so light, when death (and that in such a

terrible form too) was before him? Oh, said he, my heart is so light at my death, because Christ's was so heavy at his death.

7. To conclude, What cause have all the saints to love their dear Lord Jesus with an abounding love! Christian, open the eyes of thy faith, and fix them upon Christ, as he lay in the garden. He that suffered for us more than any creature ever did or could, may well challenge more love than all the creatures in the world. Oh what hath he suffered, and suffered upon thy account! it was thy pride, earthliness, sensuality, unbelief, hardness of heart, that laid on more weight in that day.

SERMON XXIII.

THE FIRST PREPARATION FOR CHRIST'S DEATH ON HIS ENEMIES'
PART, BY THE TREASON OF JUDAS.

MATT. XXVI. 47—49.

AND WHILE HE YET SPAKE, LO, JUDAS, ONE OF THE TWELVE, CAME, AND
WITH HIM A GREAT MULTITUDE WITH SWORDS AND STAVES, FROM THE
CHIEF PRIESTS AND ELDERS OF THE PEOPLE. NOW HE THAT BETRAYED
HIM GAVE THEM A SIGN, SAYING, WHOMSOEVER I SHALL KISS, THAT SAME
IS HE: HOLD HIM FAST. AND FORTHWITH HE CAME TO JESUS, AND SAID,
HAIL, MASTER; AND KISSED HIM.

THE former sermons give you an account how Christ improved
every moment of his time, with diligence, to make himself ready
for his death. He has commended his charge to the Father,
instituted the blessed memorial of his death, poured out his soul
to God in the garden, with respect to the grievous sufferings he
should undergo; and now he is ready, and waits for the coming
of the enemies. And think you that they were idle on their
parts? No, no, their malice made them restless. They had
agreed with Judas to betray him. Under his conduct, a band
of soldiers was sent to apprehend him. The hour, so long expected, is come. For "while he yet spake, lo, Judas, one of the
twelve, came, and with him a great multitude, with swords and
staves."

These words contain the first preparative act, on their part,
for the death of Christ, even to betray him, and that by one of
his own disciples. Now they execute what they had plotted,
ver. 14, 15. And in this paragraph you have an account, 1.
Of the traitor, who he was. 2. Of the treason, what he did.
3. Of the manner of its execution, how it was contrived and
effected. Lastly, Of the time, when they put this hellish plot in
execution.

1. We have here a description of the traitor: and it is remarkable how carefully the several evangelists have described
him, both by his name, surname, and office, " Judas—Judas
Iscariot—Judas Iscariot, one of the twelve;" that he might not
be mistaken for Jude or Judas the apostle. God is tender of
the names and reputations of his upright servants. His office,

" one of the twelve," is added to aggravate the fact, and to show how that prophecy was accomplished in him, " Yea, mine own familiar friend, in whom I trusted, which did eat of my bread, hath lifted up his heel against me," Psa. xli. 9. Lo, this was the traitor, and this was his name and office.

2. You have a description of the treason, or an account of what this man did. He led an armed multitude to the place where Christ was, gave them a signal to discover him, and encouraged them to lay hands on him, and hold him fast. This the devil put into his heart, working upon that principle, or lust of covetousness, which was predominant there. What will not a carnal heart attempt, if the devil suit a temptation to the predominant lust, and God withhold restraining grace !

3. You have here the way and manner in which the hellish plot was executed. It was managed both with force and with fraud. He comes with a multitude, armed with swords and staves, in case they should meet with any resistance. And he comes to him with a kiss, which was his signal, lest they should mistake the man. For they aimed neither at small nor great, save only at the King of Israel, the King of glory. Here was much ado, you see, to take a harmless Lamb, that did not once start from them, but freely offered himself to them.

4. And lastly, When this treasonable design was executed upon Christ. It was while he stood among his disciples, exhorting them to prayer and watchfulness, dropping heavenly and most seasonable counsels upon them. " While he yet spake, lo, Judas, and with him a multitude, came with swords and staves." Surely then it is no better than a Judas's plot, to disturb and afflict the servants of God in the discharge of their duties. This was the traitor and his treason; thus it was executed and at this time. Hence we observe,

> DOCT. THAT IT WAS THE LOT OF OUR LORD JESUS CHRIST, TO BE BETRAYED INTO THE HANDS OF HIS MORTAL ENEMIES, BY THE ASSISTANCE OF A FALSE AND PRETENDED FRIEND.

Look, as Joseph was betrayed and sold by his brethren ; David by Ahithophel, his old friend ; Samson by Delilah, that lay in his bosom ; so Christ by Judas, one of the twelve ; a man, his friend, his familiar, that had been so long conversant with him : he that by profession had lifted up his hand to Christ, now by treason lifts up his heel against him.

In the point before us, we will, I. Consider Judas, according to that eminent station and place he had under Christ.   II. We will consider his treason, according to the several aggravations of it. III. We will inquire into the cause or motives that put him upon such a dreadful, hellish design as this was. IV. And lastly, we will view the issue, and see the event of this treason, both as to Christ and as to himself. And then apply it.

I. As for the person that did this, he was very eminent by reason of the dignity to which Christ had raised him. For, he was one of the twelve; one retained not in a more general, and common, but in the nearest, and most intimate and honourable relation and service to Jesus Christ. There were in the time of Christ several sorts and ranks of persons that had relation to him. There were secret disciples; men that believed, but kept their stations, and abode with their relations in their callings. There were seventy also whom Christ sent forth; but none of these were so much with Christ or so eminent in respect of their place, as the twelve; they were Christ's family, day and night conversant with him: it was the highest dignity that was conferred upon any: and of this number was Judas.

And being one of the twelve, he was daily conversant with Christ; often joined with him in prayer, often sat at his feet, hearing the gracious words that came out of his mouth. It was one of Augustine's three wishes, that he had seen Christ in the flesh: Judas not only saw him, but dwelt with him, travelled with him, and eat and drank with him. And during the whole time of his abode with him, all Christ's carriage towards him was very obliging and winning; yea, such was the condescension of Christ to this wretched man, that he washed his feet, and that but a little before he betrayed him.

In some respect, he was preferred to the rest. For he had not only a joint commission with them to preach the gospel to others, (though, poor unhappy wretch, himself became a castaway,) but he had a peculiar office, he bare the bag, that is, he was almoner, or the steward of the family, to take care to provide for the necessary accommodations of Christ and them. Now who could ever have suspected, that such a man as this should have sold the blood of Christ for a little money? that ever he should have proved a perfidious traitor to his Lord, who had called him, honoured him, and carried himself so tenderly towards him?

II. But what did this man do? and what are the just aggravations of his fact? He most basely and unworthily sold and delivered Christ into his enemies' hands, to be put to death; and all this for thirty pieces of silver. Blush, O heavens, and be astonished, O earth, at this! In this fact, most black and horrid aggravations appear.

Judas had seen the majesty of a God in him whom he betrayed. He had seen the miracles that Christ wrought, which none but Christ could do. He knew that by the finger of God he had raised the dead, cast out devils, and healed the sick. He could not but see the beams of Divine majesty shining in his very face, in his doctrine, and in his life.

Yea, he committed this wickedness after personal warnings and premonitions given him by Christ; he had often told them in general, that one of them should betray him, Mark xiv. 18. He also denounced a dreadful woe upon him that should do it: " The Son of man indeed goeth, as it is written of him; but woe to that man by whom the Son of man is betrayed! good had it been for that man if he had never been born," ver. 21. This was spoken in Judas's presence. And one would have thought so dreadful a doom as Christ passed upon the man that should attempt this, should have affrighted him far enough from the thoughts of such a wickedness. Nay, Christ came nearer to him than this, and told him he was the man: for when Judas (who was the last that put the question to Christ) asked him, " Master, is it I ?" Christ's answer imports as much as a plain affirmation, " Thou hast said," Matt. xxvi. 25.

Moreover, he did it not out of a blind zeal against Christ, as many of his other enemies did; of whom it is said, that " had they known him, they would not have crucified the Lord of glory," 1 Cor. ii. 8 : but he did it for money. " What will ye give me, (saith he,) and I will betray him ?" Matt. xxvi. 15.

He sells him, and he sells him at a low rate too; which showed how vile an esteem he had of Christ. He is content to part with him for thirty pieces of silver. If these pieces, or shekels, were the shekels of the sanctuary, they amounted but to three pounds fifteen shillings. But it is supposed they were the common shekels, which were mostly used in buying and selling; and then his price, that he put upon the Saviour of the world, was but one pound seventeen shillings and sixpence. A goodly price (as the prophet calls it) that he was valued at ! Zech. xi. 12, 13. I confess, it is a wonder he asked no more; knowing how much they longed for his blood; and that they offered no more for him. But how then should the scriptures have been fulfilled? Oh what a sale was this! to sell that blood, which all the gold and silver in the world is not worth one drop of, for a trifle ! Still the wickedness of the fact rises higher and higher.

He left Christ in a most heavenly and excellent employment, when he went to make this soul-undoing bargain. For if he went away from the table, as some think, then he left Christ instituting and administering those heavenly signs of his body and blood: there he saw, or might have seen, the bloody work he was going about, acted as in a figure before him. If he sat out that ordinance, as others suppose he did, then he left Christ singing a heavenly hymn, and preparing to go where Judas was preparing to meet him.

Besides, what he did was not done by the persuasions of any. The high priest sent not for him, and without doubt was surprised when he came to him on such an errand. For it could never enter into any of their hearts, that any of his own disciples could ever be drawn into a confederacy against him. No, he went as a volunteer, offering himself to this work: which still heightens the sin, and makes it out of measure sinful.

The manner in which he executes his treasonable design adds further malignity to the fact. He comes to Christ with fawning words and carriage, " Hail, Master, and kissed him." Here is honey in the tongue, and poison in the heart. Let us inquire,

III. The cause and motives of this wickedness, how he came to attempt and perpetrate such a villany. Maldonate the jesuit criminates the protestant divines, for affirming that God had a hand in ordering and overruling this fact. But we say, that Satan and his own lust was the impulsive cause of it : that God, as it was a wicked treason, permitted it ; and as it was a delivering Christ to death, was not only the permitter, but the wise and holy director and orderer of it, and by the wisdom of his providence overruled it to the great good and advantage of the church. Satan inspired the motion, " Then entered Satan into Judas, surnamed Iscariot, and he went his way," &c. Luke xxii. 3, 4 ; his own lusts, like dry tinder, kindled presently : his heart was covetous. They covenanted to give him money, and he promised, &c. ver. 5, 6.

The holy God disposed and ordered all this to the singular benefit and good of his people : they did whatsoever " his hand and counsel had before determined to be done," Acts iv. 28. And by this determinate counsel of God, he was taken and slain, Acts ii. 23. Yet this in no way excuses the wickedness of the instruments : for what they did, was done from the power of their own lusts, most wickedly ; what He did, was done in the unsearchable depth of his own wisdom, most holy. God knows how to serve his own ends by the very sins of men, and yet have no communion at all in the sin he so overrules. Judas minded nothing but his own advantage, to get money :. God permitted that lust to work, but overruled the issue to his own eternal glory, and the salvation of our souls.

IV. And lastly, But what was the end and issue of this fact? As to Christ, it was his death; for the hour being come, he doth not meditate an escape, nor put forth the power of his Godhead to deliver himself out of their hands. Indeed he showed what he could do, when he made them go back and stagger with a word. He could have obtained more than twelve legions of angels to have been his life-guard; one of whom had been sufficient to have coped with all the roman legions: but how then should the scriptures have been fulfilled, or our salvation accomplished?

And what did Judas get as a reward of his wickedness? It ended in the ruin both of his soul and body. For immediately a death-pang of despair seized his conscience; which was so intolerable, that he ran to the halter for a remedy; and so falling headlong, he burst asunder, and all his bowels gushed out, Acts i. 18. As for his soul, it went to its own place, ver. 25, even the place appointed for the son of perdition, as Christ calls him, John xvii. 12. His name is to this day, and shall be to all generations, a bye-word, a proverb of reproach. This was his end; we will next improve it.

1. Hence in the first place we learn, that the greatest professors had need to be jealous of their own hearts, and look well to the grounds and principles of their profession. O professors, look to your foundation, and build not upon the sand, as this poor creature did. That is sound advice indeed, which the apostle gives, " Let him that thinks he standeth, take heed lest he fall," 1 Cor. x. 12. Oh beware of a loose foundation. If you begin your profession as Judas did, no wonder if it shall end as his did.

Beware therefore that you hold not the truth in unrighteousness. Judas did so: he knew much, but lived not up to what he knew, for he was still of a worldly spirit in the height of his profession. His knowledge never had any saving influence upon his heart; he preached to others, but he himself was a castaway. He had much light, but still walked in darkness. He had no knowledge to do himself good.

Beware you live not in a course of secret sin. Judas did so, and that was his ruin. He made a profession indeed, and carried it smoothly, but he was a thief, John xii. 6. He made no conscience of committing sin, so he could but cover and hide it from men. This helped on his ruin, and so it will thine, reader, if thou be guilty herein. A secret way of sinning, under the covert of profession, will either break out at last to the observation of men, or else slide thee down insensibly to hell, and leave thee there only this comfort, that nobody at present shall know thou art there.

Beware of hypocritical pretences of religion to accommodate self-ends. Judas was a man that had notable skill this way. He had a mind to fill his own purse, by the sale of that costly ointment which Mary bestowed upon our Saviour's feet. And what a neat cover had he fitted for it ; Why, saith he, " this might have been sold for three hundred pence, and given to the poor." Here was charity to the poor, or rather poor charity ; for this was only a blind to his base self-ends. O christian, be plain-hearted, take heed of craft and cunning in matters of religion.

Beware of self-confidence. Judas was a very confident man of himself. " Last of all, Judas said, Master, is it I ?" Matt. xxvi. 25. But he that was last in the suspicion was first in the transgression. " He that trusteth in his own heart is a fool," saith Solomon, Prov. xxviii. 26. It will be your wisdom to keep a jealous eye upon your own hearts, and still suspect their fairest pretences.

If you will not do as Judas did, nor come to such an end as he did, take heed that you live not unprofitably under the means of grace. Judas had the best means of grace that ever man enjoyed. He heard Christ himself preach, he joined often with him in prayer, but he was never the better for it all ; it was but as the watering of a dead stick, which will never make it grow, but rot it the sooner. Oh it is a sad sign, and a sad sin too, when men and women live under the gospel from year to year, and are never the better. I warn you to beware of these evils, all ye that profess religion. Let these footsteps by which Judas went down to his own place, terrify you from following him in them.

2. Learn hence also, that eminent knowledge and profession put a special and eminent aggravation upon sin. " Judas Iscariot, one of the twelve." Poor wretch ! better had it been for him, if he had never been numbered with them, nor enlightened with so much knowledge as he was endowed with : for this rent his conscience to pieces, when he reflected on what he had done, and presently ran into the gulf of despair. To sin against clear light, is to sin with a high hand. Those that had a hand in the death of Christ, through mistake and ignorance, were capable to receive the pardon of their sin by that blood

they so shed, Acts iii. 19.   Take heed therefore of abusing knowledge, and putting a force upon conscience.

3. Learn hence, that unprincipled professors will sooner or later become shameful apostates.   Judas was an unprincipled professor, and see what he came to ! Ambition invited Simon Magus to the profession of Christ, he would be " some great one," and how quickly did the rottenness of his principles discover itself in the ruin of his profession ! That which wants a root, must needs wither, Matt. xiii. 20, 21.   That which is the predominant interest, will prevail, and sway with us in the day of our trial.   Hear me, all you that profess religion, and have given your names to Christ ; if that profession be not built upon a solid and real work of grace in your hearts, you shall never honour religion, nor save your souls by it.   Oh it is your union with Christ, that, like a spring, maintains your profession.   So much as you are united to Christ, so much constancy, steadiness, and evenness, you will manifest in the duties of religion, and no more.

O brethren, when he that professes Christ for company, shall be left alone as Paul was ; when he that makes religion a stirrup to help himself into the saddle of preferment and honour, shall see that he is so advanced to be drawn forth into Christ's camp and endure the heat of the day, and not to take his pleasure ; in a word, when he shall see all things about him discouraging and threatening ; his dearest interest on earth exposed for religion's sake ; and he hath no faith to balance his present losses with his future hopes ; I say, when it comes to this, you shall then see the rottenness of many hearts discovered, and Judas may have many fellows, who will part with Christ for the world, as he did.   Oh therefore look well to your foundation.

4. Moreover, in this example of Judas you may read this truth ; that men and women are never in more imminent danger, than when they meet with temptations exactly suited to their master-lusts, to their own iniquity.   Oh pray, pray that ye may be kept from a violent suitable temptation.   Satan knows that when a man is tried here, he falls by the root.   The love of this world was all along Judas's master-sin, this was his predominant lust.   The devil found out this, and suited it with a temptation which fully hit his humour, and it carried him immediately.   This is the dangerous crisis of the soul.   Now you shall see what it is, and what it will do.   Put money before Judas, and presently you shall see what the man is.

5. Hence, in like manner, we are instructed, that no man knows where he shall stop, when he first engages himself in a way of sin.

Wickedness, as well as holiness, is not born in its full strength, but grows up to it by insensible degrees. So did the wickedness of Judas. I believe, he himself never thought he should have done what he did : and if any should have told him, in the first beginning of his profession, Thou shalt sell the blood of Christ for money, thou shalt deliver him most perfidiously into their hands that seek his life ; he would have answered as Hazael did to Elisha, " What, is thy servant a dog, that he should do this thing?" 2 Kings viii. 13. His wickedness first discovered itself in murmuring and discontent, taking a pique at some small matters against Christ, as you may find, by comparing John vi. from ver. 60 to 70, with John xii. from ver. 3 to 9. But see to what it grows at last. That lust or temptation that at first is but a little cloud as big as a man's hand, may quickly overspread the whole heaven. Our engaging in sin is as the motion of a stone down-hill, *vires acquirit eundo*, " it strengthens itself by going;" and the longer it runs, the more violent. Beware of the smallest beginnings of temptations. No wise man will neglect or slight the smallest spark of fire, especially if he see it among many barrels of gunpowder. You carry gunpowder about you, oh take heed of sparks.

6. Did Judas sell Christ for money? What a potent conqueror is the love of this world ! How many hath it cast down wounded ! What great professors have been dragged at its chariot wheels as its captives ! Hymeneus and Philetus, Ananias and Sapphira, Demas and Judas, with thousands and ten thousands, since their days, led away in triumph. It " drowns men in perdition," 1 Tim. vi. 9. In that pit of perdition this son of perdition fell, and never rose more. O you that so court and pursue it, that so love and admire it, make a stand here ; pause a little upon this example ; consider to what it brought this poor wretch, whom I have presented to you dead, eternally dead, by the mortal wound that the love of this world gave him : it destroyed both soul and body. Pliny tells us, that the mermaids delight to be in green meadows, into which they draw men by their enchanting voices ; but, saith he, there always lie heaps of dead men's bones by them. A lively emblem of a bewitching world ! Good had it been for many professors of religion, if they had never known what the riches, and honours, and pleasures of this world meant.

7. Did Judas fancy so much happiness in a little money, that he would sell Christ to get it? Learn then, that wherein men promise themselves much pleasure and contentment in the way of sin, may prove the greatest curse and misery to them that

ever befell them in the world. Judas thought it was a fine thing to get money; he fancied much happiness in it; but how sick was his conscience as soon as he had swallowed it! Oh take it again! saith he. It griped him to the heart. He knows not what to do, to rid himself of that money. Give me children, saith Rachel, or I die: she hath children, and they prove her death. Oh mortify your fancies to the world; put no necessity upon riches. "They that will be rich, fall into temptations, and many hurtful lusts, which drown men in perdition," 1 Tim. vi. 9. You may have your desires gratified with a curse. He that brings home a pack of fine clothes infected with the plague, has no such great bargain of it, how cheap soever he bought them.

8. Was there one, and but one of the twelve, that proved a traitor to Christ? Learn thence, that it is a most unreasonable thing to be prejudiced against religion, and the sincere professors of it, because some that profess it prove naught and vile.

Should the eleven suffer for one Judas? Alas, they abhorred both the traitor and his treason. As well might the high priest and his servants have condemned Peter, John, and all the rest, whose souls abhorred the wickedness. If Judas proved a vile wretch, yet there were eleven to one that remained upright: if Judas proved naught, it was not his profession made him so, but his hypocrisy; he never learned it from Christ. If religion must be charged with all the miscarriages of its professors, then there is no pure religion in the world. Name that religion among the professors whereof there is not one Judas. Take heed, reader, of prejudices against godliness on this account. The design of the devil, without doubt, is to undo thee eternally by them. "Woe to the world because of offences," Matt. xviii. 7. Blessed is he that is not offended at Christ.

9. Did Judas, one of the twelve, do so? Learn thence, that a drop of grace is better than a sea of gifts. Gifts have some excellency in them, but the way of grace is the more excellent way, 1 Cor. xii. 31. There is many a learned head in hell. Gifts are the gold that beautifies the temple; but grace is as the temple which sanctifies the gold. One tear, one groan, one breathing of an upright heart, is more than the tongues of angels.

Poor christian, thou art troubled that thou canst not speak and pray so neatly, so fluently as some others can; but canst thou go into a corner, and there pour out thy soul affectionately, though not rhetorically, to thy Father? trouble not thyself. It is better for thee to feel one divine impression from God upon thy heart, than to have ten thousand fine notions floating in thy head.

10. Did the devil win the consent of Judas to such a design as this? Could he get no other but the hand of an apostle to assist him? Learn hence, that the policy of Satan lies much in the choice of his instruments he works by. No bird (saith one) like a living bird to tempt others into the net. Austin told an ingenious young scholar, "The devil coveted him for an ornament."* He knows he hath a foul cause to manage, and therefore will get the fairest hand he can, to manage it with the less suspicion.

11. Did Judas, one of the twelve, do this? Then certainly, christians may approve and join with such men on earth, whose faces they shall never see in heaven. The apostles held communion a long time with this man, and did not suspect him. Oh please not yourselves therefore, that you have communion with the saints here, and that they think and speak charitably of you. "All the churches shall know, (saith the Lord,) that I am he that searcheth the heart and reins, and will give to every man as his work shall be," Rev. ii. 23. In heaven we shall meet many that we never thought to meet there, and miss many that we were confident we should see there.

12. Lastly, Did Judas, one of the twelve, a man so favoured, raised, and honoured by Christ, do this? Cease then from man, be not too confident, but beware of men. "Trust ye not in a friend, put no confidence in a guide, keep the door of thy lips from her that lieth in thy bosom," Mic. vii. 5. Not that there is no sincerity in any man; but there is so much hypocrisy in many men, and so much corruption in the best of men, that we may not be too confident, nor lay too great a stress upon any man. Peter's modest expression of Silvanus is a pattern for us; "Silvanus, a faithful brother unto you, as I suppose," 1 Pet. v. 12. The time shall come, saith Christ, that "brother shall betray brother to death," Matt. x. 21. Charity for others may be your duty, but too great confidence may be your snare. Fear what others may do, but fear thyself more.

* Capit abs te ornari diabolus.

SERMON XXIV.

THE SECOND AND THIRD PREPARATIVES FOR THE DEATH OF
CHRIST, BY HIS ILLEGAL TRIAL AND CONDEMNATION.

LUKE XXIII. 23, 24.

AND THEY WERE INSTANT WITH LOUD VOICES, REQUIRING THAT HE MIGHT
BE CRUCIFIED. AND THE VOICES OF THEM AND OF THE CHIEF PRIESTS
PREVAILED. AND PILATE GAVE SENTENCE THAT IT SHOULD BE AS THEY
REQUIRED.

JUDAS has made good his promise to the high priest, and delivered Jesus a prisoner into their hands. These wolves of the
evening no sooner seize the Lamb of God, but they thirst after
his precious innocent blood; their revenge and malice admit no
delay, as fearing a rescue by the people.

When Herod had taken Peter, he committed him to prison,
" intending after Easter to bring him forth to the people," Acts
xii. 4. But these men cannot sleep till they have Christ's blood,
therefore the preparation of the passover being come, they resolve in all haste to destroy him ; yet, lest it should look like a
downright murder, it shall be formalized with a trial. This his
trial and condemnation are the two last acts by which they prepared for his death, and are both contained in this context ; in
which we may observe, the indictment, and the sentence to which
the judge proceeded.

In the indictment drawn up against Christ, they accuse him
of many things, but can prove nothing. However, what is
wanting in evidence, shall be supplied with clamour and importunity. For " They were instant with loud voices, requiring
that he might be crucified ; and their voices prevailed :" when
they can neither prove the sedition and blasphemy they charged
him with, then, Crucify him, crucify him, must serve the turn,
instead of all witnesses and proofs.

The sentence pronounced upon him ; Pilate gave sentence,
that it should be as they required : from which we may observe
these two conclusions.

1. THAT THE TRIAL OF CHRIST FOR HIS LIFE WAS
MANAGED MOST MALICIOUSLY AND ILLEGALLY
AGAINST HIM, BY HIS UNRIGHTEOUS JUDGES.

2. THOUGH NOTHING COULD BE PROVED AGAINST OUR LORD JESUS CHRIST WORTHY OF DEATH, OR OF BONDS; YET HE WAS CONDEMNED TO BE NAILED TO THE CROSS, AND THERE TO HANG TILL HE DIED.

I shall handle these two points distinctly in their order, beginning with the first.

Reader, here thou mayst see the Judge of all the world standing himself to be judged; he that shall judge the world in righteousness, judged most unrighteously; he that shall one day come to the throne of judgment, attended with thousands, and ten thousands of angels and saints, standing as a prisoner at man's bar, and there denied the common right which a thief or murderer might claim, and is commonly given them.

To manifest the illegality of Christ's trial, let the following particulars be carefully weighed.

1. That he was inhumanly abused, both in words and actions, before the court met, or any examination was taken of the fact: for as soon as they had taken him, they forthwith bound him, and led him away to the high priest's house, Luke xxii. 54. And there they that held him, mocked him, smote him, blindfolded him, struck him on the face, and bid him prophesy who smote him; and many other things blasphemously spake they against him, ver. 63—65. How illegal and barbarous a thing was this? When they were but binding Paul with thongs, he thought himself abused contrary to law, and asked the centurion that stood by, "Is it lawful for you to scourge a man that is a roman, and uncondemned?" *q. d.* Is this legal? What! punish a man first, and judge him afterwards! But Christ was not only bound, but shamefully ill-treated by them all that night, dealing with him as the lords of the philistines did with Samson, to whom it was sport to abuse him. No rest had Jesus that night; oh it was a sad night to him: and this under Caiaphas's own roof.

2. As he was inhumanly abused before he was tried, so he was examined and judged by a court that had no authority to try him: "As soon as it was day, the elders of the people, and the chief priests, and the scribes came together and led him into their council," Luke xxii. 66. This was the ecclesiastical court, the great sanhedrim, which according to its first constitution, should consist of seventy grave, honourable, and learned men; to whom were to be referred all doubtful matters, too hard for inferior courts to decide. And these were to judge impartially and uprightly for God, as men in whom was the Spirit of God,

according to God's counsel to Moses, Numb. xi. 16, &c.   In this court the righteous and innocent might expect relief and protection.   And that is conceived to be the meaning of Christ's words, " It cannot be that a prophet perish out of Jerusalem," Luke xiii. 33 ; that is, there righteousness and innocency may expect protection.   But now, contrary to the first constitution, it consisted of a pack of malicious scribes and pharisees, men full of revenge, malice, and all unrighteousness : and over these Caiaphas (a head fit for such a body) at this time presided. And though there were still some face of a court among them, yet their power was so abridged by the romans, that they could not hear and determine, judge and condemn in capital matters, as formerly.   For as * Josephus their own historian informs us, Herod in the beginning of his reign took away this power from them ; and that scripture seems to confirm it, " It is not lawful for us to put any man to death," John xviii. 31 ; and therefore they bring him to Pilate's bar.   He also understood him to be a galilean ; and Herod being tetrarch of Galilee, and at that time in Jerusalem, he is sent to him, and by him remitted to Pilate.

3. As he was at first heard and judged by a court that had no authority to judge him ; so when he stood at Pilate's bar, he was accused of perverting the nation, and denying tribute to Cesar, than which nothing was more notoriously false.   For as all his doctrine was pure and heavenly, and malice itself could not find a flaw in it ; so he was always observant of the laws under which he lived, and scrupulous of giving the least just offence to the civil powers.   Yea, he not only paid the tribute himself, though he might have pleaded exemption, but charged it upon others as their duty so to do, " Give unto Cesar the things that are Cesar's," Matt. xxii. 21.   And yet with such palpable untruths is Christ charged.

4. Yea, and what is more abominable and unparalleled; to compass their malicious designs, they industriously labour to suborn false witnesses to take away his life, not sticking at the grossest perjury, and manifest injustice, so they might destroy him.   So you read, " Now the chief priests and elders, and all the council, sought false witnesses against Jesus to put him to death," Matt. xxvi. 59.   Abominable wickedness ! for such men, and so many, to complot to shed the blood of the innocent, by known and studied perjury ! What will not malice against Christ transport men to ?

5. Moreover, the conduct of the court was most insolent and

* Antiq. lib. 14. cap. 205.

base towards him during the trial; for whilst he stood before them as a prisoner, yet uncondemned, sometimes they are angry at him for his silence ! and when he speaks, and that pertinently to the point, they smite him on the mouth for speaking, and scoff at what he speaks.   To some of their light, frivolous, and insnaring questions, he is silent, not for want of an answer, but because he heard nothing worthy of one; and to fulfil what the prophet Isaiah had long before predicted of him, " He was oppressed, and he was afflicted, yet he opened not his mouth : he is brought as a lamb to the slaughter, and as a sheep before her shearers is dumb, so he opened not his mouth," Isa. liii. 7. As also to leave us an example when to speak, and when to be silent, when we for his name's sake shall be brought before governors : for such reasons as these he sometimes answers not a word, and then they are ready to condemn him for his silence.   " Answerest thou nothing? (saith the high-priest,) what is it that these witness against thee?" Matt. xxvi. 62. " Hearest thou not how many things they witness against thee?" saith Pilate, Matt. xxvii. 13.

And when he makes his defence in words of truth and soberness, they smite him for speaking : " And when he had thus spoken, one of the officers which stood by, struck Jesus with the palm of his hand, saying, Answerest thou the high priest so?" John xviii. 22.   And what had he spoken to exasperate them? What he said was but this, when they would have had him insnare himself with his own lips : " Jesus answered, I spake openly to the world, I ever taught in the synagogue, and in the temple, whither the jews always resort, and in secret have I said nothing. Why askest thou me? Ask them that heard me, behold, they know what I said." Oh who but himself could have so patiently borne such abuses ! Under all this he stands in perfect innocency and patience, making no other return to that wretch that smote him, but this, " If I have spoken evil, bear witness of the evil; but if well, why smitest thou me ? "

6. Lastly, To instance in no more: he is condemned to die by that very mouth which had once and again professed he found no fault in him. He had heard all that could be alleged against him, and saw it was a perfect piece of malice and envy. When they urge Pilate to proceed to sentence him ; " Why, (saith he,) what evil hath he done?" Matt. xxvii. 23. Nay, in the preface to the very sentence itself, he acknowledges him to be a just person : " When Pilate saw he could prevail nothing, but that rather a tumult was made, he took water, and washed his hands before the multitude, and said, I am innocent of the blood of

this just person, see ye to it," Matt. xxvii. 24. Here the innocency of Christ brake out like the sun wading out of a cloud,
convincing the conscience of his judge that he was just ; and yet
he must give sentence on him, for all that, to please the people.

Inference 1. Was Christ thus used when he stood before the
great council, the scribes and elders of Israel? Then surely
" great men are not always wise, neither do the aged understand
judgment," Job xxxii. 9. Here were many great men, many
aged men, many politic men in council ; but not one wise or
good man among them. In this council were men of parts and
learning, men of great abilities, and by so much the more per-
nicious, and able to do mischief. Wickedness in a great or
learned man, is like poison given in wine, the more operative
and deadly. Christ's greatest enemies were such as these.

2. Hence also we learn, that though we are not obliged to
answer every captious, idle, or insnaring question, yet we are
bound faithfully to own and confess the truth, when we are
solemnly called to it.

It is true, Christ was sometimes silent, and as a deaf man
that heard not ; but when the question was solemnly put, " Art
thou the Christ, the Son of the Blessed? Jesus said, I am,"
Mark xiv. 61, 62. He knew that answer would cost his life,
and yet he durst not deny it. On this account the apostle saith,
" he witnessed a good confession before Pontius Pilate," 1 Tim.
vi. 13. Herein Christ hath pointed out the way of our duty,
and by his own example, as well as precept, obliged us to a
sincere confession of him, and his truth, when we are required
lawfully so to do, that is, when we are before a lawful magistrate,
and the questions are not curious or captious ; when we cannot
hold our peace, but our silence will be interpretatively a denying of the truth ; finally, when the glory of God, the honour of
his truth, and the edification of others, are more attainable by
our open confession, than they can be by our silence ; then
must we, with Christ, give direct, plain, sincere answers.

It was the old priscillian error, to allow men to deny or dissemble their profession, when an open confession would infer
danger. But you know what Christ hath said, " Whosoever
shall deny me before men, him will I deny before my Father
which is in heaven," Matt. x. 33. It was a noble saying of
courageous Zuinglius, " What deaths would not I choose,
what punishment would I not undergo ; yea, into what
vault of hell would I not rather choose to be thrown, than to
witness against my conscience?" Truth can never be bought
too dear, nor sold cheap. The Lord Jesus, you see, owns truth

with the imminent and instant hazard of his life. The whole cloud of witnesses have followed him therein, Rev. xiv. 1. We ourselves once openly owned the ways of sin ; and shall we not do as much for Christ, as we then did for the devil ? Did we then glory in our shame, and shall we now be ashamed of our glory ? Do not we hope Christ will own us at the great day ? Why, if we confess him, he also will confess us. Oh think on the reasonableness of this duty.

3. Once more, hence it follows, That to bear the revilings, contradictions, and abuses of men, with a meek, composed, and even spirit, is excellent and Christ-like. He stood before them as a lamb; he rendered not railing for railing; he endured the contradictions of sinners against himself. Imitate Christ in his meekness. He calls you so to do, Matt. xi. 29. This will be convincing to your enemies, comfortable to yourselves, and honourable to religion : and as for your innocency, God will clear it up.

You have heard the illegal trial of Christ, how insolently it was managed against him. Right or wrong, innocent or guilty, his blood is resolved upon ; and if nothing else will do it, menaces and clamours shall constrain Pilate to condemn him.

THAT THOUGH NOTHING COULD BE PROVED AGAINST OUR LORD JESUS CHRIST WORTHY OF DEATH OR OF BONDS, YET WAS HE CONDEMNED TO BE NAILED TO THE CROSS, AND THERE TO HANG TILL HE DIED.

For the explication of this, I shall notice, I. Who gave the sentence. II. Upon whom it was given. III. What sentence it was that was given. IV. In what manner Christ received it.

I. Who, and what was he, that durst attempt such a thing as this ? Why, this was Pilate, who succeeded Valerius Gratus in the presidentship of Judea, (as * Josephus tells us,) in which trust he continued about ten years. This was in the eighth year of his government. Two years after, he was removed from his place and office by Vitellius, president of Syria, for his inhuman murdering of the innocent samaritans. This necessitated him to go to Rome to clear himself before Cesar ; but before he came to Rome, Tiberius was dead, and Caius in his room. Under him, saith † Eusebius, Pilate killed himself. ‡ " He was a man not very friendly or benevolent to the jewish nation,

* Josephus, lib. 18. Ant. Judææ, quarto, ad cap. 7.
† Euseb. Hist. Eccles. lib. 2. cap. 7.
‡ Non admodum amicus Judæorum genti, propterea quod eam suspectam haberet animo erga Cæsarem ; hunc putant sacerdotes commodum fore ipsorum proposito, &c.—*Bucer. in Matt.* xxvii.

but still suspicious of their rebellions and insurrections; this jealous humour the priests and scribes observed, and wrought upon it to compass their design against Christ." Therefore they tell him so often of Christ's sedition, and stirring up the people: and that if he let him go, he is none of Cesar's friends; which very consideration prevailed with him to do what he did. But though he had stood ill in the opinion of Cesar, how durst he attempt such a wickedness as this? What! give judgment against the Son of God? for it is evident, by many circumstances in this trial, that he had many inward fears and convictions upon him, that he was the Son of God. By these he was scared, and sought to release him, John xix. 8. 12, the fear of a Deity fell upon him; his mind was greatly perplexed, and dubious about this prisoner whether he was a God or a man. And yet the fear of Cesar prevailed more than the fear of a Deity; he proceeds to give sentence. See in this predominancy of self-interest, what man will attempt, and perpetrate, to secure and accommodate self.

II. Against whom doth Pilate give sentence? against a malefactor? No, his own mouth once and again acknowledged him innocent. Against a common prisoner? No, but one whose fame no doubt had often reached Pilate's ears, even the wonderful things wrought by him, which none but God could do: one that stood before him as the picture, or rather as the body of innocency and meekness. "Ye have condemned and killed the Just, and he resisteth you not," James v. 6. Now was that word made good, "They gather themselves together against the soul of the righteous, and condemn the innocent blood," Psa. xciv. 21.

III. But what was the sentence that Pilate gave? We have it not in the form in which it was delivered; but the sum of it was, that it should be as they required. Now what did they require? why, Crucify him, crucify him. So that in what formalities soever it was delivered, this was the substance and effect of it, I adjudge Jesus of Nazareth to be nailed to the cross, and there to hang till he be dead. Which sentence against Christ was,

1. A most *unjust* and *unrighteous* sentence; the greatest perversion of judgment and equity that was ever known to the civilized world, since seats of judicature were first set up. What! to condemn him before one accusation was proved against him? And if what they accused him of (that he said he was the Son of God) had been proved, it had been no crime, for he really was so; and therefore no blasphemy in him

to say he was. Pilate should rather have come down from his seat of judgment, and adored him, than sat there to judge him.

2. As it was an unrighteous so it was a *cruel* sentence, delivering up Christ to their wills. This was that misery which David so earnestly deprecated, "O deliver me not over to the will of mine enemies," Psa. xxvii. 12. But Pilate delivers Christ over to the will of his enemies, men full of enmity, rage, and malice. As soon as these wolves had griped their prey, they were not satisfied with that cursed, cruel, and ignominious death of the cross, to which Pilate had adjudged him, but they are resolved he shall die over and over; they will contrive many deaths in one: to this end they presently strip him; scourge him cruelly; array him in scarlet, and mock him; crown him with a bush of platted thorns; fasten that crown upon his head by a blow, which set them deep into his sacred temples; put a reed into his hand for a sceptre, spat in his face, stripped off his mock-robes again; put the cross upon his back, and compelled him to bear it. All this, and much more, they express their cruelty by, as soon as they had him delivered over to their will. So that this was a cruel sentence.

3. It was also a *rash* and *hasty* sentence. The jews are all in haste; consulting all night, and early up by the break of day in the morning, to get him to his trial. They spur on Pilate with all arguments they can to give sentence. His trial took up but one morning, and a great part of that was spent in sending him from Caiaphas to Pilate, and from Pilate to Herod, and then back again to Pilate; so that it was a hasty and headlong sentence that Pilate gave. He did not sift and examine the matter, but handled it very slightly. The trial of many a mean man hath taken up ten times more debates and time than was spent about Christ.

4. It was an *extorted, forced* sentence. They squeeze it out of Pilate by mere clamour, importunity, and suggestions of danger. In courts of judicature, such arguments should signify but little; not importunity, but proof, should carry it: but timorous Pilate bends like a willow at this breath of the people; he had neither such a sense of justice, nor spirit of courage, as to withstand it.

5. It was a *hypocritical* sentence, masking horrid murder under a pretence and formality of law. Loth he was to condemn him, lest innocent blood should clamour in his conscience; but since he must do it, he will transfer the guilt upon them, and they take it; " His blood be on us, and on our children for ever," say they. Pilate calls for water, washes his hands

before them, and tells them, "I am free from the blood of this just person." But stay; free from his blood, and yet condemn a known innocent person! Free from his blood, because he washed his hands in water! Oh the hypocrisy of Pilate! Such juggling as this will not serve his turn, when he shall stand as a prisoner before him, who now stood arraigned at his bar.

IV. And lastly, In what manner did Christ receive this cruel and unrighteous sentence? He received it like himself, with admirable meekness and patience. He doth as it were wrap himself up in his own innocency, and obedience to his Father's will, and stands at the bar with invincible patience, and meek submission. He doth not once desire the judge to defer the sentence, much less fall down and beg for his life, as other prisoners use to do at such times. No, but as a sheep he goes to the slaughter, not opening his mouth. Some apply that expression to Christ, "Ye have condemned and killed the Just, and he resisteth you not," Jam. v. 6. From the time that Pilate gave sentence, till he was nailed to the cross, we do not read that ever he said any thing, save only to the women that followed him out of the city to Golgotha: and what he said there, rather manifested his pity to them, than any discontent at what was now come upon him; "Daughters of Jerusalem, (saith he,) weep not for me, but weep for yourselves and for your children," Luke xxiii. 28, &c. Oh the perfect patience and meekness of Christ! The inferences from hence are,

Inference 1. Do you see what was here done against Christ, under pretence of law? What cause have we to pray for good laws, and righteous executioners of them? Oh! it is a singular mercy to live under good laws, which protect the innocent from injury. Laws are hedges about our lives, liberties, estates, and all the comforts we enjoy in this world. Times will be evil enough, when iniquity is not discountenanced and punished by law; but how evil are those times like to prove when iniquity is established by law! as the psalmist complains, Psa. xciv. 20. How much therefore is it our concernment to pray, that "judgment may run down as a mighty stream!" Amos v. 24. "That our officers may be peace, and our exactors righteousness!" Isa. lx. 17. It was not therefore without great reason, that the apostle exhorted, that "supplications, prayers, intercessions, and giving of thanks be made for all men; for kings, and all that are in authority, that we may lead a quiet and peaceable life in all godliness and honesty," 1 Tim. ii. 1, 2. Great is the interest of the church of God in them; they are instruments of much good or much evil.

2. Was Christ condemned in a court of judicature? How evident then is it, that there is a judgment to come after this life? Surely things will not be always carried as they are in this world. When you see Jesus condemned, and Barabbas released, conclude, that a time will come when innocency shall be vindicated, and wickedness shamed. On this very ground, Solomon concludes, and very rationally, that God will call over things hereafter at a more righteous tribunal: " And moreover, I saw under the sun the place of judgment, that wickedness was there; and the place of righteousness, that iniquity was there. I said in my heart, God shall judge the righteous, and the wicked: for there is a time there for every purpose and for every work," Eccl. iii. 16, 17. Some indeed, on this ground, have denied the Divine providence; but Solomon draws a quite contrary conclusion, God shall judge: surely, he will take the matter into his own hand, he will bring forth the righteousness of his people as the light, and their just dealing as the noon-day. It is a mercy, if we be wronged in one court, that we can appeal to another, where we shall be sure to be relieved by a just, impartial Judge. " Be patient therefore, my brethren, (saith the apostle,) until the coming of the Lord," James v. 7.

3. Again, here you see how conscience may be overborne and run down by a fleshly interest. Pilate's conscience bid him beware, and forbear: his interest bid him act; his fear of Cesar was more than the fear of God. But oh! what a dreadful thing is it for conscience to be insnared by the fear of man! Prov. xxix. 25. To guard thy soul, reader, against this mischief, let such considerations as these be ever with thee.

(1.) Consider how dear those profits or pleasures cost, which are purchased with the loss of inward peace! There is nothing in this world good enough to recompense such a loss, or balance the misery of a tormenting conscience. If you violate it for the sake of a fleshly lust, it will remember the injury you did it many years after, Gen. xlii. 21; Job xiii. 26. It will not only retain the memory of what you did, but it will accuse you for it, Matt. xxvii. 4. It will not fear to tell you that plainly, which others dare not whisper. It will not only accuse, but it will also condemn you for what you have done. This condemning voice of conscience is a very terrible voice.

You may see the horror of it in Cain, the vigour of it in Judas, the doleful effects of it in Spira. It will, from all these its offices, produce shame, fear, and despair, if God give not repentance to life. The shame it works will so confound you, that you will not be able to look up, Job xxxi. 14; Psa. i. 5. The fear it works will make you wish for a hole in the rock to hide you, Isa. ii. 9, 10. 15. 19.   And its despair is a death-pang. Oh! who can stand under such a load as this? Prov. xviii. 14.

(2.) Consider the nature of your present actions; they are seed sown for eternity, and will spring up again in suitable effects, rewards, and punishments, when you that did them are turned to dust: " What a man sows, that shall he reap," Gal. vi. 7.   And as sure as the harvest follows the seed-time, so sure shall shame, fear, and horror, follow sin, Dan. xii. 2.   What Zeuxis, the famous painter, said of his work, may much more truly be said of ours; I paint for eternity, said he, when one asked him why he was so curious in his work. Ah! how bitter will those things be in the account and reckoning, which were pleasant in the acting and committing! It is true, our actions, physically considered, are transient; how soon is a word or action spoken or done, and there is an end of it! But morally considered, they are permanent, being put upon God's book of account.   Oh, therefore, take heed what you do: so speak, and so act, as they that must give an account.

(3.) Consider, how by these things men do but prepare for their own torment in a dying hour.   There is bitterness enough in death, you need not add more gall and wormwood to increase the bitterness of it.   What is the forcing and wounding of conscience now, but the sticking so many pins or needles in your death-bed, against you come to lie down on it? This makes death bitter indeed.   How many have wished in a dying hour, they had rather lived poor and low all their days, than to have strained their consciences for the world! Ah! how is the face and aspect of things altered in such an hour!

4. Did Christ stand arraigned and condemned at Pilate's bar? Then the believer shall never be arraigned and condemned at God's bar.   This sentence that Pilate pronounced on Christ gives evidence that God will never pronounce sentence against such: for had he intended to have arraigned them, he would never have suffered Christ, their Surety, to be arraigned and condemned for them.   Christ stood at this time before a higher judge than Pilate; he stood at God's bar as well as his.   Pilate did but that which God's own hand and counsel had before determined to be done, and what God himself, at the same time, did: though God did it justly and holily, dealing with Christ as a creditor with a surety; Pilate most wickedly and basely, dealing with Christ as a corrupt judge, that shed the blood of a known innocent to pacify the people. But certain it is, that out

of his condemnation flows our justification; and had not sentence been given against him, it must have been given against us.

Oh what a melting consideration is this! that out of his agony comes our victory; out of his condemnation, our justification; out of his pain, our ease; out of his stripes, our healing; out of his gall and vinegar, our honey; out of his curse, our bless-. ing; out of his crown of thorns, our crown of glory; out of his death, our life. If he could not be released, it was that you might. If Pilate gave sentence against him, it was that the great God might never give sentence against you. And therefore, Thanks be to God for his unspeakable gift.

SERMON XXV.

CHRIST'S MEMORABLE ADDRESS TO THE DAUGHTERS OF JERU-
SALEM, IN HIS WAY TO THE PLACE OF HIS EXECUTION.

LUKE XXIII. 27, 28, &c.

AND THERE FOLLOWED HIM A GREAT COMPANY OF PEOPLE, AND OF WOMEN,
WHICH ALSO BEWAILED AND LAMENTED HIM. BUT JESUS TURNING UNTO
THEM SAID, DAUGHTERS OF JERUSALEM, WEEP NOT FOR ME, BUT WEEP
FOR YOURSELVES, AND FOR YOUR CHILDREN.

THE sentence of death being given against Christ, the execution quickly follows. The evangelist here observes a memorable passage that fell out in their way to the place of execution ;
and that is, the lamentations and wailing of some that followed
him out of the city, who expressed their pity and sorrow for
him most tenderly and compassionately : all hearts were not
hard, all eyes were not dry. " There followed him a great
company of people, and of women, which also bewailed and
lamented him," &c.

In this paragraph we have two parts, namely, the lamentation
of the daughters of Jerusalem for Christ, and Christ's reply to
them.

1. The lamentation of the daughters of Jerusalem for Christ.
Concerning them, we briefly inquire who they were, and why
they mourned.

Who they were ? The text calls them " * daughters, that is,
inhabitants of Jerusalem ; for it is a hebraism ; as daughters of
Zion, daughters of Israel." And it is likely the greatest part
of them were women ; and there were many of them, a troop of
mourners, that followed Christ out of the city towards the place
of his execution, with lamentations and wailings.

What the principle or ground of these their lamentations
was, is not agreed by those that have pondered the story. Some
are of opinion their tears and lamentations were but the effects
and fruits of their more tender and ingenuous natures, which
were moved and melted with so tragical and sad a spectacle as
was now before them. But Calvin attributes it to their faith,
looking upon these mourners as a remnant reserved by the

* Θυγατρες Ιερυσαλημ, that is, mulieres Hierosolymitanæ : Hebrais-
mus ; sic, filiæ Tsionis.—*Piscat. in loc.*

Lord in that miserable dispersion ; and though their faith was but weak, yet he judges it probable that there was a secret seed of godliness in them, which afterwards grew to a maturity, and brought forth fruit.   And to the same sense others give their opinion also.

2. Let us consider Christ's reply to them ; " Weep not for me, ye daughters of Jerusalem." Strange, that Christ should forbid them to weep for him, yea for him under such unparalleled sufferings and miseries. If ever there was a heart-melting object in the world, it was here. Oh who could hold, whose heart was not petrified, and more obdurate than the senseless rocks ? This reply of Christ undergoes a double sense and interpretation, suitable to the different construction of their sorrow. Those that look upon their sorrow as merely natural, take Christ's reply in a negative sense, prohibiting such tears as those. They that expound their sorrows as the fruit of faith, tell us, though the form of Christ's expression be negative, yet the sense is comparative. Weep rather upon your own account, than mine ; reserve your sorrows for the calamities coming upon yourselves and your children. You are greatly affected, I see, with the misery that is upon me ; but mine will be quickly over, yours will lie long. In which he shows his merciful and compassionate disposition, who was still more mindful of the troubles and burdens of others than of his own. And indeed, the days of calamity coming upon them and their children were doleful days. What direful and unprecedented miseries befell them at the breaking up and devastation of the city, who hath not read or heard ? And who can refrain from tears that hears or reads it ?

Now, if we take the words in the first sense, as a prohibition of their merely natural and carnal affections, expressed in tears and lamentations for him, just as they would have been upon any other like tragical story ; then the observation from it will be this, 1. That melting affections and sorrows, even from the sense and consideration of the sufferings of Christ, are no infallible signs of grace.

If you take it in the latter sense, as the fruit of their faith, as tears flowing from a gracious principle ; then the observation will be this, 2. That the believing meditation of what Christ suffered for us, is of great force and efficacy to melt and break the heart.

I shall rather choose to prosecute both these branches, than to decide the controversy ; especially since the notes gathered from each of them may be useful to us. And therefore I shall begin with the first, namely,

THAT MELTING AFFECTIONS AND SORROWS, EVEN
FROM THE SENSE OF CHRIST'S SUFFERINGS, ARE
NO INFALLLIBLE MARKS OF GRACE.

In this point I have two things to do, to prepare it for use.
I. To show what the melting of the affections by way of grief
and sorrow is.   II. That they may be so melted, even upon the
account of Christ, and yet the heart remain unrenewed.

I. Tears are the juice of a mind oppressed, and squeezed with
grief. Grief compresses the heart ; the heart so compressed and
squeezed, vents itself sometimes into tears, sighs, groans, &c.
And this is twofold; gracious, and wholly supernatural; or common, and altogether natural.   The gracious melting or sorrow
of the soul, is likewise two-fold ; habitual or actual. Habitual
bodily sorrow is that gracious disposition, inclination, or tendency of the renewed heart to mourn and melt, when any just
occasion is presented to the soul that calls for such sorrow. It
is expressed, by taking away the heart of stone, and giving a
heart of flesh, Ezek. xxxvi ; 26. that is, a heart impressive, and
yielding to such arguments and considerations as move it to
mourning.

Actual sorrow is the expression and manifestation of this inclination upon just occasions ; and it is expressed two ways,
either by the internal effects of it, which are the heaviness, shame,
loathing, resolution, and holy revenge begotten in the soul
upon the account of sin ; or also by more external and visible
effects, as sighs, groans, tears, &c.   The former is essential to
godly sorrow ; the latter contingent and accidental, much depending upon the natural temperature and constitution of the
body.

Natural and common meltings are nothing else but the effects
of a better temper, and the fruit of a more ingenuous spirit, and
easier constitution, which shows itself on any other, as well as
upon spiritual occasions : as Austin said, he could weep plentifully when he read the story of Dido.   The history of Christ is
a very tragical and pathetical history, and may melt an ingenuous nature, where there is no renewed principles at all.   So
that,

II. Our affections may be melted, even upon the account of
Christ ; and yet that is no infallible evidence of a gracious heart.
And the reasons for it are,

1. Because we find all sorts of affections discovered by such
as have been no better than temporary believers.   The stony-
ground hearers in Matt. xiii. 20, " received the word with joy ;"

and so did John's hearers also, who for " a season rejoiced in his light," John v. 35. Now, if the affections of joy under the word may be exercised, why not of sorrow also ? If the comfortable things revealed in the gospel may stir up the one, by a parity of reason, the sad things it reveals may answerably work upon the other. Even those israelites whom Moses told they should fall by the sword, and not prosper, for the Lord would not be with them, because they were turned away from him; yet when Moses rehearsed the message of the Lord in their ears, they mourned greatly, Numb. xiv. 39. I know the Lord pardoned many of them their iniquities, though he took vengeance on their inventions; and yet it is as true, that with many of them God was not well-pleased, 1 Cor. x. 5. Many instances of their weeping and mourning before the Lord we find in this sacred history ; and yet their hearts were not stedfast with God.

2. Because though the object about which our affections and passions are moved, may be spiritual ; yet the motives and principles that set them on work, may be but carnal and natural ones. When I see a person affected in the hearing of the word, or prayer, even unto tears, I cannot presently conclude, surely this is the effect of grace ; for it is possible, the pathetical nature of the subject-matter, the rhetoric of the speaker, the very affecting tone, and modulation of the voice, may draw tears as well as faith.

Whilst Austin was a manichee, he sometimes heard Ambrose; and, saith he, " I was greatly affected in hearing him, even unto tears many times :" howbeit, it was not the heavenly nature of the subject, but the abilities and rare parts of the speaker that so affected him. And this was the case of Ezekiel's hearers, chap. xxxiii. 32.

3. These motions of the affections may rather be a fit and mood, than the very frame and temper of the soul. Now there is a vast difference between these ; there are times and seasons, when the roughest and most obdurate hearts may be pensive and tender : but that is not its temper and frame, but only a fit, a pang, a transient passion. So the Lord complains of them, " O Ephraim, what shall I do unto thee ? O Judah, what shall I do unto thee ? for your goodness is as a morning cloud, and as the early dew, it goeth away," Hos. vi. 4. And so he complains, " When he slew them, then they sought him : and they returned and inquired early after God. And they remembered that God was their rock, and the most high God their redeemer; nevertheless they did flatter him with their lips, and lied unto him with their tongues," Psa. lxxviii. 34—36. For had this

remembrance of God been the gracious temper of their souls, it would have continued with them; they would not have been thus wavering, thus hot and cold with God, as they were. Therefore we conclude, that we cannot infer a work of grace upon the heart, simply and merely from the meltings and thaws that are sometimes upon it. And hence, for your use, I shall infer,

1. If such as sometimes feel their hearts thawed and melted with the consideration of the sufferings of Christ, may yet be deceived; what cause have they to fear and tremble, whose hearts are as unrelenting as the rocks, yielding to nothing that is proposed, or urged upon them! How many such are there, of whom we may say, as Christ said of the jews, "We have piped unto you, but ye have not danced; we have mourned unto you, but ye have not lamented!" Matt. xi. 17. They must inevitably come short of heaven, who come so short of others that do come short of heaven. If those perish that have rejoiced under the promises, and mourned under the threats of the word; what shall become of them that are as unconcerned, and untouched by what they hear, as the seats they sit on? who are given up to such hardness of heart, that nothing can affect them? One would think, the consideration of the sixth chapter of the epistle to the Hebrews should startle such men and women, and make them cry out, Lord, what will become of such a senseless, stupid, dead creature as I am? If they that have been enlightened, and have tasted of the heavenly gift, and were made partakers of the Holy Ghost, and have tasted the good word of God, and the powers of the world to come, may, notwithstanding, so fall away, that it shall be impossible to renew them again by repentance, what shall we then say, or think of the state of those to whom the most penetrating and awakening truths are no more than a tale that is told?

2. If such as these may eternally miscarry; then let all look carefully to their foundation, and see that they do not bless themselves in a thing of nought. It is manifest from 1 Cor. x. 12, that many souls stand exceeding dangerously, who are yet strongly conceited of their own safety. And if you please to consult the following scriptures, you shall find vain confidence to be a ruling folly over the greatest part of men, and that which is the utter overthrow, and undoing of multitudes of professors: Gal. vi. 3, 4; John viii. 54; Rom. ii. 18, 19. 21: Matt. xxv. 11, 12; Matt. vii. 22.

Now there is nothing more apt to beget and breed this vain soul-undoing confidence, than the stirrings and meltings of our affections about spiritual things, whilst the heart remains unrenewed all the while. For such a man seems to have all that is required of a christian, and herein to have attained the very end of all knowledge; which is operation and influence upon the heart and affections. Indeed (thinks such a poor deluded soul) if I did hear, read, or pray, without any inward affections, with a dead, cold, and unconcerned heart; or if I did make a show of zeal and affection in duties, and had it not; well might I suspect myself to be a hypocrite: but it is not so with me, I feel my heart really melted many times, when I read the sufferings of Christ; I feel my heart raised and ravished with strange joys and comforts, when I hear the glory of heaven opened in the gospel: indeed if it were not so with me, I might doubt the root of the matter is wanting; but if to my knowledge, affections be added, a melting heart joined with a knowing head, then I may be confident all is well. I have often heard ministers cautioning and warning their people not to rest satisfied with idle and unpractical notions in their understandings, but to labour for impressions upon their hearts. This I have attained, and therefore what danger of me? I have often heard it given as a mark of a hypocrite, that he hath light in his head, but it sheds not down its influence upon the heart; whereas in those that are sincere, it works on their heart and affections: so I find it with me, therefore I am in a most safe estate.

O soul! of all the false signs of grace, none more dangerous than those that most resemble true ones; and never doth the devil more surely and incurably destroy, than when transformed into an angel of light. What if these meltings of thy heart be but a flower of nature? What if thou art more indebted to a good temper of body, than a gracious change of spirit for these things? Well, so it may be. Therefore be not secure, but fear, and watch. Possibly, if thou wouldest but search thine own heart in this matter, thou mayest find, that any other pathetical, moving story, will have the like effects upon thee. Possibly too, thou mayest find, that, notwithstanding all thy raptures and joys at the hearing of heaven, and its glory, yet after that pang is over, thy heart is habitually earthly, and thy conversation is not there. For all thou canst mourn at the relations of Christ's sufferings, thou art not so affected with sin, which was the meritorious cause of the sufferings of Christ, as to crucify one corruption, or deny the next temptation, or part with any way of sin that is gainful or pleasurable to thee, for his sake.

Why now, reader, if it be so with thee, what art thou the better for the fluency of thy affections? Dost thou think in earnest that Christ hath the better thoughts of thee, because thou canst shed tears for him, when notwithstanding thou every day piercest and woundest him?   Oh! be not deceived. Nay, for ought I know, thou mayest find, upon a narrow search, that thou puttest thy tears in the room of Christ's blood, and givest the confidence and dependence of thy soul to them; and if so, they shall never do thee any good.   Therefore search thy heart, be not too confident: take not up upon such poor weak grounds as these, a soul-undoing confidence.   Always remember the wheat and tares resemble each other in their first springing up; that an egg is not liker to an egg, than hypocrisy, in some shapes and forms into which it can cast itself, is like a genuine work of grace.

There be first, that shall be last; and last, that shall be first, Matt. xix. 30.   Great is the deceitfulness of our hearts, Jer. xvii. 9.   And many are the subtleties and devices of Satan, 2 Cor. xi. 3.   Many also are the astonishing examples of self-deceiving souls recorded in the word.   Remember what you lately read of Judas.   Great also will be the exactness of the last judgment.   And how confident soever you be, that you shall speed well in that day, yet still remember that trial is not yet past.   Your final sentence is not yet come from the mouth of your Judge.   This I speak not to affright and trouble, but excite and warn you.   The loss of a soul is no small loss.

This may suffice for the first observation, built on this supposition, that the sorrow of these women was but a pang of mere natural affection in them.   But if it were the effect of a better principle, the fruit of their faith, as some judge; then I told you, the observation from it would be this,

THAT THE BELIEVING MEDITATION OF WHAT CHRIST
SUFFERED FOR US, IS OF GREAT FORCE AND EFFI-
CACY TO MELT AND BREAK THE HEART.

It is promised, that "they shall look upon him whom they have pierced, and mourn for him, as one mourneth for his only son; and shall be in bitterness for him, as one that is in bitterness for his first-born," Zech. xii. 10.   Ponder seriously, here, the spring and motive, They shall look upon me; it is the eye of faith that melts and breaks the heart.   The effect of such a sight of Christ, They shall look and mourn; be in bitterness and sorrow.   True repentance is a drop out of the eye of faith; and the measure or degree of that sorrow caused by a believing view of Christ.   To express which, two of the fullest instances of grief we read of, are borrowed; that of a tender father mourning over a dear and only son; that of the people of Israel, mourning over Josiah, that peerless prince, in the valley of Megiddo.

Now to show you how the believing meditation of Christ, and his sufferings, come kindly and savingly to break and melt down the gracious heart, I shall mention four considerations of the heart-breaking efficacy of faith, eyeing a crucified Jesus.

I. The very realizing of Christ and his sufferings by faith, is a most affecting and melting thing. Faith is a true glass, that represents all those his sufferings and agonies to the life. It presents them not as a fiction, or idle tale, but as a true and faithful narrative. This, saith faith, is a true and faithful saying, that Christ was not only clothed in our flesh—even he that is over all, God blessed for ever, the only Lord, the Prince of the kings of the earth, became a man; but it is also most certain, that in this body of his flesh, he bore the infinite wrath of God, which filled his soul with horror and amazement; that the Lord of life did hang dead upon the cross; that he went as a lamb to the slaughter, and was as a sheep dumb before the shearer; that he endured all this, and more than any finite understanding can comprehend, in my room and stead; for my sake he there groaned and bled; for my pride, earthliness, lust, unbelief, hardness of heart, he endured all this. I say, to realize the sufferings of Christ thus, is of great power to affect the coldest, dullest heart. You cannot imagine the difference there is in presenting things as realities, with convincing and satisfying evidence, and our looking on them as a fiction or uncertainty.

II. But faith can apply as well as realize; and if it do so, it must needs overcome the heart.

Ah! christian, canst thou look upon Jesus as standing in thy room, to bear the wrath of a Deity for thee; canst thou think on it, and not melt? That when thou, like Isaac, wast bound to the altar, to be offered up to justice, Christ, like the ram, was caught in the thicket, and offered in thy room. When thy sins had raised a fearful tempest, that threatened every moment to bury thee in a sea of wrath, Jesus Christ was thrown over to appease that storm! Say, reader, can thy heart dwell one hour upon such a subject as this? Canst thou, with faith, present Christ to thyself, as he was taken down from the cross, drenched in his own blood, and say, These were the wounds that he received for me; this is he that loved me, and gave himself for me; out of these wounds comes that balm that heals my soul; out of these stripes my peace? Oh you cannot hold up your hearts long to the piercing thoughts of this, but your souls will be pained, and, like Joseph, you will seek a place to vent your hearts in.

III. Faith can not only realize and apply Christ, and his death, but it can reason and conclude such things from his death as will fill the soul with affection to him, and break the heart in pieces, in his presence. When it views Christ as dead, it infers, Is Christ dead for me? then was I dead in law, sentenced and condemned to die eternally; "If one died for all, then were all dead," 2 Cor. v. 14. How woful was my case when the law had passed sentence on me! I could not be sure when I lay down, but that it might be executed before I rose; nothing but a puff of breath between my soul and hell.

Again, Is Christ dead for me? then I shall never die. If he be condemned, I am acquitted. "Who shall lay any thing to the charge of God's elect? It is God that justifieth, it is Christ that died," Rom. viii. 34. My soul is escaped as a bird out of the snare of the fowler; I was condemned, but am now cleared; I was dead, but am now alive. Oh the unsearchable riches of Christ! Oh love past finding out!

Again, Did God give up Christ to such miseries and sufferings for me? how shall he withhold any thing from me? He that " spared not his own Son, will doubtless with him freely give me all things," Rom. viii. 32. Now I may rest upon him for pardon, peace, acceptance, and glory for my soul. Now I may rely upon him safely for provision, protection, and all supplies for my body. Christ is the root of these mercies; he is more than all these, he is nearer and dearer to God than any other gift. Oh what a blessed, happy, comfortable state hath he now brought my soul into!

Once more, Did Christ endure all these things for me? then he will never leave nor forsake me: it cannot be that after he has endured all this, he will cast off the souls for whom he endured it.

IV. And lastly, Faith can not only realize, apply, and infer, but it can also compare the love of Christ in all this, both with his dealings with others, and with the soul's dealing with Christ, who loved it. To compare Christ's dealings with others, is most affecting: he hath not dealt with every one, as with me; nay, few there are that can speak of such mercies as I have from him. How many are there that have no part nor portion in his blood; who must bear that wrath in their own persons, that he bare himself for me! He espied me out, and singled me forth to be the object of his love, leaving thousands and millions still unreconciled; not that I was better than they, for

I was the greatest of sinners, far from righteousness, as unlikely as any to be the object of such grace and love: my companions in sin are left, and I am taken. Now the soul is full, too full to contain itself.

Yea, faith helps the soul to compare the love of Christ to it, with the returns it hath made to him for that love. And what, my soul! hath thy carriage to Christ been, since this grace appeared to thee? Hast thou returned love for love, love suitable to such love? Hast thou prized, valued, and esteemed this Christ, according to his own worth in himself, or his kindness to thee? Ah no, I have grieved, pierced, wounded his heart a thousand times since that, by my ingratitude; I have suffered every trifle to take his place in my heart. I have neglected him a thousand times, and made him say, Is this thy kindness to thy friend?—Is this the reward I shall have for all that I have done and suffered for thee? Wretch that I am, how have I requited the Lord! This shames, humbles, and breaks the heart. And when from such sights of faith, and considerations as these, the heart is thus affected, it affords a good argument indeed, that thou art gone beyond all the attainments of temporary believers; flesh and blood hath not revealed this.

Inference 1. Have the believing meditations of Christ, and his sufferings, such heart-melting influences? Then surely there is but little faith among men. Our dry eyes and hard hearts are evidences against us, that we are strangers to the sights of faith.

2. Have the believing meditations of Christ, and his sufferings, such heart-melting influences? Then surely the proper way of raising the affections, is to begin at the exercise of faith. It grieves me to see how many poor christians strive with their own dead hearts, endeavouring to raise and affect them, but cannot: they complain and strive, strive and complain, but can discover no love to the Lord, no brokenness of heart: they go to this ordinance and that, to one duty and another, hoping that now the Lord will fill the sails; but come back disappointed and ashamed. Poor christian, hear me one word; possibly it may do thee more service, than all the methods thou hast yet used. If thou wouldst indeed get a heart melted for sin, and broken with the kindly sense of the grace and love of Christ, thy way is not to force thy affections, nor to vex thyself, and go about complaining of a hard heart, but set thyself to believe, realize, apply, infer, and compare by faith as you have been directed; and see what this will do: "They shall look on me whom they have pierced, and mourn." This is the way to raise the heart, and break it.

3. Is this the way to get a truly broken heart? Then let those that have attained brokenness of heart this way, bless the Lord whilst they live, for so choice a mercy; and that upon a double account.

(1.) Forasmuch as a heart so affected and melted, is not attainable by any natural or unrenewed person; if they would give all they have in the world, it cannot purchase one such tear or groan over Christ. Mark, what characters of special grace it bears, in the description that is made of it, in Zech. xii. 10. Such a frame as this is not born with us, or to be acquired by us; for it is there said to be poured out by the Lord upon us, " I will pour upon them," &c. Nature is not the principle of it, but faith; for it is there said, They shall look on me; that is, believe and mourn. Self is not the end and centre of these sorrows; it is not so much for bringing condemnation upon ourselves, as for piercing Christ: " They shall look on me whom they have pierced, and shall mourn;" so that this is sorrow after God, and not an impulse of nature, as discoursed in the former point. Therefore you have cause to bless the Lord whilst you live for such a special mercy as this is. And,

(2.) It is the choicest and most precious gift that can be given you; for it is ranked among the prime mercies of the new covenant, Ezek. xxxvi. 26. This shall be the covenant; " A new heart also will I give you, and a new spirit will I put within you; and I will take away the stony heart out of your flesh, and I will give you an heart of flesh." And God himself sets no common value on it: for mark what he saith of it, " The sacrifices of God are a broken heart: a broken and a contrite spirit, O God, thou wilt not despise," Psa. li. 17. That is, God is more delighted with such a heart, than with all the sacrifices in the world; one groan, one tear, flowing from faith, and the spirit of adoption, are more to him, than the cattle upon a thousand hills. Again, " Thus saith the Lord, The heaven is my throne, and the earth is my footstool: where is the house that ye build to me? and where is the place of my rest?—But to this man will I look, even to him that is poor, and of a contrite spirit, and trembleth at my word," Isa. lxvi. 1, 2. q. d. All the magnificent temples and glorious structures in the world, give me no pleasure in comparison of such a broken heart as this. Oh then, for ever bless the Lord, who hath done that for you which none else could do, and which he has done but for few besides you.

SERMON XXVI.

OF THE NATURE AND QUALITY OF CHRIST'S DEATH.

ACTS II. 23.

HIM, BEING DELIVERED BY THE DETERMINATE COUNSEL AND FORE-KNOW-
LEDGE OF GOD, YE HAVE TAKEN, AND BY WICKED HANDS HAVE CRUCI-
FIED AND SLAIN.

HAVING considered, in order, the preparative acts for the death
of Christ, both on his own part, and on his enemies' part, we
now come to consider the death of Christ itself, which was
the principal part of his humiliation, and is the chief pillar of
our consolation.   Here we shall in order consider, First, The
kind and nature of the death he died.   Secondly, The manner
in which he bare it, namely, patiently, solitarily, and instructively; dropping divers holy and instructive lessons upon all that
were about him, in his seven last words upon the cross. Thirdly,
The funeral solemnities at his burial.   Fourthly, and lastly,
The weighty ends and great designs of his death.   In all which
particulars, as we proceed to discuss and open them, you will
have an account of the deep debasement and humiliation of the
Son of God.

First, In this text, we have an account of the kind and nature of that death which Christ died; as also of the causes of
it, both principal and instrumental.

1. The kind and nature of the death Christ died, which is
here described more generally, as a violent death, Ye have slain
him; and more particularly, as a most ignominious, cursed, dishonourable death, Ye have crucified him.

2. The causes of it are here likewise expressed: and that
both principal and instrumental.   The principal cause, permitting, ordering, and disposing all things about it, was the determinate counsel and foreknowledge of God.   There was not an
action or circumstance but came under this most wise and holy
counsel and determination of God.

The instruments affecting it were their wicked hands.   This
fore-knowledge and counsel of God, as it did no way necessitate
or enforce them to it; so neither doth it excuse their conduct

from the least aggravation of its sinfulness. It did no more
compel or force their wicked hands to do what they did, than
the mariner's hoisting up his sails, to take the wind to serve his
design, compels the wind.   And it cannot excuse their action
from one circumstance of sin ; because God's end and manner
of acting was one thing, their end and manner of acting another.
His, most pure and holy ; theirs, most malicious and daringly
wicked.   In respect of God, Christ's death was justice and
mercy.   In respect of man, it was murder and cruelty.   In respect of himself, it was obedience and humility.   Hence our
note is,

THAT OUR LORD JESUS CHRIST WAS NOT ONLY PUT
TO DEATH, BUT TO THE WORST OF DEATHS, EVEN
THE DEATH OF THE CROSS.

To this the apostle gives a plain testimony, " He became
obedient to death, even the death of the cross," Phil. ii. 8 ;
where his humiliation is both specified, he was humbled to
death ; and aggravated by a most emphatical reduplication, even
the death of the cross.   So Acts v. 30, " Jesus whom ye slew
and hanged on a tree :" *q. d.* it did not suffice you to put him
to a violent death, but you also put him to the most base, vile,
and ignominious death ; " you hanged him on a tree."

On this point we will discuss these three particulars, namely,
the nature or kind, the manner, and reasons of Christ's death
upon the tree.

I. I shall open the kind or nature of his death, by showing
you that it was a violent, painful, shameful, cursed, slow, and
unalleviated death.

1. It was a *violent* death that Christ died. Violent in itself,
though voluntary on his part.   " He was cut off out of the
land of the living," Isa. liii. 8.   And yet " he laid down his life
of himself ; no man took it from him," John x. 17.   I call his
death violent, because he died not a natural death, that is, he
lived not till nature was consumed with age, as it is in many
who live till their " radical moisture," like the oil in the lamp,
be quite consumed, and then go out like an expiring lamp.   It
was not so with Christ : for he was but in the flower and prime
of his time when he died.   And indeed, he must either die a
violent death, or not die at all ; partly, because there was no sin
in him, to open a door to natural death, as it doth in all others ;
partly, because else his death had not been a sacrifice acceptable and satisfactory to God for us.   That which died of itself
was never offered up to God ; but that which was slain, when

M 3

it was in its full strength and health. The temple was a type of the body of Christ, John ii. 19. Now, when the temple was destroyed, it did not drop down as an ancient structure decayed by time, but was pulled down by violence, when it was standing in its full strength. Therefore he is said to suffer death, and to be put to death for us in the flesh, 1 Pet. iii. 18.

2. The death of the cross was a most *painful* death. Indeed in this death were many deaths, contrived in one. The cross was a rack as well as a gibbet. The pains which Christ suffered upon the cross, are by the apostle emphatically styled " The pains of death," Acts ii. 24; but properly they signify the pangs of travail. His soul was in travail, Isa. liii. his body in bitter pangs; and being, as Aquinas speaks, optime complectionatus, of the most excellent crasis, exact and just temperament; his senses were more acute and delicate than ordinary; and so they continued all the time of his suffering, not in the least blunted by the pains he suffered.

3. The death of the cross was a *shameful* death: not only because the crucified were stripped quite naked, and so exposed as spectacles of shame; but mainly, because it was a kind of death which was appointed for the basest and vilest of men.

The free-men, when they committed capital crimes, were not condemned to the cross. No, that was looked upon as the death appointed for slaves. Tacitus calls it, Servile supplicium, the punishment of a slave: and Juvenal says, Pone crucem servo, Put the cross upon the back of a slave. And yet it is said of our Lord Jesus, He not only endured the cross, but also despised the shame, Heb. xii. 2. Obedience to his Father's will, and zeal for our salvation, made him disregard the shame of it, and despise the baseness that was in it.

4. The death of the cross was a *cursed* death. Upon that account he is said to be " made a curse for us; for it is written, Cursed is every one that hangeth on a tree," Gal. iii. 13. However, as the learned Junius hath judiciously observed, this curse is only a ceremonial curse; for otherwise it is neither in itself, nor by the law of nature, or by the civil law, more execrable than any other death. And the main reason why the ceremonial law affixed the curse to this, rather than to any other death, was principally with respect to the death Christ was to die. And therefore, reader, see and admire the providence of God, that Christ should die by a roman, and not by a judaic law. For crucifying, or hanging on a tree, was a roman punishment, and not in use among the jews. But the scriptures cannot be broken.

5. The death of the cross was a very *slow* and *lingering* death. They died leisurely. Which still increaseth and aggravateth the misery of it. If a man must die a violent death, it is a favour to be despatched : as they that are pressed to death, beg for more weight. On the contrary, to hang long in the midst of tortures, to have death coming upon us with a slow pace, that we may feel every tread of it, as it comes on, is a misery. And surely in this respect it was worse for Christ, than any other that ever was nailed to the tree. For all the while he hanged there, he remained full of life and acute sense. His life departed not gradually, but was whole in him to the last. Other men die gradually, and, towards their end, their sense of pain is much blunted. They falter, and expire by degrees, but Christ stood under the pains of death in his full strength. His life was whole in him. This was evident by the mighty outcry he made when he gave up the ghost, which showed him to be full of strength, contrary to the experience of all other men. Which made the centurion, when he heard it, to conclude, " Surely this was the Son of God," Mark xv. 37. 39.

6. It was an *unalleviated* death to Christ. Sometimes they gave to malefactors amidst their torments, vinegar and myrrh, to blunt, dull, and stupify their senses. And if they hanged long, would break their bones to despatch them out of their pains. Christ had none of this favour. Instead of vinegar and myrrh, they gave him vinegar and gall to drink, to aggravate his torments. And for the breaking of his bones, he prevented it, by dying before they came to break his legs. For the scriptures must be fulfilled, which say, Not a bone of him shall be broken.

This now was the kind and nature of that death he died. Even the violent, painful, shameful death of the cross. An ancient punishment both among the romans and carthaginians. But in honour of Christ, who died this death, Constantine the great abrogated it by law, ordaining that none should ever be crucified any more, because Christ died that death.

II. As to the manner of the execution. They that were condemned to the death of the cross, bare their cross upon their own shoulders, to the place of execution. They were stripped of all their clothes, and then were fastened to the cross with nails.

And that the equity of their proceedings might the better appear to the people, the cause of the punishment was written in capital letters, and fixed to the tree over the head of the malefactor. Of this I shall speak distinctly in the next sermon, before I come to handle the manner of his death : there being so much of providence in that circumstance, as invites us to spend more than a few transient thoughts upon it. Meanwhile, in the next place,

III. We will inquire briefly into the reasons why Christ died this, rather than any other kind of death. And amongst others, these three are obvious.

1. Because Christ must bear the curse in his death, and a curse by law was affixed to no other kind of death, as it was to this. Christ came to take away the curse from us by this death; and so must be made a curse. On him must all the curses of the moral law lie, which were due to us. And that nothing might be wanting to make it a full curse, the very death he died must also have a ceremonial curse upon it.

2. Christ died this, rather than any other kind of death, to fulfil the types and prefigurations that of old were made with respect to it.   All the sacrifices were lifted up from the earth, upon the altar.   But especially the brazen serpent prefigured this death, " Moses made a serpent of brass, and put it upon a pole," Numb. xxi. 9. And, saith Christ, " As Moses lifted up the serpent in the wilderness, so must the Son of man be lifted up," John iii. 14, that so he might correspond with that type made of him in the wilderness.

3. He died this, rather than any other death, because it was predicted of him, and in him must all the predictions, as well as types, be fully accomplished.   The psalmist spake in the person of Christ, of this death, as plainly as if he had rather been writing the history of what was done, than a prophecy of what was to be done, so many years afterwards: " For dogs have compassed me about, the assembly of the wicked have enclosed me : they pierced my hands and feet ; I may tell all my bones ; they look and stare upon me," Psa. xxii. 16, 17. Which hath a manifest reference to the distension of all his members upon the tree, which was a rack to him. So, " They shall look upon me whom they have pierced," Zech. xii. 10.   Yea, our Lord himself hath foretold the death he should die, in the forecited John iii. 14, saying, " He must be lifted up," that is, hanged between heaven and earth. And the scriptures must be fulfilled.

Thus you have a brief account both of the kind, manner, and reasons of this death of Christ.   The improvement of it you have in the following inferences of truth, deducible from it.

1. Is Christ dead ? and did he die the violent, painful, shameful, cursed death of the cross ? Then surely there is forgiveness with God, and plenteous redemption for the greatest of sinners, that by faith apply the blood of the cross to their poor guilty souls.   So speaks the apostle, " In whom we have redemption

through his blood, even the forgiveness of sins," Col. i. 14. And, " The blood of Christ cleanseth us from all sin," 1 John i. 7.   Two things will make this demonstrable.

(1.) That there is a sufficient efficacy in this blood of the cross, to expiate the greatest sins.   And, (2.) That the efficacy of it is designed and intended by God for believing sinners.

(1.) That there is sufficient efficacy in the blood of the cross, to expiate and wash away the greatest sins, is manifest, for it is precious blood, as it is called, 1 Pet. i. 18. " Ye were not redeemed with corruptible things, as silver and gold; but with the precious blood of the Son of God."   This preciousness of the blood of Christ riseth from the union it hath with that person, who is over all, God blessed for ever. And on that account is styled the blood of God, Acts xx. 28.   On account of its invaluable preciousness, it becomes satisfying and reconciling blood to God.   So the apostle speaks, " And (having made peace through the blood of his cross) by him to reconcile all things to himself; by him, I say, whether they be things in earth, or things in heaven," Col. i. 20.   The same blood which is redemption to them that dwell on earth, is confirmation to them that dwell in heaven.   Before the efficacy of this blood, guilt vanishes, and shrinks away as the shadow before the glorious sun.   Every drop of it hath a voice, and speaks to the soul that sits trembling under its guilt, better things than the blood of Abel, Heb. x. 24.   It sprinkles us from all evil, that is, an unquiet and accusing conscience, Heb. x. 22.   For having enough in it to satisfy God, it must needs have enough in it to satisfy conscience.

(2.) As there is sufficient efficacy in this blood to expiate the greatest guilt; so it is as manifest, that the virtue and efficacy of it is intended and designed by God for the use of believing sinners.   Such blood as this was shed, without doubt, for some weighty end, that some might be the better for it. Who they are for whom it is intended, is plain enough from Acts xiii. 39, " And by him all that believe are justified from all things, from which they could not be justified by the law of Moses."

That the remission of the sins of believers was the great thing designed in the pouring out of this precious blood of Christ, appears from all the sacrifices that prefigured it to the ancient church.   The shedding of that typical blood, spake a design of pardon.   And the putting of their hands upon the head of the sacrifice, spake the way and method of believing, by which that blood was then applied to them in that way ; and is still applied to us in a more excellent way.   Had no pardon been intended, no sacrifices had been appointed.

Moreover, let it be considered, this blood of the cross is the blood of a surety, that came under the same obligations with us, and in our name or stead shed it: and so of course frees and discharges the principal offender, or debtor, Heb. vii. 22.   Can God exact satisfaction from the blood and death of his own Son, the Surety of believers, and yet still demand it from believers?   It cannot be.   " Who (saith the apostle) shall lay any thing to the charge of God's elect?   It is God that justifieth. Who shall condemn? It is Christ that died," Rom. viii. 33, 34. And why are faith and repentance prescribed as the means of pardon?   Why doth God every where in his word call upon sinners to repent, and believe in this blood; encouraging them so to do, by so many precious promises of remission; and declaring the inevitable and eternal ruin of all impenitent and unbelieving ones, who despise and reject this blood?   What, I say, doth all this speak, but the possibility of a pardon for the greatest of sinners; and the certainty of a free, full, and final pardon for all believers? Oh what a joyful sound is this! What transporting voices of peace, pardon, grace, and acceptance, come to our ears from the blood of the cross !

The greatest guilt that ever was contracted upon a trembling, shaking conscience, can stand before the efficacy of the blood of Christ no more, than the sinner himself can stand before the justice of the Lord, with all that guilt upon him.

Reader, the word assures thee, whatever thou hast been, or art, that sins of as deep a dye as thine, have been washed away in this blood.   "I was a blasphemer, a persecutor, injurious; but I obtained mercy," saith Paul, 1 Tim. i. 13. But it may be thou wilt object, This was a rare and singular instance, and it is a great question whether any other sinner shall find the like grace that he did.   No question of it at all, if you believe in Christ as he did; for he tells us, ver. 16, " For this cause I obtained mercy, that in me first, Jesus Christ might show forth all long-suffering, for a pattern to them which should hereafter believe on him to life everlasting."   So that upon the same grounds on which he obtained mercy, you may obtain it also.

Those very men who had a hand in the shedding of Christ's blood, had the benefit of that blood afterwards pardoning them, Acts ii. 36.   There is nothing but unbelief and impenitency of heart can bar thy soul from the blessings of this blood.

2. Did Christ die the cursed death of the cross for believers?

Then though there be much of pain, there is nothing of curse in the death of the saints. It still wears its dart, by which it strikes; but hath lost its sting, by which it hurts and destroys. Death poured out all its poison, and lost its sting in Christ's side, when he became a curse for us.

But what speak I of the harmlessness of death to believers? It is certainly their friend and benefactor. As there is no curse, so there are many blessings in it. "Death is yours," 1 Cor. iii. 22. Yours as a special privilege and favour. Christ hath not only conquered it, but is more than a conqueror; for he hath made it beneficial, and very serviceable to the saints. When Christ was nailed to the tree, then he said as it were to death, which came to grapple with him there, "O death, I will be thy plague; O grave, I will be thy destruction:" and so he was; for he swallowed up death in victory, spoiled it of its power. So that, though it may now affright some weak believers, yet cannot hurt them at all.

3. If Christ died the cursed death of the cross for us, how cheerfully should we submit to, and bear any cross for Jesus Christ! He had his cross, and we have ours; but what are ours compared with his? His cross was a heavy cross indeed, yet how patiently and meekly did he support it! "He endured his cross:" we cannot endure or bear ours, though they be not to be named with his. Three things should marvellously strengthen us to bear the cross of Christ.

(1.) That we shall carry it but a little way. (2.) Christ bears the heaviest end of it. (3.) Innumerable blessings and mercies grow upon the cross of Christ.

(1.) We shall bear it but a little way. "It should be enough to me (saith a holy one) that Christ will have joy and sorrow halfers of the life of the saints; and that each of them should have a share of our days, as the night and day are kindly partners of time, and take it up between them. But if sorrow be the largest halfer of our days here, I know joy's day shall dawn, and will more than recompense all our sad hours. Let my Lord Jesus (since he will do so) weave my bit-and-span length of time with white and black; well and woe."—Let the rose be neighbour with the thorn. Sorrow and the saints are not married together! or suppose it was so, heaven shall make a divorce. Life is but short, and therefore crosses cannot be long. Our sufferings are but for a while, 1 Pet. v. 10. They are but the sufferings of the present time, Rom. viii. 18.

(2.) As we shall carry the cross of Christ but a little way, so Christ himself bears the heaviest end of it. He divideth

sufferings with them, and takes the largest share to himself.—
" The reproaches of them that reproached thee, are fallen upon
me," Psa. lxiv. 9.   Nay, to speak as the thing is, Christ doth
not only bear half, or the better part, but the whole of our cross
and burden. Yea, he bears all, and more than all ; for he bears
us and our burden too, or else we would quickly sink, and faint
under it.

(3.) It is reviving to think what an innumerable multitude of
blessings and mercies are the fruit and offspring of a sanctified
cross.   Since that tree was so richly watered with the blood of
Christ ; what store of choice and rich fruits doth it bear to
believers !

" I know (says one) no man hath a velvet cross, but the cross is
made of what God will have it ; yet I dare not say, Oh that I had
liberty to sell Christ's cross, lest therewith also I should sell joy,
comfort, sense of love, patience, and the kind visits of a Bridegroom.—I have but small experience of sufferings for Christ, but
I find a young heaven, and a little paradise of glorious comforts,
and soul-delighting visits of Christ in suffering for him and his
truth.—My prison is my palace, my sorrow is full of joy ; my losses
are rich losses, my pain easy pain, my heavy days are holy days
and happy days. I may tell a new tale of Christ to my friends.—
Oh what owe I to the file, and to the hammer, and to the furnace
of my Lord Jesus ! who hath now let me see how good the
wheat of Christ is, that goes through his mill, and his oven, to
be made bread for his own table.   Grace tried is better than
grace, and more than grace.   It is glory in its infancy.   Who
knows the truth of grace without a trial ?—And how soon
would faith freeze without a cross !   Bear your cross therefore
with joy."

4. Did Christ die the death, yea, the worst of deaths for us ?
Then it follows, that our mercies are brought forth with great
difficulty ; and that which is sweet to us in the fruition, was
costly and hard to Christ in the acquisition.   " In whom we
have redemption through his blood," Col. i. 14.   Upon which
a late neat writer says, " The way of grace is here to be considered ; life comes through death ; God comes in Christ ; and
Christ comes in blood : the choicest mercies come through the
greatest miseries.   Oh ! how should this raise the value of our
mercies !   What, the price of blood, the price of precious
blood, the blood of the cross !   Oh what an esteem should this
raise !

" Things (as the same ingenious author adds) are prized
rather as they come, than as they are.   Far fetched and dear

bought makes all the price, and gives all the worth with us weak creatures.   Upon this ground the scripture, when it speaks of our great fortune, tells the great price it cost ; as knowing if any thing will take with us, this will, ' To him that loved us, and washed us from our sins in his own blood,'" Rev. i. 5.

Beware then you abuse not any of the mercies that Christ brought forth with so many bitter pangs and throes.   And let all this endear Christ more than ever to you, and make you in a deep sense of his grace and love, to say, Thanks be to God for Jesus Christ.

SERMON XXVII.

OF THE SIGNAL PROVIDENCE, WHICH DIRECTED AND ORDERED
THE TITLE AFFIXED TO THE CROSS OF CHRIST.

LUKE XXIII. 38.

AND A SUPERSCRIPTION ALSO WAS WRITTEN OVER HIM IN LETTERS OF
GREEK, AND LATIN, AND HEBREW, THIS IS THE KING OF THE JEWS.

BEFORE I pass on to the manner of Christ's death, I shall consider the title affixed to the cross ; in which very much of the wisdom of Providence was discovered. It was the manner of the romans, that the equity of their proceedings might the more clearly appear to the people, when they crucified any man, to publish the cause of his death, in a table written in capital letters, and placed over the head of the crucified. And that there might be at least a show and face of justice in Christ's death, he also shall have his title or superscription.

This writing one evangelist calls the accusation, $\alpha\iota\tau\iota\alpha$, Matt. xxvii. 37. Another calls it the title, $\tau\iota\tau\lambda o\varsigma$, John xix. 19. Another the inscription or superscription, $\epsilon\pi\iota\gamma\rho\alpha\phi\eta$, so the text. And another the superscription of his accusation, $\epsilon\pi\iota\gamma\rho\alpha\phi\eta$ $\tau\eta\varsigma$ $\alpha\iota\tau\iota\alpha\varsigma$, Mark xv. 26. In short, it was a fair legible writing, intended to express the fact or crime, for which the person died.

This was their usual manner, though sometimes we find it was published by the voice of the common crier. As in the case of Attalus the martyr, who was led about the amphitheatre, one proclaiming before him, This is Attalus the christian. But it was customary and usual to express the crime in a written table, as the text expresses it. Wherein these three things offer themselves to your consideration.

1. The character or description of Christ, contained in that writing. And he is described by his kingly dignity, This is the King of the jews. The very office, which but a little before they had reproached and derided, bowing the knee to him in mockery, saying, Hail, King of the jews ; the providence of God so orders it, that therein he shall be vindicated and honoured. This is the King of the jews : or, as the other evangelists complete it, This is Jesus of Nazareth the King of the jews.

2. The person that drew his character or title. It was Pilate; he that but now condemned him : he that was his judge, shall be his herald, to proclaim his glory. For the title is honourable. Surely, this was not from himself, for he was Christ's enemy ; but rather than Christ should want a tongue to clear him, the tongue of an enemy shall do it.

3. The time when this honour was done him. It was when he was at the lowest ebb of his glory ; when shame and reproach were heaped on him by all hands. When all the disciples had forsaken him, and were fled. Not one left to proclaim his innocency, or speak a word in his vindication. Then doth the providence of God as strangely, as powerfully, overrule the heart and pen of Pilate, to draw this title for him, and affix it to his cross. Surely we must look higher than Pilate in this thing, and see how Providence serves itself by the hands of Christ's adversaries. Hence our observation is,

THAT THE DIGNITY OF CHRIST WAS OPENLY PROCLAIMED, AND DEFENDED BY AN ENEMY; AND THAT, IN THE TIME OF HIS GREATEST REPROACHES AND SUFFERINGS.

To open this mystery of Providence to you, that you may not stand idly gazing upon Christ's title, as many then did ; we must, I. Consider the nature and quality of this title. II. What hand the providence of God had in this matter. III. And then draw forth the proper uses and improvements of it.

I. To open the nature and quality of Christ's title or inscription ; let it be thoroughly considered, and we shall find,

1. That it was an *extraordinary* title, varying from all examples of that kind ; and directly crossing the main design and end of their own custom. For, as I hinted before, the end of it was to clear the equity of their proceedings, and show the people how justly they suffered those punishments inflicted on them for such crimes. But lo, here is a title expressing no crime at all, and so vindicating Christ's innocency. This some of them perceived, and moved Pilate to change it, not, This is, but, This is he that said, I am the King of the jews. In that, as they conceived, lay his crime. Oh how strange and wonderful a thing was this ! But what shall we say ? it was a day of wonders and extraordinary things. As there was never such a person crucified before, so there was never such a title affixed to the cross before.

2. It was a *public* title, both written and published with the greatest advantage of spreading itself far and near, among all

people, that could be, " for it was written in three languages, and to those most known in the world at that time." The greek tongue was then known in most parts of the world. The hebrew was the jews' native language. And the latin the language of the romans. So that it being written both in hebrew, greek, and latin, it was easy to be understood both by jews and gentiles.

And indeed, unto this the providence of God had a special eye, to make it notorious and evident to all the world ; for even so all things designed for public view and knowledge were written. Josephus tells us of certain pillars, on which was engraven in letters of greek, and latin, " It is a wickedness for strangers to enter into the holy place." So the soldiers of Gordian, the third emperor, when he was slain upon the borders of Persia, raised a monument for him, and engraved his memorial upon it, in greek, latin, persic, judaic, and egyptiac letters, that all people might read the same. And as it was written in three learned languages, so it was exposed to view in a public place ; and at a time, when multitudes of strangers, as well as jews, were at Jerusalem ; it was at the time of the passover ; so that all things concurred to spread and divulge the innocency of Christ, vindicated in this title.

3. It was an *honourable* title. Such was the nature of it, saith Bucer, that in the midst of death, Christ began to triumph by it.

4. It was a *vindicating* title ; it cleared up the honour, dignity, and innocency of Christ, against all the false imputations, calumnies, and blasphemies, which were cast upon him before, by the wicked tongues, both of jews and gentiles. They had called him a deceiver, a blasphemer, because he made himself the Son of God. But now in this, they acknowledge him to be the King of Israel.

5. Moreover it was a *predicting* and *presaging* title. Evidently foreshowing the propagation of Christ's kingdom, and the spreading of his name and glory among all kindreds, nations, tongues, and languages. As Christ hath right to enter into all the kingdoms of the earth, by his gospel, and set up his throne in every nation ; so it was presaged by this title that he should do so. And that both hebrews, greeks, and latins should be called to the knowledge of him. Nor is it a wonder, that this should be predicted by wicked Pilate, when Caiaphas himself, a man every way as wicked as he, had prophesied to the same purpose ; for " being high priest that year, he prophesied that Jesus should die for that nation ; and not for that nation only,

but that also he should gather together in one the children of God that were scattered abroad," John xi. 51, 52. Yea, many have prophesied in Christ's name, who, for all that, shall never be owned by him, Matt. vii. 22.

6. And lastly, It was an *immutable* title. The jews endeavoured, but could not persuade Pilate to alter it. To all their importunities he returns this resolute answer, " What I have written, I have written ;" as if he should say, Urge me no more, I have written his title, I cannot, I will not alter a letter thereof. Surely the constancy of Pilate at this time can be attributed to nothing but Divine special Providence. Most wonderful ! that he, who before was as unconstant as a reed shaken by the wind, is now as fixed as a pillar of brass. And yet more wonderful, that he should write down that very particular in the title of Christ, This is the King of the jews, which was the very thing that so scared him but a little before, and was the very consideration that moved him to give sentence. What was now become of the fear of Cesar? that Pilate dares to be Christ's herald, and publicly to proclaim him, The King of the jews. This was the title.

II. We shall next inquire what hand the Divine Providence had in this business. And indeed, the providence of God in this hour, acted gloriously, and wonderfully, in the following ways.

1. In overruling the heart and hand of Pilate contrary to his own inclination. I doubt not but Pilate himself was far enough from designing that which the wisdom of Providence aimed at in this matter. He was a wicked man, and had no love to Christ. He had given sentence of death against him ; yet this is he that proclaimed him to be Jesus, King of the jews. It so overruled his pen, that he could not write what was in his own heart and intention, but the quite contrary ; even a fair and public testimony of the kingly office of the Son of God, This is the King of the jews.

2. Herein the wisdom of Providence was gloriously displayed, in applying a present, proper, public remedy to the reproaches and blasphemies which Christ had then newly received in his name and honour.

3. Moreover, Providence eminently appeared at this time in keeping so timorous a person, a man of so base a spirit, that would not stick at any thing to please the people, from receding, or giving ground in the least to their importunities.

4. Herein also much of the wisdom of Providence appeared, in casting the ignominy of the death of Christ upon those very

men who ought to bear it. For it is as if Pilate had said, You have moved me to crucify your King, I have crucified him, and now let the ignominy of his death rest upon your heads, who have extorted this from me. He is righteous, the crime is not his, but yours.

5. And lastly, The providence of God wonderfully discovered itself (as before was noted) in fixing this title to the cross of Christ, when there was so great a confluence of all sorts of people to take notice of it. So that it could never have been more advantageously published, than it was at this time. So that we may say, How wonderful are the works of God! "His ways are in the sea, his paths in the great deeps; his footsteps are not known:" His providence hath a prospect beyond the understandings of all creatures.

III. We will draw forth the proper uses and improvement of it.

1. Hence it follows, That the providence of our God can, and often doth overrule the counsels and actions of the worst of men to his own glory.

It can serve itself by them that oppose it, and bring about the glory and honour of Christ, by those very men, and means, which are designed to lay it in the dust. "Surely the wrath of man shall praise thee," Psa. lxxvi. 10. The jews thought when they crowned Christ with thorns, bowed the knee, and mocked him, led him to Golgotha and crucified him; that now they had utterly despoiled him of all his kingly dignities; and yet even there he is proclaimed a King. Thus the dispersion of the jews, upon the death of Stephen, spread the gospel far and near, "For they went every where preaching the word," Acts viii. 4. Thus Paul's bonds for the gospel fell out to the furtherance of the gospel, Phil. i. 12. Oh the depth of Divine wisdom! to propagate and establish the interest of Jesus Christ, by those very means that seem to import its destruction! How great a support should this be to the faith of God's people, when all things seem to run cross to their hopes and happiness! "Let Israel therefore hope in the Lord, for with the Lord there is mercy, and with him is plenteous redemption," Psa. cxxx. 7. He is never at a loss for means to promote and serve his own ends.

2. Hence likewise it follows, That the greatest services performed to Christ undesignedly, shall never be accepted nor rewarded of God. Pilate did that for Christ that not one of his own disciples at that time durst do; and yet this service was not accepted of God, because he did it not designedly for his glory, but from the mere overruling of Providence.

" If there be first a willing mind, it is accepted according to that a man hath," saith the apostle, 2 Cor. viii. 12. The eye of God is first and mainly upon the will; if that be sincere and right for God, small things will be accepted; and if not, the greatest shall be abhorred. So 1 Cor. ix. 17. " If I do this thing (that is, preach the gospel) willingly, I have a reward; but if against my will, a dispensation is committed to me;" that is, if I upon pure principles of faith and love, from my heart, designing the glory of God, and delighting to promote it by my ministry, do cheerfully and willingly apply myself to the preaching of the gospel, I shall have acceptance and reward with God; but if my work be a burden to me, and the service of God esteemed as a bondage, why then Providence may use me for the dispensing of the gospel to others, but I myself shall lose both reward and comfort. As it doth not excuse my sin, that God can bring glory to himself out of it; so neither doth it justify an action, that God hath praise and honour accidentally by it. Paul knew that even the strife and envy in which some preached Christ, should turn to his salvation; and .yet he was not at all beholden to them for promoting his salvation that way. So Pilate here promotes the honour of Jesus Christ, to whom he had no love, and whose glory he did not at all design in this thing; and therefore hath neither acceptance nor reward with God. Oh therefore, whatever you do for Christ, do it heartily, designedly, for his glory; of a ready and willing mind; with pure and sincere aims at his glory; for this is that the Lord more respects than the greatest services by accident.

3. Would not Pilate recede from what he had written on Christ's behalf? How shameful a thing is it for christians to retract what they have said or done on Christ's behalf! When Pilate had asserted him to be King of the jews, he maintained his assertion, and all the importunity of Christ's enemies shall not move him an hair's breadth from it. Did Pilate say, " What I have written, I have written?" and shall not we say, What we have believed, we have believed; and what we have professed, we have professed? What we have engaged to Christ, we have engaged. We will stand to what we have done.

As God's election, so your profession must be irrevocable. Oh let him that is holy be holy still. That counsel given by a reverend divine in this case, is both safe and good. " Be sure (saith he) you stand on good ground, and then resolve to stand your ground against all the world. Follow God, and fear not men. Art thou godly? repent not, whatsoever thy religion cost thee. Let sinners repent, but let not saints repent. Let saints repent of their faults, but not of their faith ; of their iniquities, but not of their righteousness. Repent not of your righteousness, lest you afterward repent of your repentance.—Repent not of your zeal, or your forwardness, or activity in the holy ways of the Lord.—Wish not yourselves a step further back, or a cubit lower in your stature in the grace of God. Wish not any thing undone, concerning which God will say, Well done."

In Galen's time it was a proverbial expression, when any one would show the impossibility of a thing, "You may as soon turn a christian from Christ as do it." A true heart-choice of Christ is without reserves, and what is without reserves will be without repentance. There is a stiffness and stoutness of spirit which is our sin. But this is our glory. In the matters of God, saith Luther, I assume this title, Cedo nulli, " I yield to none."

4. Did Pilate affix such an honourable, vindicating title to the cross ? Then the cross of Christ is a dignified cross. Then the cross and sufferings of Christ are attended with glory and honour. Remember when your hearts begin to startle at the sufferings and reproaches of Christ, there is an honourable title upon the cross of Christ. And as it was upon his, so it will be upon your cross also, if ye suffer for Christ. Moses saw it, which made him esteem the very reproaches of Christ above all the treasures of Egypt, Heb. xi. 26. How did the martyrs glory in their sufferings for Christ ! calling their chains of iron, chains of gold ; and their manacles, bracelets.

It is related of Ludovicus Marsacus, a knight of France, that when he, with divers other christians of an inferior rank in the world, were condemned to die for religion, and the gaoler had bound them with chains, but did not bind him, being a more honourable person than the rest ; he was offended greatly by that omission, and said, " Why do not you honour me with a chain for Christ also, and create me a knight of that illustrious order ? "

" To you (saith the apostle) it is given in the behalf of Christ, not only to believe, but also to suffer for his sake," Phil. i. 29. There is a twofold honour attending the cross of Christ ; one in the very sufferings themselves ; another, as the reward and fruit of them. To be called out to suffer for Christ, is a great honour. Yea, an honour peculiar to the saints. The angels glorify Christ by their active, but not by their passive obedience. This is reserved as a special honour for saints.

And as there is a great deal of honour in being called forth to suffer on Christ's account ; so Christ will confer special honour upon his suffering saints, in the day of their reward; " He that confesses me before men, him will I confess also before my Father which is in heaven," Matt. x. 32.   O sirs, one of these days the Lord will break out of heaven, with a shout, accompanied with myriads of angels, and ten thousands of his saints, those glittering courtiers of heaven.   The heavens and earth shall flame and melt before him ; and it shall be very tempestuous round about him ; the graves shall open, the sea and earth shall yield up their dead.   You shall see him ascending the awful throne of judgment, and all flesh gathered before his face ; even multitudes, multitudes that no man can number.   And then to be brought forth by Christ before that great assembly of angels and saints ; and there to have an honourable mention and remembrance made of your labours and sufferings, your pains, patience, and self-denial, of all your sufferings and losses for Christ ; and to hear from his mouth, Well done, good and faithful servant : oh what honour is this ! Yet this shall be done to the man that now chooses sufferings for Christ, rather than sin ; that esteems his reproaches greater riches than the treasures of Egypt.

It is an honour the angels have not.   I make no doubt, but they would be glad (had they bodies of flesh as we have) to lay their necks on the block for Christ.   But this is the saints' peculiar privilege.   The apostles went away from the council rejoicing that they were honoured to be dishonoured for Christ ; or, as we translate it, " counted worthy to suffer shame for him," Acts v. 41.   Surely, if there be any " marks of honour," they are such as we receive for Christ's sake.   If there be any shame that hath glory in it, it is the reproach of Christ, and the shame you suffer for his name.

5. Did Pilate so stiffly assert and defend the honour of Christ ? What doubt can then be made of the success of Christ's interest, and the prosperity of his cause, when the very enemies thereof are made to serve it ?

Rather than Christ shall want honour, Pilate, the man that condemned him, shall do him honour.   And as it fared with his person, just so with his interest also. How often have the people of God received mercies from the hands of their enemies ! As in Rev. xii. 16, " The earth helped the woman," that is, wicked men did the church service.   So that this may singularly relieve us against all our despondencies and fears of the miscarriage of the interest of Christ.

Those people can never be ruined, who thrive by their losses ; conquer by being conquered ; multiply by being diminished :

whose worst enemies are made to do that for them, which friends cannot or dare not do. See you a heathen Pilate proclaiming the honour and innocency of Christ ; God will not want instruments to honour Christ by. If others cannot, his very enemies shall.

6. Did Pilate vindicate Christ in drawing up such a title to be affixed to his cross ? Then hence it follows, that God will, sooner or later, clear up the innocency and integrity of his people, who commit their cause to him. Christ's name was clouded with many reproaches ; wounded through and through, by the blasphemous tongues of his malicious enemies. He committed himself to Him that judgeth righteously, 1 Pet. ii. 23 ; and see how soon God vindicates him. That is sweet and seasonable counsel for us, when our names are clouded with unjust censures, " Commit thy way unto the Lord ; trust also in him, and he shall bring it to pass. He shall bring forth thy righteousness as the light, and thy judgment as the noon day," Psa. xxxvii. 5, 6. Joseph was accused of incontinency ; David, of treason ; Daniel, of disobedience ; Elijah, of troubling Israel ; Jeremiah, of revolting ; Amos, of preaching against the king ; the apostles, of sedition, rebellion, and alteration of laws ; but how did all these honourable names wade out of their reproaches, as the sun out of a cloud ! God cleared up their honour for them even in this world. " Slanders (saith one) are but as soap, which though it soils and daubs for the present, yet it helps to make the garment more clean and shining." Scorn and reproach is but a little cloud, that is soon blown over. But suppose ye should not be vindicated in this world, but die under a cloud upon your names ; be sure God will clear it up, and that to purpose in that great day. " Then shall the righteous (even in this respect) shine forth as the sun in the kingdom of their Father."

Be patient therefore, my brethren, unto the coming of the Lord. " The Lord cometh with ten thousand of his saints, to execute judgment upon all, and to convince all that are ungodly of all their ungodly deeds which they have ungodly committed, and of all their hard speeches which ungodly sinners have spoken against him," Jude 14, 15. Then shall they retract their censures, and alter their opinions of the saints. If Christ will be our Advocate, we need not fear who are our accusers. If your name, for his sake, be cast out as evil, and spurned in the dirt ; Christ will deliver it you again in that day whiter than the snow in Salmon.

7. Did Pilate give this title to cast the reproach of his death

upon the jews, and clear himself of it ? How natural is it to men to transfer the fault of their own actions from themselves to others ! For when he writes, This is the King of the jews, he wholly charges them with the crime of crucifying their King : and it is as if he had said, Hereafter let the blame and fault of this action lie wholly upon your heads, who have brought the guilt of his blood upon yourselves and children. I am clear, you have extorted it from me. Oh where shall we find a spirit so ingenuous, to take home to itself the shame of its own actions, and charge itself freely with its own guilt ? It is the property of renewed, gracious hearts to remember, confess, and freely bewail their own evils, to the glory of God.

SERMON XXVIII.

OF THE MANNER OF CHRIST'S DEATH, IN RESPECT TO THE SOLITARINESS THEREOF.

ZECH. XIII. 7.

AWAKE, O SWORD, AGAINST MY SHEPHERD, AND AGAINST THE MAN THAT IS MY FELLOW, SAITH THE LORD OF HOSTS: SMITE THE SHEPHERD, AND THE SHEEP SHALL BE SCATTERED: AND I WILL TURN MINE HAND UPON THE LITTLE ONES.

In the former sermons we have opened the nature and kind of death Christ died; even the cursed death of the cross. Wherein, nevertheless, his innocency was vindicated, by that honourable title providentially affixed to his cross. Method now requires that we take into consideration the manner in which he endured the cross; and that was solitarily, meekly, and instructively.

His solitude in suffering is plainly expressed in this scripture now before us. It cannot be doubted, but the prophet in this place speaks of Christ, if you consider Matt. xxvi. 31, where you shall find these words applied to Christ by his own accommodation of them: " Then said Jesus unto them, All ye shall be offended because of me this night, for it is written, I will smite the shepherd, and the sheep shall be scattered." Besides, the title here given " God's fellow," is too great for any creature in heaven or earth besides Christ.

In these words we have four things particularly to consider. 1. The commission given to the sword by the Lord of hosts. 2. The person against whom it is commissioned. 3. The dismal effect of that stroke. 4. And lastly, The gracious mitigation of it.

1. The commission given to the sword by the Lord of hosts, " Awake, O sword, and smite, saith the Lord of hosts." The Lord of hosts, at whose command all the creatures are, who, with a word of his mouth, can open all the armouries in the world, and command what weapons and instruments of death he please, calls here for the sword; not the rod, gently to chasten, but the sword, to destroy. The strokes and thrusts of the sword are mortal; and he bids it " to awake and smite." And it is as if the Lord had said, Come forth out of thy scabbard, O sword of justice; thou hast been hid there a long time, and hast,

as it were, been asleep in thy scabbard; now awake and glitter, thou shalt drink royal blood, such as thou never sheddest before.

2. The person against whom it is commissioned, "My shepherd, and the man that is my fellow." This shepherd can be no other than Christ, who is often in scripture styled "a Shepherd, yea, the chief Shepherd, the Prince of pastors." Who redeemed, feeds, guides, and preserves the flock of God's elect, 1 Pet. v. 4; John x. 11. This is he whom he also styles the man his fellow. Or his neighbour, as some render it. And so Christ is, with respect to his equality and unity with the Father, both in essence and will. His next neighbour. His other self. You have the sense of it in Phil. ii. 6. He was in the form of God, and thought it no robbery to be equal with God. Against Christ his fellow, the delight of his soul, the sword here receives its commission.

3. You have here the dismal consequence of this deadly stroke upon the Shepherd. And that is the scattering of the sheep. By the sheep understand here, that little flock, the disciples, which followed this Shepherd till he was smitten, that is, apprehended by his enemies, and they were scattered, that is, dispersed; they all forsook him and fled. And so Christ was left alone, amidst his enemies. Not one durst make a stand for him, or own him in that hour of his danger.

4. And lastly, Here is a gracious mitigation of this sad dispersion, "I will turn mine hand upon the little ones." By little ones he means the same that before he called sheep; but the expression is designedly varied, to show their feebleness and weakness, which appeared in their relapse from Christ. And by turning his hand upon them, understand God's gracious restoration, and gathering of them again after their sad dispersion, so that they shall not be lost, though scattered for the present. For after the Lord was risen, he went before them into Galilee, as he promised, Matt. xxviii. 10; and gathered them again by a gracious hand, so that not one of them was lost but the son of perdition.

I observe, suitably to the method I have proposed,

THAT CHRIST'S DEAREST FRIENDS FORSOOK AND LEFT HIM ALONE, IN THE TIME OF HIS GREATEST DISTRESS AND DANGER.

This doctrine containing only matter of fact, and that also so plainly delivered by the several faithful evangelists, I need spend no longer time in the proof of it, than to refer you to the several testimonies they have given to it. But I shall rather choose to fit and prepare it for use, by explaining these four questions.

I. Who were the sheep that were scattered from their Shepherd, and left him alone? II. What evil was there in this their scattering? III. What were the grounds and causes of it? IV. and lastly, What was the issue and event of it?

I. Who were these sheep that were dispersed and scattered from their Shepherd when he was smitten? It is evident they were those precious elect souls that he had gathered to himself, who had long followed him, and dearly loved him, and were dearly beloved of him. They were persons that had left all and followed him, and, till that time, faithfully continued with him in his temptations, Luke xxii. 28. And were all resolved so to do, though they should die with him, Matt. xxvi. 35. These were the persons.

II. But were they as good as their word? Did they indeed adhere faithfully to him? No, they all forsook him and fled. These sheep were scattered. This was not indeed a total and final apostasy, yet it was a very sinful and sad relapse; as will appear by considering the following aggravations and circumstances of it. For,

1. It was against the very articles of agreement, which they had sealed to Christ at their first admission into his service; he had told them, in the beginning, what they must resolve upon; " If any man come to me, and hate not his father, and mother, and wife, and children, and brethren, and sisters, yea, and his own life also, he cannot be my disciple. And whosoever doth not bear his cross, and come after me, cannot be my disciple," Luke xiv. 26, 27. Accordingly they submitted to these terms, and told him they had left all and followed him, Mark x. 28. Against this engagement made to Christ, they now sin. Here was unfaithfulness.

2. It was against the very principles of grace implanted by Christ in their hearts. They were holy, sanctified persons, in whom dwelt the love and fear of God. By these they were strongly inclined to adhere to Christ, in the time of his sufferings, as appears by those honest resolves they had made in the case. Their grace strongly inclined them to their duty; their corruptions swayed them the contrary way. Grace bid them stand; corruption bid them fly. Grace told them it was their duty to share in the sufferings as well as in the glory of Christ. Corruption represented these sufferings as intolerable, and bid them shift for themselves whilst they might. So that here must needs be a force and violence offered to their light, and the loving constraints thereof; which is no small evil. For though I grant it was a sudden, surprising temptation, yet

it cannot be imagined, that for so long time they were without any debate or reasonings about their duty.

3. It was much against the honour of their Lord and Master. By this their sinful flight they exposed the Lord Jesus to the contempt and scorn of his enemies. This some conceive is imported in that question which the high priest asked him; " The high priest then asked Jesus of his disciples, and of his doctrine," John xviii. 19. He asked him of his disciples, how many he had, and what was become of them now? And what was the reason they forsook their Master, and left him to shift for himself when danger appeared? But to those questions Christ made no reply. He would not accuse them to their enemies, though they had deserted him. But, doubtless, it did not a little reflect upon Christ, that there was not one of all his friends that durst own their relation to him, in a time of danger.

4. It was against their own solemn promise made to him before his apprehension, to live and die with him. They had passed their word, and given their promise that they would not flinch from him; " Peter said to him, Though I should die with thee, yet will I not deny thee. Likewise also said all the disciples," Matt. xxvi. 35. This made it a perfidious relapse. Here they break promise with Christ, who never did so with them. He might have told them when he met them afterwards in Galilee, as the roman soldier told his general, when he refused his petition after the war was ended,.I did not serve you so at the battle of Actium.

5. It was against Christ's heart-melting expostulations with them, which should have abode in their hearts while they lived. For when others that followed him went back, and walked no more with him, Jesus said to these very men, that now forsook him at last, " Will ye also go away?" John vi. 67. Will ye also forsake me? Whatever others do, I expect other things from you.

6. It was against the warning a late direful example presented to them in the fall of Judas. In him, as in a glass, they might see how fearful a thing it is to apostatize from Christ. They had heard Christ's dreadful threats against him. They were present when he called him the son of perdition, John xviii. 11. They had heard Christ say of him, " Good had it been if he had never been born." An expression able to scare the deadest heart. They saw he had left Christ the evening before. And that very day, in which they fled, he hanged himself. And yet they fly. After all this they forsake Christ.

7. It was against the law of love, which should have knit them closer to Christ, and to one another.

If to avoid the present shock of persecution, they had fled, yet surely they should have kept together, praying, watching, encouraging, and strengthening one another. But as they all forsook Christ, so they forsook one another also; for it is said, " They shall go every man to his own, and leave Christ alone," John xvi. 32; that is, saith Beza, every man to his own house, and to his own business.

8. And lastly, This their departure from Christ was accompanied with some offence at Christ. For so he tells them, " All ye shall be offended because of me this night," Matt. xxvi. 31. The word is, $\sigma\kappa\alpha\nu\delta\alpha\lambda\iota\sigma\theta\eta\sigma\epsilon\sigma\theta\epsilon$, you shall be scandalized at me, or in me. Some think the scandal they took at Christ was this, that when they saw he was fallen into his enemies' hands, and could no longer defend himself; they then began to question whether he were the Christ or no, since he could not defend himself from his enemies. Others more rightly understand it of their shameful flight from Christ, seeing it was not now safe to abide longer with him. That seeing he gave himself into their hands, they thought it advisable to provide as well as they could for themselves, and some where or other, to take refuge from the present storm, which had overtaken him. This was the nature and quality of the fact. We inquire,

III. Into the grounds and reasons of it. Which were three.

1. God's suspending wonted influences and aids of grace from them. They were not wont to do so. They never did so afterwards. They would not have done so now, had there been influences of power, zeal, and love from Heaven upon them. But how then should Christ have borne the heat and burden of the day? How should he have trod the wine-press alone? How should his sorrows have been extreme, unmixed, unmitigated, (as it behoved them to be,) if they had adhered faithfully to him in his troubles? No, no, it must not be; Christ must not have the least relief or comfort from any creature; and therefore, that he might be left alone, to grapple hand to hand with the wrath of God and of men, the Lord for a time withholds his encouraging, strengthening influences from them; and then, like Samson when he had lost his locks, they were weak as other men. " Be strong in the Lord, and in the power of his might," saith the apostle, Eph. vi. 10. If that be withheld, our resolutions and purposes melt away before a temptation, as snow before the sun.

2. The efficacy of the temptation was great, yea, much greater than ordinary. As they were weaker than they were used to be, so the temptation was stronger than any they had

yet met withal. It is called, " Their hour and the power of darkness," Luke xxii. 53. A sifting, winnowing hour, ver. 46. Oh it was a black and cloudy day. Never had the disciples met with such a whirlwind, such a furious storm before. The devil desired but to have the winnowing of them in that day, and so would have sifted and winnowed them, that their faith had utterly failed, had not Christ secured it by his prayer for them. So that it was an extraordinary trial that was upon them.

3. That which concurred to their shameful relapse, as a special cause of it, was the remaining corruptions that were in their hearts yet unmortified. Their knowledge was but little, and their faith not much. Upon the account of their weakness in grace, they were called little ones in the text. And as their graces were weak, so their corruptions were strong. Their unbelief and carnal fears grew powerfully upon them.

Do not censure them, reader, in thy thoughts, nor despise them for this their weakness. Neither say in thy heart, Had I been there as they were, I would never have done as they did. They thought as little of doing what they did, as you, or any of the saints do ; and as much did their souls detest and abhor it : but here thou mayest see, whither a soul that fears God may be carried, if his corruptions be irritated by strong temptations, and God withholds usual influences.

IV. Let us view the issue of this sad apostasy of theirs ; and you shall find it ended far better than it began. Though these sheep were scattered for a time, yet the Lord made good his promise, in turning his hand upon these little ones, to gather them. The morning was overcast, but the evening was clear. Peter repents of his perfidious denial of Christ, and never denied him more. All the rest likewise returned to Christ, and never forsook him any more. He that was afraid at the voice of a damsel, afterwards feared not the frowns of the mighty. And they that durst not own Christ now, afterwards confessed him openly before councils and rulers, and rejoiced that they were counted worthy to suffer for his sake, Acts v. 41. They that were now as timorous as hares, and started at every sound, afterward became as bold as lions, and feared not any danger, but sealed their confession of Christ with their blood. For though, at this time, they forsook him, it was not voluntarily, but by surprisal. Though they forsook him, they still loved him ; though they fled from him, there still remained a gracious principle in them ; the root of the matter was still in them, which recovered them again.

Though they forsook Christ, yet Christ never forsook them : he loved them still ; " Go tell the disciples, and tell Peter, that I go before you into Galilee," Mark xvi. 7. *q. d.* Let them not think that I so remember their unkindness, as to own them no more: no, I love them still.

The use of this is contained in the following inferences.

1. Did the disciples forsake Christ, though they had such strong persuasions and resolutions never to do it ? Then we see, that self-confidence is a sin too incident to the best of men. They little thought their hearts would have proved so base and deceitful, as they found them to be when they were tried. " Though all men forsake thee (saith Peter) yet will not I." Good man, he resolved honestly, but he knew not what a feather he should be in the wind of temptation, if God once left him to his own fears.

Little reason have the best of saints to depend upon their inherent grace, let their stock be as large as it will. The angels left to themselves, quickly left their own habitations, Jude 6. Upon which one well observes, That the best of created perfections are of themselves defective. Every excellency without the prop of Divine preservation, is but a weight which tends to a fall. The angels in their innocency were but frail, without God's sustentation ; even grace itself is but a creature, and therefore purely dependent. What becomes of the stream, if the fountain supply it not ? What continuance hath the reflection in the glass, if the man that looks into it turn away his face ? The constant supplies of the Spirit of Jesus Christ, are the food and fuel of all our graces. The best men will show themselves but men if God leave them. He who hath set them up, must also keep them. It is safer to be humble with one talent, than proud with ten ; yea, better to be an humble worm, than a proud angel. Adam had more advantage to maintain his station than any of us. But though he was created upright, and had no inherent corruption to endanger him, yet he fell.

And shall we be self-confident, after such instances of human frailty ? Alas, christian ! what match art thou for principalities and powers, and spiritual wickedness? " Be not high-minded, but fear." Consider well the instances of * Noah, Lot, David, and Hezekiah, men famous and renowned in their generations, who all fell by temptations ; yea, and that when one would think they had never been better provided to cope with them. Lot fell after, yea, presently after the Lord had thrust him out of Sodom, and his eyes had seen the direful punishment of sin ;

* Gen. ix. 21, 22, and xix. 36 ; 2 Sam. xi. 2 ; 2 Kings xx. 12.

hell, as it were, rained upon them out of heaven.   Noah, in like manner, immediately after God's wonderful and astonishing preservation of him in the ark ; when he saw a world of men and women perishing in the floods for their sins.   David, after the Lord had settled the kingdom on him, which for sin he rent from Saul, and given him rest in his house.   Hezekiah was but just up from a great sickness, wherein the Lord wrought a wonderful salvation for him.   Did such men, and at such times, when one would think no temptations should have prevailed, fall, and that so foully?   Then " let him that thinks he standeth, take heed lest he fall." Oh " be not high-minded, but fear."

2. Did Christ stand his ground, and go through with his suffering work, when all that had followed him forsook him ? Then a resolved adherence to God and duty, though left alone, without company or encouragement, is Christ-like, and truly excellent.   You shall not want better company than that which hath forsaken you in the way of God.   Elijah complains, " They have forsaken thy covenant, thrown down thine altars, and slain thy prophets with the sword ; and I, even I only, am left, and they seek my life, to take it away," 1 Kings xix. 10. And yet all this did not discourage him in following the Lord ; for still he was very jealous for the Lord God of hosts.   Paul complains, " At my first answer no man stood by me, all men forsook me : nevertheless the Lord stood with me," 2 Tim. iv. 16, 17. And as the Lord stood by him, so he stood by his God alone, without any aid or support from men.   How great an argument of integrity is this ! He that professes Christ for company, will also leave him for company.   But to be faithful to God, when forsaken of men ; to be a Lot, in Sodom ; a Noah, in a corrupted generation ; oh, how excellent is it ! It is sweet to travel over this earth to heaven, in the company of the saints, that are bound thither with us, if we can ; but if we can meet no company, we must not be discouraged from going on. It is not unlikely but before you have gone many steps farther, you may have cause to say, as one did once, " Never less alone, than when alone."

3. Did the disciples thus forsake Christ, and yet were all recovered at last ? Then, though believers are not privileged from backslidings, yet they are secured from final apostasy and ruin. The new creature may be sick, but it cannot die.   Saints may fall, but they shall rise again, Micah vii. 8.   The highest flood of natural zeal and resolution may ebb, and be wholly dried up ; but saving grace is " a well of water, still springing up into everlasting life," John iv. 14.   God's unchangeable election,

the frame and constitution of the new covenant, the meritorious and prevalent intercession of Jesus Christ, do give the believer abundant security against the danger of a total and final apostasy. " My Father, which gave them me, (saith Christ,) is greater than all : and none is able to pluck them out of my Father's hand," John x. 29.

" The foundation of God standeth sure, having this seal, The Lord knoweth who are his," 2 Tim. ii. 19. Every person committed to Christ by the Father, shall be brought by him to the Father, and not one wanting. God hath also so framed and ordered the new covenant, that none of those souls who are within the blessed clasp and bond of it can possibly be lost. It is settled upon immutable things : and we know things are as their foundations be, Heb. vi. 18, 19. Among the many glorious promises this is one, " I will not turn away from them, to do them good ; but I will put my fear in their hearts, that they shall not depart from me." As the fear of God in our hearts pleads in us against sin, so our potent Intercessor in heaven pleads for us with the Father ; and by reason thereof, we cannot finally miscarry, Rom. viii. 34, 35. Upon these grounds, we may (as the apostle does in the place last cited) triumph in that full security which God hath given us ; and say, " Who shall separate us from the love of God?" Understand it either of God's to us, as Calvin, Beza, and Martyr do ; or of our love to God, as Ambrose and Augustine do : it is true in both senses, and a most comfortable truth.

4. Did the sheep fly when the Shepherd was smitten ; did such men, and so many forsake Christ in the trial ? Then learn how sad a thing it is for the best of men to be left to their own carnal fears in a day of temptation. This was it that made those good men shrink away so shamefully from Christ in that trial. " The fear of man brings a snare," Prov. xxix. 25. In that snare these good souls were taken, and for a time held fast.

Oh what work will this unruly passion make, if the fear of God do not overrule it ! Is it not a shame to a christian, a man of faith, to see himself outdone by a heathen ? Shall natural conscience and courage make them stand and keep their places in times of danger ; when we shamefully turn our backs upon duty, because we see duty and danger together ? When the emperor Vespasian had commanded Fluidius Priscus not to come to the senate ; or, if he did, to speak nothing but what he would have him ; the senator returned this brave and noble answer, * " That as he was a senator, it was fit he should

* Charron, of Wisdom, p. 358.

be at the senate; and if, being there, he were required to give his advice, he would speak freely, that which his conscience commanded him." The emperor threatened that then he should die; he returned thus, "Did I ever tell you that I was immortal? Do you what you will, and I will do what I ought. It is in your power to put me to death unjustly, and in me to die constantly?"

Oh think, what mischiefs your fears may do yourselves, and the discovery of them to others. Learn to trust God with your lives, liberties, and comforts, in the way of your duty; and at what time you are afraid trust in him: and do not so magnify poor dust and ashes, as to be scared, by their threat, from your God and your duty. The politic design of Satan herein, is to affright you out of your coverts, where you are safe, into the net. I will enlarge on this no farther; I have * elsewhere laid down fourteen rules for the cure of this, in what of mine is public.

5. Learn hence, how much a man may differ from himself, according as the Lord is with him, or withdrawn from him. The christian does not only differ from other men, but sometimes from himself also; yea, so great is the difference between himself and himself, as if he were not the same man. And where is he that doth not so experience it? Sometimes bold and courageous, despising dangers, bearing down all discouragements in the strength of zeal and love to God; at another time faint, feeble, and discouraged at every petty thing. Whence is this but from the different administrations of the Spirit, who sometimes gives forth more, and sometimes less, of his gracious influence. These very men that fled now, when the Spirit was more abundantly shed forth upon them, could boldly own Christ before the council, and despised all dangers for his sake. We are strong or weak, according to the degrees of assisting grace. So that as you cannot take the just measure of a christian by one act, so neither must they judge of themselves, by what they sometimes feel in themselves. But when their spirits are low, and their hearts discouraged, they should rather say to their souls, " Hope in God, for I shall yet praise him;" it is low with me now, but it will be better.

6. Was the sword drawn against the Shepherd, and he left alone to receive the mortal strokes of it? How should all adore both the justice and the mercy of God so illustriously displayed herein! Here is the triumph of Divine justice, and the highest triumph that ever it had, to single forth the chief Shepherd, the

* A Saint indeed.

Man that is God's fellow, and sheathe its sword in his breast for satisfaction.

And no less is the mercy and goodness of God herein signalized, in giving the sword a commission against the Man, his fellow, rather than against us. Why had he not rather said, Awake, O sword, against the men that are mine enemies, shed the blood of them that have sinned against me, than, Smite the Shepherd, and only scatter the sheep. Blessed be God, that the dreadful sword was not drawn and brandished against our souls ; that God did not set it to our breasts, and bathe it in our blood. That his fellow was smitten, that his enemies might be spared, oh what manner of love was this ! Blessed be God therefore for Jesus Christ, who received the fatal stroke himself ; and hath now so sheathed that sword in its scabbard, that it shall never be drawn any more against any that believe in him.

7. Were the sheep scattered when the Shepherd was smitten ? Learn hence, that the best of men know not their own strength till they come to the trial. Little did these holy men imagine such a cowardly spirit had been in them, till temptation put it to the proof. Let this therefore be a caution for ever to the people of God. You resolve never to forsake Christ, you do well ; but so did these, and yet were scattered from him. You can never take a just measure of your own strength, till temptation have tried it. It is said, Deut. viii. 2, that God led the people so many years in the wilderness, to prove them ; and to know them, (that is, to make them know) what was in their hearts. Little did they think such unbelief, murmurings, discontents, and a spirit bent to backslidings, had been in them, until their straits in the wilderness gave them the sad experience of these things.

8. Did the dreadful sword of Divine justice smite the Shepherd, God's own fellow ; and at the same time the flock, from whom all its outward comforts arose, were scattered from him ? Then learn, that the holiest of men have no reason either to repine or despond, though God should at once strip them of all their outward and inward comforts together. God did take all comfort from Christ, both outward and inward ; and are you greater than he ? God sometimes takes outward, and leaves inward comfort ; sometimes he takes inward, and leaves outward comfort : but the time may come, when God may strip you of both. This was the case of Job, a favourite of God, who was blessed with outward and inward comforts ; yet a time came when God stripped him of all, and made him poor to a proverb, as to all outward comfort ; and the venom of his arrows drank up his

spirit, and the inward comforts thereof. Should the Lord deal thus with any of you, how seasonable and relieving will the following considerations be !

Though the Lord deal thus with you, yet this is no new thing; he hath so dealt with others, yea with Jesus Christ himself. If these things were done to him that never deserved it for any sin of his own, how little reason have we to complain !

Nay, for this very reason did this befall Jesus Christ before you, that the like condition might be sanctified to you, when you shall be brought into it. For Jesus Christ passed through such varieties of conditions, on purpose that he might take away the curse, and leave a blessing in those conditions, against the time that you should come into them.

Moreover, though inward comforts and outward comforts were both removed from Christ in one day, yet he wanted not support in the absence of both. How relieving a consideration is this ! "Behold, (saith he,) the hour cometh, yea, is now come, that ye shall be scattered, every man to his own, and shall leave me alone ; and yet I am not alone, because the Father is with me," John xvi. 32. Thy God, christian, can in like manner support thee, when all sensible comforts shrink away together from thy soul and body in one day.

Lastly, It deserves a remark, that this comfortless forsaken condition of Christ immediately preceded the day of his greatest glory and comfort. Naturalists observe, the greatest darkness is a little before the dawning of the morning. It was so with Christ, it may be so with thee. It was but a little while, and he had better company than theirs that forsook him. Act therefore your faith upon this, that the most glorious light usually follows the thickest darkness. The louder your groans are now, the louder your triumphs hereafter will be. The horror of your present, will but add to the lustre of your future state.

SERMON XXIX.

OF THE MANNER OF CHRIST'S DEATH, IN RESPECT OF THE PATIENCE THEREOF.

ISA. LIII. 7.

HE WAS OPPRESSED, AND HE WAS AFFLICTED, YET HE OPENED NOT HIS
MOUTH: HE IS BROUGHT AS A LAMB TO THE SLAUGHTER, AND AS A SHEEP
BEFORE HER SHEARERS IS DUMB, SO HE OPENETH NOT HIS MOUTH.

How our Lord Jesus Christ carried on the work of our redemption in his humble state, both in his incarnation, life, and death, hath in part been discovered in the former sermons. I have showed you the kind or nature of that death he died; and am now engaged, by the method proposed, to open the manner of his death. The solitariness or loneliness of Christ in his sufferings, was the subject of the last sermon. The patience and meekness of Christ in his sufferings, come in order, to be opened in this.

This chapter treats wholly of the sufferings of Christ and the blessed fruits thereof. Hornbeck tells us of a learned jew, "that ingenuously confessed this very chapter converted him to the christian faith; and such delight he had in it, that he read it more than a thousand times over." Such is the clearness of this prophecy, that he who penned it, is deservedly styled the evangelical prophet. From this seventh verse, I shall speak to these two points. The grievous sufferings of Christ, and the glorious ornament he put upon them; even the ornament of a meek and patient spirit. He opened not his mouth; but went as a sheep to be shorn, or a lamb to the slaughter. The lamb goes as quiet to the slaughter-house, as to the fold. By this lively and lovely similitude, the patience of Christ is here expressed to us. Whence the note is, That Jesus Christ supported the burden of his sufferings with admirable patience and meekness of spirit.

It is a true observation, that meekness inviteth injury, but always to its own cost. And it was evidently verified in the sufferings of Christ. Christ's meekness triumphed over the affronts and injuries of his enemies, much more than they triumphed over him.   Patience never had a more glorious triumph, than it had upon the cross.

The meekness and patience of his spirit, amidst injuries and provocations, is excellently set forth in 1 Pet. ii. 22, 23. "Who did no sin, neither was guile found in his mouth: who when he was reviled, reviled not again ; when he suffered he threatened not, but committed himself to him that judgeth righteously."

In this point we have these three things to open doctrinally.

I. The burden of sufferings and provocations that Jesus Christ was oppressed with.   II. The meekness and admirable patience with which he supported that burden.   III. The causes and grounds of that perfect patience which he then exercised.

I. The burden of sufferings and provocations which Christ supported, was very great ; for on him met all sorts and kinds of trouble at once, and those in their highest degrees and fullest strength.   Troubles in his soul, and these were the soul of his troubles. " He began to be sore amazed and very heavy," Mark xiv. 33.   The wrath of an infinite God beat him down to the dust. His body full of pain and exquisite tortures in every part. Not a member or sense but was the seat and subject of torment.

His name and honour suffered the vilest indignities, blasphemies, and reproaches that the malignity of Satan and wicked men could utter against it. Contempt was poured upon all his offices. Upon his kingly office, when they crowned him with thorns, arrayed him with purple, bowed the knee in mockery to him, and cried, " Hail, King of the jews."   His prophetical office, when they blinded him, and then bid him " prophesy who smote him."   His priestly office, when they reviled him on the cross, saying, " He saved others, himself he cannot save."   They scourged him, spit in his face, and smote him on the head and face.   Besides, the very kind of death they put him to was reproachful and ignominious ; as you heard before.

Now all this, and much more than this, meeting at once upon an innocent and dignified person ; one that was greater than all ; upon one that could have crushed all his enemies as a moth ; I say, for him to bear all this, without the least discomposure of spirit, or breach of patience, is the highest triumph of patience that ever was in the world.   It was one of the greatest wonders of that wonderful day.

II. And that is the next thing we have to consider, even this almighty patience and unparalleled meekness of Christ, supporting such a burden with such evenness and steadiness of spirit.

Christian patience, or the grace of patience, is an ability or power to suffer hard and heavy things, according to the will of God. It is a glorious power, that strengthens the suffering soul to bear. It is our passive fortitude : " Strengthened with all might, according to his glorious power, unto all patience and long-suffering with joyfulness," Col. i. 11 : that is, strengthened with the might or power of God himself; or such as might appear to be the proper impress and image of that Divine power, which is both its principle and pattern.

It is a power or ability in the soul, to bear hard, heavy, and difficult things. Such only are the objects of patience. God hath several sorts of burdens to impose upon his people. Some heavier, others lighter ; some to be carried but a few hours, others many days, others all our days : some more spiritual, bearing upon the soul ; some more external, touching or punishing the flesh immediately, and the spirit by way of sympathy ; and sometimes both sorts are laid on together.· So they were at this time on Christ. His soul full of the bitter sense and apprehension of the wrath of God : his body filled with tortures : in every member and sense grief took up its lodging. Here was the highest exercise of patience.

It is a power to bear hard and heavy things, according to the will of God. Considering it in that respect, patience, the christian grace, differs from patience, the moral virtue. So the apostle describes it, " Let them that suffer according to the will of God," &c. 1 Pet. iv. 19 ; that is, who exercise patience graciously, as God would have them.

III. In the last place, let us inquire into the grounds and reasons of this his most perfect patience. And you shall find perfect holiness, wisdom, fore-knowledge, faith, heavenly-mindedness, and obedience, at the root of this perfect patience.

1. This admirable patience and meekness of Christ, was the fruit of his perfect holiness. His nature was free from those corruptions that ours groan and labour under. Take the meek Moses, who excelled all others in that grace, and let him be tried in that very grace wherein he excels, and see how " unadvisedly he may speak with his lips," Psa. cvi. 33. Take a Job, whose famous patience is resounded over all the world—"Ye have heard of the patience of Job," and let him be tried by outward and inward troubles, meeting upon him in one day ; and even a Job may curse the day wherein he was born. Envy, revenge, discontent, despondencies, are weeds naturally springing up in the corrupt soil of our sinful natures. " I saw a little child grow pale with envy," said Austin. And the spirit that is in

us lusteth to envy, saith the apostle, Jam. iv. 5. The principles of all these evils being in our natures, they will show themselves in time of trial. The old man is fretful and passionate. But it was otherwise with Christ. His nature was like a pure crystal glass, full of pure fountain water, which though shaken and agitated never so much, cannot show, because it hath no dregs. "The prince of this world cometh, and hath nothing in me," John xiv. 30. No principle of corruption, for a handle to temptation. Our High Priest was holy, harmless, undefiled, separate from sinners, Heb. vii. 26.

2. The meekness and patience of Christ proceeded from the infinite wisdom with which he was filled. The wiser any man is, the more patient he is. Hence meekness, the fruit, is denominated from patience, the root that bears it; "The meekness of wisdom," Jam. iii. 13. And anger is lodged in folly, its proper cause; " Anger resteth in the bosom of fools," Eccl. vii. 9. Seneca would allow no place for passion in a wise man's breast. Wise men ponder, consider, and weigh things deliberately in their judgments, before they suffer their affections and passions to be stirred and enraged. Hence come the constancy and serenity of their spirits. As wise Solomon hath observed, " A man of understanding is of an excellent (or, as the hebrew is, a cool) spirit," Prov. xvii. 27.

Now wisdom filled the soul of Christ. He is wisdom in the abstract, Prov. viii. In him are hid all the treasures of wisdom, Col. ii. 3. Hence it was that he was no otherwise moved with the revilings and abuses of his enemies, than a wise physician is with the impertinences of his distempered and crazy patient.

3. His patience flowed also from his fore-knowledge. He had a perfect prospect of all those things from eternity, which befell him afterwards. They came not upon him by way of surprisal. And therefore he wondered not at them when they came, as if some strange thing had happened. He foresaw all these things long before: " And he began to teach them, that the Son of man must suffer many things, and be rejected of the elders, and chief priests, and scribes, and be killed," Mark viii. 31. Yea, he had agreed with his Father to endure all this for our sakes, before he assumed our flesh. Hence, " I gave my back to the smiters, and my cheeks to them that plucked off the hair. I hid not my face from shame and spitting," Isa. l. 6.

Just as Christ, in John xvi. 4, obviates all future offences his disciples might take at suffering for his sake, by telling them before-hand what they must expect: " These things (saith he) I told you, that when the time shall come, ye may remember that I told you of them:" so he, foreknowing what himself must suffer, and having agreed so to do, bare those sufferings with singular patience. " Jesus therefore knowing all things that should come upon him, went forth, and said unto them, Whom seek ye?" John xviii. 4.

4. His patience sprang from his faith which he exercised under all that he suffered in this world. His faith looked through all those black and dismal clouds, to the joy proposed, Heb. xii. 2. He knew that though Pilate condemned, God would justify him, Isa. l. 4—8. And he set one over-against the other: he balanced the glory, into which he was to enter, with the sufferings, through which he was to enter into it. He exercised faith in God for divine support and assistance under sufferings, as well as for glory, the fruit and reward of them, " I have set" (or, as the apostle varies it, " I foresaw) the Lord always before me; because he is at my right hand, I shall not be moved. Therefore my heart is glad, and my glory rejoiceth," Psa. xvi. 8—11. There is faith exercised by Christ, for strength to carry him through. And then it follows, " My flesh also shall rest in hope; for thou wilt not leave my soul in hell, neither wilt thou suffer thine holy one to see corruption. Thou wilt show me the path of life. In thy presence is fulness of joy; at thy right hand there are pleasures for evermore." There is his faith acting upon the glory into which he was to enter, after he had suffered these things: this filled him with peace.

5. As his faith, eyeing the glory into which he was passing, made him endure all things; so the heavenliness of his Spirit also filled him with a heavenly tranquillity and calmness of spirit under all his abuses and injuries. It is a certain truth, that the more heavenly any man's spirit is, the more sedate, composed, and peaceful. " As the higher heavens (saith Seneca) are more ordinate and tranquil; where there are neither clouds nor winds, storms nor tempests; but they are the inferior heavens that lighten and thunder, and the nearer the earth the more tempestuous and unquiet: even so the sublime and heavenly mind is placed in a calm and quiet station." Certainly that heart which is sweetened frequently with heavenly, delightful communion with God, is not very apt to be imbittered with wrath, or soured with revenge against men. The peace of God doth appease and end all strifes and differences. The heavenly Spirit marvellously affects a sedate and quiet breast.

Now, never was there such a heavenly soul on earth, since man inhabited it, as Christ was: he had most sweet and wonderful communion with God : he had meat to eat, which others, yea, and those his most intimate friends, knew not of. The Son of man was in heaven upon earth, John iii. 13; even in respect of that blessed heavenly communion he had with God, as well as in respect of his immense Deity : and that his heart was in heaven when he so patiently endured the pain and shame of the cross is evident from Heb. xii. 2, " For the joy set before him, he endured the cross, despising the shame."

6. And lastly, As his meekness and patience sprang from the heavenliness and sublimity of his spirit ; so likewise, from the complete and absolute obedience of it to his Father's will and pleasure : he could most quietly submit to all the will of God, and never regret at any part of the work assigned him by his Father.   For you must know, that Christ's death was on his part an act of obedience ; he all along eyeing his Father's command and counsel in what he suffered, Phil. ii. 7, 8 ; John xviii. 11 ; Psa. xl. 6—8.   Now, just as the eyeing and considering the hand of God in an affliction, presently becalms and quiets a gracious soul ; as you see in David, 2 Sam. xvi. 11. So much more it quieted Jesus Christ, who was privy to the design and end of his Father, with whose will he all along complied ; looking on jews and gentiles but as the instruments ignorantly fulfilling God's pleasure, and serving that great design of his Father ; this was his patience, and these the grounds of it.

In making a practical improvement of this subject I might use it in various ways; but the direct and main use of it is, to press us to a Christ-like patience in all our sufferings and troubles. And seeing in nothing we are more generally defective, and that defects of christians herein are so prejudicial to religion, and uncomfortable to themselves ; I resolve to wave all other uses, and spend the remaining time wholly upon this branch ; even a persuasive to christians unto all patience in tribulations ; to imitate their lamb-like Saviour. Unto this, christians, you are expressly called : " Because Christ also suffered for us, leaving us an example, that we should follow his steps. Who did no sin, neither was guile found in his mouth; who when he was reviled, reviled not again ; when he suffered, he threatened not ; but committed himself to him that judgeth righteously," 1 Pet. ii. 21, 22. Here is your pattern ; a perfect pattern ! a lovely and excellent pattern ! Will you be persuaded to the imitation of Christ herein? Methinks I should persuade you to it ; yea, every thing about you persuades to patience in your sufferings, as well as I : look which way you will, upward or downward, inward or outward, backward or forward, to the right hand or to the left, you shall find all things persuading and urging the doctrine of patience upon you.

1. Look upwards, when tribulations come upon you: look to that sovereign Lord, that commissionates and sends them upon you. You know troubles do not rise out of the dust, nor spring out of the ground, but are framed in heaven; "Behold I frame evil, and devise a device against you," Jer. xviii. 11. Troubles and afflictions are of the Lord's framing and devising, to reduce his wandering people to himself. In the frame of your afflictions, you may observe much of divine wisdom in the choice, measure, and season of your troubles: sovereignty, in electing the instruments of your affliction; in making them as afflictive as he pleaseth; and in making them obedient both to his call, in coming and going, when he pleaseth. Now, could you in times of trouble look up to this sovereign hand, in which your souls, bodies, and all their comforts and mercies are; how quiet would your hearts be! "I was dumb, and opened not my mouth, because it was thy doing," Psa. xxxix. 9. "It is the Lord, let him do what seemeth him good," 1 Sam. iii. 18. Oh, when we have to do with men, and look no higher, how do our spirits swell and rise with revenge and impatience! But if you once come to see that man is a rod in your Father's hand, you will be quiet, Psa. xlvi. 10. It is for want of looking up to God in our troubles, that we fret, murmur, and despond at the rate we do.

2. Look downward, and see what is below you, as well as up to that which is above you. You are afflicted, and you cannot bear it. No trouble like your trouble! never man in such a case as you are! Well, cast the eye of your mind downward, and see those who lie much lower than you. Can you see none on earth in a more miserable state than yourselves? Are you at the very bottom, and not a man below you? surely there are thousands in a sadder case than you on earth. What is your affliction? Have you lost a relation? Others have lost all. Have you lost an estate, and are become poor? Well, but there are some you read of, "who cut up mallows by the bushes, and juniper-roots for their meat. They are driven forth from among men, they cried after them as after a thief. They dwell in the cliffs of the valleys, in caves of the earth, and in the rocks. Among the bushes they brayed, under the nettles they were gathered together," Job xxx. 4—7. Are you persecuted and afflicted for Christ's sake? What think you of their sufferings,

" who had trial of cruel mockings; yea, moreover of bonds and imprisonments : they were stoned, they were sawn asunder, were tempted, were slain with the sword, they wandered about in sheep-skins and goat-skins, being destitute, afflicted, torment-ed," Heb. xi. 36, 37.   And are you better than they ? I know not what you are ; but I am sure, these were such " of whom the world was not worthy," ver. 38.

Or are your afflictions more spiritual and inward ?   Say not the Lord never dealt more bitterly with the soul of any, than he hath with yours.   What think you of the case of David, Heman, Job, Asaph, whose doleful cries, by reason of the terrors of the Almighty, are able to melt the stoniest heart that reads their complaints ?   The Almighty was a terror to them ; the arrows of God were within them ; they roared by reason of the disquietness of their hearts.   Or are your afflictions outward and inward together; an afflicted soul in an afflicted body ? Well, so it was with Paul, Job, and many other of those wor-thies gone before you.   Surely you may see many on earth who have been, and are in far lower and sadder states than yourselves. Or if not on earth, doubtless you will admit there are many in hell, who would be glad to change conditions with you, as bad as you think yours to be.   And were not all these mould-ed out of the same lump with you ?   Surely, if you can see any creature below you, especially any reasonable being, you have no reason to return so ungratefully upon your God, and accuse your Maker of severity, or charge God foolishly.   Look down, and you shall see grounds enough to be quiet.

3. Look inward, you discontented spirits, and see if you can find nothing there to quiet you.   Cast your eye into your own hearts ; consider either the corruptions or the graces that are there.   Cannot you find weeds enough there, that need such winter-weather as this to rot them ?   Hath not that proud heart need enough of all this to humble it ?   That carnal heart need of such things as these to mortify it ?   That backsliding, wandering heart need of all this to reduce and recover it to its God ?   " If need be, ye are in heaviness," 1 Pet. i. 6.   O christian ! didst thou not see need of this before thou camest into trouble ?   Or hath not God shown thee the need of it since thou wast under the rod ?   It is much thou shouldest not see it ; but be assured, if thou dost not, thy God doth : he knows thou wouldest be ruined for ever, if he should not take this course with thee.

Thy corruptions require all this to kill them. Thy lusts will take all this, it may be more than this, and all little enough.

And as your corruptions call for it, so do your graces too. Wherefore think ye the Lord planted the principles of faith, humility, patience, &c. in your souls? Were they put there for nothing? Did the Lord intend they should lie sleeping in their drowsy habits? Or were they not planted there in order to exercise? And how shall they be exercised without tribulations? Can you tell? Doth not "tribulation work patience, and patience experience, and experience hope?" Rom. v. 3, 4. Is not "the trial of your faith much more precious than of gold which perishes," 1 Pet. i. 7. Oh look inward, and you will be quiet.

4. Look outward, and see who stands by and observes your carriage under trouble. Are there not many eyes upon you? yea, many envious observers round about you. It was David's request, "Lead me, O Lord, in thy righteousness, because of mine enemies," Psa. v. 8; or, as the hebrew word there might be rendered, because of mine observers or watchers. There is many an envious eye upon you. To the wicked there can scarcely be a higher gratification and pleasure, than to see your carriage under trouble so like their own; for thereby they are confirmed in their prejudices against religion, and in their good opinion of themselves. These may talk and profess more than we, say they, but when they are tried, and put to it, it appears plainly enough, their religion enables them to do no more than we do; they talk of heaven's glory, and their future expectations; but it is only talk, for it is apparent enough their hopes cannot balance a small affliction, with all the happiness they talk of. Oh, how do you dishonour Christ before his enemies, when you make them think all your religion lies in talking of it!

5. Look backward, and see if there be nothing behind you that may hush and quiet your impatient spirits; consult the multitude of experiences past and gone, both your own and others. Is this the first strait that ever you were in? If so, you have reason to be quiet, yet to bless God that hath spared you so long, when others have had their days filled up with sorrow. But if you have been in troubles formerly, and the Lord hath helped you: if you have passed through the fire, and not been burnt; through the waters, and not drowned; if God hath stood by you, and hitherto helped you, oh what cause have you to be quiet now, and patiently wait for the salvation of God! Did he help you then, and cannot he do so now? Did he give water, and cannot he give bread also? Is he the God of the hills only, and not the God of the valleys also?

Oh call to mind the days of old, the years of the right-hand of the Most High. " These things I call to mind, therefore I have hope," Lam. iii. 21.   Have you kept no records of past experiences ?   How ungrateful then have you been to your God, and how injurious to yourselves, if you have not read them over in such a day as this; for to that end were they given you.

6. Look forward, to the end of your troubles; yea, look to a double end of them, the end of their duration, and the end of their operation.   Look ye to the end of their duration, and that is very near; they shall not be everlasting troubles, if you be such as fear the Lord.   " The God of all grace, who hath called us unto his eternal glory by Jesus Christ, after that ye have suffered a while, make you perfect," 1 Pet. v. 10.   " These light afflictions are but for a moment," 2 Cor. iv. 18 ; they are no more comparatively with that vast eternity that is before you.   What are a few days and nights of sorrows when they are past ?   Are they not swallowed up as a spoonful of water in the vast ocean ?   But more especially look to the end of their operation.   What do all these afflictions tend to and effect ?   Do they not work out an exceeding weight of glory ?   Are you not by them made " partakers of his holiness ?" Heb. xii.   Is not this all the fruit, to take away your sins?   What ! and be impatient at this; fret and repine, because God is, this way, perfecting your happiness ?   Oh ungrateful soul !

7. Look to the right-hand, and see how you are shamed, convinced, and silenced by other christians; and it may be such too, as never made that profession you have done ; and yet cannot only patiently bear the afflicting hand of God, but are blessing, praising, and admiring God under their troubles; whilst you are sinning against and dishonouring him under smaller ones.   It may be you will find some poor christians that know not where to have their next bread, and yet are speaking of the bounty of their God; while you are repining in the midst of plenty.   Ah ! if there be any ingenuousness in you, let this shame you.   If this will not, then,

8. Look to your left-hand, and there you will see a sad sight, and what one would think should quiet you.   There you may see a company of wicked, unconverted sinners, carrying themselves under their troubles but too much like yourselves. What do they more, than fret and murmur, despond and sink ; mix sin with their afflictions, when the rod of God is upon them ? It is time for thee to improve, when thou seest how near thou art come to them, whom thou hopest thou shalt never be ranked

and numbered with. Reader, such considerations as these would be of singular use to thy soul at such a time, but above all, thine eyeing the great pattern of patience, Jesus Christ; whose lamb-like carriage, under a trial, with which thine is not to be named the same day, is here recommended to thee. Oh how should this transform thee into a lamb, for meekness also !

SERMON XXX.

OF THE INSTRUCTIVENESS OF THE DEATH OF CHRIST, IN HIS SEVEN
LAST WORDS; THE FIRST OF WHICH IS HERE ILLUSTRATED.

LUKE XXIII. 34.

THEN SAID JESUS, FATHER, FORGIVE THEM, FOR THEY KNOW NOT WHAT
THEY DO.

THE manner in which Christ died hath already been opened in
the solitude and patience in which he died.   The third, to wit,
the instructiveness of his death, now follows, in these seven excellent and weighty sayings, which dropped from his blessed
lips upon the cross, whilst his sacred blood dropped on the
earth from his wounded hands and feet.   These sayings are
seven in number; three directed to his Father, and four more
to those about him.   Of the former sort this is one, "Father,
forgive them," &c.   In which we have, The mercy desired by
Christ, and that is forgiveness.   The persons for whom it is
desired; those cruel and wicked persons that were now imbru-
ing their hands in his blood.   And, The motive or argument
urged to procure that mercy from his Father, "for they know not
what they do."

The mercy prayed for is, forgiveness; "Father, forgive." Forgiveness is not only a mercy, a spiritual mercy, but one of the
greatest mercies a soul can obtain from God, without which,
whatever else we have from God, is no mercy to us.*

The persons for whom he requests forgiveness, are the same
that with wicked hands crucified him.   Their crime was the
most horrid that ever was committed by men. The best of
mercies is by him desired for the worst of sinners.

The motive or argument urged to procure this mercy for
them, is this, for they know not what they do. As if he should
say, Lord, what these poor creatures do, is not so much out of
malice to me as the Son of God; but it is from their ignorance.
To the same purpose the apostle saith, "Whom none of the
princes of this world knew; for had they known it, they would

* אשרי האיש *Fælicitates hominis*, that is, O the happiness of the man.—
Montanus.

not have crucified the Lord of glory," 1 Cor. ii. 8.   Yet this is not to be extended to all that had a hand in the death of Christ, but to the ignorant multitude, among whom some of God's elect were, who afterwards believed in him ; whose blood they spilt ; " And now, brethren, I wot that through ignorance ye did it," Acts iii. 17. For them this prayer of Christ was heard. Hence the notes are,

> DOCT. 1. THAT IGNORANCE IS THE USUAL CAUSE OF ENMITY TO CHRIST.

> DOCT. 2. THAT THERE IS FORGIVENESS WITH GOD, FOR SUCH AS OPPOSE CHRIST THROUGH IGNOR- ANCE.

> DOCT. 3. THAT TO FORGIVE ENEMIES, AND BEG FOR- GIVENESS FOR THEM, IS THE TRUE CHARACTER AND PROPERTY OF THE CHRISTIAN SPIRIT.

These observations contain so much practical truth, that it would be worth our time to open and apply them distinctly.

> DOCT. 1. THAT IGNORANCE IS THE USUAL CAUSE OF ENMITY TO CHRIST.

" These things (saith the Lord) will they do, because they have not known the Father, nor me," John xvi. 3.   What things doth he mean ? Why, kill and destroy the people of God, and therein suppose they do God good service, that is, think to oblige and gratify the Father, by their butchering his children. So Jer. ix. 3, " they proceed from evil to evil ; and have not known me, saith the Lord." *q. d.* Had they the knowledge of God, this would check and stop them in their ways of wicked- ness.   And so Psa. lxxiv. 20, " The dark places of the earth are full of the habitations of cruelty."

Three things must be inquired into, namely, I. What their ignorance of Christ was. II. Whence it was. And, III. How it disposed them to such enmity against him.

I. What was their ignorance who crucified Christ ? They knew many other truths, but did not know Jesus Christ ; in that their eyes were held.   Natural light they had ; yea, and scrip- ture light they had ; but in this particular, that this was the Son of God, the Saviour of the world, therein they were blind and ignorant. But how could that be ? Had they not heard at least of his miraculous works ? Did they not see how his birth, life, and death, agreed with the prophecies, both in time, place, and manner ? Whence should this their ignorance be when they saw, or at least might have seen, the scriptures fulfilled in him; and that he came among them in a time when they were full of expectations of the Messiah?

II. It is true, indeed, they knew the scriptures; and it cannot but be supposed the fame of his mighty works had reached their ears: but yet,

1. Though they had the scriptures among them, they misunderstood them. You find, John vii. 52, how they reason with Nicodemus against Christ; " Art thou also of Galilee? Search, and see: for out of Galilee ariseth no prophet." Here is a double mistake: they supposed Christ to arise out of Galilee, whereas he was of Bethlehem, though much conversant in the parts of Galilee; and they thought, because they could find no prophet had arisen out of Galilee, therefore none should.

Another mistake that blinded them about Christ, was from their conceit that Christ should not die, but live for ever: " We have heard out of the law, that Christ abideth for ever: and how sayest thou, the Son of man must be lifted up? who is the Son of man?" John xii. 34. That scripture which probably they urge against the mortality of Christ, is Isa. ix. 7, " Of the increase of his government and peace there shall be no end, upon the throne of David," &c. In like manner, John vii. 27, we find them in another mistake; " We know this man whence he is; but when Christ cometh, no man knoweth whence he is." This, likely, proceeded from their misunderstanding of Micah v. 2, " His goings forth have been from of old, from everlasting." Thus were they blinded about the person of Christ, by misinterpretations of scripture prophecies.

2. Another thing occasioning their mistake of Christ, was the outward meanness and despicableness of his condition. They expected a pompous Messiah, one that should come with state and glory, becoming the king of Israel. But when they saw him in the form of a servant, coming in poverty, not to be ministered unto, but to minister, they utterly rejected him: " We hid as it were our faces from him; he was despised, and we esteemed him not," Isa. liii. 3. Nor is it any great wonder these should be scandalized at his poverty, when the disciples themselves had such carnal apprehensions of his kingdom, Mark x. 37, 38.

3. Add to this, their implicit faith in the learned rabbies and doctors, who utterly misled them in this matter, and greatly prejudiced them against Christ. " Lo, (said they,) he speaketh boldly, and they say nothing to him. Do the rulers know indeed that this is the very Christ?" They pinned their faith

upon their rulers' sleeves, and suffered them to carry it whither they would.   This was their ignorance, and these its causes.

III. Let us see, in the next place, how this disposed them to such enmity against Christ.   And this it did three ways.

Ignorance disposes men to enmity and opposition to Christ, by removing those checks and rebukes of conscience, by which they are restrained from evil.   Conscience binding and reproving by the authority and virtue of the law of God, where that law is not known, there can be no reproofs ; and therefore we truly say, that ignorance is virtually every sin.

Ignorance enslaves and subjects the soul to the lusts of Satan ; he is " the ruler of the darkness of this world," Eph. vi. 12. There is no work so base and vile, but an ignorant man will undertake it.

Nay, which is more, if a man be ignorant of Christ, his truths, or people, he will not only oppose, and persecute, but he will look upon it as his duty so to do, John xvi. 3.   Before the Lord opened Paul's eyes, " he verily thought that he ought to do many things contrary to the name of Christ."   Thus you have a brief account what, and whence their ignorance was, and how it disposed and prepared them for this dreadful work.   Hence we learn these inferences.

1. How falsely is the gospel charged as the cause of discord and trouble in the world ! It is not light, but darkness, that makes men fierce and cruel.   As light increases, so doth peace : " The wolf also shall dwell with the lamb, and the leopard lie down with the kid ; and the calf and the young lion and the fatling together ; and a little child shall lead them. They shall not hurt nor destroy in all my holy mountain : for the earth shall be full of the knowledge of the Lord, as the waters cover the sea," Isa. xi. 6, 9.   What a sad condition would the world be in without gospel light ! all places would be dens of rapine, and mountains of prey.   Certainly we owe much of our civil liberty and outward tranquillity to gospel light.   If a sword, or variance, at any time, follow the gospel, it is but an accidental, not a direct and proper effect of it.

2. How dreadful is it to oppose Christ and his truths knowingly, and with open eyes ! Christ pleads their ignorance as an argument to procure their pardon.   Paul himself was once filled with rage and madness against Christ and his truths : it was well for him that he did it ignorantly : had he gone against his light and knowledge, there had been little hope of him : " I was a blasphemer, a persecutor, and injurious ; but I obtained mercy, because I did it ignorantly, and in unbelief," 1 Tim. i. 13.   I

do not say, it is utterly impossible for one that knowingly and maliciously opposes and persecutes Christ and his people, to be forgiven, but it is not usual, Heb. vi. 4, 5.   There are few instances of it.

3. What an awful majesty sits upon the brow of holiness, that few dare to oppose it that see it! There are few so daringly wicked, to fight against it with open eyes: " Who will harm you whilst ye are followers of that which is good," 1 Pet. iii. 13. *q. d.* Who dare be so hardy to set upon known godliness, or afflict and wrong the known friends of it? The true reason why many christians speed so bad, is not because they are godly, but because they do not manifest the power of godliness more than they do: their lives are so like the lives of others, that they are often mistaken for others. For holiness, manifested in its power, is so awfully glorious, that the consciences of the vilest cannot but honour it, and do obeisance to it. " Herod feared John, for he was a just man," Mark vi. 20.

4. The enemies of Christ are objects of pity. Alas, they are blind, and know not what they do. It is a pity that any other affection than pity should stir in our hearts towards them. Were their eyes but open, they would never do as they do: we should look upon them as the physician doth upon his sick distempered patient. Did they but see with the same light you do, they would be as far from hating Christ, or his ways, as you are. As soon as they cease to be ignorant, they cease to hate, saith Tertullian.

5. How needful is it before we engage ourselves against any person or way, to be well satisfied and resolved that it is a wicked person or practice that we oppose! You see the world generally runs upon a mistake in this matter. Oh beware of doing you know not what! for though you do you know not what, Satan knows what he is doing by you: he blinds your eyes, and then sets you to work. You may now do you know not what; but you may afterwards have time enough to reflect on, and lament what you have done. Oh beware what you now do!

DOCT. 2. THAT THERE IS FORGIVENESS WITH GOD, FOR SUCH AS OPPOSE CHRIST THROUGH IGNORANCE.

If all manner of sin and blasphemy shall be forgiven to men, then this, as well as others, Matt. xii. 31; even those whose wicked hands had crucified Christ, may receive remission by that blood they shed, Acts ii. 23. 38, compared.

I have two things here to do: I. To open the nature of the forgiveness, and show you what it is. II. To evince the possibility of it, for such as, mistakingly, oppose Christ.

I. Forgiveness is God's gracious discharge of a believing penitent sinner, from the guilt of all his sin, for Christ's sake.

It is *God's* discharge. None can forgive sin, but God only, Mark ii. 7. The primary and principal wrong is done to him: " Against thee, and thee only," that is, thee mainly or especially, " have I sinned," Psa. li. 4. Sins are called debts, debts to God, Matt. vi. 12; and as pecuniary debts oblige him that owes them to the penalty, if he satisfy not for it; so do our sins. And who can discharge the debtor, but the creditor?

It is a *gracious* act of discharge. " I, even I, am he that blotteth out thy transgressions for mine own sake," Isa. xliii. 25. And yet sin is not so forgiven, as that God expects no satisfaction at all; but as expecting none from us, because God hath provided a Surety for us, from whom he is satisfied: " In whom we have redemption through his blood, the forgiveness of sins, according to the riches of his grace," Eph. i. 7.

It is a gracious discharge *from the guilt of sin*. Guilt is that which pardon properly deals with. Guilt is an obligation to punishment. Pardon is the dissolving that obligation. The pardoned soul is a discharged soul: " Who shall lay any thing to the charge of God's elect? It is God that justifieth, who shall condemn? It is Christ that died," Rom. viii. 33.

It is God's discharge *of a believing penitent sinner*. Infidelity and impenitency are not only sins in themselves, but such sins as bind fast all other sins upon the soul " By him, all that believe are justified from all things," Acts x. 43. So Acts iii. 19. This " Repent therefore, that your sins may be blotted out," is the method in which God dispenseth pardon to sinners.

Lastly, It is *for Christ's sake* we are discharged; he is the meritorious cause of our remission: " As God, for Christ's sake, hath forgiven you," Eph. iv. 32. It is his blood alone that meritoriously procures our discharge. This is a brief and true account of the nature of forgiveness.

II. Now to evince the possibility of forgiveness, for such as ignorantly oppose Christ, let these things be weighed:

1. Why should any poor soul, that is now humbled for its enmity to Christ in the days of ignorance, question the possibility of forgiveness, when this effect doth not exceed the power of the cause; nay, when there is more efficacy in the blood of Christ, the meritorious cause, than is in this effect of it? There is power enough in that blood, not only to pardon thy sins, but

the sins of the whole world, were it actually applied, 1 John ii.
2. There is not only a sufficiency, but also a redundancy of
merit, in that precious blood.

2. And as this sin exceeds not the power of the meritorious
cause of forgiveness; so neither is it any where excluded from
pardon, by any word of God.   Nay, such is the extensiveness
of the promise to believing penitents, that this case is manifestly
included, and forgiveness tendered to thee in the promises: " Let
the wicked forsake his way, and the unrighteous man his
thoughts; and let him return unto the Lord, and he will have
mercy on him, and to our God, for he will abundantly pardon,"
Isa. lv. 7. Many such extensive promises there are in the scriptures: and there is not one parenthesis in all these blessed
pages, in which this case is excepted.

3. And it is yet more satisfactory; that God hath already
actually forgiven such sinners; and that which he hath done, he
may again do: yea, for this very reason he hath done it to
some, and those eminent for their enmity to Christ, that others
may be encouraged to hope for the same mercy, when they also
shall be, in the same manner, humbled for it. Take one famous
instance of many; it is that of Paul in 1 Tim. i. 13. 16. " Who
was before a blasphemer, a persecutor, and injurious: but I
obtained mercy, because I did it ignorantly in unbelief.—Howbeit for this cause I obtained mercy, that in me first Jesus
Christ might show forth all long-suffering, for a pattern to them
which should hereafter believe on him to life everlasting."

4. Moreover, it is encouraging to consider, that when God
had cut off others in the way of their sin, he hath hitherto
spared thee.   What speaks this but a purpose of mercy to thy
soul?   Thou shouldst account the long-suffering of God thy
salvation, 2 Pet. iii. 15.   Had he smitten thee in the way of
thy sin and enmity to Christ, what hope had remained? But if
he hath not only spared thee, but also given thee a heart ingenuously ashamed, and humbled for thy evils, doth not this speak
mercy for thee? surely it looks like a gracious design of love
to thy soul.

Inference 1. And is there forgiveness with God for such as
have been enemies to Christ, his truths, and gospel? Then certainly there is pardon and mercy for the friends of God, who
involuntarily fall into sin, by the surprisals of temptation, and
are broken for it, as ingenuous children for offending a good
father.   Can any doubt, if God have pardon for such enemies,
he hath it for children? If he have forgiveness for such as shed
the blood of Christ with wicked hands, hath he not much more

mercy and forgiveness for such as love Christ, and are more afflicted for their sin against him, than all other troubles they have in the world ?

How sorrowful do the dear children of God sometimes sit, after their lapse into sin ! Will God ever pardon this ? will he be reconciled again ? May I hope his face shall be to me as in former times ? Mourning soul ! if thou didst but know the largeness, tenderness, freeness of that grace, which yearns over enemies, and hath given forth thousands and ten thousands of pardons to the worst of sinners, thou wouldst not sink thus.

2. Is there pardon with God for enemies ? How inexcusable then are all they that persist and perish in their enmity to Christ ! Surely their destruction is of themselves. Mercy is offered to them, if they will receive it, Isa. lv. 7. Proclamation is made in the gospel, that if there be any among the enemies of Christ, who repent of what they have been and done against him, and are now unfeignedly willing to be reconciled, upon the word of a King, they shall find mercy : but " God shall wound the head of the enemies, and the hairy scalp of such a one as goeth on still in his trespasses," Psa. lxviii. 21. " If he turn not, he will whet his sword ; he hath bent his bow, and made it ready. He hath also prepared for him the instruments of death ; he ordaineth his arrows against the persecutors," Psa. vii. 12, 13.

This lays the blood of every man that perishes in his enmity to Christ, at his own door ; and vindicates the righteousness of God, in the severest strokes of wrath upon them. This also will be a cutting thought to their hearts eternally : I might once have had pardon, and I refused it : the gospel trumpet sounded a parley ; fair and gracious terms were offered, but I rejected them.

3. Is there mercy with God and forgiveness, even for his worst enemies, upon their submission ? How unlike to God then are all implacable spirits ! Some there are that cannot bring their hearts to forgive an enemy ; " to whom revenge is sweeter than life," 1 Sam. xxiv. 16. " If a man find his enemy, will he let him go ?" This is hell-fire, a fire that never goeth out. How little do such poor creatures consider, if God should deal by them, as they do by others, what words could express the misery of their condition ! It is a sad sin, and a sad sign, a character of a wretched state, wherever it appears. Those that have found mercy, should be ready to show mercy ; and they that expect mercy themselves, should not deny it to others. This brings us upon the third and last observation, namely,

Doct. 3. That to forgive enemies and beg forgiveness for them, is the true character and property of the christian spirit.

Thus did Christ: " Father, forgive them." And thus did Stephen, in imitation of Christ: " And they stoned Stephen, calling upon God, and saying, Lord Jesus, receive my spirit. And he kneeled down, and cried with a loud voice, Lord, lay not this sin to their charge," Acts vii. 59, 60. This suits with the rule of Christ, " But I say unto you, love your enemies; bless them that curse you, do good to them that hate you, and pray for them which despitefully use you and persecute you; that ye may be the children of God your Father which is in heaven," Matt. v. 44, 45.

I. I shall open the nature of this duty, and show you what a forgiving spirit is; and then, II. The excellency of it, how well it becomes all that call themselves christians.

I. Let us enquire what this christian forgiveness is. And that the nature of it may the better appear, I shall show you both what it is not, and what it is.

1. It consists not in a stoical insensibility of wrongs and injuries. God hath not made men as insensible, stupid blocks, that have no sense or feeling of what is done to them. Nor hath he made a law inconsistent with their very natures that are to be governed by it; but allows us a tender sense of natural evils, though he will not allow us to revenge them by moral evils: nay, the more deep and tender our resentments of wrongs and injuries are, the more excellent is our forgiveness of them; so that a forgiving spirit doth not exclude sense of injuries, but the sense of injuries graces the forgiveness of them.

2. Christian forgiveness is not a politic concealment of our wrath and revenge, because it will be a reproach to discover it; or, because we want opportunity to vent it. This is carnal policy, not christian meekness. So far from being the mark of a gracious spirit, that it is apparently the sign of a vile nature. It is not christianity to repose, but depose injuries.

3. Nor is it that moral virtue, for which we are beholden to an easier and better nature, and the help of moral rules. There are certain virtues attainable without a change of nature, such as temperance, patience, justice, &c. These are of singular use to conserve peace and order in the world; and without them, the world would soon break up, and its civil societies disband. But yet, though these are the ornaments of nature, they do not argue the change of nature. All christian graces, in the exercises of

them, involve a respect to God : and they are formed not by natural acquisition, but supernatural infusion.

4. Christian forgiveness is not an injurious giving up of our rights and properties to the pleasure of every one that hath a mind to invade them. No ; these we may lawfully defend and preserve, and are bound so to do ; though, if we cannot defend them legally, we must not avenge our wrongs unchristianly : this is not christian forgiveness. But then, positively,

It is a christian lenity, or gentleness of mind, not retaining, but freely passing by the injuries done to us, in obedience to the command of God.

It is a *lenity*, or gentleness of mind. The grace of God calms the tumultuous passions ; corrects our sour spirits, and makes them benign, gentle, and easy to be entreated : " The fruit of the Spirit is love, joy, peace, long-suffering, gentleness," &c. Gal. v. 22.

This gracious lenity *inclines the christian to pass by inju-ries ;* so to pass them by, as neither to retain them revenge-fully in the mind, or requite them when we have opportunity with the hand : yea, and that freely, not by constraint, because we cannot avenge ourselves, but willingly. We abhor to do it when we can. So that as a carnal heart thinks revenge its glory, the gracious heart is content that forgiveness should be his glory. I will be even with him, saith nature : I will be above him, saith grace : it is his glory to pass over transgres-sion, Prov. xix. 11.

And this it doth *in obedience to the command of God.* Their own nature inclines them another way. " The spirit that is in us lusteth to envy ; but he giveth more grace," Jam. iv. 5. It lusteth to revenge, but the fear of God represseth those mo-tions. Such considerations as these : God hath forbidden me ; yea, and God hath forgiven me, as well as forbidden me : they prevail upon him when nature urges to revenge the wrong. " Be kind one to another, tender-hearted, forgiving one another, even as God for Christ's sake hath forgiven you," Eph. iv. 32. This is forgiveness in a christian sense.

II. And that this is excellent, and singularly becoming the profession of Christ, is evident ; inasmuch as,

This speaks your religion excellent, that can mould your hearts into that heavenly frame, to which they are so averse, yea, contrarily disposed by nature. It is the glory of pagan morality, that it can hide and cover men's lusts and passions. But the glory of christianity lies in this, that it cannot hide, but destroy, and really mortify the lusts of nature. Would christians but live up to the excellent principles of their religion, christianity shall be no more outvied by heathenish morality. The greatest christian shall be no more challenged to imitate Socrates, if he can. We shall utterly spoil that proud boast, "that the faith of christians is outdone by the infidelity of heathens." Oh christians, yield not the day to heathens! Let all the world see the true greatness, heavenliness, and excellency of our represented pattern; and by true mortification of your corrupt natures, enforce an acknowledgment from the world, that a greater than Socrates is here. He that is really a meek, humble, patient, heavenly christian, wins this glory to his religion, that it can do more than all other principles and rules in the world. In nothing were the most accomplished heathens more defective than this forgiving of injuries: it was a thing they could not understand, or, if they did, could never bring their hearts to it; witness that rule of their great Tully: " It is the first office of justice, (saith he,) to hurt no man, except first provoked by an injury." The addition of that exception spoiled his excellent rule.

But christianity teaches, and some christians have attained it, to receive evil, and return good: " Being reviled, we bless; being persecuted, we suffer it; being defamed, we entreat," 1 Cor. iv. 12, 13. This is that meekness wrought in us by the wisdom that is from above, James iii. 17. This commends a man to the consciences of others, who, with Saul, must acknowledge, when they see themselves so outdone, " Thou art more righteous than I," 1 Sam. xxiv. 16, 17. Had we been so much injured, and had such opportunities to revenge them, we should never have passed them by, as these men did. This impresses and stamps the very image of God upon the creature, and makes us like our heavenly Father, who doth good to his enemies, and sends down showers of outward blessings upon them, that pour out floods of wickedness daily to provoke him, Matt. v. 44, 45. In a word, this christian temper of spirit gives a man the true possession and enjoyment of himself. So that our breasts shall be as the pacific sea, smooth and pleasant, when others are as the raging sea, foaming and casting up mire and dirt.

Inference 1. Hence we clearly infer, that the christian religion, exalted in its power, is the greatest friend to the peace and tranquillity of states and kingdoms. Nothing is more opposite to the true christian spirit, than implacable fierceness, strife, revenge, tumults, and uproars. It teaches men to do good, and receive evil; to receive evil, and return good. " The wisdom that is from above, is first pure, then peaceable, gentle, and easy to be entreated; full of mercy and good fruits; without partiality, and without hypocrisy; and the fruit of righteousness is sown in peace of them that make peace," Jam. iii. 17, 18. The church is a dove for meekness, Cant. vi. 9. When the world grows full of strife, christians then grow weary of the world: and sigh out the psalmist's request, "O that I had the wings of a dove! that I might fly away and be at rest."

The rule by which we are to walk, is, "If it be possible, as much as lieth in you, live peaceably with all men. Dearly beloved, avenge not yourselves, but rather give place unto wrath; for it is written, Vengeance is mine, I will repay it, saith the Lord," Rom. xii. 18, 19. It is not religion, but lusts, that make the world so unquiet, James iv. 1, 2. Not godliness, but wickedness, that makes men bite and devour one another. One of the first effects of the gospel, is to civilize those places where it comes, and settle order and peace among men. How great a mistake and evil then is it to cry out, when atheism and irreligion have broken the civil peace; This is the fruit of religion! this is the effect of the gospel! Happy would it be if religion did more obtain in all nations. It is the greatest friend in the world to their tranquillity and prosperity.

2. How dangerous a thing is it to abuse and wrong meek and forgiving christians! Their patience and easiness to forgive often invites injury, and encourages vile spirits to insult and trample upon them: but if men would seriously consider it, there is nothing in the world should more deter and affright them from such practices than this. You may abuse and wrong them, they must not avenge themselves, nor repay evil for evil: true, but because they do not, the Lord will; even the Lord to whom they commit the matter; and he will do it to purpose, except ye repent.

"Be patient therefore, brethren, unto the coming of the Lord," James v. 7. Will ye stand to that issue? had you rather indeed have to do with God than with men? When the jews put Christ to death, " he committed himself to him that judgeth righteously," 1 Pet. ii. 22, 23. And did that people get any thing by that? did not the Lord severely avenge the blood of Christ on them and their children? yea, do not they and their children groan under the doleful effects of it to this day? If God undertakes (as he always doth) the cause of this abused, meek, and peaceable people, he will be sure to avenge it seven-fold more than they could. You will get nothing by that.

3. Let us all imitate our pattern the Lord Jesus Christ, and labour for meek, forgiving spirits. I shall only propose two in-

ducements to it; the honour of Christ, and your own peace; two dear things indeed to a christian.   His glory is more than your life, and all that you enjoy in this world.   Oh do not expose it to the scorn and derision of his enemies.   Let them not say, How is Christ a lamb, when his followers are lions? how is the church a dove, when its members tear and scratch like birds of prey? Consult also the quiet of your own spirits. What is life worth, without the comfort of life? What can you have in all that you do possess in the world, as long as you have not the possession of your own souls? If your spirits be full of tumult and revenge, the Spirit of Christ will grow a stranger to you: that Dove delights in clean and quiet breasts. Oh then imitate your Lord in this excellency also!

SERMON XXXI.

THE SECOND EXCELLENT WORD OF CHRIST UPON THE CROSS,
ILLUSTRATED.

JOHN XIX. 27.

THEN SAITH HE TO THE DISCIPLE, BEHOLD THY MOTHER!

WE now pass to the consideration of the second memorable and
instructive word of our Lord Jesus Christ upon the cross, contained in this scripture.   Wherein he hath left us an excellent
pattern for the discharge of our relative duties.   It may be well
said, the gospel makes the best husbands and wives, the best
parents and children, the best masters and servants in the world ;
seeing it furnishes them with the most excellent precepts, and
proposes the best patterns.   Here we have the pattern of Jesus
Christ presented to all children for their imitation, teaching
them how to acquit themselves towards their parents, according
to the laws of nature and grace.   Christ was not only subject
and obedient to his parents whilst he lived, but manifested his
tender care even whilst he hung in the torments of death upon
the cross. " Then saith he to the disciple, Behold thy mother !"

The words contain an affectionate recommendation of his distressed mother to the care of a dear disciple, a bosom friend ;
wherein let us consider the design, manner, and season of this
recommendation.

The design and end of it, was to manifest his tender respect
and care for his mother, who was now in a most distressed, comfortless state.   For now was Simeon's prophecy, Luke ii. 35,
fulfilled in the trouble and anguish that filled her soul.   Her
soul was pierced for him, both as she was his mother, and as
she was a mystical member of him, her Head, her Lord : and
therefore he commends her to the beloved disciple, saying,
" Behold thy mother !" that is, let her be to thee as thine own
mother.   Let thy love to me be now manifested in thy tender
care for her.

The manner of his recommending her, is both affectionate
and mutual. It was very affectionate and moving, " Behold thy
mother !" *q. d.* John, I am now dying, leaving all human society

and relations, and entering into a new state, where neither the duties of natural relations are exercised, nor the pleasures and comforts of them enjoyed. It is a state of dominion over angels and men, not of subjection and obedience ; this I now leave to thee. Upon thee do I devolve both the honour and duty of being in my stead and room to her, as to all dear and tender care over her. And as it is affectionate, so it is mutual. And to his mother he said, " Woman, behold thy son !" ver. 26 ; not mother, but woman, intimating not only the change of state and conditions with him, but also the request he was making for her to the disciple with whom she was to live, as a mother with a son. And all this he designs as a pattern to others.

The season or time when his care for his mother so eminently manifested itself, was when his departure was at hand, and he could no longer be a comfort to her, by his bodily presence ; yea, his love and care then manifested themselves, when he was full of anguish both in his soul and body ; yet all this makes him not in the least unmindful of so dear a relation. Hence the doctrinal note is,

> Doct. That Christ's tender care of his mother, even in the time of his greatest distress, is an excellent pattern for all gracious children to the end of the world.

" There are three great foundations, or bonds of relation, on which all family government depends." Husbands and wives, parents and children, masters and servants. The Lord hath planted in the souls of men affections suitable to these relations ; and to his people he hath given grace to regulate those affections, appointed duties to exercise those graces, and seasons to discharge those duties. So that, as in the motion of a wheel every spoke takes its turn, and bears its stress ; in like manner, in the whole round of a christian's conversation, every affection, grace, and duty, at one season or other, comes to be exercised.

But yet grace hath not so far prevailed in the sanctification of any man's affectious, but that there will be excesses or defects in the exercise of them towards our relations ; yea, and in this the most eminent saints have been eminently defective. But the pattern set before us here, is a perfect pattern. As the church finds him the best of husbands, so to his parents he was the best of sons ; and being the best, and most perfect, is therefore the rule and measure of all others. Christ knew how those corruptions we draw from our parents are returned in their bitter fruits upon them again, to the wounding of their very hearts ; and therefore it pleased him to commend obedience and love to parents, in his own example to us.

It was anciently a proverb among the heathen, In sola Sparta, expedit senescere. It is good to be an old man, or woman, only in Sparta. The ground of it was the strict laws that were among the spartans, to punish the rebellion and disobedience of children to their aged parents. And shall it not be good to be an old father and mother in England, where the gospel of Christ is preached, and such an argument as this now set before you urged; an argument which the heathen world were never acquainted with ?

Let all that sustain the relation of children, into whose hands Providence shall cast this discourse, seriously ponder this example of Christ, proposed for their imitation in this point. Wherein we shall consider, I. What duties belong to the relation of children: II. How Christ's example enforces those duties: and then suitably apply it.

I. Let us examine what duties pertain to the relation of children, and they are as truly, as commonly branched out into the following particulars.

1. Fear and reverence are due from children to their parents, by the express command of God : " Ye shall fear every man his mother and his father," Lev. xix. 3. God hath clothed parents with his authority. They are intrusted by God with them, and are accountable to him for the souls and bodies of their children; and he expects that you reverence them, although, in respect of outward estate, or honour, you be never so much above them. Joseph, though Lord of Egypt, bowed down before his aged father, with his face to the earth, Gen. xlviii. 12.   Solomon, the most magnificent and glorious king that ever swayed a sceptre, when his mother came to speak with him for Adonijah, he rose up to meet her, and bowed himself to her, and caused a seat to be set up for the king's mother, and set her upon his right hand, 2 Kings ii. 19.

2. Dear and tender love is due from children to their parents: and to show how strong and dear that love ought to be, it is joined with the love you have for your own lives ; as it appears in that injunction, to deny both for Christ's sake, Matt. x. 37. The bonds of nature are strong and direct between parents and children.   What is the child but a piece of the parent wrapped up in another skin ? Oh the care, the cost, the pity, the tenderness, the pains, the fears they have expressed for you.   It is worse than heathenish ingratitude, not to return love for love. This filial love is not only in itself a duty, but should be the root or spring of all your duties to them.

3. Obedience to their commands is due to them, by the Lord's strict and special command: "Children, obey your parents in the Lord, for this is right; honour thy father and thy mother, which is the first commandment with promise," Eph. vi. 1. Filial obedience is not only founded upon the positive law of God, but also upon the law of nature; for though the subjection of children to parents is due to them by natural right; therefore, saith the apostle, this is right, that is, right both according to natural and positive law. However, this subjection and obedience is not absolute and universal. God has not divested himself of his own authority, to clothe a parent with it. Your obedience to them must be in the Lord, that is, in such things as they require you to do in the Lord's authority. In things consonant to that Divine and holy will, to which they, as well as you, must be subject; and therein you must obey them. Yea, even the wickedness of a parent exempts not from obedience, where his command is not so. Nor, on the other side, must the holiness of a parent sway you, where his commands and God's are opposite. Yield yourselves, therefore, cheerfully to obey all that which they lawfully enjoin, and take heed that black character fixed on the heathens who know not God, be not found upon you, " disobedience to parents," Rom. i. 30. Remember, your disobedience to their just commands rises much higher, than an affront to their personal authority; it is disobedience to God himself, whose commands second and strengthen theirs upon you.

4. Submission to their discipline and rebukes, is also your duty: "We had fathers of our own flesh that corrected us, and we gave them reverence," Heb. xii. 9. Parents ought not to abuse their authority. Cruelty in them is a great sin; wrath and rebellion in a child against his parents, is monstrous. Two considerations should especially mould children into a submissive frame, especially to godly parents; the end for which, and the manner in which they manifest their anger to their children. Their end is to save your souls from hell. They judge it better for you to hear the voice of their anger, than the terrible voice of the wrath of God. And for the manner in which they rebuke and chasten; it is with grief in their hearts, and tears in their eyes. It is no delight to them to cross, vex, or afflict you. Were it not mere conscience of their duty to God, and tender love to your souls, they would neither chide nor smite: and when they do, how do they afflict themselves in afflicting you!

5. Faithfulness to all their interests is due to them, by the natural and positive law of God. What in you lies, you are

bound to promote, not to waste and scatter their substance ; to assist, not to defraud them. " Whoso robbeth his father or mother, and saith, it is no transgression, the same is a companion of a destroyer," Prov. xxviii. 24. To dispose of their goods, much more of yourselves, without their consent, *is* (ordinarily) the greatest injustice to them.

6. And more especially, requital of all that love, care, and pains they have been at for you, is your duty so far as God enables you, and those things are requitable: " Let them learn to show piety at home, and requite their parents," 1 Tim. v. 4. It is a saying frequent among the jews, " A child should rather labour at the mill than suffer his parents to want." And to the same sense is that other saying, " Your parents must be supplied by you if you have it ; if not, you ought to beg for them, rather than see them perish." It was both the comfort and honour of Joseph, that God made him an instrument of so much succour and comfort to his aged father and distressed family, Gen. xlvii. 13. And you are also to know, that what you do for them, is not in the way of an alms, or common charity. For the apostle saith, it is but your requiting them, and that is justice, not charity. And it can never be a full requital. Indeed the apostle tells us, 2 Cor. xii. 14, that parents lay up for their children, and not children for their parents ; and so they ought ; but, surely if Providence blast them, and bless you, an honourable maintenance is their due. Even Christ himself took care for his mother.

II. You have had a brief account of this relation ; next, let us consider how the example of our Lord, who was so subject to them in his life, Luke ii. 51, and so careful to provide at his death, enforces all those duties upon children, especially upon gracious children. And this it doth two ways ; both as it hath the obliging power of a law ; and as he himself will one day sit in judgment to take an account how we have imitated him in these things.

1. His example in this hath the force and power of a law, yea, a law of love, or a law lovingly constraining you to an imitation of him. If Christ himself will be your pattern, if God will be pleased to take relations like yours, and go before you in the discharge of relative duties ; oh, how much are you obliged to imitate him, and tread in all his footsteps ! This was by him intended as a pattern, to facilitate and direct your duties.

2. He will come to take an account how you have answered the pattern of obedience and tender care he set before you in the days of his flesh. What will the disobedient plead in

that day? He that heard the groans of an afflicted father or mother, will now come to reckon with the disobedient child for them; and the glorious example of Christ's own obedience to, and tenderness of his relations, will, in that day, condemn and aggravate, silence and shame such wretched children as shall stand guilty before his bar.

Inference 1. Hath Jesus Christ given such a pattern of obedience and tenderness to parents? Then there can be nothing of Christ in stubborn, rebellious, and careless children, that regard not the good or comfort of their parents. The children of disobedience cannot be the children of God. If Divine Providence directs this to the hands of any that are so, my heart's desire and prayer for them is, that the Lord would search their souls by it, and discover their evils to them, whilst they shall read the following queries.

First query, Have you not been guilty of slighting your parents by irreverent words or conduct? To such I commend the consideration of that scripture, Prov. xxx. 17, which, methinks, should be to them as the hand-writing that appeared upon the plaster of the wall to Belshazzar: "The eye that mocketh at his father, and despiseth to obey his mother, the ravens of the valley shall pick it out, and the young eagles shall eat it." That is, they shall be brought to an untimely end, and the birds of the air shall eat that eye, that had never seen but for that parent that was despised by it. It may be you are vigorous and young, they decayed and wrinkled with age: but, saith the Holy Ghost, "Despise not thy mother when she is old," Prov. xxiii. 22. Or, when she is wrinkled, as the hebrew signifies. It may be you are rich, they poor; own, and honour them in their poverty, and despise them not. God will requite it with his hand if you do.

Second query, Have you not been disobedient to the commands of parents? A son of Belial is a son of wrath, if God give not repentance to life. Is not this the black brand set upon the heathens, Rom. i. 30. Woe to him that makes a father or mother complain, as the tree in the fable, that they are cleft asunder with the wedges that are cut out of their own bodies.

Third query, Have you not risen up rebelliously against, and hated your parents for chastening your bodies, to save your souls from hell? What is this but to resist an ordinance of God for your good? and, in rebelling against them, to rebel against the Lord; Well, if they do not, God will take the rod into his own hand, and him you shall not resist.

Fourth query, Have you not been unjust to your parents,

and defrauded them? first, help to make them poor, and then despise them because they are poor. Oh horrid wickedness! What a complicated evil is this! Thou art, in the language of the scripture, a companion with destroyers, Prov. xxviii. 24. This is the worst of theft, in God's account.

Fifth query, Are you not, or have you not been ungrateful to parents? Leaving them to shift for themselves, in those straits you have helped to bring them into. Oh consider it, children, this is an evil which God will surely avenge, except ye repent. What! to be hardened against thine own flesh; to be cruel to thine own parents, that with so much tenderness fed thee, when else thou hadst perished! If any one of my readers be guilty of these evils, to humble you for them, and reclaim you from them, I desire these five considerations may be laid to heart.

(1.) That the effects of your obedience or disobedience will stick upon you and yours to many generations. If you be obedient children in the Lord, both you and yours may reap the fruits of that your obedience, in multitudes of sweet mercies, for many generations. So runs the promise, "Honour thy father and mother, which is the first commandment with promise, that it may be well with thee, and thou mayest live long on the earth," Eph. vi. 22. You know what an eye of favour God cast upon the rechabites for this, Jer. xxxv. 8, from the 14th to the 20th verse. And as his blessings are, by promise, entailed on the obedient, so his curse upon the disobedient: "Whoso curseth his father or his mother, his lamp shall be put out in obscure darkness," Prov. xx. 20; that is, the lamp of his life quenched by death, yea, say others, and his soul also by the blackness of darkness in hell.

(2.) Though other sins do, this sin seldom escapes exemplary punishment, even in this world.

(3.) Heathens will rise up in judgment against you, and condemn you. They never had such precepts nor examples as you, and yet some of the better natured heathens would rather have chosen death, than to do as you do. You remember the story of Crœsus' dumb son, whose dear affections could make him speak when he saw Crœsus in danger: though he never spake before, yet then he could cry out, "Oh do not kill my father!" But what speak I of heathens! the stork in the heavens, yea, the beasts of the earth, will condemn the disobedience of children.

(4.) These are sins inconsistent with the true fear of God, in whomsoever they are found. A man is what indeed he is in his family, and among his relations. He that is a bad child can never be a good christian. . Either bring testimonies of your godliness from your relations, or it may be well suspected to be no better than counterfeit. Never talk of your obedience to God, whilst your disobedience to the just commands of your parents gives you the lie.

(5.) A parting time is coming, when death will break up the family; and when that time comes, oh! how bitter will the remembrance of these things be! Surely, this will be more unsupportable to you than their death, if the Lord open your eyes, and give you repentance.

2. Have you such a pattern of obedience, and tender love to parents? Then, children, imitate your pattern, as it becomes christians, and take Christ for your example. Whatsoever your parents be, see that you carry it towards them becoming such as profess Christ.

If your parents be godly, oh beware of grieving them by any unbecoming conduct. Art thou a christian indeed? thou wilt then reckon thyself obliged in a double bond, both of grace and nature, to them. Oh what a mercy would some children esteem it, if they had parents fearing the Lord, as you have!

If they be carnal, walk circumspectly, in the most precise and punctual discharge of your duties; for how knowest thou, O child, but hereby thou mayest win thy parents? Wouldst thou but humbly and seriously entreat and persuade them to mind the ways of holiness, speaking to them at fit seasons, with all imaginable humility and reverence, insinuating your advice to duties, or trouble for their evils, rather by relating some pertinent history, or proposing some excellent example, leaving their own conscience to draw the conclusion, and make application, than to do it yourselves; it is possible they may ponder your words in their hearts, as Mary did Christ's, Luke ii. 49. 51. And would you but back all this with your earnest cries to Heaven for them, and your own daily example, that they may have nothing from yourselves to retort upon you; and thus wait with patience for the desired effect; oh, what blessed instrument might you be of their everlasting good!

3. To conclude, Let those that have such children as fear the Lord, and endeavour to imitate Christ in these duties, account them a singular treasure and heritage from the Lord, and give them all due encouragement.

How many have no children at all, but are as a dry tree! and how many have such as are worse than none, the very reproach and heart-breaking of their parents, that bring down their hoary heads with sorrow to the grave! If God have given you the blessing of godly children, you can never be sufficiently sensible of, or thankful for such a favour. Oh that ever God should honour you to bring forth children for heaven ! What a comfort must this be to you, whatever other troubles you meet with abroad, when you come home among godly relations, that are careful to sweeten your own family to you by their obedience ! Especially, what a comfort is it, when you come to die, that you leave them within the covenant, entitled to Christ, and so need not be anxious how it shall be with them when you are gone ! Take heed of discouraging or damping such children from whom so much glory is likely to arise to God, and so much comfort to yourselves. Thus let Christ's pattern be improved, who went before you in such eminent holiness, in all his relations, and left you an example that you should follow his steps.

SERMON XXXII.

THE THIRD OF CHRIST'S LAST WORDS UPON THE CROSS, ILLUSTRATED.

LUKE XXIII. 43.

AND JESUS SAID UNTO HIM, VERILY I SAY UNTO THEE, TO-DAY SHALT THOU BE WITH ME IN PARADISE.

IN this scripture you have the third excellent saying of Christ upon the cross, expressing the riches of free grace to the penitent thief; a man that had spent his life in wickedness, and for his wickedness was now to lose his life. His practice had been vile and profane, but now his heart was broken for it; he proves a convert, yea, the first-fruits of the blood of the cross. In the former verse he manifests his faith; " Lord, remember me, when thou comest into thy kingdom." In this Christ manifests his pardon and gracious acceptance of him; " Verily I say unto thee, To-day shalt thou be with me in paradise." In which promise let us consider, the matter of it, the person to whom it is made, the time set for its performance, and the confirmation of it for his full satisfaction.

1. The matter or substance of the promise made by Christ, is, that he shall be with him in paradise. By paradise he means heaven itself, which is here shadowed to us by a place of delight and pleasure. This is the receptacle of gracious souls, when separated from their bodies. And that paradise signifies heaven itself, and not a third place, as some of the fathers fondly imagine, is evident from 2 Cor. xii. 2. 4; where the apostle calls the same place by the names of the third heaven, and the paradise. This is the place of blessedness designed for the people of God. So you find, Rev. ii. 7; " To him that overcometh will I give to eat of the tree of life, which is in the midst of the paradise of God;" that is, to have the fullest and most intimate communion with Jesus Christ in heaven. And this is the substance of Christ's promise to the thief: Thou, that is, thou in spirit, or thou in the noblest part, thy soul, which here bears the image of the whole person; " Thou shalt be with me in paradise."

2. The person to whom Christ makes this excellent and glorious promise was one that had lived sinfully and profanely ; a very vile and wretched man, in all the former part of his time, and, for his wickedness, now justly under condemnation. However, now at last the Lord gave him a penitent believing heart. Now, almost at the last gasp, he is soundly, in an extraordinary way, converted ; and, being converted, he owns and professes Christ amidst all the shame and reproach of his death; vindicates his innocency, and humbly supplicates for mercy ; " Lord, remember me when thou comest into thy kingdom."

3. The set time for the performance of this gracious promise is, To-day ; this very day, shalt thou be with me in glory : not after the resurrection, but immediately from the time of thy dissolution, thou shalt enjoy blessedness.

4. And lastly, You have here the confirmation and seal of this most comfortable promise to him with Christ's solemn asseveration ; " Verily I say unto thee." Higher security cannot be given. I that am able to perform what I promise, and have not out-promised myself; for heaven and the glory thereof are mine : I that am faithful and true to my promises, and have never forfeited my credit with any ; I say it, I solemnly confirm it ; " Verily I say unto thee, To-day shalt thou be with me in paradise." Hence we have three plain obvious truths, for our instruction and consolation.

DOCT. 1. THAT THERE IS A FUTURE ETERNAL STATE, INTO WHICH SOULS PASS AT DEATH.

2. THAT ALL BELIEVERS ARE, AT THEIR DEATH, IMMEDIATELY RECEIVED INTO A STATE OF GLORY AND ETERNAL HAPPINESS.

3. THAT GOD MAY, THOUGH HE SELDOM DOTH, PREPARE MEN FOR THIS GLORY, IMMEDIATELY BEFORE THEIR DISSOLUTION BY DEATH.

These are the useful truths resulting from this remarkable word of Christ to the penitent thief. We will consider and improve them in the order proposed, beginning with,

DOCT. 1. THAT THERE IS A FUTURE ETERNAL STATE, INTO WHICH SOULS PASS AT DEATH.

This is a principal foundation-stone to the hopes and happiness of souls. And seeing our hopes must needs be as their foundation and ground-work is, I shall briefly establish this truth by these five arguments. The being of a God evinces it.

The scriptures of truth plainly reveal it.   The consciences of all men have presentiments of it.   The incarnation and death of Christ is but a vanity without it.   And the immortality of human souls plainly discovers it.

Arg. 1. The being of a God undeniably evinces a future state for human souls after this life.   For, if there be a God who rules the world which he hath made, he must rule it by rewards and punishments, equally and righteously distributed to good and bad; putting a difference between the obedient and disobedient, the righteous and the wicked.   To make a species of creatures capable of a moral government, and not to rule them at all, is to make them in vain, and is inconsistent with his glory, which is the last end of all things.   To rule them, but not suitably to their natures, consists not with that infinite wisdom from which their beings proceeded, and by which their workings are ruled and ordered.   To rule them, in a way suitably to their natures, namely, by rewards and punishments, and not to perform or execute them at all, is utterly incongruous with the veracity and truth of Him that cannot lie : this were to impose the greatest cheat in the world upon men, and can never proceed from the holy and true God.   So then, as he hath made rational creatures, capable of moral government by rewards and punishments ; he rules them in that way which is suitable to their natures, promising " it shall be well with the righteous, and ill with the wicked." These promises and threatenings can be no cheat, merely intended to scare and fright, where there is no danger, or encourage where there is no real benefit ; but what he promises, or threatens, must be accomplished, and every word of God must be fulfilled.   But it is evident that no such distinction is made by the providence of God (at least ordinarily and generally) in this life; but all things come alike to all ; and as with the righteous, so with the wicked. Yea, here it goes ill with them that fear God ; they are oppressed ; they receive their evil things, and wicked men their good ; therefore we conclude, the righteous Judge of the whole earth will, in another world, recompense to every one according as his work shall be.

2. As the very being of God evinces it, so the scriptures of truth plainly reveal it.   These scriptures are the pandect, or system of the laws, for the government of man ; which the wise and holy Ruler of the world hath enacted and ordained for that purpose.   And in them we find promises made to the righteous, of a full reward for all their obedience, patience, and sufferings in the next life or world to come ; and threatenings, made

against the wicked, of eternal wrath and anguish, as the just recompence of their sin in hell for ever : " Thou treasurest up to thyself wrath against the day of wrath, and revelation of the righteous judgment of God ; who will render to every man according to his deeds : to them who, by patient continuance in well-doing, seek for glory, and honour, and immortality, eternal life : but unto them that are contentious, and obey not the truth, but obey unrighteousness, indignation and wrath, tribulation and anguish, upon every soul of man that doeth evil," &c. Rom. ii. 5—10. So 2 Thess. i. 4—7, " So that we ourselves glory in you, in the churches of God, for your patience and faith in all your persecutions and tribulations that ye endure : which is (a manifest token) of the righteous judgment of God, that ye may be counted worthy of the kingdom of God, for which ye also suffer : seeing it is a righteous thing with God to recompense tribulation to them that trouble you ; and to you who are troubled rest with us, when the Lord Jesus shall be revealed from heaven in flaming fire," &c. To these plain testimonies, multitudes might be added, if it were needful. Heaven and earth shall pass away, but these words shall never pass away.

3. As the scriptures reveal it, so the consciences of all men have some presentiments of it. Where is the man whose conscience never felt any impressions of hope, or fear, from a future world ? If it is said, these may be but the effects and force of discourse, or education ; we have read such things in the scriptures, or have heard it by preachers ; and so raise up to ourselves hopes and fears about it. I demand, how the consciences of the heathens, who have neither 'scriptures nor preachers, came to be impressed with these things ? Doth not the apostle tell us, " That their consciences in the mean while work upon these things ?" Rom. ii. 15 ; their thoughts, with reference to a future state, accuse, or else excuse, that is, their hearts are cheered and encouraged by the good they do, and terrified with fears about the evils they commit. Whereas, if there were no such things, conscience would neither accuse nor excuse for good or evil done in this world.

4. The incarnation and death of Christ, are but a vanity without it. What did he propose to himself, or what benefit have we by his coming, if there be no such future state ? Did he take our nature, and suffer such terrible things in it for nothing ? If you say, christians have much comfort from it in this life : I answer, the comforts they have are raised by faith and expectation of the happiness to be enjoyed, as the purchase of his blood, in heaven. And if there be no such heaven to which

they are appointed, no hell from which they are redeemed, they
do but comfort themselves with a fable, and bless themselves
with a thing of nought : their comfort is no greater than the
comfort of a beggar, that dreams he is a king, and when he
awakes finds himself a beggar still. Surely the ends of Christ's
death were to deliver us from the wrath to come, 1 Thess. i. 10,
not from an imaginary, but a real hell, to bring us to God,
1 Pet. iii. 18 ; to be the author of eternal salvation to them
that obey him, Heb. v. 9.

5. The immortality of human souls, puts it beyond all doubt.
The soul of man vastly differs from that of a beast, which is
but a material form, and so wholly depending on, that it must
need perish with matter.   But it is not so with us : ours are
reasonable spirits, that can live and act in a separated state from
the body. " Who knoweth the spirit of man, that goeth upward ;
and the spirit of a beast, that goeth downward to the earth ? "
Eccles. iii. 21.   For if a man dispute whether man be rational,
this his very disputing it proves him to be so : so our disputes,
hopes, fears, and apprehensions of eternity, prove our souls immortal, and capable of that state.

Inference I. Is there an eternal state, into which souls pass
after this life ? How precious then is present time, upon the
improvement whereof that state depends. Oh what a huge
weight hath God hung upon a small wire ! God hath set us
here in a state of trial : according as we improve these few hours,
so will it fare with us to all eternity. Every day, every hour,
nay, every moment of your present time hath an influence upon
your eternity. ' Do you believe this ? What ! and yet squander
away precious time so carelessly, so vainly ! How do these things
consist ? When Seneca heard one promise to spend a week with
a friend that invited him, to recreate himself with him ; he told
him, he wondered that he should make such a rash promise !
What (said he) cast away so considerable a part of your life ?
How can you do it ? Surely, our prodigality in the expense of
time, argues we have but little sense of great eternity.

2. How rational are all the difficulties and severities of religion, which serve to promote and secure a future eternal happiness ! So vast is the disproportion between time and eternity,
between things seen, and things not seen as yet, between the
present vanishing and the future permanent state, that he can
never be justly reputed a wise man, that will not let go the best
enjoyment he hath on earth, if it stand in the way of his eternal
happiness.   Nor can that man ever escape the just censure
of notorious folly, who, for the gratifying of his appetite and

present accommodation of his flesh, lets go an eternal glory in heaven. Darius repented heartily that he lost a kingdom for a draught of water; "Oh," said he, "for how short a pleasure have I sold a kingdom!" It was Moses' choice, and his choice argued his wisdom; he chose rather " to suffer afflictions with the people of God, than to enjoy the pleasures of sin, which are but for a season," Heb. xi. 25. Men do not account him a fool, that will adventure a penny, upon a probability to gain ten thousand pounds. But surely the disproportion between time and eternity is infinitely greater.

3. If there certainly be such an eternal state into which souls pass immediately after death; how great a change then doth death make upon every man and woman ! Oh what a serious thing is it to die ! It is your passage out of the swift river of time, into the boundless and bottomless ocean of eternity. You that now converse with sensible objects, with men and women like yourselves, enter then into the world of spirits. You that now see the continual revolutions of days and nights, passing away one after another, will then be fixed in a perpetual NOW. Oh what a serious thing is death !

The souls of men are, as it were, asleep now in their bodies ; at death they awake, and find themselves in the world of realities. Let this teach you, both how to carry yourselves towards dying persons when you visit them ; and to make every day some provision for that hour yourselves. Be serious, be plain, be faithful with others that are stepping into eternity ; be so with your own souls every day. Oh remember what an amazing thing eternity is ! especially considering,

DOCT. 2. THAT ALL BELIEVERS ARE, AT THEIR DEATH, IMMEDIATELY RECEIVED INTO A STATE OF GLORY AND ETERNAL HAPPINESS.

" *This day* shalt thou be with me."

This the atheist denies : he thinks he shall die, and therefore resolves to live as the beasts that perish. Beryllus, and some others after him, taught, that there was indeed a future state of happiness and misery for souls, but that they pass not into it immediately upon death and separation from the body, but shall sleep till the resurrection, and then awake and enter into it. But is not that soul asleep, or worse, that dreams of a sleeping soul till the resurrection ? Are souls so wounded and prejudiced by their separation from the body, that they cannot subsist or act separate from it ? Or have they found any such conceit in the scriptures ? Not at all. The scriptures take notice of no such interval; but plainly enough deny it: "We are confident, I say, and willing rather to be absent from the body, and present with the Lord," 2 Cor. v. 8.   No sooner parted from the body, than present with the Lord. So Phil. i. 23. "I desire to be dissolved, and to be with Christ, which is far better."   If his soul was to sleep till the resurrection, how was it far better to be dissolved, than to live?   Surely Paul's state in the body had been far better than his state after death, if this were so; for here he enjoyed much sweet communion with God by faith, but then he should enjoy nothing.   The scripture puts no interval between the dissolution of a saint, and his glorification: it speaks of the saints that are dead, as already with the Lord; and the wicked that are dead, as already in hell, calling them spirits in prison, 1 Pet. iii. 19, 20; assuring us, that Judas went presently to his own place, Acts i. 25.   And to that sense, is the parable of Dives and Lazarus, Luke xvi. 22.

But let us weigh these four things more particularly, for our full satisfaction in this point.

Arg. 1. Why should the happiness of believers be deferred, since they are immediately capable of enjoying it, as soon as separated from the body?   Alas, the soul is so far from being assisted by the body (as it is now) for the enjoyment of God; that it is either clogged or hindered by it: so speaks the apostle, 2 Cor. v. 6. 8, "Whilst we are at home in the body, we are absent from the Lord;" that is, our bodies prejudice our souls, obstruct and hinder the fulness and freedom of their communion.   When we part from the body, we go home to the Lord; then the soul is escaped as a bird out of a cage or snare. Here I am anticipated by an excellent pen,* which hath judiciously opened this point: to whose excellent observations I only add this; that if the entanglements, snares, and prejudices of the soul are so great and many in its embodied estate, that it cannot so freely dilate itself and take in the comforts of God by communion with him, then surely the laying aside of that clog, or the freeing of the soul from that burden, can be no bar to its greater happiness, which it enjoys in its separated state.

2. Why should the happiness and glory of the soul be deferred, unless God had some farther preparative work to do upon it, before it be fit to be admitted into glory?   But surely, there is no such work wrought upon it after its separation by death: all that is done of that kind, is done here. The working

* Mr. Shaw, in his Farewell to Life, reprinted by the Religious Tract Society.

day is then ended, and night comes, when no man can work, John ix. 3. To that purpose are those words of Solomon, "Whatsoever thy hand findeth to do, do it with all thy might; for there is no wisdom, nor knowledge, nor device in the grave whither thou goest," Eccles. ix. 10. So that our glorification is not deferred, in order to our fuller preparation for glory. If we are not fit when we die, we can never be fit : all is done upon us that ever was intended to be done ; for they are called, Heb. xii. 23, the spirits of the just made perfect.

3. Again, Why should our salvation slumber, when the damnation of the wicked doth not slumber? God defers not their misery, and surely he will not defer our glory. If he be quick with his enemies, he will not be slow and dilatory with his friends. It cannot be imagined, but he is as much inclined to acts of favour to his children, as to acts of justice to his enemies; See Jude, ver. 7; Acts i. 25; 1 Pet. iii. 19, 20.

4. How do such delays consist with Christ's ardent desires to have his people with him where he is, and with the vehement longings of their souls to be with Christ? You may see those reflected flames of love between the Bridegroom and his spouse in Rev. xxii. 17. 20. Delays make their hearts sick : the expectation and faith in which the saints die, is to be satisfied then ; and surely God will not deceive them. I deny not but their glory will be more complete when the body, their absent friend, is re-united, and made to share with them in their happiness ; yet that hinders not, but meanwhile the soul may enjoy its glory, whilst the body takes its rest, and sleeps in the dust.

Inference 1. Are believers immediately with God after their dissolution? Then how surprisingly glorious will heaven be to believers ! Not that they are in it before they think of it, or are fitted for it ; no, they have spent many thoughts upon it before, and been long preparing for it; but the suddenness and greatness of the change is amazing to our thoughts. For a soul to be now here in the body, conversing with men, living among sensible objects, and within a few moments to be with the Lord; this hour on earth, the next in the third heaven ; now viewing this world, and anon standing among an innumerable company of angels, and the spirits of the just made perfect : oh what a change is this ! To live as angels of God ! To live without eating, drinking, sleeping ! To be lifted up from a bed of sickness to a throne of glory ! To leave a sinful, troublesome world, a sick and pained body, and be in a moment perfectly cured, and feel thyself perfectly well, and free from all troubles and distempers ! You cannot think what this will be ! Who can tell what sights, what apprehensions, what thoughts, what frames believing souls have, before the bodies they left are removed from the eyes of their dear surviving friends !

2. Are believers immediately with God after their dissolution ? Where then shall the unbelievers be, and in what state will they find themselves immediately after death hath closed their eyes ?   Ah ! what will the case of them be that go the other way ?

To be plucked out of house and body, from among friends and comforts, and thrust into endless miseries, into the dark vault of hell ; never to see the light of this world any more ; never to see a comfortable sight ; never to hear a joyful sound ; never to know the meaning of rest, peace, or delight any more : oh what a change is here !   To exchange the smiles and honours of men, for the frowns and fury of God ; to be clothed with flames, and drink the pure unmixed wrath of God, who were but a few days since clothed in silks, and filled with the sweet of the creature !   How is the state of things altered with them ! It was the lamentable cry of poor Adrian, when he felt death approaching : " Oh my poor wandering soul ! alas ! whither art thou going !   Where must thou lodge this night !   Thou shalt never jest more, never be merry more !"

Your term in your houses and bodies is out, and there is another habitation provided for you ; but it is a dismal one !   When a saint dies, heaven above is as it were moved to receive and entertain him ; at his coming, he is received into everlasting habitations, into the inheritance of the saints in light.   When an unbeliever dies, we may say of him, alluding to Isa. xiv. 9, " Hell from beneath is moved for him, to meet him at his coming ; it stirreth up the dead for him."   No more sports, nor plays, nor cups of wine, nor beds of pleasure : the more of these you enjoyed here, the more intolerable will this change be to you. If saints are immediately with God, others are immediately with Satan.

3. How little cause have they to fear death, who shall be with God so soon after their death !   Some there are that tremble at the thoughts of death ; that cannot endure to hear its name mentioned ; that would rather stoop to any misery here, yea, to any sin, than die, because they are afraid of the exchange.   But you that are interested in Christ, need not do so ; you can lose nothing by the exchange : the words death, grave, and eternity, should have another kind of sound in your ears, and make contrary impressions upon your hearts.   If your earthly tabernacle be broken up, you shall not be found

naked; you have " a building of God, an house not made with hands, eternal in the heavens;" and it is but a step out of this into that. Oh what sweet and happy thoughts should you have of that great and last change! But what speak I of your fearlessness of death? Your duty lies much higher than that; for,

4. If believers are immediately with God, after their dissolution, then it is their duty to long for that dissolution, and cast many a longing look towards heaven. So did Paul, " I desire to be dissolved, and to be with Christ, which is far better." The advantages of this exchange are unspeakable: you have gold for brass; wine for water; substance for shadow; solid glory for very vanity. Oh! if the dust of this earth were but once blown out of your eyes, that you might see the Divine glory, how weary would you be to live, how willing to die! But then be sure your title be sound and good: leave not so great a concernment to the last; for, though it is confessed, God may do that in an hour, that never was done all your days, yet it is not common; which brings us to our third and last observation.

THAT GOD MAY, THOUGH HE SELDOM DOTH, PREPARE MEN FOR GLORY IMMEDIATELY BEFORE THEIR DISSOLUTION BY DEATH.

There is one parable, and no more, that speaks of some that were called at the last hour, Matt. xx. 9, 10. And there is this one instance in the text, and no more, that gives us an account of a person so called. We acknowledge God may do it, his grace is his own, he may dispense it how and where he pleaseth. Who shall fix bounds, or put limits to free grace, but God himself, whose it is? If he do not ordinarily show such mercies to dying sinners (as indeed he doth not); yet it is not because he cannot, but because he will not; not because their hearts are so hardened by long custom in sin, that his grace cannot break them, but because he most justly withholds that grace from them. When blessed Mr. Bilney, the martyr, heard a minister preaching thus: Oh, thou old sinner, thou hast lain these fifty years rotting in thy sin, dost thou think now to be saved? that the blood of Christ shall save thee? O, said Mr. Bilney, what preaching of Christ is this? If I had heard no other preaching than this, what had become of me? No, no, old sinners, or young sinners, great or small sinners, are not to be beaten off from Christ, but encouraged to repentance and faith; for who knows but the bowels of mercy may yearn at last upon one that hath all along rejected it? This thief was as unlikely ever to receive mercy, but a few hours before he died, as any person in the world could be.

But surely this is no encouragement to neglect the present season of mercy, because God may show mercy hereafter; or to neglect the ordinary, because God sometimes manifests his grace in ways extraordinary. Many, I know, have hardened themselves in ways of sin, by this example of mercy. But what God did at ·this time, for this man, cannot be expected to be done ordinarily for us: and the reasons thereof are,

1. Because God hath vouchsafed *us* the ordinary and standing means of grace, which this sinner had not; and therefore we cannot expect such extraordinary and unusual conversion as he had. This poor creature never heard, in all likelihood, one sermon preached by Christ, or any of his apostles: he lived the life of a highwayman, and concerned not himself about religion. But we have Christ preached freely and constantly in our assemblies: we have line upon line, precept upon precept: and when God affords the ordinary preaching of the gospel, he doth not use to work wonders. When Israel was in the wilderness, then God gave them bread from heaven, and clave the rocks to give them drink; but when they came to Canaan, where they had the ordinary means of subsistence, the manna ceased.

2. Such a conversion as this may not be ordinarily expected by any man, because such a time as that will never come again. It is possible, if Christ were to die again, and thou to be crucified with him, thou mightest receive thy conversion in such a miraculous and extraordinary way; but Christ dies no more; such a day as that will never come again.

Mr. Fenner, in his excellent discourse upon this point, tells us, That as this was an extraordinary time, Christ being now to be installed in his kingdom, and crowned with glory and honour; so extraordinary things were now done; as when kings are crowned, the streets are richly adorned, the conduits run with wine, great malefactors are then pardoned, for then they show their munificence and bounty; it is the day of the gladness of their hearts. But let a man come at another time to the conduits, he shall find no wine, but ordinary water there. Let a man be in the jail at another time, and he may be hanged; yea, and have no reason but to expect and prepare for it. What Christ did now for this man, was at an extraordinary time.

3. Such a conversion as this may not ordinarily be expected, for as such a time will never come again, so there will never be the like reason for such a conversion any more. Christ converted

him upon the cross, to give an instance of his Divine power at that time, when it was almost wholly clouded: as ·in that day the Divinity of Christ brake forth in several miracles ; the preternatural eclipse of the sun, the great earthquake, the rending of the rocks and vail of the temple ; so likewise in the conversion of this man in such an extraordinary way, and all, to give evidence of the Divinity of Christ, and prove him to be the Son of God whom they crucified : but that is now sufficiently confirmed, and there will be no more occasion for miracles to evidence it.

4. None hath reason to expect the like conversion, that enjoys the ordinary means ; because, though in this convert we have a pattern of what free grace can do, yet, as divines pertinently observe, it is a pattern without a promise ; God hath not added any promise to it, that ever he will do it for any other ; and where we have not a promise to encourage our hope, our hope can signify but little to us.

Inference 1. Let those that have found mercy in the evening of their life, admire the extraordinary grace that therein hath appeared to them. Oh that ever God should accept the bran, when Satan hath had the flour of thy days ! The fore-mentioned reverend author tells us of one Marcus Caius Victorius, a very aged man in the primitive times, who was converted from heathenism to christianity in his old age. This man came to Simplicianus, a minister, and told him, he heartily owned and embraced the christian faith. But neither he nor the church would trust him for a long time ; and the reason was, the unusualness of a conversion at such an age. But after he had given them good evidence of the reality thereof, there were acclamations and singing of psalms, the people every where crying, Marcus Caius Victorius is become a christian. This was written for a wonder ! Oh ! if God have wrought such wondrous salvation for any of you, what cause have you to do more for him than others ! To appear to you at last, when so hardened by long custom in sin, that one might say, " Can the ethiopian change his skin, or the leopard his spots ?" Oh ! what riches of mercy have appeared to you !

2. Let this convince and startle such, as even to their grey hairs remain in an unconverted state, who are where they were when they first came into the world, yea, much further off.

Bethink yourselves, ye that are full of days, and full of sin, whose time is almost done, and your great work not begun ; who have but a few sands more in the glass to run down, and then your conversion will be impossible : your sun is setting ;

your night is coming; the shadows of the evening are stretched out upon you; you have one foot in the grave. Oh think with yourselves how sad a case you are in: God may do wonders, but they are not seen every day, for then they would cease to be wondered at. O strive, strive, while you have a little time, and a few helps and means more; strive to get that work accomplished now that was never done yet; defer it no longer, you have done so too much already.

It may be (to use * Seneca's expression) you have been these sixty, seventy, or eighty years, beginning to live, about to change your practice; but hitherto you still continue the same. Do not you see how Satan hath deceived, and cheated you with vain purposes, till he hath brought you to the very brink of the grave and hell? Oh it is time now to make a stand, and pause a little where you are, and to what he hath brought you. The Lord at last give you an eye to see, and a heart to consider.

3. Lastly, Let this be a call and caution to all young ones to begin with God betimes, and take heed of delaying till the last, as many thousands have done before them to their eternal ruin. Now is your time, if you desire to be in Christ; if you have any sense of the weight and worth of eternal things upon your hearts. I know your age is voluptuous, and delights not in the serious thoughts of death and eternity: you are more inclined to mind your pleasures, and leave these serious matters to old age; but let me persuade you against that, by these considerations.

Oh set to the business of religion NOW, because this is the moulding age. Now your hearts are tender, and your affections flowing: now is the time when you are most likely to be wrought upon.

Now, because this is the freest part of your time. It is in the morning of your life, as in the morning of the day: if a man have any business to be done, let him take the morning for it; for in the after-part of the day a hurry of business comes on, so that you either forget it, or want opportunity for it.

Now, because your life is immediately uncertain; you are not certain that ever you shall attain the years of your fathers: there are graves in the church-yard just of your length; and skulls of all sorts and sizes in Golgotha, as the jews' proverb is.

Now, because God will not spare you because you are but young sinners, if you die without an interest in Christ.

Now, because your life will be the more eminently useful,

* Semper victuri. Always about to live.

and serviceable to God, when you know him betimes, and begin with him early. Austin repented, and so have many thousands since, that he began so late, and knew God no sooner.

Now, because your whole life will be the sweeter to you, when the morning of it is dedicated to the Lord. The first fruits sanctify the whole harvest : this will have a sweet influence upon all your days, whatever changes, straits, or troubles you may afterwards meet with.

SERMON XXXIII.

THE FOURTH EXCELLENT SAYING OF CHRIST UPON THE CROSS,
ILLUSTRATED.

MATT. XXVII. 46.

AND ABOUT THE NINTH HOUR JESUS CRIED WITH A LOUD VOICE, SAYING,
ELI, ELI, LAMA SABACHTHANI! THAT IS TO SAY, MY GOD, MY GOD, WHY
HAST THOU FORSAKEN ME!

THIS verse contains the fourth memorable saying of Christ upon the cross; words able to rend the hardest heart in the world: it is the voice of the Son of God in an agony: his sufferings were great, very great before, but never in that extremity as now; when this heaven-rending and heart-melting outcry brake from him upon the cross, Eli, Eli, lama sabachthani! In which observe, the time, matter, and manner of this his sad complaint.

1. The time when it was uttered was, " about the ninth hour," about three of the clock afternoon. For as the jews divided the night into four quarters, or watches; so they divided the day, in like manner, into four quarters, or greater hours; which had their names from that hour of the day that closed the quarter. So that beginning their account of their lesser hours from six in the morning, which with them was the first, their ninth hour answered to our third afternoon. And this is particularly marked by the evangelists, on purpose to show us how long Christ hung in distress upon the cross, both in soul and body, which at least was full three hours: towards the end whereof his soul was so distressed, and overwhelmed, that this doleful cry brake from his soul, in bitter anguish.

2. As to the manner of the complaint, it is not of the cruel tortures he felt in his body, nor of the scoffs and reproaches of his name; he mentions not a word of these, they were all swallowed up in the sufferings within, as the river is swallowed up in the sea, or the lesser flame in the greater. He seems to neglect all these, and only complains of what was more burdensome than ten thousand crosses; even his Father's deserting him, " My God, my God, why hast thou forsaken me?" It is a more inward trouble that burdens him, darkness upon his spirit, the hidings of God's face from him, an affliction he was totally a stranger to till now.

3. The manner in which he uttered his sad complaint, was with a remarkable vehemency, " he cried with a loud voice," not like a dying man, in whom nature was spent, but as one full of vigour, life, and sense. He stirred up the whole power of nature, when he made this grievous outcry. There is in it also an emphatical reduplication, which shows with what vehemency it was uttered ; " My God, my God."

Nay, moreover, to increase the force and vehemency of this complaint, here is an affectionate interrogation, " Why hast thou forsaken me ?" Questions, especially such as this, are full of spirits. It is as if he were surprised by the strangeness of this affliction : and rousing up himself with an unusual vehemency, turns himself to the Father, and cries, Why so, my Father ? Oh what dost thou mean by this ? What ! hide that face from me that was never hid before ! What ! and hide it from me now, in the depth of my other torments and troubles ! O what new, what strange things are these !

> DOCT. THAT GOD, IN DESIGN TO HEIGHTEN THE SUFFERINGS OF CHRIST TO THE UTTERMOST, FORSOOK HIM IN THE TIME OF HIS GREATEST DISTRESS; TO THE UNSPEAKABLE AFFLICTION AND ANGUISH OF HIS SOUL.

This proposition shall be considered in three parts : The desertion itself ; the design or end of it ; the effect and influence it had on Christ.

I. The desertion itself. Divine desertion generally considered, is God's withdrawing himself from any, not as to his essence, for that fills heaven and earth, and constantly remains the same; but it is the withdrawment of his favour, grace, and love : when these are gone, God is said to be gone. And this is done two ways, either absolutely, and wholly, or respectively, and only as to manifestation. In the first sense, devils are forsaken of God. They once were in his favour and love, but they have utterly and finally lost it. God is so withdrawn from them, as that he will never take them into favour any more. In the other sense he sometimes forsakes his dearest children, that is, he removes all sweet manifestations of his favour and love for a time.

More particularly, to open the nature of this desertion of Christ by his Father, it was,

1. A very sad desertion, the like unto which in all respects never was experienced by any, nor can be to the end of the world. All his other sufferings were but small to this ; they bore upon his body, this upon his soul ; they came from the

·hands of vile men, this from the hands of a dear Father.   He suffered both in body and soul; but the sufferings of his soul were the very soul of his sufferings.   Under all his other sufferings he opened not his mouth; but this touched the quick, so that he could not but cry out, " My God, my God, why hast thou forsaken me ?"

2. It was a penal desertion, inflicted on him for satisfaction for those sins of ours, which deserved that God should forsake us for ever, as the damned are forsaken by him.   As there lies a twofold misery upon the damned in hell, namely, pain of sense, and pain of loss; so upon Christ answerably, there was not only an impression of wrath, but also a subtraction or withdrawment of all sensible favour and love.

3. It was a desertion that was real, and not fictitious.   He doth not personate a deserted soul, and speak as if God had withdrawn the comfortable sense and influence of his love from him; but the thing was so indeed.   The Godhead restrained and kept back, for this time, all its joys, comforts, and sense of love from the manhood, yielding it nothing but support.   This bitter doleful outcry of Christ gives evidence enough of the reality of it.

4. This desertion took place in the time of Christ's greatest need of comfort that ever he had in all the time of his life on earth.   His Father forsook him at that time, when all earthly comforts had forsaken him, and all outward evils had broken in together upon him; when men, yea, the best of men stood afar off, and none but barbarous enemies were about him. When pains and shame, and all miseries even weighed him down; then, to complete and fill up his suffering, God stands afar off too.

5. It was such a desertion as left him only to the supports of his faith.   He had nothing else now but his Father's covenant and promise to rest upon.   And indeed, the faith of Christ did manifest itself, in these very words of complaint in the text. For though all comfortable sights of God and sense of love were obstructed, yet you see his soul cleaves fiducially to God for all that : " My God," &c.   His faith laid hold on God, under a most suitable title, or attribute, Eli, Eli, " My strong One, my strong One," *q. d.*   O thou, with whom is infinite and everlasting strength; thou that hast hitherto supported my manhood, and according to thy promise upheld thy servant; what ! wilt thou now forsake me ? My strong One, I lean upon thee. To these supports and refuges of faith this desertion shut up Christ : by these things he stood, when all other visible and sensible

comforts shrunk away, both from his soul and body. This is the brief account of the nature and quality of Christ's desertion.

II. In the next place, let us consider the designs and ends of it; which were principally satisfaction and sanctification. Satisfaction for those sins of ours which deserved that we should be totally and everlastingly forsaken of God. This is the desert of every sin, and the damned do feel it, and shall to all eternity. God is gone from them for ever: not essentially; the just God is with them still, the God of power is still with them, the avenging God is ever with them; but the merciful God is gone, and gone for ever. And thus would he have withdrawn himself from every soul that sinned, had not Christ borne that punishment for us in his own soul.

And as satisfaction was designed in this desertion of Christ, so also was the sanctification of all the desertion of the saints designed in it. For he having been forsaken before us, and for us, whenever God forsakes us, that very forsaking of his is sanctified, and thereby turned into a mercy to believers. Hence are all the precious fruits and effects of our desertions: such are the earnest excitations of the soul to prayer, Psa. lxxvii. 2; lxxxviii. 1, 9. The fortifying the tempted soul against sin. The reviving of ancient experiences, Psa. lxxvii. 5. Enhancing the value of the Divine presence with the soul, and teaching it to hold Christ faster than ever before. These, and many more, are the precious effects of sanctified desertion; but how many, or how good soever these effects are, they all owe themselves to Jesus Christ, as the author of them; who, for our sakes, would pass through this sad and dark state, that we might find those blessings in it.

III. Let us consider the effects and influence this desertion had upon the spirit of Christ.

And though it did not drive him to despair, yet it even amazed him, and almost swallowed up his soul in the deeps of trouble and consternation. This cry is a cry from the deeps, from a soul oppressed even to death. Let but five particulars be weighed, and you will say, never was there any darkness like this; no sorrow like Christ's sorrow in this deserted state. For,

1. Apprehend, reader, this was a new thing to Christ, and that which he never was acquainted with before. From all eternity until now there had been constant and wonderful outlets of love, delight, and joy, from the bosom of the Father, into his bosom. He never missed his Father before; never saw a frown, or a veil, upon that blessed face before. This made it a heavy burden indeed.

2. Again, as it was a new thing, and therefore the more amazing, so it was a great thing to Christ; so great, that he scarce knew how to support it. · Had it not been a great trial indeed, so great a spirit as his was would never have so drooped under it, and made so sad a complaint of it. It was so sharp, so heavy an affliction to his soul, that it caused him, who was meek under all other sufferings as a lamb, to roar under this like a lion; for so much those words of Christ signify; " My God, my God, why hast thou forsaken me ? Why art thou so far from the voice of my roaring ?" Psa. xxii. 1.

3. It was too a burden laid on in the time of his greatest distress; when his body was in tortures, and all about him was black, dismal, and full of horror and darkness. He suffered this desertion at a time when he never had the like need of Divine supports and comforts, and that aggravated it.

4. So heavy was this pressure upon Christ's soul, that in all probability it hastened his death; for it was not usual for crucified persons to expire so soon; and those that were crucified with him were both alive after Christ was gone. Some have hanged more than a day and a night, some two full days and nights, in those torments alive; but never did any feel inwardly what Christ felt. He bare it till the ninth hour, and then makes a fearful outcry and dies.

Inference 1. Did God forsake Christ upon the cross as a punishment to him for our sins ? Then it follows, that as often as we have sinned, so oft have we deserved to be forsaken of God. This is the just recompence and desert of sin. And, indeed, here lies the principal evil of sin, that it separates between God and the soul. This separation is both the moral evil that is in it, and the penal evil inflicted by the righteous God for it. By sin we depart from God, and, as a due punishment of it, God departs from us. This will be the dismal sentence in the last day, " Depart from me, ye cursed," Matt. xxv. Thenceforth there will be a gulf fixed between God and them, Luke xix. 20. No more friendly intercourse with the blessed God for ever. Beware, sinners, how you say to God now, Depart from us, we desire not the knowledge of thy ways, lest he say, Depart from me, you shall never see my face.

2. Did Christ never make such a sad complaint and outcry, till God hid his face from him ? Then the hiding of God's face is certainly the greatest misery that can possibly befall a gracious soul in this world. When they scourged, buffeted, and smote Christ, yea, when they nailed him to the tree, he opened not his mouth; but when his Father hid his face from him, then he

cried out; yea, his voice was the voice of roaring: this was more to him than a thousand crucifyings. And, surely, as it was to Christ, so is it to all gracious souls, the saddest stroke, the heaviest burden that ever they felt. When David forbade Absalom to come to Jerusalem, to see his father, he complains, in 2 Sam. xiv. 32, " Wherefore (saith he) am I come from Geshur, if I may not see the king's face?" So doth the gracious soul bemoan itself; Wherefore am I redeemed, called, and reconciled, if I may not see the face of my God?

It is said of Tully, when he was banished from Italy, and of Demosthenes, when he was banished from Athens, that they wept every time they looked towards their own country: and, is it strange that a poor deserted believer should mourn every time he looks heaven-ward? Say, christian, did the tears never trickle down thy cheeks when thou lookedst towards heaven, and couldst not see the face of thy God, as at other times? If two dear friends cannot part, though it be but for a season, but that parting must be in a shower; blame not the saints if they sigh and mourn bitterly when the Lord, who is the life of their life, depart, though but for a season, from them; for if God depart, their sweetest enjoyment on earth, the very crown of all their comforts is gone: and what will a king take in exchange for his crown? What can recompense a saint for the loss of his God? Indeed, if they had never seen the Lord, or tasted the incomparable sweetness of his presence, it were another matter; but the darkness which follows the sweetest light of his countenance, is double darkness.

And that which doth not a little increase the horror of this darkness is, that when their souls are thus benighted, and the sun of their comfort is set; then doth Satan, like the wild beasts of the desert, creep out of his den, and roar upon them with hideous temptations. Surely this is a sad state, and deserves tender pity! Pity is a debt due to the distressed, and the world shows not a greater distress than this. If ever you have been in troubles of this kind yourselves, you will never slight others in the same case: nay, one end of God's exercising you with troubles of this nature, is to teach you compassion towards others in the same case. Do they not cry to you, as Job xix. 21, " Have pity, have pity upon me, O ye my friends, for the hand of God hath touched me." Draw forth bowels of mercy and tender compassion to them; for, either you have been, or are, or may be in the same case yourselves: however, if men do not, most certainly Christ, who hath felt it before them, and for them, will pity them.

3. Did God really forsake Jesus Christ upon the cross? Then from the desertion of Christ, singular consolation springs up to the people of God; yea, manifold consolation. Principally it is a support in these two respects, as it is preventive of your final desertion, and a comfortable pattern to you in your present sad desertions.

(1.) Christ's desertion is preventive of your final desertion : because he was forsaken for a time, you shall not be forsaken for ever, for he was forsaken for you ; and God's forsaking him, though but for a few hours, is equivalent to his forsaking you for ever. It is every way as much for the dear Son of God, the delight of his soul, to be forsaken of God for a time ; as if such a poor inconsiderable thing as thou art, should be cast off to eternity. Now this being equivalent, and borne in thy room, must needs give thee the highest security in the world, that God will never finally withdraw from thee : had he intended to have done so, Christ had never made such a sad outcry as you hear this day, " My God, my God, why hast thou forsaken me ? "

(2.) Moreover, this sad desertion of Christ becomes a comfortable pattern to poor deserted souls in divers respects ; and the proper business of such souls, at such times, is to eye it believingly, in these six respects.

[1.] Though God deserted Christ, yet at the same time he powerfully supported him : his omnipotent arms were under him, though his face was hid from him : he had not indeed his smiles, but he had his supports. So, christian, just so shall it be with thee : thy God may turn away his face, but he will not pluck away his arm. When one asked holy Mr. Baines, how the case stood with his soul, he answered, Supports I have, though suavities I want.

[2.] Though God deserted Christ, yet he deserted not God: his Father forsook him, but he could not forsake his Father, but followed him with this cry, " My God, my God, why hast thou forsaken me ? "

And is it not even so with you ? God goes off from your souls, but you cannot go off from him. No, your hearts are mourning after the Lord, seeking him carefully with tears ; complaining of his absence, as the greatest evil in this world.

[3.] Though God forsook Christ, yet he returned to him again. It was but for a time, not for ever. In this also doth his desertion parallel yours. God may, for several wise and holy reasons, hide his face from you, but not so as it is hid from the damned, who shall never see it again. This cloud will pass away ; this night shall have a bright morning : " For (saith thy God) I will not contend for ever, neither will I be always wroth; for the spirit shall fail before me, and the souls which I have made." ·

[4.] Though God forsook Christ, yet at that time he could justify God. So you read, Psa. xxii. 2, 3, " O my God, (saith he,) I cry in the day-time, but thou hearest not; and in the night-season, and am not silent: but thou art holy." Is not thy spirit, according to the measure, framed like Christ's in this; canst thou not say, even when he writes bitter things against thee, he is a holy, faithful, and good God for all this? There is not one drop of injustice in all the sea of my sorrows. Though he condemn me, I must and will justify him.

[5.] Though God took from Christ all visible and sensible comforts, inward as well as outward; yet Christ subsisted, by faith, in the absence of them all: his desertion put him upon the acting of his faith. My God, my God, are words of faith; the words of one that wholly depends upon his God: and is it not so with you too? Sense of love is gone, sweet sights of God shut up in a dark cloud: well, what then? must thy hands presently hang down, and thy soul give up all its hopes? what! is there no faith to relieve in this case? Yes, yes, and blessed be God for faith. " Who is among you that feareth the Lord, and obeyeth the voice of his servants, that walketh in darkness, and hath no light; let him trust in the name of the Lord, and stay himself upon his God," Isa. l. 10. To conclude,

[6.] Christ was deserted a little before the glorious morning of light and joy dawned upon him. It was a little, a very little while, after this sad cry, before he triumphed gloriously: and so it may be with you; heaviness may endure for a night, but joy and gladness will come in the morning.

But, reader, perhaps you are saying, I fear I am absolutely and finally forsaken.

Why so? Do you find the characters of such a desertion upon your soul? Examine and tell me, whether you find a heart willing to forsake God? Is it indifferent to you whether God ever return again or no? Are there no mournings, meltings, or thirstings after the Lord? Indeed, if you forsake him, he will cast you off for ever; but can you do so? Oh, no, let him do what he will, I am resolved to wait for him, cleave to him, mourn after him, though I have no present comfort from him, no assurance of my interest in him; yet will I not exchange my poor weak hopes for all the good in this world.

Again, you say God hath forsaken you, but hath he taken away from your souls all conscientious tenderness of sin, so that now you can sin freely, and without any regret ?   If so, it is a sad token indeed : tell me, soul, if thou, indeed, judgest God will never return in loving-kindness to thee any more ; why dost thou not then give thyself over to the pleasures of sin, and fetch thy comforts from the creature, since thou canst have no comfort from thy God ?   Oh, no, I cannot do so ; even if I die in darkness and sorrow, I will never do so : my soul is as full of fear and hatred of sin as ever, though empty of joy and comfort. Surely, these are no tokens of a soul finally abandoned by its God.

4. Did God forsake his own Son upon the cross ? Then the dearest of God's people may, for a time, be forsaken of their God.   Think it not strange, when you, that are the children of light, meet with darkness, yea, and walk in it ; neither charge God foolishly, nor say he deals hardly with you.   You see what befell Jesus Christ, whom his soul delighted in. It is doubtless your concernment to expect and prepare for days of darkness.   You have heard the doleful cry of Christ, " My God, my God, why hast thou forsaken me ? "   You know how it was with Job, David, Heman, Asaph, and many others, the dear servants of God, what heart-melting lamentations they made upon this account ; and are you better than they ?   Oh, prepare for spiritual troubles ; I am sure you do enough every day to involve you in darkness.   Now, if at any time this trial befall you, mind these two seasonable admonitions, and lay them up for such a time.

(1.) Exercise the faith of adherence, when you have lost the faith of evidence.   When God takes away that, he leaves this : that is necessary to the comfort, this to the life of his people. It is sweet to live in views of your interest, but if they be gone, believe and rely on God, for an interest. Stay yourselves on your God when you have no light, Isa. l. 10.   Drop this anchor in the dark, and do not reckon all gone when evidence is gone : never reckon yourselves undone whilst you can adhere to your God.

(2.) Take the right method to recover the sweet light which you have sinned away from your souls.   Do not go about from one to another complaining ; nor yet sit down desponding under your burden.   But,

Search diligently after the cause of God's withdrawment : urge him importunately by prayer, to show thee wherefore he contends with thee, Job x. 2. Say, Lord, what evil is it which thou so rebukest ?   I beseech thee show me the cause of thine anger : have I grieved thy Spirit in this thing, or in that ?

Was it my neglect of duty, or my formality in duties? Was I not thankful for the sense of thy love, when it was shed abroad in my heart? O Lord, why is it thus with me?

Humble your souls before the Lord for every evil you shall be convinced of: tell him, it pierces your hearts that you have so displeased him, and that it shall be a caution to you, whilst you live, never to return again to folly: invite him again to your souls, and mourn after the Lord till you have found him : If you seek him, he will be found of you, 2 Chron. xv. 2.

Wait on in the use of means till Christ return. Oh be not discouraged ; though he tarry, wait you for him ; for, blessed are all they that wait for him.

SERMON XXXIV.

THE FIFTH EXCELLENT SAYING OF CHRIST UPON THE CROSS,
ILLUSTRATED.

JOHN XIX. 28.

AFTER THIS, JESUS KNOWING THAT ALL THINGS WERE NOW ACCOMPLISHED,
THAT THE SCRIPTURE MIGHT BE FULFILLED, SAITH, I THIRST.

THIS is the fifth word of Christ upon the cross, spoken a little before he bowed the head and yielded up the ghost. It is recorded only by this evangelist; and, there are four things remarkable in this complaint of Christ, namely, The person complaining; the complaint he made; the time when, and the reason why he so complained.

1. The person complaining is Jesus. This is a clear evidence, that it was no common suffering: great and resolute spirits will not complain for small matters. Let us therefore see next,

2. The affliction, or suffering, he complains of; and that is, thirst. There are two sorts of thirst, one natural and proper, another spiritual and figurative: Christ felt both at this time. His soul thirsted, in vehement desires and longings, to accomplish and finish that great and difficult work he was now about; and his body thirsted, by reason of those unparalleled agonies it laboured under, for the accomplishing thereof: but it was the proper natural thirst he here intends, when he said, "I thirst." Now, "this natural thirst," of which he complains, "is the raging of the appetite for moist nourishment, arising from scorching up of the parts of the body for want of moisture." And, amongst all the pains and afflictions of the body, there can scarcely be named a greater, and more intolerable one, than extreme thirst. The most mighty and valiant have stooped under it. Mighty Samson, after all his conquests and victories, complains thus; " And he was sore athirst, and called on the Lord, and said, Thou hast given this great deliverance into the hand of thy servant: and now shall I die for thirst, and fall into the hands of the uncircumcised ?" Judges xv. 18. Hence, Isa. xli. 17, thirst is put to express the most afflicted state: " When the poor and needy seek water, and there is none, and their

tongue faileth for thirst, I the Lord will hear them;" that is, when my people are in extreme necessities, under any extraordinary pressures and distresses, I will be with them, to supply and relieve them. Thirst causes a most painful compression of the heart, when the body, like a spunge, sucks and draws for moisture, and there is none. And this may be occasioned, either by long abstinence from drink, or by the labouring and expense of the spirits under grievous agonies and extreme tortures; which, like a fire within, soon scorch up the very radical moisture.

Now, though we find not that Christ tasted a drop since he sat with his disciples at the table; after that no more refreshments for him in this world; yet that was not the cause of this raging thirst; but it is to be ascribed to the extreme sufferings which he so long had conflicted with, both in his soul and body. These preyed upon him, and drank up his very spirits. Hence came this sad complaint, " I thirst."

3. The time when he thus complained was, " when all things were now accomplished," that is, when all things were even ready to be accomplished in his death; a little, a very little while before his expiration, when the pangs of death began to be strong upon him: and so it was both a sign of death at hand, and of his love to us, which was stronger than death, that would not complain sooner, because he would admit of no relief, nor take the least refreshment, until he had done his work.

4. The design and end of his complaint was, " that the scripture might be fulfilled," that is, that it might appear, for the satisfaction of our faith, that whatsoever had been predicted by the prophets, was exactly accomplished, even to a circumstance, in him. Now it was foretold of him, " They gave me gall for my meat, and, in my thirst, they gave me vinegar to drink," Psa. lxix. 21; and herein it was verified. Hence the note is,

> Doct. That such were the agonies and extreme sufferings of our Lord Jesus Christ upon the cross, as drank up his very spirits, and made him cry, " I thirst."

"If I (said one) should live a thousand years, and every day die a thousand times the same death for Christ that he once died for me, yet all this would be nothing to the sorrows Christ endured in his death." At this time the Bridegroom Christ might have borrowed the words of his spouse, the church, " Is it nothing to you, all ye that pass by ? See and behold, if there be any sorrow like unto my sorrow which is done unto me, wherewith the Lord hath afflicted me in the day of his fierce anger," Lam. i. 12.

Here we are to inquire into, and consider the extremities and agonies Christ laboured under upon the cross, which occasioned this sad complaint of thirst; and then make application, in the several inferences of truth deducible from it.

The sufferings of our Lord Jesus Christ upon the cross were twofold, namely, his corporeal, and spiritual sufferings. We shall open them distinctly, and show how both these meeting together upon him in their fulness and extremity, must needs consume his very radical moisture, and make him cry, " I thirst." To begin with the first.

I. His corporeal and more external sufferings were exceeding great, acute, and extreme sufferings ; for they were sharp, universal, continual, and unrelieved by any inward comfort.

1. They were *sharp* sufferings ; for his body was racked in those parts where sense more eminently dwells : in the hands and feet the veins and sinews meet, and their pain and anguish meet with them; " They digged my hands and my feet," Psa. xxii. 16. Now Christ, by reason of his exact and excellent temper of body,* had doubtless more quick, tender, and delicate senses than other men. Sense is, in some, more delicate and tender, and in others dull and blunt, according to the temperament and vivacity of the body and spirits; but in none as it was in Christ, whose body neither sin nor sickness had any way enfeebled or dulled.

2. His pains also were *universal,* not affecting one, but every part ; they seized every member ; from head to foot, no member was free from torture : for, as his head was wounded with thorns, his back with bloody lashes, his hands and feet with nails, so every other part was stretched and distended beyond its natural length, by hanging upon that cruel engine of torment, the cross. And as every member, so every particular sense was afflicted.

3. These universal pains were *continual,* not by fits, but without any intermission. He had not a moment's ease by the cessation of pains ; wave came upon wave, one grief driving on another, till all God's waves and billows had gone over him. To be in extremity of pain, and that without a moment's intermission, will quickly pull down the stoutest nature in the world.

4. And lastly, his pains were altogether *unrelieved.* If a

* His body was of a most excellent contexture when it was miraculously formed.—*Aquin. pars tertia. Art.* 6.

man have sweet comforts flowing into his soul from God, they will sweetly demulce and allay the pains of the body: this made the martyrs shout amidst the flames. Yes, even inferior comforts and delights of the mind, will greatly relieve the oppressed body. But now Christ had no relief this way in the least; not a drop of comfort came from heaven into his soul to relieve it, and the body by it: but, on the contrary, his soul was filled up with grief, and had a heavier burden of its own to bear than that of the body; so that instead of relieving, it increased unspeakably the burden of its outward man. For,

II. Let us consider these inward sufferings of his soul, how great they were, and how quickly they spent his natural strength, and turned his moisture into the drought of summer.

1. His soul felt the wrath of an angry God, which was terribly impressed upon it. The wrath of a king is as the roaring of a lion; but what is that to the wrath of God? See what a description is given of it in Nahum i. 6. "Who can stand before his indignation? and who can abide in the fierceness of his anger? His fury is poured out like fire, and the rocks are thrown down by him." Had not the strength that supported Christ been greater than that of rocks, this wrath had certainly overwhelmed and ground him to powder.

2. And as it was the wrath of God that lay upon his soul, so it was the pure wrath of God, without any allay or mixture: not one drop of comfort came from heaven or earth; all the ingredients in his cup were bitter ones: "For God spared not his own Son," Rom. viii. 32. Had Christ been abated or spared, we had not.

3. Yea, all the wrath of God was poured out upon him, even to the last drop; so that there is not one drop reserved for the elect to feel. Christ's cup was deep and large, it contained all the fury and wrath of an infinite God in it! and yet he drank it up: he bare it all.

III. It is evident that such extreme sufferings as these, meeting together upon him, must needs exhaust his very spirits, and make him cry, "I thirst." For let us consider,

1. What mere external pains and outward afflictions can do. These prey upon, and consume our spirits. So David complains, "When thou with rebukes correctest man for iniquity; thou makest his beauty to consume away as a moth," Psa. xxxix. 11; that is, as a moth frets and consumes the most strong and well-wrought garment, and makes it seary and rotten without any noise, so afflictions waste and wear out the strongest bodies. They make bodies of the firmest constitution like an

old rotten garment : they shrivel and dry up the most vigorous and flourishing body, and make it like a bottle in the smoke, Psa. cxix. 83.

2. Consider what mere internal troubles of the soul can do upon the strongest body; they spend its strength, and devour the spirits. So Solomon speaks, Prov. xvii. 22, "A broken spirit drieth the bones," that is, it consumes the very marrow with which they are moistened. So Psa. xxxii. 3, 4, "My bones waxed old, through my roaring all the day long. For day and night thy hand was heavy on me: my moisture is turned into the drought of summer." What a spectacle of pity did Francis Spira become, merely through the anguish of his spi it! A spirit sharpened with such troubles, like a keen knife, cuts through the sheath. Certainly, whoever hath had any acquaintance with troubles of soul, knows, by sad experience, how, like an internal flame, it feeds and preys upon the very spirits, so that the strongest stoop and sink under it. But,

3. When outward bodily pains shall meet with inward spiritual troubles, and both in extremity shall come in one day; how soon must the firmest body fail and waste away ! Now strength fails apace, and nature must fall flat under this load. The soul and body sympathize with each other under trouble, and mutually relieve each other. If the body be sick and full of pain, the spirit supports, cheers, and relieves it by reason and resolution all that it can ; and if the spirit be afflicted, the body sympathizes and helps to bear up the spirit : but if the one be overladen with strong pains, more than it can bear, and calls for aid from the other; and the other be oppressed with intolerable anguish, and cries out under a burden greater than it can bear, so that it can contribute no help, but instead thereof adds to its burden, which before was above its strength to bear, then nature must needs fail, and the friendly union between soul and body suffer a dissolution by such an extraordinary pressure as this. So it was with Christ, when outward and inward sorrows met in one day in their extremity upon him. Hence the bitter cry, " I thirst."

Inference 1. How horrid a thing is sin ! How great is that evil of evils, which deserves that all this should be inflicted and suffered for the expiation of it !

The sufferings of Christ for sin give us the true account, and fullest representation of its evil. Oh then, let not thy vain heart slight sin, as if it were but a small thing ! If ever God show thee the face of sin in this glass, thou wilt say, there is not such another horrid representation to be made to a man in all the world. Fools make a mock at sin, but wise men tremble at it.

2. How afflictive and intolerable are inward troubles! Did Christ complain so sadly under them, and cry, "I thirst?" Surely then they are not such light matters as many are apt to make of them. If they so scorched the very heart of Christ, preyed upon his very spirits, and turned his moisture into the drought of summer, they deserve not to be slighted, as they are by some. The Lord Jesus was fitted to bear and suffer as strong troubles as ever befell the nature of man, and he did bear all other troubles with admirable patience; but when it came to this, when the flames of God's wrath scorched his soul, then he cries, "I thirst."

David's heart was, for courage, as the heart of a lion; but when God exercised him with inward troubles for sin, then he roars out under the anguish of it: "I am feeble, and sore broken; I have roared, by reason of the disquietness of my heart. My heart panteth, my strength faileth me: as for the light of mine eyes, it is also gone from me," Psa. xxxviii. 8. 10. "A wounded spirit who can bear?" Many have declared that all the torments in the world are nothing to the wrath of God upon the conscience. What is the worm that never dies but the efficacy of a guilty conscience? This worm feeds upon, and gnaws the very inwards, the tender and most sensible part of man; and is the principal part of hell's horror. In bodily pains, a man may be relieved by proper medicines; here nothing but the blood of sprinkling relieves. In outward pains, the body may be supported by the resolution and courage of the mind; here the mind itself is wounded. Oh let none despise these troubles, they are dreadful things!

3. How dreadful a place is hell, where this cry is heard for ever, "I thirst!" There the wrath of the great and terrible God flames upon the damned for ever, in which they thirst, and none relieves them. If Christ complained, "I thirst," when he had conflicted but a few hours with the wrath of God; what is their state then, that are to grapple with it for ever? When millions of years are past and gone, ten thousand millions more are coming on. There is an everlasting thirst in hell, and it admits of no relief. Think on this, ye that now add drunkenness to thirst, who wallow in all sensual pleasures, and drown nature in an excess of luxury. Remember what Dives said in Luke xvi. 24. "And he cried and said, Father Abraham, have mercy on me, and send Lazarus that he may dip the tip of his finger in water, and cool my tongue, for I am tormented in this flame." If thirst in the extremity of it be now so insufferable, what is that thirst

which is infinitely beyond this in measure, and never shall be relieved?   Say not it is hard that God should deal thus with his poor creatures.   You will not think it so, if you consider what he exposed his own dear Son to, when sin was but imputed to him; and what that man deserves to feel, that hath not only merited hell, but, by refusing Christ the remedy, the hottest place in hell.

4. How much do nice and wanton appetites deserve to be reproved!   The Son of God wanted a draught of cold water to relieve him, and could not have it.   God hath given us variety of refreshing creatures to relieve us, and we despise them. We have better things than a cup of water to refresh and delight us when we are thirsty, and yet are not pleased.   Oh that this complaint of Christ on the cross, "I thirst," were but believingly considered; it would make you bless God for what ye now despise, and beget contentment in you for the meanest mercies, and most common favours in this world.   Did the Lord of all things cry, "I thirst," and had nothing in his extremity to comfort him; and dost thou, who hast a thousand times over forfeited all temporal as well as spiritual mercies, contemn and slight the good creatures of God? What! despise a cup of water, who deservest nothing but a cup of wrath from the hand of the Lord! Oh lay it to heart, and hence learn contentment with any thing.

5. Did Jesus Christ upon the cross cry, "I thirst?" Then believers shall never thirst eternally. Their thirst shall be certainly satisfied.

So it is promised, "Blessed are they which hunger and thirst after righteousness; for they shall be filled," Matt. v. 6.   In heaven they shall then depend no more upon the stream, but drink from the overflowing fountain itself: " They shall be abundantly satisfied with the fatness of thy house, and thou shalt make them drink of the river of thy pleasures : for with thee is the fountain of life, and in thy light shall we see light," Psa. xxxvi. 8.   There they shall drink and praise, and praise and drink for evermore ; all their thirsty desires shall be filled with complete satisfaction.   Oh how desirable a state is heaven upon this account! and how should we be restless till we come thither, as the thirsty traveller is until he meet that cool, refreshing spring he wants and seeks for! This present state is a state of thirsting; that to come, of refreshment and satisfaction. Some drops indeed come from the fountain by faith, but they quench not the believer's thirst ; rather, like water sprinkled on the fire, they make it burn the more : but there the thirsty soul hath enough.

6. Did Christ in the extremity of his sufferings cry, " I thirst ?" Then how great, beyond all compare, is the love of God to sinners, who for their sakes exposed the Son of his love to such extreme sufferings !

Oh the height, length, depth, and breadth of that love which passeth knowledge !   The love of God to Jesus Christ was infinitely beyond all the love we have for our children, as the sea is more than a spoonful of water : and yet, as dearly as he loved him, he was content to expose him to all this, rather than we should perish eternally.

And it should never be forgotten, that Jesus Christ was exposed to these extremities of sorrow for sinners, the greatest of sinners, who deserved not one drop of mercy from God.   This commends the love of God singularly to us, in that " whilst we were yet sinners, Christ died for us," Rom. v. 1.   Thus the love of God in Jesus Christ still rises higher and higher in every discovery of it.   Admire, adore, and be transported with the thoughts of this love !   Thanks be to God for his unspeakable gift.

SERMON XXXV.

JOHN XIX. 30.

WHEN JESUS THEREFORE HAD RECEIVED THE VINEGAR, HE SAID, IT IS
FINISHED: AND HE BOWED HIS HEAD, AND GAVE UP THE GHOST.

"It is finished." This is the sixth remarkable word of our Lord Jesus Christ upon the cross, uttered as a triumphant shout when he saw the glorious issue of all his sufferings now at hand.

It is but one word in the original; but in that one word is contained the sum of all joy, the very spirits of all divine consolation. The ancient greeks reckoned it their excellency to speak much in a little; " to give a sea of matter in a drop of language." What they only sought, is here found. I find some variety, (and indeed variety rather than contrariety) among expositors about the relation of these words. Some are of opinion, that the antecedent is the legal types and ceremonies; and so make this to be the meaning: It is finished; that is, all the types and prefigurations that shadowed forth the redemption of souls, by the blood of Christ, are now fulfilled and accomplished. And, doubtless, as this is itself a truth, so it is such a truth as may not be excluded, as foreign to the true scope and sense of this place. And though it be objected, that many types and prefigurations remained at this time unsatisfied, even all that looked to the actual death of Christ, his continuance in the state of the dead, and his resurrection; yet it is easily removed, by considering that they are said to be finished, because they were just finishing, or ready to be finished: and it is as if Christ had said, I am now putting the last hand to it, a few moments of time more will complete and finish it; I have the sum now in my hand, which will fully satisfy and pay God the whole debt. It is now but bow the head, and the work is done, and all the types therein fulfilled. So that we cannot exclude the fulfilling of the types in the death of Christ, from their just claim to the sense of this place. But yet, though we cannot here exclude this sense, we cannot allow it to be the whole or principal sense: for lo! a far greater truth is contained herein, even the finishing or completing of the whole design and plan of our redemption, and therein of all the types that prefigured it. Both these judicious Calvin conjoins, making the completing of redemption the principal, and the fulfilling of all the types the collateral and secondary sense of it. Yet it must be observed, when we say, Christ finished redemption work by his death, the meaning is not that his death alone did finish it; for his abode in the grave, resurrection, and ascension, had all of them their joint influence therein. According then to the principal scope of the place, we observe,

> THAT JESUS CHRIST HATH PERFECTED AND COMPLETELY FINISHED THE GREAT WORK OF REDEMPTION, COMMITTED TO HIM BY GOD THE FATHER.

To this great truth the apostle gives a full testimony, "By one offering he hath perfected for ever them that are sanctified," Heb. x. 14. And to the same purpose speaks Christ, "I have glorified thee on earth; I have finished the work thou gavest me to do," John xvii. 4. Concerning this work, and the finishing thereof by Jesus Christ upon the cross, we shall inquire, what this work was; how Christ finished it; and what evidence can be produced for the finishing of it.

I. What was the work which Christ finished by his death?

It was the fulfilling the whole law of God in our room, and for our redemption, as a sponsor or surety for us. The law is a glorious thing; the holiness of God is engraven or stamped upon every part of it; "From his right hand went a fiery law," Deut. xxxiii. 2. The jealousy of the Lord watched over every point and tittle of it, for his dreadful and glorious name was upon it; it cursed every one that continued not in all things contained therein, Gal. iii. 10. Two things, therefore, were necessarily required in him that should perfectly fulfil it, and both found in our Surety, and in him only, namely, a subjective and effective perfection.

1. A subjective perfection. He that wanted this, could never say, "It is finished." Perfect working always follows a perfect Being. That he might therefore finish this great work of obedience, and therein the glorious design of our redemption; lo! in what shining and perfect holiness was he produced! "That holy thing that shall be born of thee, shall be called the Son of God," Luke i. 35. And indeed, "such an High Priest became us, who is holy, harmless, undefiled, separate from sinners," Heb. vii. 26. So that the law could have no exception against his person; nay, it was never so honoured since its first pro-

mulgation, as it was by having such a perfect and excellent person as Christ to stand at its bar, and give it due reparation.

2. There must be also an effective perfection, or a perfection of working and obeying, before it could be said, " It is finished." This Christ had ; for he continued in all things written in the law, to do them : He fulfilled all righteousness, as it behoved him to do, Matt. iii. 15. He did all that was required to be done, and suffered all that was requisite to be suffered : he did and suffered all that was commanded or threatened, in such perfection of obedience, both active and passive, that the pure eye of Divine justice could not find a flaw in it ; and so finished the work his Father gave him to do : and this work finished by our Lord Jesus Christ was both a necessary, difficult, and precious work.

The work which Christ finished upon the cross was *necessary*, upon a threefold account.

It was necessary on the Father's account. I do not mean that God was under any necessity, from his nature, of redeeming us this or any other way ; for our redemption is an act of the free counsel of God ; but when God had once decreed and determined to redeem and save poor sinners by Jesus Christ, then it became necessary that the counsel of God should be fulfilled : " To do whatsoever thy hand and counsel had before determined to be done," Acts iv. 28.

It was necessary with respect to Christ, upon the account of that precious compact that was between the Father and him about it. Therefore it is said by Christ himself, " Truly the Son of man goeth as it was determined," Luke xxii. 22 ; that is, as it was fore-agreed and covenanted. Under the necessity of fulfilling his engagement to the Father, he came into the world ; and being come, he still minds his engagement, " I must work the works of him that sent me," John ix. 3.

Yea, and it was no less necessary upon our account that this work should be finished ; for, had not Christ finished this work, sin had quickly finished all our lives, comforts, and hopes. Without the finishing this work, not a son or daughter of Adam could ever have seen the face of God. Therefore it is said, " As Moses lifted up the serpent in the wilderness, so must the Son of man be lifted up ; that whosoever believeth in him should not perish, but have everlasting life," John iii. 14, 15. On all these accounts the finishing of this work was necessary.

As it was necessary this work should be finished, so the finishing of it was exceeding *difficult :* it cost many a cry, many a groan, and many a tear, before Christ could say, " It is finished."

All the angels in heaven were not able, by their united strength, to lift that burden one inch from the ground, which Christ bare upon his shoulders, yea, and bare it away. But how heavy a burden this was, may in part appear by his agony in the garden, and the bitter outcries he made upon the cross, which in their proper places have been opened.

And lastly, It was a most *precious* work which Christ finished by his death; that work was despatched and finished in few hours, which will be the matter of everlasting songs and triumphs to the angels and saints to all eternity. Oh it was a precious work! The mercies that now flow out of this fountain, namely, justification, sanctification, adoption, &c. are not to be estimated; besides the endless happiness and glory of the world to come, which cannot enter into the heart of man to conceive. If the angels sang when the foundation-stone was laid, what shouts, what triumphs should there be among the saints, when this voice is heard, " It is finished !"

II. Let us next inform ourselves how, and in what manner Jesus Christ finished this glorious work; and if you search the scriptures upon that account, you will find that he finished it obediently, freely, diligently, and fully.

1. This blessed work was finished by Jesus Christ most *obediently*, " He became obedient to death, even the death of the cross," Phil. ii. 8. " His obedience was the obedience of a servant, though not servile obedience."* So it was foretold of him, before he entered upon his work, " The Lord God hath opened mine ear, and I was not rebellious, neither turned away back," Isa. l. 5.

2. As Christ finished it obediently, so he finished it *freely*. Freedom and obedience in acting are not at all opposite to, or exclusive of each other. Moses' mother nursed him in obedience to the command of Pharaoh's daughter, yet most freely with respect to her own delight and contentment in that work. So it is said of Christ, and that by his own mouth, " Therefore doth my Father love me, because I lay down my life, that I might take it again. No man taketh it from me, but I lay it down of myself : I have power to lay it down, and I have power to take it up again. This commandment have I received of my Father," John x. 17, 18. He liked the work for the end's sake. When he had a prospect of it from eternity, then were his delights with the sons of men : then he rejoiced in the habitable parts of the earth, Prov. viii. 30, 31. And when he came into the world, about it, with what a full and free consent did his

* Obedientia servi, non servilis.

heart echo to the voice of his Father calling him to it ! "Lo, I come : I delight to do thy will : thy law is within my heart," Psa. xl.   He finished the work freely.

3. He finished it also *diligently ;* he was never idle wherever he was, but "went about doing good," Acts x. 38. Sometimes he was so intent upon his work, that he "forgat to eat bread," John iv. 30, 31.   As the life of some men is but a diversion from one trifle to another, from one pleasure to another ; so the whole life of Christ was spent and taken up between one work and another : never was a life so filled up with labour : the very moments of his time were all employed for God to finish this work.

4. He finished it *completely* and *fully*. All that was to be done by way of meritorious redemption is fully done ; no hand can come after his ; angels can add nothing to it. That is perfected to which nothing is wanting, and to which nothing can be added. Such is the work which our Lord Jesus Christ finished. Whatever the law demanded is perfectly paid ; whatever a sinner needs, is perfectly obtained and purchased ; nothing can be added to what he hath done ; he put the last hand to it, when he said, "It is finished."

III. Let us consider what evidence we have that Christ hath so finished redemption-work : and if you pursue that inquiry, you will find these, among other plain evidences of it.

1. When Christ died, the work of redemption must needs be finished, inasmuch as the blood, as well as the obedience of Christ, was of infinite value and efficacy, sufficiently able to accomplish all the ends for which it was shed : when that therefore is actually shed, justice is fully paid, and, consequently, the souls for whom, and in whose names it is paid, are fully redeemed from the curse by the merit thereof.

2. It is apparent that Christ finished the work, by the discharge or acquittance God the Father gave him, when he raised him from the dead, and set him at his own right hand. If Christ, the sinner's Surety, be, as such, discharged by God the Creditor, then the debt is fully paid. Now Christ was justified, and cleared at his resurrection, from all charges and demands of justice ; therefore it is said, 1 Tim. iii. 16, that he was justified in the spirit, that is, openly discharged by that very act of the Godhead, his raising him from the dead. For when the grave was opened, and Christ arose, it was to him as the opening of the prison doors, and setting a surety at liberty, who was confined for another man's debt. To the same sense Christ speaks of his ascension, "The Spirit (saith he) shall convince the

world of righteousness," John xvi. 10 ; that is, of a complete and perfect righteousness in me, imputable to sinners for their perfect justification. And whereby shall he convince and satisfy them that is so ? Why, by this, " Because I go to the Father, and ye see me no more." There is a great deal of force and weight in those words, " because ye see me no more :" for it amounts to this much ; by this you shall be satisfied I have fully and completely performed all righteousness, and that, by my active and passive obedience, I have so fully satisfied God for you, as that you shall never be charged or condemned ; because, when I go to heaven, I shall abide there in glory with my Father, and not be sent back again, as I should, if any thing had been omitted by me. And this the apostle gives you also in so many plain words, " After he had offered one sacrifice for sins, for ever sat down on the right hand of God," Heb. x. 12—14. And what doth he infer from that, but the very truth before us, that " by one offering he hath perfected for ever them that are sanctified ?"

3. It is evident Christ hath finished the work, by the blessed effects of it upon all that believe in him : for by virtue of the completeness of Christ's work, finished by his death, their consciences are now pacified, and their souls, at death, actually received into glory ; neither of which could be, if Christ had not in this world finished the work. If Christ had done his work imperfectly, he could not have given rest and tranquillity to the labouring and burdened souls that come to him, as now he doth, Matt. xi. 28. Conscience would still be hesitating, trembling, and unsatisfied ; and had he not finished his work, he could not have had entrance through the veil of his flesh into heaven, as all that believe in him have, Heb. x. 19, 20. And thus you see briefly the evidences, that the work is finished.

Inference 1. Hath Christ perfected and completely finished all his work for us? How sweet a relief is this to us that believe in him against all the defects and imperfections of all the works for God, that are wrought by us ! There is nothing finished that we do : all our duties are imperfect duties. Oh there is much sin and vanity in the best of our duties : but here is the grand relief, and that which answers to all our doubts and fears upon that account ; Jesus Christ hath finished all his work, though we can finish none of ours : and so, though we be defective, poor, imperfect creatures, in ourselves, yet, notwithstanding, we are complete in him, Col. ii. 9, 10. Though we cannot perfectly obey, or fulfil one command of the law, yet is " the righteousness of the law fulfilled in us that believe," Rom.

viii. 4. Christ's complete obedience being imputed to us, makes us complete, and without fault before God. It is true, we ought to be humbled for our defects, and troubled for every failing in obedience ; but we should not be discouraged, though multitudes of weaknesses be upon us, and many infirmities compass us about, in every duty we put our hand to : though we have no righteousness of our own ; yet of God, Christ is made unto us righteousness ; and that righteousness of his is infinitely better than our own : instead of our own, we have his. Oh blessed be God for Christ's perfect righteousness !

2. Did Christ finish his work with his own hand ? How dangerous and dishonourable a thing is it to join any thing of our own to the righteousness of Christ, in point of justification before God ! Jesus Christ will never endure this ; it reflects upon his work dishonourably : he will be all, or none, in your justification.   If he have finished the work, what need of our additions ? And if not, to what purpose are they ? Can we finish that which Christ himself could not ? But we would fain be sharing with him in this honour, which he will never endure. Did he finish the work by himself, and will he ever divide the glory and praise of it with us ? No, no, Christ is no half Saviour.   Oh it is a hard thing to bring these proud hearts to live upon Christ for righteousness. God humbles proud nature, by calling sinners wholly from their own righteousness to Christ for their justification.

3. Did Christ finish his work for us ? then there can be no doubt, but he will also finish his work in us.   As he began the work of our redemption, and finished it ; so he that hath begun the good work in you, will also finish it upon your souls. And of this the apostle saith, " he is confident," Phil. i. 6.   Jesus Christ is not only called the author, but also the finisher of our faith, Heb. xii. 2.   If he begin it, no doubt he will finish it. And indeed the finishing of his own work of redemption without us, gives full evidence that he will finish his work of sanctification within us ; and that because these two works of Christ have a respect and relation to each other ; and such a relation, that the work he finished by his own death, resurrection, and ascension, would be in vain to us, if the work of sanctification in us should not in like manner be finished.   Therefore, as he presented a perfect sacrifice to God, and finished redemption-work ; so will he present every one perfect and complete, for whom he offered up himself; for he will not lose the end of all his sufferings at last.   To what purpose would his meritorious impetration be, without complete and full application ? Therefore

be not discouraged at the defects and imperfections of your inherent grace: be humbled for them, but be not dejected by them: this is Christ's work as well as that: that work is finished, and so will this.

4. Is Christ's work of redemption a complete and finished work? How excellent and comfortable beyond all compare, is the method and way of faith! Surely the way of believing is the most excellent way in which a poor sinner can approach God; for it brings before him a complete, entire, perfect righteousness; and this must needs be most honourable to God, as well as most comfortable to the soul that draws nigh to God. Oh what a complete, finished, perfect thing is the righteousness of Christ! the searching eye of the holy and jealous God cannot find the least flaw or defect in it. Let God or conscience look upon it; turn it every way; view it on every side; thoroughly weigh and examine it; it will appear a pure, a perfect piece, containing in it whatsoever is necessary for the reconciling of an angry God, or pacifying of a distressed and perplexed soul. How pleasing therefore, and acceptable to God, must be that faith, which presents so complete and excellent an atonement to him! Hence the acting of our faith upon Christ for righteousness, the approaches of faith to God with such an acceptable present, is called the work of God; " This is the work of God, that ye believe," John vi. 29. One act of faith pleases him more, than if you should toil all your lives at a task of obedience to the law. As it is more for God's honour and thy comfort, to pay all thou owest him at one payment, in one full sum, than to be paying by very small degrees, and never be able to make full payment, or see the bond cancelled; so this perfect work only produces perfect peace.

5. Did Christ work, and work out all that God gave him to do, till he had finished his work? How necessary then is a laborious working life to all that call themselves christians! The life of Christ, you see, was a laborious life. Shall he work and we play? Oh work, and work out your own salvation with fear and trembling, Phil. ii. 12.

Will any one say, But if Christ wrought so hard, we may sit still. If he finished the work, nothing remains for us to do.

I answer, Nothing of that work which Christ did remains for you to do, but there is other work for you to do; yea, store of work lying upon your hands. You must work as well as Christ, though not for the same ends Christ did. He wrought all his life long, to work out a righteousness to justify you before God. But you must work, to obey the commands of Christ, into whose right ye are come by redemption : you must work to testify your thankfulness to Christ, for the work finished for you : you must work, to glorify God by your obedience ; let your light so shine before men. For these, and divers other such ends and reasons, your life must be a working life. May God preserve all his people from the gross and vile opinions of antinomian libertines, who cry up grace and decry obedience.

Reader, be thou a follower of Christ, imitate thy pattern ; yea, let me persuade thee, as ever thou hopest to clear up thine interest in him, imitate him in such particulars as these that follow.

(1.) Christ began early to work for God ; he took the morning of his life, even the very beginning of it, to work for God : " How is it (said he to his parents, when he was but a child of about twelve years old) that ye sought me ? Wist ye not that I must be about my Father's business ?" Reader, if the morning of thy life be not gone, oh devote it to the work of God as Christ did : if it be, ply thy work the closer in the afternoon of thy life.

(2.) As Christ began by time, so he followed his work closely ; he was early up, and he wrought hard, so hard, that " he forgat to eat bread," John iv. 31, 32. So zealous was he in his Father's work, that his friends thought " that he had been beside himself," Mark iii. 21. So zealous, that " the zeal of God's house eat him up."

(3.) Christ often thought upon the shortness of his time, and wrought diligently because he knew his working-time would be but little. So you find it, John ix. 4, " I must work the works of him that sent me whilst it is day ; the night cometh, when no man can work." Oh in this be like Christ : rouse your hearts to diligence with this consideration. If a man have much to write, and he be almost come to the end of his paper, he will write close, and thereby put much matter in a little room.

(4.) He did much work for God in a very silent manner : he laboured diligently, but did not spoil his work, when he had wrought it, by vain ostentation. When he had expressed his charity in his acts of mercy and bounty to men, he would humbly seal up the glory of it, with this charge, " See ye tell no man of it," Matt. viii. 4. He affected no popular air. Oh imitate your pattern ; work hard for God, and let not pride blow upon it, when you have done. It is difficult for a man to do much, and not value himself for it too much.

(5.) Christ carried on his work for God resolvedly : no discouragements would beat him off, though never any work met with more from first to last.   How did scribes and pharisees, jews, gentiles, yea, devils set upon him, by persecutions, and reproaches, violent oppositions, and subtle temptations ; but yet, he goes on with his Father's work for all that : he is deaf to all discouragements.   So it was foretold of him, " He shall not fail, nor be discouraged," Isa. xlii. 4.   Oh that more of this spirit of Christ were in his people : oh that, in the strength of love to Christ, and zeal for the glory of God, you will pour out your hearts in service, and, like a river, sweep down all discouragements before you.

(6.) He continued working whilst he continued living : his life and labour ended together : he fainted not in his work : nay, the greatest work he did in this world, was his last work.   Oh be like Christ in this, be not weary of well-doing : give not over the work of God, while you can move hand and tongue to promote it, and see that your last works be more than your first. Oh let the motions of your soul after God be, as all natural motions are, swiftest when nearest the centre.   * Say not it is enough, whilst there is any capacity of doing more for God. In these things, christians, be like your Saviour.

6. Did Christ finish his work?   Look to it christians, that ye also finish your work which God hath given you to do ; that you may with comfort say, when death approaches, as Christ said, " I have glorified thee on earth, I have finished the work thou gavest me to do ; and now, O Father, glorify thou me with thine own self," John xvii. 4.   Christ had a work committed to him, and he finished it ; you have a work also committed to you : oh see that you may be able to say, It is finished, when your time is so : oh work out your own salvation with fear and trembling ; and, that I may persuade you to it, I beseech you lay these considerations close to heart.

If your work be not done before you die, it can never be done. " There is no work, nor knowledge, nor device in the grave, whither thou goest," Eccl. ix. 5. 10.   They that go down to the pit cannot celebrate the name of God, Isa. xxxviii. 18. Death binds up the hand from working any more ; strikes dumb the tongue that it can speak no more ; for then the composition is dissolved.   The body, which is the soul's instrument to work by, is broken and thrown aside : the soul itself presented immediately before the Lord, to give an account of all its works. Oh therefore, seeing the night cometh when no man can work, make haste and finish your work.

* Si dixisti sufficit, periisti. If thou once say it is enough, thou art lost.

If you finish not your work, as the season of working, so the season of *mercy* will be over at death. Do not think, you that have neglected Christ all your lives, you that could never be persuaded to a laborious holy life, that ever your cries and entreaties shall prevail with God for mercy, when your season is past. No, it is too late; " Will God hear his cry, when troubles come upon him?" Job xxvii. 9. The season of mercy is then over; as the tree falls, so it lies; then he that is holy shall be holy still, and he that is filthy shall be filthy still. Alas, poor souls, you come too late; " The master of the house is risen up, and the door is shut," Luke xiii. 25. The season is over: happy had it been if ye had known the day of your visitation.

If your work be not finished when you come to die, you can never finish your lives with comfort. He that hath not finished his *work* with *care*, can never finish his *course* with *joy*. Oh what a dismal case is that soul in, that finds itself surprised by death in an unready posture! To lie shivering upon the brink of the grave, saying, Lord, what will become of me! Oh I cannot, I dare not die! For the poor soul to shrink back into the body, and cry, Oh, it were better for me to do any thing than die! Why, what is the matter? Oh, I dare not go before the awful judgment-seat. If I had in season made Christ sure, I could then die with peace. Lord, what shall I do? How dost thou like this, reader? Will this be a comfortable close? When one asked a christian that constantly spent six hours every day in prayer, why he did so? He answered, Oh, I must die, I must die. Well then, look to it that you finish your work as Christ also did his.

SERMON XXXVI.

**THE SEVENTH AND LAST WORD WITH WHICH CHRIST BREATHED
OUT HIS SOUL, ILLUSTRATED.**

LUKE XXIII. 46.

AND WHEN JESUS HAD CRIED WITH A LOUD VOICE, HE SAID, FATHER, INTO
THY HANDS I COMMEND MY SPIRIT: AND HAVING SAID THUS, HE GAVE
UP THE GHOST.

THESE are the last of the last words of our Lord Jesus Christ
upon the cross, with which he breathed out his soul. They
were David's words before him, Psa. xxxi. 5, and for substance,
Stephen's after him, Acts vii. 59. They are words full both
of faith and comfort; fit to be the last breathings of every gracious soul in this world. They are resolved into these five
particulars:

1. The person depositing, or committing: The Lord Jesus
Christ, who in this, as well as in other things, acted as the Head
of the church. This must be remarked carefully, for therein
lies no small part of a believer's consolation. When Christ commends his soul to God, he doth as it were bind up all the souls
of the elect in one bundle with it, and solemnly presents them
all with his, to his Father's acceptance. To this purpose one
aptly renders it: " This commendation made by Christ, turns
to the singular profit and advantage of our souls; inasmuch as
Christ, by this very prayer, hath delivered them into his Father's
hand, as a precious treasure, whenever the time comes that they
are to be loosed from the bodies which they now inhabit."
Jesus Christ neither lived nor died for himself, but for believers:
what he did in this very act, refers to them as well as to his
own soul: you must look therefore upon Christ, in this last
and solemn act of his life, as gathering all the souls of the elect
together, and making a solemn tender of them all, with his own
soul, to God.

2. The depository, or person to whom he commits this precious treasure, and that was to his own Father: " Father, into
thy hands I commend my spirit." *Father* is a sweet, encouraging, assuring title: well may a son commit any concernment,

how dear soever, into the hands of a father, especially such a Son into the hands of such a Father.

3. The *depositum*, or thing committed into this hand: *my spirit*, that is, my soul, now instantly departing, upon the very point of separation from my body. The soul is the most precious of all treasures. A whole world is but a trifle, if weighed, for the price of one soul, Matt. xvi. 26. This inestimable treasure he now commits into his Father's hands.

4. The act by which he puts it into that faithful hand of the Father, παραθησομαι, I commend. We rightly render it in the present tense, though the word be future ; for with these words he breathed out his soul. This word is of the same import with συνιστημι, I present, or tender it into thy hands. It was in Christ an act of faith, a most special and excellent act intended as a precedent for all his people.

5. The last thing observable is, the manner in which he uttered these words, and that was with a loud voice ; he spake it that all might hear it, and that his enemies, who judged him now destitute and forsaken of God, might be convinced that he was not so, but that he was dear to his Father still, and could put his soul confidently into his hands : " Father, into thy hands I commend my spirit." Taking then these words, not only as spoken by Christ, the Head of all believers, and so commending their souls to God with his own, but also as a pattern, teaching them what they ought to do themselves, when they come to die ; we observe,

THAT DYING BELIEVERS ARE BOTH WARRANTED, AND ENCOURAGED, BY CHRIST'S EXAMPLE, BELIEVINGLY TO COMMEND THEIR PRECIOUS SOULS INTO THE HANDS OF GOD.

Thus the apostle directs christians, to commit their souls to God's fatherly protection, when they are either going into prisons, or to the stake for Christ : " Let them (saith he) that suffer according to the will of God, commit the keeping of their souls to him in well-doing, as unto a faithful Creator," 1 Pet. iv. 19.

This proposition we will consider in these two main branches of it, namely, what is implied in the soul's commending itself to God by faith, when the time of separation is come; and what warrant or encouragement gracious souls have for so doing.

I. What is implied in this act of a believer, his commending, or committing, his soul into the hands of God at death ?

1. It implies this evidently in it, That the soul outlives the

body, and fails not, as to its being, when its body fails; it feels the house in which it dwelt, dropping into ruins, and looks out for a new habitation with God.   "Father, into thy hands I commend my spirit."   The soul knows itself to be a more noble being than that corruptible body, to which it was united, and is now to leave in the dust: it understands its relation to the Father of spirits, and from him it expects protection and provision in its unbodied state; and therefore into his hands it puts itself. If it vanished, or breathed into air, and did not survive the body; if it were annihilated at death, it were but a mocking of God to say, when we die, "Father, into thy hands I commend my spirit."

2. It implies the soul's true rest to be in God.   See which way its motions and tendencies are, not only in life, but in death also.   "Father, into thy hands."   God is the centre of all gracious spirits.   While they tabernacle here, they have no rest but in the bosom of their God: when they go hence, their expectation and earnest desires are to be with him.   It had been working after God by gracious desires before, it had cast many a longing look heaven-ward before; but when the gracious soul comes near its God, (as it doth in a dying hour,) "then it even throws itself into his arms;" as a river, that after many turnings and windings, at last is arrived to the ocean.   "Nothing but God can please it in this world, and nothing but God can give it content when it goes hence."   Whom have I in heaven but thee? And on earth there is none that I desire in comparison of thee, Psa. lxxiii. 25.

3. It also implies the great value believers have for their souls. That is the precious treasure; and their main solicitude and chief care, is to see it secured in a safe hand: "Father, into thy hands I commit my spirit." These words express the believer's care for his soul, that it may be safe, whatever becomes of the vile body. A believer, when he comes nigh to death, spends but few thoughts about his body, where it shall be laid, or how it shall be disposed of; he trusts that in the hands of friends: but as his great care all along was for his soul, so he expresses it in these his very last breathings, in which he commends it into the hands of God. It is not, Lord Jesus, receive my body, take care of my dust; but, Receive my spirit; Lord, secure the jewel, when the casket is broken.

4. These words imply the deep sense that dying believers have of the great change that is coming upon them by death; when all visible and sensible things are shrinking away from them, and failing. They feel the world and the best comforts

of it failing; every creature and creature-comfort failing; for, at death we are said to fail, Luke xvi. 9. Hereupon the soul clasps the closer about its God, cleaves more close than ever to him: "Father, into thy hands I commend my spirit." Not that a mere necessity puts the soul upon God; or that it cleaves to God, because it hath then nothing else to take hold on. No; it chose God for its portion, when it was in the midst of all its outward enjoyments, and had as good security as other men have for the long enjoyment of them. But my meaning is, that although gracious souls have chosen God for their portion, and do truly prefer him to the best of their comforts; yet in this compounded state, they live not wholly upon their God, but partly by faith, and partly by sense; partly upon things seen, and partly upon things not seen. The creatures had some interest in their hearts; alas, too much: but now all these are vanishing. I shall see man no more, with the inhabitants of the world (said sick Hezekiah): hereupon the soul turns itself from them all, and casts itself upon God for all its subsistence, expecting now to live upon its God entirely, as the blessed angels do.

5. It implies faith in the atonement of God, and his full reconciliation to believers, by the blood of the great Sacrifice; else they durst never commit their souls into his hands: " For it is a fearful thing to fall into the hands of the living God," Heb. x. 31; that is, of God unatoned by the offering up of Christ. The soul dare no more cast itself into the hand of God, without such an atoning sacrifice, than it dares approach to a consuming fire. And, indeed, the reconciliation of God by Jesus Christ, as it is the ground of all acceptance with God; for we are made accepted in the Beloved; so it is plainly implied in the order or manner of the reconciled soul's committing itself to him: for, it first casts itself into the hands of Christ, then into the hands of God by him. So Stephen, when dying, "Lord Jesus, receive my spirit." And by that hand it would be put into his Father's hands.

6. And lastly, It implies both the efficacy and excellency of faith, in supporting and relieving the soul at a time when nothing else is able to do it. Faith is its conductor, when it is at the greatest loss and distress that ever it met with: it secures the soul when it is turned out of the body; when heart and flesh fail, this leads it to the Rock that fails not: it remains by that soul till it sees it safe through all the territories of Satan, and safe landed upon the shore of glory; and then is swallowed up in vision. Many a favour it hath shown the soul while it dwelt in its body. The great service it did for the soul was in the time of its espousals to Christ. This is the marriage-knot, the

blessed bond of union between the soul and Christ. Many a relieving sight and sweet support hath faith afforded since that; but, surely, its first and last works are its most glorious works. By faith it first ventured itself upon Christ; threw itself upon him in the deepest sense of its own vileness and utter unworthiness, when sense, reason, and multitudes of temptations stood by, contradicting and discouraging the soul; by faith it now casts itself into his arms, when it is launching out into vast eternity. They are both noble acts of faith; but the first, no doubt, is the greatest and most difficult: for, when once the soul is interested in Christ, it is no such difficulty to commit itself into his hands, as when it had no interest at all in him. It is easier for a child to cast himself in the arms of his own father, in distress, than for one that hath been both a stranger and an enemy to Christ, to cast itself upon him, that he may be a Father and a Friend to it. And this brings us upon the second inquiry, namely,

II. What warrant or encouragement have gracious souls to commit themselves at death into the hands of God? I answer, Much every way; all things encourage and warrant their so doing: for,

1. This God, to whom the believer commits himself at death, is its Creator, the Father of its being: he created and inspired it, and so it hath the relation of a creature to a Creator; yea, of a creature now in distress, to a faithful Creator: "Let them that suffer according to the will of God, commit the keeping of their souls to him in well-doing, as to a faithful Creator," 1 Pet. iv. 19. It is very true, this single relation, in itself, gives little ground of encouragement, unless the creature had conserved that integrity in which it was originally created. And they that have no more to plead with God for acceptance, but their relation to him as creatures to a Creator, will doubtless find that word made good to their little comfort, "It is a people of no understanding, therefore he that made them, will not have mercy on them, and he that formed them, will show them no favour," Isa. xxvii. 11. But now, grace brings that relation into repute: holiness ingratiates us again, and revives the remembrance of this relation; so that believers only can plead this.

2. Again, as the gracious soul is his creature, so it is his redeemed creature; one that he hath bought, and that with a great price, even with the precious blood of Jesus Christ, 1 Pet. i. 18, 19. This greatly encourages the departing soul to commit itself into the hands of God; so you find, Psa. xxxi. 5. "Into thy hands do I commend my spirit, thou hast redeemed it, O

Lord God of truth." Lord, I am not only thy creature, but thy redeemed creature ; one that thou hast bought with a great price : for my sake Christ came from thy bosom, and is it imaginable, that after that thou hast in such a costly way, even by the expense of the precious blood of Christ, redeemed me, thou shouldst at last exclude me ? Shall the ends both of creation and redemption of this soul be lost together ? will God form such an excellent creature as my soul is, in which are so many wonders of the wisdom and power of its Creator ; will he be content, when sin has marred the frame, and defaced the glory of it, to recover it to himself again, by the death of his own dear Son ; and after all this, cast it away, as if there were nothing in all this ? " Father, into thy hands I commend my spirit :" I know thou wilt have a respect to the work of thy hands ; especially to a redeemed creature, upon which thou hast expended so great sums of love.

3. Nay, that is not all ; the gracious soul may confidently and securely commit itself into the hands of God, when it parts with its body at death, not only because it is his creature, his redeemed creature, but because it is his renewed creature also : and this lays a firm ground for the believer's confidence and acceptance ; not that it is the proper cause, or reason of its acceptance, but as it is the soul's best evidence, that it is accepted with God, and shall not be refused by him, when it comes to him at death : for, in such a soul, there is a double workmanship of God, both glorious pieces, though the last exceeds in glory. A natural workmanship, in the excellent frame of that noble creature, the soul ; and a gracious workmanship upon that again ; a new creation upon the old ; glory upon glory. " We are his workmanship, created in Christ Jesus," Eph. ii. 10. The Holy Ghost came down from heaven on purpose to create this new workmanship, to frame this new creature ; and indeed it is the top and glory of all God's works of wonder in this world ; and must needs give the believer encouragement to commit himself to God, whether it shall reflect either upon the end of the work, or upon the end of the workman ; both which meet in the salvation of the soul so wrought upon. The end of the work is our glory. By this " we are made meet to be partakers of the inheritance of the saints in light," Col. i. 12. It is also the design and end of him that wrought it : " Now he that hath wrought us for the self-same thing, is God," 2 Cor. v. 5. Had he not designed thy soul for glory, the Spirit should never have come upon such a sanctifying design as this : surely it shall not fail of a reception into glory, when it is cast out of this

tabernacle : such a work was not wrought in vain, neither can it ever perish. When once sanctification comes upon a soul, it so roots itself in the soul, that where the soul goes, it goes : gifts indeed, they die ; all natural excellency and beauty, that goes away at death, Job iv. 21 ; but grace ascends with the soul ; it is a sanctified, when a separate soul. And will God shut the door of glory upon such a soul, that by grace is made meet for the inheritance ? Oh, it cannot be !

4. As the gracious soul is a renewed soul, so it is also a sealed soul; God hath sealed it in this world for that glory, into which it is now to enter at death. All gracious souls are sealed objectively, that is, they have those works of grace wrought on their souls, which evidence their title to glory ; and many are sealed formally ; that is, the Spirit helps them clearly to discern their interest in Christ, and all the promises. This both secures heaven to the soul in itself, and becomes also an earnest or pledge of that glory in the unspeakable joys and comforts that it produces in the soul. So you find, 2 Cor. i. 22, " Who hath sealed us, and given us the earnest of the Spirit in our hearts." How can the soul that hath found all this, fear in the least a rejection by its God, when at death it comes to him ? Surely, if God have sealed, he will not refuse you ; if he have given his earnest, he will not shut you out.

5. Moreover, every gracious soul may confidently cast itself into the arms of its God, when it goes hence, with, " Father, into thy hands I commit my spirit ;" forasmuch as every gracious soul is in covenant with God, and God stands obliged by his covenant and promise to such, not to cast them out, when they come unto him. As soon as ever thou didst become his, by regeneration, that promise became thine, " I will never leave you, nor forsake you," Heb. xiii. 5. And will he leave the soul at a time when it has more need of God to stand by it, than it ever had ? Every gracious soul is entitled to that promise, " I will come again, and receive you to myself," John xiv. 3. And will he fail to make it good when the time of the promise is come, as at death it is? It cannot be. When he sees a poor soul that he hath made, redeemed, sanctified, sealed, and by solemn promise engaged himself to receive, coming to him at death, firmly depending upon his faithfulness that hath promised, saying, as David, 2 Sam. xxiii. 5, Though, Lord, there be many defects in me, " yet thou hast made a covenant with me, well ordered in all things, and sure ; and this is all my salvation, and all my hope ;" how can God refuse such a soul ? How can he put it off, when it so puts itself upon him ?

6. But this is not all; the gracious soul sustains many intimate and dear relations to that God into whose hands it commends itself at death.   It is his spouse, and the consideration of such a day of espousals may well encourage it to cast itself into the bosom of Christ, its Head and Husband. It is a member of his body, flesh, and bones, Eph. v. 30.   It is his child, and he its everlasting Father, Isa. ix. 6. It is his friend: " Henceforth (saith Christ) I call you not servants, but friends," John xv. 15. What confidence may these, and all other the dear relations Christ owns to the renewed soul, beget, in such an hour as this is ! What husband can throw off the dear wife of his bosom, who in distresses casts herself into his arms ? What father can shut the door upon a dear child that comes to him for refuge, saying, Father, into thy hands I commit myself?

7. The unchangeableness of God's love to his people, gives confidence that they shall in no wise be cast out.   They know Christ was the same to them at last as he was at first ; the same in the pangs of death, as he was in the comforts of life : " having loved his own which were in the world, he loved them unto the end," John xiii. 1.   He doth not love as the world loves, only in prosperity ; but they are as dear to him when their beauty and strength are gone, as when they were in the greatest flourishing.   If we live, we live to the Lord ; and if we die, we die to the Lord ; so then, whether we live or die, we are the Lord's, Rom. xiv. 8.   Now consider all these things, and weigh them both apart, and together, and see whether they amount not to a full evidence of the truth of this point, that dying believers are warranted and encouraged to commend their souls into the hands of God ; whether they have not every one of them cause to say, as the apostle did, " I know whom I have believed, and am persuaded that he is able to keep that which I have committed to him against that day," 2 Tim. i. 12.

The improvement of all this you have in the following practical deductions.

1. Are dying believers only warranted and encouraged thus to commend their souls into the hands of God ? What a sad strait then must all dying unbelievers be in about their souls ! Such souls will fall into the hands of God, but that is their misery, not their privilege: they are not put by faith into the hands of mercy, but fall by sin into the hands of justice : not God, but the devil is their father, John viii. 44. Whither should the child go but to its own father ? They have not one of those forementioned encouragements to cast themselves into the hands of God, except the naked relation they have to God

as their Creator, and that is as good as none, without the new creation. If they have nothing but this to plead for their salvation, the devil hath as much to plead as they. It is the new creature that brings the first creation into repute again with God.

Oh dismal, oh deplorable case! A poor soul is turning out of house and home, and knows not where to go ; it departs, and immediately falls into the hands of justice. Little, ah little do the friends of such a one think, whilst they are honouring his dust by a splendid and honourable funeral, what a case that poor soul is in that lately dwelt there, and what fearful straits and extremities it is now exposed to! He may cry, indeed, Lord! Lord! open to me, as in Matt. vii. 22 ; but to how little purpose are these vain cries! Will God hear him when he cries? Job xxvii. 9. It is a lamentable case!

2. Will God graciously accept, and faithfully keep what the saints commit to him at death? How careful then should they be to keep what God commits to them, to be kept for him while they live! You have a great trust to commit to God when you die, and God hath a great trust to commit to you whilst you live : you expect that he should faithfully keep what you shall then commit to his keeping, and he expects you should faithfully keep what he now commits to your keeping. If you keep his truths, he will keep your souls. " Because thou hast kept the word of my patience, I also will keep thee," &c. Rev. iii. 10. Be faithful to your God, and you shall find him faithful to you. None can pluck you out of his hand ; see that nothing wrest his truths out of your hands. " If we deny him, he also will deny us," 2 Tim. ii. 12. Take heed lest those estates you have gotten as a blessing, attending the gospel, prove a temptation to you to betray the gospel. " Religion (saith one) brings forth riches, but the daughter devours the mother." How can you expect acceptance with God, who have betrayed his truth, and dealt perfidiously with him.

3. If believers may safely commit their souls into the hands of God, how confidently may they commit all lesser interests and lower concernments into the same hand! Shall we trust him with our souls, and not with our lives, liberties, or comforts? Can we commit the treasure to him and not a trifle? Whatever you enjoy in this world, is but a trifle to your souls. Sure, if you can trust him for eternal life for your souls, you may much more trust him for the daily bread for your bodies. I know it is objected, that God hath made over temporal things to his people upon conditional promises, and an absolute faith

can never be grounded upon conditional promises. But what means this objection? Let your faith be but suitable to these conditional promises, that is, believe they shall be made good to you so far as God sees them good for you; do you but labour to come up to those conditions required in you, and thereby God will have more glory, and you more comfort. If your prayers for these things proceed from pure ends, the glory of God, not the satisfaction and gratification of your lusts; if your desires after them be moderate as to the measure, content with that proportion the Infinite Wisdom sees fittest for you : if you take God's way to obtain them, and dare not strain conscience, or commit a sin, though you should perish for want; if you can patiently wait God's time for enlargements from your straits, and not make any sinful haste; you shall be surely supplied : and he that remembers your souls will not forget your bodies. But we live by sense, and not by faith; present things strike. our affections more powerfully than the invisible things that are to come.   The Lord humble his people for this.

4. Is this the privilege of believers, that they can commit their souls to God in a dying hour ? Then how precious, how useful a grace is faith to the people of God, both living and dying ! While we live and converse here in the world, all our comfort and safety is from it ; for all our union with Christ, the fountain of mercies and blessings, is by faith, " that Christ may dwell in your hearts by faith," Eph. iii. 17. All our communion with Christ is by it: "he that cometh to God must believe," Heb.. xi. 6. The soul's life is wrapt up in this communion with God, and that communion in faith. All communications from Christ depend upon faith ; for as all communion is founded in union, so from our union and communion are all our communications. All communications of quickenings, comforts, joy, strength, and whatsoever serves to the well-being of the life of grace, are all through that faith which first knits us to Christ, and still main-. tains our communion with Christ ; believing, we rejoice, 1 Pet.. i. 8.   The inner man is renewed, whilst we look to the things that are not seen, 2 Cor. iv. 18.   And as our life, and all its supports and comforts here, are dependent on faith, so in our death, the safety and comfort of our souls then depends upon our faith : he that hath no faith, cannot commit his soul to God, but rather shrinks from God.   Faith can do many sweet offices for your souls upon a death-bed, when the light of this world is gone, and all joy ceases on earth : it can give us sights of invisible things in the other world, and those sights will breathe life into your souls, amidst the very pangs of death.

Reader, do but think what a comfortable foresight of God, and the joys of salvation, will be to thee, when thine eye-strings are breaking : faith cannot only see that beyond the grave, which will comfort, but it can cleave to its God, and clasp Christ in a promise, when it feels the ground of all sensible comforts trembling, and sinking under thy feet : " My heart and my flesh fail, but God is the strength (or rock) of my heart, and my portion for ever."   Reeds fail, but the rock is firm footing ; yea, and when the soul can no longer tabernacle here, it can cast itself upon God, with, " Father, into thy hands I commend my spirit." Oh precious faith !

5. Do the souls of dying believers commend themselves into the hands of God? Then let not the surviving relations of such sorrow as those that have no hope. A husband, a wife, a child, is rent by death out of your arms : well, but consider into what arms, into what bosom they are commended. Is it not better for them to be in the bosom of God, than in yours ? Could they be spared so long from heaven, as to come back again to you but an hour, how would they say to you, as Christ said to the daughters of Jerusalem, " Weep not for me, but weep for yourselves, and for your children."   I am in a safe hand, I am out of the reach of all storms and troubles. Oh did you but know what their state is, who are with God, you would be more than satisfied about them.

6. I will close all with a word of counsel. Is this the privilege of dying believers, to commend their souls into the hands of God? Then as ever you hope for comfort or peace in your last hour, see that your souls be such, as may be then fit to be commended into the hands of a holy and just God : see that they be holy souls ; God will never accept them if they be not holy : " Without holiness no man shall see God," Heb. xii. 14. " He that hath this hope, (namely, to see God,) purifieth himself, even as he is pure," 1 John iii. 3.   Endeavours after holiness are inseparably connected with all rational expectations of blessedness.   Will you put an unclean, filthy, defiled thing into the pure hand of the most holy God ? Oh see that thy soul be holy, and already accepted in the Beloved ; or woe to it when it shall take its leave of the tabernacle it now dwells in ! The gracious soul may confidently say then, Lord Jesus ! into thy hand I commend my spirit. O let all that can say so then, now say, Thanks be to God for Jesus Christ.

SERMON XXXVII.

CHRIST'S FUNERAL ILLUSTRATED, IN ITS MANNER, REASONS,
AND EXCELLENT ENDS.

JOHN XIX. 40—42.

THEN TOOK THEY THE BODY OF JESUS, AND WOUND IT IN LINEN CLOTHES
WITH THE SPICES, AS THE MANNER OF THE JEWS IS TO BURY. NOW IN THE
PLACE WHERE HE WAS CRUCIFIED THERE WAS A GARDEN; AND IN THE
GARDEN A NEW SEPULCHRE, WHEREIN WAS NEVER MAN YET LAID. THERE
LAID THEY JESUS THEREFORE BECAUSE OF THE JEWS' PREPARATION DAY;
FOR THE SEPULCHRE WAS NIGH AT HAND.

You have heard the last words of dying Jesus commending his
spirit into his Father's hands. And now the Life of the world
hangs dead upon a tree. The Light of the world, for a time,
muffled up in a dismal cloud. The Sun of righteousness set in
the region and shadow of death. The Lord is dead, and he
that wears the keys of the grave at his girdle, is now himself to
be locked up in the grave. All you that are the friends and
lovers of Jesus, are this day invited to his funeral. " Come, see
the place where the Lord lay." There are six remarkable particulars about his funeral, in these three verses.

1. The preparations that were made for it; and those were
mainly in two particulars, namely, the begging and perfuming
of the body. His body could not be buried, till, by begging,
his friends had obtained it as a favour from his judge. The
dead body was by law in the power of Pilate, who adjudged it
to death, as the bodies of those that are hanged are in the power
of the judge to dispose of them as he pleases. And when they
had gotten it from Pilate, they wound it in fine linen clothes
with spices. But what need of spices to perfume that blessed
body? His own love was perfume enough to keep it sweet in
the remembrance of his people to all generations : however, by
this they will manifest, as far as they are able, the dear affection
they have for him.

2. The bearers that carried his body to its grave, were Joseph
of Arimathea, and Nicodemus, two secret disciples ; both men
of estate and honour. None could imagine that these would

have appeared at a time of so much danger, with such boldness for Christ ; that ever they would have gone openly and boldly to manifest their love to Christ, when dead, who were afraid to come to him (except by night) when he was living. But now a spirit of zeal and courage is come upon them, when those that made greater and more open confessions of him are gone.

3. The attendants who followed the bier, were the women that followed him out of Galilee ; among whom the two Marys and the mother of Zebedee's children (whom Mark calls Salome) are only named.

4. The grave, or sepulchre, where they laid him : it was in Joseph's new tomb, which he had prepared in a garden near Golgotha, where our Lord died. Two things are remarkable about this tomb ; it was another's tomb, and it was a new tomb. It was another's ; for as he had not a house of his own to live in, so he had not a tomb of his own to lay his body in when dead. And it was a new tomb, wherein never man was yet laid. Doubtless there was much of providence in this ; for had any other been laid there before him, it might have proved an occasion both to shake the credit and slur the glory of his resurrection, by pretending it was some former body, and not the Lord's, that rose out of it. In this also Divine Providence had a respect to that prophecy, Isa. liii. 9, which was to be fulfilled at his funeral: " He made his grave with the rich."

5. The disposition of the body in that tomb. It is true, there is no mention made of the groans and tears with which they laid him in his sepulchre ; yet we may well presume, they were not wanting in plentiful expressions of their sorrow that way ; for as they wept and smote their breasts when he died, Luke xxiii. 48 ; so, no doubt, they laid him with melting hearts and flowing eyes in his tomb, when dead.

6. The last remarkable particular in the text, is the solemnity with which his funeral rights were performed, and they were all suitable to his humbled state. It was, indeed, a funeral as decently ordered, as the straits of time and the state of things would then permit ; but there was nothing of pomp or outward state : few marks of honour set by men upon it : only the heavens adorned it with divers miraculous works, which in their proper place will be spoken of. Thus was he laid in his grave, where he continued for three incomplete days and nights in the territories of death, in the land of darkness and forgetfulness ; partly to correspond with Jonah his type, and partly to ascertain the world of the reality of his death. Whence our observation is,

THAT THE DEAD BODY OF OUR LORD JESUS CHRIST WAS DECENTLY INTERRED BY A SMALL NUMBER OF HIS OWN DISCIPLES, AND CONTINUED IN THE STATE OF THE DEAD FOR A TIME.

This observation containing matter of fact, and that so plainly and faithfully delivered to us by the pens of the several evangelists, we need do no more to prepare it for our use, than to satisfy these two inquiries : Why had Christ any funeral at all, since his resurrection was so soon to follow his death ? and, What manner of funeral Christ had ?

I. Why had Christ any funeral at all, since he was to rise again from the dead within that space of time that other men commonly have to lie before their interment; and had his body continued longer unburied, it could see no corruption, having never been tainted by sin ? Why, though there was no need of it at all upon that account, yet there were these four weighty ends and reasons for it.

1. It was necessary Christ should be buried, to ascertain his death ; else it might have been looked upon as a cheat: for, as they were ready enough to impose so gross a cheat upon the world at his resurrection, " That the disciples came by night, and stole him away," much more would they have denied at once the reality, both of his death and resurrection, had he not been so perfumed and interred. But this cut off all pretensions ; for in their kind of embalming, his mouth, ears, and nostrils were all filled with their spices and odours ; bound up in linen, and laid long enough in the tomb to give full assurance to the world of the certainty of his death; so that there could be no latent principle of life in him. Now, since our eternal life is wrapt up in Christ's death, it can never be too firmly established. To this, therefore, we may well suppose Providence had special respect in his burial, and the manner of it.

2. He must be buried, to fulfil the types and prophecies that went before. His abode in the grave was prefigured by Jonah's abode three days and nights in the belly of the whale : " So shall the Son of man be three days and three nights in the heart of the earth," Matt. xii. 40. Yea, the prophet had described the very manner of his funeral, and, long before he was born, foretold in what kind of tomb his body should be laid : " He made his grave with the wicked, and with the rich in his death," Isa. liii. 9 ; pointing, by that expression, at this tomb of Joseph, who was a rich man ; and the scriptures cannot be broken.

3. He must be buried, to complete his humiliation ; this

being the lowest step he could possibly descend to in his abased state. " They have brought me to the dust of death ;" lower he could not be laid.

4. But the great end and reason of his interment was the conquering of death in its own dominion and territories ; which victory over the grave furnished the saints with that triumphant song of deliverance, " O death ! where is thy sting? O grave ! where is thy destruction ?" 1 Cor. xv. 55. Our graves would not be so sweet and comfortable to us, when we come to lie down in them, if Jesus had not lain there before us and for us. Death is a dragon, the grave its den ; a place of dread and terror ; but Christ goes into its den, there grapples with it, and for ever overcomes it ; disarms it of all its terror ; and not only makes it cease to be inimical, but to become exceeding beneficial to the saints ; a bed of rest, and a perfumed bed ; they do but go into Christ's bed, where he lay before them.

II. Let us inquire what manner of funeral Christ had ? And if we intently observe it, we shall find many remarkable properties in it.

1. We shall find it to be a very obscure and private funeral. Here was no external pomp : Christ affected it not in his life, and it was no way suitable to the ends and manner of his death. Humiliation was designed in his death ; and state is inconsistent with such an end : besides, he died upon the cross ; and persons so dying do not use to have much ceremony and state at their funerals. Three things show it to be a very humble and obscure funeral as to what concerned outward glory, with which the great ones of the earth are usually interred. For,

The dead body of the Lord was not brought from his own house, as other men's commonly are, but from the cross. They begged it of his judge. Had they not obtained this favour from Pilate, it must have been buried in Golgotha ; it had been cast into a pit digged under the cross. And when buried, it was attended with a very poor train : a few sorrowful women followed the bier. Other men are accompanied to their graves by their relations and friends : the disciples were all scattered from him, afraid to own him dying, and dead. And these few that were resolved to give him a funeral, are forced, by reason of the straits of time, to do it in great haste ; for the preparation for the passover was at hand. This was the obscure funeral which the body of the Lord had. Thus was the Prince of the kings of the earth, who has the keys of death and hell, laid into his grave.

2. Yet though men could bestow little honour upon it, the

heavens bestowed several marks of honour upon it; adorned it with divers miracles, which wiped off the reproach of his death. These miracles were antecedent to his interment, or concomitants of it.

There was an extraordinary and preternatural eclipse of the sun; such an eclipse as was never seen since it first shone in heaven: the sun fainted at the sight of such a rueful spectacle, and clothed the whole heaven in black. The sight of this caused a great philosopher, who was then far from the place where this unparalleled tragedy was acting, to cry out upon the sight of it, " * Either the God of nature now suffers, or the frame of the world is now dissolved." The same Dionysius, writing to Apollophanes, a philosopher, who would not embrace the christian faith, thus goes about to convince him. " † What thinkest thou (saith he) of the eclipse when Christ was crucified? Were we not both of us at Heliopolis, and standing in the same place? Did we not see the moon in a new manner following the sun; and not in the conjunction, but from the ninth hour until the evening, by a reason unknown in nature, directly opposite to the sun? Didst thou not then, being greatly terrified, say unto me, Oh my Dionysius, what strange communications of the heavenly bodies are these?"

Such a preternatural eclipse is remembered in no other history; for it was not in time of conjunction, but opposition, the moon being then at full. From the sixth to the ninth hour, the sun and moon were together in the midst of heaven; but in the evening she appeared in the east, her own place, opposite to the sun. And then miraculously returning from east to west, did not pass by the sun, and set in the west before it, but kept it company for the space of three hours, and then returned to the east again. And whereas in all other natural eclipses, the shadow always begins on the western parts of the body of the sun, and that part is also first cleared; it was quite contrary to this; for though the moon was opposite to the sun, and distant from it in the whole breadth of heaven, yet with a miraculous swiftness it overtook the sun, darkened first the eastern part of it, and soon prevailed over its whole body; which caused " darkness over all the land;" that is, say some, over the whole earth; or, as others, over the whole land of Jewry; or, as others, over the whole horizon, and all places of the same altitude and latitude, which is most probable.

And as Christ's funeral was attended with such a miraculous

---

* Aut Deus naturæ patitur, aut mundi machina dissolvitur.—*Dionysius Areopag.*

† Theod. Metochit. Hist. Rom. p. 39.

eclipse, which put the heavens and earth into mourning; so the rocks did rend; the veil of the temple rent in twain from top to bottom; the graves opened, and the dead bodies of many saints arose and went into the holy city, and were seen of many. The rending of the rocks was a sign of God's fierce indignation, Nahum i. 6, and a discovery of the greatness of his power; showing them what they deserved, and what he could do to them that had committed this horrid fact; though he rather chose at this time to show the dreadful effects of it upon inanimate rocks, than rocky-hearted sinners: but especially it served to convince the world, that it was none other but the Son of God that died; which was further manifested by these concomitant miracles. .

As for the rending in twain of the veil, it was a notable miracle, plainly showing that all ceremonies were now accomplished and abolished; no more veils now: as also that believers have now most free access into heaven. At that very instant when the veil rent, the high priest was officiating in the most holy place, and the veil which hid him from the rest of the people being rent, they might freely see him about his work in the holy of holies; a lively emblem of our High Priest, whom now we see by faith in the heavens, there performing his intercession-work for us.

The opening of the graves, plainly showed the design and end of Christ's going into the grave; that it might not have dominion over the bodies of the saints, but being vanquished and destroyed by Christ, it lets go all that are his whom he ransomed from the grave; a specimen whereof was given in those holy ones that rose at that time and appeared to many in the holy city. Thus was the funeral of our Lord performed by men; thus was it attended by miracles from heaven.

And now we have seen Jesus interred; He that wears at his girdle the keys of hell and death, himself locked up in the grave. What shall I say of him whom they now laid in the grave? shall I undertake to tell you what he was, what he did, suffered, and deserved? Alas! the tongues of angels must pause and stammer in such a work. He is a Sun of righteousness, a Fountain of life. Of him it might be said in that day, Here lies the adorable Jesus, in whom is treasured up whatsoever an angry God can require for his satisfaction, or an empty creature for his perfection; before him was none like him, and after shall none arise comparable to him. "If every leaf and spire of grass," saith one,* " nay, all the stars, sands, and atoms, were

* Mr. Jenkin.

so many souls and seraphims, whose love should double in them every moment to all eternity, yet would it fall infinitely short of what is due to his worth and excellency. Suppose a creature composed of all the choice endowments that ever dwelt in the best of men since the creation of the world, and added to this, the understanding, strength, splendour, and holiness of all the angels, it would all amount but to a dark shadow of this incomparable Jesus."

Come and see, believing souls, look upon dead Jesus in his winding-sheet, by faith, and say, Lo, this is he, of whom the church said, " My Beloved is white and ruddy:" his ruddiness is now gone, and a death-paleness hath prevailed over all his body, but still as lovely as ever, yea, altogether lovely. If David, lamenting the death of Saul and Jonathan, said, " Daughters of Jerusalem, weep over Saul, who clothed you in scarlet, with other delights ; who put ornaments of gold upon your apparel ;" much rather may I say, Children of Zion, weep over Jesus, who clothed you with righteousness, and the garments of salvation.

This is he who quitted the throne of glory ; left the bosom of unspeakable delights ; came in a body of flesh, produced in perfect holiness ; brake through many and great impediments, (thy great unworthiness, the wrath of God and man,) by the strength of love to bring salvation home to thy soul. Can he that believingly considers this, do less than faint at the sense of that love that brought him to the dust of death, and cry out with that father, " My Lord was crucified !" But without insisting any longer upon generals, I will draw down the particulars of Christ's funeral to your use, in the following inferences.

1. Was Christ buried in this manner ? Then a decent and mournful funeral, where it can be had, is very laudable among christians.

I know the souls of the saints have no concern for their bodies, nor are they solicitous how the body is treated here ; yet there is a respect due to them, as they are the temples wherein God hath been served and honoured by those holy souls that once dwelt in them ; as also on account of their relation to Christ, and the glory that will be one day put upon them, when they shall be changed, and made like unto Christ's glorious body. Upon such special accounts as these, their bodies deserve an honourable treatment, as well as upon the account of humanity, which owes this honour to the bodies of all men.

To have no funeral is accounted a judgment, Eccles. vii. 4 ; or to be tumbled into a pit without any to lament us, is as lamentable. We read of many solemn and mournful funerals in scripture,* wherein the people of God have affectionately paid their respects and honours to the dust of the saints, as men that were deeply sensible of their worth, and how great a loss the world sustains by their removal. Christ's funeral had as much of decency and solemnity in it, as the time would permit; though he was a stranger to all pomp, both in life and death.

2. Did Joseph and Nicodemus so boldly appear at a time of so much danger, to beg the body, and give it a funeral? Let it be for ever a caution to strong christians, not to despise or glory over the weak. You see here a couple of timorous persons, that were afraid to be seen in Christ's company, when the other disciples professed their readiness to die with him: yet those flee, and these appear for him when the trial comes indeed. If God desert the strong, and assist the weak, the feeble shall be as David, and the strong as tow. I speak not this to discourage any man from striving to improve inherent graces to the utmost; for it is ordinarily found in experience, that the degrees of assisting grace are given out according to the measures of inherent grace: but I speak it to prevent a sin incident to strong christians, of despising the weak, which God corrects by such instances and examples as this before us.

3. Hence we may be assisted in discerning the depths of Christ's humiliation for us, by seeing from what, and to what his love brought him. It was not enough, that he who was in the form of God, became a creature, which was an infinite stoop, nay, to be made a man, an inferior order of creatures; nay, to be a poor man, to spend his days in poverty and contempt; but also to be a dead corpse for our sakes. Oh what manner of love is this!

Now, the deeper the humiliation of the Son of God was, the more satisfactory to us it must needs be; for as it shows us the heinousness of sin that deserves all this, so the fulness of Christ's satisfaction, whereby he makes up that breach. Oh, it was deep humiliation indeed! How unlike himself is he now become! Doth he look like the Son of God? What! the Son of God, whom all the angels adore, to be hurried by three or four persons into his grave in an evening! to be carried from Golgotha to the grave in this manner, and there lie as a captive to death for a time! Never was the like change of conditions; never such an abasement heard of in the world.

4. From this funeral of Christ results the purest and strongest consolation and encouragement to believers, against the fears of

* Gen. xxiii. 2; xxxv. 19; 1. 10; 2 Chron. xxxv. 24; John xi. 31; Acts viii. 2.

death and the grave. If this be so, that Jesus hath lain in the grave before you ; let me say then to you as the Lord spake to Jacob, " Fear not to go down into Egypt, for I will go down with thee, and I will also surely bring thee up again," Gen. xlvi. 3, 4. So here, fear not, believer, to go down to the grave, for God will be with thee there, and will surely bring thee up thence. This consideration, that Jesus Christ hath lain in the grave himself, gives manifold encouragements to the people of God, against the terrors of the grave.

(1.) The grave received, but could not destroy Jesus Christ: and as it fared with Christ's body personal, so it shall with Christ's body mystical : it could not retain him ; it shall not for ever retain them. This resurrection of Christ out of his grave, is the very ground of our hope for a resurrection out of our graves. " Christ is risen from the dead, and become the first-fruits of them that slept," 1 Cor. xv. 20.

(2.) As the union between the body of Christ and the Divine nature was not dissolved when that body was laid in the grave, so the union between Christ and believers is not, cannot be dissolved, when their bodies shall be laid in their graves. It is true, the natural union between his soul and body was dissolved for a time ; but the hypostatical union was not dissolved, no, not for a moment: that body was the body of the Son of God, when it was in the sepulchre. In like manner the natural union between our souls and bodies is dissolved by death; but the mystical union between us and Christ can never be dissolved.

(3.) As Christ's body, when it was in the grave, did there rest in hope ; so it shall fare with the dead bodies of the saints when they lay them down also in the dust: " My flesh also shall rest in hope," saith Christ, Psa. xvi. 9. In like manner the saints commit their bodies to the dust in hope: " The righteous hath hope- in his death," Prov. xiv. 32. And as Christ's hope was not a vain hope, so neither shall their hope be vain.

(4.) Christ's lying in the grave before us, hath quite changed and altered the nature of the grave ; so that it is not what it was. It was once a part of the curse. " Dust thou art, and unto dust thou shalt return," was a part of the threatening and curse for sin. The grave had the nature and use of a prison, to keep the bodies of sinners against the great assizes, and then deliver them up into the hands of a great and terrible God ; but now it is no prison, but a bed of rest, where Christ lay before us ; which is a sweet consideration of the grave indeed : " They shall enter into peace, they shall rest in their beds,"

Isa. lvii. 2. Oh then let not believers stand in fear of the grave. He that hath one foot in heaven need not fear to put the other into the grave. " Though I walk through the valley of the shadow of death, I will fear no evil, for thou art with me," Psa. xxiii. 4.

Indeed, the grave is a terrible place to them that are out of Christ: death is the Lord's officer to arrest them; the grave is the Lord's prison to secure them. When death draws them into the grave, it draws them thither as a lion doth his prey into the den to devour it. So you read, Psa. xlix. 14, " Death shall feed" or prey " upon them." Death there reigns over them in its full power, Rom. v. 14. And though at last it shall render them again to God, yet it were better for them to lie everlastingly where they were, than to rise to such an end; for they are brought out of their graves as a condemned prisoner out of the prison, to go to execution. But the case of the saints is not so; the grave (thanks be to our Lord Jesus Christ!) is a privileged place to them, whilst they sleep there; and when they awake, it will be with singing. When they awake, they shall be satisfied with his likeness.

5. Since Christ was laid in his grave, and his people reap such privileges by it; as ever you expect rest or comfort in your graves, see that you get union with Christ now.

It was an ancient custom of the jews, to put rich treasures into the graves with their friends, as well as to bestow much upon their sepulchres. It is possible that you have no great matter to bestow upon your funerals, nor are they likely to be splendid; no stately monuments; no hidden treasure; but if Christ be yours, you carry that with you to your graves which is better than all the gold and silver in the world. What would you be the better if your coffin were made of beaten gold, or your grave-stone set thick with glittering diamonds? But if you die in the Lord, that is, interested in and united to the Lord, you shall carry six grounds of comfort with you to your graves, the least of which is not to be purchased with the wealth of both the Indies.

(1.) The first ground of comfort which a believer carries with him to the grave, is, that the covenant of God holds firmly with his very dust, all the days of its appointed time in the grave. So much Christ tells us, Matt. xxii. 31, 32. " I am the God of Abraham, and the God of Isaac, and the God of Jacob: God is not the God of the dead, but of the living:" *q. d.* Abraham, Isaac, and Jacob, are naturally dead; but inasmuch as God, long after their deaths, proclaimed himself their God still, therefore they are federally alive to God : they live, that is, their covenant relation lives still. " Whether we live, or whether we die, (saith the apostle,) we are the Lord's," Rom. xiv. 7—9. Now, what an encouragement is here ! I am as much the Lord's in the state of the dead, as I was in the state of the living : death puts an end to all other relations and bonds, but the bond of the covenant rots not in the grave : our dust is still the Lord's.

(2.) As God's covenant with our very bodies is indissolvable, so God's love to our very dust is inseparable. " I am the God of Abraham."   The apostle is express, Rom. viii. 38, 39, that death separates not the believer from the love of God. As at first it was not our natural comeliness or beauty that engaged his love to us ; so neither will he cease to love us when that beauty is gone, and we become objects of loathing to all flesh. When a husband cannot endure to see his wife, or a wife her husband ; but saith of them that were once dear and pleasant, as Abraham of his beloved Sarah, " Bury my dead out of my sight ;" yet then the Lord delights in it as much as ever.

(3.) As God's love will be with you in the grave, so God's providence shall take order about your graves, when they shall be digged for you.   And be sure he will not order your graves to be dug till you are fit to be put into them : he will bring you thither in the best time ; " Thou shalt come to thy grave as a shock of corn in its season," Job v. 26 ; you shall be ripe and ready before God house you there. It is said of David, that " after he had served his generation by the will of God, he fell asleep," Acts xiii. 36. Oh what a holy and wise will is that will of God, that so orders our death ! And how proper is it, that our will should be concluded by it !

(4.) If you be in Christ, God's pardons have loosed all the bonds of guilt from you, before you lie down in the grave ; so that you shall not die in your sins. It is a grievous threatening, " Ye shall die in your sins," John viii. 24. Better be cast alive into a pit among dragons and serpents, than dead in your graves among your sins. Oh what a terrible word is that, " His bones are full of the sins of his youth, which shall lie down with him in the dust !" Job xx. 11. But from the company of sin, in the grave, all the saints are delivered. God's full, free, and final pardons have shut guilt out of your graves.

(5.) Whenever you come to your graves, you shall find the enmity of the grave slain by Christ : it is no enemy ; nay, you will find it friendly, a privileged place to you : it will be as sweet to you that are in Christ, as a soft bed in a still, quiet

chamber to one that is weary and sleepy.   Therefore it is said,
" Death is yours," 1 Cor. iii. 22 ; yours as a privilege ; your
friend : there you shall find sweet rest in Jesus ; be hurried,
pained, troubled no more.

(6.) To conclude : if in Christ, know this for your comfort,
that your own Lord Jesus Christ keeps the keys of all the cham-
bers of death ; and as he unlocks the door of death, when he
lets you in, so he will open it again for you when you awake,
to let you out ; and from the time he opens to let you in, till
the time he opens to let you out, he himself watches over you
while you sleep there.   " I (saith he) have the keys of death,"
Rev. i. 18.   Oh then, as you expect peace or rest in the cham-
bers of death, get union with Christ.   A grave with Christ is
a comfortable place.

SERMON XXXVIII.

WHEREIN FOUR WEIGHTY ENDS OF CHRIST'S HUMILIATION ARE
OPENED, AND PARTICULARLY APPLIED.

ISA. LIII. 11.

HE SHALL SEE OF THE TRAVAIL OF HIS SOUL, AND SHALL BE SATISFIED.

WE are now arrived at the last particular place which we designed
to speak to in Christ's state of humiliation, namely, the designs
and blessed ends for which he was so deeply abased. It is inconsistent with the prudence of a common agent, to be at vast
expenses of time, pains, and cost, and not to propound to himself
a design worthy of all those expenses. And it is much less
imaginable, that Christ should so stupendously abase himself,
by stooping from the bosom of his Father to the state of the
dead, where our last discourse left him, if there had not been
some excellent and glorious thing in his eye, the attainment
whereof might give him a content and satisfaction, equivalent
to all the sorrows and abasements he endured for it. And so
much is plainly held forth in this scripture, " He shall see of
the travail of his soul, and shall be satisfied." In which words
three things fall under our consideration.

1. The travailing pangs of Christ. So the agonies of his
soul and torments of his body are fitly called, not only because
of the sharpness and acuteness of them, being in that respect
like birth-pangs of a travailing woman, for so this word signifies,
but also because they forerun, and make way for the birth,
which abundantly recompenses all those labours. I shall not
here enlarge upon the pangs and agonies endured by Christ in
the garden, or upon the cross, which the prophet styles " the
travail of his soul," having, in the former sermons, opened it
largely in its particulars, but pass to the

2. Thing considerable in these words, and that is, the assured
fruits and effects of this his travail; " He shall see of the travail
of his soul." By seeing, understand the fruition, obtainment, or
enjoyment of the end of his sufferings. He shall not shed his
blood upon a hazard; his design shall not miscarry; but he
shall certainly see the ends he aimed at accomplished.

3. This shall yield him great satisfaction; as a "woman forgets her sorrow, for joy that a man is born into the world," John xvi. 21; he shall see it and be satisfied. As God, when he had finished the work of creation, viewed his work with pleasure and satisfaction; so doth our exalted Redeemer, with great contentment, behold the happy issues of his sufferings. It affords pleasure to a man to see great affairs, by orderly conduct, brought to happy issues. Much more doth it yield delight to Jesus Christ to see the results of the most profound wisdom and love wherein he carried on redemption-work. All runs into this proposition,

THAT ALL THE BLESSED DESIGNS AND ENDS FOR WHICH THE LORD JESUS CHRIST HUMBLED HIMSELF TO THE DEATH OF THE CROSS, SHALL CERTAINLY BE ATTAINED, TO HIS FULL CONTENT AND SATISFACTION.

My present business is not to prove, that Christ shall certainly obtain what he died for, nor to open the great satisfaction and pleasure which will arise to him out of those issues of his death; but to point at the principal ends of his death; making some brief improvement as we pass along.

Let us inquire into the designs and ends of Christ's humiliation, at least the main and principal ones; and we shall find, that as the sprinkling of the typical blood in the Old Testament was done for four weighty ends or uses, so the precious and invaluable blood of the testator and surety of the New Testament is shed for four weighty ends also.

I. That blood was shed and applied to deliver from danger: "And the blood shall be to you for a token upon the houses where you are; and when I see the blood, I will pass over you, and the plague shall not be upon you, to destroy you when I smite the land of Egypt," Exod. xii. 13.

II. That blood was shed to make an atonement betwixt God and the people: "And he shall do with the bullock as he did with the bullock for a sin-offering, so shall he do with this; and the priest shall make an atonement for them, and it shall be forgiven them," Lev. iv. 20.

III. That blood was shed to purify persons from their ceremonial pollutions: "He shall dip the cedar-wood, and the scarlet, and the hyssop, with the living bird, in the blood of the bird that was killed over the running water: and he shall sprinkle upon him that is to be cleansed from the leprosy seven times,*

* Seven times, signifies perfect expiation; this number was consecrated to denote perfection.—*Menoch.*

and shall pronounce him clean, and shall let the living bird loose in the open field," Lev. xiv. 6, 7.

IV. That blood was shed to ratify and confirm the testament or covenant of God with the people: " And Moses took the blood, and sprinkled it on the people, and said, Behold the blood of the covenant, which the Lord hath made with you concerning all these words," Exod. xxiv. 8.

These were the four main ends for shedding and sprinkling that typical blood ; and in like manner there are four principal ends for shedding and applying Christ's blood. As that typical blood was shed to deliver from danger, so this was shed to deliver from wrath, even the wrath to come. That was shed to make an atonement, so was this. That was shed to purify persons from uncleanness, so was this. That was shed to confirm the testament, so was this. As will appear in the following particulars more at large.

I. One principal design and end of shedding the blood of Christ, was to deliver his people from danger, the danger of that wrath which burns down to the lowest hell. So you find, 1 Thess. i. 10. " Even Jesus, who delivered us from the wrath to come." Here our misery is both specified and aggravated. Specified, in calling it wrath, a word of deep and dreadful signification. The damned best understand the import of that word. And aggravated, in calling it wrath to come, or coming wrath. *Wrath to come* implies both the futurity and perpetuity of this wrath. It is wrath that shall certainly and inevitably come upon sinners. As surely as the night follows the day, as surely as the winter follows the summer, so shall wrath follow sin, and the pleasures thereof. Yea, it is not only certainly future, but when it comes it will be abiding wrath, or wrath still coming. When millions of years and ages are past and gone, this will still be wrath to come ; ever coming, as a river ever flowing.

Now from this wrath to come, Jesus hath delivered his people by his death. For that was the price laid down for their redemption from the wrath of the great and terrible God : " Much more then, being justified by his blood, we shall be saved from wrath through him," Rom. v. 9. The blood of Jesus was the price that ransomed man from this wrath. And it was shed not only to deliver them from wrath to come, but to deliver them freely, fully, distinguishingly, and wonderfully from it.

1. *Freely*, by his own voluntary interposition and undertaking of the mediatorial office, moved thereunto by his own pity and compassion, which yearned over his elect in their misery.

The saints were once a lost generation, that had sold themselves, and their inheritance also ; and had not wherewithal to redeem either: but there was One who became their near kinsman, to whom the right of redemption did belong ; who being the Heir of all things, undertook to be their God ; and out of his own proper substance to redeem both them and their inheritance : them, to be his own inheritance, Eph. i. 11; and heaven, to be theirs, 1 Pet. i. 4.   All this he did most freely, when none made supplication to him.   No sighing of the prisoners came before him.   He designed it for us before we had a being.   And when the purposes of his grace were come to their parturient fulness, then did he freely lay out the infinite treasures of his blood to purchase our deliverance from wrath.

2. Christ by death hath also delivered his people *fully*.   A full deliverance it is, both in respect of time and degrees.   A full deliverance in respect of time.   It was not a reprieve, but a deliverance.   Therefore is he become " the Author of eternal salvation to them that obey him," Heb. v. 9.   And as it is full in respect of time, so likewise in respect of degrees.   He died not to procure a mitigation or abatement of the rigour or severity of the sentence, but to rescue his people fully from all degrees of wrath.   So that there is no condemnation to them that are in Christ, Rom. viii. 1.

3. This deliverance obtained for us by the death of Christ, is a *special* and distinguishing deliverance.   Not common to all, but peculiar to some ; and they by nature no better than those that are left under wrath.   Yea, as to natural disposition, moral qualifications, and external endowments, oftentimes far inferior to them that perish.   " You see your calling, brethren," 1 Cor. i. 26.

4. It is a *wonderful* salvation.   It would weary the arm of an angel to write down all the wonders that are in this salvation. That ever such a design should be laid, such a project of grace contrived in the heart of God, who might have suffered the whole species to perish :—that it should only concern man, and not the angels, by nature more excellent than us—that Christ him-self should go forth upon this glorious design—that he should effect it in such a way, by taking our nature and suffering the penalty of the law therein—that our deliverance should be wrought out and finished when the Redeemer and his design seemed both to be lost and perished—these, with many more, are such wonders as will take up eternity itself to search, admire, and adore them.

Before I part from this first end of the death of Christ, give me leave to deduce two useful inferences from it, and then proceed to a second.

(1.) Hath Christ by death delivered his people from the wrath to come ? How ungrateful and disingenuous a thing must it be then for those that have obtained such a deliverance as this, to repine and grudge at those light afflictions they suffer for a moment upon Christ's account in this world !

Alas ! what are these sufferings, that we should grudge at them ? Are they like those which the Redeemer suffered for our deliverance ? Did ever any of us endure for him what he endured for us ? Or is there any thing you can suffer for Christ in this world, comparable to this wrath to come, which you must have endured, had he not, by the price of his own blood, rescued you from it ?

Reader, wilt thou but make the comparison in thine own thoughts, in the following particulars, and then pronounce when thou hast duly compared. What is the wrath of man to the wrath of God ? What is the arm of a creature to the anger of a Deity ? Can man thunder with an arm like God ? What are the sufferings of the vile body here, to the tortures of a soul and body in hell ? The torments of the soul are the very soul of torments. What are the troubles of a moment, to that wrath, which, after millions of years are gone, will still be called wrath to come ? Oh, what comparison between a point of hasty time, and the interminable duration of vast eternity ? What comparison is there between the intermitting sorrows and sufferings of this life, and the continued, uninterrupted wrath to come ? Our troubles here are not constant ; there are gracious relaxations, lucid intervals here ; but the wrath to come allows not a moment's ease or mitigation. What light and easy troubles are those, which work, under the blessing of God, to the everlasting good of them that love him, compared with that wrath to come, out of which no good effects or issues are possible to proceed to the souls on which it lies ! And lastly, How much more comfortable is it, to suffer in fellowship with Christ and his saints for righteousness' sake, than to suffer with devils and reprobates for wickedness' sake ! Grudge not then, O ye that are delivered by Jesus from wrath to come, at any thing ye do suffer, or shall suffer from Christ, or for Christ, in this world.

(2.) If Jesus Christ hath delivered his people from the wrath to come, how little comfort can any man take in his present enjoyments and accommodations in the world, whilst it remains a question with him whether he be delivered from the wrath to come? It is well for the present, but will it be so always! Man is a prospecting creature, and it will not satisfy him that his present condition is comfortable, except he have some hopes it shall be so hereafter. It can afford a man little content that all is easy and pleasant about him now, whilst such terrible hints of wrath to come are given him by his own conscience daily. Oh, methinks such a thought as this, What if I am reserved for the wrath to come? should be to him as the fingers appearing upon the plaster of the wall were to Belshazzar in the height of a festivity. Give not sleep therefore to thine eyes, reader, till thou hast got good evidence that thou art of that number whom Jesus hath delivered from the wrath to come, till thou canst say he is a Jesus to thee. This may be made out to thy satisfaction three ways.

[1.] If Jesus have delivered thee from sin, the cause of wrath, thou may conclude he hath delivered thee from wrath, the effect and fruit of sin. Upon this account the sweet name of Jesus was given to him, " Thou shalt call his name Jesus, for he shall save his people from their sins," Matt. i. 21. Whilst a man lies under the dominion and guilt of sin, he lies exposed to wrath to come; and when he is delivered from the guilt and power of sin, he is certainly delivered from the danger of this coming wrath. Where sin is not imputed, wrath is not threatened.

[2.] If thy soul do set an inestimable value on Jesus Christ, and be endeared to him on account of that inexpressible grace manifested in this deliverance, it is a good sign thy soul hath a share in it. Mark what an epithet the saints give Christ upon this account; " Giving thanks unto the Father, who hath delivered us from the power of darkness, and translated us into the kingdom of his dear Son," Col. i. 12, 13. Christ is therefore dear, and dear beyond all compare to his saved ones.

I remember it is related of the poor enthralled grecians, that when Titus Flaminius had restored their ancient liberties, and proclamation was to be made in the market-place by an herald; they so pressed to hear it, that the herald was in great danger of being stifled and pressed to death among the people; but when the proclamation was ended, there were heard such shouts and joyful acclamations, that the very birds of the air fell down astonished with the noise, while they continued to cry, Σωτηρ, Σωτηρ, a Saviour, a Saviour; and all the following night they continued dancing and singing about his pavilion. If such a deliverance so endeared them to Titus, how should the great deliverance from wrath to come, endear all the redeemed to love their dear Jesus! This is the native effect of mercy, upon the soul that hath felt it.

[3.] A disposition and readiness of mind to do or endure any thing for Christ's sake, on account of his deliverance from the wrath to come, is a good evidence you are so delivered. " That we may walk worthy of the Lord unto all pleasing, being fruitful in every good work," Col. i. 10. There is readiness to *do* for Christ. " Strengthened with all might, according to his glorious power, unto all patience and long-suffering with joyfulness," ver. 11. There is a cheerful readiness to *endure* any thing for Christ. And how both these flow from the sense of this great deliverance from wrath the 12th verse will inform you, which was but now cited. Oh then, be serious and assiduous in the resolution of this grand point. Till this be resolved, nothing can be pleasant to thy soul.

II. As the typical blood was shed and sprinkled to deliver from danger, so it was shed to make atonement: " He shall expiate (we translate, atone) the sin," Lev. iv. 20. The word imports both. And the true meaning is, that by the blood of the bullock, all whose efficacy stood in its relation to the blood of Christ, signified and shadowed by it, the people, for whom it was shed, should be reconciled to God by the expiation and remission of their sins. And what was shadowed in this typical blood, was really designed and accomplished by Jesus Christ, in the shedding of his blood.

Reconciliation of the elect to God, is therefore another of those glorious results which Christ travailed for. So you find it expressly, Rom. v. 10. " If when we were enemies, we were reconciled to God by the death of his Son." This *if* is not a word of doubting, but argumentation. The apostle supposes it is a known truth, or principle yielded by all christians, that the death of Christ was to reconcile the elect to God. And again he affirms it with like clearness, " And having made peace through the blood of his cross, by him to reconcile all things," Col. i. 20. And that this was a main and principal end designed both by the Father and Son in the humiliation of Christ, is plain from 2 Cor. v. 19, " God was in Christ reconciling the world unto himself." God filled the humanity with grace and authority. The Spirit of God was in him to qualify him. The authority was in him by commission, to make all he did valid. The grace and love of God to mankind was in him, and one of the principal effects in which it was manifested, was this design upon which he came, namely, to reconcile the world to God. Upon which ground Christ is called the " propitiation for our sins," 1 John ii. 2. * " Now reconciliation or atonement is nothing else but the making up of the ancient friendship between God and men which sin had dissolved, and so to reduce these enemies into a state of concord, and sweet agreement." And the means by which this blessed design was effectually compassed was by the death of Christ, which made complete satisfaction to God for the wrong we had done him. There was a breach made by sin between God and the fallen angels, but that breach is never to be repaired or made up ; since, as Christ took not on him their nature, so he never intended to be a Mediator of reconciliation between God and them. But that which Christ designed, as the end of his death, was to reconcile God and man. Not the whole species, but a certain number, who were given to Christ. We shall now make some improvements of this, and pass on to the third end of the death of Christ.

Inference 1. If Christ died to reconcile God and man, how horrid an evil then is sin ! And how terrible was that breach made between God and the creature by it, which could be made up no other way but by the death of the Son of God ! I remember to have read, that when a great chasm or breach was made in the earth by an earthquake, and the oracle was consulted how it might be closed, this answer was returned, That breach can never be closed except something of great worth be thrown into it. Such a breach was that which sin made, it could never be reconciled but by the death of Jesus Christ, the most excellent thing in all the creation.

2. How sad is the state of all such as are not comprised in the articles of peace with God ! The impenitent unbeliever is excepted. God is not reconciled to him ; and if God be his enemy, how little avails it who is his friend ! For, if God be a man's enemy, he hath then an almighty enemy, whose very frown is destruction : " I lift up my hand to heaven and say, I live for ever. If I whet my glittering sword, and my hand take hold on judgment ; I will render vengeance to my enemies, and will reward them that hate me. I will make mine arrows drunk with blood, and my sword shall devour flesh ; and that with the blood of the slain and of the captives, from the beginning of revenges upon the enemy," Deut. xxxii. 40—42.

Yea, he is an unavoidable enemy. Fly to the utmost parts of the earth, there shall his hand reach thee, as it is Psa. cxxxix. 10. The wings of the morning cannot carry thee out of his reach. If God be your enemy, you have an immortal enemy,

* Daven. in Col. i. 20.

who lives for ever to avenge himself upon his adversaries. And what wilt thou do when thou art in Saul's case? 1 Sam. xxviii. 15, 16. Alas, whither wilt thou turn? To whom wilt thou complain? But what wilt thou do when thou shalt stand at the bar and see that God, who is thine Enemy, upon the throne? Sad is their case indeed, who are not comprehended in the articles of peace with God.

3. If Christ died to reconcile us to God, give diligence to clear up to your own souls your interest in this reconciliation. If Christ thought it worth his blood to purchase it, it is worth your care and pains to clear it. And what can better evidence it than your conscientious tenderness of sin, lest you make new breaches. Ah, if reconciled, you will say, as Ezra ix. 13, 14, " And now our God, seeing thou hast given us such a deliverance as this, should we again break thy commandments?" If reconciled to God, his friends will be your friends, and his enemies your enemies. If God be your Friend, you will be diligent to please him, John xv. 10. 14. He that makes not peace with God is an enemy to his own soul. And he that is at peace, but takes no pains to clear it, is an enemy to his own comfort.

III. But I must pass from this to the third end of Christ's death, namely, The sanctification of his people. Typical blood was shed, as you heard, to purify them that were unclean; and so was the blood of Christ shed to purge away the sins of his people : so speaks the apostle expressly, " Christ gave himself for the church that he might sanctify and cleanse it," Eph. v. 25, 26. And so he tells us himself, " And for their sakes I sanctify myself," that is, consecrate or devote myself to death, " that they also might be sanctified through the truth," John xvii. 19. Upon the account of this benefit received by the blood of Christ, is that doxology, which, in a lower strain, is now sounded in the churches, but will be matter of the Lamb's song in heaven; " To him that loved us, and washed us from our sins in his own blood,—be glory and honour for ever," Rev. i. 5, 6. Now, there is a twofold evil in sin, the guilt of it, and the pollution of it. Justification properly cures the former, sanctification the latter ; but both justification and sanctification flow unto sinners out of the death of Christ. And though it is proper to say the Spirit sanctifies, yet, it is certain, it was the blood of Christ that procured for us the Spirit of sanctification. Had not Christ died, the Spirit had never come down from heaven upon any such design.

The pouring forth of Christ's blood for us, obtained the pouring forth of the Spirit of holiness upon us. Therefore the Spirit is said to come in his name, and to take of his, and show it unto us. Hence it is said, " he came both by blood and by water," 1 John v. 6; by blood, washing away the guilt; by water, purifying from the filth of sin. Now this fruit of Christ's death, even our sanctification, is a most incomparable mercy. For, do but consider a few particular excellencies of holiness.

1. Holiness is the image and glory of God. His image, Col. iii. 10, and his glory, Exod. xv. 11. " Who is like unto thee, O Lord, glorious in holiness?" Now, when the guilt and filth of sin are washed off, and the beauty of God put upon the soul in sanctification, oh what a beautiful creature is the soul now! It is a beam of Divine glory upon the creature.

2. And as it is the soul's highest beauty, so it is the soul's best evidence for heaven. " Blessed are the pure in heart : for they shall see God," Matt. v. 8. " And without holiness, no man shall see God," Heb. xii. 14. No gifts, no duties, no natural endowments will evidence a right in heaven, but the least measure of true holiness will secure heaven to the soul.

3. Again, as holiness is the soul's best evidence for heaven, so it is a continual spring of comfort to it in the way thither. The purest and sweetest pleasures in this world are the results of holiness. Till we come to live holily, we never live comfortably. Heaven is epitomized in holiness.

4. And, to say no more, it is the peculiar mark by which God hath visibly distinguished his own from other men : " The Lord hath set apart him that is godly for himself," Psa. iv. 3. Oh holiness, how surpassingly glorious art thou !

Inference 1. Did Christ die to sanctify his people? How deep then is the pollution of sin, that nothing but the blood of Christ can cleanse it ! All the tears of a penitent sinner, should he shed as many as there have fallen drops of rain since the creation to this day, cannot wash away one sin. The everlasting burnings in hell cannot purify the flaming conscience from the least sin.

2. Did Christ die to sanctify his people ? Behold then the love of a Saviour. " He loved us, and washed us from our sins in his own blood." He did not shed the blood of beasts, as the priests of old did, but his own blood, Heb. ix. 12. And that not common, but precious blood, 1 Pet. i. 19. The blood of God ; one drop of which outvalues the blood that runs in the veins of all Adam's posterity. And not some of that blood, but all, to the last drop. And thus liberal was he of his blood to us when we were enemies. Oh what manner of love is this ! But I must hasten.

IV. As Christ died to sanctify his people; so he died also to confirm the new testament to all those sanctified ones. So it was in the type, Exod. xxiv. 8, and so it is in Matt. xxvi. 28, " This is the new testament in my blood," that is, ratified and confirmed by my blood. For, where a testament is, there must also of necessity be the death of the testator, Heb. ix. 16. So that now all the blessings and benefits bequeathed to believers in the last will and testament of Christ, are abundantly confirmed and secured to them by his death. Yea, he died on purpose to make that testament of force to them. Men make their wills and testaments; and Christ makes his. What they bequeath, and give in their wills, is a free and voluntary act, they cannot be compelled to do it. And what is bequeathed to us in this testament of Christ, is altogether a free and voluntary donation. Other testators usually bequeath their estates to their wives and children, and near relations; so doth this testator; all is settled upon his spouse, the church, upon believers, his children. A stranger intermeddles not with these mercies. Men give all their goods and estates that can that way be conveyed, to their friends that survive them. Christ giveth to his church, in the new testament, three sorts of goods.

1. All temporal good things, 1 Tim. vi. 6; Matt. vi. 33; that is, the comfort and blessing of all, though not the possession of much. " As having nothing, and yet possessing all things," 2 Cor. vi. 10.

2. All spiritual good things, as remission of sin, and acceptance with God, which are contained in their justification, Rom. iii. 24—26. Sanctification of their natures, both initial and progressive, 1 Cor. i. 30. Adoption into the family of God, Gal. iii. 26. The ministry of angels, Heb. i. 14. Interest in all the promises, 2 Pet. i. 4.

3. All eternal good things. Heaven, glory, and eternal life, Rom. viii. 16, 17. No such bequests as these were ever found in the testaments of princes. That which kings and nobles settle by will upon their heirs, are but trifles to what Christ hath conferred in the new testament upon his people. And all this is confirmed and ratified by the death of Christ; so that the promise is sure, and the estate indefeasible to all the heirs of promise.

How the death of Christ confirmed the new testament is worth our inquiry. The socinians, as they allow no other end of Christ's death, but the confirmation of the new testament, so they affirm he did it only by way of testimony, or witness-bearing in his death. But this is a vile derogation from the efficacy of Christ's blood, to bring it down into an equality with the blood of martyrs. As if there were no more in it than was in their blood. But know, reader, Christ died not only, or principally, to confirm the testament by his blood, as witness to the truth of those things, but his death ratified it as the death of a testator, which makes the new testament irrevocable; just as when a man hath made his will, and is dead, that will is presently in force, and can never be recalled. Besides, the will of the dead is sacred with men; they dare not cross it. It is certain the last will and testament of Christ is most sacred, and God will never annul or make it void. Moreover, it is not with Christ as with other testators, who die, and must trust the performance of their wills with their executors; but as he died to put it in force, so he lives again to be the executor of his own testament. And all power to fulfil his will is now in his own hands, Rev. i. 18.

Inference 1. Did Christ die to confirm the new testament, in which such legacies are bequeathed to believers? How are all believers concerned then to clear their title to the mercies contained in this blessed testament! And this may be done two ways: by clearing to ourselves our covenant relations to Christ; and by discovering those special covenant-impressions upon our hearts, to which the promises therein contained do belong.

(1.) Examine your relations to Christ. Are you his spouse? Have you forsaken all for him? Psa. xlv. 10, 11. Are you ready to take your lot with him, as it falls in prosperity or adversity? Jer. ii. 2. And are you loyal to Christ? " Thou shalt be for me, and not for another," Hos. iii. 3. Do you yield obedience to him as your Head and Husband? Eph. v. 23; then you may be confident you are interested in the benefits and blessings of Christ's last will and testament; for can you imagine Christ will make a testament and forget his spouse? It cannot be. If he so loved the church as to give himself for her, much more what he hath is settled on her. Again, are you his spiritual seed, his children by regeneration? Are you born of the Spirit? John iii. Do you resemble Christ in holiness? 1 Pet. i. 15, 16. Do you find a reverential fear of Christ carrying you to obey him in all things? Mal. i. 6. Are you led by the Spirit of Christ? " As many as are so led, they are the sons of God," Rom. viii. 14. To conclude, Have you the Spirit of adoption, enabling you to cry, Abba, Father? Gal. iv. 6; that is, helping you in a gracious manner, with reverence mixed with filial confidence, to open your hearts spiritually to your Father on all occasions? If so, you are children; and if children, doubt not but you have a rich legacy in Christ's last will and testament.

(2.) You may also discern your interest in the new testament or covenant (for they are substantially the same thing) by the new covenant impressions that are made on your hearts, which are so many clear evidences of your right to the benefits it contains. Such are spiritual illuminations, Jer. xxxi. 34, gracious softness and tenderness of heart, Ezek. xi. 19, the awful dread and fear of God, Jer. xxxii. 43, the copy or transcript of his laws on your hearts in gracious correspondent principles, Jer. xxxi. 33. These things speak you the children of the covenant, on whom all these great things are settled.

2. To conclude, it is the indispensable duty of all on whom Christ hath settled such mercies, to admire his love, and walk answerably to it.

(1.) Admire the love of Christ. Oh how intense and ardent was the love of Jesus, who designed for you such an inheritance, with such a settlement of it upon you ! Before this love let all the saints fall down astonished, humbly professing that they owe themselves, and all they are, or shall be worth, to eternity, to this love.

(2.) And be sure you walk becoming persons for whom Christ hath done such great things. Comfort yourselves under present abasures with your spiritual privileges, James ii. 5, and let all your rejoicing be in Christ, and what you have in him, whilst others are blessing themselves in vanity.

Having finished what I designed to speak to, about the work of redemption, so far as it was carried on by Christ in his humble state, we shall now view that blessed work as it is further advanced and perfected in his state of exaltation.

The whole of that work was not to be finished on earth in a state of suffering and abasure, therefore the apostle makes his exaltation, in order to the finishing of the remainder of his work, so necessary a part of his priesthood, that without it he could not have been a priest. "If he were on earth he should not be a priest," Heb. viii. 4 ; that is, if he should have continued always here, and had not been raised again from the dead, and taken up into glory, he could not have been a complete and perfect priest. For just as it was not enough for the sacrifice to be slain without, and his blood left there ; but after it was shed without, it must be carried within the veil, into the most holy place before the Lord, Heb. ix. 7 ; so it was not sufficient that Christ shed his own blood on earth, except he carry it before the Lord into heaven, and there perform his intercession-work for us.

Moreover, God the Father stood engaged in a solemn covenant to reward him for his deep humiliation, with a most glorious and illustrious advancement, Isa. xlix. 5—7. And how God (as it became him) made this good to Christ, the apostle very clearly expresses, Phil. ii. 9. Yea, justice required it should be so. For how could our Surety be detained in the prison of the grave, when the debt for which he was imprisoned was by him fully discharged, so that the law of God must acknowledge itself to be fully satisfied in all its claims and demands? His resurrection from the dead was, therefore, his discharge or acquittance upon full payment, which could not in justice be denied him.

And, indeed, God the Father lost nothing by it, for there never was a more glorious manifestation made of the name of God to the world, than was made in that work. Therefore it is said, Phil. ii. 11, speaking of one of the designs of Christ's exaltation, it was, (saith the apostle,) "That every tongue should confess that Jesus Christ is Lord, to the glory of God the Father." Oh how is the love of God to poor sinners illustriously, yea, astonishingly, displayed in Christ's exaltation! When, to show the complacency and delight which he took in our recovery, he hath openly declared to the world, that his exalting Christ to all that glory, such as no mere creature ever was or can be exalted to, was bestowed upon him as a reward for that work, that most grateful work of our redemption, "Wherefore God also hath highly exalted him," Phil. ii. 9. There is an emphatical pleonasm in that word; our english is too flat to deliver out the elegancy of the original, it is super-exaltation. A greater argument of his high satisfaction and content in the recovery of poor sinners cannot be given. For this, therefore, God the Father shall have glory and honour ascribed to him in heaven to all eternity.

Now this singular exaltation of Jesus Christ, as it properly respects his human nature, which alone is capable of advancement; for, in respect of his Divine nature, he never ceased to be the Most High; so it was done to him as a common person, and as the Head of all believers, their Representative in this as well as in his other works. God therein showing what, in due time, he intends to do with the persons of his elect, after they, in conformity to Christ, have suffered awhile. Whatever God the Father intendeth to do in us, or for us, he hath first done it to the person of our Representative, Jesus Christ. And this, if you observe, the scriptures carry in very clear and plain expressions, through all the degrees and steps of Christ's exaltation, namely, his resurrection, ascension, session at the right hand of God, and returning to judge the world; of which I purpose to speak distinctly in the following discourses.

He arose from the dead as a public person: "If ye then be risen with Christ," saith the apostle, Col. iii. 1; so that the saints have communion and fellowship with him in his resurrection.

He ascended into heaven as a public person; for so it is said in Eph. ii. 6, " He hath raised us up," or exalted us together with Christ; "and hath made us sit together in heavenly places in Christ Jesus." We sit there in our Representative. And when he shall come again to judge the world, the saints shall come with him. So it is prophesied, " The Lord my God shall come, and all the saints with thee," Zech. xiv. 5. And as they come with Christ from heaven, so they shall sit on thrones with him. They shall be assessors with the Judge, 1 Cor. vi. 2. This deserves a special remark, that all this honour is given to Christ, as our Head and Representative, for thence results abundance of comfort to the people of God. Carry it therefore along with you in your thoughts, throughout the whole of Christ's advancement. Think, when you hear that Christ is risen from the dead, and is in all that glory and authority in heaven, how sure the salvation of his redeemed is. " For if, when we were enemies, we were reconciled to God, by the death of his Son; much more, being reconciled, we shall be saved by his life." Surely it cannot be supposed but " he is able to save them to the uttermost that come unto God by him, seeing he ever lives to make intercession," Heb. vii. 25. Think how safe the people of God in this world are, whose Head is in heaven. It was a comfortable expression of one of the fathers, encouraging himself and others with this truth in a dark day; " Come, (said he,) why do we tremble thus? Do we not see our Head above water?" If he live, believers cannot die; " Because I live, ye shall live also," John xiv. 19.

And let no man's heart suggest a suspicious thought to him, that this wonderful advancement of Christ may cause him to forget his poor people, groaning here below under sin and misery. For the temper and disposition of his faithful and tender heart is not changed with his condition. He bears the same respect to us as when he dwelt among us. For indeed he there lives and acts upon our account, Heb. vii. 25; 1 John ii. 1, 2.

And how seasonable and comfortable will the meditations of

Christ's exaltation be to thee, O believer, when sickness hath wasted thy body, withered its beauty, and God is bringing thee to the dust of death! Think then, that that "vile body shall be conformed to the glorious body of Christ," Phil. iii. 21. As God hath glorified, and highly exalted his Son, "whose form was marred more than any man's," so will he exalt thee also. I do not say, to an equality in glory with Christ, for in heaven he will be discerned and distinguished by his peculiar glory, from all the angels and saints; as the sun is known by its excellent glory from the lesser stars. But we shall be conformed to this glorious Head, according to the proportion of members. Oh whither will love mount the believer in that day!

Having spoken thus much of Christ's exalted state, to cast some general light upon it, and engage your attentions to it, I shall now, according to the degrees of this his wonderful exaltation, briefly open it, under the fore-mentioned heads, namely, his resurrection, ascension, session at the Father's right-hand, and his return to judge the world.

SERMON XXXIX.

WHEREIN THE RESURRECTION OF CHRIST, WITH ITS INFLUENCES UPON THE SAINTS' RESURRECTION, IS CLEARLY OPENED, AND COMFORTABLY APPLIED, BEING THE FIRST STEP OF HIS EXALTATION.

MATT. XXVIII. 6.

HE IS NOT HERE: FOR HE IS RISEN, AS HE SAID. COME, SEE THE PLACE WHERE THE LORD LAY.

WE have finished the doctrine of Christ's humiliation, wherein the Sun of righteousness appeared to you as a setting sun, gone out of sight; but as the sun when it is gone down to us, begins a new day in another part of the world, so Christ, having finished his course and work in this world, rises again, and that, in order to the acting another glorious part of his work in the world above. In his death, he was in a sense totally eclipsed; but in his resurrection, he begins to recover his light and glory again. An angel descends from heaven, to roll away the stone, and, with it, the reproach of his death ; and to announce his resurrection to the two Maries, whose love to Christ had, at this time, drawn them to visit the sepulchre, where they lately left him.

At this time (the Lord being newly risen) the keepers were trembling, and become as dead men. So great was the terrible majesty and awful solemnity attending Christ's resurrection; but, to encourage these pious souls, the angel anticipates them with these good tidings; " He is not here; for he is risen, as he said: come, see the place where the Lord lay:" *q. d.* Be not troubled, though you have not the end you came for, one sight more of your dear, though dead Jesus; yet you have not lost your labour; for, to your eternal comfort, I tell you, "he is risen, as he said." And to put it out of doubt, come hither and satisfy yourselves, " See the place where the Lord lay."

In which words we have both a declaration and confirmation of the resurrection of Christ from the dead.

1. " He is not here." Here indeed you laid him, here you left him, and here you thought to find him as you left him; but you are happily mistaken, He is not here. He is risen,

ηγερθη; the word imports, the active power or self-quickening principle, by which Christ raised himself from the state of the dead. It was the Divine nature, or Godhead of Christ, which revived and raised the manhood.

2. Here is also a plain confirmation of Christ's resurrection, and that, first, from Christ's own prediction. "He is risen, as he said." He foretold that which I declare to be now fulfilled. Let it not therefore seem incredible to you. Secondly, by their own sight. "Come, see the place where the Lord lay." The grave hath lost its guest; it is now empty; death hath lost its prey. It received, but could not retain him; "Come, see the place where the Lord lay." Hence our observation is,

THAT OUR LORD JESUS CHRIST, BY THE ALMIGHTY POWER OF HIS OWN GODHEAD, REVIVED, AND ROSE FROM THE DEAD; TO THE TERROR AND CONSTERNATION OF HIS ENEMIES, AND THE UNSPEAKABLE CONSOLATION OF BELIEVERS.

That our Lord Jesus Christ, though laid, was not lost in the grave; but the third day revived and rose again, is a truth confirmed to us by many infallible proofs, as Luke witnesseth, Acts i. 3. We have testimonies of it, both from heaven and earth, and both infallible. From heaven, we have the testimony of angels, and to the testimony of an angel all credit is due; for angels are holy creatures, and cannot deceive us. The angel tells the two Maries, in the text, "He is risen." We have testimonies of it from men, holy men, who were eye-witnesses of this truth, to whom he showed himself alive by the space of forty days after his resurrection, by no less than * nine solemn apparitions to them. At one time five hundred brethren saw him at once, 1 Cor. xv. 6. These were holy persons, who durst not deceive, and who confirmed their testimony with their blood. So that no point of religion is of more confessed truth and infallible certainty than this before us.

And blessed be God it is so. For if it were not, then were the " gospel in vain," 1 Cor. xv. 14, seeing it hangs the whole weight of our faith, hope, and salvation, upon Christ as risen from the dead. If this were not so, then would the holy and divinely inspired apostles be found false witnesses, 1 Cor. xv. 15; for they all, with one mouth, constantly, and to the death affirmed it. If Christ be not risen, "then are believers yet in their sins," 1 Cor. xv. 17. For our justification is truly ascribed

* John xx. 14. Mark xvi. 12. John xx. 19. 1 Cor. xv. 5—7. 1 Cor. xv. 8. John xx. 26. John xxi. 1, 2. Luke xxiv. 36.

to the resurrection of Christ, Rom. iv. 25.　Whilst Christ was dying, and continued in the state of the dead, the price of our redemption was all that while in paying; the payment was completed, when he revived and rose again.　Therefore for Christ to have continued always in the state of the dead, had been never to have completely satisfied; hence the whole force and weight of our justification depends upon his resurrection.　Nay, had not Christ risen, "the dead had perished," 1 Cor. xv. 18. Even the dead who died in the faith of Christ, and of whose salvation there now remains no ground to doubt.

Moreover, had he not revived and risen from the dead, how could all the types that prefigured it have been satisfied?　Surely they must have stood as insignificant things in the Scriptures; and so must all the predictions of his resurrection, by which it was so plainly foretold.　See Matt. xii. 40; Luke xxiv. 46; Psa. xvi. 10; 1 Cor. xv. 4.　Had he not risen from the dead, how could he have been installed in that glory whereof he is now possessed in heaven, and which was promised him before the world was, upon the account of his death and sufferings?　"For to this end Christ both died, and rose, and revived, that he might be Lord both of the dead and living," Rom. xiv. 9; and that, in this state of dominion and glorious advancement, he might powerfully apply the virtues and benefits of his blood to us.　So then, there remains no doubt at all of the certainty of Christ's resurrection.　I need spend no more words to confirm it; but rather choose to explain and open the nature and manner of his resurrection, which I shall do by showing you several properties of it.

1. Christ rose from the dead with awful majesty.　So you find it in Matt. xxviii. 2—4.　"And, behold, there was a great earthquake; for the angel of the Lord descended from heaven, and came and rolled back the stone from the door, and sat upon it.　His countenance was like lightning, and his raiment white as snow: and for fear of him the keepers did shake, and became as dead men."　Human infirmity was not able to bear such heavenly majesty as attended the business of that morning. Nature sank under it.　This earthquake was, as one calls it, a sign of triumph, or token of victory, given by Christ, not only to the keepers, and the neighbouring city, but to the whole world, that he had overcome death in its own dominions, and, like a conqueror, lifted up his head above all his enemies.

2. And to increase the splendour of that day, and carry on the triumph, his resurrection was attended with the resurrection of many of the saints; who had slept in their graves till then, and then were awakened and raised to attend the Lord at his rising.

So you read, Matt. xxvii. 52, 53. " And the graves were opened; and many bodies of the saints which slept arose, and came out of the graves after his resurrection, and went into the holy city, and appeared unto many." This wonder was designed, both to adorn the resurrection of Christ, and to give a specimen or pledge of our resurrection; which also is to be in the virtue of his. This indeed was the resurrection of saints and none but saints, the resurrection of many saints, yet it was but a special resurrection, intended only to show what God will one day do for all his saints; and for the present, to give testimony of Christ's resurrection from the dead. They were seen, and known of many in the city, who doubtless never thought to have seen them any more in this world. To inquire curiously, as some do, who they were, what discourse they had with those to whom they appeared, and what became of them afterwards, is a vain thing. God hath cast a veil of silence and secrecy upon these things, that we might content ourselves with the written word; and he that " will not believe Moses and the prophets, neither will he believe though one rise from the dead," as these saints did.

3. As Christ rose from the dead with those attendants, who accompanied him at his resurrection; so it was by the power of his own Godhead that he quickened and raised himself; and by the virtue of his resurrection were they raised also, who accompanied him. It was not the angel who rolled back the stone, that revived him in the sepulchre, but he resumed his own life ; so he tells us, John x. 17, " I lay down my life, that I may take it again." Hence, 1 Pet. iii. 18, he is said to be put to death in the flesh, but quickened by the Spirit, that is, by the power of his Godhead, or Divine nature, which is opposed there to flesh, or his human nature. By the eternal Spirit he offered himself up to God, when he died, Heb. ix. 14; that is, by his own Godhead, not the third Person in the Trinity, for then it could not have been ascribed to him as his own act, that he offered up himself. And by the same Spirit he was quickened again. Therefore, the apostle well observes, " That he was declared to be the Son of God with power, by his resurrection from the dead," Rom. i. 4. Now if he had been raised by the power of the Father, or of the Holy Spirit only, and not by his own, how could he be declared by his resurrection to be the Son of God? What more had appeared in him than in others ? For others are raised by the power of God, if that were all. So that in this respect also it was a marvellous resurrection. Never any did, or shall rise as Christ rose, by a self-quickening principle. For though many dead saints rose at that time also, yet it was by

the virtue of Christ's resurrection that their graves were opened, and their bodies quickened. In which respect he saith, when he raised dead Lazarus, " I am the resurrection and the life," John xi. 25.

4. And therefore it may be truly affirmed, that though some dead saints are raised to life before the resurrection of Christ, yet that Christ is " the First-born from the dead," as he is called, Col. i. 18. For though Lazarus and others were raised, yet it was not by themselves, but by Christ. It was by his virtue and power, not their own. And though they were raised to life, yet they died again ; but Christ dieth no more. " Death hath no dominion over him." He was the First-born from the dead, that in all things he might have the pre-eminence.

5. But lastly, Christ rose as a public person ; " As the First-fruits of them that slept," 1 Cor. xv. 20. I desire this may be well understood ; for upon this account it is that our resurrection is secured to us by the resurrection of Christ ; and not a resurrection only, but a blessed and happy one, for the First-fruits both assured and sanctified the whole crop or harvest.

Now that Christ did rise, as a public person, representing and comprehending all the elect, who were called the children of the resurrection, is plain from Eph. ii. 6, where we are said to be risen with, or in him. So that, as we are said to die in Adam, (who also was a common person,) as the branches die in the death of the root ; so we are said to be raised from death in Christ, who is the Head, Root, and Representative, of all his elect seed. And why is he called the First-born, and First-begotten from the dead, but with respect to the whole number of the elect, that are to be born from the dead in their time and order also ; and as sure as the whole harvest follows the first-fruits, so shall the general resurrection of the saints to life eternal follow this birth of the First-born from the dead. It shall surely follow it, and that not only as a consequent follows an antece-dent, but as an effect follows its proper cause. Now there is a three-fold causality, or influence that Christ's resurrection hath upon the saints' resurrection, of which it is at once the merito-rious, efficient, and exemplary cause.

The resurrection of Christ is a *meritorious* cause of the saints' resurrection, as it completed his satisfaction, and finished his payment, and so our justification is properly assigned to it, as before was noted from Rom. iv. 25.

And as it is the meritorious cause of our resurrection, so it is the *efficient* cause of it also. For when the time shall come that the saints shall rise out of the dust, they shall be raised by

Christ, as their Head, in whom the effective principle of their life is. " Your life is hid with Christ in God," as it is Col. iii. 3. So in Rom. viii. 10, " And if Christ be in you, the body indeed is dead because of sin; but the spirit is life because of righteousness:" that is, Though you are really united to Christ by the Spirit, yet your bodies must die as well as other men's ; but your souls shall be presently, upon your dissolution, swallowed up in life. And then it follows, ver. 11, " But if the Spirit of him that raised up Jesus from the dead, dwell in you, he that raised up Christ from the dead, shall also quicken your mortal bodies by his Spirit that dwelleth in you;" that is, though your bodies must die, yet they shall live again in the resurrection ; and that by virtue of the Spirit of Christ which dwelleth in you, and is the bond of your mystical union with him your Head. You shall not be raised as others are, by a mere word of power, but by the Spirit of life dwelling in Christ your Head, which is a choice prerogative indeed.

Christ's resurrection is not only the meritorious and efficient cause, but it is also the exemplary cause or pattern of our resurrection. " He being the first and best, is therefore the pattern and measure of all the rest." So you read, Phil. iii. 21, " Who shall change our vile body that it may be fashioned like unto his glorious body." Now the conformity of our resurrection to Christ's stands in the following particulars. Christ's body was raised substantially the same ; so will ours. His body was raised first ; so will ours be raised before the rest of the dead. His body was wonderfully improved by the resurrection ; so will ours. His body was raised to be glorified ; and so will ours.

(1.) Christ's body was raised substantially the same that it was before ; and so will ours. Not another, but the same body. Upon this very reason the apostle uses that identical expression, " This corruptible must put on incorruption, and this mortal, immortality," 1 Cor. xv. 53. Pointing, as it were, to his own body when he spake it ; the same body, not another body in its stead. For should God prepare another body to be raised instead of this, it would not be a resurrection, but a creation.

(2.) His body was raised, not by a word of power from the Father, but by his own Spirit. So the resurrection of the saints is to be effected, as I opened to you, by his Spirit which now dwelleth in them. That very Spirit of Christ which effected their spiritual resurrection from sin, shall effect their corporal resurrection also from the grave.

(3.) His body was raised first, he had in this, as well as in other things, the pre-eminence ; so shall the saints, in respect of the wicked, have the pre-eminence in the resurrection, " The dead in Christ shall rise first," 1 Thess. iv. 16.   They are to attend the Lord at his coming, and will be brought forth sooner than the rest of the world, to attend on that service.

(4.) Christ's body was marvellously improved by the resurrection ; and so will ours.   It fell in weakness, but was raised in power, no more capable of sorrows, pains, and dishonours.   In like manner our bodies are " sown in weakness, but raised in power ; sown in dishonour, raised in glory.   Sown natural bodies, raised spiritual bodies," as the apostle speaks, 1 Cor. xv. 43, 44.   No distempers hang about glorified bodies, nor are they henceforth subject to any of those natural necessities to which they are now tied.   There are no defects, or deformities, in the children of the resurrection.   What members are now defective or deformed, will then be restored to their perfect being and beauty ; " for, if the universal death of all parts be rescinded by the resurrection, how much more the partial death of any single member ! " as Tertullian speaks ; and from thenceforth they are free from the law of mortality, " They can die no more," Luke xx. 35, 36.   Thus shall they be improved by their resurrection.

(5.) To conclude, Christ's body was raised from the dead to be glorified and crowned with honour.   Oh it was a joyful day to him ; and so will the resurrection of the saints be to them, the day of the gladness of their hearts.   It will be said to them in that morning, " Awake and sing, ye that dwell in the dust," as Isa. xxvi. 19.   Oh how comfortable will be the meeting between the glorified soul and its new-raised body.   And there are three things will make it so.

[1.] The gratifications of the soul, by the satisfaction of its natural desire of union with its own body.   For even glorified souls in heaven have such a desire of re-union.   We are all sensible of the soul's affection to the body now, in its compounded state, we feel the tender care it hath for the body, the sympathy with it, and lothness to be separated from it.   It is said to be " at home in the body," 2 Cor. v. 6.   And had not God implanted such an inclination to this its tabernacle in it, it would not have paid that due respect it owes the body while it inhabited in it, nor have regarded what became of it when it left it.   This inclination remains still with it in heaven, it reckons not itself completely happy till its old dear companion and partner be with it.   Now, when this its inclination to its own body, its longings after it, are gratified with a sight and enjoyment of it again, oh what a comfortable meeting will this make it! especially if we consider,

[2.] The excellent temper and state in which they shall meet each other. For, as the body shall be raised with all the improvements and endowments imaginable, which may render it amiable, and every way desirable, so the soul comes down immediately from God out of heaven, shining in its holiness and glory. And thus it re-enters its body, and animates it again. But,

[3.] And principally, that wherein the chief joy of this meeting consists, is the end for which the glorified soul comes down to quicken and repossess it, namely, to meet the Lord, and ever to be with the Lord; to receive a full reward for all the labours and services it performed to God in this world. This must needs make that day a day of triumph and exaltation. It comes out of the grave, as Joseph out of his prison, to be advanced to the highest honour. Oh do but imagine what an ecstasy of joy it will be for a soul thus to resume its own body, and say, as it were, unto it, Come away, my dear, my ancient friend, who servedst and sufferedst with me in the world; come along with me to meet the Lord, in whose presence I have been ever since I parted with thee. Now thy bountiful Lord hath remembered thee also, and the day of thy glorification is come. Surely it will be a joyful awaking. For do but imagine, what a joy it is for dear friends to meet after long separation, how they usually give demonstrations of their love and delight in each other, by embraces, kisses, tears, &c. Or frame but to yourselves a notion of perfect health, when a sprightly vivacity runs through every part, and the spirits do, as it were, dance before us, when we go about any business; especially to such a business as the business of that day will be, to receive a crown, and a kingdom. Do but imagine then what a sun-shine morning this will be, and how the pains and agonies, cold sweats, and bitter groans at parting will be recompensed by the joy of such a meeting!

Thus I have showed you the certainty of Christ's resurrection, the nature and properties of it, the threefold influence it hath on the saints' resurrection, and the conformity of ours unto his, in these five respects. From the consideration of all which,

We infer, 1. That if Christ was thus raised from the dead, then death is fairly overcome, and swallowed up in victory: were it not so, it had never let Christ escape out of the grave. Death is a dreadful enemy, it defies all the sons and daughters of Adam. None durst cope with this king of terrors but Christ.

and he, by dying, went into the very den of this dragon, fought with it, and foiled it in the grave, its own territories and dominions, and came off a conqueror. For, as the apostle says, " It was impossible it should hold or detain him," Acts ii. 24. Never did death meet with its over-match before it met with Christ; and he conquering it for us, and in our names, rising as our Representative, now every single saint triumphs over it as a vanquished enemy: "O death, where is thy sting? O grave, where is thy victory? Thanks be to God, who hath given us the victory through our Lord Jesus Christ," 1 Cor. xv. 55. 57. Thus, like Joshua, they set the foot of faith upon the neck of that king.

2. Has Christ, and hath his resurrection such a potent and comfortable influence upon the resurrection of the saints? Then it is the duty, and will be the wisdom of the people of God, so to govern, dispose, and employ their bodies, as becomes those that understand what glory is prepared for them at the resurrection of the just. Particularly,

(1.) Be not fondly tender of them, but employ and use them for God here. How many good duties are lost and spoiled by sinful indulgence to our bodies! Alas! we are generally more solicitous to live long, than to live usefully. How many christians have active, vigorous bodies, yet God hath little service from them! If your bodies were animated by some other souls that love God more than you do, and burn with holy zeal to his service, more work would be done for God by your bodies in a day, than is now done in a month. To have an able, healthy body, and not use it for God, for fear of hurting it, is as if one should give you a strong and stately horse, upon condition you must not work or ride him. Wherein is the mercy of having a body, except it be employed for God? Will not its reward at the resurrection be sufficient for all the pains you now put it to in his service?

(2.) See that you preserve the due honour of your bodies. " Possess them in sanctification and honour," 1 Thess. iv. 4. Oh, let not those eyes be now defiled with sin, by which you shall see God,—those ears be inlets to vanity, which shall hear the hallelujahs of the blessed. God hath designed honour for your bodies, oh, make them not either the instruments or objects of sin. There are sins against the body, 1 Cor. vi. 18. Preserve your bodies from those defilements, for they are the temple of God; " If any man defile the temple of God, him shall God destroy," 1 Cor. iii. 17.

(3.) Let not the contentment and accommodation of your

bodies draw your souls into snares, and bring them under the power of temptations to sin.   This is a very common case.   Oh how many thousands of precious souls perish eternally for the satisfaction of a vile body for a moment !   Their souls must suffer, because their bodies cannot.   It is recorded to the immortal honour of those worthies, in Heb. xi. 35, " That they accepted not deliverance, that they might obtain a better resurrection."   They might have had a temporal resurrection from death to life, from reproach to honour, from poverty to riches, from pains to pleasure ; but upon such terms they judged it not worth acceptance. They would not expose their souls to secure their bodies.   They had the same natural affections that other men have.   They were made of as tender flesh as we are, but such was the care they had of their souls, and the hope of a better resurrection, that they listened not to the complaints of their bodies.   Oh that we were all in the same resolutions with them.

(4.)   Withhold not, upon the pretence of the wants your own bodies may be in, that which God and conscience bid you to communicate for the refreshment of the saints, whose present necessities require your assistance.   Oh, be not too indulgent to your own flesh, and cruel to others.   Certainly, the consideration of that reward which shall be given you at the resurrection, for every act of christian charity, is the greatest incentive in the world to it.   And to that end it is urged as a motive to charity: " When thou makest a feast, call the poor, the maimed, the lame, the blind ; and thou shalt be blessed; for they cannot recompense thee : for thou shalt be recompensed at the resurrection of the just," Luke xiv. 13, 14.   It was the opinion of an eminent modern divine, that no man living fully understands and believes that scripture, " Inasmuch as ye have done it unto one of the least of these my brethren, ye have done it unto me," Matt. xxv. 40.   How few saints would be exposed to daily wants and necessities, if that scripture were but fully understood and believed !

3. Is Christ risen from the dead, and that as a public Person and Representative of believers? How are we all concerned then to secure to ourselves an interest in Christ, and consequently in this blessed resurrection !   What consolation would be left in this world, if the hope of the resurrection were taken away ?   It is this blessed hope that must support you under all the troubles of life, and in the agonies of death.   The securing of a blessed resurrection to yourselves, is therefore the deepest concernment you have in this world.   And it may be secured to yourselves,

if, upon serious heart-examination, you can discover the following evidences.

(1.) If you are regenerated creatures, brought forth in a new nature to God, for we are " begotten again to a lively hope, by the resurrection of Jesus Christ from the dead."   Christ's resurrection is the ground-work of our hope.   And the new birth is our title or evidence of our interest in it.   So that until our souls are partakers of the spiritual resurrection from the death of sin, we can have no assurance that our bodies shall be partakers of that blessed resurrection to life.   " Blessed and holy (saith the Spirit) is he that hath part in the first resurrection, on such the second death hath no power," Rev. xx. 6.   Let not unregenerate souls expect a comfortable meeting with their bodies again.   Rise they shall by God's terrible citation, at the sound of the last trump, but not to the same end that the saints arise, nor by the same principle.   They to whom the Spirit is now a principle of sanctification, to them he will be the principle of a joyful resurrection.   See then that you get gracious souls now, or never expect glorious bodies then.

(2.) If you be dead with Christ, you shall live again by the life of Christ.   If we have been planted together in the likeness of his death, we shall be also in the likeness of his resurrection, Rom. vi. 5. 8 ; συμφυτοι, planted together. Some refer it to believers themselves ; jews and gentiles are planted together in Christ.   So Erasmus, " Believers grow together like branches upon the same root," which should powerfully enforce the great gospel duty of unity among themselves.   But I would rather understand it with reference to Christ and believers, with whom believers are in other scriptures said to suffer together, and be glorified together ; to die together, and live together ; to be crucified together, and buried together ; all noting the communion they have with Christ, both in his death, and in his life.   Now, if the power of Christ's death, that is, the mortifying influence of it, have been upon our hearts, killing their lusts, deadening their affections, and subduing their appetites to the creature, then the power of his life, or resurrection, shall come upon our dead, withered bodies, to revive and raise them up to live with him in glory.

(3.) If your hearts and affections be now with Christ in heaven, your bodies in due time shall be there also, and conformed to his glorious body.   So you find it, Phil. iii. 20, 21. " For our conversation is in heaven, from whence also we look for the Saviour, the Lord Jesus Christ : who shall change our vile body, that it may be fashioned like unto his own glorious body."   The body is here called vile, or the body of our vileness.   Not as God made it, but as sin hath marred it.   Not absolutely, and in itself, but relatively, and in comparison of what it will be at the resurrection.   Then those scattered bones and dispersed dust, like pieces of old broken, battered silver, will be new cast, and wrought in the best and newest fashion, even like to Christ's glorious body.   Whereof we have this evidence, that our conversation is already heavenly.   The temper, frame, and disposition of our souls is already so; therefore the frame and temper of our bodies in due time shall be so.

(4.) If you strive now to attain the resurrection of the dead, no doubt but you shall then attain what you now strive for. This was Paul's great ambition, "that by any means he might attain unto the resurrection of the dead," Phil. iii. 11.   He means not simply a resurrection from the dead, for that all men shall attain, whether they strive for it or no; but by a metonymy of the subject for the adjunct, he intends that complete holiness and perfection, which shall attend the state of the resurrection; so it is expounded, ver. 12.   So then, if God have raised in your hearts a vehement desire, and assiduous endeavour after a perfect freedom from sin, and full conformity to God, in the beauties of holiness; that very love of holiness, your present pantings, and tendencies after perfection, speak you to be the persons designed for it.

(5.) If you are such as do good in your generation.   If you be fruitful and useful men and women in the world, you shall have part in this blessed resurrection: "All that are in the graves shall hear his voice and shall come forth; they that have done good unto the resurrection of life," John v. 28, 29.   Now it is not every act materially good, that entitles a man to this privilege; but the same requisites that the schoolmen assign to make a good prayer, are also necessary to every good work. The person, matter, manner, and end, must be good.   Nor is it any single good act, but a series and course of holy actions, that is here meant.   What a spur should this be to us all, (as indeed the apostle makes it, closing up the doctrine of the resurrection with this solemn exhortation, 1 Cor. xv. 58, with which I also close mine,) "Therefore, my beloved brethren, be ye stedfast, unmovable, always abounding in the work of the Lord, for as much as ye know that your labour is not in vain in the Lord."

Thanks be to God for his unspeakable gift.

SERMON XL.

THE ASCENSION OF CHRIST ILLUSTRATED, AND VARIOUSLY IM-
PROVED, BEING THE SECOND STEP OF HIS EXALTATION.

JOHN XX. 17.

JESUS SAITH UNTO HER, TOUCH ME NOT; FOR I AM NOT YET ASCENDED TO
MY FATHER: BUT GO TO MY BRETHREN, AND SAY UNTO THEM, I ASCEND
UNTO MY FATHER, AND YOUR FATHER; AND TO MY GOD, AND YOUR GOD.

IN the former sermons, we have been following Christ through
his humiliation, from the time that he left the blessed bosom of
the Father: and now, having finished the whole course of his
obedience on earth, and risen again from the dead, we must, in
this discourse, follow him back again into heaven, to that bosom
of ineffable delight and love, which, for our sakes, he so freely
left. For it was not his end in rising from the dead, to live such
a low, animal life as this is, but to live a most glorious life, as an
enthroned King in heaven: upon which state he was now ready
to enter, as he tells Mary in the text, and bids her tell it to the
disciples; " Go, tell my brethren, that I ascend to my Father," &c.
In which injunction we have,

1. The persons to whom this message was sent, my "brethren,"
so he calls the disciples. A sweet compellation, and full of love.
Much like that of Joseph to his brethren, Gen. xlv. 4, save only
that there is much more tenderness in this than that; for he reminds them in the same breath of what they had done against
him; " I am Joseph your brother, whom ye sold: " but in this
it is, " Go tell my brethren," without the least mention of their
cowardice or unkindness. And,

2. The message itself, " Tell my brethren, I ascend to my
Father, and your Father; to my God, and your God." It is
put in the present tense, as if he had been ascending; though
he did not ascend for some weeks after this ; but he so expresses
it, to show what was the next part of his work, which he was to
act in heaven for them; and how much his heart was set upon
it, and longed to be about it: " I ascend to my Father, and your
Father; to my God, and your God." This is the substance of
that comfortable message, sent by Mary to the pensive disciples.
Hence the observation is,

THAT OUR LORD JESUS CHRIST DID NOT ONLY RISE
FROM THE DEAD, BUT ALSO ASCENDED INTO HEAVEN;
THERE TO DESPATCH ALL THAT REMAINED TO BE
DONE FOR COMPLETING THE SALVATION OF HIS
PEOPLE.

So much the apostle plainly witnesseth, " He that descended
is the same also that ascended up far above all heavens," Eph.
iv. 10.   A full and faithful account whereof the several evangelists have given us, Mark xvi. 19; Luke xxiv. 51.   This is
sometimes called his going away, as John xvi. 7.   Sometimes
his being exalted, Acts ii. 33.   Sometimes his being made higher
than the heavens, Heb. vii. 26.   And sometimes his entering
within the veil, Heb. vi. 19, 20.

Now for the opening this act of Christ, we will bind up the
whole in the satisfaction of these six questions.   I. Who ascended?   II. Whence did he ascend?   III. Whither?   IV.
When?   V. How?   VI. Why did he ascend?   And these
will take in what is needful for you to be acquainted with in
this point.

I. Who ascended? This the apostle answers, " the same that
descended," Eph. iv. 9, 10, namely, Christ.   And himself tells
us, "I ascend."   And though the ascension were of Christ's whole
person, yet it was only a figurative expression, with respect to his
Divine nature, but it agrees most properly to the humanity of
Christ, which really changed places and conditions by it.   And
hence it is that he said, "I came forth from the Father, and am
come into the world; again, I leave the world, and go to the
Father," John xvi. 28.   He goes away, and we see him no more.
As God, he is spiritually with us still, even to the end of the world.
But as man, " the heavens must contain him till the restitution
of all things," Acts iii. 21.

II. Whence did Christ ascend?   I answer, more generally,
he is said to ascend from this world, to leave the world, John
xvi. 28; but more particularly, it was from mount Olivet, near
Jerusalem, the very place where he began his last sufferings.
Oh, what a difference was there between the frame Christ was
in, in that mount, before his passion, and this he is now in, at
his ascension! But,

III. Whither did he ascend? It is manifest it was into the
third heavens ; the throne of God, and place of the blessed;
where all the saints shall be with him for ever.   It is said to be
far above all heavens, that is, the heavens which we see, for
they are but the pavement of that stately palace of the great

King. He is gone (saith the apostle) within the veil, that is, into the most holy place. And into his Father's house, John xiv. 2. And he is also said to go to the "place where he was before," John vi. 62, from whence at his incarnation he came.

IV. When did Christ ascend? Was it presently as soon as he arose from the dead? No, not so, for, "after his resurrection (saith Luke) he was seen of them forty days, speaking of the things pertaining to the kingdom of God." And truly the care and love of Christ to his people was very manifest in this his stay with them. He had ineffable glory prepared for him in heaven, and awaiting his coming, but he will not go to possess it, till he had settled all things for the good of his church here. For in this time he confirmed the truth of his resurrection, gave charge to the apostles concerning the discipline and order of his house or kingdom; which was needful, since he intended that their acts should be rules to future churches. So long it was necessary he should stay. And when he had set all things in order, he would stay no longer. He had work of great concernment to do for us in the other world. He desired to be no longer here, than he had work to do for God and souls; a good pattern for the saints.

V. How did Christ ascend into heaven?

1. Here it is worthy our observation, that Christ ascended as a public Person or Forerunner, in our names, and upon our account. So it is said expressly, Heb. vi. 19, 20, speaking of the most holy place within the veil; whither (saith he) the Forerunner is for us entered. His entering into heaven as our Forerunner implies both his public capacity and precedency.

His *public capacity*, as one that went upon our business to God. So he himself speaks, " I go before to prepare a place for you, " John xiv. 2, to take possession of heaven in your names. The Forerunner hath respect to others that were to come to heaven after him, in their several generations; for whom he hath taken up mansions, which are kept for them against their coming.

It notes *precedency;* he is our Forerunner, but he himself had no forerunner. Never any entered into heaven before him, but such as entered in his name, and through the virtue of his merits. He was the first that ever entered into heaven directly, immediately, in his own name, and upon his own account. But all the fathers who died before him entered in his name.

2. He ascended *triumphantly* into heaven. To this some expositors refer that which in the type is spoken of David, when he lodged the ark in its own place, with musical instruments and shoutings; but to Christ, in the antitype, when he was received

up triumphantly into glory: "God is gone up with a shout, the Lord with the sound of a trumpet. Sing praises to God, sing praises; sing praises unto our King, sing praises," Psa. xlvii. 5, 6.

A cloud is prepared, as a royal chariot, to carry up the King of glory to his princely pavilion. "A cloud received him out of their sight," Acts i. 9. And then a royal guard of mighty angels surrounded the chariot, if not for support, yet for greater state and solemnity of their Lord's ascension. And oh what jubilations of the blessed angels were heard in heaven! How was the whole city of God moved at his coming! For, as when "he brought his First-begotten into the world, he said, Let all the angels of God worship him," Heb. i. 6; so at his return thither again, when he had finished the work of redemption, there were no less demonstrations given by those blessed creatures of their delight and joy in it. The very heavens echoed and resounded on that account. Yea, the triumph is not ended at this day, nor ever shall.

It is said, "I saw, in the night visions, and behold one like the Son of man came with the clouds of heaven, and came to the Ancient of days, and they brought him near before him. And there was given him dominion, and glory, and a kingdom, that all people, nations, and languages, should serve him," Dan. vii. 13, 14. This vision of Daniel's was accomplished in Christ's ascension, when *they*, that is, the angels, brought him to the Ancient of days, that is, to God the Father, who to express his welcome to Christ, gave him glory and a kingdom. Therefore God is said to "receive him up into glory," 1 Tim. iii. 16. He went up, and the Father received him; yea, received so as none ever was received before him, or shall be received after him.

3. Further, Christ ascended *munificently*, shedding forth, abundantly, inestimable gifts upon his church at his ascension. "Wherefore he saith, When he ascended up on high, he led captivity captive, and gave gifts unto men." The place to which the apostle refers, is Psa. lxviii. 17, 18, where you have both the triumph and magnificence with which Christ went up excellently set forth together. "The chariots of God (saith the psalmist) are twenty thousand, even thousands of angels: the Lord is among them, as in Sinai, in the holy place. Thou hast ascended on high, thou hast led captivity captive: thou hast received gifts for men; yea, for the rebellious also, that God might dwell among them." Which words, in their primary and literal sense, were a celebration of that famous victory and triumph of David over the enemies of God, recorded 2 Sam. viii. These conquered enemies bring him several sorts of presents, all which

he dedicated to the Lord. The spiritual sense is, that just so our Lord Jesus Christ, when he had overcome by his death on the cross, and now triumphed in his ascension, takes the parts and gifts of his enemies, and gives them, by their conversion to the church, for its use and service: thus he received gifts, even for the rebellious, that is, sanctifies the natural gifts and faculties of such as hated his people before, dedicating them to the Lord, in his people's service. Thus, as one observes, Tertullian, Origen, Augustine, and Jerome, came into Canaan, laden with egyptian gold; meaning, they came into the church richly laden with natural learning and abilities. Augustine was a manichee, Cyprian a magician, learned Bradwardine a scornful, proud naturalist, who once said, when he read Paul's epistles, Dedignabar esse parvulus; he scorned such childish things, but afterwards became a very useful man in the church of God. And even Paul himself was as fierce an enemy to the church as breathed on earth, till Christ gave him into its bosom by conversion, and then no mere man ever did the Lord and his people greater service than he. Men of all sorts, greater and smaller lights, have been given to the church. Officers of all sorts were given it by Christ. Extraordinary and temporary, as prophets, apostles, evangelists; ordinary and standing, as pastors and teachers, which remain to this day, Eph. iv. 11. And those stars are fixed in the church-heaven by a most firm establishment, 1 Cor. xii. 28. Thousands now in heaven, and thousands on earth also, are blessing Christ at this day for these his ascension gifts.

4. Our Lord Jesus Christ ascended most *comfortably*, for whilst he was blessing his people, he was parted from them, Luke xxiv. 50, 51. Therein making good to them what is said by him, " Having loved his own, he loved them unto the end," John xiii. 1. There was a great deal of love manifested by Christ in this very last act of his in this world. The last sight they had of him in this world was a most sweet and encouraging one. They heard nothing from his lips but love, they saw nothing in his face but love, till he mounted his triumphant chariot, and was taken out of their sight.

Surely these blessings at parting were sweet and rich ones. For the matter of them, they were the mercies which his blood had so lately purchased for them. And for their extent, they were not only intended for them who had the happiness to be upon the place with him from whence he ascended; but they reach us as well as them; and will reach the last saint that shall be upon the earth till he come again. For they were but representatives of the future churches, Matt. xxviii. 20. And in blessing them, he blesseth us also. And by this we may be satisfied that Christ carried a heart full of love to his people away with him to heaven; since his love so abounded in the last act that ever he did in this world, and left such a demonstration of his tenderness with them at parting.

5. He ascended, as well as rose again, by his own power. He was not merely passive in his ascension, but it was his own act. He went to heaven. Therefore it is said, Acts i. 10, he went up, namely, by his own Divine power. And this plainly evinceth him to be God, for no mere creature ever mounted itself from earth, far above all heavens, as Christ did.

VI. Why did Christ ascend?

I answer, His ascension was necessary upon many and great accounts. For,

1. If Christ had not ascended, he could not have interceded, as now he doth, in heaven for us; and do but take away Christ's intercession, and you starve the hope of the saints. For what have we to succour ourselves with, under the daily surprises of sin, but this, " That if any man sin, we have an Advocate with the Father:" mark that, " *with* the Father ;" a Friend upon the place; one that abides there, on purpose to transact all our affairs, and as a Surety for the peace between God and us.

2. If Christ had not ascended, you could not have entered into heaven when you die; for he went to " prepare a place for you," John xiv. 2. He was, as I said before, the first that entered into heaven directly, and in his own name; and had he not done so, we would not have entered when we die, in his name. The Forerunner made way for all that are coming on, in their several generations, after him. Nor could your bodies have ascended after their resurrection but in virtue of Christ's ascension. For he ascended, as was said before, in the capacity of our Head and Representative; to his Father, and our Father; for us, and himself too.

3. If Christ had not ascended, he could not have been inaugurated and installed in the glory he now enjoys in heaven. This world is not the place where perfect felicity and glory dwell. And then, how had the promise of the Father been made good to him? Or our glory, which consists in being with, and conformed to him, where had it been? " Ought not Christ to suffer, and to enter into his glory?" Luke xxiv. 26.

4. If Christ had not ascended, how could we have been satisfied, that his payment on the cross made full satisfaction to God? How is it that the Spirit convinceth the world of righteousness,

John xvi. 8. 10, but from Christ's going to the Father, and returning hither no more? which gives evidence of God's full satisfaction, both with his person and work.

5. Further, How should we have enjoyed the great blessings of the Spirit and ordinances, if Christ had not ascended? And surely, we could not have been without either. If Christ had not gone away, " the Comforter had not come," John xvi. 7 ; he begins where Christ had finished. For he takes of his, and shows it to us, John xvi. 14. And therefore it is said, " The Holy Ghost was not given, because Jesus was not yet glorified," John xvii. 39. He was then given as a sanctifying Spirit, but not given in that measure, as afterwards he was, to furnish and qualify men with gifts for service. And indeed, by Christ's ascension, both his sanctifying and his ministering gifts were shed forth, more commonly and more abundantly upon men ; so that whatsoever good of conversion, edification, support, or comfort you receive from spiritual ordinances, he hath shed forth that, which you now see and feel. It is the fruit of Christ's ascension.

6. If Christ had not ascended, how had all the types and prophecies, that prefigured and foretold it, been fulfilled? " And the scriptures cannot be broken," John x. 35.

So that, upon all these accounts, it was expedient that he should go away. It was for his glory, and for our advantage. Though we lost the comfort of his bodily presence by it, yet if " we loved him, we would rejoice, because he went to the Father," John xiv. 28. We ought to have rejoiced in his advancement, though it had been to our loss ; but when it is so much for our benefit, as well as his glory, it is a matter of joy on both sides, that he is ascended to his Father, and our Father ; to his God, and to our God. From the several blessings flowing to us out of Christ's ascension, it was that he charged his people not to be troubled at his leaving them, John xiv. And hence learn,

Inference 1. Did Christ ascend into heaven? Is our Jesus, our treasure indeed there? Where then should the hearts of believers be, but in heaven, where their Lord, their Life is? Surely, saints, it is not good that your love and your Lord should be in two different countries, said one that is now with him. Up, and hasten after your Lover, that he and you may be together. Christians, you ascended with him virtually, when he ascended; you shall ascend to him personally, hereafter; oh that you would ascend to him, spiritually, in acts of faith, love, and desires daily. Sursum corda, Up with your hearts, was the form used by the ancient church at the sacrament. How good were it, if we could say with the apostle, " Our conversation is in heaven, from whence we look for the Saviour," Phil. iii. 20. A heart ascendant, is the best evidence of your interest in Christ's ascension.

2. Did Christ go to heaven as a Forerunner? What haste should we make to follow him? Come, christians, " Lay aside every weight, and the sin that so easily besets you, and run with patience the race set before you, looking unto Jesus," Heb. xii. 1, 2. The Captain of our salvation is entered within the gates of the new Jerusalem, and calls to us out of heaven to hasten to him; proposing the greatest encouragements to them that are following after him, saying, " He that overcomes shall sit with me in my throne, as I also overcame, and am set down with my Father in his throne," Rev. iii. 21. How tedious should it seem to us, to live so long at a distance from our Lord Jesus!

3. Did Christ ascend so triumphantly, leading captivity captive? How little reason then have believers to fear their conquered enemies! Sin, Satan, and every enemy, were in that day led away in triumph, dragged at Christ's chariot-wheels, brought after him as it were in chains. It is a lovely sight to see the necks of those tyrants under the foot of our Joshua. He made at that day " an open show of them," Col. ii. 15. Their strength is broken for ever. In this he showed himself more than a conqueror; for he conquered and triumphed too. Satan was then trod under his feet, and he hath promised to tread him under our feet also, and that shortly, Rom. xvi. 20. Some power our enemies yet retain, the serpent may bruise our heel, but Christ hath bruised his head.

4. Did Christ ascend so munificently, shedding forth so many mercies upon his people; mercies of inestimable value, reserved on purpose to adorn that day? Oh then see that you abuse not those precious ascension-gifts of Christ, but value and improve them as the choicest mercies. Now, the ascension-gifts, as I told you, are either the ordinances and officers of the church, (for he then gave them pastors and teachers,) or the Spirit that furnished the church with all its gifts. Beware you abuse not either of these.

Abuse not the ordinances and officers of Christ. This is a sin that no nation is plunged deeper into the guilt of, than this nation. Surely God hath written to us the great things of his law, and we have accounted them small things.

But in the next place, see that you abuse not the Spirit, whom God sent from heaven at his ascension, to supply his bodily absence among us, and is the great pledge of his care for, and tender love to his people.   Take heed that you do not vex Him by your disobedience; nor grieve Him by your unkindnesses; nor quench Him by your sinful neglects of duty, or abuse of light.   Oh behave dutifully towards the Spirit, and obey his voice; comply with his designs, and yield up yourselves to his guidance and conduct.   Methinks, to be entreated by the love of the Spirit, Rom. xv. 30, should be as great an argument as to be entreated for Christ's sake.   Now, to persuade all the saints to be tender of grieving the Spirit by sin, let me urge a few considerations proper to the point under hand.

(1.) He was the first and principal mercy that Christ received for you at his first entrance into heaven.   It was the first thing . he asked of God when he came to heaven. So he speaks, "I will pray the Father, and he shall give you another Comforter, that he may abide with you," John xiv. 16.   So that the Spirit is the first-born of mercies; and deserves the first place in our hearts and esteem.

(2.) The Spirit comes not in his own name to us, (though, if so, he deserves a dear welcome for his own sake, and for the benefits we receive by him, which are inestimable,) but he comes to us in the name, and in the love, both of the Father and the Son; as one authorized and delegated by them: "But when the Comforter is come, whom I will send unto you from the Father," John xv. 26.   Mark, I will send him from the Father; and in John xiv. 26, the Father is said to " send him in Christ's name."

(3.) But that is not the only consideration that should cause you to beware of grieving the Spirit, but he deserves better entertainment than any of the saints give him, for his own sake, and upon his own account, and that upon a double score, namely, of his nature and office.

On account of his *nature;* for he is God co-equal with the Father and Son in nature and dignity : "The Spirit of the Lord spake by me, and his word was in my tongue.   The God of Israel said, the Rock of Israel spake to me," 2 Sam. xxiii. 2, 3. So that you see he is God; the Rock of Israel. God omnipotent, for he created all things, Gen. i. 31.   God omnipresent, filling all things, Psa. cxxxix. 7.   God omniscient, who knows your hearts, Rom. viii. 27.   Beware therefore of . grieving him, for in so doing you grieve God.

Also on account of his *office,* and the benefits we receive by him.   We are obliged, even on the score of gratitude and ingenuity, to obey him; for he is sent in the quality of an Advocate to help us to pray; to indite our requests for us; to teach us what and how to ask of God, Rom. viii. 26.   He comes to us as a Comforter, John xiv. 16. And none like him. His work is to take of Christ's and show it to us; that is, to take of his death, resurrection, ascension, yea, of his present intercession in heaven, and show it to us. It was he that formed the body of Christ in the womb, and so prepared him to be a sacrifice for us. He filled that humanity with his unexampled fulness, Luke i. 35; Isa. lxi. 1; Col. i. 19. So fitting and anointing him for the discharge of his office. It is he that puts efficacy into the ordinances, and without him they would be a dead letter. It was he that blessed them to your conviction and conversion, 2 Cor. ix. 6; John xvi. 9; 1 Pet. i. 12; 1 John iii. 24; Rom. viii. 9. 26; John xiv. 26; Ezek. xxxvi. 25—27. Without Him you could never have had an interest in Christ, or communion with Christ. It was he that so often hath helped your infirmities, when you knew not what to say; comforted your hearts, when they were overwhelmed within you, and you knew not what to do; preserved you many thousand times from sin and ruin, when you have been upon the slippery brink of it in temptations. It is he, in his sanctifying work, that is the best evidence your souls have for heaven. It were endless to enumerate the mercies you have by him. And now, reader, dost thou not blush to think how unworthily thou hast treated such a Friend? Oh grieve not the Holy Spirit, whom Christ sent as soon as ever he went into heaven, in his Father's name, and in his own name, to perform all these offices for you.

5. Is Christ ascended to the Father as our Forerunner? Then the door of salvation stands open to all believers, and by virtue of Christ's ascension, they also shall ascend after him, far above all visible heavens. O my friends, what place hath Christ prepared for you! what a splendid habitation hath he provided for you! "God is not ashamed to be called your God; for he hath prepared for you a city," Heb. xi. 16. In that city Christ hath provided mansions, and resting-places for your everlasting abode, John xiv. 2, and keeps them for you till your coming. Oh how august and glorious a dwelling is that, where sun, and moon, and stars, shall shine as much below your feet, as they are now above your heads! May God send us a joyful meeting within the veil with our Forerunner, and sweeten our passage into it, with many a foresight and foretaste thereof. And, in the mean time, let the love of a Saviour inflame our hearts, so that whenever we cast a look towards that place, where our Forerunner is for us entered, our souls may say, with melting affections, Thanks be to God for Jesus Christ; and again, Blessed be God for his unspeakable gift.

SERMON XLI.

THE SESSION OF CHRIST AT GOD'S RIGHT HAND EXPLAINED AND
APPLIED, BEING THE THIRD STEP OF HIS GLORIOUS EXALTATION.

HEB. I. 3.

WHEN HE HAD BY HIMSELF PURGED OUR SINS, SAT DOWN ON THE RIGHT
HAND OF THE MAJESTY ON HIGH.

CHRIST being returned again to his Father, having finished
his whole work on earth, is there bid by the Father to sit down
in the seat of honour and rest : a seat prepared for him at God's
right hand—that makes it honourable ; and all his enemies as
a footstool under his feet—that makes it easy.   How much is
the state and condition of Jesus Christ changed in a few days !
Here he groaned, wept, laboured, suffered, and found no rest in
this world ; but when he comes to heaven, there he enters into
rest, sits down for ever in the highest throne, prepared by the
Father for him when he had done his work.

The scope of this epistle to the Hebrews, is to demonstrate
Christ to be the fulness of all legal types and ceremonies, and
that whatever light glimmered to the world through them, yet it
was but as the light of the day-star to the light of the sun.   In
this chapter, Christ, the subject of the epistle, is described ; and
particularly, in this third verse, he is described three ways.

1. By his essential and primeval glory and dignity ; he is the
brightness of his Father's glory, the very refulgency of that Sun
of glory.   * " The primary reason of that appellation is with
respect to his eternal and ineffable generation, light of light, as
the Nicene creed expresses it ; as a beam of light proceeding
from the sun.   And the secondary reason of it is with respect
to men;" for as the sun communicates its light and influence to
us by its beams ; so doth God communicate his goodness, and
manifest himself to us, by Christ.   " Yea, he is the express
image, or character of his person.   Not as the impressed image
of the seal upon the wax, but as the engraving in the seal itself."†
Thus he is described by his essential glory.

* Glass. Rhet. p. 174.   † Glass. Rhet. sac. p. 159.

T 3

2. He is described by the work he wrought here on earth, in his humbled state; and it was a glorious work, and that wrought out by his own single hand, "When he had by himself purged our sins." A work that all the angels in heaven could not do, but Christ did it.

3. He is described by his glory, which, as a reward of that work, he now enjoys in heaven. "When he had by himself purged our sins, he sat down on the right hand of the Majesty on high;" that is, the Lord clothed him with the greatest power, and highest honour, that heaven itself could afford; for so much this phrase of "sitting down on the right hand of the Majesty" imports, as will appear in the explication of this point, which is the result of this clause, namely,

THAT WHEN OUR LORD JESUS CHRIST HAD FINISHED HIS WORK ON EARTH, HE WAS PLACED IN THE SEAT OF THE HIGHEST HONOUR AND AUTHORITY AT THE RIGHT HAND OF GOD IN HEAVEN.

This truth is transformingly glorious. Stephen had but a glimpse of Christ at his Father's right hand, and it caused "his face to shine, as it had been the face of an angel," Acts vi. 15. This, his high advancement, was foretold and promised before the work of redemption was taken in hand: "The Lord said unto my Lord, Sit thou at my right hand, until I make thine enemies thy footstool," Psa. cx. 1. And this promise was punctually performed to Christ, after his resurrection and ascension, in his supreme exaltation, far above all created beings, in heaven and earth, Eph. i. 20—22. We shall here open two things in the doctrinal part, namely, What is meant by God's right hand; and What is implied in Christ's sitting there, with his enemies for a footstool.

I. What are we to understand here by God's right hand? It is obvious enough, that the expression is not proper, but figurative and borrowed. God hath no hand, right or left; but it is a condescending expression, wherein God stoops to the creature's understanding, and by it he would have us understand honour, power, and nearness.

1. The right hand is the hand of *honour*, where we place those whom we highly esteem and honour. So Solomon placed his mother in a seat at his right hand, 1 Kings ii. 19. So in token of honour, God sets Christ at his right hand; which, on that account, in the text, is called the right hand of Majesty. God hath therein expressed more favour, delight, and honour to Jesus Christ, than ever he did to any creature. "To which of

the angels said he at any time, Sit thou on my right hand?"
Heb. i. 13.

2. The right hand is also the hand of *power;* and the setting
of Christ there, imports his exaltation to the highest authority,
and most supreme dominion. Not that God the Father hath
put himself out of his authority, and advanced Christ above himself; no, "for in that he saith he hath put all things under him,
it is manifest that he is excepted which did put all things under
him," 1 Cor. xv. 27. But to sit as an enthroned King at God's
right hand, imports power, yea, the most sovereign and supreme
power; and so Christ himself calls the right hand at which he
sits; "Hereafter shall ye see the Son of man sitting on the right
hand of power," Matt. xxvi. 64.

3. And as it signifies honour and power, so *nearness* in place,
and so it is applied to Christ, in Psa. cx. 5. "The Lord at thy
right hand shall strike through kings in the day of his wrath;"
that is, the Lord, who is very near thee, present with thee, he
shall subdue thine enemies. This then is what we are to understand by God's right hand, honour, power, and nearness.

II. Let us see what is implied in Christ's sitting at God's
right hand, with his enemies for his footstool.

1. It implies the perfecting and completing of Christ's work,
for which he came into the world. After his work was ended,
then he sat down and rested from those labours. "Every priest
standeth daily ministering and offering oftentimes the same sacrifices, which can never take away sins: but this man, when he
had offered one sacrifice for sins, for ever sat down on the right
hand of God," Heb. x. 11, 12. Here he assigns a double difference between Christ and the levitical priests; they stand,
which is the posture of servants; he sits, which is the posture
of a Lord. They stand daily, because their sacrifices cannot
take away sin; he did his work fully, by one offering; and after
that, sits or rests for ever in heaven.

2. His sitting down at God's right hand, notes the high content and satisfaction of God the Father in him, and in his work.
"The Lord said to my Lord, Sit thou on my right hand;" the
words are brought in as the words of the Father, welcoming
Christ to heaven; and, as it were, congratulating the happy
accomplishment of his most difficult work. He delighted greatly to behold him here in his work on earth, and by a voice from
the excellent glory he told him so, when he spake from heaven
to him, saying, "Thou art my beloved Son, in whom I am well
pleased," 2 Pet. i. 17. And himself tells us, "Therefore doth
my Father love me, because I lay down my life," &c. John x. 17;

for it was a work that the heart of God had been set upon from eternity; he took infinite delight in it.

3. Christ's sitting down at God's right hand in heaven, notes the advancement of Christ's human nature to the highest honour; even to be the object of adoration to angels and men. For it is properly his human nature that is the subject of all this honour and advancement; and being advanced to the right hand of Majesty, it is become an object of worship and adoration. Not simply, as it is flesh and blood, but as it is personally united to the Second Person, and enthroned in the supreme glory of heaven.

Oh here is the mystery, that flesh and blood should ever be advanced to the highest throne of Majesty, and being there installed in that glory, we may now direct our worship to him as God-man; and to this end was his humanity so advanced, that it might be adored and worshipped by all. "The Father hath committed all judgment unto the Son: that all men should honour the Son, even as they honour the Father." And the Father will accept of no honour divided from his honour. Therefore it is added, "He that honoureth not the Son, honoureth not the Father which hath sent him," John v. 22, 23. Hence the apostles, in the salutations of their epistles, beg for grace, mercy, and peace, from God the Father, and our Lord Jesus Christ; and in their valedictions, they desire the grace of our Lord Jesus Christ to the churches.

4. It imports the sovereignty and supremacy of Christ over all. The investiture of Christ with authority over the empire of both worlds: for this belongs to him that sits down upon his throne. When the Father said to him, Sit at my right hand, he did therein deliver to him the dispensation and economy of the kingdom. He put the awful sceptre of government into his hand, and so the apostle interprets and understands it, "He must reign till he hath put all his enemies under his feet," 1 Cor. xv. 25. And to this purpose, the same apostle accommodates (if not expounds) the words of the psalmist, "Thou madest him a little lower than the angels," that is, in respect of his humbled state on earth, "thou crownedst him with glory and honour, and didst set him over the works of thy hands; thou hast put all things in subjection under his feet," Heb. ii. 7, 8. He is over the spiritual kingdom, the church, absolute Lord there, Matt. xxviii. 18—20. He is also Lord over the providential kingdom, the whole world, Psa. cx. 2; and this providential kingdom, being subordinate to his spiritual kingdom, he orders and rules this, for the advantage and benefit thereof, Eph. i. 22.

5. To sit at God's right hand, with his enemies for a foot-

stool, implies Christ to be a Conqueror over all his enemies. To have his enemies under his feet, denotes perfect conquest and complete victory. They trampled his name and his saints under their feet, and Christ will tread them under his feet. It is true indeed this victory is incomplete as yet ; for now " we see not yet all things put under him, (saith the apostle,) but we see Jesus crowned with glory and honour," and that is enough. Enough to show the power of his enemies is now broken ; and though they make some opposition still, yet it is to no purpose at all; for he is so infinitely above them, that they must fall before him; and all the power of God stands ready bent to strike through his enemies, as it is, Psa. cx. 5.

6. Christ sitting in heaven notes to us the great and wonderful change that is made upon the state and condition of Christ, since his ascension into heaven. Ah, it is far otherwise with him now, than it was in the days of his humiliation here on earth. It were good, as a worthy * of ours says, to compare in our thoughts the abasement of Christ, and his exaltation together, as it were in columns, one over against the other. He was born in a stable, but now he reigns in his royal palace. Then he had a manger for his cradle, but now he sits on a chair of state. Then in contempt, they called him the carpenter's son; now he obtains a more excellent name than angels. Then he was led away into the wilderness to be tempted of the devil; now it is proclaimed before him, " Let all the angels of God worship him." Then he had not a place to lay his head on ; now he is exalted to be Heir of all things. In his state of humiliation, " he endured the contradiction of sinners ;" in his state of exaltation, " he is adored and admired by saints and angels." Then " he had no form or comeliness ; and when we saw him, there was no beauty, why we should desire him :" now the beauty of his countenance shall send forth such glorious beams, as shall dazzle the eyes of all the celestial inhabitants round about him, &c.

7. Christ's sitting at God's right hand, implies the advancement of believers to the highest honour: for this session of Christ's respects them, and there he sits as our Representative, in which respect we are made to sit with him in heavenly places, as the apostle speaks, Eph. ii. 6. How secure may we be (saith Tertullian) who do now already possess the kingdom ! meaning in our Head, Christ. Surely, it is matter of exceeding joy to believe that Christ our Head, our flesh and blood, is in all this glory at his Father's right hand. Thus we have opened

* T. Case, Mount Pisgah, part 3. p. 21. An abridgement of it is published by the Religious Tract Society.

the sense and import of Christ's sitting at his Father's right hand. Hence we infer,

1. Is this so great an honour to Christ, to sit enthroned at God's right hand? What honour then is reserved in heaven for those that are faithful to Christ, now on earth! Christ prayed, and his prayer was heard, " that we may be with him to behold the glory that God hath given him," John xvii. 24 ; and what heart can conceive the felicity of such a sight ? It made Stephen's face shine as the face of an angel, when he had but a glimpse of Christ at his Father's right hand. " Thine eyes shall see the king in his beauty," Isa. xxxiii. 17 ; which respected Hezekiah in the type, Christ in the truth. But this is not all, though this be much, to be spectators of Christ in his throne of glory ; we shall not only see him in his throne, but also sit with him enthroned in glory. To behold him is much, but to sit with him is more. This sight you shall have of Christ, will change you into his likeness. " We shall be like him, (saith the apostle,) for we shall see him as he is," 1 John iii. 2. He will place us as it were in his own throne with him. So runs the promise, " To him that overcometh will I grant to sit with me in my throne ; even as I also overcame, and am set down with my Father in his throne," Rev. iii. 21 : and so 2 Tim. ii. 12, " If we suffer we shall also reign with him." The Father set Christ on his right hand, and Christ will set the saints on his right hand. So, you know, the sheep are placed by the angels at the great day, Matt. xxv., and so the church, under the figure of the daughter of Egypt, whom Solomon married, is placed " on the king's right hand, in gold of Ophir," Psa. xlv. This honour have all the saints. Oh what manner of love is this ! These expressions indeed do not intend that the saints shall have a parity of glory with Christ, for in all things he must have the pre-eminence : but they note the great honour that Christ will put upon the saints ; as also, that his glory shall be their glory in heaven ; as the glory of the husband redounds to the wife ; and again, their glory will be his glory, 2 Thess. i. 10, and so it will be a social glory. Oh, it is admirable to think, whither free grace hath already mounted up poor dust and ashes ! to think how nearly related now to this royal, princely Jesus ! But how much higher are the designs of grace, that are not yet come to their parturient fulness, they look beyond all this that we now know ! " Now are we the sons of God, but it doth not yet appear what we shall be," 1 John iii. 2. Ah what reason have you to honour Christ on earth, who is preparing such honours for you in heaven!

2. Is Christ Jesus thus enthroned in heaven ? Then how impossible is it, that ever his interest should miscarry or sink on earth ! The church hath many subtle and potent enemies. True, but as Haman could not prevail against the jews, whilst Esther their friend spake with them to the king, no more can they, whilst our Jesus sits at his and our Father's right hand. Surely, they that touch his people touch the very " apple of his eye," Zech. ii. 8. " He must reign till his enemies are put under his feet," 1 Cor. xv. 25. The enemy under his feet shall not destroy the children in his arms. He sits in heaven on purpose to manage all to the advantage of his church, Eph. i. 22. Are our enemies powerful ? lo, our King sits on the right hand of power. Are they subtle and deep in their contrivance ? He that sits on the throne, overlooks all they do. " He that sits in heaven beholds," and derides their attempts, Psa. ii. 4. He may permit his enemies to straiten them in one place, but it shall be for their enlargement in another. For it is with the church, as it is with the sea; what it loses in one place, it gets in another, and so really loses nothing. He may suffer them also to distress us in outwards, but we shall be recompensed with inward and better mercies ; and so we shall lose nothing by that. A footstool, you know, is useful to him that treads on it, and serves to lift him up higher ; so shall Christ's enemies be to him and his, albeit they think not so. What singular benefits the oppositions of his enemies occasion to his people, I have * elsewhere discovered, to which I may refer my reader ; and pass to,

3. Is Christ set down on the right hand of the Majesty in heaven ? Oh with what awful reverence should we approach him in the duties of his worship ! Away with light and low thoughts of Christ. Away with formal, irreverent, and careless frames in praying, hearing, yea, in conversing and speaking of Christ. Away with all deadness and drowsiness in duties ; for he is a great King with whom you have to do ; a King, to whom the kings of the earth are but as little bits of clay. Lo, the angels cover their faces in his presence. He is an adorable Majesty.

When John had a vision of this enthroned King, about sixty years after his ascension ; such was the overpowering glory of Christ, as the sun when it shineth in its strength, that when he saw him, he fell at his feet as dead ; and died it is likely he had, if Christ had not laid his hand on him, and said, " Fear not ; I am the first and the last ; I am he that liveth, and was dead ; and, behold, I am alive for evermore," Rev. i. 17, 18. When

* A Saint indeed, published by the Religious Tract Society.

he appeared to Saul in the way to Damascus, it was in glory above the glory of the sun, which overpowered him also, and laid him as one dead upon the ground.

Oh that you did but know what a glorious Lord you worship and serve, who makes the very place of his feet glorious, wherever he comes. Surely He is greatly to be feared in the assembly of his saints, and to be had in reverence of all that are round about him. There is indeed a boldness or free liberty of speech allowed to the saints, Eph. iii. 12; but no rudeness or irreverence. We may indeed come, as the children of a king come to their father, who is both their awful Sovereign, and tender Father; which double relation causes a due mixture of love and reverence in their hearts, when they come before him. Though he be your Father, Brother, Friend, yet the distance between him and you is infinite.

4. If Christ be so gloriously advanced in the highest throne, then none need to reckon themselves dishonoured, by suffering the vilest things for his sake. The very chains and sufferings of Christ have glory in them. Hence Moses " esteemed the very reproaches of Christ greater riches than the treasures in Egypt," Heb. xi. 26. He did not, (as one saith,) only endure the reproaches of Christ, but counted them treasures, to be reckoned among his honours and things of value. So Thuanus reports of Ludovicus Marsacus, a noble knight of France, when he was led with other martyrs, that were bound with cords, to execution, and he for his dignity was not bound, he cried, Give me my chain too, let me be a knight of the same order. Disgrace itself is honourable, when it is endured for the Lord of glory. And surely there is (as one says) a little paradise, a young heaven, in sufferings for Christ. If there were nothing else in it, but that they are endured on his account, it would richly reward all we can endure for him; but if we consider how exceeding kind Christ is to them, that count it their glory to be abased for him; that though he be always kind to his people, yet (if we may so speak) he overcometh himself in kindness, when they suffer for him; it will almost make us in love with his reproaches.

5. If Christ sat not down to rest in heaven, till he had finished his work on earth; then it is in vain for us to think of rest, till we have finished our work, as Christ also did his.

How willing are we to find rest here! To dream of that, which Christ never found in this world, nor any ever found before us. Oh think not of resting, till you have done working and done sinning. Your life and your labours must end together. "Write, (saith the Spirit,) Blessed are the dead that die in the Lord, for they rest from their labours," Rev. xiv. 13. Here you must be content to dwell in the tents of Kedar; hereafter you shall be within the curtains of Solomon. Heaven is the place of which it may be truly said, that there the weary be at rest. Oh think not of sitting down on this side heaven. There are four things will keep the saints from sitting down on earth to rest, namely, grace, corruption, devils, and wicked men.

Grace will not suffer you to rest here. Its tendencies are beyond this world. It will be looking and longing for the blessed hope. A gracious person takes himself for a pilgrim, seeking a better country, and is always suspicious of danger in every place and state. It is still beating up the sluggish heart with such language as that, " Arise, depart, this is not thy rest, for it is polluted," Mic. ii. 10. Its further tendencies and continual jealousies, will keep you from sitting long still in this world.

Your *corruptions* also will keep you from rest here. They will continually exercise your spirits, and keep you upon your watch. Saints have their hands filled with work by their own hearts every day, sometimes to prevent sin, and sometimes to lament it; and always to watch and fear, to mortify and kill it. Sin will not long suffer you to be quiet, Rom. vii. 21—23. And if a bad heart will not break your rest here, then,

Satan will do it. He will find you work enough with his temptations and suggestions, and except you can sleep quietly in his arms as the wicked do, there is no rest to be expected. " Your adversary the devil goeth about as a roaring lion, seeking whom he may devour; whom resist," 1 Pet. v. 8.

Nor will his servants and instruments let you be quiet on this side heaven. Their very name speaks their turbulent disposition. " My soul (saith the holy man) is among lions: and I lie even among them that are set on fire, even the sons of men, whose teeth are spears and arrows," Psa. lvii. 4. Well, then, be content to enter into your rest, as Christ did into his.

SERMON XLII.

CHRIST'S ADVENT TO JUDGMENT, BEING THE FOURTH AND LAST DEGREE OF HIS EXALTATION, ILLUSTRATED AND IMPROVED.

ACTS x. 42.

AND HE COMMANDED US TO PREACH UNTO THE PEOPLE, AND TO TESTIFY THAT IT IS HE WHICH WAS ORDAINED OF GOD TO BE THE JUDGE OF QUICK AND DEAD.

CHRIST, enthroned in the highest glory in heaven, is there to abide for the effectual and successful government, both of the world, and of the church, until the number given him by the Father, before the world was, and purchased by the blood of the cross, be gathered in ; and then cometh the judgment of the great day, which will perfectly separate the precious from the vile ; put the redeemed in full possession of the purchase of his blood in heaven ; and " then shall he deliver up the kingdom to his Father, that God may be all in all."

This last act of Christ, namely, his judging the world, is a special part of his exaltation and honour bestowed upon him, " because he is the Son of man," John v. 27. In that day shall his glory, as King, and supreme Lord, shine forth as the sun when it shineth in its strength. Oh what an honour will it be to the man Christ Jesus, who stood arraigned and condemned at Pilate's bar, to sit upon the great white throne, surrounded with thousands and ten thousands of angels ; men and devils waiting upon him to receive the final sentence from his mouth ! In this will the glory of Christ's sovereignty and power be illustriously displayed before angels and men. And this is that great truth which he commanded to be preached and testified to the people, namely, that it is " he which is ordained of God to be the Judge of quick and dead."

Wherein we have three things to be distinctly considered, namely, the subject, object, and fountain of the supreme judiciary authority.

1. The subject of it is Christ, he is ordained to be Judge. Judgment is the act of the whole undivided Trinity. The Father and Spirit judge, as well as Christ, in respect of authority

and consent; but it is the act of Christ, in respect of visible management and execution.

2. The object of Christ's judiciary authority, is the quick and dead, that is, all that at his coming do live, or ever had lived. This is the object personal; all men and women that ever sprang from Adam; all the apostate spirits that fell from heaven, and are reserved in chains to the judgment of this great day. And in this personal object, is included the real object, namely, all the actions, both secret and open, that ever they did, 2 Cor. v. 10; Rom. ii. 16.

3. The Fountain of this delegated authority is God the Father; for he hath ordained Christ to be the Judge. "He is appointed," as the Son of man, to this honourable office and work. The word denotes, a firm establishment of Christ in that office by his Father. He is now, by right of redemption, Lord and King. He enacts laws for government, then he comes to judge of men's obedience and disobedience to his laws.

Hence the point of doctrine is plainly this,

THAT OUR LORD JESUS CHRIST IS ORDAINED BY GOD THE FATHER TO BE THE JUDGE OF QUICK AND DEAD.

This truth stands upon the firm basis of scripture authority. You have it from his own hand, " The Father judgeth no man, but hath committed all judgment unto the Son," John v. 22. And so the apostle, " He hath appointed a day, in the which he will judge the world in righteousness by that man whom he hath ordained," Acts xvii. 31. And again, "In the day when God shall judge the secrets of men by Jesus Christ," Rom. ii. 16. Three things will be opened here. I. The certainty of a judgment to come. II. The quality and nature of it. III. That it is a special part of Christ's exaltation to be appointed Judge in this day.

I. The certainty of a judgment. This is a truth of firmer establishment than heaven and earth. It is no devised fable, no cunning artifice to keep the world in awe; but a thing as confessedly true as it is awfully solemn. For,

1. As the scriptures aforementioned (with these, 2 Cor. v. 10; Eccles. xii. 14; Matt. xii. 36; and many other, the true and faithful sayings of God) do very plainly reveal it; so the justice and righteousness of God require it should be so. For the Judge of all the earth will do right, Gen. xviii. 25. Now righteousness itself requires that a difference be made between the righteous and the wicked : " Say ye to the righteous, It shall

be well with him ; woe to the wicked, it shall be ill with him," Isa. iii. 10, 11. But no such distinction is generally and fully made between one and another in this world. Yea, rather the wicked prosper, and the righteous perish : " There is a just man that perisheth in his righteousness, and there is a wicked man that prolongeth his life in his wickedness," Eccles. vii. 15. Here the " wicked devoureth the man that is more righteous than himself," Hab. i. 13 ; as the fishes of the sea, where the great and strong swallow up the small and weak. And even in courts of judicature, where the innocent might expect relief, there they often meet with the worst oppressions. How fairly and justly therefore doth the wise man infer a judgment to come from this consideration : " I saw under the sun the place of judgment, that wickedness was there ; and the place of righteousness, that iniquity was there. I said in my heart, God shall judge the righteous and the wicked : for there is a time there for every purpose and for every work," Eccles. iii. 16, 17 ; which denotes that the judgment to come is the only relief and support left to poor innocents, to quiet and comfort themselves withal. To the same purpose also is that, " Ye have condemned and killed the just ; and he doth not resist you. Be patient therefore, brethren, unto the coming of the Lord," Jam. v. 6, 7. It is confessed, that sometimes God vindicates his providence against the atheism of the world, by particular strokes upon the wicked ; but this is but rare. And as one of the fathers well observes, " if no sin were punished here, no providence would be believed ; again, if every sin were openly punished here, no judgment hereafter could be expected."

2. Besides, man is a reasonable being, and every reasonable being is an accountable being. He is a subject capable of moral government. His actions have a relation to a law. He is swayed by rewards and punishments. He acts by counsel, and therefore of his actions he must expect to give an account, as it is Rom. xiv. 12, " So then every one of us shall give an account of himself to God." Especially if we add, that all the gifts of body, mind, estate, time, &c. are so many talents, committed and intrusted to him by God, and every one of us hath one talent at least ; therefore a time to render an account for all these talents will come, Matt. xxv. 14, 15. We are but stewards, and stewards must give an account, in order whereto, there must be a great audit day.

3. And what need we seek evidence of this truth, further than our own conscience ? Lo, it is a truth engraven legibly upon every man's own breast. Every one hath a kind of little

tribunal in his own conscience, which both accuses and excuses, for good and evil, which it could never do, were there not a future judgment, of which it is now conscious to itself. In this court, records are now kept of all we do, even of our secret actions and thoughts, which never yet took air. But if no judgment, what need of records? Nor let any imagine, that this may be but the fruit of education and discourse; that we have heard of such things, and so are scared by them. For if so, how comes it to obtain so universally? Who could be the author of such a common deception?

But I shall rather choose, in the

II. place, To open the nature and manner of this judgment, than to spend more time in proving a truth that cannot be denied without violence offered to a man's own light. If then the question be, What manner of judgment will this be? I answer,

1. It will be a great and awful day. It is called the "judgment of the great day," Jude 6. Three things will make it so; the manner of Christ's coming; the work he comes about; and the issues, or events of the work. The manner of Christ's coming will be awfully solemn, "For the Lord himself shall descend from heaven with a shout, with the voice of the archangel, and with the trump of God; and the dead in Christ shall rise first: then we which are alive and remain, shall be caught up together with them in the clouds, to meet the Lord in the air," &c. 1 Thess. iv. 16, 17. Christ shall come forth out of heaven, with the shouts of angels. Above all which (as some expound it) shall the voice of the archangel be distinctly heard. And after this shout, the trump of God shall sound. The dead being raised, they shall be gathered before the great throne on which Christ shall sit in his glory; and there be divided exactly to the right and left hand of Christ, by the angels. Here will be the greatest assembly that ever met; where Adam may see his numerous offspring, even as the sand upon the sea-shore, which no man can number. And never was there such a perfect division made, (how many divisions soever have been in the world,) none was ever like it. The saints shall meet the Lord in the air, and there the Judge shall sit upon the throne, and all the saints round about him; the wicked remaining below upon the earth, there to receive their final doom and sentence.

These preparatives will make it awful; and much more will the work itself, that Christ comes about, make it so. For it is " to judge the secrets of men," Rom. ii. 16; to sever the tares from the wheat ; to make every man's whites and blacks appear ; and according as they are found in that trial, to be sentenced to their everlasting and immutable states. Oh what a solemn thing is this ! And no less will the execution of the sentence on both parts make it a great and solemn day. The heart of man cannot conceive what impressions the voice of Christ, from the throne, will make, both upon believers and unbelievers.

Imagine Christ upon his glorious throne, surrounded with myriads and legions of angels, his royal guard ; a poor unbeliever trembling at the bar ; an exact scrutiny made into his heart and life ; the dreadful sentence given ; and then a cry ; and then his delivering him over to the executioners of eternal vengeance, never, never to see a glimpse of hope or mercy any more.

Imagine Christ, like the general of an army, mentioning with honour, at the head of all the hosts of heaven and earth, all the services that the saints have done for him in this world : then sententially justifying them by open proclamation ; then mounting with him to the third heavens, and entering the gates of that city of God, in that noble train of saints and angels intermixed ; and so for ever to be with the Lord. Oh what a great day must this be !

2. As it will be an awful and solemn judgment, so it will be a critical and exact judgment. The name of the Judge is, the " Searcher of hearts." The Judge hath eyes as flames of fire, which pierce to the dividing of the heart and reins. It is said, Matt. xii. 36, that men shall then " give an account of every idle word that they shall speak." It is a day that will perfectly discriminate the world. No hypocrite can escape. Justice holds the balances in an even hand.

3. It will be a universal judgment, " We must all appear before the judgment-seat of Christ," 2 Cor. v. 10. And, " Every one of us shall give an account of himself to God," Rom. xiv. 12. Both those that are under the law, " and those that, having no law, were a law unto themselves," Rom. ii. 14. Those that had many talents, and he that had but one talent, must appear at this bar ; those that were carried from the cradle to the grave, with him that stooped for age : the rich and poor ; the father and the child ; the master and servant ; the believer and the unbeliever, must stand forth in that day. " I saw the dead, small and great, stand before God, and the books were opened," Rev. xx. 12.

4. It will be a judgment full of convictive clearness. All things will be so sifted to bran, (as we say,) that the sentence

of Christ, both on saints and sinners, shall be applauded. "Righteous art thou, O Lord, because thou hast judged thus." His judgments will be as the light that goeth forth. So that those poor sinners whom he will condemn, shall be first self-condemned. Their own consciences shall be forced to confess, that there is not one drop of injustice in all that sea of wrath, into which they are to be cast.

5. It will be a supreme and final judgment, from which lies no appeal. For it is the sentence of the highest and only Lord. "For as the ultimate resolution of faith is into the word and truth of God, so the ultimate resolution of justice is into the judgment of God." * This judgment is supreme and imperial. For Christ is the only Potentate, 1 Tim. vi. 5; and therefore the sentence once passed, its execution is infallible. And so you find it in that judicial process, Matt. xxv. 46, just after the sentence is pronounced by Christ, it is immediately added, "These shall go away into everlasting punishment, but the righteous into life eternal." This is the judgment of the great day.

III. In the last place, I must inform you, that God, in ordaining Christ to be the Judge, has very highly exalted him. This will be very much for his honour; for in this, Christ's royal dignity will be illustrated, beyond whatever it was since he took our nature, till that day; now he will appear in his glory. For,

1. This act of judging pertaining properly to the kingly office, Christ will be glorified as much in his kingly office, as he hath been in either of the others. We find but some few glimpses of the kingly office breaking forth in this world: as, his riding with hosannas into Jerusalem; his whipping the buyers and sellers out of the temple, his title upon the cross, &c. But these were but faint beams: now that office will shine in its glory, as the sun in the midst of the heavens. For what were the hosannas of little children, in the streets of Jerusalem, to the shouts and acclamations of thousands of angels, and ten thousands of saints? What was his whipping the profane out of the temple, to his turning the wicked into hell, and sending his angels to gather out of his kingdom every thing that offendeth? What was a title written by his judge, and fixed on the ignominious tree, to the name that shall now be seen on his vesture, and on his thigh, King of kings, and Lord of lords.

2. This will be a display of his glory in the highest, before the whole world. For there will be present at once, and together,

* Ad Dei verbum sit ultima resolutio fidei, ad Dei tribunal ultima resolutio judicii.

all the inhabitants of heaven, and earth, and hell: angels must be there to attend and minister; those glittering courtiers of heaven must attend his person; so that heaven will, perhaps, for a time, be left empty of all its inhabitants: men and devils must be there to be judged: and before this great assembly, will Christ appear in royal majesty. He will (to allude to that text, Isa. xxiv. 23) reign before his ancients gloriously. "For he will come to be glorified in his saints, and to be admired in all them that believe," 2 Thess. i. 10.

3. This will roll away for ever the reproach of his death: for Pilate and the high priest, that judged him at their bars, shall now stand quivering at his bar; with Herod that set him at nought, the soldiers and officers that traduced and abused him: there they that reviled him on the cross, wagging their heads, will stand, with trembling knees, before his throne. "For every eye shall see him, and they also that pierced him," Rev. i. 7. So that this will be a full and universal vindication of the death of Christ, from all that contempt and ignominy that had attended it. We next improve it.

Inference 1. Is Jesus Christ ordained of God to be the Judge of quick and dead? Great then is the security believers have, that they shall not be condemned in that day. Who shall condemn, when Christ is Judge? If believers be condemned in judgment, Christ must give sentence against them; yea, and they must condemn themselves too. I say, Christ must give sentence, for that is the proper and peculiar office of Christ. And certainly, no sentence of condemnation shall in that day be given by Christ against them. For,

He died to save them, and he will never cross and overthrow the designs and ends of his own death. That cannot be imagined.

Nay, they have been cleared and absolved already. And being once absolved by Divine sentence, they can never be condemned afterward; for one Divine sentence cannot cross and rescind another. He justified them here in this world by faith; declared in his word, (which shall then be the rule of judgment, Rom. ii. 16,) that "there is no condemnation to them that are in Christ," Rom. viii. 1. And surely he will not retract his own word, and give a sentence quite cross to his own statute-book, out of which he hath told us that they shall be judged.

Moreover, the far greatest part of them will have passed their particular judgment, long before that day, and being therein acquitted by God the Judge of all, and admitted into heaven upon the score and account of their justification, it cannot be imagined that Christ should now condemn them with the world.

Nay, he that judged them, is their Head, Husband, Friend, and Brother; who loved them, and gave himself for them. Oh then, with what confidence may they go, even unto his throne! and say, with Job, "Though he try us as fire, we know we shall come forth as gold." We know that we shall be justified. Especially if we add, that they themselves shall be the assessors with Christ in that day. No, it is not the business of that day to condemn them, but to absolve and pronounce them pardoned and justified, according to the sentence of Acts iii. 19. So that it must needs be a time of refreshing (as all scriptures call it) to the people of God. You that now believe, shall not come into condemnation, John v. 24. You that now judge yourselves, shall not be condemned with the world, 1 Cor. xi. 31, 32.

2. If Christ be ordained of God to be the Judge of quick and dead, how miserable a case will Christless souls be in at that day! They that are Christless now, will be speechless, helpless, and hopeless then. How will their hands hang down, and their knees knock together! Oh what pale faces, quivering lips, fainting hearts, and roaring consciences will be among them in that day! Oh dreadful day! Oh astonishing sight! to see the world in a dreadful conflagration, the elements melting, the stars falling, the earth trembling, the judgment set, the prisoners brought forth! Oh who shall endure this day, but those that by union with Christ are secured against the danger and dread of it!

Let me demand of poor Christless souls, whom this day is likely to take unawares, do you think it possible to avoid appearing, after that terrible citation is given to the world by the trump of God? Alas, how can you imagine it? is not the same power that revived your dust, able to bring you before the bar? There is a necessity that you must come forth, "We *must* all appear," 2 Cor. v. 10. It is not in the sinner's choice, to obey the summons or not.

And if you must appear, are there no accusers, nor witnesses, that will appear against you, and confront you in the court? What think you, was Satan so often a tempter to you here, and will he not be an accuser there? Yes, nothing surer; for that was the main design of all his temptations. What think you of your own consciences? are they not privy to your secret wickedness? do not they now sometimes whisper in your ears, what you do not like to hear of? If they whisper now, they will thunder then, Rom. ii. 15, 16. Will not the Spirit accuse you, for resisting his motions, and stifling thousands of his convictions? Will not your companions in sin accuse you, who drew or were drawn by you to sin? Will not your teachers be your accusers? How many times have you made them complain, Lord, they are iron and brass, they have made their faces harder than a rock; they refuse to return! Will not your very relations be your accusers, to whom you have failed in all your relative duties? Yea, and every one whom you have tempted to sin, abused, defrauded, overreached; all these will be your accusers. So that it is without dispute, you will have accusers enough to appear against you.

Then being accused before Jesus Christ, what will you plead for yourselves? will you confess, or will you deny the charge? If you confess, what need more? "Out of thine own mouth will I judge thee," saith Christ, Luke xix. 22. If you deny, and plead not guilty, thy Judge is the Searcher of hearts, and knows all things. So that it will not at all help thee to make a lie thy last refuge. This will add to the guilt, but not cover it.

If no defence or plea be left thee, then what canst thou imagine should retard the sentence? Why should not Christ go on to that dreadful work? "Must not the Judge of all the earth do right?" Gen. xviii. 25. Must not he render to every man according to his deeds? 2 Cor. v. 10. Yes, no question but he will proceed to that sentence, how terrible soever it be to you to think on it now, or hear it then.

If sentence be once given by Christ against thy soul, what in all the world canst thou imagine should hinder the execution? Will he alter the thing that is gone out of his mouth? No, Psa. lxxxix. 34. Dost thou hope he is more merciful and pitiful than this? Thou mistakest, if you expect mercy out of that way in which he dispenses it. There will be thousands, and ten thousands that will rejoice in, and magnify his mercy then; but they are such as obey his call, repented, believed, and obtained union with his person here; but for unbelievers, it is against the settled law of Christ, and constitution of the gospel, to show mercy to them. But it may be, you think your tears, your cries, your pleadings with him, may move him. These, indeed, might have done somewhat in time, but they come out of season now. Alas! too late. What the success of such pleas and cries will be, you may see if you will but consult two scriptures: Job xxvii. 8, 9, "What is the hope of the hypocrite, though he hath gained, when God taketh away his soul? Will God hear his cry when trouble cometh upon him?" No. And Matt. vii. 22, 23, "Many will say unto me in that day, Lord, Lord, have we not prophesied in thy name, and in thy name have cast out devils, and in thy name have done many wonderful works? And then will I profess unto them, I never knew you; depart from me, ye that work iniquity."

And must it come to this dismal issue with you indeed? God forbid it should. Oh then,

3. If Christ be appointed of God to be the Judge of all, how are all concerned to secure their interest in him, and therein an eternity of happiness to their own souls, by the work of regeneration! Of all the business that men and women have in this world, there is none so solemn, so necessary, and important as this. O, my brethren, this is a work able to drink up your spirits, when you do but think of the consequence of it.

Summon in then thy self-reflecting and considering powers: get alone, reader, and, forgetting all other things, ponder with thyself this deep, dear, eternal concernment of thine. Examine the state of thy own soul. Look into the scriptures, then into thine own heart, and then to heaven, saying, Lord, let me not be deceived in so great a concernment to me as this. Oh let not the trifles of time wipe off the impressions of death, judgment, and eternity from thy heart. Oh that solemn word *eternity*, that it might be night and day with thee; 'that the awe of it may be still upon thy spirit. A lady of this nation, having spent the whole afternoon and a great part of the evening at cards, in mirth and jollity, came home late at night, and finding her waiting maid reading, she looked over her shoulder upon the book, and said, Poor melancholy soul, why dost thou sit here poring so long upon thy book? That night she could not sleep, but lay sighing and weeping: her servant asked her once and again what ailed her; at last she burst out into tears, and said, Oh! it was one word that I cast my eye upon in thy book, that troubles me; there I saw that word, eternity. How happy were I, if I were provided for eternity! Sure it concerns us, seeing we look for such things, to be diligent that we may be found of him in peace. Oh let not that day come by surprise upon you. Remember, that as death leaves, so judgment will find you.

4. Is Jesus Christ appointed Judge of quick and dead? Then look to it, all you that hope to be found of him in peace, that you avoid those sins, and live in the daily practice of those duties, which the consideration of that day powerfully persuades you to avoid or practise. Do you indeed expect such a day? Oh then,

See that you be meek and patient under all injuries and abuses for Christ's sake. Avenge not yourselves, but leave it to the Lord, who will do it. Do not anticipate the work of God. " Be patient, my brethren, to the coming of the Lord," Jam. v. 7, 8. Be communicative, public-hearted christians, studying and devising liberal things for Christ's distressed members ; and you shall have both an honourable remembrance of it, and a full reward of it in that day, Matt. xxv. 34—36. Be watchful and sober, keep the golden bridle of moderation upon all your affections ; and see that you be not overcharged with the cares and love of this present life, Luke xxi. 34, 35. Will you that your Lord come and find you in such a posture? Oh " let your moderation be known unto all men. The Lord is at hand," Phil. iv. 5. Improve all your Master's talents diligently and carefully. Then must you make up your account for them all.

But, above all, be sincere in your profession. Let your hearts be found in God's statutes, that you may never be ashamed ; for this day will be the day of manifestation of all hidden things. And nothing is so secret, but that day will reveal it : " Beware of hypocrisy ; for there is nothing covered, that shall not be revealed ; neither hid, that shall not be known," Luke xii. 1, 2.—Thus I have finished, through Divine aids, the whole doctrine of the impetration of redemption by Jesus Christ ; we shall wind up the whole in a general exhortation, and I have done.

And now, to close up all, let me persuade all those for whom the dear Son of God came from the blessed bosom of the Father ; assumed flesh ; and laid down his own life a ransom for their souls ; for whom he lived, died, rose, ascended, and lives for ever in heaven to intercede—to live wholly to Christ, as Christ lived and died wholly for them.

Oh brethren, never was the heathen world acquainted with such arguments to deter them from sin, never acquainted with such motives to urge them to holiness, as I shall now acquaint you with. My request is, to give up both your hearts and lives to glorify the Father, Son, and Spirit, whose you are, by the holiness and heavenliness of them. Greater things are expected from you than from other men. See that you turn not all this grace into wantonness. Think not because Christ hath done so much for you, you may sit still ; much less indulge yourselves in sin, because Christ offered up such an excellent sacrifice for the expiation of it. No, though Christ came to be a curse, he did not come to be a cloak for your sins. " If one died for all, then were all dead ; that they that live, should not henceforth live to themselves, but unto him that died for them," 2 Cor. v. 14, 15. Oh keep your lives pure and clean. " If you live in the Spirit, see that you walk in the Spirit," Gal. v. 25 ; that is, (saith

Cornelius a Lapide,) " Let us shape and order our lives and actions according to the dictates, instinct, and impulses of the Spirit, and of that grace of the Spirit put within us, and planted in our hearts, which tendeth to practical holiness."   Oh let the grace which is in your hearts, issue out into all your religious, civil, and natural actions.   Let the faith that is in your hearts appear in your prayers ; the obedience of your hearts, in hearing ; the meekness of your hearts, in suffering ; the mercifulness of your hearts, in distributing ; the truth and righteousness of your hearts, in trading ; the sobriety and temperance of your hearts, in eating and drinking.   These are the fruits of Christ's sufferings indeed, they are sweet fruits.   Let grace refine, ennoble, and elevate all your actions ; that you may say, " Truly our conversation is in heaven."   Let grace have the ordering of your tongues, and of your hands ; the moulding of your whole conversation.   Let not humility appear in some actions, and pride in others ; holy seriousness in some companies, and vain frothiness in others.   Suffer not the fountain of corruption to mingle with, or pollute the streams of grace.   But be you in the fear of the Lord all the day long.   Let there be a due proportion between all the parts of your conversation.   Approve yourselves the servants of Christ in all things.   " By pureness, by knowledge, by long-suffering, by the Holy Ghost, by love unfeigned, by the word of truth, by the power of God, by the armour of righteousness on the right hand and on the left," 2 Cor. vi. 6, 7. See then how accurately you walk.—Cut off occasion from them that desire occasion ; and in well doing commit yourselves to God, and commend religion to the world.   That this is your great concernment and duty, I shall evidence to your consciences, by these following considerations.   That of all persons in the world, the redeemed of the Lord are most obliged to be holy ; and most assisted for a life of holiness ; and that God intends to make great use of their lives, both for the conviction and conversion of others.

I. Consider, God hath more obliged them to live pure and strict lives.   I know the command obliges all men to it : even those that cast away the cords of the commands, and break Christ's bonds asunder, are yet bound by them ; and cannot plead a dispensation to live as they do.   Yea, and it is not unusual for them to feel the obligations of the command upon their consciences, even when their impetuous lusts hurry them on to the violation of them.   But there are special ties upon your souls, that oblige you to holiness more than others. Many special and peculiar engagements you are under from

God, from yourselves, from your brethren, and from your enemies.

1. God hath peculiarly obliged you to purity and strictness of life. Yea, every Person in the blessed Trinity hath cast his cord over your souls, to bind up your hearts and lives to the most strict and precise obedience of his commands.

(1.) The Father hath obliged you, and that not only by the common tie of creation, which is yet of great efficacy in itself; for, is it reasonable that God should create and form so excellent a piece, and that it should be employed against him? that he should plant the tree, and another eat the fruit of it? But, besides this common engagement, he hath obliged you to holiness of life,

[1.] By his wise and merciful designs and counsels for your recovery and salvation by Jesus Christ. It was he that laid the corner-stone of your salvation with his own hands. The first motion sprang out of his breast. If God had not designed the Redeemer for you, the world had never seen him. It was the act of the Father to give you to the Son to be redeemed, and then to give the Son to be a Redeemer to you. Both of them stupendous and astonishing acts of grace. And in both God acted as a most free Agent. Oh how much owest thou to the Lord for this! And what an engagement doth it leave upon thy soul, to obey, please, and glorify him!

[2.] By his bountiful remunerations of your obedience, which have been wonderful. What service didst thou ever perform for him, for which he hath not paid thee a thousand times more than it is worth. Didst thou ever seek him diligently, and not find him a bountiful Rewarder? Didst thou ever give a cup of cold water in the name of a disciple, and not receive a disciple's reward? Matt. x. 42. Hast thou not found inward peace and comfort flowing into thy soul, upon every piece of sincere obedience? Oh what a good Master do the saints serve! You that are remiss and inconstant in your obedience, you that are heartless and cold in duties, hear how your God expostulates with you: "Have I been a wilderness to Israel, a land of darkness?" Jer. ii. 31. *q. d.* Have I been a hard Master to you? Have you any reason to complain of me? Are fruits of sin like fruits of obedience? Do you know where to find a better master? Why then are you so shuffling and inconstant, so sluggish and remiss in my work? Surely God is not behind-hand with any of you. May you not say with David, "This I had, because I kept thy precepts?" Psa. cxix. 56. There are fruits in holiness, even present fruit. It is a high favour to be employed for God; reward enough that he will accept any thing thou dost. But to return every duty thou dost perform to him with such comforts, such quickenings, such inward and outward blessings into thy bosom, so that thou mayest open the treasury of thine own experiences, view the variety of encouragements and tokens of his love, at several times received in duties; and say, This I had, and that I had, by waiting on God and serving him—oh what an engagement is this upon thee to be ever abounding in the work of the Lord! Though thou must not work for wages, yet God will not let thy work go unrewarded. For he is not unrighteous to forget your work and labour of love.

[3.] Your Father hath further obliged you to holiness and purity of life, by signifying to you (as he hath frequently done) the great delight and pleasure he hath therein. He hath told you, " that such as are upright in the way are his delight," Prov. xi. 20. That he would have you " forget not to do good, and to communicate, for with such sacrifices he is well pleased," Heb. xiii. 16. You know you cannot " walk worthy of the Lord to all pleasing," except " ye be fruitful in every good word and work," Col. i. 10. And what a bond is this upon you to live holy lives! Can you please yourselves in displeasing your Father? If you have the hearts of children in you, surely you cannot. Oh you cannot grieve his Spirit by loose and careless walking, but you must grieve your own spirits too. How many times hath God pleased you, gratified and contented you, and will you not please and content him? In many things the Lord hath wonderfully condescended to please you, and now there is but one thing that he desires of you, and that most reasonable, yea, beneficial for you, as well as pleasing to him; " Only let your conversation be as it becometh the gospel of Jesus Christ," Phil. i. 27. This is the one thing, the great and main thing he expects from you in this world; and will not you do it? Can you expect he should gratify your desires, when you make no more of grieving and displeasing him? Well, if you know what will please God, and yet resolve not to do it, but will rather please your flesh, and gratify the devil than him; pray pull off your vizards, fall into your own rank among hypocrites, and appear as indeed you are.

[4.] The Father hath further obliged you to strictness and purity of conversation, by his gracious promises made to such as so walk. He hath promised to do great things for you, if you will " order your conversation aright," Psa. l. 23. He will be your sun and shield, if you walk before him and be upright, Gen. xv. 1. " He will give grace and glory, and no good thing will he withhold from him that walketh uprightly," Psa. lxxxiv. 11

And he promises no more to you than he hath made good to others that have thus walked, and stands ready to perform to you also.   If you look to enjoy the good of the promise, you are obliged by all your expectations and hopes to order your lives purely and uprightly.   This hope will set you on work to purge your lives, as well as your hearts, from all pollutions: " Having these promises, let us cleanse ourselves from all filthiness of the flesh and spirit, perfecting holiness in the fear of God," 2 Cor. vii. 1.

[5.] Yea, He hath yet more obliged you to strict and holy lives, by his confidence in you, that you thus walk and please him.   He expresseth himself in scripture, as one that dares trust you with his glory, knowing that you will be tender of it, and dare not do otherwise.   But if a man repose confidence in you, and trust you with his concerns, it greatly obliges you to be faithful.   What an engagement was that upon Abraham to walk uprightly, when God said of him, " I know him, that he will command his children and his household after him, and they shall keep the way of the Lord," Gen. xviii. 19 : *q. d.* As for this wicked generation, whom I will speedily consume in my wrath, I know they regard not my laws, they will trample my commands under their feet, they care not how they provoke me, but I expect other things from Abraham, and I am confident he will not fail me. I know him, he is a man of another spirit, and what I promise myself from him, he will make good.   And to the like purpose is that in Isa. lxiii. 7.   " I will mention the loving-kindness of the Lord, and the praises of the Lord, according to all that the Lord hath bestowed on us, and the great goodness toward the house of Israel, which he hath bestowed on them, according to his mercies, and according to the multitude of his loving-kindnesses.   For he said, Surely they are my people, children that will not lie (or fail me) : so he was their Saviour."   Here you have an ample account of the endearing mercies of God to that people, ver. 7, and the Lord's confident expectations of suitable returns from them, ver. 8. I said, that is, (speaking after the manner of men in like cases,) I made a full account, that after all these endearments and favours bestowed upon them, they would not offer to be disloyal and false to me. I have made them sure enough to myself, by so many bonds of love.   Like to which is that expression, " I said, Surely thou wilt fear me, thou wilt receive instruction," Zeph. iii. 7.   Oh how great are the expectations of God from such as you !

(2.) You are further engaged to this precise and holy life, by what the Son hath done for you. Is not this pure and holy life the very aim and next end of his death? Did he not shed his blood to " redeem you from your vain conversations?" 1 Pet. i. 18. Was not this the design of all his sufferings? " That being delivered out of the hands of your enemies, you might serve him in righteousness and holiness all the days of your life," Luke i. 74, 75. And is not the apostle's inference, 2 Cor. v. 14, 15, highly reasonable? " If one died for all, then were all dead: and that he died for all, that they which live should not henceforth live unto themselves, but unto him that died for them." Did Christ only buy your persons, and not your services also? No, whoever hath thy time, thy strength, or any part of either, I can assure thee, christian, that Christ hath paid for it, and thou givest away what is none of thine own to give. Every moment of thy time is his; every talent, whether of grace or nature, is his; and dost thou defraud him of his own? Oh how liberal are you of your precious words and hours, as if Christ had never made a purchase of them! Oh think of this, when thy life runs muddy and foul. When the fountain of corruption flows out at thy tongue, in idle, frothy discourse; or at thy hand, in sinful, unwarrantable actions; doth this become the redeemed of the Lord? Did Christ come from the bosom of his Father for this? Did he endure the cross, and lay down his life for this? Was he so well pleased with all his sorrows and sufferings, his pangs and agonies, upon the account of that satisfaction he should have in seeing the travail of his soul? Isa. liii. 11. And doth not this engage you to look to your lives, and keep them pure? Oh! what will engage you if this will not? But,

(3.) This is not all; as a man, when he weigheth a thing, casteth in weight after weight, till the scales are counterpoised; so doth God cast in engagement after engagement, and argument upon argument, till thy heart, christian, be weighed up and won to this heavenly light. And therefore, as Elihu said to Job, " Suffer me a little, and I will show thee what I have yet to speak on God's behalf," chap. xxxvi. 22. Some arguments have already been urged on the behalf of the Father and Son, for purity and holiness of life; and next I have something to plead on the behalf of the Spirit. I plead now on his behalf, who hath so many times helped you to plead for yourselves with God. He that hath so often refreshed, quickened, and comforted you, he will be quenched, grieved, and displeased by an impure, loose, and careless conversation; and what will you do then? Who shall comfort you when the Comforter is departed from you? When he that should relieve your souls is far off? Oh " grieve not the holy Spirit of God, whereby you are sealed to the day of redemption," Eph. iv. 30. There is nothing grieves him more than impure practices, for he is a holy Spirit. As water damps and quenches the fire, so doth sin quench the Spirit, 1 Thess. v. 19. Will you quench the warm affections and burning desires which he hath kindled in your bosoms? If you do, it is a question whether ever you may recover them again to your dying day. The Spirit is grieved when thy corruptions within are stirred by temptations, and break out to the defiling of thy life; then is the holy Spirit of God, as it were, made sad and heavy within thee, as that expression, μη λυπειτε, Eph. iv. 30, may be rendered. Eor thereby thou resistest his motions, whereby in the way of a loving constraint he would lead and guide thee in the way of thy duty; yea, thou not only resistest his motions, but crossest his grand design, which is to purge and sanctify thee wholly, and build thee up more and more to the perfection of holiness. And when thou thus forsakest his conduct, and crossest his design in thy soul, then doth he usually withdraw as a man that is grieved by the unkindness of his friend.

This is the fruit of careless and loose walking. To this sad issue it will bring thee at last, and when it is come to this, thou shalt go to ordinances, and duties, and find no good in them; no life-quickening comfort there. When thy heart, which was wont to be enlarged, and flowing, shall be clung up and dry; when, like Samson, thou shalt go forth and shake thyself, as at other times, but thy strength is gone; then tell me, what thou hast done in resisting, quenching, and grieving the holy Spirit of God by impure and offensive practices? And thus you see what engagements lie upon you from the Spirit also to walk uprightly, and keep the issues of life pure. Thus God hath obliged you to circumspect and holy lives.

2. You are under great engagements to keep your lives pure, even from yourselves, as well as from your God. As God hath bound you to purity of conversation, so you have bound yourselves. And there are several things in you, and done by you, which wonderfully increase and strengthen your obligations to practical holiness.

(1.) Your clearer illumination is a strong bond upon your souls: " Ye were sometimes darkness, but now ye are light in the Lord; walk as children of light," Eph. v. 8. You cannot pretend or plead ignorance of your duty. You stand convinced in your own consciences before God, that this is your unquestionable duty. Christians, will you not all yield to this? I know you readily yield. We live, indeed, in a contentious, disputing age. In other things, our opinions are different. One chris-

tian is of this judgment, another of that ; but in this we all meet
and close in oneness of mind and judgment, that it is our indis-
putable duty to live pure, strict, and holy lives.   The grace of
God, which hath appeared to you, hath taught you this truth
clearly, and convincingly, Tit. ii. 11, 12.   "You have received
how you ought to walk, and to please God," 1 Thess. iv. 1.
Well then, this being yielded, the inference is plain and undeniable; that you cannot walk as others, in the vanity of their
mind, but you must offer violence to your own light. You cannot suffer the corruptions of your hearts to break forth into practice, but you must slight and put by the notices and rebukes of
your own consciences : " He that knoweth to do good, and doeth
it not, to him it is sin," Jam. iv. 17 ; yea, aggravated sin ;
sin of a deeper tincture than that of heathens ; sin that sadly
wastes and violates conscience.   Certainly, whoever hath, you
have no cloak for your sin.   Besides, what pleasure in sin can
you have ? Indeed, such as for want of light know not what
they do, or such, whose consciences are seared, and past feeling ;
they may seek a little pleasure (such as it is) out of sin; but
what content or pleasure can you have, so long as your light is
ever breaking in upon you, and smiting you for what you do ? '
This greatly increases your obligation to a precise, holy life.

(2.) Again, you are professors of holiness. You have given in
your names to Christ, to be his disciples; and by this your engagements to a life of holiness are yet further strengthened :
" Let every one that nameth the name of Christ, depart from
iniquity," 2 Tim. ii. 19.   The name of Christ is called upon
you, and it is a worthy name, Jam. ii. 7.   It is called upon you,
as the name of the husband is called upon his wife : " Let thy
name be called upon us," Isa. iv. 1.   Or, as the name of a
Father is called upon his child : " Let my name be called on
them, and the name of my fathers," Gen. xlviii. 16. Well then,
you bear the name of Christ as his spouse or children ; and will
you not live suitably to your name ? Oh how will that worthy
name of Christ be blasphemed through you, if you adorn it not
with becoming deportment ? Better you had never professed any
thing, than to set yourselves by your profession in the eye and
observation of the world, and then to pour contempt on Jesus
Christ, by your scandalous conversation, before the eyes of the
world. Oh, that is a heavy charge, " Through you is the name
of God blasphemed among the heathens," Rom. ii. 24.   Unhappy man ! that ever thou shouldst be a reproach to Christ !
The herd of wicked men are men of no note or observation.
They may sin, and sin again ; drink, swear, and tumble in all

uncleanness, and it passes away silently; the world takes little notice of it. Their wicked actions make but little noise in the world; but the miscarriages of professors are like a blazing comet, or an eclipsed sun, which all men gaze at, and make their observations upon. Oh then, what manner of persons ought you to be, who bear the worthy name of Christ upon you!

(3.) But more than this, you have obliged yourselves to this life of holiness by your own prayers. How many times have you lifted up your hands to heaven, and cried with David, "O that my ways were directed to keep thy statutes! Order my steps in thy word: and let not any iniquity have dominion over me," Psa. cxix. 5. 133. Were you in earnest with God, when you thus prayed? Did you mean as you said? Or did you only compliment with God? If your hearts and tongues agreed in this request, doubtless it is as much your duty to endeavour, as to desire those mercies; and, if not, yet do all these prayers stand on record before the Lord, and will be produced against you as witnesses to condemn you, for your hypocrisy and vanity. How often also have you in your prayers lamented and bewailed your careless and uneven walkings! You have said with Ezra, "O my God, I am ashamed, and even blush to look up unto thee," chap. ix. 6. And do not your confessions oblige you to greater circumspection and care for time to come? Will you confess and sin; and sin and confess? go to God and bewail your evils, and when you have bewailed them, return again to the commission of them? God forbid you should thus dissemble with God, play with sin, and dye your iniquities with a deeper tincture.

(4.) To add no more, you have often reproved or censured others for their miscarriages and falls, which adds to your own obligation, to walk accurately, and evenly. Have you not often reproved your erring brethren? or at least privately censured them, if not duly reproved them, (for to these left-handed blows of secret censurings, we are more apt, than to the fair and open strokes of just and due reproofs,) and will you practise the same things you criminate and censure others for? "Thou that teachest another," saith the apostle, "teachest thou not thyself?" Rom. ii. 21. So say I, thou that censurest or rebukest another, condemnest thou not thyself? Will your rebukes ever do good to others, whilst you allow in yourselves what you condemn in them? And as these reproofs and censures can do them no good, so they do you much evil: by reason of them you are self-condemned persons; and out of your own mouths God will judge you. For you need no other witness than yourselves in this case. Your own tongues will fall upon you. Your censures and reproofs of others will leave you without plea or apology, if you look not to your lives with greater care. And yet will you be careless still? Fear you not the displeasure of God; nor the wounding and disquieting your own consciences? Surely, these things are of no light value with you, if you be christians indeed.

3. You are yet further engaged to practical holiness upon the account of your brethren, who are not a little concerned and interested therein. For if, through the neglect of your hearts, your lives be defiled and polluted, this will be thrown in their faces, and many innocent and upright ones both reproached. and grieved upon your account. This mischievous effect holy David earnestly deprecated: " O God, thou knowest my foolishness, and my sins are not hid from thee. Let not them that wait on thee, O Lord God of hosts, be ashamed for my sake : let not those that seek thee, be confounded for my sake, O God of Israel," Psa. lxix. 5, 6. *q. d.* Lord, thou knowest what a weak and foolish creature I am, and how apt to miscarry, if left to myself; and should I, through my foolishness, act unbecoming a saint, how would this shame the faces and sadden the hearts of thy people ! They will be as men confounded at the report of my fall. The fall of one christian is matter of trouble and shame to all the rest. Thy loose and careless life will cause them to estrange themselves from thee, and look shy upon thee, as being ashamed to own thee, and canst thou bear that ? will it not grieve and pierce your very hearts to see a cloud of strangeness and trouble over the countenances of your brethren ; to see yourselves disowned and lightly esteemed by them ?

This very consideration struck a great favourite in the persian court to the very heart. * It was Ustazanes, who had been governor to Sapores in his minority. And this man for fear denied the christian faith, and complied with the idolatrous worship of the king. And one day (saith the historian) sitting at the court-gate, he saw Simon, the aged archbishop of Seleucia, drawn along to prison, for his constancy in the christian faith ; and, though he durst not openly own the christian faith he had so basely denied, and confess himself a christian, yet he could not choose but rise, and express his reverence to this holy man, in a respectful and honourable salutation ; but the zealous good man frowned upon him, and turned away his face from him, as thinking such an apostate unworthy of the least respect from him. This presently struck Ustazanes to the heart, and drew from him many tears and groans ; and thus he reasoned with himself:

* Sozomen, lib. 2. cap. 8.

Simon will not own me, and can I think but that God will disclaim me, when I appear before his tribunal? Simon will not speak unto me, will not so much as look upon me, and can I look for so much as a good word or look from Jesus Christ, whom I have so shamefully betrayed and denied? Hereupon he threw off his rich courtly robes, and put on mourning apparel, and professed himself a christian, and died a martyr. Oh it is a piercing thing to an honest heart, to be cast out of the favour of God's people. If you walk loosely, neither God nor his people will look kindly upon you.

4. Your very enemies engage you to this pure and holy life, upon a double ground, namely, as they are your bold censurers, and your watchful observers. They censure you as hypocrites, and will you give them ground and matter for such a charge? They say, only your tongues are more holy then other men's; and shall they prove it from your practice? They also observe you diligently, and are highly gratified by your miscarriages. If your lives be loose and defiled, you will not only be a shame to your friends but the song of your enemies. You will gratify all the enemies of God. This is that they watch for. They are curious observers of your goings. And that which makes them triumph at your falls and miscarriages, is not only that deep-rooted enmity between the two seeds, but because all your miscarriages and evils are so many absolutions to their consciences, and justifications (as they think) of their ways and practices. For, as your strictness and holiness doth, as it were, condemn them, as Noah, by his practice, condemned the world, Heb. xi. 7; so when you fall, you, as it were, absolve their consciences, loose the bonds of conviction you had made fast upon them, and now there is matter of joy put before them. Oh, say they, whatever these men talk, we see they are no better than we. They can do as we do. They can cozen and cheat for advantage. They can comply with any thing for their own ends: it is not conscience, as we once thought, but mere stomach and humour, that made them so precise. And oh! what a sad thing is this! hereby you shed soul-blood. You fasten the bonds of death upon their souls. You kill those convictions, which, for any thing you know, might have made way to their conversion. When you fall, you may rise again; but they may fall at your example, and never rise more, never have a good opinion of the ways of God, or of his people any more. Upon this consideration, David begs of God, " Lead me, O Lord, in thy righteousness, because of mine enemies," (or, as the hebrew, my observers,) " make thy way straight before my face,"

Psa. v. 8. And thus you see how your very enemies oblige you to this holy and pure conversation also.

Now put all this together, and see to what these particulars will amount. What think you of all this? Are you obliged or not to this purity of life? Are all these bonds so tied, that you can get loose, and free yourselves at pleasure from them? If all these things are of no force with you, if none of these bonds can hold you, may it not be questioned, (notwithstanding your profession,) whether any spiritual principle, any fear of God, or love to Christ, be in your souls or no? Oh, you could not play fast and loose with God, if so; you could not, as Samson, snap these bonds asunder at your pleasure.

II. Consider, as you are more obliged to keep the issues of life pure than others are, so God hath given you greater assistances and advantages for it than others have. God hath not been wanting to any in helps and means. Even the heathen, who are without the gospel, will be yet speechless and inexcusable before God; but how much more will you be so, who, besides the light of nature, and the general light of the gospel, have,—such a principle put within you,—such patterns set before you,—such an Assistant ready to help you,—so many rods to quicken you and prevent your wandering; if notwithstanding all these helps, your life be still unholy.

1. Shall men of such *principles* walk as others do? Shall we lament for you, as David once did for Saul, saying, " There the shield of the mighty was vilely cast away, the shield of Saul; as though he had not been anointed with oil." There the honour of a christian was vilely cast away, as though he had not been anointed with the Spirit? " You have received an unction from the Holy One, which teacheth you all things," 1 John ii. 20; another Spirit, far above that which is in other men, 1 Cor. ii. 12. And as this spirit which is in you, is fitted for this life of holiness, (" for ye are his workmanship, created in Christ Jesus unto good works," Eph. ii. 10,) so this holy spirit, or principle, infused into your souls, hath such a natural tendency to this holy life, that if you live not purely and strictly, you must offer violence to your own principles and new nature.

This principle affords you a twofold help for a life of holiness. It pulls you back from sin, as in Joseph; " How can I do this great wickedness, and sin against God?" And it also inclines you powerfully to obedience. It is a curb to sin, and a spur to holiness. It is impossible for others to live spiritually and heavenly, because they have no new nature to incline them hereunto. And, methinks, it should be hard for you to live carnally, and sensually, and therein cross the very bent and tendency of the new creature, which is formed in you. How can you neglect prayer, as others do, whilst the Spirit, by divine pulsations, is awaking and rousing up your sluggish hearts with such inward motions and whispers, as that, Psa. xxvii. 8, "Seek my face;" yea, whilst you feel (during your omissions of duty) something within that bemoans itself, and, as it were, cries for food, and will not let you be quiet, till it be relieved? How can you let out your hearts to the world, as other men do, when all that while your spirit is restless, and aches like a bone out of joint? And you can never be at ease, till you come back to God, and say, as Psa. cxvi. 7, "Return unto thy rest, O my soul." Is it not hard, yea, naturally impossible, to fix a stone, and make it abide in the fluid air? Doth not every creature, in a restless motion, tend to its proper centre, and desire its own perfection? So doth this new creature also. You see how the rivers in their course will not be checked, but bear down all the obstacles in their way; a stop doth but make them rage the more, and run the swifter afterwards.

There is a central force in these natural motions, which cannot be stopped. And the like may you observe, in the motions of a renewed soul: "It shall be in him a well of water springing up," John iv. 14. And is it not hard for you to keep it down, or turn its course? How hard did Jeremiah and David find that work? If you do not live holy lives, you must cross your own new nature, and violate the law that is written in your own hearts. To this purpose a late * writer speaks: Till you were converted, (saith he,) the flesh was predominant, and therefore it was impossible for you to live any other than a fleshly life; for every thing will act according to its predominant principle. Should you not therefore live a spiritual life? Should not the law of God, written in your hearts, be legible in your lives? Oh should not your lives be according to the tendency of your hearts? Doubtless this is no small advantage to practical holiness. But,

2. Besides this principle within, you have no small assistance for the purity of life, by these excellent patterns before you. The path of holiness is no untrodden path. Christ and his servants have beaten it before you. The life of Christ is your copy, and it is a fair copy indeed, without a blot. Oh what an advantage is this, to draw all the lines of your actions ac-

* Mr. T. Mall's Exhortation to Holy Living.

cording to his example ! This glorious, grand example is often pressed upon for your imitation : "Looking unto Jesus," Heb. xii. 2; he hath left you an example, that ye should tread in his steps, 1 Pet. ii. 21. His life is a living rule to his people; and besides Christ's example, (for you may say, Who can live as Christ did ? his example is quite above us,) you have a cloud of witnesses ; and these men of like passions, temptations, and constitutions with you ; who have gone before you in exemplary holiness. The Holy Ghost (intending therein your special help and advantage) hath set many industrious pens to work, to write the lives of the saints, and preserve for your use their holy sayings and heavenly actions. He bids you " take them for an example," James v. 10. Oh ! what excellent men are passed on before you ! what renowned worthies have led the way ! Men, whose conversations were in heaven, whilst they tabernacled on earth. Whilst this lower world had their bodies, the world above had their hearts, and their affections. Their actions and their designs were all for heaven. Men that improved troubles and comforts, losses and gains, smiles and frowns, and all for heaven; their hearts were full of heavenly meditations, their mouths of heavenly communications, and their practices of heavenly inclinations. Oh what singular help is this ! Where they followed Christ, and kept the way, they are propounded for your imitation ; and where any of them turned aside, you have a mark set upon that action for your caution and prevention. Doth any strange or unusual trial befall you ? Here you may see " the same affliction accomplished in your brethren," 1 Pet. v. 9. Here is a store of good company to encourage you. Do the world and the devil endeavour to turn you from your duty, by loading it with shameful scoffs, or sufferings ? In this case you may look to Jesus, who despised the shame ; and to your brethren, who counted it their honour to be dishonoured for the name of Christ, Acts v. 41. Is it a dishonour to thee, to be ranked with Abraham, Moses, David, and such as were the glory of the ages they lived in ? Art thou at any time under a fit of discouragement, and ready to despond under any burden ? Oh, how mayest thou be animated by such examples, when such a qualm comes over thy heart ! Some sparks of their holy courage cannot but steal into thy breast, whilst thou considerest them. In them God hath set before thee the possibility of overcoming all difficulties ; thou seest men of the same mould, who had the same trials, discouragements, and fears, that now thou hast, and yet overcame all. How is thy unbelief checked, when thou sayest, Oh ! I shall never reach the end, I shall one day utterly perish! Why dost thou say so? Why may not such a poor creature as thou art, be carried through as well as they? Had not they the same temptations and corruptions with you? Were they not all troubled with an evil heart, an insnaring world, and a busy devil, as well as you? Alas! when they put on the divine, they did not put off the human nature; but complained, and feared, as you do; and yet were carried through all.

Oh what an advantage have you this way! They that first trusted in Christ, had not such helps as you. You have the benefit of their experiences. You that are fallen into the last times, have certainly the best helps to holiness; and yet, will not you live strictly and purely? Will you put on the name and profession of christians, and yet be lofty in your spirits, earthly in your designs, negligent of duty, frothy in your communications? Pray, from which of all the saints did you learn to be proud? Did you learn that from Christ, or any of his? From which of his saints did you learn to be earthly and covetous, passionate or censorious, overreaching and crafty? If you have read of any such evils committed by them, have you not also read of their shame and sorrow, their repentance and reformation? If you have found any such blots in their lives, it was left there designedly to prevent the like in yours. Oh what a help to holiness is this!

3. You have not only a principle within you, and a pattern before you, but you have also an omnipotent Assistant to help, and encourage you throughout your way. Are you feeble and infirm? and is every temptation, even the weakest, strong enough to turn you out of the way of your duty? Lo, God hath sent his Spirit to help your infirmities, Rom. viii. 26. No matter then how weak you are, how many and mighty your difficulties and temptations are, as long as you have such an Assistant to help you. Great is your advantage for a holy life this way also. For,

(1.) When a temptation to sin presses sore upon you, he pleads with your conscience within, whilst Satan is tempting without. How often hath he brought such scriptures to your remembrance, at the very opportunity, as have saved you out of the temptation! If you attend to his voice, you may hear such a voice within you, as that, " Oh, do not this abominable thing which I hate, " Jer. xliv. 4. To this purpose is that promise, " Thine eyes shall behold thy teachers: and thine ears shall hear a word behind thee, saying, This is the way, walk ye in it, when ye turn to the right hand, and when ye turn to the left,"

Isa. xxx. 20, 21.   Here you have a twofold help to holiness, the outward teaching of the word, verse 20, and the inward teachings of the Spirit, verse 21.   He shall say, This is the way, when ye are turning aside to the right hand, or to the left.   Alluding to a shepherd, saith one, who, driving his sheep before him, whistles them in, when he sees them ready to stray.

(2.) When ye walk holily and closely with God in your duties, and the Spirit encourages you to go on, by those inward comforts, sealings, and joys, you have from him at such times ; how often does he entertain your souls in public ordinances, in private duties, with his hidden manna, with marrow and fatness, with incomparable and unspeakable comforts, and all this to strengthen you in your way, and encourage you to hold on.

(3.) When you are indisposed for duties, and find your hearts empty and dry, he is ready to fill them, quicken and raise them ; so that oftentimes the beginning and end of your prayers, hearing, or meditations, are as vastly different, as if one man had begun, and another ended the duty.   Oh then, what assistances for a holy life have you ! Others indeed are bound to resist tempt-'ations, as well as you; but, alas ! having no special assistance from the Spirit, what can they do ? It may be, they reason with temptation a little while, and in their own strength resolve against it ; but how easy a conquest doth Satan make where no greater opposition is made to him than this ! Others are bound to hear, meditate, and pray, as well as you ; else the neglect of those duties would not be their sin ; but, alas ! what pitiful work do they make of it, being left to the hardness and vanity of their own hearts ! When you spread your sails, you have a gale, but they lie wind-bound, heart-bound, and can do nothing spiritually in a way of duty.

4. You have a further advantage to this holy life, by all the rods of God that are at any time upon you.   I might show you in many particulars, your advantages in' this way also, but I shall only present these three to your observation at this time.

(1.) By these you are clogged to prevent your straying and wandering.   Others may wander even as far as hell, and God will not spend a sanctified rod upon them, to reduce or stop them ; but saith, " Let them alone," Hos. iv. 17.   But if you wander out of the way of holiness, he will clog you with one trouble or other to keep you within bounds. " Lest I should be lifted up, a thorn in the flesh, a messenger of Satan, was sent to buffet me," 2 Cor. xii. 7. So David, " Before I was afflicted I went astray ; but now have I kept thy word," Psa. cxix. 67. Afflictions are used by God, as thorns by husbandmen, to stop the gaps, and keep you from breaking out of God's way: " I will hedge up her way with thorns, and build a wall, that she shall not find her paths," Hos. ii. 6.   A double allusion: 1. To cattle that are apt to stray; I will hedge up thy way with thorns. 2. To the sea, which is apt to overflow the country; I will build a wall to prevent inundations.   Holy Basil was a long time sorely afflicted with an inveterate head-ache; he often prayed for the removal of it: at last God removed it, but in the room of it, he was sorely exercised with the motions and temptations of lust; which, when he perceived, he heartily desired his head-ache again, to prevent a worse evil.   You little know the ends and uses of many of your afflictions.   Are you exercised with bodily weakness? It is a mercy you are so; and if these pains and infirmities were removed, these clogs taken off, you may, with Basil, wish for them again, to prevent worse evils.   Are you poor? why, with that poverty God hath clogged your pride. Are you reproached? with these reproaches God hath clogged your ambition.   Corruptions are prevented by your afflictions. And is not this a marvellous help to holiness of life.

(2.) By your afflictions, your corruptions are not only clogged, but purged.   By these God dries up and consumes that spring of sin that defiles your lives: " By this therefore shall the iniquity of Jacob be purged; and this is all the fruit to take away his sin," Isa. xxvii. 9. God orders your wants to kill your wantonness; and makes your poverty poison to your pride.   They are God's physic, to purge ill humours out of your souls.   " When they fall by the sword, and by famine, and by captivity, and by spoil, it is to try them, and to purge them, and to make them white?"   Dan. xi. 33—35.   They are both purges and lavatories to your souls.   Others have the same afflictions that you have, but they do not work on them as on you; they are to you as fire for purging, and water for cleansing: and yet, shall not your lives be clean? It is true, (as one well observes upon that place of Daniel,) Christ is the only lavatory, and his blood the only fountain to wash away sin; but, in the virtue and efficacy of that blood, sanctified afflictions are cleansers and purges too.   A cross without a Christ never made any man better, but with Christ, saints are much the better for the cross.   Hath God put you so many times into the furnace, and yet is not the dross separated? The more afflictions you have been under, the more assistance you have had for this life of holiness.

(3.) By all your troubles, God hath been weaning you from the world, the lusts and pleasures of it, and drawing out your souls to a more excellent life and state than this.   He makes your sorrows in this life give a lustre to the glory of the next. Whoever hath, be sure you shall have no rest here; and all, that you may long more ardently for that to come. He often makes you groan, "being burdened, to be clothed with your house from heaven," 2 Cor. v. 2. 4. And yet will you not be weaned from lusts, customs, and evils of it? Oh what manner of persons should you be for heavenly and holy conversation! You stand upon the higher ground. You have, as it were, the wind and tide with you. None are assisted for this life as you are. Put all this together, and see what this second argument contributes toward your further conviction, and persuasion to holy life. Have you received a supernatural principle, fitting you for, and inclining you to holy actions, resisting and holding you back from sin? Hath God also set before you such eminent patterns to encourage and quicken you in your way? Doth the Spirit himself stand ready, so many ways, to assist and help you in all difficulties, and hath God hedged up the way of sin with the thorns of affliction, to prevent your wandering; and yet will you turn aside? Will you offer violence to your own principles and new nature? refuse to follow such leaders as have beaten the way before you? resist, or neglect his gracious assistance of the blessed Spirit, which he offers you in every need, and venture upon sin, though God hath hedged up your way with afflictions? Oh, how can you do such great wickedness, and sin against such grace as this!

Methinks, I need say no more to convince you how much you are concerned to keep the issues of life pure, none being so much obliged to it, or assisted for it, as you are. But when I remember that Joash lost the complete victory over the syrians, because he smote not his arrows often enough upon the ground, 2 Kings xiii. 19, I shall level one arrow more at this mark; for, indeed, that can never be enough pressed, which can never be enough practised. And therefore,

III. Consider, it will yet further appear to be your high concernment, to exact holiness in your conversations, because of the manifold and great uses which God hath to make of the visible holiness and purity of your lives, both in this world and that to come. The uses God puts the conversation-holiness of his people in this world unto, are these among others.

1. To win over souls to Christ, and bring them in love with religion. Practical holiness is a very lovely, attractive, and constraining thing. If the heathen could call moral virtue *verticordia*, turn-heart, from that constraining and winning power it exercises upon the hearts of men; if they could say of it, that

were it visible to human eyes, all men would adore it, and fall in love with it ; how much rather may we say so of true holiness, made visible in the lives of saints ! This is the turn-heart indeed. So much of God as appears in men, so much drawing excellency there is in them. And this is the apostle's argument: " That ye may have fellowship with us," 1 John i. 3. Why, what is there in your fellowship to invite men to you ? " Truly our fellowship is with the Father, and with his Son Christ Jesus." Who can but covet their company, that keep company every day with God? Great is the efficacy of visible holiness to work upon the hearts of men ; either working in fellowship with the word, or working solitarily without the word.

Where God is pleased to afford the word unto men, there the practical holiness of saints is of singular use, to assist and help it in its operation upon the hearts of men. When the lives of christians sensibly experience that to the eyes of men, which the gospel doth to their ears ; when so we preach, and so ye believe and live ; when we draw by our doctrines, and you draw with us by your examples; when we hold forth the word of life doctrinally, and you hold it forth practically, as Phil. ii. 16; where is the heart that can stand before us ? Oh ! when the plain and powerful gospel pierces the ears of men, and, at the same time, the visible holiness of professors shines so full in their faces, that they must rather put out their own eyes, or else be forced to acknowledge, that God is in you of a truth ; then it will work to purpose upon souls ; then will Christ see of the travail of his soul daily.

Yea, if God deny the word to men, yet this practical holiness, I am speaking of, may be to them an ordinance for conversion. This way, souls may be won to Christ without the word, as the apostle speaks, 1 Pet. iii. 1. Though pulpits should be silent, and vision fail; yet, if you would this way turn preachers, if your lives may but preach the reality, excellency, and sweetness of Jesus Christ and his ways ; and, if you would this way preach down the love of the word, and let men see what poor vanities these are ; and preach up the necessity and beauty of holiness ; surely you, even you might be honoured to bring many souls to Christ, to turn many to righteousness, and cause many to bless God, on your behalf, in the day of visitation. This is the use God hath for the holiness and purity of your lives ; and doth not this engage you strongly to it ? What, not when it may prove the means of eternal life to others ? Surely, if you have any bowels of mercy in you, you cannot hide from others that whereby they may be saved. How can you, instead of holding forth the word of life, (which is your manifest duty,) visibly hold forth the works of death before men? Have you been beholden to others, and shall none be beholden to you for help towards heaven? Dare you say, Let others shift as well as they can, find the way to heaven by themselves as they can, they shall have no benefit by your light? If you be christians, you are christians of a different stamp and spirit from all those we find described in scripture. Should you not rather say as the lepers did, " Do we well to hold our peace," 2 Kings vii. 9, whilst others are perishing? Shall the lips of ministers, and the lives of christians, be both silenced together? Shall poor sinners neither hear any thing from us, nor see any thing from you, that may help them to Christ? The Lord have mercy then upon the poor world, and pity it, for its case is desperate. Oh put on, as the elect of God, bowels of mercy. Destroy not, by the looseness of your conversation, so many souls; for your scandalous miscarriages are like a bag of poison put into the spring which supplies the whole city with water.

2. Another use God hath for it, is to recover the credit of religion, which by the apostasies of hypocrites, and scandalous falls of careless christians, is wounded and exposed to contempt. Much reproach by this means is brought upon religion, and how shall that reproach be rolled away, but by your strictness and purity? By this the world must be convinced that all are not so. Though some be a blot to the name of Christ, yet others are his glory. The more others slur and disgrace religion, the more God expects you to honour and adorn it. I remember Chrysostom brings in the persecutors speaking to two renowned martyrs, after this manner, Why are you so nice and scrupulous? See you not that others of your rank and profession have done these things? To which they returned this brave answer, " For that very reason we will stand out like men, and will never yield to it." There is a holy antiperistasis in the zeal of a christian, which makes it, like fire, burn most vehemently in the coldest weather. If men make void God's law, therefore will David love his commandments above gold, Psa. cxix. 127.

3. God makes use of it for the encouragement of his ministers who labour among you. And indeed it is of no small use to refresh their hearts, and strengthen their hands in their painful work: " Now we live, (saith the apostle,) if ye stand fast in the Lord," 1 Thess. iii. 8. He speaks as if their very life lay at the very mercy of the people, because so much of the joy and comfort of it is wrapt up in their regularity and stedfastness. God knows what a hard duty his poor ministers have, and how many

discouragements attend them in their work ; hear how one * of them expresses it: " Ministers would not be grey-headed so soon, nor die so fast, notwithstanding their great labours, if they were but successful ; but this cuts to the heart, and makes us bleed in secret, that though we do much, yet it comes to nothing. Our work dies, therefore we die. Not so much that we labour, as that we labour in vain."

Christians, you hear our case, you see our work. Now a little to cheer our spirits in the midst of our hard and killing labours, God sends us to you for a little refreshment, that, by beholding your holy and heavenly conversation, your cheerful obedience, and sweet agreement in the ways of God, we may be comforted over all these troubles, 2 Thess. i. 3, 4.

4. God hath further use for the holiness of your lives ; this serves to daunt the hearts, and overawe the consciences of his and your enemies. And sometimes it hath had a strange influence and effect upon them. There is a great deal of awful majesty in holiness, and when it shines upon the conscience of a wicked man, it makes him stoop and do obeisance to it, which turns to a testimony for Christ and his ways before the world. Thus Herod was overawed by the strict and holy life of John ; he feared him, knowing that he was a just and holy man, and observed (or preserved and saved) him. That bloody tyrant was convinced in his conscience of the worth and excellency of that servant of God, and was forced to reverence him for his holiness. How much is this for the honour of holiness, that it conquers the very persecutors of it, and makes them stoop to the meanest servant of God ! It is said of Henry II. of France, that he was so daunted by the heavenly majesty of a poor tailor that was burnt before him, that he went home sad, and vowed that he would never be present at the death of such men any more. When Valence the emperor came in person to apprehend Basil, he saw such majesty in his very countenance, that he reeled at the very sight of him ; and had fallen backward to the ground, had not his servants stepped in to support him. O holiness, holiness, thou art a conqueror ! So much, O christians, as you show of it in your lives, so much you preserve your interest in the consciences of your enemies : cast off this, and they despise you presently.

5. God will use the purity of your conversations to judge and convince the world in the great day. It is true, the world shall be judged by the gospel, but your lives shall also be produced as a commentary upon it ; and God will not only show them by

* Lockyer upon the Colossians, p. 528, 529.

the word how they ought to have lived, but bring forth your lives and ways to stop their mouths, by showing how others did live. And this I suppose is intended in that text, " The saints shall judge the world, yea, we shall judge angels," 1 Cor. vi. 2, 3, that is, our examples are to condemn their lives and practices; as Noah, Heb. xi. 7, is said to condemn the world by building the ark, that is, his faith in the threatening, and obedience to the command, condemned their supineness, infidelity, and disobedience. They saw him every day about that work, diligently preparing for a deluge, and yet were not moved with the like fear that he was; this left them inexcusable. So when God shall say in that day to the careless world, Did you not see the care, and diligence, the holy zeal, watchfulness, and self-denial of my people, who lived among you ? How many times have they been watching and praying, when you have been drinking or sleeping ! Was it not easy to reflect when you saw their pains and diligence, Have not I a soul to look after as well as they ; a heaven to win or lose, as well as they ? Oh how speechless and inexcusable will this render wicked men ! Yea, it shall not only be used to judge them, but angels also. How many shocks of temptations have poor saints stood ; whereas they fell without a tempter ! They stood not in their integrity, though created in such excellent natures. How much then are you concerned on this very account also to walk exactly ! if not, instead of judging them, you shall be condemned with them.

And thus you see what use your lives and actions shall be put to. Oh then, since you are thus obliged to holiness of life, thus singularly assisted for it ; and since there are such great dependences upon it, and uses for it, both now and in the world to come, see that ye be holy in all manner of conversation. See that, " as ye have received Christ Jesus the Lord, so ye walk in him ;" always remembering, that for this very end, Christ hath redeemed, or " delivered you out of the hands of your enemies, that you might serve him without fear, in holiness and righteousness all the days of your lives," Luke i. 74, 75. And to how little purpose will be all that I have preached, and you have heard of Christ, if it be not converted into practical godliness ! This is the scope and design of it all.

And now, reader, thou art come to the last leaf of this treatise of Christ ; it will be but a little while, and thou shalt come to the last page or day of thy life, and thy last moment in that day. Woe to thee, woe and alas for ever, if an interest in this blessed Redeemer be then to get. The world affords not a sadder sight,

x

than a poor Christless soul shivering upon the brink of eternity. To see the poor soul that now begins to awake out of its long dream, at its entrance into the world of realities, shrink back into the body, and cry, Oh, I cannot, I dare not die. And then the tears run down. Lord, what will become of me? Oh what shall be my eternal lot? This, I say, is as sad a sight as the world affords. That this may not be thy case, reflect upon what thou hast read in these sermons. Judge thyself in the light of them. Obey the calls of the Spirit in them. Let not thy slight and formal spirit float upon the surface of these truths, like a feather upon the water; but get them deeply fixed upon thy spirit, by the Spirit of the Lord; turning them into life and power upon thee; and so animating the whole course and tenor of thy conversation by them, that it may proclaim to all that know thee, that thou art one who esteemest all to be but dross, that thou mayest win Christ.

THE END.